Educational Gameplay and Simulation Environments:
Case Studies and Lessons Learned

David Kaufman
Simon Fraser University, Canada

Louise Sauvé
Télé-université, Canada

Information Science REFERENCE

INFORMATION SCIENCE REFERENCE
Hershey · New York

Director of Editorial Content:	Kristin Klinger
Director of Book Publications:	Julia Mosemann
Development Editor:	Julia Mosemann
Publishing Assistant:	Kurt Smith
Typesetter:	Callie Klinger
Quality control:	Jamie Snavely
Cover Design:	Lisa Tosheff
Printed at:	Yurchak Printing Inc.

Published in the United States of America by
Information Science Reference (an imprint of IGI Global)
701 E. Chocolate Avenue
Hershey PA 17033
Tel: 717-533-8845
Fax: 717-533-8661
E-mail: cust@igi-global.com
Web site: http://www.igi-global.com/reference

Library of Congress Cataloging-in-Publication Data

Educational gameplay and simulation environments : case studies and lessons learned / David Kaufman and Louise Sauve, editors.
p. cm.
Includes bibliographical references and index.
Summary: "This book covers theoretical, social, and practical issues related to educational games and simulations, contributing to a more effective design and implementation of these activities in learning environments"--Provided by publisher.
ISBN 978-1-61520-731-2 (hardcover) -- ISBN 978-1-61520-732-9 (ebook) 1. Educational games--Canada--Case studies. 2. Simulation games in education--Canada--Case studies. I. Kaufman, David, 1945- II. Sauve, Louise, 1953-
LB1029.G3E34 2010
371.39'7--dc22

2009044844

British Cataloguing in Publication Data
A Cataloguing in Publication record for this book is available from the British Library.

Editorial Advisory Board

Table of Contents

Detailed Table of Contents

Section 3
Learning Efficacy

Section 3, acknowledging the need for clear evidence to support claims about the effects of games and simulations on learning, focuses on literature and evaluation studies that demonstrate or question their learning impacts.

This chapter presents a synthesis of the literature (1998-2008) on the efficacy of games and simulations for learning. Based on definitions and sets of essential attributes for games and for simulations, the authors examine the contributions of each to knowledge structuring and the development of problem-solving skills. Noting that games and simulations have positive learning outcomes in various situations, the authors present variables to measure the knowledge and skills developed by learners who use games and simulations.

This chapter describes the development, implementation, and evaluation of a Collaborative Online Multimedia Problem-based Learning Simulation (COMPS) instructional model designed for students and practitioners in the health professions to develop clinical reasoning and diagnostic skills. COMPS was developed to support a case-based tutorial model where learners can work together online to solve authentic problems no matter where they may be located, bringing together the engagement and immersiveness of simulations with the social interaction of face-to-face learning.

This chapter presents a framework of game motivational constructs that are applicable to the design of interactive health software. A platform based on this framework that supports a variety of games is described, and an evaluation presented, that examines the impact of these interactions on children with long-term health disorders. The project goal was to determine if games developed with health-related

Section 4
Special In-Depth Section on Game Shell and Game Creation

Section 4 is a special section that outlines the development process used by a research team at the research center SAVIE (Société d'apprentissage à vie – www.savie.qc.ca) at the Télé-université in Quebec, Canada, to develop a generic educational game shell (GEGS) for a series of online educational frame games for their Educational Games Central online community (http://egc.savie.ca). The section's five chapters describe the analysis, design, interface specification, and validation of the GEGS and the formative evaluation of a specific game created with the shell. Section 4 differs from others in this volume in that it illustrates the practical process of creating a GEGS, using the game Parcheesi™ as a framework. Taken together, the chapters in Section 4 provide the reader with a comprehensive "how-to" picture of one educational game project, complete with detailed steps, design criteria, explanations for the choices made, and validation guidelines and results.

As the first of five chapters describing the development process for a generic educational game shell, this chapter discusses how the authors analyzed 40 computerized educational games and interviewed teachers to determine the main characteristics built into digital educational games. The analysis allowed comparison of game attributes with the pedagogic and technical needs of target populations (i.e., primary and secondary school teachers and students) and their learning contexts.

This chapter describes the design phase of the creation of a generic educational game shell (GEGS) for the frame game Parcheesi. The frame game structure was adapted through modifications to the game board, materials, and game scenario, and navigation aids were added to guide players. Learning content was integrated into the game, and pedagogical aspects of the game (e.g., objectives, target learners, school learning material) were specified. Mechanisms were added to create various question types and to provide for feedback, debriefing, and game evaluation. The chapter provides suggestions for avoiding common errors in the design of online educational games.

This chapter discusses usability rules for avoiding defects in the media design for generic educational game shell (GEGS) components, including visual interfaces, text, and sound. These rules served as a

Foreword

David Kaufman and Louise Sauvé have bridged theory and practice to create a uniquely informative, evidence-based, and abundantly practical volume on educational simulation and gaming environments. The book promises to become an essential reference for academics, designers, teachers, and students of games, simulations, and simulation games when fundamental educational aims and learning outcomes are uppermost in their minds.

The four sections of this volume draw upon the contributions and the expertise of academics, researchers, teachers, health professionals, technicians, and students to cover a vast territory related to simulations and gaming. The diversity of examples provided is extensive and will provide guidance for those involved in researching, creating, and using games or simulations in education.

The first section deals with foundations and theory, the second with game design and prototyping, the third section with learning efficacy, and the fourth with specific generic educational game shell and game creation. Taken together, the four sections provide an in-depth examination of theoretical models and original applications as well as a sound rationale and guidelines for the pursuit of educational aims through judicious use of games and simulations. The interest of this volume lies, in part, with the authors' successful demonstration that their orientation is in tune with school curriculum goals and basic tenets of effective teaching and learning practices.

The section on foundations and theory begins with working definitions of games, simulations, and simulation games. It goes on to provide a rationale for the overall project and the writers' efforts to better define the field itself. In discussing the notion of effectiveness of games and simulations, the authors make a compelling case for supporting learning through the effective use of sound, image, and animation as well as mechanisms and structures involving repetition, frequent feedback, challenge and competition, active learning, and teamwork. Also included in the section on foundations and theory are chapters devoted to simulation in the education of health professionals, the role of narrative, the potential of the concept of fantasy to enhance games, the issue of gender and games, the response of pre-service teachers to games, and the place of video games for the "net" generation. One of these chapters introduces the reader to new software environments and applications designed for patients and medical students and professionals navigating the health care system. Another offers a fascinating account of well-established, traditional narrative structures and describes to what extent they can be adapted to the interactive experience, while other chapters discuss notion of fantasy as well as the controversial issue of gender in games.

The second section of the book deals with design and prototyping. It includes a lead chapter linking theory and practice, showing how inter-related elements and structures of a game are mobilized to create a meaningful educational experience. Other chapters describe in turn the use of a simulator for teaching ethical decision-making, the harnessing of the popular socioconstructivist approach to education to develop healthy life habits through a game, the potential team work and communication benefits of multi-player games, new tools for researchers studying the impact of gaming, the development of a character-based system in gaming, and, finally, a promising model of treating mental health patients through learning-oriented simulations.

The five chapters in the third section of this book deal with the critical issue of learning efficacy. The authors first explore variables measuring knowledge gains and the development of skills such as problem solving. A second chapter considers the application of multimedia games as a means for children with long-term health problems to take increased responsibility for managing their condition. A third considers the potential development of positive attitudes towards animals through games involving virtual pets. Parents and educators will be interested in both the overview, provided in subsequent chapters, of research on the impact of violent video games with respect to aggressive behaviors in children, and the results of a study of the application of biofeedback in a gaming environment. In summary, the third section of the volume raises key issues concerning the potential efficacy of games on the development of a range of skills, attitudes, and competencies among children and youth with a variety of social, health and cognitive needs.

The concluding section of the book serves as a model for those researchers and practitioners seeking to develop games for educational ends. Chapters in the final section report on the critical analysis of 40 computerized educational games and the design and development of a "generic educational game shell," the integration of content and pedagogical objectives into the game environment, the adoption of "usability guidelines' to make the games come alive for users, the validation of generic educational game shells by teachers creating the games, and formative evaluation of an educational game on sexually transmitted diseases intended to inform and increase awareness among secondary students. This section is substantively different from the others, as it could stand alone as a basic text on the five stages of creating a generic educational game shell and developing online games using the shell.

David Kaufman and Louise Sauvé are to be commended for their considerable efforts to assemble and tie together a wide variety of perspectives on the educational use of simulation and gaming. This book succeeds in addressing basic research questions as well as offering many practical lessons derived from trials and validation exercises in a variety of clinical and educational settings. *Educational Gameplay and Simulation Environments: Case Studies and Lessons Learned* promises to become a staple reference for professionals in the health and education sectors across North America and beyond for years to come.

Alan Wright
University of Windsor, Canada

***Alan Wright** is Vice-provost, Teaching and Learning, at the University of Windsor. In this role he is responsible for the overall academic direction and management of the Centre for Teaching & Learning and leads the development of learning-centered policies, practices, and programs in the university. Prior to his appointment, Dr. Wright was Director of Undergraduate Studies at the University of Quebec and an Associate Professor of Education at its Lévis Campus He is a graduate of Mount Allison University, the University of New Brunswick (B.A., English and French Literature); McGill University, Montreal (Education and M.A. degrees); and the University of Montreal (Ph.D. in Foundations of Education). His work in the field of educational development includes workshop facilitation and curriculum development in a number of countries as well as significant contributions to the professional literature on improving university teaching and learning.*

Preface

Games and simulations are growing entertainment and cultural forces in our world. Players embrace games and simulations on game machines, PCs, mobile phones and online; they develop quick-reaction and motor skills, engage cognitive processes, enter into complex fantasy environments, play with peers across the planet, and even create entire new social lives in simulated environments. Meanwhile, educators struggle ever-harder to engage their students who are more drawn to these attractive new activities than to more traditional learning. Using games and simulations as learning tools could help, but how can we conceptualize, design, and implement them effectively?

Educational Gameplay and Simulation Environments: Case Studies and Lessons Learned presents a collection of papers based on research arising from Canada's *Simulation and Advanced Gaming Environments (SAGE) for Learning* Project (2003-2008). Covering theoretical, social, and practical issues related to educational games and simulations, these chapters contribute to a strong foundation, clearer understanding, and more effective design and implementation of these activities in learning environments. This volume should both help and challenge educators, researchers, and game developers wishing to broaden their work to effectively include games and simulations.

THE *SAGE FOR LEARNING* PROJECT

Aimed at better understanding and supporting learning in these environments, the bilingual, Pan-Canadian *SAGE for Learning* initiative addressed the interplay among the exploding popularity of technology-based simulations and games for entertainment; new technologies for appealing, immersive, engaging simulations and games; and growing evidence that learning works best when people collaborate, practice and reflect on their learning.

Focusing on health-related learning, the initiative investigated:

a. how people learn through technology-based simulations and games
b. which cognitive, human and social factors, as well as which game and simulation characteristics, contribute to making simulations and games engaging, motivating, and effective for learning
c. how to integrate new technologies and our theoretical knowledge of learning to create effective learning simulations and games in real-world settings (e.g., schools, hospitals, businesses, communities)
d. how to improve our methods and tools for research and evaluation on learning with simulations and games

The project was funded for approximately $3 million by Canada's Social Sciences and Humanities Research Council (SSHRC) through its Initiative on the New Economy - Collaborative Research Initiative Program. Thirty-six Canadian and international university-based researchers in education, psychology, computer science, educational technology, new digital media, and research/ evaluation methodologies participated. The project also included over thirty Canadian and international partner organizations, many of which supported and collaborated on SAGE research projects.

SAGE for Learning members worked to transform health-related learning through the study, development, and application of technology-based games and simulations. The network's research objectives were to:

- build and validate a *common multidimensional taxonomy and conceptual framework* to guide SAGE research
- describe the *types and characteristics of learning* that take place through the use of SAGEs
- identify, observe, document and model *key cognitive and social processes* that develop, promote or hinder learning in SAGEs
- study the capacity of SAGEs to *support learning as described by key learning theories* through adaptation and creation of simulations and games for specific learner groups and tasks
- develop and implement *research methodologies and tools* appropriate for describing and assessing SAGE learning processes and outcomes
- demonstrate the *application of knowledge* resulting from our research on SAGE impacts in the development, implementation, and testing of prototype SAGEs
- pilot the *implementation* of SAGEs in authentic contexts, e.g. schools, businesses, and community settings

These research objectives were addressed through a multi-methodological approach consisting of descriptive, developmental, and evaluative research phases, using a mixed quantitative-qualitative methodology. SAGE research was conceptually grouped into *foundation* and *application* domains, with specific loosely integrated projects addressing theoretical as well as practical issues involved in translating game and simulation entertainment technologies into effective learning tools and in evaluating their learning impact.

NEW-GENERATION LEARNING

Understanding games and simulations for learning is important because we face major questions about how our technology-supported education approaches should evolve. As noted above, simulations and games are now significant entertainment vehicles. The statistics are staggering; global video game sales are expected to reach 68.3 billion by 2012, approximately 65% of American households play video games, and 63% of parents believe that games are a positive part of their children's lives. Massively Multiplayer Online Games attract millions of players; for example, 11.5 million were playing *World of Warcraft*® in late 2008, and the *Second Life*® virtual environment, which includes virtual college classrooms, is said to have more than 1.5 million registered users.

As they have become more widely accepted, games and simulations have emerged as tools for learning outside and within academia; educators and trainers reason that the popularity, engagement characteristics, and wide accessibility of digital games and simulations can provide powerful learning tools if understood and properly exploited, particularly for newer generations of learners. Several writers have suggested that the "gamer generation" has developed a new cognitive style characterized by multitasking, a relatively short attention span, and a preference for learning through investigation and discovery, all characteristics of game-based learning. Others believe that, inspired by a constructivist approach, the use of video games has changed young people's way of learning: the learner plays first, then learns and later generalizes to apply experiences in new situations, while the teacher's role has changed to supporting active learning and the construction of knowledge. Some writers describe the profile of current teenagers as "born communicators" who prefer their learning to be interactive, visual, kinesthetic, immediate, and involve "doing" rather than thinking or talking. Finally, some believe that online games offer the "digital native" generation the opportunity for inductive reasoning, allowing players to resolve cognitive conflicts through a constant cycle of hypotheses, test and revision.

Games and simulations, often embodying established learning theories, should be excellent learning tools. Their exploration, collaboration, complex problem solving, practice and feedback through "safe" failure and learner decision-making, have led to claims that they can support constructivist learning, situated cognition, cognitive apprenticeship, experiential learning, development of self-efficacy and learner-centeredness. However, educational institutions have not yet deeply investigated their potential, and much research remains to be done to establish effective ways to design, develop and integrate them into educational settings.

IN THIS VOLUME

Educational Gameplay and Simulation Environments: Case Studies and Lessons Learned addresses this need in a diverse collection of papers arising from individual SAGE research projects, linked by their common concern with effective learning-related theory and applications for games and simulations. This volume covers specific issues and examples in theoretical foundations, design, prototyping, application, and evaluation, complemented by a detailed look at the planning, design, development and validation of a specific online generic educational game shell and game application.

Section 1: Foundations and Theory

The recent rush to study and apply games and simulations to learning has produced studies with varying conceptual frameworks and methodologies. As a result, their results are often conflicting or inconclusive, limiting their value. Section 1 is intended to help clarify the theory and fundamental concepts of the field and to support educators and learners in understanding these fundamentals.

Games, Simulations and Simulation Games for Learning: Definitions and Distinctions (Chapter 1), presents the results of a systematic review of the literature from 1998 through 2008 to develop a conceptual definition of games, simulation and simulation games based on their essential attributes. The authors describe their motivation for the analysis, their methodological approach, databases reviewed, analysis grid and the results of the review, differentiating among the three categories. This analysis is intended to improve the precision of future studies concerning the effects of games, simulations and simulation games on learning by contributing to a common language for current and future research.

Chapter 2, *Effective Educational Games,* argues that educational games have not always been taken seriously but are, in fact, highly interactive (and playful) supports for communication and interaction that should be employed more fully in 21st century education. The chapter summarizes studies highlighting mechanisms that motivate and support learning, including competition, challenge, feedback, active learner participation, teamwork, interaction, repetition and segmentation of learning content. These are illustrated with examples of health-related game applications. This work should reduce educators' concern about using games and simulations for learning by clearly describing their demonstrated benefits and providing supporting evidence and examples.

Simulation in Health Professional Education (Chapter 3), provides background and orientation for the use of simulations in health-related learning. It defines "simulations" and outlines their attributes, goals, advantages and limitations, suggesting ways of overcoming the latter. After distinguishing and illustrating categories and forms of simulations and explaining elements that make simulations effective, the chapter examines the contributions of various types of simulations to the training of health professionals and briefly describes examples developed within the framework of the SAGE project.

The next two chapters in Section 1 discuss how specific game or simulation elements influence learning. Chapter 4, *The Role of Narrative in Educational Games and Simulations,* discusses the major role which narrative components play in supporting learning in interactive games and simulations. Applied correctly, these components have the capacity to improve the interactive experience and to support learning that is rich in significance.

Chapter 5, *Does Fantasy Enhance Learning in Digital Games?* examines how digital games have the potential to create environments that increase motivation, engage learners, and support learning. The authors explore the relationship between digital games, imagination and learning, and describe key factors which make digital games motivating. They argue that these factors are important in the design of games for learning because motivation plays a major role in engaging players in learning activities. They then describe the contribution of fantasy in the context of digital games and the importance of creating types of fantasy adapted to different sexes. Finally, they examine how learning content is integrated into fantasy-based digital games.

In Chapter 6, *Gender and Digital Gameplay: Theories, Oversights, Accidents, and Surprises,* the authors criticize and challenge game studies researchers, arguing that faulty assumptions and biases have distorted research in game studies. They identify norms and assumptions that lead to difficulties and briefly present a three-year study on gender and digital games, explaining more precisely the effects of some of these too-frequent "traps." Their work should help to expand our research vision, improve study design, and increase our understanding of girls and gameplay.

Chapter 7, *Games in Health Education: A Survey of Pre-service Teachers,* presents background data on the need for effective health education in the schools and describes a field study evaluating student teachers' perceptions of the use of games for health-related learning. This survey, carried out with 300 pre-service teachers in New Brunswick and Quebec, studied respondent familiarity with games, their perceptions of the utility of games for learning, and the games they preferred to play. The results of this study informed a specific educational game project and, more generally, provide us with insights into the gap between "desire" and "practice" in the use of educational games.

Chapter 8, *Video Games and the Challenge of Engaging the "Net" Generation*, changes perspective to discuss the use of videogames in education from the viewpoint of a professional game developer. Noting that educational games are often criticized for stressing learning to the detriment of their playful, engaging aspects, the author describes for educators the aspects of modern personal computer games that create and retain player interest. He argues in favor of more communication and cooperation between education specialists and commercial game developers to improve the quality and learning impact of their digital games.

Section 2: Design and Prototyping

Section 2 presents research and application software prototypes for educational games, simulations, and simulation games, as well as tools to support their delivery and evaluation. These chapters expand our understanding of good design and the game/ simulation creation process. They also broaden our knowledge of the potential for games and simulations to support learning in new ways and content domains.

Educational Games: Moving from Theory to Practice (Chapter 9) presents a creative process for the game *Contagion* in which, in contrast to traditional approaches, players are involved in all stages of game creation; avoiding a formal framework of "learning outcomes" for the game, the authors instead worked to embed useful knowledge from a teaching point of view in all aspects of game design and play. This chapter challenges our beliefs about simulation game development.

Chapter 10, *Designing a Simulator for Teaching Ethical Decision-Making,* presents the design of a multimedia simulation-based learning environment the *Ethical Advisor*, which support the scenario-based teaching of ethical decision-making. The case-based environment challenges learners to identify relevant information, to analyze decisions in light of theoretical models, and to manage and filter information flow.

In Chapter 11, *Design of a Socioconstructivist Game for the Classroom: Theoretical and Empirical Considerations*, the authors describe the use of literature reviews, a field study, and an analysis of multimedia educational games to develop theoretical and empirical foundations for the design of new types of educational multi-media games that support the socio-constructivist approach recommended in new primary and secondary school curricula. The study results informed a comprehensive set of requirements guiding the choice of a game framework.

Online Multiplayer Games: A Powerful Tool for Learning Communication and Teamwork (Chapter 12) describes the design of a communication and groupware platform, *ENJEUX-S*, that increases the learning impact of online games and simulations by allowing gameplay with integrated video and voice real-time communication. The learning contributions of the platform are emphasized, showing the learning advantages of online, multimedia, multiplayer games. The *ENJEUX-S* testing methodology and results offer an example for developers of online environments.

Advancing the Study of Educational Gaming: A New Tool for Researchers (Chapter 13) describes *OpenVULab,* an Internet-based system supporting flexible, remote data collection and analysis for the formative and summative evaluation of online games and simulations. An initial field trial of the tool is presented, providing a useful approach for similar studies and a clear illustration of *OpenVULab's* research and practical value.

Chapter 14, *Designing Socially Expressive Character Agents to Facilitate Learning,* moves farther into the future with a description of *FaceSpace,* an expressive but easy-to-author 3D character-based system that makes possible simulated face-to-face collaboration, adaptive socially-based presentations for informal learning, and multi-user, avatar-based distance education scenarios.

In a specific health domain, *The Use of Virtual Reality in Clinical Psychology Research: Focusing on Approach and Avoidance Behaviors* (Chapter 15) described how simulations using immersive virtual reality technologies, combined with the analysis of recorded ocular and physical movements, can help to improve our understanding and treatment of psychopathologies. Experiments treating phobias and pedophilia show how this simulation-based learning approach might be applied in practice.

Section 3: Learning Efficacy

Section 3 acknowledging the need for clear evidence to support claims about the effects of games and simulations on learning, focuses on literature and evaluation studies that demonstrate or question their learning impact. Chapter 16, *The Efficacy of Games and Simulations for Learning,* reviews the game and simulation literature (1998-2008) on learning effectiveness, drawing on the foundational work presented in Chapter 1 to base the review on clear game and simulation definitions. Concentrating on knowledge structuring and the development of problem-solving skills, the chapter is a major contribution to arguments for the use of games and simulations as tools for complex learning.

Collaborative Online Multimedia Problem–Based Simulations (COMPS) (Chapter 17) describes an innovative online problem-based learning application that incorporates multimedia elements and a video narrative into a medical case. The results of a preliminary evaluation show that this approach is effective in developing critical reasoning skills.

Chapter 18, *Games for Children with Long-Term Health Problems,* describes the development and testing of a game framework and series of handheld and PC-based videogames for children in with chronic health problems. Their results show great promise in using videogames for these types of applications.

An unusual study examining learning effects of a virtual dog simulation is presented in Chapter 19, *Handheld Games: Can Virtual Pets Make a Difference?* The study examined whether children's' empathy toward animals, and attitudes toward the humane treatment of animals, could be improved through using a handheld videogame that allows them to play with and care for a virtual dog. Results support the use of gameplay to develop and enhance children's caring attitudes and behavior.

Chapter 20, *The Learning Impact of Violent Video Games*, attempts to answer queries posed by parents to the SAGE project about whether they should be concerned about violence in games played by their children. Through a review of current literature on the topic, the authors address the issue of violence in videogames and summarize evidence for and against its harmful effects. Although research to date has not produced a clear conclusion, the chapter should contribute to our understanding of the concepts, controversies, practical research issues, and conflicting evidence surrounding this question.

Chapter 21, *A Study of Biofeedback in a Gaming Environment,* reports on an innovative study conducted in a neuro-educational laboratory that examines the issue of learning biofeedback through a videogame. This exploratory work lays a path for further work that could eventually lead to innovative methods of learning enhancement, as well as treatment for problems such as learning anxiety.

Section 4: Special In-Depth Section on Game Shell and Game Creation

Section 4 is a special section that outlines the development process used by a research team at the research center SAVIE (*Société d'apprentissage à vie* – www.savie.qc.ca) at the Télé-université in Quebec, Canada, to develop a generic educational game shell (GEGS) for a series of online educational framegames for their *Educational Games Central* online community (http://egc.savie.ca). The section's five chapters describe the analysis, design, interface specification, and validation of the GEGS and the formative evaluation of a specific game created with the shell. Section 4 differs from others in this volume in that it illustrates the practical process of creating a GEGS, using the game *Parcheesi* as a framework. Taken together, the chapters in Section 4 provide the reader with a comprehensive "how-to" picture of one educational game project, complete with detailed steps, design criteria, explanations for the choices made, and validation guidelines and results.

CONCLUSION

This collection should be useful in many ways to researchers, practitioners and students of games and simulations for learning. For researchers, it adds to the theoretical and practical knowledge of game- and simulation-based learning and suggests many directions for future work. For educators hoping to use games and simulations, it provides helpful examples, guidelines, evaluation techniques and results, and lessons learned. For education and learning technology students, this collection provides foundation knowledge, identifies key questions and implementation considerations, and should stimulate further discussion and curiosity. For game developers, it provides theoretical background for design choices; resources to support design, development, and evaluation; and extensive examples and guidelines to apply in practice.

It is our hope that all readers will be encouraged to consider more deeply the relationships among games and simulations, learning theory, and practice, ultimately advancing their skill in creating and implementing effective and engaging environments for today's and tomorrow's learners.

David Kaufman and Louise Sauvé,
Vancouver and Quebec City
July, 2009

Acknowledgment

Dozens of people were involved in contributing to the enormous effort required to produce a book of this size and complexity. We thank them all as they are too numerous to be named here. However, there are some 'special' individuals who played an essential role in this book project. First, we express our deepest gratitude to Dr. Alice Ireland, who served for five years as Executive Director of the SAGE project on which this book is based, and then spent another year (and many hours) serving as the coordinator and major editor of this volume. Thanks are also due to Sandra McKenzie, who served as editor in the final stage, for her hard work and dedication. We also wish to thank Dany Vallerand and Annie Lachance for their logistical support during the editing process and their coordination of the translation of the chapters and figures into the French language for the French chapter peer reviews and French book version. Of course, this volume could not have come together without the hard work and commitment of the other chapter authors, who all served as researchers in the SAGE project. We offer our warm thanks and gratitude for their friendship, collegiality and excellent chapters.

We are particularly grateful to Dr. Alan Wright for taking the time out of his hectic schedule as Vice-Provost, Teaching & Learning at the University of Windsor to write the Foreword to this volume. As both an educator and author, Dr. Wright appreciates the importance of continually searching for ways of improving our educational methods.

We wish to acknowledge the contribution of the members of our Editorial Board, who are listed elsewhere in this book. All members served as peer reviewers for the chapters in this volume, and their helpful suggestions contributed greatly to improving the quality of the chapters.

Thanks are due to Julia Mosemann, the development editor for this book. Ms. Mosemann's positive energy, helpful suggestions and expert guidance throughout the development process were invaluable.

We gratefully acknowledge the Social Sciences and Humanities Research Council of Canada (SSHRC) for providing funding for almost five years (2003-08) through its Initiative on the New Economy: Collaborative Research Initiative program. The $3 million grant we received supported the *Simulation and Advanced Gaming Environments (SAGE) for Learning* project. This book is a result of that project.

We also offer our thanks to the Canadian Advanced Network And Research for Industry and Education (CANARIE) for funding of the development and testing of *ENJEUX-S,* the multimedia communications platform that supported our national and international online collaboration during the SAGE project.

Last but not least, we gratefully acknowledge Simon Fraser University for providing a grant to partially support the costs of the final editing of this book.

David Kaufman
Simon Fraser University, Canada

Louise Sauvé
Télé-université, Canada

Section 1
Foundations and Theory

Chapter 1
Games, Simulations, and Simulation Games for Learning:
Definitions and Distinctions

Louise Sauvé
Télé-université, Canada

Lise Renaud
University of Quebec in Montreal, Canada

David Kaufman
Simon Fraser University, Canada

ABSTRACT

The authors of this chapter carried out a systematic review of the literature from 1998 to 2008 with the goal of developing conceptual definitions of game, simulation, and simulation game based on their essential attributes. This chapter first describes the motivation for this project and its methodological approach. It then introduces the databases consulted, and the analysis grid used. Finally, it presents the review results, which suggest a differentiation among games, simulations and simulation games. This analysis is intended to improve the precision of future research studies concerning the effects on learning of games, simulations, and simulation games.

INTRODUCTION

It is striking to note that, despite many studies, researchers and theoreticians do not always agree on precise meanings for the concepts of *game*, *simulation* and *simulation game*. Research to date on the learning efficacy of games, simulations and simulation games has suffered from an absence of clear concept definitions, comparing very different tools and activities without distinguishing among them. This has produced indecisive and sometimes divergent results. To attempt to remedy this methodological weakness, we carried out a systematic literature review to establish definitions and articulate the essential attributes of games, simulations, and simulation games (Sauvé et al., 2005), relating these definitions to the learning-oriented concept of *serious games*.

As seen in the examples of Crookall (1995); de Freitas, Savill-Smith, and Attewell (2006); Feinstein, Mann, and Corsun (2002); Kirriemuir and Mc-

DOI: 10.4018/978-1-61520-73 -2.ch001

Farlane (2004); Jones (1998); Sauvé (1985); Sauvé and St-Pierre (2003); and Wolfe and Crookall (1998), it is clear that the absence of consensus on terminology has led to contradictory research results on learning from games, simulations and simulation games. Since our larger project aims at examining the efficacy of games, simulations, and simulation games for learning, it is important to clearly define these concepts and to articulate their essential attributes.

It is not, however, easy to establish the critical attributes of these three types of activities when we are confronted with a plethora of definitions. Certain authors, notably supporters of *serious games* (e.g., Alvarez, 2007) opt for treating games and simulations as similar activities, emphasizing their technological attributes and the application domains in which they are used. Others identify certain characteristics (e.g., competition, risk, fantasy and suspense) which are more relevant to the spirit of game (Lhôte, 1986) or to motivation[1] (Rieber, 1996) than to the concept itself. Others describe them from a purely technology or mathematical perspective (Landry, 2003)[2]. Finally, many authors experiment with activities that they describe as games or simulations without defining them (e.g., Hunsaker, 2007; Mzoughi, Herring, Foley, Morris, & Gilbert, 2007). These practices reaffirm the importance and relevance of proposing essential attributes for games, simulations, and simulation games (Sauvé, Renaud, Kaufman, & Marquis, 2007).

To attempt to remedy this methodological weakness, we carried out a systematic literature review to establish definitions and articulate the essential attributes of games, simulations and simulation games (Sauvé et al., 2005). According to Larousse en-ligne (www.larousse.fr), an attribute is defined as *"that which belongs, that which is inherent to something."* We understand an essential attribute to be a characteristic or specific property which describes the element; without this property, the element is no longer recognized as such. We address the essential attributes in this chapter. In the first section, six critical attributes of educational games are examined: (1) player(s), (2) conflict, (3) rules, (4) predetermined goal(s), (5) artificial character, and (6) educational character. In the second section, five attributes of educational simulations are explained: (1) a model of reality defined as a system, (2) dynamic, (3) simplified, (4) having validity, and (5) having an educational purpose. In the third part, four attributes of educational simulation games are described: (1) a simulation (model of a real or fictitious, simplified and dynamic system); (2) players in competition or cooperation; (3) rules; and (4) educational character. Simulation games are then related to "serious games" as the term is now being used in the literature. In conclusion, a distinction will be made among the three concepts.

EDUCATIONAL GAMES

The literature on video games and serious games does not distinguish between games, simulations and simulation games[3] (Usta, Akbas, Cakir, & Ozdemir, 2008). Acknowledging that the essential attributes of a game are still very controversial, and that many authors define games to include attributes of a simulation, we base our argument, for the purposes of this chapter, on the authors who distinguish among the terms "game," "simulation," and "simulation game."

According to Stolovitch (1983), four essential properties define a game: *contrivance, conflict, control,* and *closure*. In other words, a game describes a fictitious (contrived) situation in which players are in position of conflict either with others or against outside forces, where rules provide a control structure for player actions, and where players pursue the purpose of winning (closure). Chamberland, Lavoie and Marquis (1995) define a game as an "interaction of learners in an activity with artificial character, where they are subjected to rules and steered towards the achievement of a purpose." Dempsey, Lucassen and Rasmussen

(1996) assert that a game is a set of activities driven by rules, presenting certain artificial aspects, a purpose, constraints and consequences, and implying one or several players in a competition or training of the mental faculties and various skills. Prenksy (2001) describes six structural elements of electronic games: rules; goals and objectives to be accomplished; feedback allowing players to measure their progress toward game goals; conflict, competition, and challenge; opposition to the computer or other players; and a representation or story, such as recognition and construction of a specific drawing in the game *Tetris*®. Feinstein, Mann, and Corsun (2002) describe a game as a set of interactions between players in a compulsory framework, directed by a set of rules and procedures. Atake (2003) identifies three essential characteristics of a game: rules, a purpose, and an element of pleasure. Facer et al. (2004) include competition and challenge or the pursuit of a purpose as essential characteristics of a game. Gradler (2004) states that games are exercises in competition with the objective of winning, in which players have to display knowledge of a specific subject to advance in the game and obtain victory.

Beaufils (2006) defines a game as a situation in which individuals (players) are driven to choose among a certain number of possible actions within a framework defined in advance (rules of the game); the result of these choices establishes an exit from the game associated with gains or losses for each of the participants. For Schuytema (2007), a game is an activity which includes a series of actions and decisions; the activity, governed by rules, takes place in a defined context and is directed to a goal. Juul (2003) describes a game as a system where the players engage in an artificial conflict defined by rules and giving a quantifiable result. Wikipédia (2008a) defines a game as an activity of physical or mental leisure, subject to conventional rules, in which we participate for diversion and to achieve some pleasure and amusement. Finally, Abaza and Steyn (2008) summarize the characteristics of a game or *serious game* as being digital with strong computer constituents, including a challenge and objectives, while offering entertainment, a scorekeeping system, and the development of competence, knowledge, and attitude change.

These definitions of game used in an educational context have in common six essential attributes: (1) one or several players, (2) conflict, (3) rules, (4) a purpose predetermined by the game, (5) artificial character and (6) the educational character. We now examine each in more detail.

One or Several Players

Player(s) are one or several persons assuming roles or making decisions within the game framework. A game cannot work without at least one player (Griffiths, 2002) or several players (Gosen & Wabush, 1999). A person can play only against oneself, where the purpose of the game is to achieve a perfect performance or improve a point score from one play to the next; with others, which gives the game a cooperative character; or against the other players or the computer, which gives the game a competitive character. Although the number of players can theoretically vary from one to infinity, for a given game it is usually fixed or variable inside a narrow range. Studies also describe player and team characteristics and their efficacy for learning (see Chapter 16 of this volume). In an educational game, the player is also a learner who takes actions to achieve learning, and for whom a feedback mechanism acts to validate his learning.

Conflict, Competition or Cooperation

Conflict is represented in a game by dynamic, human or computer-controlled obstacles that prevent the easy realization of the objective by the player(s). The obstacles must be active, even "intelligent" in order to create a conflict and at least give the illusion of a response determined by player actions (Kasvi, 2000). Conflict also implies the notions of fight, competition, and challenge, which motivate individuals to hold their roles in the game and to make decisions. ("Fight" is often used as synonym for conflict and is defined in the same way.) In games such as *Chess*, *Monopoly®*, and *Bridge*, this fight or competition exists between players or between teams.

Competition is a key feature of games with a single player (who opposes himself in order to improve his performance with every challenge) and those that include several players (who oppose each other to achieve the same purpose). In solitary games, conflict takes the shape of a confrontation between the player and chance (e.g., dice, roulette, etc.) or another opponent, such as the computer, using a decision algorithm. Finally, challenge occurs when actions taken by a player engender reactions in opponent(s), creating a competition or a fight (Kirriemur & MacFarlane, 2004).

Cooperation takes place when players join other players to achieve a common purpose. Always present in a team game, cooperation requires group tasks (Gray, Topping, & Carcary, 1998) that are governed by rules. In team games, degrees of cooperation and competition vary and consequently must be balanced by rules to make sure that all team members master the learning content. For example, in the game *Earth Ball* (Brand, 1968), the challenge sets the players against certain obstacles or difficulties which can be surmounted only by the pooling of player resources.

Rules

Rules are a set of simple or complex conditions that describe the relations between players and the game environment. They specify the extent and nature of the players' justifiable actions and establish the sequence and structure in which participant actions will take place (Gray, Topping, & Carcary, 1998). Rules serve three types of functions (Stolovitch & Thiagarajan, 1980):

- Rules of *procedure* describe the constituents of the game, i.e., the number of players or the number of teams, the role of each of the participants, their activities, and the movements or actions which can be made.
- Rules of *closure* specify the results expected for each player, as well as the constraints; for example, the first player who reaches a score of 100 within a row wins.
- Rules of *control* describe the consequences for a player who does not respect the preceding rules. For example, in the game *Mille bornes®*, a player who saves a Security card until the end forfeits the 100 point bonus for his team.

Brougère (1999) notes that rules result either from external regulations accepted by the players, or from an agreement or negotiation between the players as part of the game. In every case, rules must be clear, organized, complete, pre-established, and accepted by the players before gameplay begins. Without pre-established rules known by the player(s), the game becomes a playful activity in which players are free to create rules or to modify them according to their whim and to the activity's progress (De Grandmont, 2005). However, in a growing number of electronic games, the player is called to deduce rules by playing, adjusting decisions as he refines his understanding of the gameplay.

A Predetermined Goal

The predetermined goal of a game refers to the end of the game, and to the notion of victory, gain, or reward (Salopek, 1999). It indicates how the game ends, and for educational games, it includes the learning objectives pursued by the player(s). The goal is governed by rules which determine (1) one or more winners, and often one or more losers, and (2) when and how various game-ends can arise. These rules can also contain time limits and scoring objectives leading to player success or elimination. The desire to achieve the goal conditions choices made by players during the gameplay. According to the type of game, it can involve overcoming opponents by competing in engagement and cleverness, triumphing over fate, or surmounting an obstacle with the aim of gaining a victory or reward.

Artificial Character

The artificial character of a game refers to two rather different notions, according to various authors. For Sauvé and Chamberland (2000), a game is a fictitious activity without reference to reality, or that operates outside the usual standards of reality (for example, the games *Tic Tac Toe*, *Bingo*, and *Checkers*). Set in a fictitious situation, the player can reach a playful, unreal, and sometimes absurd dimension. If the constraints of reality applied, the activity would become a simulation game rather than a game. Malone and Lepper (1987, p. 240) refer to this fanciful aspect as a built environment "of mental, physical or social images which do not exist."

Some authors omit this attribute from the definition of a game, defining game attributes to include the notion of reality (Crawford, 1999; Eyraud, 1998; Kasvi, 2000).

Educational Character

An activity is a game when it possesses the attributes described previously, as is the case for *Checkers*. Playing this game regularly makes us better at it, but this does not make *Checkers* an educational game. De Grandmont (2005) states that a game that is not used in an educational or pedagogical context is said to be a playful ("ludic") game. She further distinguishes between an *educational* game, in which a learning-centered purpose is implicit and hidden from the player, and the pleasure which the game engenders is more extrinsic, and a *pedagogical* game, in which the purpose is clearly directed toward the need to learn, is explicitly identified as such, and appeals to the intrinsic pleasure of performing well. In both cases, the game must contribute to learning, which we define as a process of acquiring knowledge or new behavior as a result of interactions with the environment.

This learning through games is described in the literature; according to these authors, learning through games takes place through acquisition of new knowledge, development of intellectual skills (e.g., abstraction, anticipation, strategic thinking, problem resolution, lateral thinking, spatial representation, hand-eye coordination), and development of behavior and attitudes.

Finally, others focus on the characteristics which educational (or pedagogical) games develop in the learner. Asakawa and Gilbert (2003), Bain and Newton (2003) and Prensky (2005a, 2005b, 2006) suggest that the "game generation" has developed a new cognitive style characterized by multitasking, a relatively short attention span during learning, and a way of learning which emphasizes investigation and discovery. They argue that the use of digital games will motivate learning in this new generation. Saethang and Kee (1998) and Shaffer, Squire, Halverson, & Gee (2004) state that the use of video games has changed young people's way of learning and inspires a constructivist approach; the learner plays at first, understands later, and generalizes by applying the learning in new situations. These authors also assert that the learner actively participates in the construction of his knowledge. Oblinger and Oblinger (2005) describe today's adolescents as born intuitive and visual communicators. They have strong visual and spatial capacities, doubtless supported by their practice with video games. They prefer to learn by experimenting rather than by following assignments, moving easily from one task or activity to the next if one does not sustain their interest. They respond energetically to questions and demand fast answers in return. In brief, the young Internet user prefers learning with interactivity, visualization, sensation, and im-

Figure 1. It's going to kill you in Canada!

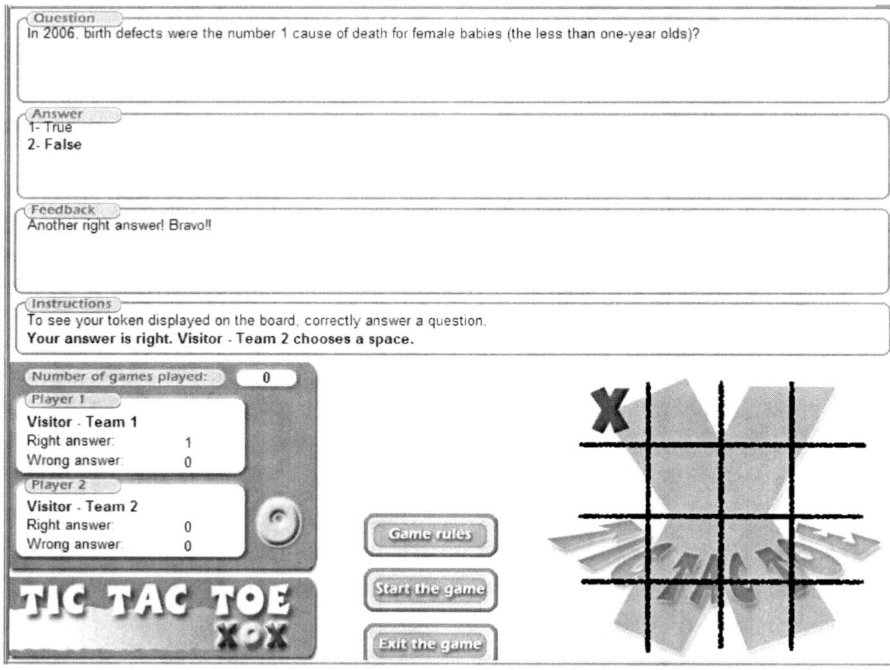

mediacy. Finally, Van Eck (2006) adds that online games offer to the "digital native" generation the opportunity to reason inductively and to increase their visual skills and capacity to relate various sources of information. A game allows the player to resolve cognitive conflicts, requiring a constant cycle of hypotheses, test and revision.

For a further discussion of the efficacy of games for learning, we refer the reader to Chapter 16.

A Game Example to Illustrate Our Definition

The game *It's going to kill you in Canada!*, adapted from Stolovitch & Thiagarajan (1980), aims to teach the main causes of mortality of Canadians according to age groups. The principle of the game is similar to that of *Tic Tac Toe*. However, to achieve the game's goal, its size and rules were modified to use a four-by-four or six-by-six square matrix, as shown in Figure 1.

The goal of the game is to align four or six identical symbols vertically, horizontally or diagonally. Two teams of players compete (interaction). To occupy a square of the matrix, a team has to state a correct cause of mortality. For example, let us imagine that the first team chooses the top left square. To occupy this compartment, they must identify the first cause of mortality for Canadians in the 1-to-24-year-old age group, which in this particular case is "accidents". Opposing teams can challenge the answer of the first team and so win the square. Various rules govern this competition. Two other teams proceed in turn in the same way.

In our experience, although the activity is completely artificial and the subject is rather dry, the participants commit to it energetically, reflecting seriously, actively exchanging hypotheses, and justifying their choices to other team members. Answers arouse reactions and the discussion quickly centers on the differences between age groups and between sexes as to the incidence of causes such as accidents, cancer, or cardiovascular illness. It is in these discussions that the educational character of the game is completely realized.

In this example, we must emphasize that the game's structure (i.e., board, player movement, rules, goal) is artificial and does not represent a reality. The learning content in the game is inspired by real facts (e.g., statistics on the causes of mortality), but they are not reproduced in a model of reality.

EDUCATIONAL SIMULATIONS

Simulations are generally grouped into two broad categories: simulations in the sciences and engineering that are used to experiment and test hypotheses, and training simulations that offer environments that simplify reality and allow learning without the risks inherent in certain "live" situations. In this chapter, we shall focus on this second type of simulation, for which the identification of key attributes seems less controversial.

Sauvé (1985, p. 109) defines the concept of simulation to include the following essential properties: (1) a model of representation, (2) simplification, (3) dynamism, and (4) reality defined as a system. This definition is echoed by Garris, Ahlers and Driskell (2002), Gorman (2000), Romme (2002), and Swanson and Ornelas (2001), who define the simulation as a simplified and dynamic, highly realistic and representative model of an element or elements of reality. Peters, Vissers and Heijne (1998) add to this definition an educational aspect, defining a simulation as a simplified model of reality used in education to study and understand reality. Borges and Baranauskas (1998) refine this definition to include computer simulation, described as computer techniques that facilitate the creation of models to experiment, investigate the consequences of building the models, and verify knowledge about the systems and phenomena which they represent.

Certain authors ascribe particular importance to the dynamic aspect of simulations, notably with respect to feedback. Gorman (2000) notes that an effective simulation puts learning into real situations, in which the learner executes actions and makes decisions with the aim of obtaining real-time feedback. Based on Alessi and Trollip (2001), Maier and Grobler (2000) also identify system feedback, in their terms, "human-computer interaction." In computer terminology, a simulation is a program which models an artificial or natural system or process, allowing the players to interact with the system, make various decisions and reflect their actions upon its results (Nurmi, 2004). Linsk and Tunney (1997) and Milrad (2002) clarify that effective feedback has to be done in a positive way so that participants reap benefits from educational simulations and transfer their experiences to other spheres of activity.

More recently, Bean (2006) defined "simulation" using three essential attributes: (1) imitation of something real, (2) knowledge that it is not real, and (3) the possibility of modifying it. He argues that imitating something real is the element that distinguishes a simulation from a game. He states that a simulation allows one to practice something outside the real situation in order to develop or strengthen experience and knowledge. The simulation is a simplification of elements of reality that can be more enriching than the real experience, notably through reduction of time and distance from details which are not necessary for the learning. A simulation differs from "real" life; it allows participants to become responsible for their own learning without any inherent danger. Bradley (2006) defines a simulation as the technique of imitating the behavior of some situation or process by means of a suitable analogous situation, especially for the purpose of study or personnel training. Yilmaz, Ören, and Aghaee (2006) identify two attributes of a simulation: (1) it is an imitation of reality, and (2) it is an experiment with dynamic models directed at a purpose. Finally, Wikipedia (2007) defines a simulation as an imitation of a reality, or a process in which the act of simulation requires the representation of the key elements of a physical or abstract system; it can also include elements which are not real or which are not yet in existence.

To identify the essential attributes of the educational simulation, we focus on authors who use the simulation for learning purposes. We identify five relevant attributes: (1) a model of the reality defined as a system; (2) a dynamic model; (3) a simplified model; (4) a faithful, accurate, and valid model; and (5) an educational purpose.

A Model of Reality Defined as a System

Reality is generally defined as an individual's perception of a system, an event, a person, or an object; perceptions can differ from one individual to another, or have varied interpretations. The reality described in a simulation represents one or more elements of a more complex real system; consequently, the choice of elements depends on what the designer chooses to put at the forefront in the educational simulation model (Swanson & Ornelas, 2001). Milrad (2002) states that a model which supports learning must simulate real situations and give feedback to the participant, allowing him to improve his knowledge of reality. The reality can take multiple forms, but in the context of an educational simulation, it generally reproduces a dynamic system (Arthur, Malone, & Nir, 2002).

A model is a mental image that is made of the world (Forrester, 1971). This simplified image of reality is based on concepts or relations which help each individual to establish his representation of the real system. Landry (2005) identifies three points of convergence which define a model: its representation, its resemblance to reality, and its simplification.

There are various forms of model representation: physical, schematic, symbolic, and role-playing. In the simulation literature the model is often defined as an abstract (digital) or concrete (analog) representation of a real system, the constituents of which are clearly defined and exhibit behavior towards a phenomenon that is similar to that of the system being studied (Arthur et al., 2002). The system defines itself through a set of elements, each of which has appropriate rules, and which have rules of interaction to achieve a goal. A system evolves in an environment which reacts and influences it (Sauvé, 1985, p. 64). Cioffi, Purcal, and Arundell (2005) state that a simulation offers a miniature version of a sphere of concrete activity in real life. Aldrich (2004) and Medley and Horne (2005) confirm this, stating that a simulation is a realistic model which can imitate authentic and appropriate scenarios taken from reality, e.g., by offering situations under pressure that allow participants to discover their feelings and ability to act.

A Dynamic Model

Identifying a critical factor which differentiates a simulation of other types of models, Swanson and Ornelas (2001) explain that simulations copy the essential elements of reality in a dynamic model and allow the participant to control this reality to study it at a desired pace and convenient time. By definition, a model is static when its components are not designed to be modified. A simulation uses a dynamic model when it reproduces, to a certain extent, the behavior of the real system in time through the movement of its components. In other words, the model is manipulated by the combination of various selected variables. An effective simulation places the learner in real situations, in which he executes actions and makes decisions with the aim of obtaining real-time feedback (Maier & Grobler, 2000).

A Simplified Model

A simplified model has a distance between itself and reality, introducing a degree of abstraction necessary to understand the system's functions and tasks (Borges & Baranauskaus, 1998). This simplification can be defined for a specific aspect of reality (Kriz & Hense, 2006) or an incomplete representation of a larger reality that reproduces its essential characteristics (Blasi & Alfonso, 2006; Garris et al., 2002). These essential characteristics are considered to be relevant by the designer for reaching the objectives for which the simulation is built, whether or not it is educational. The simulation is thus a mockup of reality, certain elements of which are removed to emphasize others in order to better capture the interest of learners or to achieve particular educational goals.

A Faithful, Accurate and Valid Model

"Fidelity" is defined as "the degree of similarity between the training situation and the operational situation which is simulated. It is a two-dimensional measurement of this similarity in terms of: (1) physical characteristics, for example visual, spatial, kinesthetic; and (2) functional characteristics, for example the informational, stimulus, and response options of the training situation" (Hays & Singer, 1989, p.50). Garris et al. (2002) add to this definition the validity of the structure, the processes explained in the simulation, and its capacity to predict reality. From a learning perspective, Claudet (1998) notes that simulations have to reproduce as faithfully as possible their situations, dilemmas, and actors in order to allow learners to practice and to transfer their experiences in "almost real" situations.

The notion of validity refers to the degree of uniformity and coherence of the specifications of the environment with respect to reality (Garris et al., 2002). Pegden, Shannon, and Sadowski (1995) state that the results obtained by the simulation have to be the same as those obtained in the real world, with the real-world system serving as the model for the simulation. Although simplified, the simulation must be accurate because its essential function is to allow a better understanding of reality. This is particularly important for an educational simulation. This notion of an accurate representation of reality is intimately connected with the previous idea of a simplification of reality. Indeed, the simpler the model, the greater the risk of falsifying the reality under study. To choose the characteristics of the reality to be included in the model, the simulation designer thus has to determine which phenomena will be accurately reproduced.

Educational Character

Research in education (including continuing education) has demonstrated that simulation supports the development of simple and complex competencies. For example, competencies required by health professionals are better acquired in an environment using varied realistic examples and supplying learning activities in situations that imitate the real world (Demetriadis, Karoulis, & Pombortis, 1999; Swanson & Ornelas, 2001; Zhu, Zhou & Yin, 2001). Simulations are particularly suited to creating such environments because they are highly interactive, can reinforce concepts and theories, and because they place an object or a system at the center of learning (Charrière & Magnin, 1998; Johnson et al., 1998).

Regardless of the type or format of the simulation, its main objective is to offer an environment that (1) supports the learner's development of mental models; (2) allows the learner to test the effectiveness of these models in explaining or predicting events in the system; (3) optimizes the discovery of relationships among variables and the confrontation of divergent approaches; and (4) offers the opportunity to create, evaluate, or demonstrate intangible ideas or dangerous experiences, or to show that which does not exist (Milrad, 2002; Wikipedia, 2007). Chapter 16 examines in more depth the efficacy of simulations for learning.

A Simulation Example to Illustrate Our Definition

In the simulation *DxR Clinician®*, developed at the University of Illinois and used worldwide, the reality is a situation requiring diagnosis and

Figure 2. Example of a clinical case simulation (source:Bryce,King, Graebner, & Myers (1998)(open access))

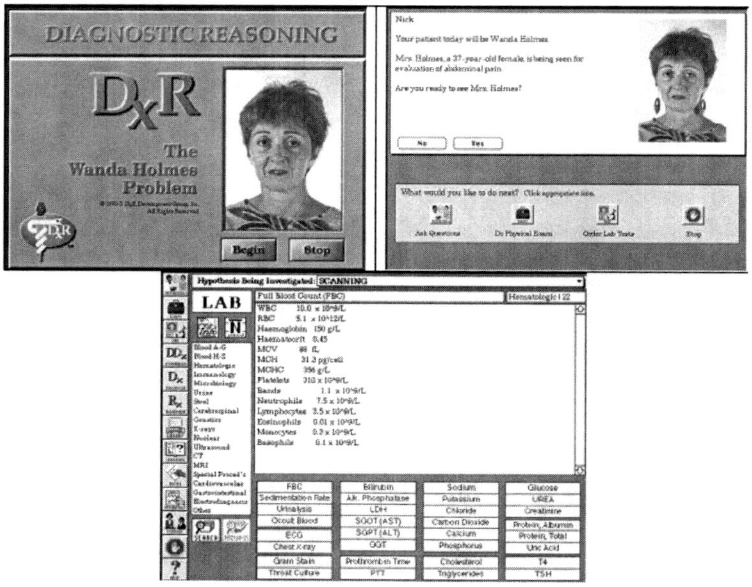

treatment of a simulated patient based on multiple data sources (e.g., X-Rays, heart test results, blood analyses) without risk to the patient (Figure 2).

The **simplified model** is constructed from a database of 260 questions on the patient's life history, 425 physical examination procedures and 440 laboratory tests. The patient's description and behaviors are very close to reality. The model dynamics translate student actions to the simulated patient, producing reactions that are representative of reality: good diagnosis and treatment lead to healing, while poor diagnosis and treatment lead to complications, degeneration, or worse. To allow the apprentice physician to learn useful lessons from the simulation, the model is accurate in that it reacts in similar ways to reality. For each case, feedback is given to the student to allow him to compare his solution with that recommended by the case author, who based the simulation on real cases (Bryce et al., 1998).

Although the simulation does not replicate an actual patient meeting, it teaches interpersonal communication skills related to patient questioning and examination while having the technological advantages of online simulation: the ability to train large numbers of students cost-effectively and without risk.

To summarize, Greenblat (1998) notes that to simulate is to model reality. Reality is easier to understand when it is stripped of some elements which make it complex, highlighting only certain aspects considered important. This exercise of simplification helps us to describe, analyze, and understand the facts, laws, and behaviors that constitute our world.

SIMULATION GAMES

This last type of activity is discussed on two tracks; some authors (e.g., Bloomer, 1973) define a simulation game as a combination of game characteristics with elements of reality, while others (e.g., Sawyer, 2004; Zyda, 2005) call the activities "serious games" rather than "simulation games."

Working generally in the domain of education, supporters of the first track combine "game" and "simulation" into a tool called a "simulation game" (Bloomer, 1973; Gillispie, 1973). Evans (1979) defines a simulation game as a combination of game elements with characteristics of a simulation. He describes a simulation game as an activity in which players, subjected to a set of rules, work to change the variables in a model to reach certain objectives. Rules define the various actions which the players can make. The model, or the structure of the simulation game, determines the results of these actions and indicates to the players how to measure their progress through the simulation game objectives.

Renaud (1987) establishes the essential properties of a simulation game, describing it as a simplified and dynamic model of a real or hypothetical system in which players are in position of competition or cooperation, rules structure player actions, and the goal is to win. Greenblat (1988) defines a simulation game by explaining that its environment and participant activities have the characteristics of a game: players have a role to perform and a goal to achieve, with actions needed to succeed, constraints to be respected and results (positive or negative) ensuing from their actions and from the other elements of the system. All this is modeled on real life. In other words, the simulation game is a hybrid involving the characteristics of a game in simulated contexts. Christopher (1999) defines a simulation game as an activity having at least two persons and four essential attributes (which she calls key components): (1) a framework, or a real but not necessarily realistic environment; (2) for each participant, a role to be played or an objective to be reached (a program), distinguished from actions of the game, which can be spontaneous; (3) rules and roles that limit player actions within the game; and finally (4) a system of scorekeeping, monitoring, or another form of "systematic observation" so that all involved have a better overall view of the game.

Finally, other authors approach the presence of elements of reality within a game without necessarily calling it a simulation game, notably Hostetter and Madison (2002), Griffiths (2002) and Usta et al. (2008). For example, Salen and Zimmerman (2004) describe a simulation game as type of game having "...a system in which the players undertake an artificial conflict, defined by rules, resulting in a quantifiable result" (p. 96). Like the previous authors, they integrate the notion of reality into the game by referring to the notion of system. They even categorize the type of system to which their definition refers as mathematical, social, or representational.

Sandford and Williamson (2005) define a simulation games as an imitation of the real word with the goal of capturing the attention of the player through immersive gameplay, attempting to motivate him through scoring, performance rating, conflict, and payoff. These motivating factors give the player an incentive to learn the mechanics of the game through exploration and experimentation in a risk-free environment. Similarly, Legendre (2005) defines the education simulation game as "a process in the form of a game which simulates a situation or an activity corresponding to an aspect of reality" (p. 815). Finally, Apperley (2006) states that a simulation incorporates a model of reality at different levels, which distinguishes it from a game and from a simulation game. The level of correspondence can vary from a strict correspondence to reality to pure whim (absence of simulation). However, strict adherence to reality kills the game, and too much freedom within the game kills the simulation. The simulation game is a genre that is difficult to define because the designer has to satisfy contradictory demands to both adhere to reality and to amuse.

The concept of *serious game,* while generally agreed to involve the use of video games for training, appears to have critical attributes characteristic of simulation games. Coming more from the domain of computer engineering and video games, supporters of the serious game define one as "a mental contest, played with a computer in accordance with specific rules, that uses entertainment to further government or corporate training, education, health, public policy, and strategic communication objectives" (Zyda, 2005, p. 26). The video game takes "any form of computer-based entertainment software, either textual or image-based, using any electronic platform such as personal computers or consoles and involving one or multiple players in a physical or networked environment" (Frasca, 2001, p. 4). In other words, a serious game is a video game with an educational component. Michael and Chen (2006) list serious game applications in the domains of politics, religion, art and industry. Sawyer (2007) has popularized the term, noting that it refers to computer applications realized by "developers, researchers, and manufacturers who see how to use using video games and technologies for purposes beyond entertainment" (video 6502, 0.32 to 0.39 minutes).

Based on an analysis of the various types of games included under the term, Alvarez (2007) defines a serious game as "a computer application, the initial intention of which is to coherently combine serious aspects including, but not limited to, education, learning, communication, and information, with playfulness stemming from the video game. Such an association, involving the implementation of a computerized 'educational scenario' including a sound and graphic presentation, a history, and appropriate rules, thus aims at going beyond simple entertainment. This distance seems to increase with the depth of the educational scenario" (p. 51). He defines the "educational scenario" as a "function," with the intention of supporting learning or practice, separately or together, the property of which is to arouse motivation to learn and the realization of which depends on its integration into a video game" (p. 109).

Finally, Wikipédia (2008b) reiterates the previous comments by defining the serious game as "a computer application which combines a serious educational, informative, communication-oriented, marketing, ideological or training intention, with playfulness stemming from a video game or a computer simulation. The vocation of a *Serious Game* is to make the serious dimension attractive by adding a framework, interaction, rules and possibly playful objectives."

It is, however, necessary to qualify our definition, since certain authors, notably Abaza and Steyn (2008) and Bergeron (2006), use the notion of serious games without including the realism aspect of simulation games. The latter defines a serious game as "an interactive computer application, with or without a significant hardware component, that has a challenging goal, is fun to play, incorporates some concept of scoring, and imparts to the user a skill, knowledge or attitude that can be applied in the real world" (page xvii).

Whether we use the term "simulation game" or "serious games" [4] to refer to these diverse applications, seven attributes are common to the various definitions. We will examine them briefly in this section, since they have already been discussed earlier in sections 1 and 2. These are: (1) a model of a real or fictitious system that is (2) simplified and (3) dynamic, with (4) players in (5) competition or cooperation, (6) rules, and (7) an educational character. We now look at these in more detail.

A Model of a Real or Fictitious, Simplified and Dynamic System

In articles on simulation games, the notion of model is identified by various terms: "imitation of real life situations" (Nassar, 2002); "mock-created" and "a core of knowledge, situations and environment similar or common to the real world" (Newmann & Twigg, 2000), and "realistic, interactive and effective environment in time" (Jacobs et al., 2003). Simulation games allow the learning of central or essential elements of a situation without being "blocked" by the more trivial aspects (Crooks & Eucker, 2001); they offer both a general view and various perspectives on the same problem (Christopher, 1999). Salen and Zimmerman (2004) state that systems included in games share at least four elements:

- objects, which represents the parts, elements, or variables of the system;
- attributes, which represent the qualities or the properties of the system or its objects;
- internal relations among objects; and
- the environment, which represents the context of the system.

Greenblat (1998) defines a simulation game as "a dynamic model of the central characteristics of a system, a process, or real or hypothetical environment," implying that less important characteristics are omitted in the model. The model thus becomes a simplified representation of reality. This simplification allows the learner to focus on certain elements of the model that might have escaped his attention in reality (Lieberman, 1998; Apkan, 2002).

"Reality" in a simulation game is emphasized by various authors (e.g., Ebner & Efron, 2005; Perez & Gallardo, 2004). Lainema and Makkonen (2003) note that the transfer of learning increases with the game's similarity to reality.

Christopher (1999) adds that the reality of a simulation game is established by the environment in which the player acts in the game. For example, the simulation game *Contagion*, identified as a serious game by its authors (de Castell & Jensen, 2006), reproduces a city threatened by disease (Figure 3). The player acts in this environment to earn points and check the epidemic.

Players

Players of varying numbers are also considered an essential attribute by Corbeil (1999). Sauvé (2004) mentions that in a simulation game, a person or a group of persons (the players) have to assume a role or make decisions. Researchers have tended to emphasize simulations involving several players and cooperation between the players, because of the impacts which this cooperation will have on learning. Cooperation intensifies learning (Romme, 2002), improves communication and teamwork skills, and fosters a spirit of community (Fertig, 2001). Morton and Tarvin (2001) intro-

Figure 3. Contagion

duce the notion of "peer teachers," where every participant contributes directly to others' learning. Crooks and Eucker (2001) advance the idea of "group knowledge" through collective problem solving: "As groups work together effectively, they arrive at synergetic insights and solutions that transcend the accumulative knowledge of individual group members" (p. 118).

In addition, researchers note that participants each play a role and that shifting of roles offers multiple perspectives (Crooks & Eucker, 2001; Gaba, Howard, Fish, Smith, & Sowb, 2001; Jacobs et al., 2003). This allows a player to experience situations not corresponding to his hierarchical level within an organization (Eaves & Flagg, 2001).

Rules

Simulation games are systems where the properties of the game emerge from the collection of rules which govern the action (Squire et al., 2003). The use of the simulation game as research mechanism into theories of behaviorism, organizational structure, analysis of information and other domains requires that we must be able to control parameters and rules, and participant roles must be well established (Yeo & Tan, 1999). A form of "systematic observation" allows players to see the entire game; this type of observation will be empirical or at least will propose a point of view outside the simulation game. Without this, the person who presents the simulation game and carries out the research will have to influence the results to confirm his hypotheses (Christopher, 1999). Therefore, game actions can be spontaneous and improvised but they must appear in a carefully built context, as when rule-based, allowing the researcher to obtain the type of behavior required for the study (Christopher, 1999).

Educational Character

A simulation game structures knowledge by supporting the creation of a mental model and development of "shared knowledge." The social aspect of knowledge structuring, in particular feedback from others, is highlighted by numerous authors. Direct feedback from learners' actions in the simulation game strengthens theoretical understanding. The simulation game offers a broad vision of concepts presented (Anderson & Stafford, 2006). Participants also become aware of the importance of the simulation game's educational objectives, and build their own "empirical database."

A simulation game develops skills in problem resolution connected with decision-making, planning, knowledge transfer, and creativity (linked to cognition), as well as in flexibility of reflection. The player learns to use systematic, operational, strategic, critical thought and analysis in the development of problem resolution skills. He also becomes more confident and displays more initiative and imagination (Kiili, 2007; Scherpereel, 2005).

Through repetition and variation of actions on realistic problems, the simulation game sets up conditions supporting information integration, ensuring acquisition, understanding and retention with regard to game content (Coles, Strickland, Padgett & Bellmoff, 2007).

Motivation is defined as the captivating aspect of simulation games, and it supports learners' receptivity and engagement (Asal, 2005). It is especially seen with, but not dependent on, simulation game computerization. Motivation shows as a positive attitude to the learning material that persists after playing the simulation game; it is influenced by competition, the simulation game's resemblance to reality, and by recognition and reward to successful players (Casile & Wheeler, 2005).

Simulation games improve face-to-face and Internet communication among learners and create a more egalitarian context for players. Players learn to trust others, work in teams, and consider others' opinions. Simulation games can make it possible to build collective knowledge (Corson, Young, McManus, & Erdem, 2006; Krolikowska,et al., 2007; Marks, Lehr & Brastow, 2006).

Knowledge transfer is a rather vague concept among the authors reviewed, described as vertical or horizontal, close or distant. Researchers examine it in the context of application of theoretical notions learned before the simulation game is played, as well as player awareness of knowledge used in a real context. Some conclude that knowledge transfer increases with the degree of reality of the simulation game's model (Coles et al., 2007; Shaffer, 2006).

Authors such as Yaoyuenyong, Hadikusumo, Ogunlana, and Siengthai (2005) emphasize the active participation encouraged by simulation games, noting that the realism present in the simulation game increases participation and favors the internalization of learning, as well as the possibility of making responsible decisions.

Other impacts are also identified. The simulation game favors development of the critical sense and of attitude change. The effects of the technology, in particular its visual aspects, improve learning in the simulation game. Also, a player's preparation before playing a simulation game has an effect on the level of his post-game learning (Kashibushi & Sakamoto, 2001).

A Simulation Game Example to Illustrate Our Definition

In the simulation game *PeaceMaker*®Impact Games, 2008), players develop their understanding of the Israel-Palestinian conflict using an environment represented as a map of Israel and of the Palestinian territories. (Figure 4), along with pictures and video documentaries describing previous key events involving the main characters—the Israeli prime minister and the Palestinian president (Figure 5). *PeaceMaker* models the **real world** and incorporates the essential attributes of simulation; players must react to Middle East events constructed from authentic documentaries. Each player can choose the degree of difficulty of the game (i.e., peace, tension, or violence). Players make economic, diplomatic, and security decisions to accomplish a peace agreement and to create a Palestinian state (**goal**) in a war which puts two people into **conflict** within a game of chance (based on actual past scenarios and events between Israel and Palestinians), within clearly defined constraints (**rules**). The more the player makes decisions which allow conflict to progress towards peace, the more the player will collect points (from popular opinion polls evaluating his efforts). Rules are added to manage the conflict, determine the end of the simulation game and the winner(s); however, all the rules must reflect the laws of the simulated system, for example, the effect of a decision on the direction of conflict.

As seen in this example, the boundary is sometimes thin between simulations and simulation games. We argue that a simulation game combines properties of both games and simulations and that the efficacy of this type of activity for learning will also tend to combine those of games and of simulations, as discussed further in Chapter 16.

CONCLUSION

According to Jones (1998), many game and simulation researchers do not distinguish between games and simulations, and even fewer distinguish between them and the concept of simulation game. "Usually the words are used interchangeably. In addition, simulation/game—a combination of game and simulation—is employed as yet another interchangeable term. The most common term is game, which seems to mean 'the event I am referring to and similar events.' Thus, game is used to cover not only simulations, simulation/games, exercises, role-plays, and puzzles but also genuine games. The result is the abolition of categories. Words and meanings are treated contemptuously.

Figure 4. PeaceMaker Environment (used with permission)

Figure 5. PeaceMaker game characters and authentic documentary (used with permission)

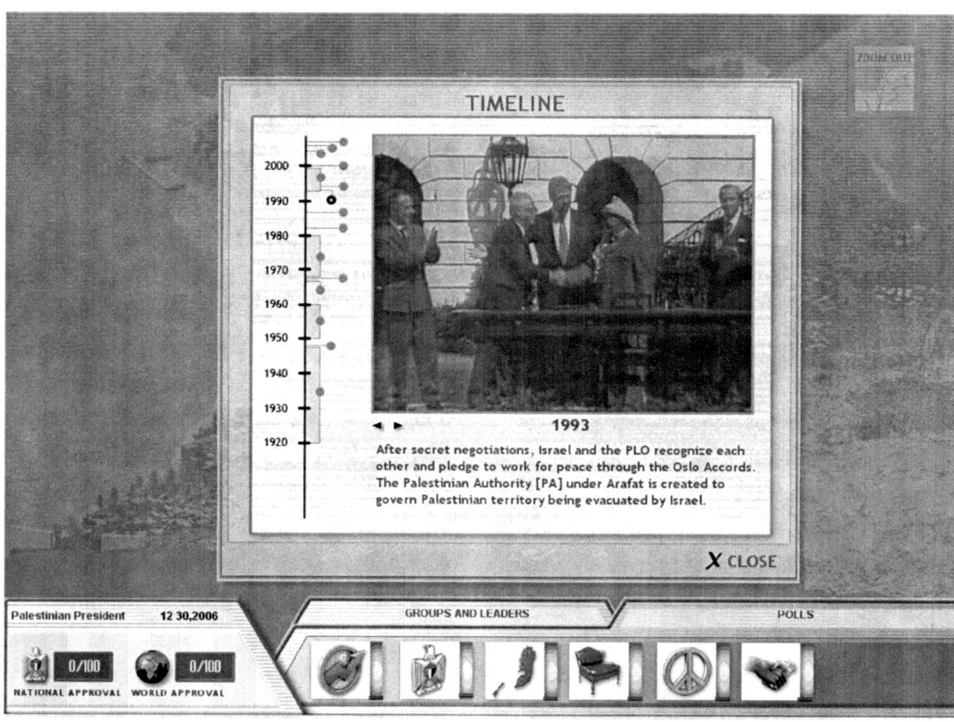

Table 1. Essential attributes of a game, simulation and simulation game

GAME	SIMULATION	SIMULATION GAME
Artificial character	**Reality defined as a system**	**Reality defined as a system**
	• Model • Simplified • Dynamic • Faithful, accurate and valid	• Model • Simplified • Dynamic
• Player(s) • Conflict (competition) • Rules • Predetermined goal (to win)		• Player(s) • Conflict (competition) • Rules • Predetermined goal (to win)

From this, it follows that most designers and facilitators are in no position to detect or prevent a clash of methodologies that damages personal relations, friendships, and reputations. They lack the concepts needed for diagnosis" (p. 165).

If one examines the essential attributes discussed here (Table 1), it is clear that a game is not a simulation. A game is a fictitious, fanciful or artificial situation in which players, put in position of conflict with others or against other forces, are governed by rules which structure their actions to reach both a game goal (win) and to achieve learning objectives. Also, the value of a game is not judged by its resemblance to reality.

In contrast, a simulation requires a simplified, dynamic and valid representation of reality defined as a system. It is distinguished from a game by its model, which is judged in comparison with reality, and by its correspondence with the system that it represents during play. A game is created without reference to reality, which is never the case for a simulation. Simulation does not inevitably imply conflict or competition, and the person who uses it does not try to win, as is the case in a game.

In a game, there is always at least one player and one winner, which is not the case for certain simulations that work without human intervention and do not aim at winning. When one or several players are a part of a simulation, interact with other simulation constituents, and have a notion of winner and loser, the concept of simulation game appears. Also, if conflict appears in a simulation as an essential attribute and not as part of its content, again the concept of simulation game surfaces. Finally, it is clear that the notions of simulation game and serious game, both of which include the critical attributes of a game together with those of a simulation, do not make it easier to classify or differentiate among various game- and simulation-related activities.

Considering the increasing interest in the educational milieu in using active learning approaches, including games, simulations, and simulation games, together with the growing role of video games for the digital generation, it becomes crucial to know the real efficacy of these activities for learning. This will help teachers to choose activities wisely according to their learning objectives. By using a conceptual classification which is based on the essential attributes of a game, simulation, and simulation game, it becomes easier for researchers to identify studies which apply to each activity and to compare results with research hypotheses, leading to better convergence and more comparable results in terms of learning efficacy.

ACKNOWLEDGMENT

We would like to thank all the students who contributed to the analysis for this study, including Mahboubeh Asgari, Shaoleh Bigdeli, Julie Bourbonnière, Pascal Bujold, Véronique Doré-Bluteau,

Catherine Dumais, Jean-Simon Marquis, Frédéric Sibomana, and Amélie Trépanier.

REFERENCES

Abaza, M., & Steyn, O. (2008). Role of computer serious games in education and training. In K. McFerrin, R. Weber, R. Carlsen, & D. A. Willis (Eds), *Proceedings of 19th International Conference Annual of Society for Information Technology & Teacher Education* (pp. 1592-1599). Chesapeake, VA: AACE.

Aldrich, C. (2004). *Simulations and the future of learning.* San Francisco: Pfeiffer.

Alessi, S., & Trollip, S. (2001*). Multimedia for learning: Methods and development* (3rd ed.). Boston, MA: Allyn & Bacon.

Alvarez, J. (2007). *Du jeu video au serious game: Approches culturelle, pragmatique et formelle* [Video games as serious games: Cultural, pragmatic and formal approaches]. Unpublished Ph.D. dissertation, Université Toulouse, Toulouse, France.

Anderson, L. R., & Stafford, S. L. (2006). Does crime pay? A classroom demonstration of monitoring and enforcement. *Southern Economic Journal*, *72*(4), 1016–1025.

Apkan, J. P. (2002). Which comes first: Computer simulation of dissection or a traditional laboratory practical method of dissection? *Electronic Journal of Science Education, 6*(4). Available at http://wolfweb.unr.edu/homepage/crowther/ejse/akpan2.pdf.

Apperley, T. H. (2006). Genre and game studies: Toward a critical approach to video game genres. *Simulation & Gaming*, *37*(1), 6–23. doi:10.1177/1046878105282278

Arthur, D., Malone, S., & Nir, O. (2002). Optimal overbooking. *The UMAP Journal*, *23*(3), 283–300.

Asakawa, T., & Gilbert, N. (2003). Synthesizing experiences: Lessons to be learned from Internet-mediated simulation games. *Simulation & Gaming*, *34*(1), 10–22. doi:10.1177/1046878102250455

Asal, V. (2005). Playing games with international relations. *International Studies Perspectives*, *6*, 359–373. doi:10.1111/j.1528-3577.2005.00213.x

Atake, K. (2003). *Using games to teach English in a Japanese junior high school.* ERIC Document Reproduction Service No. ED47948.

Bain, C., & Newton, C. (2003). Art games: Pre-service art educators construct learning experiences for the elementary art classroom. *Art Education*, *56*(5), 33–40.

Bean, M. (2006). *What is a simulation*? Staff article for Forio Business Simulations. Retrieved from http://forio.com/resources/what-is-a-simulation

Beaufils, B. (2006). *Intelligence artificielle et intelligence collective: Théorie des jeux* [Artificial intelligence and collective intelligence: Theory of games. Lille: Laboratoire d'Informatique Fondamentale de Lille. Retrieved from http://www2.lifl.fr/~beaufils/mri/theorie_des_jeux.bruno-3.pdf

Becta (2006). *Engagement and motivation in games development processes.* Research report. Available at www.becta.org.uk.

Bergeron, B. (2006). *Developing serious games.* Hingham, MA: Charles River Media.

Blasi, L., & Asfonso, B. (2006). Increasing the transfer of simulation technology from R&D into school settings: An approach to evaluation from overarching vision to individual artifact in education. *Simulation & Gaming*, *37*(2), 245–267. doi:10.1177/1046878105284449

Bloomer, J. (1973). What have simulation and gaming got to do with programmed learning and educational technology? *Programmed Learning and Educational Technology*, *10*(4), 224–234.

Borges, M. A. F., & Baranauskas, M. C. C. (1998). A user-centred approach to the design of an expert system for training. *British Journal of Educational Technology*, *29*(1), 25–34. doi:10.1111/1467-8535.00043

Bradley, P. (2006). The history of simulation in medical education and possible future directions. *Medical Education*, *40*(3), 254–262. doi:10.1111/j.1365-2929.2006.02394.x

Brand, S. (1968). *Whole earth catalog*. Menlo Park, CA: Portola Institute.

Brougère, G. (1999). Some elements relating to children's play and adult simulation/gaming . *Simulation & Gaming*, *30*(2), 134–146. doi:10.1177/104687819903000204

Bryce, D. A., King, N. J., Graebner, C. F., & Myers, J. H. (1998). Evaluation of a diagnostic reasoning program (DxR): Exploring student perceptions and addressing faculty concerns. *Journal of Interactive Media in Education, 98*(1). Available at www-jime.open.ac.uk/98/1

Casile, M., & Wheeler, J. V. (2005). The magnetic sentences industry game: A competitive in-class experience of business-level strategy. *Journal of Management Education*, *29*(5), 696–713. doi:10.1177/1052562905277315

Chamberland, G., Lavoie, L., & Marquis, D. (1995). *20 formules pédagogiques* [20 pedagogical forms]. Quebec, QC, Canada: Presses de l'Université du Québec.

Charriere, P., & Magnin, M. C. (1998). Simulations globales avec Internet: un atout majeur pour les départements de langues [Global simulations with the Internet: A major trump card for language departments]. *The French Review*, *72*(2), 320–328.

Christopher, E. M. (1999). Simulations and games as subversive activities. *Simulation & Gaming*, *30*(4), 441–455. doi:10.1177/104687819903000403

Cioffi, J., Purcal, N., & Arundell, F. (2005). A pilot study to investigate the effect of a simulation strategy on the clinical decision making of midwifery students. *The Journal of Nursing Education*, *44*(3), 131–134.

Claudet, J. G. (1998). Using multimedia case simulations for professional growth of school leaders: Administrator Case Simulation Project. *T.H.E. Journal*, *25*(11), 82–86.

Coles, C. D., Strickland, D. C., Padgett, L., & Bellmoff, L. (2007). Games that "work": Using computer games to teach alcohol-affected children about fire and street safety. *Research in Developmental Disabilities*, *28*(5), 518–530. doi:10.1016/j.ridd.2006.07.001

Corbeil, P. (1999). Learning from the children: Practical and theoretical reflections on playing and learning. *Simulation & Gaming*, *30*(2), 163–180. doi:10.1177/104687819903000206

Corson, D. L., Young, C. A., McManus, A., & Erdem, M. (2006). Overcoming managers' perceptual shortcuts through improvisational theater games. *Journal of Management Development*, *25*(3-4), 298–315. doi:10.1108/02621710610655792

Crawford, D. B. (1999). Managing the process of review: Playing "Baseball" in class. *Intervention in School and Clinic*, *35*(2), 93–95. doi:10.1177/105345129903500205

Crookall, D. (1995) Simulation/ Gaming: A guide to the literature. In D. Crookall & K. Arai (Eds.), *Simulation and gaming across disciplines and cultures: ISAGA at a watershed* (pp. 151-177). Thousand Oaks, CA: Sage Publications.

Crooks, S. M., & Eucker, T. R. (2001). "Fab 13": The learning factory. *Performance Improvement Quarterly*, *14*(2), 108–124.

de Castell, S., & Jenson, J. (2006). Contagion: A preview of content design. In *Proceedings of the IMAGINE Network Conf.*, Banff, AB, Canada.

de Freitas, S., Savill-Smith, C., & Attewell, J. (2006). *Computer games and simulations for adult learning: Case studies from practice*. London: Learning and Skills Research Centre, University of London.

De Grandmont, N. (2005). *Pédagogie du jeu... philosophie du ludique* [Game pedagogy…ludic philosophy]. Available at http://cf.geocities.com/ndegrandmont/index.htm.

Demetriadis, S., Karoulis, A., & Pombortis, A. (1999). "Graphical" jog through: Expert based methodology for user interface evaluation, applied in the case of an educational simulation interface. *Computers & Education*, *32*(4), 285–299. doi:10.1016/S0360-1315(99)00009-3

Dempsey, J. V., Haynes, L. L., Lucassen, B. A., & Casey, M. S. (2002). Forty simple computer games and what they could mean to educators. *Simulation & Gaming*, *33*(2), 157–168. doi:10.1177/1046878102332003

Dempsey, J. V., Lucassen, B., & Rasmussen, K. (1996). *The instructional gaming literature: Implications and 99 sources*. Technical Report 96-1. College of Education, University of South Alabama. Retrieved March 7, 2001, from http://www.coe.usouthal.edu/TechReports/notes.html

Eaves, R. H., & Flagg, A. J. (2001). The U.S. Air Force pilot simulated medical unit: A teaching strategy with multiple applications. *The Journal of Nursing Education*, *40*(3), 110–115.

Ebner, N., & Efron, Y. (2005, July). Using tomorrow's headlines for today's training: Creating pseudo-reality in conflict resolution simulation games. *Negotiation Journal*, *21*(3), 377–393. doi:10.1111/j.1571-9979.2005.00070.x

Evans, D. R. (1979). *Games and simulations in literacy training*. Teheran: Hulton Educational Publications.

Eyraud, E. (1998). Le jeu dans l'apprentissage d'une langue vivante: Application à l'espagnol [The game in learning a living language: Application to Spanish]. *Bulletin APLV* – Strasbourg summary no. 60. Summary of unpublished master's thesis, LCE (Langue et Civilisation Etrangère) d'espagnol, Université Paris X Nanterre. Available from http://averreman.free.fr/aplv/num60-jeu-espagnol.htm

Facer, K., Stanton, D., Joiner, R., Reid, J., Hull, R., & Kirk, D. (2004). Savannah: Mobile gaming and learning? *Journal of Computer Assisted Learning*, *20*(6), 399–409. doi:10.1111/j.1365-2729.2004.00105.x

Feinstein, A. H., Mann, S., & Corsun, D. L. (2002). Charting the experiential territory: Clarifying definitions and uses of computer simulation, games, and role play. *Journal of Management Development*, *21*(10), 732–744. doi:10.1108/02621710210448011

Fertig, G. (2001). Hard times and new deals: Teaching fifth graders about the Great Depression. *Social Education*, *65*(1), 34–40.

Forrester, J. W. (1971). *World dynamics*. Cambrige, MA: Wright Allen Press.

Frasca, G. (2001). *Videogames of the oppressed: Videogames as a mean for critical thinking and debate*. Unpublished master's thesis, Georgia Institute of Technology, Atlanta GA.

Gaba, D. M., Howard, S. K., Fish, K. J., Smith, B. E., & Sowb, Y. A. (2001). Simulation-based training in anesthesia crisis resource management (ACRM): a decade of experience. *Simulation & Gaming*, *32*(2), 175–193. doi:10.1177/104687810103200206

Garris, R., Ahlers, R., & Driskell, J. E. (2002). Games, motivation, and learning: A research and practice model. *Simulation & Gaming*, *33*(4), 441–467. doi:10.1177/1046878102238607

Gillespie, P. H. (1973). *Learning through simulation games.* Paramus, NJ: Paulist Press.

Gorman, P. J. (2000). The future of medical education is no longer blood and guts, it is bits and bytes. *American Journal of Surgery, 180*(5), 353–356. doi:10.1016/S0002-9610(00)00514-6

Gosen, J., & Wabush, J. (1999). As teachers and researchers, where do we go from here? *Simulation & Gaming, 30*(3), 292–303. doi:10.1177/104687819903000305

Gradler, M. E. (2004). Games and simulations and their relationships to learning. In D. H. Jonassen (Ed.), *Handbook of research for educational communications and technology* (2nd ed, pp. 571-581). Hillsdale, NJ: Lawrence Erlbaum Associates Inc.

Gray, A. R., Topping, K. J., & Carcary, W. B. (1998). Individual and group learning of the Highway Code: Comparing board game and traditional methods. *Educational Research, 40*(1), 45–53.

Greenblat, C. S. (1988). Designing games and simulations. Thousand Oaks, CA: Sage Publications.

Griffiths, M. (2002). The educational benefits of videogames. *Education and Health, 20*(3), 47–51.

Hays, R. T., & Singer, M. J. (1989). *Simulation fidelity in training system design: Bridging the gap between reality and training.* New York: Springer-Verlag.

Hostetter, O., & Madison, J. (2002). *Video games - The necessity of incorporating video games as part of constructivist learning, Department of Educational Technology.* Retrieved November 5, 2004 from http://www.game-research.com/art_games_contructivist.asp

Hunsaker, P. L. (2007). Using social simulations to assess and train potential leaders to make effective decisions in turbulent environments. *Career Development International, 12*(4), 341–360. doi:10.1108/13620430710756744

Impact Games. (2008). *Peacemaker game.* Retrieved April 25, 2008 from http://www.peacemakergame.com/game.php

Jacobs, J., Caudell, T., Wilks, D., Keep, M. F., Mitchell, S., Buchanan, H., et al. (2003). Integration of advanced technologies to enhance problem-based learning over distance: Project TOUCH. *The Anatomical Record (Part B: New Anatomy), 270B*, 16-22

Johnson, L. A., Wohlgemuth, B., Cameron, C. A., Caughman, F., Koertge, T., & Barna, J. (1998). Dental interactive simulations corporation (DISC): Simulations for education, continuing education, and assessment. *Journal of Dental Education, 62*(11), 919–928.

Jones, K. (1998). Hidden damage to facilitators and participants. *Simulation & Gaming, 29*(2), 165–172. doi:10.1177/1046878198292003

Juul, J. (2003). *The game, the player, the world: Looking for a heart of gameness.* Keynote presentation at DiGRA Level-up Conference, Utrecht, Belgium.

Kaptelinin, V., & Cole, M. (2001). Individual and collective activities in educational computer game playing. In T. Koschmann & R. Hall (Eds), *CSCL2 Carrying forward the conversation* (pp. 303-316). Mahwah, NJ: Lawrence Erlbaum Associates Inc.

Kashibuchi, M., & Sakamoto, A. (2001). The educational effectiveness of a simulation/game in sex education. *Simulation & Gaming, 32*(3), 331–343. doi:10.1177/104687810103200304

Kasvi, J. J. (2000). Not just fun and games - Internet games as a training medium. In P. Kymäläinen & L. Seppänen (Eds.), *Cosiga - Learning with computerised simulation games* (pp. 23-34). HUT: Espoo.

Kiili, K. (2007). Foundation for problem-based gaming. *British Journal of Educational Technology, 38*(3), 394–404. doi:10.1111/j.1467-8535.2007.00704.x

Kirriemuir, J., & McFarlane, A. (2004). *Literature review in games and learning.* Bristol, UK: NESTA Futurelab.

Kriz, W. C., & Hense, J. U. (2006). Theory-oriented evaluation for the design of and research in gaming and simulation. *Simulation & Gaming*, *37*(2), 268–283. doi:10.1177/1046878106287950

Krolikowska, K., Kronenberg, J., Maliszewska, K., Sendzimir, J., Magnuszewski, P., & Dunajski, A. (2007). Role-playing simulation as a communication tool in community dialogue: Karkonosze Mountains case study. *Simulation & Gaming*, *38*(2), 195–210. doi:10.1177/1046878107300661

Lainema, T., & Makkonen, P. (2003). Applying a constructivist approach to educational business games: Case REALGAME. *Simulation & Gaming*, *34*(1), 131–149. doi:10.1177/1046878102250601

Landry, R. (2003). La simulation sur ordinateur [Computer simulation]. In B. Gauthier (Ed), *Recherche sociale. De la problématique à la collecte de données* (pp. 469-501). Québec, QC, Canada: Presses de l'Université du Québec.

Legendre, R. (2005). *Dictionnaire actuel de l'éducation.* Montréal, QC, Canada: Guérin.

Lhôte, J.-M. (1986). *Dictionnaire des jeux de société* [Dictionary of games in society]. Paris: Flammarion.

Lieberman, D. A. (1998). *Health education video games for children and adolescents: Theory, design, and research findings.* Paper presented at the annual meeting of the International Communication Association, Jerusalem.

Linsk, N. T., & Tunney, K. (1997). Learning to care: Use of practice simulation to train health social workers. *Journal of Social Work Education*, *33*(3), 473–489.

Maier, F. H., & Grobler, A. (2000). What are we talking about? A taxonomy of computer simulations to support learning. *System Dynamics Review*, *16*(2), 135–148. doi:10.1002/1099-1727(200022)16:2<135::AID-SDR193>3.0.CO;2-P

Malone, T. W., & Lepper, M. R. (1987). Making learning fun: A taxonomy of intrinsic motivations for learning. In R. E. Snow & M. J. Farr (Eds.), *Aptitude, Learning and Instruction. Volume 3: Conative and Affective Process Analyses* (pp. 223-253). Hillsdale, NJ: Lawrence Erlbaum Associates Inc.

Marks, M., Lehr, D., & Brastow, R. (2006). Cooperation versus free riding in a threshold public goods classroom experiment. *The Journal of Economic Education*, *37*(2), 156–170. doi:10.3200/JECE.37.2.156-170

Medley, C. F., & Horne, C. (2005). Using simulation technology for undergraduate nursing education. *The Journal of Nursing Education*, *44*(1), 31–34.

Michael, D., & Chen, S. (2006). *Serious games: Games that educate, train, and inform.* Boston MA: Thomson.

Milrad, M. (2002). Using construction kits, modeling tools and system dynamics simulations to support collaborative discovery learning. *Educational Technology and Society*, *5*(4), 76–87.

Morton, P. G., & Tarvin, L. (2001). The pain game: Pain assessment, management, and related JCAHO Standards. *Journal of Continuing Education in Nursing*, *32*(5), 223–227.

Mzoughi, T., Herring, S. D., Foley, J. T., Morris, M. J., & Gilbert, P. J. (2007). WebTOP: A 3D interactive system for teaching and learning optics. *Computers & Education*, *49*(1), 110–129. doi:10.1016/j.compedu.2005.06.008

Nassar, K. (2002). Simulation gaming in construction: ER, the Equipment Replacement Game. *Journal of Construction Education*, *7*(1), 16–30.

Newmann, W. W., & Twigg, J. L. (2000). Active engagement of the intro IR student: A simulation approach. *PS: Political Science and Politic*, *33*(4), 835–842. doi:10.2307/420926

Nurmi, S. (2004). *Are simulations useful for learning?* Review article for ERNIST research project. Retrieved October 25, 2007, from http://insight-old.eun.org/eun.org2/eun/en/Insight_Research&Development/content.cfm?ov=33695&lang=en

Oblinger, D. G., & Oblinger, J. L. (2005). *Educating the net generation.* Washington, DC: Educause.

Pegden, C. D., Shannon, R. E., & Sadowski, R. P. (1995*). Introduction to simulation using SIMAN* (2nd ed.). Singapore: McGraw-Hill.

Perez, B. E., & Gallardo, A. L. (2004, September). *Empleo de juegos de simulación empresarial como herramienta para la innovación docente: Experiencia en control de gestión de la Diplomatura de Turismo* [Managerial use of simulation games as tool for teaching innovation: Experience in a tourism diploma course]. Paper presented at the Asociación Española de Profesores Universitarios de Contabilidad (ASEPUC) IV Jornada de Docencia en Contabilidad, Seville.

Peters, V., Vissers, G., & Heijne, G. (1998). The validity of games. *Simulation & Gaming*, *29*(1), 20–30. doi:10.1177/1046878198291003

Prensky, M. (2001). *Digital game-based learning.* New York and London: McGraw Hill.

Prensky, M. (2005a, December). Adopt and adapt: 21st-century schools need 21st-century technology. *Edutopia.* Available at http://www.edutopia.org/adopt-and-adapt

Prensky, M. (2005b). Engage me or enrage me: What today's learners demand. *EDUCAUSE Review*, (September-October): 60–64.

Prensky, M. (2006). *Don't bother me Mom - I'm learning!* St Paul, MN: Continuum.

Renaud, L. (1987). *Impact de certains éléments, à l'intérieur du jeu de simulation, sur les attitudes, les comportements et le transfert d'apprentissage des jeunes enfants face à la sécurité routièr* [The impact of certain simulation game elements on the attitudes, behaviors, and transfer of learning in young children about road safety]. Unpublished Ph.D. dissertation, Université de Montréal, Montreal, QC, Canada.

Rieber, L. P. (1996). Seriously considering play: Designing interactive learning environments based on blending of microworlds, simulations and games. *Educational Technology Research and Development*, *44*(1), 43–58. doi:10.1007/BF02300540

Romme, A. G. L. (2002). *Microworlds for management education and learning.* Working paper. Tilburg University, Tilburg, Netherlands. Available at http://www.unice.fr/sg/resources/articles/romme_2002_microworlds-management-ed-learning.pdf

Saethang, T., & Kee, C. C. (1998). A gaming strategy for teaching the use of critical cardiovascular drugs. *Journal of Continuing Education in Nursing*, *29*(2), 61–65.

Salen, K., & Zimmerman, E. (2004). *Rules of play.* Cambridge, MA: The MIT Press.

Salopek, J. J. (1999). Stop playing games. *Training & Development*, *53*(2), 28–38.

Sandford, R., & Williamson, B. (2005). *Games and learning.* Bristol, UK: futurelab. Available at http://www.futurelab.org.uk/resources/publications_reports_articles/handbooks/Handbook133.

Sauvé, L. (1985). *Simulation et transfert d'apprentissage. Une étude sur les niveaux de fidélité pour le transfert d'apprentissage* [Simulation and the transfer of learning: A study of the level of fidelity for the transfer of learning. Unpublished Ph.D. dissertation, University of Montreal, Montreal, QC, Canada. Sauvé, L (2004). *Guide de recension des écrits. ApprentisSAGE par les jeux* [Guide for a literature review: Learning with games].Québec, QC, Canada: SAVIE.

Sauvé, L., & Chamberland, G. (2000). *Jeux, jeux de simulation et jeux de rôle: une analyse exploratoire et pédagogique* [Games, simulation games and role-playing games: An exploratory pedogical analysis. Cours TEC 1280: Environnement d'apprentissage multimédia sur l'inforoute. Québec, QC, Canada: Télé-université. Sauvé, L., Renaud, L., Kaufman, D., & Marquis, J.-S. (2007). Distinguishing between games and simulations: A systematic review of the literature. *Journal of Educational Technology & Society, 10*(3), 244–256.

Sauvé, L., Renaud, L., Kaufman, D., Samson, D., Bluteau-Dore, V., Dumais, C., et al. (2005). *Revue systématique des écrits (1998-2004) sur les fondements conceptuels du jeu, de la simulation et du jeu de simulation.* [Systematic review of the literature (1998-2004) on the conceptual foundations of games, simulations, and simulation games]. Québec, QC, Canada: SAGE and SAVIE.

Sauvé, L., & St-Pierre, C. (2003). *Recension des écrits sur les jeux éducatifs* [Review of the literature on educational games]. Research report. Québec, QC, Canada: Télé-université and SAVIE.

Sawyer, B. (2004, April) So what are serious games? Paper presented at the Computer Game Technology Conference 2004, Toronto, ON, Canada.

Sawyer, B. (2007, May). *Ben Sawyer talks about Serious Games at E3. Online*: http://seriousgames.ning.com/video/video/show?id=630751:Video:6502 (0'32" to 0'39").

Scherpereel, C. M. (2005). Changing mental models: Business simulation exercises. *Simulation & Gaming, 36*(5), 388–403. doi:10.1177/1046878104270005

Schuytema, P. (2007). *Game design: A practical approach.* Boston, MA: Charles River Media.

Shaffer, D. W. (2006). Epistemic frames for epistemic games. *Computers & Education, 46*(3), 223–234. doi:10.1016/j.compedu.2005.11.003

Shaffer, D. W., Squire, K. R., Halverson, R., & Gee, J. P. (2004). *Video games and the future of learning,* Research report, University of Wisconsin-Madison and Academic Advanced Distributed Learning Co-Laboratory. Available at http://www.academiccolab.org/resources/gappspaper1.pdf.

Squire, K., Jenkins, H., Holland, W., Miller, H., O'Driscoll, A., & Tan, K. P. (2003). Design principles of next-generation digital gaming for education. *Educational Technology, 43*(5), 17–23.

Stolovitch, H. D. (1983). *Notes de cours: jeux de simulation* [Course notes: Simulation games]. Montreal, QC, Canada: Université de Montréal, Section de technologie éducationnelle.

Stolovitch, H. D., & Thiagarajan, S. (1980). *Frame games.* Englewood Cliffs, NJ: Educational Technology Publications.

Swanson, M. A., & Ornelas, D. (2001). Health jeopardy: A game to market school health services. *The Journal of School Nursing, 17*(3), 166–169. doi:10.1177/10598405010170030901

Usta, E., Akbas, O., Cakir, R., & Ozdemir, S. (2008). The effects of computer games on high school students' perception of confidence. In K. McFerrin et al. (Eds.), *Proceedings of Society for Information Technology and Teacher Education International Conference 2008* (pp. 1833-1840). Chesapeake, VA: AACE.

Van Eck, R. (2006). The effect of contextual pedagogical advisement and competition on middle-school students' attitude toward mathematics and mathematics instruction using a computer-based simulation game. *Journal of Computers in Mathematics and Science Teaching*, *25*(1), 165–195.

Wikipédia. (2008a). *Jeu* [Game]. Retrieved September12, 2008 from http://fr.wikipedia.org/wiki/Jeu.

Wikipédia. (2008b). *Serious Game*. Retrieved January 7, 2008 from http://fr.wikipedia.org/wiki/Serious_game

Wikipedia (2007). *Simulation*. Retrieved November 8, 2007 from http://en.wikipedia.org/wiki/Simulation

Wolfe, J., & Crookall, D. (1998). Developing a scientific knowledge of simulation/gaming. *Simulation & Gaming*, *29*(1), 7–19. doi:10.1177/1046878198291002

Yaoyuenyong, C., Hadikusumo, B. H. W., Ogunlana, S. O., & Siengthai, S. (2005). Virtual construction negotiation game – An interactive learning tool for project management negotiation skill training. *International Journal of Business & Management Education*, *13*(2), 21–36.

Yeo, G. K., & Tan, S. T. (1999). Toward a multilingual, experiential environment for learning decision technology. *Simulation & Gaming*, *30*(1), 70–82. doi:10.1177/104687819903000108

Yilmaz, L., Ören, T., & Aghaee, N.-G. (2006). Intelligent agents, simulation and gaming. *Simulation & Gaming*, *37*(3), 339–349. doi:10.1177/1046878106289089

Zhu, H., Zhou, X., & Yin, B. (2001). Visible simulation in medical education: Notes and discussion. *Simulation & Gaming*, *3*(3), 362–369. doi:10.1177/104687810103200306

Zyda, M. (2005). From visual simulation to virtual reality to games. *Computer*, *38*(9), 25–32. doi:10.1109/MC.2005.297

ADDITIONAL READING

Sauvé, L., Renaud, L., Kaufman, D., Samson, D., Bluteau-Dore, V., Dumais, C., et al. (2005). *Revue systématique des écrits (1998-2004) sur les fondements conceptuels du jeu, de la simulation et du jeu de simulation.* [Systematic review of the literature (1998-2004) on the conceptual foundations of games, simulations, and simulation games]. Québec, QC, Canada: SAGE and SAVIE.

Sauvé, L., Renaud, L., Kaufman, D., & Sibomana, F. (2008). *Revue systématique des écrits (1998-2008) sur les impacts du jeu, de la simulation et du jeu de simulation sur l'apprentissage: rapport final*. [Systematic review on the impact of games, simulations, and simulation games on learning: Final report] (Research report). Québec, QC, Canada: SAGE and SAVIE.

KEY TERMS AND DEFINITIONS

Conflict: Represented in a game by dynamic, human or computer-controlled obstacles that prevent the easy realization of the objective by the player(s). The obstacles must be active, even intelligent, to create a conflict and give the illusion of a response determined by player actions.

Educational Game: A fictitious, fantasy or imaginary situation in which players, placed in conflict with others or assembled in a team against an external opponent, are governed by rules determining their actions with a view to achieving learning objectives and a goal determined by the game, either to win or to seek revenge.

Fidelity: The degree of similarity between the training situation and the operational situation which is simulated. It is a two dimensional measurement of this similarity in terms of: (1) the physical characteristics, for example visual, spatial, kinesthetic, etc; and (2) the functional characteristics, for example the informational, stimulus, and response options of the training situation.

Reality: Generally defined as an individual's perception of a system, an event, a person, or an object. Perceptions can differ from one individual to another, or have varied interpretations.

Rules: A set of simple or complex conditions that describe the relations between players and the game environment. They specify the extent and nature of the players' justifiable actions, and establish the sequence and structure in which participant actions will take place.

Serious Game: A mental contest, played with a computer in accordance with specific rules, which uses entertainment to further government or corporate training, education, health, public policy, and strategic communication objectives.

Simulation: A simplified, dynamic, and accurate representation of a reality, represented as a system.

Simulation Game: A simplified and dynamic model of a real or hypothetical system in which players are in position of competition or cooperation, rules structure player actions, and the goal is to win.

ENDNOTES

1 In this scheme, "game" is generally defined with the following characteristics: 1) it is usually voluntary; 2) it is intrinsically motivating; 3) it involves active and often physical engagement; and 4) it is distinguished from other activities by having an imaginary quality (Rieber, 1996).

2 "Simulation" is a digital technique for carrying out experiments on a computer using models that describe sequentially the behavior of real systems (Landry, 2003).

3 Citing Kaptelinin and Cole (2001) and Becta (2006), Usta et al. (2008) list these different types of games: action games, adventure games, fight games, platform games (the characters in the game run on or along the platform and jump), knowledge games, simulation /modeling /roleplay games (for instance, management and strategy games), drill-and-practice games, logical games and mathematical games.

4 Certain supporters of serious games might refute that these are simulation games. However, their definition and attributes allow us to integrate them into the simulation game category.

Chapter 2
Effective Educational Games

Louise Sauvé
Télé-université, Canada

ABSTRACT

This chapter argues that although educational games have not always been taken seriously, they are forms of play that offer strong interactive communication support and should be a component of 21st century education. It reports on a systematic review of studies highlighting the game elements that support motivation and learning: repetition, learning content segmentation, feedback, challenge and competition, active participation in learning, teamwork, and interaction, and illustrates these mechanisms with examples.

INTRODUCTION

The game as a learning tool was first defended by thinkers such as Aristotle and Plato. It is to the latter that we owe this advice to teachers: "Do not use violence on children, but rather see that they educate themselves through play" (Rabecq-Maillard, 1969, p. 4). "It is interesting to note that the Romans gave to *school* the same name that they game to *game*, that is *ludus*." (Chamberland & Provost, 1996, p. 8).

Educational games are not always taken seriously. While they do involve play, today's games are highly interactive, communication-supported tools that should not be dismissed in 21st -century education. For example, their sound, image and animation capabilities are very useful for illustrating complex situations while maintaining playfulness. In addition, online games offer to the digital generation opportunities to practice inductive reasoning, increase visual skills, and improve their capacity to integrate information from various sources. Games also allow players to resolve cognitive conflicts through a constant cycle of hypothesis, testing and revision, (Van Eck, 2006). It appears that there are numerous game mechanisms that can lead to learning.

This chapter presents a synthesis of studies highlighting game characteristics which motivate

DOI: 10.4018/978-1-61520-731-2.ch002

and support learning, responding to the cognitive styles of digital-era students. These characteristics include, notably: practice, segmentation of learning content, feedback, competition and challenge, active learner participation, teamwork, and interaction. These mechanisms make possible the use of a socioconstructivist pedagogy (De Grandmont, 2005), as outlined in Quebec's new primary and secondary education program.

The notion of "game," along with simulation and simulation game, is defined and discussed in Chapter 1 of this volume. This chapter focuses specifically on games, with emphasis on those delivered online. Unless noted otherwise, our examples are frame games developed for the *Carrefour virtuel de jeux éducatifs / Educational Games Central* (http://egc.savie.ca) at la Société pour l'Apprentissage à VIE (SAVIE) (www.savie.qc.ca).

DEFINITIONS

Before discussing game mechanisms and learning, we define what we understand by learning and motivation.

Learning

"Game" and "learning" are terms that are regularly linked in the research literature. Games are studied from multiple perspectives in connection with knowledge acquisition and transfer; they are considered as favoring learning (described as tools for active participation by the learner, knowledge structuring and integration, information gathering and communication, etc.), or, conversely, as obstacles to learning. To unravel this controversy, we must understand what we mean by learning through games.

Learning is the acquisition of knowledge, attitudes and skills with the help of experience, practice, or study. Learning is a particularly complex act; a learning situation includes not only a specific environment, but also a person's individual characteristics. Learning means not only modifying behavior, but also, and especially, changing the meaning which we give to our experience. Cognitive psychology helps us to better understand the active role played by the person in a learning situation, as much in the effectiveness of his learning strategies as in the representations used to give meaning to activity. The socioconstructivist approach also demonstrates the important roles of both knowledge organization in memory and social interactions in the elaboration of new knowledge. All these aspects of learning are supported in an effective educational game.

INTERNAL AND EXTERNAL CONDITIONS

Among various learning activities, the game joins the case study, simulation, simulation game, project approach, and collaborative learning as an active educational method. Game mechanisms can create powerful conditions for individual learning. Motivation is the preliminary condition and foundation for the learner's engagement in the learning process; we examine motivation in more detail below. Aside from motivation, two sets of conditions for learning are important: internal and external (Sauvé & Chamberland, 2000).

Internal Conditions

Three sets of internal conditions refer to factors that the learner brings to the learning process. First are the user's *prior knowledge and experience,* which provide knowledge, competencies, and behaviors that must be exploited for learning. The more a game requires the learner to draw from and apply this prior learning, the more knowledge will be strengthened. For example, a game on sexually transmitted infections will appeal to the player's knowledge and experience to answer various closed and open questions dealing with the subject, thereby allowing the player to move on the game board and to win points and possibly the entire game. Throughout the game play, learners will consider as more useful the knowledge that allows them to succeed in the game, which will have the effect of strengthening their acquired knowledge

Second are *intellectual skills* that must be exercised. Intellectual skills are frequently refined and improved when used in a game. For example, games offer situations or problems to be resolved that stimulate intellectual skills during game play; the repeated challenge of using these skills helps to assure the player's energetic participation.

A third set of internal conditions is the *learning strategies* that the player develops as she learns, which allow her to approach and gain the most from new situations. A game can establish a rich environment with stimuli new to the learner, contributing to the development of new learning strategies. To the extent that the learner plays and acquires new knowledge and skills, she realizes that she learns in ways other than the usual lecture, listening, note taking, etc. The game thus contributes to widening the player's repertoire of learning strategies, and to make her aware of other strategies, notably metacognitive ones.

External Conditions

Four external conditions activate and support the internal conditions. First, repetition, or the practice of exercises and similar tasks, is doubtless one of the best ways to help a learner to retain information. Reread the previous sentence five times—there is a good chance that you will remember it! On the other hand, repetition generally engenders boredom. A game is a rare occasion to use the mechanism of repetition without monotony. Frequently in a game the player must repeat the same information, procedure, or reasoning, and accumulated points or improved position are powerful incentives that overcome the avoidance usually associated with practice.

Second, the positive reinforcement that follows successful learning produces a pleasant and satisfactory effect for the learner. Games generally contain numerous reinforcement mechanisms that encourage learning; for example, the accumulation of points, bonuses, or resources increases the respect toward and self-confidence of players, which helps them to stay interested in game play. The opposite is also true, that is, errors committed during a game often cause negative reinforcement (loss of points or other resources). Negative reinforcement is recognized as less effective than positive reinforcement, because of loss of self-respect. However, in the artificial context of an educational game, negative reinforcement is perceived with a certain detachment that mitigates the loss of self respect.

Third, feedback is a mechanism that indicates whether or not an answer is satisfactory. Precise feedback is very effective, while vague feedback is of limited usefulness. Digital games set up feedback mechanisms that assure precision and immediacy, which are ideal for learning.

Fourth, dividing content into small segments is more effective than concentrated learning (Le Ny, 1968). Content segmentation helps learners understand complexity. Educational games usually proceed by dividing learning content into questions or small modules that draw the player's attention to key elements of the material, contributing to learning quality and retention.

MOTIVATION

Games are intrinsically rewarding (Sauvé & Chamberland, 2000); that is, the player finds pleasure in the activity, independent of the learning gains which he might achieve. This distinguishes games from other educational forms, which are often seen by the learner as monotonous, even tiring. We often observe that a learner who is interested in a certain subject is annoyed by the way teachers approach it (e.g., the expert's lecture). A game sometimes achieves the opposite, attracting initially-resistant learners to a given subject. Play is, in itself, a satisfying activity.

According to Sauvé and Viau (2002), motivation is defined as "…the effort or energy that the person is ready to expend to carry out a given learning task" (p.9). Motivation to learn depends on the importance which the learner attaches to the final goal, her interest in the task, and her perception of its difficulty. This definition is repeated by most authors who study games in a learning context. Griffin and Butler (2005), as well as Moyer and Bolyard (2003), state that this feeling of commitment is enhanced by learners' active involvement; a game arouses in them the desire to persevere and to carry out the task, which in turn motivates them to learn. But what are the game mechanisms that stimulate motivation?

First of all, the pleasure offered by the game and the excitement and enthusiasm with which players participate are important factors in motivating learners to play (Lawrence, 2004). Also, games' pleasant atmosphere, their capacity to reduce stress, and the tendency of team games to encourage teamwork and collaboration all arouse motivation. Finally, the challenge contained in games, as well as their competitive aspect, are elements that increase motivation to learn (Asakawa & Gilbert, 2003).

In addition to these elements we have the "domino" effect of a game: players are motivated to learn because their opponents are doing the same. Also, feedback is considered by Virvou, Katsionis and Manos (2005) as an important motivational condition for learning in digital games. Finally, Sedig (2007) identifies four variables that favor intrinsic motivation, called " flow," in a mathematics game: interest, control, challenge and attention.

In summary, games favor motivation for learning in various ways. Research has clearly demonstrated that games positively support players' respect and self-confidence, pleasure in play, and commitment as well as the desire to persevere and to carry out a task. Various game mechanisms arousing this motivation are examined later in this chapter, including challenge and competition, active participation in the game, teamwork, the degree of interaction offered by the game, and feedback.

REPETITION

Repetition is found in most applications with exercises, in which questions are often introduced in the form of repetitive tasks to be carried out, e.g., to answer multiple choice questions, complete sentences, or match objects correctly. We have all experienced repetition when learning spelling or arithmetic. However, repetition quickly means monotony, stifling motivation. Games offer an opportunity to take advantage of repetition without the usual inconveniences; indeed, chance and rivalry in a game counter the boredom usually associated with repetition.

Unlike drills and other forms of systematic repetition, games contain an element of unpredictable, disrupted repetition (as when drawing cards) that includes an unexpected element. To ensure this repetition, it is necessary to set up questions or learning activities in a game so that they often return to the same material, for example, by limiting the number of questions or activities. Then a player who sees the same information reappearing recognizes it and considers it useful for the purpose of progress in the game. Outside the play context, this redundancy would be boring to the learner.

The game is thus an ideal context for learning based on repetition. This modality in a game corresponds particularly to the phase of operation ("de rodage") described by Brien (2006). During this phase, recently acquired knowledge must be used to anchor it more solidly in memory and give it some permanence.

The game *Concentration* consists in making pairs from a series of cards which are arranged in rows with hidden faces. In turn, each player

Figure 1. Cards in the game Mémor-os

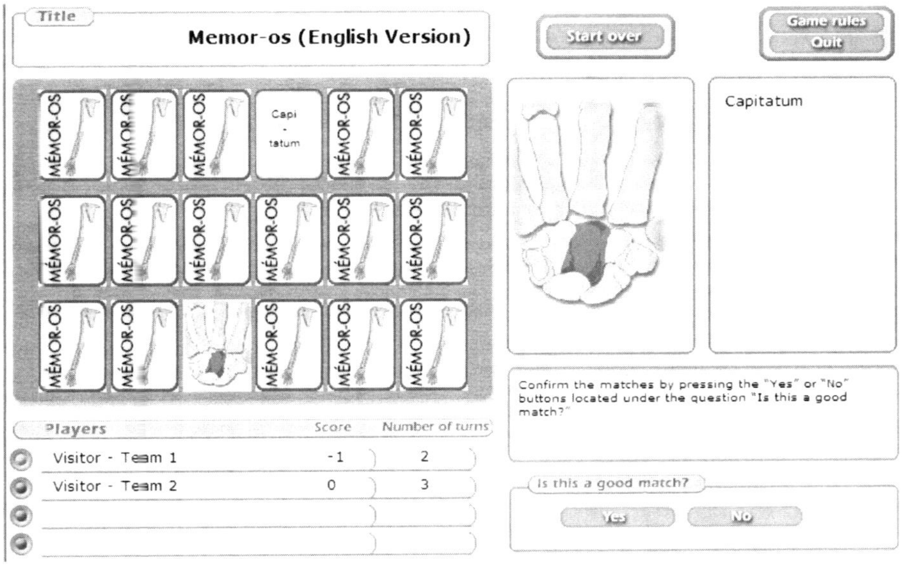

turns two cards and takes the pair if both cards are identical. In the *Educational Games Central* adaptation of this game, *Mémor-os*, every card has an equivalent, rather than a twin, providing a typical game application for repetition. This example works, for example, in learning the names of each bone of the human skeleton. At the start, there is a large component of chance in this game; learners turn several cards before a pair is formed. However, a learner gains an advantage by remembering the cards which were unsuccessfully turned. The information recurs; the card with the term "Phalange proximale" will be turned over perhaps three or four times before being correctly associated with the corresponding illustration (Figure 1). This repetition helps to reinforce the relationship between the term and the bone in the player's memory.

CONTENT SEGMENTATION

Studies show that an appropriate balance between game time and learning time is needed to maintain motivation (Sauvé & Samson, 2004). It is common, however, for designers of educational games to reduce game time in favor of learning activities, demotivating learners, particularly those of the "game generation."

Few studies on games consider the notion of encapsulating content. In general, educational game designers follow these steps to segment the content of an educational game:

- Determine the subject content to teach according to the general learning objective and the target population.
- Define the major content segments according to specific learning objectives and the target population.
- Describe the content elements in relation to the specific objectives and the larger segments, in the form of a table or flowchart.
- Formulate questions or items for every content element.

To illustrate this, we present an example of the steps in structuring game content for an online educational game about sexually transmitted infections called *STIs: Stopping the Transmission*.

Table 1. Content segmentation example

Segment	Content Elements
Prevention	Information about how to break the STI cycle of transmission: types of condoms, identification of at-risk behavior and effective behavior
Prevalence	State of situation on the number infected or carrying an STI; information about infection factors—their nature, their visible or invisible effects
Transmission	Information about how various infections can be sexually transmitted. This part allows players to question myths that are wide-spread and well-anchored in the general population.
Treatment	Information about how to be cured (or to live with) STIs: how to prevent their transmission—for example, to refrain from engaging in certain high-risk behaviors —and about the actions to be taken when a person believes that she has been exposed to an infection

First, the subject content was determined in with regard to the target population, teenagers from 14 to 17 years old who typically misunderstand certain sexually transmitted infections (STIs) and their treatment. Therefore, the young people who will be playing the game should develop an understanding of the problem of sexually transmitted infections, their prevalence, their transmission, their treatment, and ways to prevent them.

Second, to attain the general learning objective, the game helps players identify the risks of contracting an STI and learn strategies for self-protection, understand the significance of STIs in order to to sensitize them to the importance of sexual protection for their own health and that of others, address misunderstandings and myths that could compromise healthy behavior, and learn ways of preventing and treating these infections. The game content underlying these four specific objectives was therefore grouped into the categories of prevention, prevalence, transmission, and treatment.

Third, for each part of the game, content elements were described in relation to the specific objectives and the larger segments (Table 1).

Fourth, for every content element, questions or game items were formulated It was important to vary the type and degree of difficulty of questions in the game: true/ false, multiple choice with one or several answers, a logical sequence, short or long open questions, questions involving performance, overview, role play, etc. (Figure 2).

For the game *STIs: Stopping the Transmission*, the authors used 84 questions grouped into the four major content categories.

FEEDBACK

In an educational game, the player is also a learner, who acts to realize learning goals and for whom a feedback mechanism must be in place so that he can validate his learning. This feedback must be immediate, well adjusted to the learner's actions, and consistent with the content to be learned (Lemay, 2008). According to social cognitive theory (Bandura, 1977), humans show a variety of behaviors which are learned from events caused by outside stimuli, decoded by an internal information system, and strengthened by feedback. If this feedback is received immediately following an answer and is directly connected to behavior, the individual will adjust his behavior. Also, the feedback must be continuing; it must follow the learner's answer at once, often creating the next stimulus to which he has to react, creating a continuous flow stimulus and answers. In a game, feedback is omnipresent and continually responsive to player actions, tactics, and strategies (ErgoLab, 2003; Koster, 2004).

Inspired by the definition provided by Rodet (2000) and adapted by Sauvé and Chamberland (2000), we describe effective feedback as follows: it comes in response to an action by the

Figure 2. Types of questions on the transmission of STIs

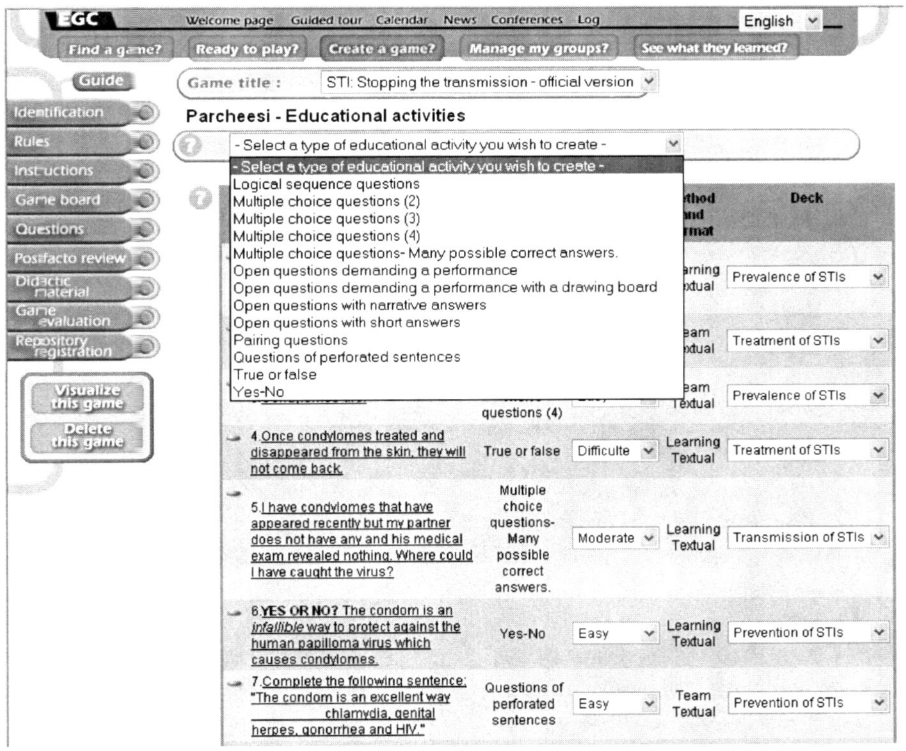

learner, suggests a correction, and expresses a value judgment which should be well-reasoned and argued. Its purpose is to help the learner deepen her knowledge or change her behavior and to show her how to do so. Feedback in a game must allow the learner to measure her progress towards attaining the learning objectives (Schwabe & Göth, 2005). Feedback has two components (Paquelin, 2002):

- *Verification* gives a judgment of exactness or error. It allows the user to verify the appropriateness of her action.
- *Explanation* brings additional information (Kulhavy & Stock, 1989; Pridemore & Klein, 1991). When an explanation is given, the emphasis is placed on understanding and correcting errors through acquiring new declarative knowledge. This feedback role arises from a constructivist concept of learning.

Effective feedback stimulates learners to draw their own conclusions. Educational games must thus integrate feedback mechanisms in the form of messages which immediately respond to player actions under specific conditions (Shneiderman, 2004; Woltjer, 2005). Let us now examine types of feedback that are useful in a game.

Feedback Connected to Navigation

This feedback allows the player to see the result of his action in the game:

- If the player points at or clicks an element or an object, the game generates a sign (i.e., text, sound or visual) allowing him to see the result of the action, such as: movement of a token, movement of the die, a button that lights up or changes color when activated, reaction of an avatar, or posting of a new page.

Figure 3. Feedback example recommending complementary references in the game 'Motivation in Games!'

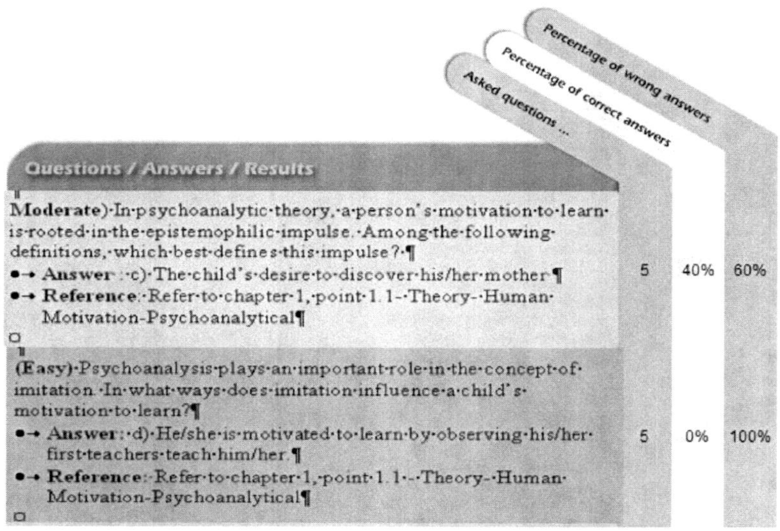

- If a player action is against the game rules, instructions or an error message appear. Error messages are rarely written or revised by the game designer, however, it is necessary to pay particular attention to these types of messages, which return the user to the desired path. In our *Educational Games Central* games, for example, error messages are often revised after testing to identify incorrect operations and indicate correct ways of proceeding, these often being simpler than the maneuvers that led the user to erroneous actions.

Just-in-time Feedback Linked to Each Learning Task

This feedback allows the player to identify successful activities and those where he failed. Examples include:

- text, visual or sound feedback on the contents of a learning activity which corrects and comments on the player's incorrect answer;
- feedback on the content of a learning activity, offering further information on a player's correct answer;
- feedback at the end of the game, which allows the learner to examine her results with regard to the game's learning activities and provides an opportunity to review missed material through easily accessible online resources (Figure 3).

Motivational Feedback

Feedback not only highlights errors; it can also include encouragement and validation of successful learning. This type of feedback should be included to maintain the user's motivation which, according to Viau (1994), is the central element influencing learning effectiveness. Messages could include, for example, a visual or sound item on the "success or failure" results of every learning activity in the shape of a thumb raised or pointing downward (Figure 4), a positive or negative sound, or points added to the player's score.

Figure 4. Example of iconographic feedback

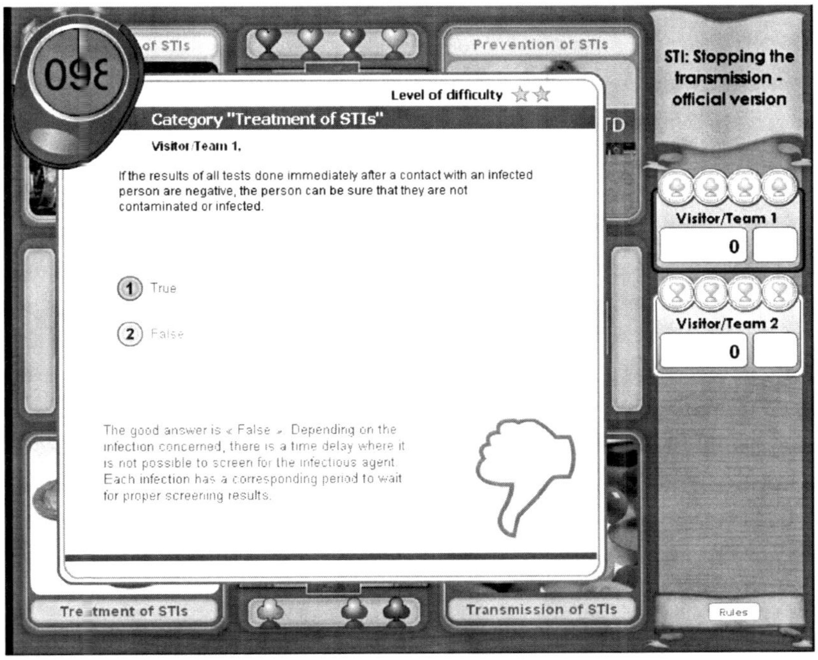

Peer Feedback on the Experience and Learning Results

Returning an oral or written synthesis to the learner augments his learning (Petranek, 2000) by allowing him to reflect on the activity and his own feelings. "the phase of returning a synthesis is essential and must not be omitted because most of the learning happens at this moment" (Medley & Horne, 2005, p. 32). "In the discussion which follows the activity *(debriefing)*, the performance of the teams is compared and the participants are invited to describe the strategies which they followed. It leads them to a clear understanding of the meaning of the 'critical path' and the impact of the activities arising on the critical path" (Van Houcke, Vereecke, & Gemmel, 2005, p. 55).

In an educational game, it is necessary to reserve5-10% of the total duration of the game for synthesis (debriefing), which includes the following elements:

- *catharsis,* in order to release tensions, feelings, perceptions, attitudes, and reactions of the participants about the experience. During this stage, players freely express their feelings and react with their emotions. No one is forced to do so, but all must feel that they have the opportunity.
- *description* of both the learning content and the lived experience, in other words, what took place, when, and how. Through lived experience, we understand what the learners achieved, recapitulating the gameplay experience and transferring it into a solidly integrated element of the participant's structured consciousness. The recapitulation includes: the initial perception of the participants on the progress of the game and their own progress; the results achieved, including the acquisition of knowledge, attitudes and skills; factual, psychological and symbolic descriptions

of what took place in the game; problems experienced; and the relations of cause and effect.

- *analysis* that establishes the relationship between the game's learning contents, learners' prior knowledge, and knowledge developed through learning in the game.
- *generalization,* leading learners to draw general conclusions on the lived experience and to release some reflections, better integrating the learning in their context.
- *critique* of the game is sometimes added as the last stage of debriefing. It is especially useful when a game is being tested with a sample of the learners for which it was conceived (see Chapter 26). Feedback offers to the teacher who has adapted a frame game in a new educational context the opportunity to watch player behavior in the game, obtain their suggestions and proposals to perfect the game (formative evaluation), and assess their interest and desire to continue this type of experience;

Feedback on the Result of Learning Activities

To increase retention and long-term learning, an educational game must integrate a feedback mechanism which offers to each learner a summary of the results that she obtained in the game's learning activities, as well as an outline of content or learning resources for revisiting material that was not successfully learned.

In summary, any online educational game must include feedback on the player's actions to facilitate learning and maintain learners' commitment to the tasks to be completed in the game. Unfortunately, we have found that few designers of digital educational games include learning-related feedback mechanisms (Sauvé et al., 2005).

COMPETITION AND CHALLENGE

In digital games, elements of competition and challenge are present in different degrees. They motivate learners to play their roles in game and to make decisions (Facer et al., 2004).

Competition is less intense in games involving only a single player (who opposes herself to improve her performance) than in games with several players (who compete to be the first to reach the same goal). In solitary games, conflict takes the shape of a confrontation between the player and fate (*Solitaire*, *Dice*, *Roulette*, etc.) or another opponent such as the computer possessing a decision algorithm. Challenge occurs when the player's actions engender reactions from an opponent, creating a competition or a fight (Kirriemur & MacFarlane, 2004).

During our analysis (Sauvé et al., 2005), we noticed that the designers of digital educational games often reduce or eliminate chance in their games, so that players' actions are concentrated on learning a given subject. This process results in a lack of motivation in learners toward the game as the means of learning. To avoid this type of situation, various mechanisms were found in the literature (Sauvé, Renaud, Kaufman, & Sibomana, 2008b) and validated (Sauvé, Renaud & Hanca, 2008a) to ensure challenge and healthy competition in online educational games.

Integrating Game Goals with Attaining New Levels, Multiple Environments or Paths

Levels and multiple game environments are a central element of video games. Access to a new level represents achievement for the player. The global purpose of the game is broken into more limited objectives, maintaining the motivation of player as he achieves each in turn. Typically, levels offer growing challenges as the player reaches new ones. Indeed, as the player increases his competence, new levels or environments suggest new

Figure 5. Example of a game with two different paths

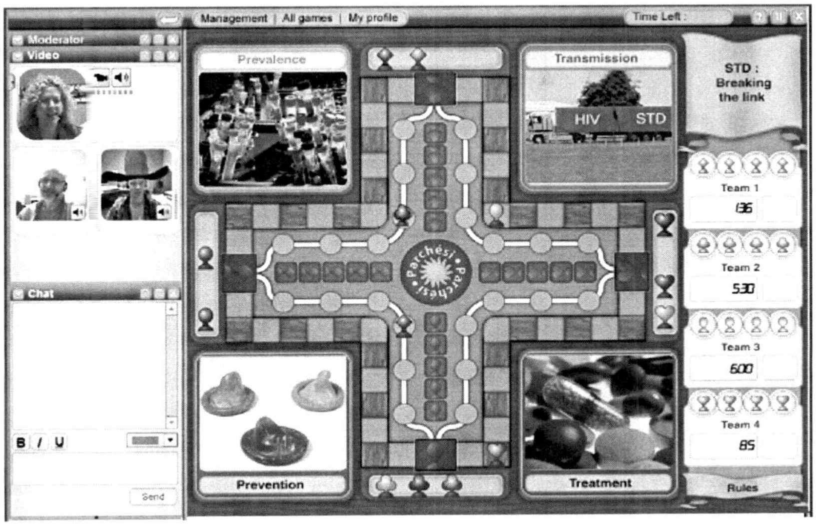

challenges at the limit of her skills. There is no doubt that this phenomenon of difficult-to-access levels in educational games will have the same psychological effect on learners as on players of video games. As they stumble on a difficulty several times, achievement of the following level seems at first impossible, then becomes practically an obsession, following which the player reaches this new landing the first time, then again, then repeatedly, with surprising ease.

Multiple paths are also present in table games. Some allow players to complete a route more quickly, to win the game (Figure 5). Others extend a player's path by returning him to the starting point. Shorter paths are generally accessed by formulating a correct answer or by executing an expected action. A correct answer allows the player to take the fast route, while an incorrect answer moves the token to a slower route.

Hiding Information

Players' interest in video games is often based on the phenomenon of hidden information. Unlike most conventional games, for which players have to know the rules before beginning the game, many video games have few or no explicit rules; rules must be deduced by the player in the course of game play. Learning the rules which govern the game becomes a process of continuous investigation, during which the player elaborates hypotheses, verifies their value, adjusts the hypothesis, and tests it again until he comes to a complete understanding of the game's rules. This method of discovery is very attractive to the player.

Maintaining a Sense of Uncertainty About the Game's Outcome

Facing a partner who is too strong or too weak, or viewing a game's learning activities as too difficult or too easy, reduces the game's challenge and the pleasure arising from uncertainty about the game's outcome. Certain conditions help to make an educational game's challenge similar to that of video games: the learning content must take into account the prior knowledge of its intended learners, and its learning activities must offer varying degrees of difficulty that encourage the participation of all players, even those without much knowledge of the subject of the game (Salen & Zimmerman, 2005).

Mechanisms must also be included to ensure that the end of the game remains uncertain. Examples include:

- controlled execution of unpredictable events, for example, cards for good luck and adversity distributed randomly by the computer system to reduce the differences between opponents who are sometimes too strong or too weak;
- varying the number of points to be won in a learning activity in the game for players who have weaker scores;
- fixing the end of a part of the game by predetermining a time period added to the highest score.

A succession of unexpected, randomly-linked situations can play a regulating role in a game (Falstein, 2004). For example, within a certain game level, chance can be non-existent, while in a subsequent level chance intervenes, making the task of the player more difficult. In this respect, the importance of the place granted a player at random becomes a contributory element in the progress of the game. If chance has a role in ending a game, even the least-endowed with a group, those who have few occasions to excel in other school contexts, can emerge as winners and so know an hour of glory.

Reinforcement Mechanisms

A well-conceived educational game offers a player multiple occasions to make choices and relevant decisions with regard to learning objectives. Rules of the game leading to accumulated points, advancing or retreating on the game path, and activities that help learners evaluate their own rate of success while completing a given task, are examples of reinforcement that push the player to adopt desired behavior and avoid making errors (Goldenberg, Andrusyszyn & Iwasiw, 2005).

These reinforcements allow the learner to know exactly where in the game she is and where she is going. Online digital games represent a formidable breakthrough in the speed and precision of reinforcement available to the player. The richness of visual and sound stimuli and their high level of interactivity are major trump cards for these types of games. In these games, the player not only has to react correctly to the environment into which she is plunged, but also must deduce for herself most of the laws which govern the game. Although our research did not explore this specific game aspect, it is logical to suppose that the capacity of the individuals to handle several sets of information simultaneously and to respond appropriately is favored.

Contrary to most other educational forms, games provide immediate and frequent reinforcement. For example, the learner is informed at once about the quality of his performance, rather than after a delay as with exams. This real-time feedback is a continual source of reinforcement, which the player uses to refine decisions and strategy.

Our game *Thin or Fat?,* an educational version of *Snakes and Ladders,* perfectly illustrates the concept of immediate reinforcement (Figure 6). The player's arrival in a square with the tail of a snake requires the player to answer a question. If the answer is correct, the player moves her token to the head of the snake (always higher than the tail, in this case), which constitutes positive reinforcement through an immediate gain in the race toward the final square. The game also has negative reinforcement; a player falling on a square with a snake's head must answer a question; a good answer allows the player to remain on the spot but a bad answer will cause her to slide towards the tail of the snake—an immediate negative reinforcement.

Figure 6. Example of the game Thin or Fat?, adapted from Snakes and Ladders

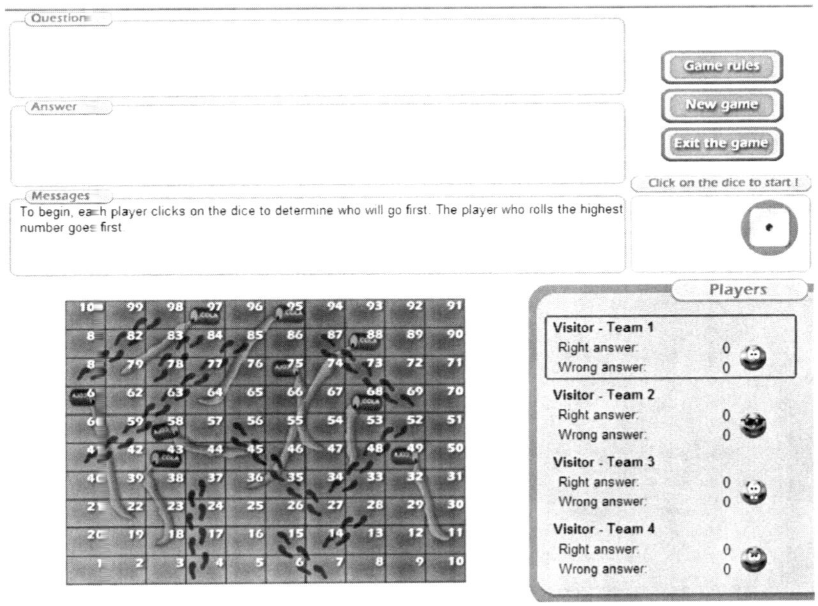

ACTIVE PARTICIPATION

Active participation places learners in situations of action rather than passive observation, allowing them to practice in a concrete context the knowledge or skills to be developed. In other words, activities have to provide situations in which learners must use their new knowledge or skills just as they would in "real" life.

Generally, researchers emphasize the importance of learner commitment and the active role that learners must play during a game in order to maintain their motivation and stimulate their learning. For example, Stadler (1998) refers to the active learning engendered by games; Wissman and Tankel (2001) note that learner participation in a game gives them the opportunity to play an active role in their learning. The degree of stimulation and pleasure that participants feel while playing are also apparently variables that favor active participation and motivation. Markey, Power and Booker (2003) confirm that motivation and excitement are important elements of player participation in a game. In this respect, the more stimulating a game is, the more the participants will be active, the more pleasure they will have, and the more they will be motivated to play and learn.

Various authors, including De Grandmont (2005), describe active participation by referring to the cognitive or physical skills which are developed or enhanced during a game. For example, Gee (2003) examines psychomotor skills and cognitive processes, and Kasvi (2000) analyzes creative skills, induction, reasoning, and flexibility in the internal knowledge representations. Armory, Naicker, Vincent, and Adams (1999) study visualization, reflexes, and memorization, and Hamalainen, Nanninen, Jarvela, and Hakkinen (2006) observe the production of questions and elaborated reasoning. All these skills are developed in game-based learning activities; the more the activities are diversified, the more these skills can be developed. For example, in the game *Attention Wanders (Attention vagabonde)*, adapted from *Parcheesi*™, more than thirteen interactive multimedia activities are offered to university students so that they can become aware

Figure 7. Example of learning activity with video in the game Attention Wanders

of difficulties experienced by those with attention deficit disorder and learn about ways to reduce these difficulties. Figure 7 shows a learning activity in this game.

Sauvé and Chamberland (2006) include as forms of active learner participation manipulation of the game to achieve a better position (e.g., advancing a piece on a game board), appropriating resources (e.g., obtain points in *Scrabble®* by making a word) or, more simply, progressing on a path (e.g., throwing a die and moving a piece on the *Mother Goose* game board). These manipulations can be more or less complex, either because of the rules which govern them (or because of the number of options offered to the player (e.g., some words are worth very high points in *Scrabble*, depending on where they are placed).

In the context of online educational games, designers must also consider the motor skills needed for game manipulation. Young people who are used to video games demand that speed of execution affect the quality of a player's performance. For example, in the game *STIs: Stopping the Transmission*, a quick positive answer allows a player to win more points. Also, a more time-consuming performance in a game, such as drawing or drafting a short text, can require manipulation with some dexterity with the keyboard, mouse or joystick. These requirements must be taken into account so that a player having less dexterity than others is not penalized. In *Parcheesi*, for example, points obtained in the learning activities that require a certain dexterity are not based on the time needed to realize the activity but rather on the completion of the activity within a given time period.

In summary, the notion of active participation has no single explanation in game research, but is discussed in two ways: one referring to learner commitment arising from active game play, and the other considering the development of cognitive and psychomotor skills through game participation.

TEAMWORK AND PARTICIPANT COOPERATION

Teamwork is often described in game studies as cooperation, which is defined as the capacity to enter into relationships with others, negotiate, discuss, collaborate, share feelings and ideas, develop links and friendships, and, finally, develop team spirit (including a desire for competitiveness).

Cooperation happens when players join together to achieve a common goal. Always present in a team game, it requires group tasks (Gray, Topping, & Carcary, 1998) which are governed by rules. In team learning games, degrees of cooperation and competition vary and must be balanced by rules to ensure that all the members of the team master the contents. For example, in the game *Earth Ball* (Brand, 1968), the challenge sets players against certain obstacles or difficulties which can be surmounted only by pooling the players' resources.

The addition of web communication tools (e.g., chat, audio- or videoconferencing) in online educational games (Figure 8) allow real-time exchanges during gameplay, permitting implementation of techniques supporting cooperation; group discussions, in particular, improve the degree of player involvement and contribution, the degree of reflection on others' points of view, and decision-making based on consensus. We review these tools in Chapter 12.

Integration of an unpredictable system that encourages the participation of every team member in attaining a game goal favors social interdependence, listening and confidence in others. Players find that it is impossible for them to resolve problems alone, so they have to collaborate to succeed. The implementation of rules or instructions in the game can favor mutual aid by, for example, encouraging members of a team to help their team-mate who cannot answer a question or complete a task to move forward on the game board or to gain points. These mechanisms, when implemented, help players to build their common knowledge, remain motivated, and generate ideas. Peters and Vissers (2004) speak of "distributed cognition," "collective learning," and "organizational learning" to underline the impact of team collaboration.

Figure 8. Example of a game integrated into a communication space with the aid of the ENJEUX-S environment

INTERACTION

Interaction is commonly defined as action or mutual influence established between two or more objects. An interaction is always followed by one or more effects as, for example, the unwanted effects of a drug interaction (Wikipédia, 2008). Online digital games offer an elevated degree of interaction between the user and the system (i.e., player to player or against the computer), between several users and the system (i.e., two or more players interacting with the game in teams) and/or between players themselves (i.e., in games that integrate a tool such as videoconferencing that supports real-time exchanges among learners). The first two types of interaction refer to intentional interactivity, whereas the third type results from relational interactivity.

In digital games, intentional interactivity allows and facilitates consultation, exploration, and manipulation of the various constituents of the online game with the aim of reappropriation, reorganization, and reconstruction of the message and its meaning (Boulet, 2002). In other words, the individual learns when he is placed in a relationship with an environment in which he can act, and that reacts, by modifying some of its characteristics. In this definition, two types of interactivity are at play (Mallender, 1999):

- *Interactivity connected to navigation* is the property of an application (for example, a digital game) that allows the learner to interact with the system to start different actions: movements in the game, the choice of route, posting a picture, release of a video, or completion of an exercise (Chassé & Lefebvre, 2001; Thoa, 2004). It is not an integral part of the process of learning, but it allows the player to access learning activities by throwing a die, turning a roulette wheel, moving a piece on a game board, returning to the start, etc.
- *Pedagogical interactivity* refers to the active participation of the learner in the process of learning. Varied activities are proposed to the learner within the framework of one or several precise learning objectives, for example, completing an exercise, answering a closed or open question, drawing, discovering information, or obtaining feedback.

Kinzie et al. (1996) note that the Internet constitutes one of the most effective distribution means to date to offer a high level of intentional interactivity and to increase the level of retention and satisfaction of learners by means of games. Maier and Grobler (2000) state that feedback in games facilitates human- computer interaction. (See above for more detail on feedback mechanisms.) Hingston, Combes, and Masek (2006) add that educational games which exploit current technological possibilities encourage learner interaction with educational content.

Relational interactivity arises in the context of human-to-human or human-to-computer communication in which the computer becomes the game vehicle, transmission channel and a physical link between two persons. Hourst and Thiagiarajan (2001) note that games encourage the development of better group cohesion among learners. Shapiro and Shapiro (2001) conclude that the use of games encourages interaction, discussion, and coordination of ideas between learners. The game therefore becomes a means of communication and collaboration that supports active learning. We emphasize that this type of learning increases motivation for the majority of students (Reuss & Gardulski, 2001). Several studies in education underline the utility of new technologies to promote collaborative learning (e.g., see Marton, 1994; Ritchie & Hoffman, 1996).

The literature, however, does not give enough information about the interaction mechanisms of digital games. To illustrate them in the context of

Figure 9. Example of a question shown over the game board

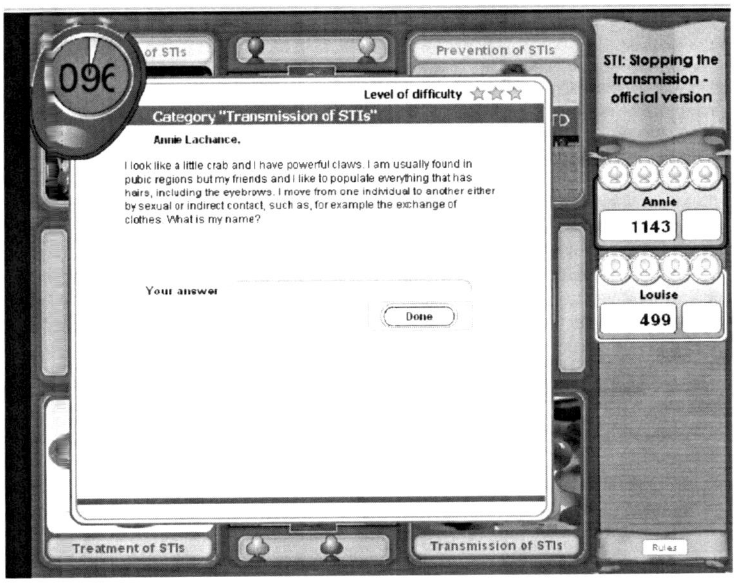

online games, we are inspired by strategies that Bergeron (2007) considers as integral to the effective management and dynamics of interactivity:

- present the computer task in as transparent a way as possible by using a metaphor (for example, illustrate a task of completing an incomplete statement with a puzzle that is missing a piece);
- use consistent indicators across the different game components to facilitate knowledge transfer (for example, indicate wrong answers in red and correct answers in blue);

Figure 10. An error message

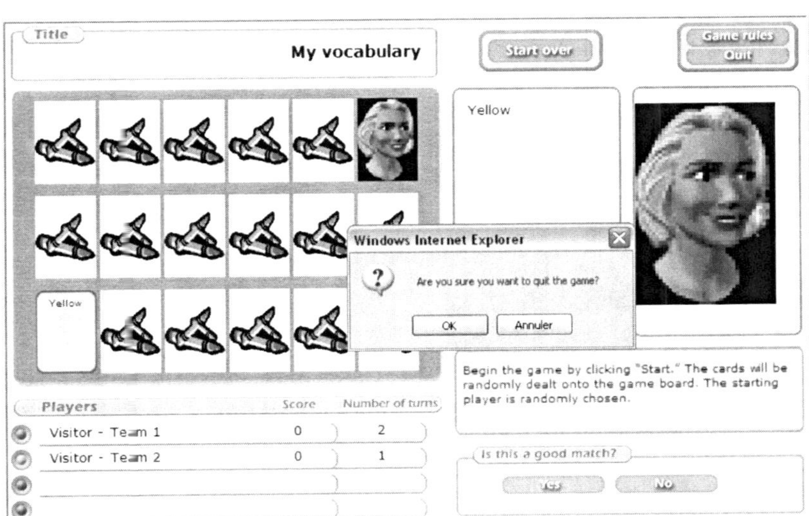

Table 2. Summary of mechanisms supporting learning in online educational games

Conditions for Learning	Game Mechanisms
Repetition	• Insert a mechanism in the game to randomly repeat activities to provide an element of novelty. • Limit the number of questions or learning activities in the game so that they are revisited during play. • Use repetition of information to increase points in the game so that the player recognizes the importance of repetition in winning the game.
Content Segmentation	• Establish a balance between game time and learning time to maintain participants' motivation. • Limit the game content to a specific subject and offer varied and numerous exercises. We propose four steps to establish content boundaries: 1. Determine subject content to teach according to the general objective and the target population. 2. Define the major content segments according to specific learning objectives and the target population. 3. Describe the content elements in relation to the specific objectives and larger segments. 4. Formulate questions or items for every content element.
Feedback	• Insert feedback messages linked to navigation so that players can see in real time the results of their game actions. • Integrate just-in-time feedback with each learning task so that players can identify their successes and failures. • Insert motivational feedback messages that encourage the player and value his learning achievements. • Include oral or written synthesis mechanisms with peers who support the learning to allow the learner to reflect on the activities and his feelings. • Include content review mechanisms to enhance feedback on learning realized in the game and access to supplemental material for learning that was not achieved.
Reinforcement	• Include game rules that have players accumulate points or move forward or back on the game path according to whether answers are correct or incorrect. • Include activities that have learners evaluate their success rate during completion of a given task. • Integrate a real-time feedback mechanism so that the player can gauge the quality of her performance.

- use visual cues (e.g., icons and pictograms) to help the user locate information (for example, use tokens to represent players, a die for token movement, a loudspeaker to hear the pronunciation of a word, a hook to validate an answer, one X to leave a page or a module, etc.);
- reduce the cognitive or mnemonic load by ensuring that the learner's attention centers on one thing at a time, inserting details and nuances later (for example, post the most important information over the game board to focus the attention on the activity to be completed) (Figure 9);
- inform the learner of her current standing in the game by showing the stages of her game route and the results achieved so far (for example, use displays throughout the progress of the game to inform the player about the state of play);
- confirm any action that could result in the loss of data (for example, if the player inadvertently clicks on the "Exit the game" button, a message "Are you sure you want to leave the current game?" pops up to verify that the action is intended);
- offer the possibility of cancelling an action or correcting an error with a simple click; for example, a player must click OK or Cancel in response to a message after an error in manipulation requesting an end to the game, as shown in Figure 10.

CONCLUSION

To ensure that educational games are effective from the point of view of learning and motivation, we have identified certain conditions that must be respected and for which mechanisms must be

Table 3. Summary of mechanisms favoring motivation in online educational games

Conditions for Learner Motivation	Game Mechanisms
Challenge and Competition	• Include goals associated with attaining multiple levels, environments, or routes through the game. • Hide information. • Maintain a feeling of uncertainty about the game outcome.
Active Participation in Learning	• Place learners in active rather than passive situations during the progress of the game by allowing them to manipulate elements of the game: roll dice, turn a roulette wheel, move a token or object, etc. • Insert varied learning activities supporting the development of cognitive or physical skills.
Teamwork	• Use web-based communication tools (chat, audio- or videoconferencing) during game play. • Use an unpredictable system, encouraging every team member to compete to achieve the game's goals. • Include rules to encourage mutual aid.
Interaction	• Integrate features such as movement, choice of route, pictures, video, or completion of exercises to set up intentional interactivity connected to navigation. • Include varied activities requiring the learner to accomplish specific learning objectives: for example, completing an exercise, answering a closed or open question, drawing, discovering information, or obtaining feedback. • Set up mechanisms for player communication: • Use consistent color coding to show correct and incorrect answers; • Use visual cues to help players locate information • Reduce cognitive or mnemonic load by focusing the player's attention on one item at a time and incorporating details and nuances later; • Keep the learner aware of her current status by showing the stages of her path, as well as her results so far.

set up. Table 2 summarizes these mechanisms under the major categories of repetition, content segmentation, feedback, and reinforcement.

Table 3 summarizes mechanisms that favor learner motivation, grouped according to challenge and competition, active participation in learning, teamwork, and interaction

We hope that the use of these two grids will help game designers, teachers and education professionals make informed decisions in their choices, design, and reviews of educational games.

REFERENCES

Armory, A., Naicker, K., Vincent, J., & Adams, C. (1999). The use of computer games as an educational tool: Identification of appropriate game types and game elements. *British Journal of Educational Technology*, *30*(4), 311–321. doi:10.1111/1467-8535.00121

Asakawa, T., & Gilbert, N. (2003). Synthesizing experiences: Lessons to be learned from Internet-mediated simulation games. *Simulation & Gaming*, *34*(1), 10–22. doi:10.1177/1046878102250455

Bandura, A. (1977). *Social learning theory*. Englewood Cliffs, NJ: Prentice-Hall.

Bergeron, G. (2007). La richesse pédagogique de l'interactivité [The learning richness of interactivity]. *Correspondance, 13* (2), Available at http://www.ccdmd.qc.ca/correspo/Corr13-2/Richesse.html

Boulet, G. (2002). *Interactivité et communication médiatisée* [Interactivity and media communication]. Retrieved June 12, 2005 from http://cueep100.univ-lille1.fr/utic/Enseigner,%20 Former/interactivite.pdf

Brand, S. (1968). *Whole Earth Catalog*. Menlo Park, CA: Portola Institute.

Brien, R. (2006). *Science cognitive et formation* [Training and cognitive science]. Québec, QC, Canada: Presses de l'Université du Québec.

Chamberland, G., & Provost, G. (1996). *Jeu, simulation et jeu de rôle* [Games, simulations, and role-playing games]. Québec, QC, Canada: Presses de l'Université du Québec.

Chasse, D., & Lefebvre, S. (2001). *ABC des notes de cours.* BAP- COSTIC. Available at http://www.cours.polymtl.ca/costic/atel_ndec_elec/sld001.htm

De Grandmont, N. (2005). *Pédagogie du jeu... philosophie du ludique* [Game pedagogy... philosophy of gaming]. Available at http://cf.geocities.com/ndegrandmont/index.htm

Ergolab (2003). *Feedback et rapport homme-ordinateur* [Human-computer feedback and rapport]. Retrieved April 27, 2008 from http://www.ergolab.net/articles/feedback-erogonomie.html

Facer, K., Stanton, D., Joiner, R., Reid, J., Hull, R., & Kirk, D. (2004). Savannah: Mobile gaming and learning? *Journal of Computer Assisted Learning, 20*(1), 399–409. doi:10.1111/j.1365-2729.2004.00105.x

Falstein, N. (2004, May). The flow channel. *Game Developer Magazine, 11*(5), 52a.

Gee, J. P. (2003). *What video games have to teach us about learning and literacy.* New York: Palgrave.

Goldenberg, D., Andrusyszyn, M. A., & Iwastw, C. (2005). The effect of classroom simulation on nursing students' self-efficacy related to health teaching. *The Journal of Nursing Education, 44*(7), 310–314.

Gray, A. R., Topping, K. J., & Carcary, W. B. (1998). Individual and group learning of the highway code: Comparing board game and traditional methods. *Educational Research, 40*(1), 45–53.

Griffin, L. L., & Butler, J. I. (2005). *Teaching games for understanding.* Champaign, IL: Human Kinetics.

Hamalainen, R., Manninen, T., Jarvela, S., & Hakkinen, P. (2006). Learning to collaborate: Designing collaboration in a 3-D game environment. *The Internet and Higher Education, 9*(1), 47–61. doi:10.1016/j.iheduc.2005.12.004

Hingston, P., Combes, B., & Masek, M. (2006). Teaching an undergraduate AI course with games and simulation. In Z. Pan, R. Aylett, H. Diener, X. Jin, S. Gobel, & L. Li (Eds.), *Technologies for E-Learning and Digital Entertainment* (LNCS 3942, pp. 494-506). New York: Springer-Verlag.

Hourst, B., & Thiagarajan, S. (2001) *Les jeux-cadres de Thiagi: techniques d'animation à l'usage du formateur* [Thiagi frame games: Animation techniques for trainers]. Paris: Les Éditions d'Organisation.

Kasvi, J. J. J. (2000). Not just fun and games - Internet games as a training medium. In P. Kymäläinen & L. Seppänen (Eds.), *Cosiga - Learning with computerised simulation games* (pp. 23-34). HUT: Espoo.

Kinzie, M. B., Larsen, V. A., Bursh, J. B., & Baker, S. M. (1996). Frog dissection via the World-Wide Web: Implications for widespread delivery of instruction. *Educational Technology Research and Development, 44*(2), 59–69. doi:10.1007/BF02300541

Kirriemuir, J., & McFarlane, A. (2004). *Literature review in games and learning.* Bristol, UK: NESTA Futurelab.

Koster, R. (2004). *A theory of fun for game design.* Scottsdale, AZ: Paraglyph Press.

Kulhavy, R., & Stock, W. (1989). Feedback in written instruction: The place of the response certitude. *Educational Psychology Review, 1*, 279–308. doi:10.1007/BF01320096

Lawrence, R. (2004). Teaching data structures using competitive games. *IEEE Transactions on Education, 47*(4), 459–467. doi:10.1109/TE.2004.825053

Le Ny, J. F. (1968). L'apprentissage [Learning] [Chicago: Encyclopædia Britannica.]. *Encyclopaedia Universalis, 2*, 173–175.

LeMay, P. (2008). Game and flow concepts for learning: some considerations. In K. McFerrin, R. Weber, R. Carlsen, & D. A. Willis (Eds), *Proceedings of the Society for Information Technology and Teacher Education International Conference 2008* (pp. 510-515). Chesapeake, VA: AACE.

Losier, M. (2003). *My vocabulary* (online game). Quebec, QC, Canada: Carrefour virtuel de jeux éducatifs. Available at http://www.savie.qc.ca/CarrefourJeux2/Site/Jeux/Concentration/Info_Concentration.asp?NoPartie=379

Maier, F. H., & Grobler, A. (2000). What are we talking about? A taxonomy of computer simulations to support learning. *System Dynamics Review, 16*(2), 135–148. doi:10.1002/1099-1727(200022)16:2<135::AID-SDR193>3.0.CO;2-P

Mallender, A. (1999). *Écrire pour le multimédia* [Writing for multimedia]. Montreal: Editions DUNOD. Retrieved July 17, 2002 from http://mediamatch.derby.ac.uk/french/design/default.htm

Markey, C., Power, D., & Booker, G. (2003). Using structured games to teach early fraction concepts to students who are deaf or hard of hearing. *American Annals of the Deaf, 148*(3), 251–258. doi:10.1353/aad.2003.0021

Marton, P. (1994). La conception pédagogique de systèmes d'apprentissage multimédia interactif: fondements, méthodologie et problématique [Learning design for systems of interactive multimedia training: Foundations, methodology and problems]. *Éducatechnologique, 1*(3), 5-12.

Medley, C. F., & Horne, C. (2005). Using simulation technology for undergraduate nursing education. *The Journal of Nursing Education, 44*(1), 31–34.

Moyer, P. S., & Bolyard, J. J. (2003). Classify and capture: Using Venn diagrams and Tangrams to develop abilities in mathematical reasoning and proof. *Mathematics Teaching in the Middle School, 8*(6), 325–330.

Paquelin, D. (2002). Analyse d'applications multimédias pour un usage pédagogique [Analysis of multimedia applications for pedagogic use]. *Apprentissage des langues et systèmes d'information et de communication (ALSIC), 5*(1), 3-32.

Peters, V., & Vissers, G. (2004). A simple classification model for debriefing simulation games. *Simulation & Gaming, 35*(1), 70–84. doi:10.1177/1046878103253719

Petranek, C. F. (2000). Written debriefing: The next vital step in learning with simulations. *Simulation & Gaming, 31*(1), 108–118. doi:10.1177/104687810003100111

Pridemore, D., & Klein, J. (1991). Control of feedback in computer-based instruction. *Educational Technology Research and Development, 39*(4), 27–32. doi:10.1007/BF02296569

Rabecq-Mallard, M. M. (1969). *Histoire des jeux éducatifs* [History of educational games]. Paris: Nathan.

Reuss, R. L., & Gardulski, A. F. (2001). An interactive game approach to learning in historical geology and paleontology. *Journal of Geoscience Education, 49*(2), 120–129.

Ritchie, D. C., & Hoffman, B. (1996, June). *Using instructional design principles to amplify learning on the World Wide Web*. Paper presented at SITE 96 (Society for Information Technology and Teacher Education 7th World Conference). Retrieved Nov. 1, 2002 from http://edweb.sdsu.edu/clrit/learningtree/DCD/WWWInstrdesign/WWWInstrDesign.html

Rodet, J. (2000). La rétroaction, support d'apprentissage? [Feedback – a learning support?] *Revue du Conseil québécois de la formation à distance, 4*(2), 45-74.

Salen, K., & Zimmerman, E. (2004). *Rules of play*. Cambridge, MA: The MIT Press.

Sauvé, L., & Chamberland, G. (2000). *Jeux, jeux de simulation et jeux de rôle: une analyse exploratoire et pédagogique* [Games, simulation games and role-playing games: An exploratory pedogical analysis. Cours TEC 1280:Environnement d'apprentissage multimédia sur l'inforoute. Québec, QC, Canada: Télé-université.

Sauvé, L., Renaud, L., & Hanca, G. (2008a). *Étude de cas auprès des élèves du secondaire: apprentissage des ITS à l'aide d'un jeu éducatif en ligne* [Case study of secondary school students: Learning about STIs with the aid of an online educational game]. Research report. Québec, QC, Canada: SAGE and SAVIE.

Sauvé, L., Renaud, L., Kaufman, D., & Sibomana, F. (2008b). *Revue systématique des écrits (1998-2007) sur les impacts du jeu, de la simulation et du jeu de simulation sur l'apprentissage* [Systematic review of the literature (1998-2007) on the impacts of games, simulations, and simulation games on learning]. Research report. Québec, QC, Canada: SAGE and SAVIE.

Sauvé, L., Renaud, L., & Kazsap, M. IsaBelle, C., Gauvin, M., & Simard, G. (2005). *Analyse de 40 jeux éducatifs (en ligne ou sur cédérom)* [Analysis of 40 educational games (on line and on CD-ROM)]. Research report. Québec, QC, Canada: SAGE and SAVIE.

Sauvé, L., & Samson, D. (2004). *Rapport d'évaluation de la coquille générique du Jeu de l'oie du projet Jeux génériques: multiplicateurs de contenu multimédia éducatif canadien sur l'inforoute* [Evaluation report on the Mother Goose generic game shell for the project Generic games: Multipliers of Canadian multimedia educational content on the Internet]. Québec, QC, Canada: SAVIE and Fonds Inukshuk inc.

Sauve, L., & Viau, R. (2002). L'abandon et la persévérance dans l'enseignement à distance: l'importance de la relation enseignement – apprentissage [Abandonment and perseverance in distance education: The importance of relation education – training]. In *Nouveau centenaire - nouveaux modèles. Acte du Colloque de l'ACDE.* Available at http://www.cade-aced.ca/icdepapers/sauveviau.htm

Schwabe, G., & Goth, C. (2005). Mobile learning with a mobile game: Design and motivational effects. *Journal of Computer Assisted Learning, 21*(3), 204–216. doi:10.1111/j.1365-2729.2005.00128.x

Sedic, K. (2007). Toward operationalization of `flow' in mathematics learnware. *Computers in Human Behavior, 23*(4), 2064–2092. doi:10.1016/j.chb.2006.11.001

Shapiro, R., & Shapiro, R. G. (2001, April). *Games to explain aspects of psychology.* Paper presented at the Annual Convention of the National Association of School Psychologists, Washington, DC.

Shneiderman, B. (2004). Designing for fun: How to make user interfaces more fun. *Interactions (New York, N.Y.), 11*(5), 48–50. doi:10.1145/1015530.1015552

Stadler, M. A. (1998). Demonstrating scientific reasoning. *Teaching of Psychology, 25*(3), 205–206. doi:10.1207/s15328023top2503_11

Thoa, E. (2004). *Ergonomie et jeu vidéo* [Ergonomics of video games]. Retrieved April 27, 2008 from http://www.usabilis.com/articles/2004/ergonomie-jeu.htm

Van Eck, R. (2006). The effect of contextual pedagogical advisement and competition on middle-school students` attitude toward mathematics and mathematics instruction using a computer-based simulation game. *Journal of Computers in Mathematics and Science Teaching, 25*(1), 165–195.

Vanhoucke, M., Vereecke, A., & Gemmel, P. (2005). The project scheduling game (PSG): Simulating time/cost trade-offs in projects. *Project Management Journal*, *36*(1), 51–59.

Viau, R. (1994). *La motivation en contexte scolaire* [Motivation in the school context] (Édition québécoise). Montréal, QC, Canada: Éditions du Renouveau pédagogique.

Virvou, M., Katsionis, G., & Manos, K. (2005). Combining software games with education: Evaluation of its educational effectiveness. *Educational Technology & Society*, *8*(2), 54–65.

Wikipédia. (2008). *Interaction*. Retrieved January 3, 2008 from http://fr.wikipedia.org/wiki/Interaction

Wissmann, J. L., & Tankel, K. (2001). Nursing student's use of a psychopharmacology game for client empowerment. *Journal of Professional Nursing*, *17*(2), 101–106. doi:10.1053/jpnu.2001.22274

Woltjer, G. B. (2005). Decisions and macroeconomics: Development and implementation of a simulation game. *The Journal of Economic Education*, *36*(2), 139–144. doi:10.3200/JECE.36.2.139-144

ADDITIONAL READING

Adams, E., & Rollings, A. (2003). *On game design*. Indianapolis IN: New Riders Publishing.

Salen, K., & Zimmerman, E. (2004). *Rules of play*. Cambridge, MA: The MIT Press.

Shneiderman, B., & Plaisant, C. (2004). *Designing the user interface: Strategies for effective Human-Computer Interaction* (4th ed.). Boston, MA: Addison Wesley.

KEY TERMS AND DEFINITIONS

Active Participation: Places learners in situations of action, allowing them to practice in a concrete context the knowledge or skills to be developed. Activities provide situations in which learners must use their new knowledge or skills just as they would in real life.

Competition: A key feature of games with a single player (who opposes himself to improve his performance with every challenge) and those that include several players who oppose each other to achieve the same purpose.

Cooperation: The capacity to enter into relationships with the others, to negotiate, to discuss, to collaborate, to share feelings and ideas, to develop links and friendships and, finally to develop team spirit, including a desire to compete.

Educational Game: A fictitious, fantasy or imaginary situation in which players, placed in conflict with others or assembled in a team against an external opponent, are governed by rules determining their actions with a view to achieving learning objectives and a goal determined by the game, either to win or to seek revenge.

Feedback: A mechanism that indicates to the learner whether or not he has a satisfactory answer, suggests a correction, and expresses a value judgment which should be well-reasoned and argued. Its purpose is to help the learner to deepen her knowledge or to change her behavior and to indicate how to do so.

Interaction: An action or mutual influence between two or more objects. An interaction is always followed by one or several effects as, for example, the unwanted effects of a drug interaction

Learning: The acquisition of knowledge or skills with the help of experience, practice or study. Learning results include knowledge, attitudes and skills acquired by students.

Motivation: The effort or energy needed to carry out a given learning task. Motivation to learn depends on the importance which the learner attaches to the final goal, her interest in the task, and her perception of its difficulty.

Negative Reinforcement: Recognized as less effective than positive reinforcement, because of the anxiety it causes the player.

Positive Reinforcement: Produces a pleasant and satisfactory effect for the learner.

Chapter 3
Simulation in Health Professional Education

David Kaufman
Simon Fraser University, Canada

ABSTRACT

This chapter begins with a definition of "simulation" and outlines simulation attributes. It then discusses the purpose of simulations distinguishing and illustrating their various categories and forms in medical and health professional education, and describes their benefits, limitations, and ways to use them effectively. The elements of effective simulations for learning, and why these are important, are then explained. To illustrate these concepts, the chapter concludes by describing health-related simulations developed in the SAGE for Learning project, including COMPS, a collaborative online multimedia problem-based simulation; COMPSoft, a software environment for creating cases and allowing learners to work through them online; HealthSimNet, a simulation for HIV/AIDS patients and professionals to experience navigating the health care system; and MIRAGE, a psychiatry prototype for medical students.

INTRODUCTION

Simulations have long been used as training tools in many health disciplines in which "live" repetitive practice is difficult, costly, or risky; examples include simulated patients for medical diagnosis and treatment, organ dissection models, and computer-based clinical cases. This chapter presents an overview and examples of simulations for health professional education. It begins with a general definition and purpose of simulations, distinguishing and illustrating their various categories and forms in medical and health education and describing their benefits, limitations, and ways to overcome the latter. It then reviews the elements of effective simulations for learning and explains why these are important. To illustrate these concepts, it describes several health-related simulations developed in the *SAGE for Learning* project. These examples include *COMPS*, a collaborative online multimedia

DOI: 10.4018/978-1-61520-731-2.ch003

problem-based simulation; *COMPSoft*, a software environment for creating cases and allowing learners to work through them online; *HealthSimNet*, a simulation for HIV/AIDS patients and professionals to experience navigating the health care system; and *MIRAGE*, a psychiatry prototype for medical students.

BACKGROUND

Definition of Simulation

As noted in Chapter 1, there has long been a conceptual confusion about, and consequent misuse of, the terms game, simulation, and simulation game. To distinguish clearly among these often-confused ideas, we begin with the following definitions (Crookall, Greenblat, Coote, Klabbers & Watson, 1987; Garris, Ahlers, & Driskell, 2002; Sauvé, et al, 2005a; Sauvé, Renaud, Kaufman, & Sibomana, 2008; Stolovitch, 1981):

- **Games:** Activities that do not attempt to replicate reality, have clearly defined sets of rules including scoring systems, and produce winners and losers
- **Simulations:** Activities that include exploration and practice within models of reality, but without competition, scoring, and winners/ losers
- **Simulation games:** Games that are based on simplified but dynamic models of aspects of reality

We have found that these distinctions are necessary for a conceptual framework that relates these distinct types of activities to their impacts on learning.

Prensky (2004) asserts that simulation is, by definition, pretending (p. 1), and that the one universal truth about any simulation is that at its center lies a model (p. 2). Sauvé, Renaud, and Kaufman, in Chapter 1 of this book, elaborate by explaining that the essential attributes of educational simulations are the following: a model of reality defined as a system; a dynamic model, a simplified, precise and valid model, and a potential for fostering the understanding of the reality that the model represents. A model is first defined as an abstract or concrete representation of a real system in which components are clearly specified. Such a model is based on reality as defined by the perception which an individual has of a system, an event, a person or an object.

However, McGee (2006) asserts that a simulation is more than simply a model with which the learner interacts. Simulations provide a framework for learners to build on their existing knowledge and augment existing cases that they already have stored in their memory. They provide an experience where learning is both interactive and dynamic. It is difficult, if not impossible, to model the world completely in enough detail to replicate reality. However, Schank and Cleary (1995) note that the technology is becoming advanced enough that in a specific context it can make learners believe that they have encountered an accurate representation of reality, allowing them to act virtually in a way that is similar to how they would act in the real world.

As noted in Chapter 1, "fidelity" is defined as "the degree of similarity between the training situation and the operational situation which is simulated." It is a two-dimensional measurement of this similarity in terms of: (1) physical characteristics - visual, spatial, kinesthetic, etc.; and (2) functional characteristics, for example, "the informational, stimulus, and response options of a training situation" (Hays & Singer, 1989, p.50). The notion of validity refers to the degree of uniformity and coherence in the environment specifications in comparison to reality (Garris et al., 2002). In other words, the results obtained by simulations have to be the same as those obtained in the real world, with the system serving as a model for the simulation.

Purpose of a Simulation

Regardless of the type or size of simulation used, Milrad (2002) asserts that the main purpose of a simulation is to create an environment to: (1) encourage the development of cognitive models in learners; (2) allow for testing of the models used in a system, and (3) discover the relationships between variables in the model. Research in education (including continuing education) has demonstrated that simulations promote competency development, both basic and complex. For instance, the level of competency required by medical professionals is better acquired in an environment which uses varied examples in a realistic context, and which provides educational activities through situations that imitate the real world (Swanson & Ornelas, 2001; Zhu, Zhou & Yin, 2001). Simulations are particularly appropriate for creating such environments because they offer high-level interactivity, strengthen concept and theory acquisition, and place objects or systems at the center of learning (Charrière & Magnin, 1998; Johnson et al., 1998).

Paper-based "in-basket" simulations have been used in education and training settings for many years, but advances in computers, networks and bandwidth have created a range of new possibilities for the use of simulations for teaching and learning. Current tools make it more feasible to build complex models, and the online, multiplayer capability in many of the current software platforms allows students and teachers to be in different locations while working together online. The high levels of fidelity and realism available are also creating more believable interactions for learners.

The medical profession has expanded its use of educational simulations into a range of areas. This is partly a response to the number of medical errors, projected shortages in medical professionals, and the need to quickly train workers to deal with newly-evolving threats such as pandemics and bioterrorism (Eder-Van Hook, 2004). There is also a growing awareness that medical graduates do not have the critical thinking skills necessary to work in an increasingly complex clinical environment (Jeffries, 2005). It is difficult, if not impossible, to teach in a traditional classroom setting the knowledge and procedures needed to address all of these issues effectively in practice (Hamilton, 2005). In order to teach these skills, many medical schools in the United States are using an apprenticeship model that requires students to work under realistic conditions to gain the skills they will need to work on real patients. Until recently, this has mainly focused used cadavers, laboratory animals, or real patients (Eder-Van Hook, 2004); this is based on a belief that working on analogous animal structures, preserved tissue, and real cases will translate into increased competency in the physician's real world practice (Liu, Tendick, Cleary, & Kaufmann, 2003). Although cadavers and laboratory animals are helpful, real patients provide the majority of the learning opportunities for students.

This model is beginning to suffer under changing delivery methodologies. The financial drivers that are reducing the amount of inpatient time and moving patients quickly through the medical system are limiting student exposure to a variety of diseases and physical findings (Issenberg, McGaghie, Petrusa, Gordon, & Scalese, 2005). This is affecting the amount of time students can devote to maintaining and improving their skills. In addition to these constraints, the pace of innovation in medicine has left medical students with a requirement to know even more, while having less time to actually learn (Shaffer, Gordon, & Bennett, 2004).

Medical simulation is being viewed as an innovation that will change the current approach to training while addressing these issues. It is seen as both a new training tool and a way of evaluating skills and assessing competency years after students have graduated (Knapp, 2004).

Health care workers learn through observation and repetition. In clinical settings, this means that they are only able to learn from the cases that present themselves during the short period that they are in school. Simulation-based approaches allow the learner to engage in realistic training in communication, leadership, and team interaction, as well as observation and repetition as many times as is necessary to achieve mastery. The overall benefit of allowing students to use training simulations, with appropriate pedagogical scaffolding, is considerable. Simulations are believed to provide better-trained health care workers, reduce medical errors, save money due to lower malpractice rates, and improve the quality of patient care overall (Eder-Van Hook, 2004; Hamilton, 2005; Issenberg et al., 2005). Several studies have already shown that learners who use computer-based and physical simulations make fewer mistakes (Gallagher & Cates, 2004). Simulations can gather quantitative data about student performance that can be stored for later evaluation (Knoll, Trojan, Haecker, Alken, & Michel, 2005). There is also a higher level of student satisfaction in those groups who were able to use simulations rather than traditional, lecture-based material (Docherty, Hoy, Topp, & Trinder, 2005). This higher satisfaction level is because simulation-based approaches are more motivating and interesting than traditional work assignments (Spinello & Fischbach, 2004).

SIMULATION CATEGORIES AND FORMS

Simulations can be classified into seven categories:

1. **Software simulations:** Used for IT and application training
2. **Business simulations:** Generally employed to develop management skills, accounting practices, often by running simulated companies
3. **Situational simulations:** Used to promote communication skills, problem-solving, and decision-making
4. **Technical simulations:** Which allow learners to practice on models of physical systems to learn equipment operation, rather than practicing on expensive or dangerous systems
5. **Procedural simulations:** Useful for learning step-by-step processes that require a defined set of steps that should be practiced many times to achieve mastery
6. **Virtual worlds:** Recreate workplaces and other environments to allow practice of organizational and social interactions
7. **Hybrid simulations:** Combinations of the above categories.

Simulations in medical and health education can be grouped into six forms, depending on the learning objectives and context. The first two forms use humans without the need for technology, while the next two forms are multimedia-based simulators. The final two forms, called simulators, represent a subclass of the simulation domain. These forms include:

1. **Role-play, small group "in-basket" activities:** Cases based on authentic situations that the learner must resolve by making decisions and/or taking action
2. **Simulated or standardized patients:** Trained volunteers or actors who play the role of the patient in interviews and/or physical examinations, and who have been trained to respond in specific ways, based on the actions of the learner
3. **Computer-based clinical simulations:** Typically interactive, multimedia-based cases that require an individual learner or team to work through clinical problems and receive feedback
4. **Video-based simulations:** Scenarios shown on video that present dilemmas

to the learner(s), often in areas such as ethics, professionalism, or doctor-patient relationships

5. **Realistic interactive simulations:** Plastic models and high-tech modeling of various body parts such as the female pelvis (for a pelvic exam) or the male prostate (for a prostate exam)
6. **Complex interactive simulations:** An expensive yet highly realistic form of simulation. These comprise a realistic model of a full human body to allow learners to conduct complex procedures, sometimes in a simulated emergency or operating room. These are sometimes referred to as human patient simulators

Forms 5 and 6 allow learners to practice procedures such as venepuncture, endoscopy, ultrasounds, and even surgery. Their more complex forms are described below in more detail.

Realistic Interactive Simulators

The need for safe and effective health care education has acted as a catalyst for the development of medical simulators (Committee on Quality of Health Care in America (CQHCA) Institute of Medicine, 1999). Medical simulators may be relatively simple or extremely complex, and capable of teaching and evaluating either a specific task or a linked series of tasks. Simulators range from low-tech, simple plastic models of infants, children, or adults to realistic, high-tech simulators. They can be integrated into the medical curriculum to teach and evaluate three levels of skills that range from basic, uni-dimensional, individual skills through higher level, multidimensional, individual skills to very complex, multidimensional, teamwork skills. An example of the first skill level would be how to correctly place a stethoscope for a cardiac examination. An example of the second skill level would be how to perform a full cardiac examination, interpret the findings, and prescribe medication. An example of the third skill level would be how to work in a team to manage a patient in cardiac arrest and then give bad news to the family (Lane, Slavin, & Ziv, 2001).

Task-Specific Simulators

Lane et al. (2001) provide two good examples of task-specific simulators: *CathSim®* and *UltraSim®*. *CathSim* is used for phlebotomy and IV insertion training (www.ht.com). *UltraSim*, an ultrasound simulator developed by MedSim in 1996, operates like an actual ultrasound system and has a fully functional control panel (Nisenbaum, Arger, Derman, & Ziv, 2000). The system includes performance assessment features, a built-in instructor, and an extensive library of clinical cases (Meller, 1997). The clinical cases are based on real-patient 3D ultrasound images, covering a wide range of organ systems and conditions such as abdominal, obstetrics/ gynecology, breast, and vascular pathologies. The authors explain that many systems have been installed worldwide in training programs for ultrasound technicians, radiologists, and obstetrics/gynecology specialists. In addition, the simulator is increasingly used for training surgeons and emergency room physicians in the acute care setting (Lane et al., 2001).

Complex Interactive Simulators

High-tech simulators are sophisticated, computer-driven platforms that model human anatomy and physiology and allow trainees to manage complex clinical situations in a realistic setting (Lane et al., 2001). This generation includes sophisticated mannequin platforms with humanlike tactile and visual appearance, and virtual reality devices and simulators that replicate virtual or simulated clinical settings. The patient simulators are versatile and sophisticated, incorporating responsive eyes, anatomic airways, patient voices, arm movements, and heart and breath sounds. They feature physiological modeling of ventilation and gas exchanges, cardiopulmonary functions, and the pharmacological actions of more than 80 agents, including anesthesia gases. The mannequin's internal components can interface with various types of patient monitors and medical devices, including anesthesia machines, ventilators, and defibrillators. The mannequin may be used to teach basic sciences such as pharmacology and physiology, as well as complex medical management of a patient case, including drug administration, cardiopulmonary resuscitation, endotracheal intubation, tracheostomy, and insertion of chest tubes. These patient simulators are often used as the core platforms of simulation centers. Simulation centers attempt to replicate fully functioning operating rooms, intensive care units, emergency departments, or patient rooms (Lane et al., 2001).

SIMULATION BENEFITS AND LIMITATIONS

Why Use Simulations?

There are many benefits to the appropriate and effective use of simulations for learners, patients, and organizations. Benefits for learners include the provision of practice and feedback, higher levels of engagement and enjoyment, learning as much from mistakes as from correct actions, and reduced learning time. Learners can receive their training in chunks, and tasks can be presented with increasing complexity, all in a context that approaches reality. Benefits to patients are clear, as these lead to better trained health professionals who will make fewer errors. Finally, health care institutions benefit as risks to patients are decreased, fewer errors are reported, and expensive equipment is used less but more effectively. In addition, competency standards can be set and monitored. In clinical training environments it is becoming increasingly difficult to find appropriate placements, clinical rotations are shorter, and working time restrictions are limiting the availability of staff. Simulations can serve as a complement to direct patient experience and seminars with clinicians.

Eder-Van Hook (2004, p. 6) asserts that "students have the opportunity to practice, make mistakes, and improve their skills and knowledge on the simulated patient *without consequence to the patient*. Medical simulation-based training provides better-trained health care providers, reduces medical errors, saves money, and improves the quality of patient care overall." She summarizes eloquently the argument in support of using simulations in health education:

> *Currently, there are hundreds of schools in the United States providing "hands on" healthcare education to medical, nursing, and allied health students. These schools predominately use the apprenticeship model as their main teaching style, often referred to in medicine as "do one, see one, teach one." ... A health care provider's ability to react prudently in an unexpected situation is one of the most critical factors in creating a positive outcome in a medical emergency, regardless of whether it occurs on the battlefield, freeway, or hospital emergency room. This ability, however, is not a skill that one is born with, but rather it is learned and developed with time, training, practice, and repetition. Today, advances in technology have created new and better, methods for teaching the practice of medicine and reinforcing best practices. One of the most exciting innovations in health care is in the field of medical simulation. Employing medical simulation techniques can help move medicine from the old "see one, do one, teach one" method to a "see one, practice many, do one" model for success. (p. 2)*

These benefits can be seen in a number of potential applications of simulations in healthcare. These include areas such as routine learning and rehearsal of clinical and communication skills at all levels, routine basic training of individuals and teams, practice of complex clinical situations, training of teams in crisis resource management, and rehearsal of serious and/or rare events requiring intervention. Another aspect involves the induction of trainees into new clinical environments and the use of equipment, as well as the design and testing of new clinical equipment. Finally, performance assessment of staff at all levels and maintenance of competence through refresher training of staff at all levels can be an important application (Ker & Bradley, 2007).

More generally, research has focused on how the Internet, handheld devices, and immersive environments can be used to support the delivery and evaluation of theory-based, often collaborative learning experiences. Simulations can employ sophisticated, detailed virtual reality representations of physical settings, as in many of today's commercial video games (e.g., *The Sims®*), wireless handheld devices or cell phones that allow instant communication and feedback (e.g., Naismith, Lonsdale, Vavoula, & Sharples, 2004), game boxes to bring simulations (and games) to the family living room (e.g., *Wii Fit®*, *Guitar Hero®*), Internet-based multiplayer simulations (e.g., *COMPS)*, head-mounted displays, 3D immersive CAVE environments, or "exergaming" devices that sense and translate to the screen players' physical movements (Wikipedia, 2006). Moreover, digital simulations have become attractive, even addictive, fixtures of popular culture and vehicles for commercially and politically-motivated "learning" (e.g., Skyworks Interactive, 2009; Soussi, 2003).

There are a number of arguments that would seem to support simulations as learning tools, including:

- **Engagement:** Simulations are highly engaging. They can offer motivating, absorbing, interactive, collaborative experiences that draw in users and keep them interacting for many hours, learning in order to succeed in the simulation and often developing complex social networks in the process (Asgari & Kaufman, 2004). Some educators ask what we can learn from simulations about engagement that can be brought to learning activities.
- **Experience:** Simulations have long been popular and proven tools for trainers and educators in various venues (Stolovitch, 1981; Stolovitch & Thiagarajan, 1980). Examples using newer technologies are emerging as powerful tools for learning complex concepts and behaviors (e.g., *Cornell Management Game*, 2006; Sawyer, 2002).
- **Potential for integrating theory, experience and best practice:** Simulations appear to offer many opportunities to improve learning engagement and effectiveness by embodying accepted learning theories. Networked, collaborative simulation environments can provide interactivity, immersion, motivation, learner control, repeated practice, feedback, and opportunity for reflection, especially useful where authentic experiential learning is infeasible for reasons of cost, access or safety (Kinzie, Larsen, Bursh, & Baker, 1996; Ruben, 1999; Schank & Neaman, 2001).
- **Learning outcomes:** A number of studies have demonstrated the effectiveness of simulations for cognitive, emotional and psychomotor learning (e.g. Baranowski et al., 2003; Kirriemuir & McFarlane, 2004; Sauvé et al., 2005a, 2008). According to these studies, simulations motivate learning, offer immediate feedback, consolidate knowledge, support skills development and application, aid learning transfer, and influence changes in behavior and attitudes, all pointing to greater learning effectiveness with simulations.

Limitations of Simulations

Of course, there are limitations to using simulations in education, as there are for any learning modality. From the developer's perspective, simulations can be expensive and difficult to create, with lengthy development times. If the content changes often, the simulation may no longer be useful or may require resources to continue updating it. From a learner's perspective, the inputs required are sometimes not very lifelike, a limited set of choices may be presented, and there is often too much time for reflection on the part of the learner. Finally, simulation assumptions or rules are usually implicit rather than explicit, which limits their learning potential.

Lane et al. (2001) provide a caution that is worthy of consideration:

There is always a danger that educators might be seduced into using simulation to achieve educational goals that are easily and effectively met using non-simulation modalities. It is essential, therefore, to evaluate critically whether educational goals can be better met in traditional clinical settings using innovative teaching techniques rather than simulation techniques. The use of rigorous qualitative and quantitative measures of educational outcomes to demonstrate the value added by simulation techniques and programs is also essential. Finally, it must be remembered that simulation is not real life, that simulated performance does not completely correlate with performance with real patients, and that even in the age of advanced simulation, the value of instruction and learning at the bedside is still critically important. (p. 309)

Using Simulations Effectively

Ker & Bradley (2007) have provided guidelines for effective simulation-based education. As with any educational medium, a designer of simulations must first understand the learner's needs and requirements. This is typically accomplished through a needs assessment (Grant, 2002) and/or environmental scan (Hatch & Pearson, 1998). After establishing learning outcomes or addressing existing ones, scenarios can be created based on them. The designer will work to establish both psychological and cognitive fidelity in the simulation, and this is greatly enhanced by creating synergy between content experts (clinicians) and process experts (educationalists). Finally, and contrary to common practice, the evaluation design should be completed at the design stage, using all levels of the Kirkpatrick hierarchy (Kirkpatrick, 1994).

In order to ensure that learning is enhanced, the scenarios should be presented in a progressive, staged manner, moving from the specific to general. Of course, timely feedback needs to be provided. It is important that the practice is guided, including mistakes and providing resources and support to seek improvement. Finally, performance measurement (technical and non-technical) should be embedded for individuals and teams.

The gold standard for simulation-based education is to transfer learning to authentic settings. Transfer can be enhanced in several ways. The easiest way is to link the timing of the simulation as closely as possible to workplace experience. Placing the learning in context by recreating a real clinical environment to help suspension of disbelief will then assist in transfer of learning to performance. Throughout the simulation experience, the role of a facilitator and/or tutor is crucial for ensuring integration, reflection-in-action and reflection-on-action [often called a 'debrief'] (Schön, 1983).

Based on a systematic review of simulation literature from 1969-2003, Issenberg et al. (2005) have identified a number of features that promote learning, including:

- feedback
- repetitive practice
- integration within curriculum

- range of difficulties
- adaptable, multiple learning strategies
- range of clinical scenarios
- safe, educationally supportive learning environment
- active learning based on individualized needs
- defining outcomes
- ensuring simulator validity (realistic recreation of complex clinical situations).

It is clear that most of these features are consistent with the guidelines given above and provide a succinct checklist for educators wishing to evaluate potential simulations for their learning-support potential.

SAGE SIMULATION PROJECTS

SAGE simulation research and development addressed a variety of specific health and medical education applications and foundational issues. Projects included the following:

***Collaborative Online Multimedia Problem-based Simulations (COMPS)*:** This project team explored the potential of *COMPS* to support problem-based learning (PBL) for medical student education and for continuing medical education for health professionals. They designed, developed, and tested a set of full scale, media-rich, narrative-based simulations in which learners role-play medical professionals and access realistic resources to guide their diagnoses and treatments (see Chapter 17). This project especially emphasized patient-centered health care. Simulations were developed and tested in different forms in *WebCT*® and in the *ENJEUX-S* software platform (see Chapter 12). It falls into the category of situational simulation, described earlier. Its form is a *role-play, small group "in-basket" activity,* which is a case based on an authentic situation that the learner must resolve by making decisions and/or taking action; however, it also has elements of a *video-based simulation* with scenarios shown on video that present dilemmas to the learner(s).

The study addressed a well-known medical education pedagogy, problem-based learning (PBL), implemented in an online distributed environment. In medical education, the Internet is being used increasingly as a learning tool and as a venue for delivering online education (McKimm, Jollie, & Cantillon, 2003). This move to the web has been propelled by changes such as the decentralization of health care and a decrease in opportunities for face-to-face encounters with patients. This has led to a search for new opportunities for learning that enable students to collaborate no matter where they work or study.

This research was aimed at expanding PBL into a kind of online role-playing simulation where medical students could work together in a distributed environment to resolve authentic problems and situations, thereby promoting their professional development (Albanese, 1993). The study's hypothesis was that problem-based learning in medical education can benefit from techniques found in online simulations and computer game environments. In order to learn more, the team developed a model that:

- built upon a framework of PBL theory and practice
- supported collaborative learning
- moved towards an online simulation to create an authentic environment for learning in a risk-free setting
- incorporated the benefits of multimedia
- integrated a strong narrative line to create a more holistic picture of the patient

Although there has been little work done on effective design of online simulation environments, design criteria based on a constructivist or situated framework suggests problem-solving skills can be promoted (Hawley & Duffy, 1998).

COMPS is described in detail in Chapter 17. Its major design components include:

Figure 1. Case resources for a COMPS scenario

- Course Menu - Homepage > Case Presentation > **Resources**

Case Resources: Use these resources for your research assignment.

Image: Mononucleuosis Rash	Image: Mononucleosis rash in face
Image: Tonsils with infectious Mononucleosis	An Example of Mono Test Results
3D Model: Neck and throat	Video: How to palpate the cervical node: Part 1
Epstein Barr: Recent Advances	Article: Evaluation of 12 Commercial Tests for Detection of Epstein-Barr Virus-Specific and Heterophile Antibodies
Article: Infectious Mononucleosis web sites	Pharyngitis, Tonsillitis, and other Throat Problems: Web Sites

- **A case scenario:** Instructors can present narrative-based case information to students at the beginning of the case
- **Patient information:** Students get information, gain basic patient-centered skills, and acquire clinical reasoning skills through interaction in an authentic clinical setting
- **Physical exam tools:** Students use physical exam information and tools to refine their diagnostic and clinical reasoning skills
- **Lab & medical records:** Students examine records to improve their diagnostic skills
- **Resource center:** Students use self-directed approaches to researching information. The resource center (Figure 1) provides resources such as articles and audio/video clips as well as access to digital libraries
- **Synchronous communication:** Students discuss clinical topics or collaborate with each other directly
- **Asynchronous communication:** Students share learning resources and post their personal opinions and reflections

***COMPSoft*:** Based on the *ENJEUX-S* platform, this project developed an advanced multimedia, online, multi-user simulation environment (Sauvé et al., 2005b). The web environment integrates multimedia components (i.e., video, audio, voice, graphics) with 2D / 3D simulations, allowing for instantaneous and simultaneous interaction so that users in any location can collaborate (see Chapter 12). The *ENJEUX-S* environment is composed of three spaces distinguishable at several levels. Its *Management* space, allowing the creation and modification of game and simulation sessions, is user-friendly, simple and flexible. The *Team* space makes it easy for group players to exchange in text and audio modes before the start of a game. The *Games and Simulations* space exhibits an excellent display quality, stability, and fluidity in the audio and video exchanges. *COMPSoft* also has several video screen display modes (up to 12 participants individually, fixed for the coordinator or in alternation). In addition to providing the coordinator with ancillary work tools that facilitate his teaching (PowerPoint and video viewer, application sharing, white board, polling), the *Games and Simulations* space supports his supervision by means of a control panel that allows him to direct all aspects related to the communication between participants. Finally, collaborative learning is enhanced with the creation of private audio and video rooms where participants can work or communicate in parallel for a length of time, predetermined or not by the supervisor.

The *COMPSoft* platform has been configured specifically for online problem-based learning simulations (Figure 2), using functions for present-

Figure 2. COMPSoft interface example

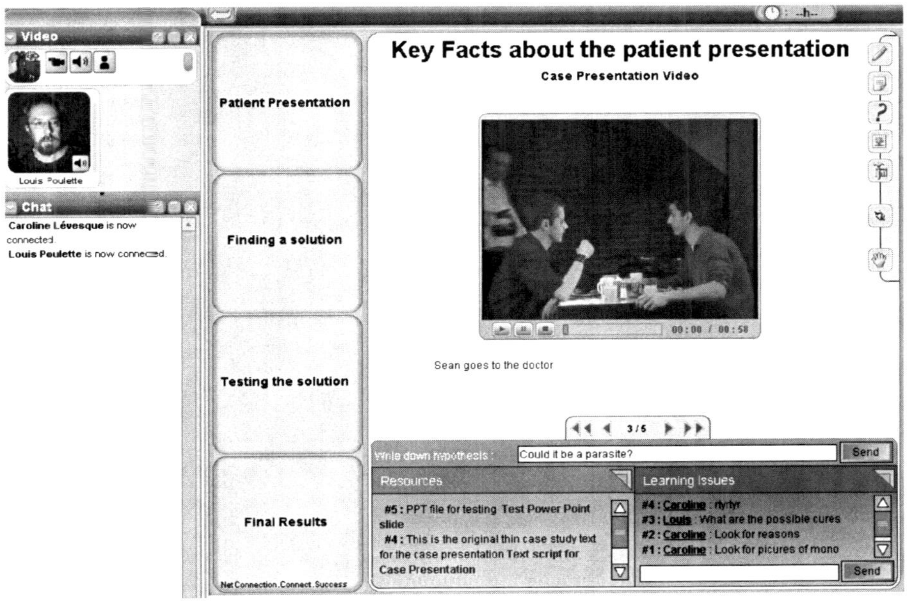

Figure 3. HealthSimNet example screen

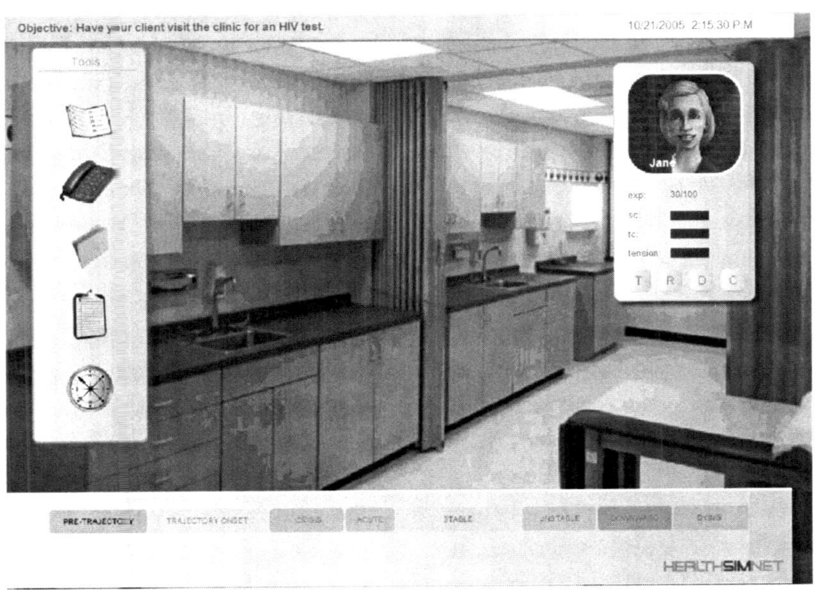

ing a case through text, audio or video; allowing group discussion about the case with concurrent recording for later reference; and accessing online text or media resources including links to external websites.

HealthSimNet: Researchers in this project explored how to create and apply tools to facilitate learning based on activity-theory-based models of complex sets of interactions among inter-professional teams. The result was *HealthSimNet*

Figure 4. MIRAGE example screen (Martian character)

software to model team interactions and simulate complex interdisciplinary case scenarios for use in medical and professional education (Dobson, Burgoyne, & LeBlanc, 2004). This is an example of a hybrid simulation, combining a situational simulation with a virtual world. Its form allows users to combine a role-play, in-basket simulation with a computer-based clinical simulation. Using the tool to model a set of communications about an HIV/AIDS case revealed competencies and gaps in the professional practices of nurses, physicians, and child welfare workers, as well as legal obstacles and areas in which public health outcomes could be improved through more effective interactions (Figure 3).

***MIRAGE* psychiatry simulation:** This project was a collaborative effort between researchers in the Simon Fraser University Faculty of Education and the Psychiatry Department in the Faculty of Medicine at the University of Toronto. The project team created and tested a simulation that could be used to discuss psychotic symptoms in order to assist students to reflect and confront their own attitudes and increase empathy for people suffering from psychotic illness. This was accomplished by showing a situation from different points of view, and why actions from the point of view of someone who is psychotic makes sense to that person. Each player controls a 3D avatar in the clinical environment and sees the other characters differently from their counterparts. For example, the doctor sees a psychotic patient, while the patient sees the doctor as an alien who is trying to capture him (Figure 4). (Technically, this was accomplished through some innovative programming using the *Unreal Tournament®* software engine.) Different causes of psychosis can be simulated and then discussed in a debriefing session (e.g., schizophrenia, bipolar disorder, manic episode, drug induced) elements. The simulation involves a doctor and nurse as well as a patient. It emphasizes the importance of inter-professional cooperation to help create better team work and thus better care for patients. This innovative simulation falls into the category of a hybrid simulation combining a situational simulation with a virtual world. Its form combines a computer-based clinical situation in psychiatry with a role-play activity based on an authentic situation that the learner must resolve by making decisions and/or taking action.

CONCLUSION

Thanks to the rapid advances in information technology, the field of technology-based simulation is exploding. This is particularly evident in the domain of health care, for a variety of reasons. First and foremost, simulation-based training in healthcare can provide better-trained healthcare providers, reduce medical errors, improve the quality of patient care, and save money. Second, simulations have been shown to be effective and efficient learning tools, especially when combined with other methods and supported by a debriefing process. Third, there are many simulation resources already available, and these can be extremely cost-effective. As more research demonstrates the benefits of using simulations for learning and transfer to authentic settings, healthcare practitioners, teachers, administrators, and policy-makers will increase their support and use of these tools.

REFERENCES

Albanese, M. A. (1993). Problem-based learning: A review of literature on its outcomes and implementation issues. *Academic Medicine*, *68*(1), 52–81. doi:10.1097/00001888-199301000-00012

Arthur, D., Malone, S., & Nir, O. (2002). Optimal overbooking. *The UMAP Journal*, *23*(3), 283–300.

Asgari, M., & Kaufman, D. M. (2004, September). *Intrinsic motivation and game design*. Paper presented by the first author at the 35th Ann. Conf. of the International Simulation and Gaming Association (ISAGA) and Conjoint Conference of Swiss, Austrian, German Simulation & Gaming Association (SAGSAGA), Munich, Germany.

Baranowski, T., Baranowski, J., Cullen, K. W., Marsh, T., Islam, N., & Zakeri, I. (2003). Squire's Quest! Dietary outcome evaluation of a multimedia game. *American Journal of Preventive Medicine*, *24*(1), 52–61. doi:10.1016/S0749-3797(02)00570-6

Borges, M. A. F., & Baranauskas, M. C. C. (1998). A user-centred approach to the design of an expert system for training. *British Journal of Educational Technology*, *29*(1), 25–34. doi:10.1111/1467-8535.00043

Charriere, P., & Magnin, M. C. (1998). Simulations globales avec Internet: un atout majeur pour les départements de langues [Global simulations with the Internet: A major trump card for language departments]. *The French Review*, *72*(2), 320–328.

Cioffi, J., Purcal, N., & Arundell, F. (2005). A pilot study to investigate the effect of a simulation strategy on the clinical decision making of midwifery students. *The Journal of Nursing Education*, *44*(3), 131–134.

Claudet, J. G. (1998). Using multimedia case simulations for professional growth of school leaders: Administrator Case Simulation Project. *T.H.E. Journal*, *25*(11), 82–86.

Committee on Quality of Health Care in America (CQHCA) Institute of Medicine. (1999). *To err is human: Building a safer health system*. Washington, DC: National Academy Press.

Cornell Management Game. (2006). Retrieved August 31, 2006 from http://www.cms-training.com/

Crookall, D., Greenblat, C. S., Coote, A., Klabbers, J. H. G., & Watson, D. R. (1987). *Simulation-gaming in the late 1980s*. Oxford, UK: Pergamon Press.

Dobson, M., Burgoyne, D., & Le Blanc, D. (2004). Transforming tensions in learning technology design: Operationalizing activity theory. *Canadian Journal of Learning Technologies*, *30*(1), 20–45.

Docherty, C., Hoy, D., Topp, H., & Trinder, K. (2005). eLearning techniques supporting problem based learning in clinical simulation. *International Journal of Medical Informatics*, *74*(7-8), 527–533. doi:10.1016/j.ijmedinf.2005.03.009

Eder-Van Hook, J. (2004). *Building a national agenda for simulation-based medical education.* Fort Detrick, MD: Telemedicine and Advanced Technology Research Center (TATRC), U.S. Army Medical Research and Materiel Command. Available at http://www.medsim.org/articles/AIMS_2004_Report_Simulation-based_Medical_Training.pdf

Gallagher, A. G., & Cates, C. U. (2004). Approval of virtual reality training for carotid stenting: What this means for procedural-based medicine. *Journal of the American Medical Association*, *292*(24), 3024–3026. doi:10.1001/jama.292.24.3024

Garris, R., Ahlers, R., & Driskell, J. E. (2002). Games, motivation, and learning: A research and practice model. *Simulation & Gaming*, *33*(4), 441–467. doi:10.1177/1046878102238607

Goldenberg, D., Andrusyszyn, M.-A., & Iwasiw, C. (2005). The effect of classroom simulation on nursing students' self-efficacy related to health teaching. *The Journal of Nursing Education*, *44*(7), 310–314.

Grant, J. (2002). Learning needs assessment: Assessing the need. *British Medical Journal*, *324*(7330), 156–159. doi:10.1136/bmj.324.7330.156

Hamilton, R. (2005). Nurses' knowledge and skill retention following cardiopulmonary resuscitation training: A review of the literature. *Journal of Advanced Nursing*, *51*(3), 288–297. doi:10.1111/j.1365-2648.2005.03491.x

Hatch, T. F., & Pearson, T. G. (1998). Using environmental scans in educational needs assessment. *The Journal of Continuing Education in the Health Professions*, *18*(3), 179–184. doi:10.1002/chp.1340180308

Hawley, C. L., & Duffy, T. M. (1998). Design model for learner-centered, computer-based simulations. In N. J. Maushak & C. Schlosser (Eds.). *20th annual proceedings: Selected research and development presentations at the 1998 convention of the Association for Educational Communications and Technology* (pp. 159-166). Ames, IA: Iowa State University.

Hays, R. T., & Singer, M. J. (1989). *Simulation fidelity in training system design: Bridging the gap between reality and training.* New York: Springer-Verlag.

Hung, D., Chee, T. S., & Hedberg, J. G. (2005). A framework for fostering a community of practice: Scaffolding learners through an evolving continuum. *British Journal of Educational Technology*, *36*(2), 159–176. doi:10.1111/j.1467-8535.2005.00450.x

Issenberg, S. B., Mcgaghie, W. C., Petrusa, E. R., Gordon, D. L., & Scalese, R. J. (2005). Features and uses of high-fidelity medical simulations that lead to effective learning: A BEME systematic review. *Medical Teacher*, *27*(1), 10–28. doi:10.1080/01421590500046924

Jeffries, P. R. (2005). A framework for designing, implementing, and evaluating simulations used as teaching strategies in nursing. *Nursing Education Perspectives*, *26*(2), 96–103.

Johnson, L. A., Wohlgemuth, B., Cameron, C. A., Caughman, F., Koertge, T., & Barna, J. (1998). Dental interactive simulations corporation (DISC): Simulations for education, continuing education, and assessment. *Journal of Dental Education*, *62*(11), 919–928.

Ker, J., & Bradley, P. (2007). *Simulation in medical education.* Edinburgh, UK: Association for the Study of Medical Education (ASME).

Kinzie, M. B., Larsen, V. A., Bursh, J. B., & Baker, S. M. (1996). Frog dissection via the world-wide web: Implications for widespread delivery of instruction. *Educational Technology Research and Development*, *44*(2), 59–69. doi:10.1007/BF02300541

Kirkpatrick, D. L. (1994). *Evaluating training programs: The four levels.* San Francisco, CA: Berrett-Koehler.

Kirriemuir, J., & McFarlane, A. (2004). *Literature review in games and learning.* Bristol, UK: NESTA FutureLab. Retrieved August 31, 2006 from http://www.nestafuturelab.org/research/reviews/08_01.htm

Knapp, B. (2004). Competency: An essential component of caring in nursing. *Nursing Administration Quarterly*, *28*(4), 285–287.

Knoll, T., Trojan, L., Haecker, A., Alken, P., & Michel, M. S. (2005). Validation of computer-based training in ureterorenoscopy. *BJU International*, *95*(9), 1276–1279. doi:10.1111/j.1464-410X.2005.05518.x

Lane, J. L., Slavin, S., & Ziv, A. (2001). Simulation in medical education: A review. *Simulation & Gaming*, *32*(3), 297–314. doi:10.1177/104687810103200302

Liu, A., Tendick, F., Cleary, K., & Kaufmann, C. (2003). A survey of surgical simulation: Applications, technology, and education. *Presence (Cambridge, Mass.)*, *12*(6), 599–614. doi:10.1162/105474603322955905

Maier, F. H., & Grobler, A. (2000). What are we talking about? A taxonomy of computer simulations to support learning. *System Dynamics Review*, *16*(2), 135–148. doi:10.1002/1099-1727(200022)16:2<135::AID-SDR193>3.0.CO;2-P

McGee, M. (2006). *Simulation in education: State of the field review.* Ottawa, ON, Canada: Canadian Council on Learning. Available at http://www.ccl-cca.ca/NR/rdonlyres/C3CB4C08-F7D3-4915-BDAA-C41250A43516/0/SFRSimulationinEducationJul06REV.pdf

McKimm, J., Jollie, C., & Cantillon, P. (2003). ABC of learning and teaching: Web based learning. *British Medical Journal*, *326*(7394), 870–873. doi:10.1136/bmj.326.7394.870

Medley, C. F., & Horne, C. (2005). Using simulation technology for undergraduate nursing education. *The Journal of Nursing Education*, *44*(1), 31–34.

Meller, G. (1997). A typology of simulators for medical education. *Journal of Digital Imaging*, *10*(3), 194–196. doi:10.1007/BF03168699

Milrad, M. (2002). Using construction kits, modeling tools and system dynamics simulations to support collaborative discovery learning. *Educational Technology and Society*, *5*(4), 76–87.

Naismith, L., Lonsdale, P., Vavoula, G., & Sharples, M. (2004). *Literature review in mobile technologies and learning.* Bristol, UK: Futurelab. Retrieved August 21, 2006 from http://www.futurelab.org.uk/download/pdfs/research/lit_reviews/futurelab_review_11.pdf

Nisenbaum, H. L., Arger, P. H., Derman, R. M., & Ziv, A. (2000). Ultrasound simulator (UltraSim) as an evaluation tool of residents' scanning skills: pilot study. *Journ. of Ultrasound in Med.*, *19*(suppl), S13.

Prensky, M. (2004) Interactive pretending: An overview of simulation. Retrieved November 28, 2008 from http://www.marcprensky.com/writing/Prensky-Interactive_Pretending.pdf.

Ruben, B. D. (1999). Simulations, games, and experience-based learning: The quest for a new paradigm for teaching and learning. *Simulation & Gaming*, *30*(4), 498–505. doi:10.1177/104687819903000409

Sauvé, L., Renaud, L., Kaufman, D., & Marquis, J. S. (2007). Distinguishing between games and simulations: A systematic review. *Educational Technology & Society*, *10*(3), 247–256.

Sauvé, L., Renaud, L., Kaufman, D., Samson, D., Bluteau-Dore, V., Dumais, C., et al. (2005a). *Revue systématique des écrits (1998-2004) sur les fondements conceptuels du jeu, de la simulation et du jeu de simulation.* [Systematic review of the literature (1998-2004) on the conceptual foundations of games, simulations, and simulation games]. Québec, QC, Canada: SAGE and SAVIE.

Sauvé, L., Renaud, L., Kaufman, D., & Sibomana, F. (2008). *Revue systématique des écrits (1998-2008) sur les impacts du jeu, de la simulation et du jeu de simulation sur l'apprentissage. Rapport final* [Systematic review of the literature on the impacts of games, simulations and simulation games. Final report]. Québec, QC, Canada: SAGE and SAVIE.

Sauvé, L., Villardier, L., Probst, W., Sanchez Arias, V., Kaufman, D., & Power, M. (2005b). World play: Playing internationally in real time. In P. Kommers & G. Richards (Eds.), *Proceedings of World Conference on Educational Multimedia, Hypermedia and Telecommunications 2005* (pp. 4059-4065). Chesapeake, VA: AACE.

Sawyer, B. (2002). Serious games: Improving public policy through game-based learning and simulation. Washington, DC: Foresight and Governance Project, Woodrow Wilson International Center for Scholars. Retrieved Sept. 8, 2008 from http://www.seriousgames.org/images/seriousarticle.pdf

Schank, R., & Cleary, C. (1995). *Engines for education.* Hillsdale, NJ: Lawrence Erlbaum Associates Inc.

Schank, R., & Neaman, A. (2001). Motivation and failure in educational simulation design. In K. D. Forbus & P. J. Feltovich (Eds.), *Smart machines in education: The coming revolution in educational technology* (pp. 37-69). Cambridge, MA: The MIT Press.

Schnotz, W., & Rasch, T. (2005). Enabling, facilitating, and inhibiting effects of animations in multimedia learning: Why reduction of cognitive load can have negative results on learning. *Educational Technology Research and Development, 53*(3), 47–58. doi:10.1007/BF02504797

Schön, D. A. (1983). *The reflective practitioner: How professionals think in action.* New York: Basic Books.

Shaffer, D. W., Gordon, J. A., & Bennett, N. L. (2004). Learning, testing, and the evaluation of learning environments in medicine: Global performance assessment in medical education. *Interactive Learning Environments, 12*(3), 167–178. doi:10.1080/10494820512331383409

Skyworks Interactive® (2009). *Skyworks advergame development.* Hackensack, NJ: Skyworks Interactive. Retrieved February 13, 2009 from http://www.skyworks.com.

Soussi, A. (2003, March 9). War games becoming all too real. *Sunday Herald.* Retrieved August 31, 2006 from http://www.sundayherald.com/31960.

Spinello, E. F., & Fischbach, R. (2004). Problem-based learning in public health instructions: A pilot study of an online simulation as a problem-based learning approach. *Education for Health, 17*(3), 365–373. doi:10.1080/13576280400002783

Stolovitch, H. D. (1981). Technology of simulation gaming for education and training. Retrieved May 13, 2003 from http://www.hsa-ltd.com/Articles.htm#2.

Stolovitch, H. D., & Thiagarajan, S. (1980). *Frame games.* Englewood Cliffs, NJ: Educational Technology Publications.

Swanson, M. A., & Ornelas, D. (2001). Health Jeopardy: A game to market school health services. *The Journal of School Nursing, 17*(3), 166–169. doi:10.1177/105984050101700301

Wikipedia (2006). *Exergaming.* Retrieved September 2, 2006 from http://en.wikipedia.org/wiki/Exertainment

Zhu, H., Zhou, X., & Yin, B. (2001). Visible simulation in medical education: Notes and discussion. *Simulation & Gaming, 3*(3), 362–369. doi:10.1177/104687810103200306

ADDITIONAL READING

Aldrich, C. (2004). *Simulations and the future of learning: An innovative (and perhaps revolutionary) approach to e-learning*. San Francisco: Pfeiffer.

Aldrich, C. (2005). *Learning by doing*. San Francisco: John Wiley & Sons.

Issenberg, S. B., Mcgaghie, W. C., Petrusa, E. R., Gordon, D. L., & Scalese, R. J. (2005). Features and uses of high-fidelity medical simulations that lead to effective learning: A BEME systematic review. *Medical Teacher*, *27*(1), 10–28. Available at http://www.bemecollaboration.org/beme/pages/reviews/issenberg.html. doi:10.1080/01421590500046924

Issenberg, S. B., & Scalese, R. J. (2008). Simulation in health care education. *Perspectives in Biology and Medicine*, *51*(1), 31–46. doi:10.1353/pbm.2008.0004

Ker, J., & Bradley, P. (2007). *Simulation in medical education*. Edinburgh, UK: Association for the Study of Medical Education (ASME).

McFetrich, P. (2006). A structured literature review on the use of high fidelity patient simulators for teaching in emergency medicine. *Emergency Medicine Journal*, *23*(7), 509–511. doi:10.1136/emj.2005.030544

KEY TERMS AND DEFINITIONS

Computer-Based Clinical Simulations (Interactive): Multimedia-based, computerized cases that require an individual learner or team to work through clinical problems and receive feedback.

Fidelity: The degree of similarity between the training situation and the operational situation which is simulated.

Games: Activities that do not attempt to replicate reality, have clearly defined sets of rules including scoring systems, and produce winners and losers.

Interactive Simulations (Simulators): These use plastic models and/or high- tech modeling of various body parts such as the female pelvis (for a pelvic exam) or the male prostate (for a prostate exam). Complex interactive simulations (human patient simulators) comprise a realistic model of a full human body to allow learners to conduct complex procedures, sometimes in a simulated emergency or operating room.

Procedural Simulations: Simulations used for learning step-by-step processes that require a defined set of steps that should be practiced many times to achieve mastery.

Simulated or Standardized Patients: Trained volunteers or actors who play the role of patient in interviews and/or physical examinations, and who have been trained to respond in specific ways based on the actions of the learner.

Simulations: Activities that include exploration and practice within models of reality but without competition, scoring, and winners/ losers.

Simulation Games: Games that are based on simplified but dynamic models of aspects of reality.

Situational Simulations: Simulations used to promote the learning of communication skills, problem-solving, and decision-making.

Technical Simulations: Simulations that allow learners to practice on models of physical systems to learn equipment operation, rather than practicing on expensive or dangerous systems.

Video-Based Simulations: Video scenarios that present dilemmas to the learner(s), often in areas such as ethics, professionalism, or doctor-patient relationships.

Chapter 4
The Role of Narrative in Educational Games and Simulations

Jim Bizzocchi
Simon Fraser University, Canada

ABSTRACT

This chapter examines the relationship of story, interaction, and learning through a close view of the role of narrative in two SAGE for Learning projects: Contagion and COMPS. The combination of narrative with an interactive multi-mediated environment can enhance the learning experience. In interactive environments, the standard narrative arc has limited analytical utility; in its place, we use a framework of more focused and particular narrative components, with the following components: storyworld, character, emotion, narrativized interface, micro-narrative and narrative progression. This framework is used to analyze Contagion and COMPS, revealing the underlying narrative dynamics that drive the design, and support the learning experiences that they make possible.

INTRODUCTION AND BACKGROUND

The combination of narrative and well-constructed media-rich digital environments has the capacity to support learning in a variety of ways. Well-designed games and simulations do provide this opportunity for multi-mediated and engaging learning environments. Mayer and Chandler (2001) point out that multimedia presentations can support both retention and transfer. Malone and Lepper (1987) maintain that games tap into increased motivation through mechanisms such as challenge, fantasy, curiosity, and learner agency. The author's work with Brad Paras (Paras & Bizzocchi, 2005) indicates that a key connection between games and learning is the powerful effect of Csikszentmihalyi's "flow state" on building the intrinsic motivation to maximize immersion within the learning experience (Csikszentmihalyi, 1990). Scholars such as James Gee (Gee, 2003) and Marc Prensky (Prensky, 2001) maintain that even existing commercial games have significant learning outcomes in their own right. The relationship between games and learning has been identified by scholars internationally

DOI: 10.4018/978-1-61520-731-2.ch004

as a significant opportunity to be explored and developed. Some of the many concentrations for research into games and learning include the MIT- University of Wisconsin *Education Arcade*[1], the *Serious Games*[2] conferences and websites, and the Canadian *Imagine*[3] and *SAGE*[4] research networks.

Narrative has a similar and well-recognized potential to support and enhance learning. Narrative is an extremely powerful personal, social, and cultural phenomenon. Donald Polkinghorne's (1988) extensive overview of the role of narrative in the social sciences relies on Barthes to remind us that narratives are everywhere, and that they have the power to shape us as individuals and as cultures. Polkinghorne (1988), Alvarez and Risko (1989) and Grady (2002) maintain that narrative helps provide learners with conceptual schema, which enable them to understand better and learn more. The unifying power of storytelling can support the juncture of new knowledge with old, and the connection that underlies constructivist learning experiences (Mott, Callaway, Zettlemoyer, Lee, & Lester, 1999). Narrative can also unify learner and content. Character and plot actions in stories increase learner commitment and involvement through identification, and can therefore facilitate transformative learning experiences (Rossiter, 2002). Laurillard (1998) holds that narrative structure is central to comprehension, and its absence can severely inhibit learning.

Media-rich narrative-based simulations and games can offer learners the richest of mediated experience – immersion. Immersion is a much-used and even overused term, but its utility as an analytical filter is enhanced by giving it more specificity. It is possible to recognize at least three quite different forms of user immersion. The oldest, and most closely tied to narrative, is Coleridge's, who describes the immersion of "suspension of disbelief" and the WILLING surrender to the pleasure of story (Coleridge, 1817). Csikszentmihalyi's (1990) is the immersion of active engagement with dynamic process— the immersion of "flow." Cinema, the dominant cultural medium of the 20th century, is the benchmark for Coleridge's immersion. Games are the current benchmark for Csikszentmihalyi's immersion, and may well develop into the dominant cultural medium of the early part of this century. Ermi and Mäyra (2007) parse immersion into distinct types that include the two immersions described above. Their "challenge-based immersion" corresponds to Csikszentmihalyi's flow, and they term the second type "imaginative immersion," which corresponds to Coleridge's "suspension of disbelief." They then go beyond this simple dualistic model, adding a third immersion, "sensory immersion," related to the sensory outputs of the game system. This third immersion may correspond to certain aspects of Gunning's "cinema of attractions," which he saw as one pole of an early and persistent cinematic dialectic between spectacle and narrative (Gunning, 1990). Educational games and simulations can give learners educational experiences complete with all three forms of immersive rewards: imaginative, sensory-rich, and challenging. This is indeed a compelling vision. Janet Murray argues that digital environments which combine immersion and agency have the additional potential of providing transformative experience – surely a heady goal for educators (Murray, 1997).

"Narrative": A Slippery Term

Eric Zimmerman (2004) maintains that "narrative," when considered in combination with concepts such as "game" or "interactivity," becomes a "naughty" term. "Naughtiness" is his sly way of reminding us that the use of such terms requires discipline if we are to avoid misleading conflations and false contradictions. Certainly the undisciplined collision of the concepts of game and narrative led to several years of intellectual sound and fury (and probably more smoke than light) in the game studies discourse (Pearce, 2005). Underneath this unfortunate scholarly melodrama are some fundamental conceptual traps worth recognizing and carefully avoiding. The one that concerns this chapter is the fact that "narrative," like any other powerful and pervasive cultural phenomenon, means many things to many people. I believe that the problem stems from the fact that when theorists write about narrative, what they often mean is really the narrative arc. This is a natural mistake. The narrative arc refers to the causal and emotional connections and implications driven by the carefully designed sequencing of narrative events in time and space. Control over the narrative arc is an incredibly powerful tool for shaping the reception and experience of story. First identified by Aristotle, the narrative arc continues to provide the framework for the design of the plots we see, and for the resulting stories we build in our heads (Aristotle & Janko, 1987).

A typical version of the narrative arc sequence of events is the following formulation: setup, complication, development, resolution, and denouement (Thompson, 1999, pp. 28-29). Each stage has a distinct function, and the authors of traditional narrative works agonize over the order, timing, and exact details of each step:

- the setup introduces the characters and the storyworld they inhabit
- the complication introduces a challenge to be overcome
- the development is the long phase that dominates the bulk of the storytelling, as the protagonist works towards her goal
- the resolution or climax is the culmination of the struggles of the development phase, often resulting in some form of victory or defeat
- the denouement or falling action ties up the story's loose ends, and allows the narrative experience to finish gracefully

This has proven to be an efficient engine for the creation of satisfying narrative works. However, the difficulty with this model is that its power depends in large part on tight control over the design and implementation of details. With tight authorial control, each narrative event can work in tight conjunction with every other narrative event. Because of that, the expressive synergy of the whole far exceeds the individual contributions. The power of the carefully designed narrative arc has enabled media forms such as the novel to dominate the culture of the nineteenth century, and the cinema to dominate the twentieth.

Yet tight control over details is precisely what the interactive process does not afford. In an interactive experience a share of control is ceded to the interactor, and a critical degree of fine authorial control is lost. It is therefore impossible to reconcile the traditional full-blown narrative arc with interactive experience, including educational games and simulations. Laurillard recognizes this in her paper on interactive multi-media in education (Laurillard, 1998). The author of this chapter concurs, and takes the position that there is a fundamental inconsistency between the narrative arc and the interactive experience (Bizzocchi, 2001, 2003; Bizzocchi & Woodbury, 2003). User (or learner) interaction must compromise or even confound the author's complete control over the sequence of narrative events.

However, if we ignore the siren song of the narrative arc, we are free to examine other parameters of story that may be more limited conceptually, but more useful in reaching our goal of understanding the role of narrative in interactive educational games and simulations. This approach avoids a direction that, although intriguing, has complicated our understanding of the relationship of narrative and interactivity.

A Narrative Framework

A more modest framework of relevant narrative parameters can include the examination of the following components:

- **Storyworld:** The environment within which the game unfolds
- **Character:** The beings that populate this game world
- **Emotion:** Both the emotions shown by the games characters and those elicited in the player
- **Narrative interface:** How the narrative sensibilities are instantiated in the appearance and the functionality of the interface design
- **Micro-narrative:** Smaller moments of narrative flow and coherence that occur within a broader context of game play
- **Narrative progression:** A softer, fuzzier version of a narrative path than the traditional narrative arc such as the ordered progression through levels found in commercial electronic games

Storyworld

We stand on firm theoretical ground in our consideration of storyworld as a critical narrative parameter in the experience of interactive game and simulation environments. Jesper Juul (2005, pp. 130-132) develops a four-level hierarchy of abstraction and representationalism in the construction of game worlds. He identifies the levels as "Abstract," as in *Tetris*®; "Iconic," as in face cards in a standard deck; "Incoherent," which he sees as an incomplete (or even self-contradictory) storyworld such as chess or *Donkey Kong*®; and "Coherent," as we find in a more complete and well-articulated storyworld. He argues that current adventure games, for example, typically fall into the final category of coherent and complete storyworlds. (Juul also includes a fifth level of sophistication that is marked by the nesting of game worlds within each other.) Henry Jenkins (2004, pp. 121 - 124) connects storyworlds to a concept of spatial storytelling that has roots in the histories of both narrative and pre-digital games. "Environmental storytelling," to use his term, not only provides a stage where story and interactive environment can play together, but can also evoke pre-existing narrative associations, embed narrative information within the mise-en-scene, and provide necessary resources for the interaction itself. The author of this chapter has argued that a diffusion of "narrative texture" throughout the storyworld can help to suture any disconnection between interaction and the pleasure of narrative. He sees "narrative texture" as the consistent expressive use of all of the subsidiary crafts of a mediated design (i.e., lighting, costume, props, location, music, sound effects) to reinforce narrative themes and the experience of a unified storyworld (Bizzocchi, 2001, 2003).

Character

Within the interactive game and simulation worlds, the characters (i.e., heroes, villains, player-avatars, and non-player characters) live the enactment of the experience and the resultant story. In the broader world of narrative construction, character is seen as the key to reader identification, and beginning writers are strongly urged to construct "character-driven" drama. Salen and Zimmerman rely on the narrative theory of J. Hillis Miller in their take on the role of narrative in games (Salen & Zimmerman, 2004, p. 380). Miller identifies "personification" as a key component of the definition of narrative, and Salen and Zimmerman favor this formulation as consistent with the active construction of character and meaning that occurs in the process of game play.

In traditional narrative, character traits are designed by the author, and find expression in the actions of the story's plot. Readers see the actions and deduce their sense of the character's traits from the actions they observe. In games there are, broadly speaking, two types of characters. The first type are those driven by the game's artificial intelligence (AI) rather than by player actions; these are commonly called "non-player characters" (NCPs). The second type is the character who is the avatar for the player herself. The relationship between character trait and character action is complicated in interactive games. For NPCs, the game's AI is designed to trigger NPC actions that respond to the game state and the player's actions in a manner consistent with a coherent set of traits that define the NPC's character. The player, on the other hand, determines the actions of her avatar, thereby defining the personality traits and character of her own in-game proxy.

Emotion

Emotion in games is a complicated phenomenon. The oft-used benchmark is a lament that we haven't seen "a video game that can make you cry," to which Hal Barwood, a LucasArts game designer, once replied, "I have — tears of boredom." Barwood's cynical interjection at the 1999 MIT "Video Games Come of Age" conference (Barwood, 2000) was contested by several other conference participants who cited moments of deep sadness in games such as *Zelda®*, *Fantasmagoria®*, and *Planetfall®*.

Perron (2004) examines this subject closely, initially separating our identification with the narrative emotion expressed by the characters within the game, which he calls "fiction/witness" emotions from the ludic emotions generated by the process of play. He later cites Philip Tan to include a third type: artifact emotion, or the "aesthetics of astonishment" (Perron, 2005). It is interesting that this three-fold schema of game emotion ("fiction emotion," "artifact emotion," and "game play emotion") maps directly onto Ermi and Mäyra's (2007) three dimensions of immersion (imaginative, sensory, and challenge-based).

If our concern is the relationship of emotion to the experience of narrative in educational games and simulations, it is the narrative "fiction/witness" emotion that will yield the most relevant analysis and conclusions. For our purposes, it will be even more useful to separate this narrative emotion into its two components: the expressed narrative emotion shown by the characters within the game or simulation, and the empathic narrative emotion felt by the players or interactors when participating in the experience.

Narrative Interface

In an earlier series of papers (Bizzocchi, 2001, 2003; Bizzocchi & Woodbury, 2003), the author examined the question of narrative within the design of the interface. In these papers I address the potential disconnection between the pleasure of story and the experience of interaction. I use as my example a lost masterpiece of interactive design and experience, the interactive CD-ROM *Ceremony of Innocence* (Bantock, 1997). This piece is an interesting case study because it combines a deep experience of story with the playing of a series of 60 puzzle-games. *Ceremony* is based on the *Griffin and Sabine* trilogy by Nick Bantock, a love story told in 60 post-cards and letters (Bantock, 1991; 1992; 1993). In *Ceremony*, each post-card and letter is transformed into a puzzle-game which must be solved for the narrative to proceed.

I argue that in this work the incorporation of narrative into the design of the interface has the effect of helping to suture any potential narrative disconnection due to interaction. The analysis here concentrates on two purposeful remediations of the cursor within the overall interactive design. The first remediation is a purely visual one. I argue that the look of the cursors associated with Sabine's puzzle-games reinforce certain of her character traits, and that the look of the cursors associated with Griffin's puzzle-games reinforce his character traits. The second cursor remediation is a more interesting one. In several of the puzzle-games, the standard operational functionality of the mouse-cursor has been changed or "subverted." I claim that the specific transformations of cursor functionality can be seen to correspond to the protagonist's personality. In the process of struggling with the cursor to solve the puzzles, the player is forced to physically enact the protagonist's struggles and ultimately embody the personality traits.

Ben Lin (2007) extends this analysis of narrative interface. He has developed a model of interface design with four quadrants that examine player input and game-state output in both hardware and software forms (Lin, Bizzocchi, & Budd, 2005). Using this model as a reference scheme, he has identified specific strategies for the incorporation of narrative into the design of the interface functionality. Lin's list includes behavioral mimicry interfaces, behavioral metaphor interfaces, narrativization of game metric displays, narrativization of visual perspectives, and mixed reality interfaces (Lin, 2007).

Narrative Progressions and Micro-Narratives

This chapter has argued that the classic (and tightly controlled) Aristotelian narrative arc does not provide utility in the context of interactive forms such as games and simulations. However, there are related, but less rigid formulations that recognize modified forms of narrative progression and coherence consistent with an interactive environment. Let's consider again the simple and classic description of the narrative arc: setup, challenge, development, resolution or climax. We can identify a rough progression of the player and the characters working through an overall game play or simulation arc leading to the resolution of success or failure. The difficulty for interactive experience with respect to the traditional concept of the narrative arc lies in the loss of complete authorial control over the details of the progression. However, there are design strategies that support a softer and more limited level of authorial control over the arc of the experience. Often this arc is expressed as Jenkins formulated – progress across a carefully designed storyworld and game space. This progress can be further articulated and segmented through the use of game levels, which function as guidelines for the player experience of subsidiary arcs, each level with its own version of setup, complications, development and resolution. However, the exercise of authorial control over an interactive narrative arc is problematic at best. Crawford refers in rather derogatory terms to various authorial strategies to control narrative progress: "foldback," "obstructionist," and "kill 'em if they stray" (Crawford, 2003, pp. 79-81).

However, as we go deeper into the interactive experience, and examine smaller individual moments of user actions, the concept of a localized arc takes on considerable force. The changing context for play is constantly set up with fresh complications and challenges, the user's interaction itself is an instantiation of the narrative development phase, and intermediate successes and failures act as interim resolutions and localized climaxes. Jenkins connects this phenomenon to a concept he calls "micro-narrative" in more traditional contexts (Jenkins, 2004, p. 125). By this, he refers to moments of brief, self-contained, and coherent moments of narrative progression embedded within a longer narrative development, such as the fate of the mother and the baby carriage in *The Battleship Potemkin*.

It is possible to see the process of micro-narrative at work throughout the experience of interactive play. In this perspective, one can frame game design as a process that sets the stage and the conditions for a series of micro-narrative events that are triggered and completed (or not) by the player's success or failure in the moment of play. In this framing, we no longer draw a distinction between game and narrative, but we see the two conjoined in an ongoing process of engagement. Insofar as this view is accurate, we have added to the two classic narrative modes of diegesis - the story as told, and mimesis - the story as shown. In moments of micro-narrative engagement within an immersive interactive experience, we are engaged in praxis - the story as enacted (Bizzocchi, 2001, 2003).

The analytical framework for understanding the role of narrative in games, simulations and related interactive works is now complete. The components of this framework are: storyworld, character, protagonist emotion, user emotion, narrative interface, micro-narrative, and narrative progression. The next step is to use these components as analytical tools for observing, understanding and explicating the role of narrative in two interactive projects: the educational simulation *COMPS* and the educational game *Contagion*. This process is a modified form of close reading, a humanities methodology that closely examines a creative artifact. Like any such reading, this is an act of interpretation that first observes and deconstructs the artifact and its experience, and then builds an analysis based on these observations (Van Looy and Baetans, 2003).

NARRATIVE IN *COMPS*

COMPS Overview

COMPS (Collaborative Online Multimedia Problem-based Simulation) is a multi-mediated and networked simulation designed to support collaborative problem-based learning (PBL) for professionals in the health sector. Its goal is to develop both diagnostic skills and clinical reasoning. It is designed to do so in an effective distance-based model that will enable health professionals to learn together regardless of their physical location. *COMPS* combines the immersion and engagement of multi-media simulations with the rich social interaction that is the strength of face-to-face learning. The details of *COMPS* are described in Chapter 17, but for the purposes of this chapter the key questions are the nature and sequencing of the presentations and interactions, and the qualities of the narrative experience.

The heart of cooperative PBL training in the health profession is the use of patient case studies as the prime vehicle for the learning process. Health professionals are given a patient's history plus access to background medical information and simulated test results. They proceed to work through a series of brainstorming processes to identify first the key learning variables, to construct the clinical process and finally to determine a diagnosis and treatment. The process of reviewing the case, planning the research and the diagnostics, and reaching the shared conclusions is as important as the results themselves.

A critical factor in the *COMPS* design was the team's early decision to incorporate "thick" narrative at the core of this process. Typical PBL case studies are based on "thin" narratives, with relatively complete medical descriptions, but little else. These "thin" narratives have little or no sense of the patient as a fully rounded human being – as someone with a rich personal context that includes non-medical factors such as personality, outside life and history.

Kenny and Beagan argue for two approaches to help thicken the case histories of PBL simulations (Kenny & Beagan, 2004). The first approach is to incorporate a series of "narrative components" within these thicker case histories. The components they list switch the case study writing from a narrow medical perspective to a broader patient's perspective. The components include the use of vernacular language, active voice, direct dialogue, extension of the time frame beyond the narrow window of symptoms, presentation of more of the patient's full life, and a broader sense of narrative progression and resolution. The difficulty with the instantiation of this thicker narrative in print cases is that it increases the size of the writing, and can lose the focus, becoming messy. They suggest the use of video components and interactive web-based technologies to make these richer cases more compelling for the PBL participants.

The *COMPS* design team at Simon Fraser University has incorporated Kenny and Beagan's suggestions in their design. *COMPS* is committed to a thick-narrative, video-enhanced, multi-mediated design. The *COMPS* team first augmented the standard thin narrative with a two-stage writing process. An experienced medical case-writer wrote the first version, incorporating more personal information than a standard case would contain. This thicker case was then given to a professional script writer, who turned the case into a series of short video scripts. These video scripts included the standard medical examinations, but also had a glimpse into the life of the patient outside the medical setting. The finished scripts were given to a professional director working with community theater actors. They were then rehearsed, shot, and edited. Finally, the finished clips were combined with standard medical reference material and incorporated within a standard web-based networked instructional environment (*WebCT*®). A second standard web environment (*e-Live*®) was used for the networked problem-solving sessions. *e-Live* allowed the use of both voice-over-Internet protocol audio (VoIP) and an associated whiteboard for shared visual communication.

At a higher level, it seems clear that the *COMPS* team is committed to a fabric of personal, educational, and social values. The foundation is a holistic view of the patient as a human being, not a bundle of symptoms to be solved. This is coupled with an educational commitment to the value of group-based cooperative learning, and a social commitment to the provision of education at a distance. This combination of values has driven the stories they have designed and the weaving of their story components within an educational framework and a software environment.

COMPS Video Segments

The initial *COMPS* test case, "Sean and Kelly," presented a young male with unidentified symptoms. Six video clips are presented to the participants:

- **Scene 1:** Apartment or house: Sean (patient) and Kelly (his girlfriend) have a fight about his symptoms. He lists them and accuses her of giving him a sexually-transmitted disease
- **Scene 2:** Doctor's office: Doctor interviews Sean about his symptoms
- **Scene 3:** Doctor's office: Doctor further interviews Sean about his symptoms and his history
- **Scene 4:** Doctor's office: Doctor interviews Sean about his medical history
- **Scene 5:** Doctor's office: Doctor gives Sean a physical exam
- **Scene 6:** Doctor's office: Doctor administers lab tests on Sean

Each video clip presentation is accompanied by individual and group-based student tasks, online discussion sessions, and the development of interim group conclusions that move the collaborative problem-solving process towards its conclusion. The students make use of related medical information available online as part of the *COMPS* environment. They are also free to augment the *COMPS* medical material with open internet searches for medical information.

This process follows Kenny and Beagan's suggestions. The case history is richer than normal thin case studies, both in terms of amount of information and the form of the information. The participants learn some of the patient's direct history through the scene with his girlfriend, which would normally be outside a standard (thin) case study. The video format allows participants to form their own sense of the patient's personality, lifestyle, and emotional makeup.

Application of the Narrative Component Model to *COMPS* Environment

The *COMPS* experience can be usefully analyzed with the components of the narrative model developed earlier in this article: Storyworld, Character, Emotion, Narrative Interface, and Narrative Progression.

Storyworld: The *COMPS* storyworld is a simple one, but it gives the participants a more grounded look at both the patient's world and the doctor's world. This effect is most pronounced with respect to the doctor. The "apartment" where Sean and Kelly fight in the opening video presentation is bare and without much visual information about who lives there. In the words of one participant it looked "generic." The doctor's office, on the other hand, adds authenticity and impact to the narrative. (The office used in the video was in fact the actual office of the on-screen doctor - a practicing physician who also was a member of a community theatre group). During the first *COMPS* evaluation, participants remarked that this setting made the encounter with the doctor more real.

Character: The characters developed by the *COMPS* team were generally believable and well-rounded. They benefited from the veracity of the original medical case-writer, the depth of the project's professional script writer, the direction of an experienced film and theater director, and the reasonably well-honed performances of three community theater actors. Participants noted that the girlfriend was believable, but her role was brief. Sean was seen as more problematic. He played his part with a degree of emotion, especially in his early encounter with Kelly when he accused her of cheating and giving him an STD. Participants noted that his early performance was not realistic and seemed a bit over the top. However, they felt that his performances with the doctor (the bulk of the video scenes) were more natural and believable. One participant was put off by his early performance which seemed "weird," but noted that this improved in the scenes with the doctor. The doctor's performance, on the other hand, was universally enjoyed by the participants. To them, she seemed competent, professional, skilled and empathetic.

Emotion: The play of emotion in the characters was rich, but generally believable. Kelly trusted her own emotions, vigorously rejecting Sean's accusations, and storming out of the room when he wouldn't stop. Sean changed emotional tenor. He was belligerent and accusatory with Kelly, but much more subdued and concerned with the doctor. This change in emotional flavor seemed to underlie his change in both believability and likeability with the participants. One participant stated that he didn't like Sean — or believe in him — when he was defensive with Kelly, but that he was more sympathetic and believable when he was acting "a bit scared" with the doctor. Sean's fear in the doctor's office was due to his worry over his condition, not to the character of the doctor, who was not only competent, but consistently supportive of Sean. Her character was deemed "motherly" by one of the participants — all of whom liked her.

Interestingly, the participants seemed to deny any significant emotional connections on their own part. This may have been due in part to the difficulty of even a competent and professional video production to compete with either the slick production values of television or cinema works or the visceral impact of an actual documentary. However, it may also be due to the role the participants were playing. Their job in the simulation is to act as the extension of the screen doctor, and figure out the disease. As one of them said: "Once I got into problem-solving, the emotion disappeared and my mind took over." It is somewhat ironic, but in this regard, the participants modeled the emotionally-constricted doctor that Kenny and Beagan – and the *COMPS* researchers – strive to enrich.

Narrative interface: The interface of the *COMPS* environment is not as complex as the sophisticated interface of CGI-based games or simulations. However, it does perform the two specific and narrative-rich communications functions necessary for the PBL process to succeed. It allows the participants to share voice interactions with each other, and therefore share the nuanced communication capabilities of the human voice. This is a practical advantage in the ability of participants at a distance to form a cohesive group and efficiently address their joint task. Its second function is the ability to deliver the narrative-rich video segments which carry not only basic information, but the thicker sense of the full case and the person within.

Narrative progression and micro-narratives: This category is critical to the effectiveness of the *COMPS* simulation. A basic definition of narrative is "a sequence of events in time and space, joined by a cause-and-effect relationship" (Bordwell & Thompson, 1996). Teasing out the significance of this sequence of events, and determining the cause-and-effect relationship is precisely what a doctor must do, and it is precisely what the participants in the PBL simulation must do. In this regard, any doctor's diagnosis is in itself an exercise in narrative construction. *COMPS* endeavors to enrich the narrative progression in order to render the process more human and the results more robust and effective. The participants' role in this process replicates one of the most pervasive narrative forms in popular culture – the mystery. There is a solution to this mystery, and the process is to trace the narrative progression from reported symptom, to observation, to testing, to conclusion and diagnosis. This narrative progression is built around repeated cycles of discussion and problem-solving, cycles which are in fact exercises in solving a complex mystery about a real character. Micro-narrative plays a critical role in this process – each of the videos is a micro-narrative, and each carries not only its own factual and emotional weight, but is also part of the overall progression towards resolution.

NARRATIVE IN *CONTAGION*

Overview of the Game

Contagion is a single-player online simulation game developed by a team at Simon Fraser and York Universities. The project is discussed by the researchers in Chapter 9. This chapter will confine itself to the analysis of the role of narrative in the design and experience of the game. Here we present a brief overview of the game to provide the context within which the narrative plays out.

The ostensible goal of the game is to save a city-state, Pyramidea, from the effects of plague and disease. A higher-level goal is to give senior secondary, college, and university students a chance to live out public health decision-making at various levels of responsibility, and perhaps learn whether they are in fact interested in a health-related career. In the game, the players learn some fundamental facts about the dynamics of infection and public health. More importantly, they act out a process of decision-making in an environment designed to make explicit the complex dynamics of individual responsibility and competing social values.

As with *COMPS*, the *Contagion* team has instantiated educational, social, and personal values within their narrative and interactive systems. On one level, it is clear that they are committed to increasing understanding about what underlies a rational, humane, and effective system of public and personal health. They are also anxious to have young people engage with the challenges of public health, and consider a career in that area. These aims are reinforced by a still broader set of values around gender, race, power, and social justice. As we see in the analysis below, the skillful design of narrative enabled them to incorporate a complex set of values and value-laden decision-making, within a playable and interesting game system.

Application of the Narrative Component Model to *Contagion*

Storyworld: The storyworld of Pyramidea is exquisitely designed. The city-state is organized into three domains, arranged in a hierarchical pyramid. The bottom of the society is Lower Pyramidea, where the mass of ordinary citizens of the lower class struggle to survive both economically and medically. They are beset by various illnesses and diseases, whose virulence is barely kept in check by the front-line medical workers who share this bottom rung of the social ladder with them. The middle of the pyramid contains the forces of the state, the Pyramidea Inoculation Network (PIN), whose job is to enforce control and quarantine against the lower orders and their constant threat of overwhelming plague and contagion. Their real job is to protect the elite of Upper Pyramidea from the disease and social threat in Lower Pyramidea. The elite at the top of the social pyramid are engaged in rarified activities which include the pursuit of pure knowledge – such as medical research.

This storyworld purposely reflects one of the oldest models in western culture. The design team modeled this world on the dynamics of Plato's *Republic*. The three levels of Pyramidea mirror Plato's triple hierarchy of ordinary citizens, warriors, and the philosopher-king. The pervasive threat to public health in Pyramidea has channeled that dynamic into a society based on the maintenance of the narrow health interests of the ruling class through the enforced quarantine and related measures perpetrated by the middle level enforcers against the disease-ravaged lower class.

In the context of *Contagion*, this storyworld is at the same time a narrative frame, a game-play space, and a representation of a culture and a society that, like our own in the western world, is beset with contradictions of class, privilege, and power.

Character: The storyworld is populated with a number of characters, but there are four that are most richly drawn: the three player-avatars, and the mythical hero from the past. Each of the three player-avatars is drawn from a different level of Pyramidea. "Dox" is a front-line health worker living and working in Lower Pyramidea. "Pin" is a PIN medical and quarantine enforcer from the quasi-military Middle Pyramidea state offices. "Virus Hunter" is a member of the Upper Pyramidea ruling elite whose goal is to be a great scientist and medical researcher.

Social values are embedded in the design decisions about characters. Typical stereotypes about gender and race are broken or confounded in the look of the non-player characters (NPCs). Racial and gender markers are there, but the associated roles are cast against type. The state enforcers are not necessarily male; Asians and females have positions of responsibility; and the lower classes tend to appear Caucasian. Color is present, but is never realistic.

The look of the player avatars has a measure of user control, including choice of gender and costume color. Players also have the option of changing the names of their avatars from the defaults to names of their own choice. These customization functions are designed to help players to identify more closely with the avatars they are controlling. The three characters are drawn from their respective classes, but as player avatars, their actions reflect the choices of the game players. Through a sophisticated scoring system, the player accumulates either "ignorance" or "enlightenment" points. It is possible to play, and ultimately to win, the game in either direction, depending on the choices the player has her avatar make. In the process, the player enacts her own version of a value system through the choices she makes. She can either act in a way consistent with a sense of general responsibility for the entire social structure of Pyramidea, or she can act out of narrow self and class interests.

Emotion: The game takes place in an emotion-laden world. Fear is a major driver for the entire game. All classes fear Contagion and disease, the lower classes fear the PIN enforcers, and the upper and middle classes are terrified of the lower ones. In addition, arrogance and brutality typify the PIN mentality, and pride and hubris typify the upper class. The health workers in the lower city at least have a measure of compassion that drives their mission.

It is questionable whether the players ultimately reach the same level of identification and empathy for these characters that one might expect in other media such as film or novels. It is a characteristic of most game play that although narrative pleasure is part of the experience, ludic pleasure, or displeasure, is the core of the experience. User testing of *Contagion* confirmed this. For the young players (12 to 16 years old) tested, emotions were tied to the game play, not to the story. Players were thrilled when they won, frustrated when they were losing, and generally experienced pleasure and satisfaction in the context of game play success. In this regard, *Contagion* is similar to most games in that user emotion is primarily the emotion of play, not story.

Narrative interface: The look and feel of the *Contagion* screens provide an effective framework for the experience of narrative in the characters and the storyworld. Gameplay instructions are delivered in narrative-reinforcing channels such as a simple notebook for the lower-level health worker, or a more expensive and sophisticated PDA for the PIN enforcers. The world itself is richly represented, and the characters appear consistent with their individual roles and with the overall storyworld. (See *Contagion* images in Chapter 9.) A sophisticated interactive touch is the design and functionality of the two framing graphics that form a boundary shell on either side of the game play frame. At the same time they both reinforce narrative theme and function as readout indicators for critical game play metrics. On the left is a PIN enforcer with a club holding back the lower classes. If the player's ignorance level increases, the club becomes more and more menacing. On the right is a frieze of a person being helped up a ladder by medical workers. As the player's enlightenment level increases the person is handed up higher and higher by the supporting helpers.

Narrative progression and micro-narratives: As the game play proceeds, micro-narratives, level narratives, and the larger storyworld narrative are successively developed. In order to finish the game, the player must complete one game cycle within each of the three levels of Pyramidea. Each cycle has its own beginning and setup, its own series of actions and mini-games that must be performed, and its own interim winning state. In the lower level, the "Dox" avatar must administer medical advice and support in her station, navigate through the streets, avoid the PIN operatives, administer more medical aid in the neighborhood, and return to her station. Starting in the middle level enforcement office, the "PIN" avatar must complete a biohazard cleanup game, and then travel down to the lower level to perform mini-missions in both the urban neighborhoods and the farming sections. In the process, the player has a choice to act in a brutal manner and build her ignorance level, or act more benevolently and build her enlightenment level. The upper level game play centers on the researcher "Virus Hunter" avatar. The player performs a combination of medical and historical research activities, culminating in the disinfecting of a PIN hospital in the lower level of the game.

The actions and mini-games are moments of micro-narrative development that drive the intermediate narrative of the level play, which in turn builds the larger narrative of the storyworld. This leads to the culminating endgame segment. Here the player must coordinate the three avatars, allocate various resources, and respond to a combination of widespread civil strife and rampant plague and *Contagion*, both of which wrack the entire city. At this point, a legendary figure from the city's historic past appears in holographic form, reminiscent of Hari Seldon's appearances in Asimov's *Foundation* series (Asimov, 1951), and offers guidance in this moment of crisis. The player manipulates resources and actions to meet the crisis, maneuvering towards one of two possible winning states. The player can crush the riots through the use of overwhelming force, accumulating more ignorance points in the process of turning the city into an even more authoritarian and repressed police-state. Conversely, the player can accumulate enlightenment and open up the city's social barriers, accepting the risk of some short-term losses for the protected classes in order to build a new social structure where the free mingling of all people leads to the ultimate development of natural immunities throughout society.

The goal of the researchers is to build a gameworld that is interesting and fun to play on its own terms, that provides the opportunity to make a range of both action and moral choices, and is situated within a storyworld compelling enough that the player will choose to evaluate the consequences of these choices.

CONCLUSION

This chapter began with the recognition that the traditional, rigidly-controlled narrative arc is not an appropriate analytical match with the interactive nature of educational games and simulations. It maintains that a broader, less restrictive framework of narrative components is a better tool for the description and analysis of the role of narrative within interactive environments. These components are: storyworld, character, emotion, narrativized interface, micro-narrative and narrative progression. This framework of narrative components was applied in the analysis of the role of story in an education simulation (*COMPS*) and an educational simulation game (*Contagion*). This analysis shows that well-designed and integrated narrative components have the power to enhance interactive experience, giving it a depth and a resonance that can better engage learners. This will increase the motivation to commit and remain committed within the learning process. Effective narrative design can also harness the cognitive power of story, and allow interactive participants to recognize and create schema to contextualize and integrate their own learning.

Equally striking is the relationship of narrative design and story to the values that educational designers embed within the interactive environments they build. Narrative constructions have values embedded in the core of their design. The complex play of character, theme, setting and action is driven at a deep level by the value system of the authors. One cannot read *War and Peace* and avoid coming to terms with Tolstoy's deep values about family and society. In a less exalted example from contemporary culture, nor can you read one of Michael Crichton's novels without confronting his sharp ambivalence towards the promise and the threat of technology in modern society. In the same way, the values of the creators of *COMPS* and *Contagion* are reflected in the interactive systems they designed and amplified by the narratives they have incorporated.

ACKNOWLEDGMENT

This paper is built on the original work of the researchers of the *SAGE COMPS* team and *Contagion* team. My thanks especially to *COMPS* principal investigator David Kaufman and graduate student Robyn Schell and to *Contagion* principal investigators Suzanne De Castell and Jennifer Jenson and graduate students Nis Bojin and Nicholas Taylor. The narrative framework that is the foundation of this paper grew out of my paper in *Loading*, the Journal of the Canadian Games Studies Association, vol. 1, issue 1. My analysis of games and narrative has benefited from the insights and work of my graduate students Krystina Madej, Ben Lin, Douglas Grant, Kirsten Johnson, and Josh Tanenbaum.

NOTE

The Jenkins and Zimmerman articles in this text are cited in the chapter, but the entire book has valuable articles from the leading theorists in game studies, interactive narrative and digital culture.

This text is cited directly in the chapter, but is also an excellent text on a wide range of game theory, practice and culture.

REFERENCES

Alvarez, M. C., & Risko, V. J. (1989). *Schema activation, construction, and application.* ERIC Document Reproduction Service No. ED312611. Retrieved from ERIC database.

Aristotle, , & Janko, R. (1987). [*With the tractatus coislinianus: A hypothetical reconstruction of poetics II, the fragments of the on poets.*] [R. Janko Trans.] [. Indianapolis, IN: Hackett Publishing Company.]. *Poetics*, I.

Asimov, I. (1951) *The Foundation trilogy: Three classics of science fiction.* New York: Doubleday Books

Bantock, N. (1991). *Griffin & Sabine: An extraordinary correspondence.* San Francisco: Chronicle Books.

Bantock, N. (1992). *Sabine's notebook: In which the extraordinary correspondence of Griffin & Sabine continues.* Vancouver, BC, Canada: Raincoast Books.

Bantock, N. (1993). *The golden mean: In which the extraordinary correspondence of Griffin & Sabine concludes.* Vancouver, BC, Canada: Raincoast Books.

Bantock, N. (1997). *Ceremony of innocence* (Macintosh/Windows edition). Wiltshire: Real World Multimedia.

Barwood, H. (2000). *Games as interactive storytelling.* Message posted to http://web.mit.edu/cms/games/storytelling.html

Bizzocchi, J. (2001). *Ceremony of innocence: A case study in the emergent poetics of interactive narrative.* Unpublished M.Sc. thesis, Comparative Media Studies, Massachusetts Institute of Technology, Cambridge, MA.

Bizzocchi, J. (2003, May). *Ceremony of innocence and the subversion of interface: Cursor transformation as a narrative device.* Paper presented at the Digital Arts and Culture 2003: Streaming Wor(l)Ds, Royal Melbourne Institute of Technology, Melbourne, Australia.

Bizzocchi, J., & Woodbury, R. F. (2003). A case study in the design of interactive narrative: The subversion of the interface. *Simulation & Gaming, 34*(4), 550–568. doi:. doi:10.1177/1046878103258204

Bordwell, D., & Thompson, K. (1996). *Film art: An introduction* (5th ed.). New York: McGraw-Hill.

Coleridge, S. T. (1817). *Biographia literaria or, biographical sketches of my literary life and opinions.* New York: Kirk and Mercein.

Crawford, C. (2003). *The art of interactive design: A euphonious and illuminating guide to building successful software.* San Francisco: No Starch Press.

Csikszentmihalyi, M. (1990). *Flow: The psychology of optimal experience* (1st ed.). New York: Harper & Row.

Ermi, L., & Mäyra, F. (2007). Fundamental components of the game play experience: Analyzing immersion. In S. de Castell, & J. Jenson (Eds.), *Worlds in play: International perspectives on digital games research* (pp. 37-53). New York: Peter Lang Publishing.

Gee, J. P. (2003). *What video games have to teach us about learning and literacy.* New York: Palgrave Macmillan.

Grady, K. (2002). *Adolescent literacy and content area reading.* ERIC Document Reproduction Service No. ED469930. Retrieved from ERIC database.

Gunning, T. (1990). The cinema of attractions. In A. Barker, & T. Elsaesser (Eds.), *Early cinema: Space, frame, narrative* (pp. 56-67). London: BFI Publishing.

Jenkins, H. (2004). Game design as narrative architecture. In N. Wardrip-Fruin, & P. Harrigan (Eds.), *First person: New media as story, performance, and game* (pp. 118-130). Cambridge, MA: The MIT Press.

Juul, J. (2005). *Half-real: Video games between real rules and fictional worlds*. Cambridge, MA: The MIT Press.

Kenny, N. P., & Beagan, B. L. (2004). The patient as text: A challenge for problem-based learning. *Medical Education*, *38*(10), 1071–1079. doi:10.1111/j.1365-2929.2004.01956.x

Laurillard, D. (1998). Multimedia and the learner's experience of narrative. *Computers & Education*, *31*(2), 229. doi:10.1016/S0360-1315(98)00041-4

Lin, B. (2007). *Games, narrative and interface design*. Unpublished M.Sc. thesis, Simon Fraser University, Burnaby, BC, Canada.

Lin, B., Bizzocchi, J., & Budd, J. (2005, June). *Interface and narrative texture.* Paper presented at the 2005 conference of the Digital Games Research Association (DiGRA), Changing Views: Worlds in Play, Vancouver BC, Canada. Retrieved October 25, 2007 from http://www.digra.org/dl/

Looy, V. Jan and Baetans, Jan. (2003). *Close reading new media: Analyzing electronic literature.* Leuven, Belgium: Leuven University Press.

Malone, T. W., & Lepper, M. R. (1987). Intrinsic motivation and instructional effectiveness in computer-based education. In R. E. Snow & M. J. Farr (Eds.), *Aptitude, learning, and instruction*: *III. Conative and affective process analysis* (pp. 255-286). Hillsdale, NJ: Lawrence Erlbaum Associates, Inc.

Mayer, R. E., & Chandler, P. (2001). When learning is just a click away: Does simple user interaction foster deeper understanding of multimedia mes-*SAGEs*? *Journal of Educational Psychology*, *93*(2), 390. doi:10.1037/0022-0663.93.2.390

Mott, B., Callaway, C., Zettlemoyer, L., Lee, S., & Lester, J. (1999). Towards narrative centered learning environments. In M. Mateas & P. Sengers (Eds.), *Narrative Intelligence: Papers from the 1999 Fall Symposium*, Technical Report FS-99-01 (pp. 78-82). Menlo Park, CA: American Association for Artificial Intelligence.

Murray, J. H. (1997). *Hamlet on the holodeck: The future of narrative in cyberspace*. New York: Free Press.

Paras, B. S., & Bizzocchi, J. (2005, June). *Game, motivation, and effective learning: An integrated model for educational game design.* Paper presented at the 2005 conference of the Digital Games Research Association (DiGRA), Changing Views: Worlds in Play, Vancouver, BC, Canada. Retrieved October 25, 2007 from http://www.digra.org/dl/db/06276.18065.pdf

Pearce, C. (2005) Theory wars: An argument against arguments in the so-called ludology/narratology debate. In S. DeCastell & J. Jenson (Eds.), *Changing Views - Worlds in Play, Selected Papers of the 2005 Digital Games Research Association's Second International Conference* (pp. 41-45). Vancouver, BC, Canada: Simon Fraser University.

Perron, B. (2004). Sign of a threat: The effects of warning systems in survival horror games. In A. Clarke (Ed.), *Proceedings, the Fourth International Conference on Computational Semiotics for Games and New Media (COSIGN 2004)* (pp. 132-141).

Perron, B. (2005, June). *A cognitive psychological approach to gameplay emotions.* Paper presented at the 2005 conference of the Digital Games Research Association (DiGRA), Changing Views: Worlds in Play, Vancouver BC, Canada. Retrieved October 25, 2007 from http://www.digra.org/dl/db/06276.58345.pdf

Polkinghorne, D. (1988). *Narrative knowing and the human sciences*. Albany NY: State University of New York Press.

Prensky, M. (2001). *Digital game-based learning*. New York: McGraw-Hill.

Rossiter, M. (2002). *Narrative and stories in adult teaching and learning.* ERIC Document Reproduction Service No. ED473147. Retrieved from ERIC database.

Salen, K., & Zimmerman, E. (2004). *Rules of play: Game design fundamentals*. Cambridge, MA: The MIT Press.

Thompson, K. (1999). *Storytelling in the new Hollywood: Understanding classical narrative technique*. Cambridge, MA: Harvard University Press.

Zimmerman, E. (2004). Narrative, interactivity, play and games - four naughty concepts in need of discipline. In N. Wardrip-Fruin, & P. Harrigan (Eds.), *First person: New media as story, performance, and game* (pp. 154-155). Cambridge, MA: The MIT Press.

ADDITIONAL READING

Bizzocchi, J. (2007). Games and narrative: An analytical framework. *Loading: The Journal of the Canadian Games Studies Association, 1*(1), 5-10. Available at http://journals.sfu.ca/loading/index.php/loading/article/view/1/1

Bordwell, D. (1985). *Narration in the fiction film*. Madison WI: University of Wisconsin Press.

Kenny, N. P., & Beagan, B. L. (2004). The patient as text: A challenge for problem-based learning. *Medical Education, 38*(10), 1071–1079. doi:10.1111/j.1365-2929.2004.01956.x

Salen, K., & Zimmerman, E. (2004). *Rules of play: Game design fundamentals*. Cambridge, MA: The MIT Press.

Wardrip-Fruin, N., & Harrigan, P. (Eds.). (2004). *First person: New media as story, performance, and game*. Cambridge, MA: The MIT Press.

KEY TERMS AND DEFINITIONS

Interactive Narrative: A narrative that unfolds within an interactive environment such as hypertext, electronic game, or virtual world.

Interface: The hardware and software that carry information between the user and a computer system.

Media-Rich Narrative: Narrative that has been enriched through the addition of component media forms such as graphics, photographs, video, and/or audio.

Micro-Narrative: A smaller and relatively self-contained unit of narrative coherence and flow within a larger narrative experience.

Narrative: A sequence of events in time and space, typically involving characters, storyworld, and some form of dramatic progression.

Storyworld: The general environment as described or depicted in the telling or presentation of a narrative.

"Thick" Narrative: In the context of this chapter, medical case studies that give a holistic view of the patient and his/her life, rather than a "thin" description confined to listing medical symptoms.

ENDNOTES

1 http://www.educationarcade.org
2 http://www.seriousgames.org
3 http://www.ierg.net/
4 http://www.*SAGE*forlearning.ca/

Chapter 5
Does Fantasy Enhance Learning in Digital Games?

Mahboubeh Asgari
Simon Fraser University, Canada

David Kaufman
Simon Fraser University, Canada

ABSTRACT

Digital games have the potential to create environments that increase motivation, engage learners, and support learning. This chapter focuses on fantasy as one of the motivational features of games, and explores the relationships among digital games, fantasy, and learning. The authors describe game characteristics and the key factors that make digital games motivational and compelling – important factors in designing games for learning. Motivation is critical in engaging students in learning activities, and this chapter explores fantasy as an important motivational feature in digital games, the popular genre of fantasy role-playing games such as Dungeons & Dragons, and the importance of creating different kinds of fantasies for males and females. Finally, the authors explore the integration of learning content in fantasy contexts in digital games.

INTRODUCTION

Digital games have the potential to create environments that increase motivation, engage learners, and support learning (e.g., see Shaffer, Squire, Halverson, & Gee, 2005; Stewart, 1997). Research suggests that imagination plays a large part in this. Digital games allow learners to explore their imagination comfortably (Millians, 1999). Using fantasies, mental images, and non-real situations in digital games can stimulate learners' behavior (Vockell, 2004), making learning more motivating and appealing by presenting the material either in an imaginary context that is familiar to them or in a fantasy context that is emotionally attractive (Malone & Lepper, 1987). Creating environments that absorb learners in a fantasy world can motivate and engage them in learning activities (Cordova, 1993). Past empirical research suggests that embedding material in a fantasy context can enhance learning more than a generic, non-contextual environment (Cordova, 1993; Garris, Ahlers, & Driskell, 2002,

DOI: 10.4018/978-1-61520-731-2.ch005

citing Druckman, 1995). However (as discussed in more detail later in the chapter), recent research (Habgood, 2007) challenges the established fantasy-based integration of learning material with games and proposes an alternative perspective that identifies game mechanics as more critical than fantasy to effective integration.

This chapter focuses on the relationship between fantasy and learning in computer-based instructional games. Since learning is believed to be one of the benefits of play which is related to factors such as increased motivation (Rieber, 2001), and digital games are reported to increase motivation, we first review the features that make such games motivational. We discuss the relationship between motivation and learning in order to show that including motivational features in educational games affects students' learning. Among such motivational features, we focus on the element of fantasy. The popular genre of fantasy role-playing games such as *Dungeons & Dragons* and the importance of creating different kinds of fantasies for different genders are also explained. Finally, we explore the integration of learning content in fantasy contexts in digital games.

BACKGROUND

Game Definition

Generally, a game is defined as a set of voluntary activities which has participants, goals, rules, and some kind of (physical or mental) competition. Dempsey, Haynes, Lucassen, & Casey (2002) define a game as "a set of activities involving one or more players. It has goals, constraints, payoffs, and consequences. A game is rule-guided and artificial in some respects. Finally, a game involves some aspect of competition, even if that competition is with oneself" (p. 159). The term "digital game" usually refers to games played using a personal computer or personal game machine. Prensky (2001) defines digital games by a set of key characteristics including: rules, goals and objectives, outcomes and feedback, conflict/ competition/ challenge/ opposition, interaction, and representation or story. (see Chapter 1 for a complete discussion). Digital games can be categorized as adventure, simulation, competition, cooperation, programming, puzzles, and business management games (Hogle, 1996, citing Dempsey, Lucassen, Gilley, & Rasmussen, 1993; Jacobs & Dempsey, 1993).

During the past 40 years, digital games have been played with a variety of technologies and on many devices: from a sealed console, floppy disk, CD-ROM, with email, on the Internet, and with handheld machines such as the *Game Boy*®, mobile phones, and game consoles such as the Sony *PlayStation*® 2/3 or Nintendo's *Gamecube*®. Digital games can be played individually, against the computer, or against other people, either face-to-face or online. The terms computer game and video game are usually used interchangeably and the term "digital game" incorporates both.

Game Characteristics

Digital games share a number of essential features. Good games are fun and intrinsically motivating. The best games, as Prensky (2001) asserts, are easy to learn while providing many challenges. Some features that help players learn a game and get immersed in it include clear and concise instructions (Gee, 2003), help functions, tips, and 'winning prototypes' (examples of how to play the game) (Dempsey, Lucassen, Haynes, & Casey, 1996), and clear, constructive, and encouraging feedback (Malone, 1980; Reeve, 1992). Motivating games also incorporate an optimal challenge (Csikszentmihalyi, 1990), have an appropriate and clear goal (Dempsey et al., 1996; Malone, 1980), and offer clear and meaningful rules (Becta, 2001, cited by Mitchell & Savill-Smith, 2004; Garris et al., 2002; Prensky, 2005).

More motivating features include elements of curiosity and fantasy (Malone, 1980), having an intermediate number of choices, and giving players an intermediate control over the features of the game (Malone & Lepper, 1987; Snider, 2003; Waal, 1995). Interactivity (Salen & Zimmerman, 2004; Waal, 1995, citing Myers, 1990), and competition (Malone & Lepper, 1987; Vockell, 2004; Vorderer, Hartmann, & Kilmmt, 2003) are other essential features of motivating games. As well, good video games reward innovative thinking (Gee, 2003) and reward players within the rules and game structures (de Castell & Jenson, 2003).

With regard to fantasy, Waal (1995, citing Myers, 1990) says that fantasy, unlike challenge and interactivity, is not powerful enough to keep the player motivated and engaged; however, it is influential in engaging the player in the first stages of playing the game, when the player is deciding whether or not to play. In other words, fantasy can be the hook that motivates the player. Malone (1980) notes that digital games that involve fantasies such as war, destruction, and competition seem to be more compelling than less emotionally engaging games.

Technical game features also motivate and engage players. Players like to have high quality screen design, color, animation, a high level of detail, textural depth, and immersive experience, as well as sounds, visuals, and situations that attract them (Dempsey et al., 1996; Malone, 1980; Prensky, 2001; Waal, 1995). Rieber (1991) states that instructional computer activities containing animated graphics are more appealing to students than those without dynamic graphics. According to interviews with four game development companies done by the British Educational Communications and Technology Agency (Becta, 2006), high quality graphics and sounds may not only develop players' initial interest, but they may also foster an emotional response in players. As well, players like to see the game as a real- time performance. Therefore, fast and more responsive games engage their players (Dempsey et al., 1996; Prensky, 2001; Rosas et al., 2003).

In addition to the above features, the concept of identity is an important consideration in designing motivating games. Games, especially role-playing video games, can motivate their players through the characters that the players develop—characters with whom players can identify and create emotional bonds. These fantasy virtual characters need to have a high degree of personal relevance so that they can reach people of different ages, gender, class, race, and ethnicity. According to Gee (2004), motivated players make connections with their characters, care for their characters as an extension of themselves, and project their own identities onto those imaginary virtual characters. Motivational games can produce powerful identities through the emotions and efforts that players put into the game. In educational contexts, digital games can offer opportunities for students to practice; automate their skills; and trigger deep learning through creating simulated worlds, developing fantasy characters for different players, and recruiting identities (Gee, 2003, 2004; Squire, 2004, 2006).

Emotions are the basis for our motivation to become engaged in activities (Deci & Ryan, 1985). Deci and Ryan declare that emotions, including interest-excitement (citing Izard, 1977) and joy (citing Csikszentmihalyi, 1975), are the basis of intrinsically motivated behavior. Interest-excitement can play an important role in the direction and strength of attention and also in the adaptation, development, and coordination of human behavior. According to Deci and Ryan, "interest and excitement are central emotions that accompany intrinsic motivation, and the concept of flow represents a descriptive dimension that may signify some of the purer instances of intrinsic motivation" (p. 29). Thus, games with features that invite emotions, including interest-excitement, are motivating for players.

MOTIVATION AND LEARNING

The features which make digital games motivating and engaging need to be taken into account while designing games for learning. Learners' motivation is an important evidence-based psychological principle reported by the American Psychological Association (APABEA, 1997), influencing both what is learned, and to what degree. According to APABEA, positive emotions such as curiosity can increase motivation and facilitate learning; however, negative emotions such as anxiety and worrying about competence or failure can decrease motivation and interfere with learning. In addition, learners' intrinsic motivation can be stimulated by tasks that are personally relevant, appropriate in complexity and difficulty, provide personal choice and control, and allow learners to believe that they can succeed. An opportunity for learners to interact and collaborate with others also enhances motivation and learning.

Increased intrinsic motivation may heighten the learner's attention toward instruction; enhanced motivation may change the learner's "depth of processing" or active involvement in the activity, or change the learner's mood state. Finally, a learner may recall or transfer abstract problems better when such problems are presented in familiar ways (Malone & Lepper, 1987).

Motivation has a direct effect on learning outcomes, the desire to continue to learn, and in general, what and how to learn. With this in mind, we need to include motivating, engaging features in designing digital games for learning. One of these features, as mentioned before, is fantasy.

Fantasy and Digital Games

Fantasy is a popular genre that uses supernatural forms. One fantasy genre has taken the form of video games. Lepper and Malone (1987) define fantasy as an environment that "evokes mental images of physical or social situations not actually present" (p. 240). Such objects or situations include physical or social impossibilities that motivate and attract players. Garris et al. (2002) assert that including "imaginary or fantasy context, themes, or characters" and providing "optimal level of informational complexity" can make computer games motivational (p. 447). Fantasy role-playing games are appealing and motivating because they engage players' imagination and fantasies.

Fantasy role-playing video games have evolved from *Dungeons & Dragons (D&D)*. Wikipedia (http://en.wikipedia.org/wiki/) notes that *"Dungeons & Dragons* is a tabletop fantasy role-playing game (RPG) originally designed by E. Gary Gygax and Dave Arneson, and first published in 1974 by the Gygax-owned company Tactical Studies Rules, Inc. (TSR)." They are now the leader in the role-playing game market, with millions of people playing the game. The name *Dungeons & Dragons* has sometimes been used as a generic term for fantasy role-playing games. Experienced *D&D* players have an advantage when it comes to playing other fantasy video games.

Fantasy and Control

In *D&D*, players create imaginary characters within a fantasy context. Based on their characterization, they decide how they want their characters to act and play and can improvise freely within the rules of the game. In fantasy role-playing games, players can take on different identities; they can play their virtual character, they can play their real-world character, or they can switch between the two. While playing, they can talk about their in-game fantasy roles or their real-world identity (Gee, 2003).

Likewise, Evry (2004) explains the relationship between fantasy and control. In a fantasy role-playing game, players can experience a strong sense of agency and feel that they truly are their characters. The more control they have, the stronger their sense of agency. A great sense of control comes from a highly responsive character. An unrealistic and crude character can decrease the player's sense of agency. A sense of agency affects the player's feeling of power and personal connection to the character he or she is playing, or to the entire game.

Fantasy and Identity

Fantasy environments may increase intrinsic motivation in players through satisfying their needs. Through fantasies, players can interact in situations that are not part of their real life. Fantasies can include situations and activities that are unlikely or impossible to happen in reality and in people's daily lifestyle. Role-playing games such as *Dungeons & Dragons* provide the opportunity for the players to live out their fantasies. Players create characters that inhabit strange worlds and have unusual abilities. Through role-playing, players identify with their characters, which can develop and evolve over months. The characters trigger fantasies that satisfy players' emotional needs. For instance, players can experience power, success, or fame within the context of the game (Cordova, 1993; Malone & Lepper, 1987). Sometimes, players can take their imaginary characters so seriously that they blur the lines between fantasy and reality.

Gee (2003) also discusses the concept of fantasy and the imaginary virtual identity in fantasy role-playing games. Explaining the three types of identity—real-world identity, virtual identity, and projective identity—Gee argues that a player can imagine a newborn identity at the intersection of the player's real-world identity and his/her fantasy virtual identity. While playing, some players play outside their "real" identity, projecting values and desires onto the virtual identity. For example, a player may play their fantasy virtual character as someone who takes risks, is creative, or is resilient in the face of failure, though in real life the player may have completely different traits.

Fantasy and Gender

There are significant differences among individuals in the fantasies they find compelling (Malone & Lepper, 1987). Fantasies that girls find compelling appear to be different from those of boys (Cassell & Jenkins, 1998). This is because the dialogues that define likes and dislikes for girls and boys are, on the whole, substantively different and so provide them with specific sets of values, tastes, and interests. Cassell & Jenkins (1998) make an important point in saying that "the binary opposition between masculine and feminine is a purely cultural construct" (p. 1). Men and women's interests can differ from one culture to another based on how they are defined in that culture.

In general, since most of the roles and positions that media offer to males and females are predefined—protagonists roles for women but competitive and violent roles, and the like, for males—fantasies that girls and boys find appealing differ accordingly. Role-playing video games can provide the opportunity for females and males to change roles, positions, or powerful gender stereotypes, and redefine themselves through different fantasies, roles, and characters that they act out.

While it is necessary that different and more neutral images be projected through the media for both males and females, it is important to design games that appeal to female interests and tastes. According to Hartmann and Klimmt (2006), research on media genre preference (citing Slater, 2003) indicates that males are more interested in violent and competitive games than females, due to the media model that encourages boys to identify with those images. Few digital games address females' preferences, similarly reinforced by popular media, for non-violent content, which leads to girls' lack of interest in playing such games (Hartmann & Klimmt, 2006, citing Jansz, 2005; Subrahmanyam & Greenfield, 1998).

This was observed in Cassell and Jenkins' (1999) study. In their analysis of two game design contexts, Cassell and Jenkins found that gender differences were consistent. Boys showed more propensity for violence in their game-playing than did girls. Many girls commented that they did not like the content or the violent nature of the games. Cassell and Jenkins argued that it is the lack of models that is responsible for the girls' aversion to violent games. Instead, girls tend to enjoy games that employ narrative. Girls are not uninterested in video games; they are just attracted to different game designs and features than the ones that comprise the dominant game genre.

Therefore, to motivate girls, it is necessary to design role-playing video games that include girls' fantasies and desires. An example of an existing one (actually a simulation game, see chapter 1) is *The Sims®*. *The Sims* (first published in 2000) is successful because it appeals to girls' preferences while also attracting males. The game is not about being faster, winning, eliminating one's competitors, or having more explosions—the type of content that tends to be more male-oriented. Rather, it is about gradual processes, developing explorations, establishing friendships, and extending social status (Jenkins, 2001).

In this section, we have discussed the fantasy role-playing game genre and explained that suitable fantasies and interests for girls and boys need to be included in games to engage both. Now we focus on the element of fantasy as a motivational factor in digital games, and discuss it in relation to learning.

FANTASY AND LEARNING

The concept of fantasy-based integration of learning material and digital games comes from early research by Malone (1981) and Malone and Lepper (1987). They stated that the educational effectiveness of a digital game relates to the way in which learning material is integrated into the fantasy context of the game. If the learning content is intrinsically integrated into the fantasy context, greater learning will occur than with extrinsic integration. Most of the research in this area since has used Malone, and Malone and Lepper's work.

However, a study by Habgood and his colleagues (2005), followed by Habgood's Ph.D. dissertation (2007), criticize the works of the above-mentioned researchers and propose an alternative perspective on the intrinsic integration of learning content. In this section we will first review the literature on fantasy and learning, and then describe briefly Habgood and his colleagues' criticism.

Experimental research on fantasy and learning has shown that instructional material presented in a fantasy context that is of interest leads to increases in both students' motivation and learning (Cordova, 1993; Cordova & Lepper, 1996; Parker & Lepper, 1992). In these studies, those who learned from an embellished fantasy context learned more than those in an unembellished program. According to Malone (1980), an emotionally appealing fantasy needs to be intrinsically related to the skill learned in the activity. Games with no fantasies involve only abstract symbols.

Endogenous vs. Exogenous Fantasy

Fantasy contexts can be intrinsic/endogenous and extrinsic/exogenous to the game content (Lepper & Malone, 1987; Rieber, 1996). In endogenous fantasy, the content to be learned is embedded in the fantasy context; that is, the skill to be learned and the fantasy are related to each other. In exogenous fantasy, the relationship between the content of the study and the fantasy is purely arbitrary. While traditional educational games have relied on exogenous fantasy games such as *Hangman*, more recent examples such as *SimCity®* and others in the *Sim®* series use endogenous fantasy contexts in which the content of learning is embedded into the game content. As Rieber (1996) notes, players in a game with endogenous fantasy are more interested in the fantasy and so in the learning content. On the other hand, exogenous fantasy can be considered as educational "sugar coating." There are many educational games that use exogenous fantasies.

In their study, Malone and Lepper (1987) describe endogenous and exogenous fantasy using two types of instructional games. In the first type (exogenous), students learn about prefixes; whenever they perform successfully, a cavorting dragon breathing smoke and fire appears on the screen. In this context, the content of the game can be replaced with any subject, and the dancing dragon does the same. However, in the second type of instructional game (endogenous), learners need to solve problems about fractions presented to them in the form of requests from customers in a pizza shop. In this context, the skills to be learned, i.e., fractions, are integrated with the context. Malone and Lepper believe that the use of these two different types of fantasy contexts have different effects in the learner's long-term interest in the material being presented. They also believe that endogenous fantasies are preferred to exogenous fantasies because in endogenous fantasy, the feedback is not just right or wrong, but is both specific and constructive. Both Lepper and Malone (1987) and Rieber (1996) find endogenous fantasies more interesting and educational than exogenous fantasies.

Curiosity

Fantasy in educational games stimulates curiosity and motivates students to play and learn. Curiosity is the result of knowledge gaps. Malone and Lepper (1987) explain that curiosity can be stimulated by making individuals think that their existing knowledge lacks one or more of three characteristics: completeness, consistency, and parsimony. In a game, mystery can evoke curiosity. For example, adventure themes, or activities in fantasy contexts can stimulate curiosity.

Cognitive Aspects of Fantasy

Fantasy can be studied from two perspectives: cognitive and emotional (Lepper & Malone, 1987; Malone & Lepper, 1987). The use of fantasy in instructional design has cognitive advantages. For instance, presenting new information to learners by relating it to their past knowledge through endogenous fantasies can help them better understand the information. On the other hand, in simulations, new information can be embedded in an imaginary context which learners will later apply to their real-life situations. Fantasy may also improve memory for instructional material. Malone and Lepper (1987) state that "fantasies should provide appropriate metaphors or analogies for the material presented for learning" (p. 249).

Malone and Lepper argue that goals in fantasy activities should reinforce instructional goals, not compete with them. For instance, the consequences of failure should not be more interesting and exciting than the consequences of success (e.g., as in the *Hangman* game). Moreover, achieving instructional goals should take precedence over subjective success; they say that "fantasy should not permit the learner to experience subjective success without the achievement of instructional goals" (p. 247).

Emotional Aspects of Fantasy

Fantasy fulfills emotional needs, especially when it provides imaginary characters that are familiar to the learner (Malone & Lepper, 1987). In the emotional aspects of fantasy, two factors are related: personalization and learners' prior interests. The fantasy context can be personalized by incorporating information about learners' backgrounds and interests into the fantasy environment (Cordova, 1993; Malone & Lepper, 1987). Malone and Lepper believe that personalizing fantasies might be beneficial in increasing intrinsic motivation.

For instance, asking about the learners' favorite sport or books, and then presenting instructional problems in relation to those interests, can increase learners' motivation and engagement.

The second approach is to relate fantasy elements to learners' tastes and preferences. In this regard, differences between girls and boys need to be considered. As explained before, girls' tastes and interests should be reflected in games so that they are emotionally satisfied when playing. This is not easy since game designers are mostly male; one solution may be to bring more female designers into the game industry to include more of the types of fantasies that females would prefer in games. This would have the added benefit, as Jenkins (2001) suggests, of helping to develop a new generation of game designers with a broader perspective.

Games and Player Identity

Gee (2003) discusses the relationship between digital games and learning through the fantasy characters and identities that the players develop. Video games, especially role-playing games, can recruit identities and encourage players to take on a new identity. According to Gee, deep learning occurs through identity engagement. For learning to happen, students need to be able to bridge their real-world identities with the new identity that they make. For instance, in a science classroom in which the new identity might be that of a scientist, a student who comes from a family that identifies themselves as not "into" science is at a disadvantage because the student must see and make connections between the new identity that she is forming and the other identities that she has already formed and brings into the classroom.

According to Gee, role-playing video games are good at allowing players to take on new identities through the fantasy roles they play. They can provide environments for players that include new sets of roles, actions and values. Through the development of fantasy characters, players can participate in certain actions, perform in new practices, and adopt new attitudes and values through their fantasy roles. Their fantasy characters and roles can help players see themselves in those new ways of being, and see themselves capable of taking on the new identity. Fantasy role-playing games can help learners bridge their old identities with new ones.

Criticisms of the Role of Fantasy in Learning

Not all game researchers support the above arguments. In particular, Habgood, Ainsworth, and Benford (2005) and Habgood (2007) challenge the fantasy-based approach to integrating learning material into digital games. They criticize Malone's conclusion that endogenous fantasy, or the "integral and continuing relationship" of fantasy with the learning content, can improve the educational effectiveness of a digital game. Examining both the theoretical and empirical foundations of endogenous fantasy, Habgood argues that including intrinsic/endogenous fantasies in digital games does not necessarily improve their educational effectiveness. Rather, he proposes an alternative approach based on integrating learning content into the game's underlying rule systems or game mechanics. Based on the construction of, and experimentation with, two versions of the game *Zombie Division*, he argues that, compared to game mechanics, fantasy is only a superficial way of integrating learning content within a game because any specific learning content can be changed without changing the nature of flow in the game. In general, Habgood and his colleagues' alternative perspective on the intrinsic integration of learning content focuses on and incorporates the elements of game mechanics, flow, and representations rather than fantasy.

CONCLUSION

This chapter has reviewed the literature and theoretical perspectives on the influence of fantasy in game-based learning. While the recent work by Habgood and his colleagues challenges the established fantasy-based perspective on effective integration of learning content with digital games, the past professional literature, as well as discussions with game designers, support the argument that fantasy plays a key role in successful digital games for enhancing both motivation and learning. Creating a fantasy context is emotionally appealing, can motivate and engage, and can lead to greater learning.

From a practical viewpoint, a few basic guidelines can go a long way towards using fantasy to help in creating effective digital games. These guidelines suggest that educational game developers:

1. use fantasy to reinforce instructional goals, not compete with them
2. provide appropriate metaphors and analogies for learning
3. provide imaginary characters that are familiar to the learner
4. accommodate gender differences in fantasies
5. relate the fantasy to the content to be learned

Although fantasy is a key component of a good digital game, it is important to emphasize that it alone is not powerful enough to sustain motivation and engagement. However, fantasy can serve as a hook to engage the learner so that other game features such as interactivity, competition, control, curiosity, challenge and feedback can be activated (Asgari & Kaufman, 2008).

REFERENCES

American Psychological Association's Board of Educational Affairs (APABEA). (1997). *The 14 learning-centred psychological principles*. Retrieved December 8, 2006 from http://www.apa.org/ed/lcp.html

Asgari, M., & Kaufman, D. (2008). Motivation, learning, and game design. In R.E. Ferdig (Ed.), *Handbook of research on effective electronic gaming in education*. Hershey, PA: Information Science Reference.

British Educational Communications and Technology Agency (Becta). (2001). *Computer games in education project: Report*. Coventry, UK: Becta. Retrieved July 12, 2007, from http://partners.becta.org9.uk/index.php?section=rh&rid=13595.

British Educational Communications and Technology Agency (Becta). (2006). *Engagement and motivation in games development processes*, Version 1. Retrieved from http://partners.becta.org.uk/page_documents/partners/cge_games_development.pdf

Cassell, J., & Jenkins, H. (Eds.). (1998). *From Barbie to Mortal Kombat*. Cambridge, MA: The MIT Press.

Cordova, D. I. (1993). *The effects of personalization and choice on students' intrinsic motivation and learning*. Unpublished Ph.D. dissertation, Stanford University.

Cordova, D. I., & Lepper, M. R. (1996). Intrinsic motivation and the process of learning: Beneficial effects of contextualization, personalization, and choice. *Journal of Educational Psychology*, *88*(4), 715–730. doi:10.1037/0022-0663.88.4.715

Csikszentmihalyi, M. (1975). Play and intrinsic rewards. *Journal of Humanistic Psychology*, *15*(3), 41–63. doi:10.1177/002216787501500306

Csikszentmihalyi, M. (1990). *Flow: The psychology of optimal experience*. New York: Harper & Row.

de Castell, S., & Jenson, J. (2003). Serious play. *Journal of Curriculum Studies*, *35*(6), 649–665. doi:10.1080/0022027032000145552

Deci, E. L., & Ryan, R. M. (1985). *Intrinsic motivation and self-determination in human behavior.* New York: Plenum.

Dempsey, J., Lucassen, B., Gilley, W., & Rasmussen, K. (1993). Since Malone's theory of intrinsically motivating instruction: What's the score in the gaming literature? *Journal of Educational Technology Systems*, *22*(2), 173–183.

Dempsey, J. V., Haynes, L. L., Lucassen, B. A., & Casey, M. S. (2002). Forty simple computer games and what they could mean to educators. *Simulation & Gaming*, *33*(2), 157–168. doi:10.1177/1046878102332003

Dempsey, J. V., Lucassen, B. A., Haynes, L. L., & Casey, M. S. (1996). *Instructional applications of computer games.* New York: American Educational Research Association.

Evry, H. (2004). *Beginning game graphics.* Boston: Course Technology, Incorporated.

Garris, R., Ahlers, R., & Driskell, J. E. (2002). Games, motivation, and learning: A research and practice model. *Simulation & Gaming*, *33*(4), 441–467. doi:10.1177/1046878102238607

Gee, J. P. (2003). *What video games have to teach us about learning and literacy.* New York: Palgrave Macmillan.

Gee, J. P. (2004). *Learning by design: Good video games as learning machines.* Madison, WI: University of Wisconsin Academic ADL Co-Lab. Available at: http://www.academiccolab.org/resources/documents/Game%20Paper.pdf

Habgood, M. P. J. (2005, June). *Zombie Division: Intrinsic integration in digital learning games.* Paper presented at the 2005 Human Centred Technology Workshop, Brighton, UK.

Habgood, M. P. J. (2007). *The effective integration of digital games and learning content.* Unpublished Ph.D. dissertation, University of Nottingham. Retrieved from http://etheses.nottingham.ac.uk/archive/00000385/

Habgood, M. P. J., Ainsworth, S. E., & Benford, S. (2005). Endogenous fantasy and learning in digital games . *Simulation & Gaming*, *36*(4), 483–498. doi:10.1177/1046878105282276

Habgood, M. P. J., Ainsworth, S. E., & Benford, S. (2005, July). *Intrinsic fantasy: Motivation and affect in educational games made by children.* Paper presented at the AIED 2005 workshop on motivation and affect in educational software, Amsterdam. Available at http://www.informatics.sussex.ac.uk/users/gr20/aied05/index.htm

Hartmann, T., & Klimmt, C. (2006). Gender and computer games: Exploring females' dislikes. *Journal of Computer-Mediated Communication, 11*(4), article 2. Available at http://jcmc.indiana.edu/vol11/issue4/hartmann.html

Hogle, J. G. (1996). *Considering games as cognitive tools: In search of effective "Edutainment"* (working paper). University of Georgia Department of Instructional Technology. Retrieved June 11, 2008 from http://twinpinefarm.com/pdfs/games.pdf.

Jacobs, J. W., & Dempsey, J. V. (1993). Simulation & gaming: Fidelity, feedback, and motivation. In J. V. Dempsey & G. C. Sales (Eds.), *Interactive instruction and feedback* (pp.197-227). Englewood Cliffs, NJ: Educational Technology Publications.

Jenkins, H. (2001). *From Barbie to Mortal Kombat: Further reflections.* Available at http://culturalpolicy.uchicago.edu/conf2001/papers/jenkins.html.

Lepper, M. R., & Malone, T. W. (1987). Intrinsic motivation and instructional effectiveness in computer-based education. In R. E. Snow & M. J. Farr (Eds.), *Aptitude, learning, and instruction: Vol. 3. Conative and affective process analyses* (pp. 255-286). Hillsdale, NJ: Lawrence Erlbaum Associates Inc.

Malone, T., & Lepper, M. (1987). Making learning fun: A taxonomy of intrinsic motivations of learning. In R. E. Snow & M. J. Farr (Eds.), *Aptitude, learning, and instruction: Vol. 3. Conative and affective process analyses* (pp. 223-253). Hillsdale, NJ: Lawrence Erlbaum Associates Inc.

Malone, T. W. (1980). *What makes things fun to learn? A study of intrinsically motivating computer games.* Unpublished Ph.D. dissertation, Stanford University.

Millians, D. (1999). Thirty years and more of simulations and games. *Simulation & Gaming, 30*(3), 352–355. doi:10.1177/104687819903000311

Mitchell, A., & Savill-Smith, C. (2004). *The use of computer and video games for learning: A review of the literature*. London, UK: Learning and Skills Development Agency.

Parker, L. E., & Lepper, M. R. (1992). Effects of fantasy contexts on children's learning and motivation: Making learning more fun. *Journal of Personality and Social Psychology, 62*(4), 625–633. doi:10.1037/0022-3514.62.4.625

Prensky, M. (2001). *Digital game-based learning*. New York: McGraw-Hill.

Prensky, M. (2005). Computer games and learning: Digital game-based learning. In J. Raessens & J. Goldstein (Eds.), *Handbook of computer game studies* (pp. 97-122). Cambridge, MA: The MIT Press.

Reeve, J. (1992). *Understanding motivation and emotion.* Fort Worth: Harcourt Brace Jovanovich.

Rieber, L. P. (1991). Animation, incidental learning, and continuing motivation. *Journal of Educational Psychology, 83*(3), 318–328. doi:10.1037/0022-0663.83.3.318

Rieber, L. P. (1996). Seriously considering play: Designing interactive learning environments based on the blending of microworlds, simulations, and games. *Educational Technology Research and Development, 44*(2), 43–58. doi:10.1007/BF02300540

Rieber, L. P. (2001). Designing learning environments that excite serious play. In G. Kennedy, M. Keppell, C. McNaught, & T. Petrovic (Eds.), *Meeting at the crossroads. Proceedings of the 18th Annual Conference of the Australian Society for Computers in Learning in Tertiary Education* (pp. 1-10). Melbourne: Biomedical Multimedia Unit, the University of Melbourne.

Rosas, R., Nussbaum, M., Cumsille, P., Marianov, V., Correa, M., & Flores, P. (2003). Beyond Nintendo: Design and assessment of educational video games for first and second grade students. *Computers & Education, 40*(1), 71–94. doi:10.1016/S0360-1315(02)00099-4

Salen, K., & Zimmerman, E. (2004). *Rules of play.* Cambridge, MA: The MIT Press.

Shaffer, D. W., Squire, K. R., Halverson, R., & Gee, J. P. (2005). *Video games and the future of learning.* WCER (Wisconsin Center for Education Research) Working Paper, No. 2005-4. Available at http://www.wcer.wisc.edu/publications/workingPapers/Working_Paper_No_2005_4.pdf

Snider, M. (2003, March 3). Wired to another world: Online games like EverQuest and The Sims have become a new addiction. *Maclean's, 116*(9), 23–25.

Squire, K. (2004). *Replaying history: Learning world history through playing Civilization III.* Unpublished PhD dissertation, Indiana University. Retrieved June 11, 2008 from http://website.education.wisc.edu/kdsquire/dissertation.html

Squire, K. (2006). From content to context: Videogames as designed experience. *Educational Researcher*, *35*(8), 19–29. doi:10.3102/0013189X035008019

Stewart, K. M. (1997). Beyond entertainment: Using interactive games in web-based instruction. *Journal of Instruction Delivery Systems*, *1*(2), 18–20.

Vockell, E. (2004). *Educational psychology: a practical approach.* Retrieved January 20, 2009 from http://education.calumet.purdue.edu/Vockell/EdPsyBook/

Vorderer, P., Hartmann, T., & Klimmt, C. (2003). *Explaining the enjoyment of playing video games: The role of competition.* In *Proceedings of the second international conference on entertainment computing.* Available at http://portal.acm.org/citation.cfm?id=958735

Waal, B. D. (1995). *Motivations for video game play: A study of social, cultural and physiological factors.* Unpublished Master's thesis, School of Communication, Simon Fraser University

ADDITIONAL READING

Ferdig, R. E. (Ed.) (2009). *Handbook of research on effective electronic gaming in education*. Hershey, PA: Information Science Reference.

KEY TERMS AND DEFINITIONS

Computer/Video Games: These terms are usually used interchangeably. Key characteristics of computer/video games include rules, goals and objectives, outcomes and feedback, fantasy, conflict/competition/challenge/opposition, curiosity, interaction, and representation or story.

Digital Games: Usually refers to games played using a personal computer or personal game machine. Digital games can be played individually, against the computer, or against other people face-to-face or online. The term '*digital games*' incorporates both computer games and video games.

Dungeons and Dragons: A tabletop fantasy role-playing game (RPG) originally designed by E. Gary Gygax and Dave Arneson, and first published in 1974 by the Gygax-owned company Tactical Studies Rules, Inc. (TSR)" (Wikipedia). The term *Dungeons & Dragons* has sometimes been used as a generic term for fantasy role-playing games.

Educational Games: Games whose design and play are based on a set of educational objectives or learning outcomes.

Fantasy: Creations of the imaginative faculty and mental images which are unrealistic or improbable, and not actually present. In regards to digital games, fantasy contexts can be intrinsic/endogenous or extrinsic/exogenous to the game content.

Game: A set of voluntary activities which has participants, goals, rules, and some kind of competition (physical or mental). The competition can be against oneself, others, or a computer.

Motivation: The willingness or desire to satisfy a need or to engage in an activity. The two types of motivation commonly recognized in the literature are intrinsic and extrinsic.

Chapter 6
Gender and Digital Gameplay:
Theories, Oversights, Accidents, and Surprises

Jennifer Jenson
York University, Canada

Suzanne de Castell
Simon Fraser University, Canada

ABSTRACT

In this chapter, we take a fresh look at gender and digital gameplay. Rather than repeat the stereotypes of who plays what, how, and why, we show how our own preconceptions about gender keep surprises at bay, reinforcing, instead, oft-cited ideologies. As researchers, we are entitled to be surprised by our findings. Serious interpretive work, in conjunction with alternative methodologies, promise very different findings from the expected, and accepted, assumptions about women and girls and their involvement in gameplay.

INTRODUCTION

If someone returns from work one night and announces he has accidentally run over a cat on the way home, that's one thing. If he comes home night after night having accidentally run over one cat after another, it's reasonable to question his affection for cats, and to dispute the extent to which this can be rightly called an 'accident' anymore. (D. W. Hamlyn, class notes, c. 1977)

DOI: 10.4018/978-1-61520-731-2.ch006

This chapter is about an apparent inability to give centre stage to the concept of "equity" in theorizing, analyzing, or interpreting research on gender and gameplay, an inability that is, in fact, so frequent as to no longer appear accidental. This is an issue that has been brewing in our minds for some time. Several years ago, similarly baffled at the apparent inability of otherwise well-informed, sophisticated educational researchers and scholars to comprehend any but the most outdated definition of gender equity as "equal numbers of males and females in all subjects," it began to dawn on us that something was going persistently and systematically wrong with work on this issue (Bryson & de Castell, 1993). To be clear, there is unquestionably theoretically insightful, radical, intellectually exciting ground being broken in gender studies. There is, for example, brilliant work in queer theory from the likes of Eve Sedgewick, Judith Butler, Michel Foucault, and Donna Haraway; work that amply testifies to the advances in conceptualization that can be and have been made. But what happens in the move from gender-based theory to application, in sociology, in design, in research, in equity policy, in game studies, or in any other arena of "progressive" gender-centric practice?

In this chapter, we call on some of that insightful and innovative theoretical work in questioning the apparent mistakes of contemporary work on gender and digital gameplay. We re-consider deficiencies as "e-fficiencies," as deeply-rooted forms of productive "bio-power" (Foucault, 1990) that induce a perception of the constructed and artificial as natural and essential, so as to render profound inquiry inconceivable, thus disabling critical inquiry. In other words, this chapter is an attempt to rethink long-held assumptions and presumptions of work on gender and gameplay in an effort to demarcate more clearly how they have not only biased our analyses to date, but have also obscured what might well be present if we employed a different framework for viewing. In some sense, this is, as Iris Marion Young (among many others) has pointed out, a struggle over language, the very words we use to describe events, to encode practices, to shape the stories we tell as researchers (Young, 1998/2005). In this attempt to re-think persistent and repetitive "accidents" of theory, we will touch briefly on a longitudinal study (three years) of gender and digital gameplay with more than 100 girls and boys aged 12-15 (for a fuller description of the study, see Jenson, de Castell, & Fisher, 2007) to illustrate more fully the workings of some of these all too familiar discursive traps.

A useful beginning in nearly all contemporary work on gender is with Butler's analysis of gender performativity, which invites us to distinguish between what appears to be an essential truth of gender from the conventions that, through their repeated embodiment, appear both necessary and natural. Echoing earlier arguments by feminist sociologist Dorothy Smith that explanations invoking women's roles are in actuality ideological moves which reify conventions, imposing expectations and obligations which ought to be critically exposed, Butler writes that "gender cannot be understood as a role which either expresses or disguises an interior 'self,' whether that 'self' is conceived as sexed or not. As performance which is performative, gender is an 'act,' broadly construed, which constructs the social fiction of its own psychological interiority" (Butler, 1990, p.22).

In this view, what the repetition of conventional gender performances accomplishes is hegemony. Repetition is far from a mistake, or an unhappy accident of scholarship gone wrong. Instead, what we are looking at are the deepest epistemic roots of scholarly inquiry in an extremely important cultural area. This would be a different vision altogether, a vision of something working very well indeed, working so well, in fact, that even experienced and accomplished researchers find themselves, ourselves, steering, mesmerized, to aporia. What repetition signals, then, is not an accident, but something quite purposeful: a deeply-structured process which naturalizes convention and makes it impossible to see or hear anything other than an inner truth of gender that does not seem capable of dislodging when discussions move from the esoteric domains of high theory into applied areas like social, technological, and educational research, design, policy, and practice.

In the next section we begin by enumerating some of the conventions and norms that are often repeated when writing and talking about women/girls and playing digital games and then show

how those norms are often misinterpreted, indeed mislabeled as evidence for a stable fact about gender. As Butler reminds us, "Whether gender or sex is fixed or free is a function of a discourse which seeks to set certain limits to analysis or safeguard certain tenets of humanism as presuppositional to any analysis of gender" (Butler, 1999, p.12). Here we examine those limits and presuppositions which delimit gender analysis in relation to digital games.

COOPERATION VS. COMPETITION

There is a timeworn orthodoxy in "girl-friendly" game design that girls like to cooperate, whereas boys prefer to compete (Cassells & Jenkins, 1998). What is far less clear is what "competition" and "cooperation" mean; whose definitions of these terms are running this show? In the work we have done observing and interviewing girls about how they play, and what they like and dislike in video and computer gameplay, it soon becomes clear that the very idea of "competition," for example, is both gendered and contestable. If we think we know what competition means, then we probably have not observed, analyzed, or talked to very many girls playing games. It is commonplace that many female athletes, for example, are highly competitive, so why would we not expect girls who play computer games to be competitive? It's time we expended some intellectual effort de-coding competition, before blithely invoking the term as a marker of gendered play preferences.

There seems to be a systematic need to theorize the axiomatic concepts within which research is attempting to study gender and digital gameplay. Theoretical work, for example, on competition demonstrates its "essentially contested" character (M. Fielding, 1976, after W. B. Gallie, 1956); its meaning is neither transparent nor consistent, so it's important to sort out what "competition" really means. The term obviously does not refer to the structure of the games played, since many of the games girls choose to play are competitive in their structure. In *Super Monkey Ball™*, for example, you have to fly more accurately, race faster, roll over more bananas, and so on, than your fellow players. Even if you are playing solo, you are challenged by the game itself to keep improving on your own score. Wherever there is scoring, there is competition. Is there any video game that doesn't have some form of competition built into it? (see Chapter 1 for a full discussion of definitions).

Of course many girls do like, even love, competitive gameplay. Many of the more than 80 girls we interviewed said that they enjoy the same kinds of competitive gameplay that boys do: fighting, beating, racing against one another, building higher, faster, deeper, longer, accumulating the most points, knocking out opponents, all of that. Many other girls seem to love to play with others, but their competition takes a different, not necessarily gender-specific, form —what one of our research assistants designated as "benevolent competition." When girls in our study played in this benevolently competitive way, they were still very much competing, but they are also supporting, encouraging and even helping their playmates to succeed in the game. The point is that they *are* competing. They are playing competitively in the ways enabled and supported for girls. That means only that these girls, and others like them, are competing in ways socially regulated as appropriate to and acceptable for them as girls. If their competition took the same form as that of their brothers, this might be cause for trouble on all sides. What this account doesn't do —and unless we attain equality of access and experience, never can do — is tell us about "gender differences in girl-friendly game design" (Graner Ray, 2004). If the very terms of our calculations, our axiomatic concepts and foundational practices, embody and express hegemonic rules, we will continue to define for women and girls activities, dispositions, aspirations and accomplishments in terms of what these mean for boys and men. The problem is one of terms and turf. If we define the matter from the outset in terms that describe only what happens on male turf, we are unlikely to illuminate much about the situation as it is possible for women. As Butler elsewhere explained, the state accords rights to those that it then goes on to represent. This is always already a hegemonic performance, however worthy or progressive our intentions. So our first interpretation of benevolent competition was in some sense already predefined and put in binary opposition to how the boys were playing, and led to us mistakenly trying to attribute something about how girls play to our repertoire of findings.

An example of research intended to challenge and invert the usual way that work on gender and gameplay has been reported is the work of Valerie Walkerdine, who strongly argues that:

> *...many games are the site for the production of contemporary masculinity because they both demand and appear to ensure performances such as heroism, killing, winning, competition, and action, combined with technological skill and rationality. In relation to girls, this constitutes a problem because contemporary femininity demands practices and performances which bring together heroics, rationality, etc. with the need to maintain a femininity that displays care, co-operation, concern and sensitivity to others. (2007, p. 48)*

It is one thing to acknowledge and work with the gender constructions within which the children in our studies play games. But to theorize our own findings from this standpoint is another thing, demanding that we take into account how the gender imperatives work within and against our analytical and interpretive efforts. It is inscribed in both our concepts (e.g., an unquestioned concept of competition as a masculine trait which is then, necessarily, not found in girls' play), and in our methods, which misconstrue normatively constrained gendered performances as data from which we might literally read truths about what girls like, what they can do, what they are interested in, and how they play. If researchers are prepared to acknowledge that the boys in their studies come into the research situation with more experience and greater gender-investment in performing gaming interest and ability—and, with that, competitiveness—they surely must also acknowledge the necessity to bring girls to a comparable experience/investment level before reaching any conclusions about gender-based differences in digital game play. Experience and investment are not variables to be acknowledged and then summarily dismissed from consideration. All that can leave us with is re-citation and re-inscription: boys necessarily always perform masculinity and girls practice femininity. This is probably part of the reason that gender and gameplay studies have told us little in the past 10 years that we had not already discovered in the first–generation gender research.

So when we say that girls play competitively in the ways enabled and supported for girls, what we are saying is not that girls are thereby channeling some kind of hardwired femininity; rather we are trying to draw attention to the irrefutable importance of context and knowledge to their play performances. It is absolutely significant, for example, that in each of the years we studied girls' play that in the first weeks of the club, there was much more helping dialogue than direct competition as they familiarized themselves with the games. Later on, for most players who attended regularly, this dialogue decreased, and they began taking up positions as experts in particular games. Instead of reading this as "help vs. competition," we see it as moving from novice to expert roles, a factor often overlooked in commentary on competition versus cooperation.

The approach we propose to this kind of research takes into account the work of theorists like Butler (1990, 1999), Foucault (1990) and Smith (1989) and begins with a very different premise: given that games have been and continue to be a popular cultural site for play, especially for men and boys, who and what supports their play, and under what conditions, and when, how, with whom and under what conditions do girls and women play games? This might shake loose some limiting binary readings of masculinity and femininity that past studies have replicated (c.f. Graner Ray, 2004; Walkerdine, 1998, 2007).

FROM NOVICE TO EXPERT: ANOTHER ACCOUNT OF GENDERED DIFFERENCES

In our own work on gender and gameplay, taking differences in experience and investment into account has radically altered our own perceptions of our subjects, our data, and our methods.

As we observed adolescents between 12 and 13 as they learned and played console games, we saw a wide range of performances, from hypermasculinity to hyperfemininity, in both girls and boys. So we came to see games less as a site for the production of contemporary masculinity than as a leisure site in which, given time and permission, girls were as eager to spend time as boys. Performance, under these conditions, was very much regulated by technological skill: the better the player, the less performance per se.

For example, in the final year the girls decided to hold a game tournament and compete directly with one another over a period of a few months (interestingly, the boys did not want the option of competing either among themselves or, later, with experienced girl-players) to see who could achieve the highest overall score. One of the games chosen for the tournament was *Guitar Hero®* (GH) which they played on the Playstation 2®, using a plastic guitar as a controller. For those not familiar with the game, the goal of *Guitar Hero* is to accurately press the keys on the guitar in time with the music; the more accurately a song is played, the higher the score.

Observing the girls play, we noted that initially there was a lot of chatter: how to hold the guitar, how to play, encouragement from onlookers, exclamations when missing notes, and quite a lot of self-effacing commentary like "I suck/ I can't do this/ This is too hard." However, as the girls began to master the game, the chatter died away, and we observed many play sessions with very little talk, other than "I missed/ Oh crap/ That sucked." All of the self-deprecating talk had nearly vanished, and the girls eagerly checked their final scores to see who had won in head to head competition. Interestingly, because GH was a game that none of the boys had at home (at least to begin with, although after the first few weeks, three of the boys had acquired GH for their homes; none of the girls purchased GH) we observed the same cycle in their play as we did with the girls – a cycle that we had not fully recognized before as being related so directly to game familiarity. We had, in years past, commented on how little the boys spoke to one another in many of the play sessions, unless it was to show off and brag about their skills, put down another player, or ask for or receive help. We attributed some of this behaviour as unique to the groups of boys playing, however, it could just as easily be attributed to the difference between experienced game players and novices. In other words, the more skilled the players, the less collaboration, less talk, less self-deprecating commentary, less help offered, all performances which could be (and have been) attributed to girls playing games. So what we've been (mis)reading as research about girls and gameplay, as we've said before, could actually be research about novices and gameplay.

In fact, Dianne Carr's (2005) work on gender and play preferences maps neatly onto the work we document here. Hers was a study of a girls' game club in an all-girls' school, in which she examined the "relationships between taste, content, context and competence, in order to explore the multiple factors that feed into users' choices and contribute to the formation of gaming preferences" (Carr, 2005, p. 466). She concludes, not with a reinscription of gendered gameplay preferences (e.g., what games the girls in her study most preferred to play), but instead by acknowledging that while it is possible to "map patterns" for play preferences, to do so assumes that they are stable instead of preferences being "an assemblage, made up of past access and positive experiences and subject to situation and context" (p. 479). Finally, and importantly, Carr states, "What did become apparent was that the girls' increasing gaming competencies enabled them to identify and access the different potential play experiences offered by specific games, and to selectively actualize these potentials according to circumstance and prerogative. This indicates that forms of competency underlie and inform our gaming preferences—whatever our gender" (p. 478). It might well be, then, that competency has been too often misrecognized as some factual attribute for gender.

RE-CITING GENDER RESEARCH

Here we attempt to give examples of how research in this area is used to re-entrench gender norms.

That research data embody hegemonic conventions about gender should come as no surprise. Since research is itself a socially situated practice, so must be the data it elicits. In the face of this intransigent fact, what have we done to take acknowledged bias into account in such a way that it is still possible for our research to surprise us (Jenson & de Castell, 2005; Smith, 1989)? In *Tricks of the Trade* (Becker, 1998), research methodologist Anselm Strauss argues persuasively for building "*contra*-factual possibilities" into our research design, from contexts to characters to questions. How is it, then, that we appear to forget to substantively control for greater investment and prior experience in studies of what games "girls like best" (Carr, 2005; Walkerdine, 1998; Walkerdine, Thomas, & Studdert, 1998) or most typically choose to create (Denner, Werner, Bean, & Campe, 2005; Kafai, 1995)?

It is well-understood that the responses people give to questions about what and how they most like to play necessarily vary according to several factors: their immediate situation; their understanding of the intent of the questions, who is asking the questions, etc. All of these factors shape the range and nature of their responses. For example, one respondent early in our study commented that: "If a guy asks another guy, " do you play video games?" he'll pretty much always say yes, because guys know video games are about competing with other guys, and about winning. But if a girl asks a guy if he plays, he'll say no, so she doesn't think he's a social misfit who only likes to stare at a computer screen."

And yet almost all the girls we asked responded that they played with brothers or male relatives, even though none of the boys reported that they played with sisters or other female relatives. These discrepancies only make sense if what we have are not informative answers to our questions, but informative performances of gender-normativity, unless we alter the conditions so as to make something other than that response possible, thus allowing ourselves as researchers to be surprised by our own findings. Bakhtin's (1981, 1986) insightful analysis of "addressivity" and "dialogicality" would go a long way towards redressing the resiliently stereotypical research findings about girls and gaming. But improving the analysis of gender-focused research is only a part, and perhaps the lesser part, of what is at stake here.

Often, for example, when we interviewed girls about the games they play, most of them named a few titles, sometimes not accurately, and then indicated that they play but they do not always get to choose the game. Interestingly, in one focus group interview, after going round the table and naming games, one girl asked if computer games counted, and the researcher responded "Yes," to which everyone replied by talking at once, naming off their favorite, free, online games. We had initially asked the wrong question, or they had perceived it as a question simply about console gameplay. A similar incident is reported in Walkerdine (2007), but she interprets the question as being "too difficult" for the respondent to answer, instead of speculating on why that question might have produced an awkward silence on the part of the female participant (the question was "What are your favorite game characters?"). The interpretation that seems most direct in both these situations is that what girls like best are, for the most part, girl games like *The Sims®* or broadly, racing games, but those stock answers miss the surprising fact that, by and large, the games that these girls are playing are puzzle, online, free games when they have computer time, while their brothers and cousins and male peers are playing console games that cost money, and to which their sisters often do not enjoy equal access.

RE-CITING STEREOTYPICAL PRACTICE: OTHER DISCOURSES?

One way out of this stranglehold might be to enlist a different methodological approach, one that was present both in our study and Carr's (2005) (though not explicitly stated); that is to take context, actors, and tools into consideration. Actor network theory (ANT) (e.g., see Latour, 2005), a conceptual framework which investigates human agency as always already "networked" across an intersecting landscape of affordances, both human and non-human, of context, tools, symbols, plants, and animals, is of particular interest to digital games researchers, for whom ANT offers a full voice, so to speak, to artificial intelligence in its varied forms and functions. Seth Giddings (2007) explains why actor network theory appears particularly well-suited to digital games studies, promising as a standpoint from which to carry out studies in a field that is, as yet, new and under construction. He argues that digital gameplay "transgresses" the boundaries between subject and object through its conflation of game, machine, and player, in particular that: "a full understanding of both the playing of digital games, and the wider technocultural context of this play, is possible only through a recognition and theorization of the reality of technological agency" (p. 115). Employing ANT as a theoretical lens makes this possible, as it "claims both the agency of non-humans and, moreover, the *symmetry* of agency between humans and non-humans in any ICT network" (p.118).

It is our contention that ANT seems as well a highly suitable approach to studying gender and gameplay. Take, for example, the description earlier in the chapter of the girls playing *Guitar Hero*; there we reported that a shift in controllers actually contributed to an overall gain in competence on the part of the girls. In other words, the change in controllers (i.e., a technology change) actually enabled, for those particular girls, a way into one of the cultures of gameplay. ANT seems, as well, a highly suitable approach to studying changes in technology design, in this case, new forms of game controllers, affordances that are restructuring users' interaction with digital gameplay. We argue that the way this restructuring of interactivity is happening suggests considerable changes for both theories and practices of serious play, and invites major shifts in the design of games for education and training. By contrast with the intense interest and attention (and fan base!) that has been devoted to game design and designers across all sectors of game culture, the things players directly interact with, the objects they use to play, and, in particular, the end user's hardware, has not enjoyed comparable airtime. It's an understandable human failing to accord primacy of place to human agents in explaining innovation, though it may in fact be user interface design that turns out to be far more significant for advancing new audiences, inviting new players, and thereby affording new possibilities to those previously marginalized.

The difficulty with studies of gender and gameplay has most frequently been the regular attribution of gender norms and characteristics to actors, contexts and artifacts which are always in flux. It is not that previous research has been inadequate or wrong; it is simply that in telling those stories (Visweswaran, 1994), researchers, in recounting their findings, have fixed gender in order to stabilize the network of interactions, and the possibilities for troubling gender shifts. Carr's work resists this fixing: she does not enumerate a list of games that girls prefer, nor does she attempt to label what girls like best. However, there is a whole other stream of work that has been popularized and is recounted again and again at both academic and commercial games conferences, in which Freud's old question of "what women want" has somehow become the holy grail of how to make more money in the industry. While money is less an object on the academic side of the question, it gets a no less contested response; at the 2007 DiGRA conference in Tokyo, a prominent European academic sitting in the audience at a panel discussion on women in games, in which the panelists had detailed the gender stereotypes that keep women out of the lucrative games industry, asked pointedly: "Don't you want to try to present your stuff in a way that doesn't burn bridges?" What we think he was really asking was, "If you think that it is a problem that more women and girls don't play games and aren't in the industry, can't you just play nice and tell us we are doing a good job?"

CONCLUSION

Gender is, and has been for some time, a contested site: it is "at play" and "in play" in radically different ways, given different contexts, actors and tools/technologies. What we are calling for here is a way of holding tight to that complexity – to, in some sense, live in the eye of the storm in a way that opens up possibilities for telling stories in ways that are more faithful to action and interaction. Identity recast in such a way, taking in earnest Butler's (1999) claim that "gender is a complexity whose totality is permanently deferred, never fully what it is at any given juncture in time" (p. 151), might begin to loosen the noose that hetero-normative sentiment has had on gender and gameplay research.

The main problem with flawed research is that it can drive flawed practice. Going back to the catastrophic driver described in the introduction to this chapter, neither better night-vision lenses, nor improved headlights, nor any other intervention directed at improving his ability to see cats on the road could prove effective if the real problem was a particular perception about cats and a consequent deep-seated desire to rid the world of the feline species. In a not-dissimilar way, when girl-friendly principles derived from research that misperceives itself as an inner truth about gender, drive intervention efforts to engage girls in game play, or with game design, or with games as a route to computer programming, those interventions will themselves entrench the very inequities they seek to remediate. We cannot look to practical work, no matter how well supported, whose very foundations are flawed, to address problems that remain undetected and unacknowledged. Good first steps would be to resuscitate interpretation as an indispensable tool for gender research in game studies, unlearn the stereotypical assumptions, and challenge covertly stereotyped concepts (such as "competition") that have thus far driven research in this field. By these simple means, we begin to make it possible to discover something other than what we assume we already "know" about girls and video gameplay, and to be surprised about "what girls like best."

ACKNOWLEDGMENT

We gratefully acknowledge the work of research assistants Jeff Zweifl, Claire Fletcher, Sheryl Vasser and Stephanie Fisher on this project as well as funding from the Social Sciences and Humanities Research Council (SSHRC) of Canada.

Earlier drafts of this paper are to be found in the 2005 Digital Games Research Association (DiGRA) conference proceedings and the online journal *Eludamos: Journal for Computer Game Culture*.

REFERENCES

Bakhtin, M. M. (1981). *The dialogic imagination: Four essays by M. M. Bakhtin.* M. Holquist (Ed.), C. Emerson & M. Holquist (Trans.). Austin, TX: University of Texas Press.

Bakhtin, M. M. (1986). *Speeck Genres and other late essays.* C. Emerson & M. Holquist (Eds.), V. W. McGee (Trans.). Austin, TX: University of Texas Press.

Becker, H. S. (1998). *Tricks of the trade: How to think about your research while you're doing it.* Chicago: University of Chicago Press.

Bryson, M., & de Castell, S. (1993). En/Gendering equity. *Educational Theory, 43*(4), 341–355. doi:10.1111/j.1741-5446.1993.00341.x

Butler, J. (1990). Performative acts and gender constitution: An essay in phenomenology and feminist theory. In S. Case (Ed.), *Performing feminisms: Feminist critical theory and theatre.* Baltimore: Johns Hopkins University Press.

Butler, J. (1999). *Gender trouble: Feminism and the subversion of identity.* New York: Routledge.

Carr, D. (2005). Context, gaming pleasures and gendered preferences. *Simulation & Gaming, 36*(4), 464–482. doi:10.1177/1046878105282160

Cassells, J., & Jenkins, H. (Eds.). (1998). *From Barbie to Mortal Kombat.* Boston: The MIT Press.

Denner, J., Werner, L., Bean, S., & Campe, S. (2005). The Girls Creating Games Program: Strategies for engaging middle school girls in information technology. *Frontiers: A Journal of Women's Studies . Special Issue on Gender and IT, 26*(1), 90–98.

Fielding, M. (1976). Against competition: In praise of malleable analysis and the subversion of philosophy. *Journal of Philosophy of Education, 10*(1), 124–146. doi:10.1111/j.1467-9752.1976.tb00008.x

Foucault, M. (1990). *The history of sexuality, an introduction: Volume I.* New York: Vintage.

Gallie, W. B. (1956). Essentially contested concepts. In . *Proceedings of the Aristotelian Society, 56*, 167–198.

Giddings, S. (2007). Playing with non-humans: Digital games as technocultural form. In S. de Castell & J. Jenson (Eds.), *Worlds in play: International perspectives on digital games research* (pp. 115-128). New York: Peter Lang.

Graner Ray, S. G. (2004). *Gender inclusive game design: Expanding the market.* Hingham, MA: Charles River Media, Inc.

Jenson, J. de Castell, S., & Fisher, S. (2007). Girls playing games: Rethinking stereotypes. In *Proceedings of the 2007 conference on Future Play,* Toronto, Canada (pp. 9-16). New York: ACM.

Jenson, J., & de Castell, S. (2005). Her own boss: Gender and the pursuit of incompetent play. In S. de Castell & J. Jenson (Eds.), *Proceedings, 2005 Conference of the Digital Games Research Association (DiGRA), Changing Views: Worlds in Play.* Vancouver, Canada. Available at http://www.digra.org/dl/display_html?chid=http://www.digra.org/dl/db/06278.27455.pdf

Kafai, Y. B. (1995). *Minds in play: Computer game design as a context for children's learning.* Hillsdale, NJ: Lawrence Erlbaum Associates, Inc.

Latour, B. (2005). *Reassembling the social: An introduction to Actor-Network-Theory* Oxford, UK: Oxford University Press.

Smith, D. E. (1989). *The everyday world as problematic.* Lebanon, NH: Northeastern University Press.

Visweswaran, K. (1994) *Fictions of feminist ethnography*. Minneapolis, MN: University of Minnesota Press.

Walkerdine, V. (1998). Children in cyberspace: A new frontier? In K. Lesnik-Oberstein (Ed.), *Children in culture: Approaches to childhood* (pp. 231-247). New York: St. Martin's.

Walkerdine, V. (2007). *Children, gender, video games: Towards a relational approach to multimedia*. New York: Palgrave Macmillan.

Walkerdine, V., Thomas, A., & Studdert, D. (1998). *Young children and video games: Dangerous pleasures and pleasurable danger.* Available at http://creativetechnology.salford.ac.uk/fuchs/projects/downloads/young_children_and_videogames.htm.

Young, M. I. (1998/2005). Five faces of oppression. In A. E. Cudd & R. O. Andreasen (Eds.), *Feminist theory: A philosophical anthology*. Malden, MA: Blackwell Publishing.

ADDITIONAL READING

de Castell, S. & Jenson, J. (2007). *Worlds in play: International perspectives on digital games research*. New York: Peter Lang.

Kafai, Y., Heeter, C. Denner, J., & Sun, J. Y. (2008). *Beyond Barbie and Mortal Kombat: New perspectives on gender and gaming*. Cambridge, MA: The MIT Press.

Peters, R. S. (1977). *Education and the education of teachers*. London: Routledge & Kegan Paul.

KEY TERMS AND DEFINITIONS

Actor Network Theory (ANT): A conceptual framework developed by Michel Callon (1991) and Bruno Latour (1992) which investigates human agency as always already "networked" across an intersecting landscape of affordances, both human and non-human, of context, tools, symbols, plants, and animals.

Gameplay: Refers here to any kind of digital game play, whether computer-based, console-based (e.g. X-Box 360, Wii, or Playstation 3) or handheld (Nintendo DS/DSi or PSP).

Gender: Not to be confused with biological markers for sex, gender indicates a range of social and cultural 'norms' and behaviours that are attributed to people, most often along a masculine and feminine binary.

Hegemony: Cultural and social predominance.

Heteronormativity: Those rules, constructs and laws that naturalize and institutionalize heterosexuality as universal.

Performativity: A term, at least in this paper, taken from the work of Judith Butler, and here meant to indicate that gender identity is not fixed, that it is continually "performed", and that performance is dependent on context, history, and conventions.

Remediation: A term coined by Bolter and Gruisin (1999) which refers to the tendency of 'new media' to modify and/or reshape past media. In other words, to refashion older media, making it new.

Sex: The biological marker for male/female.

Chapter 7
Games in Health Education: A Survey of Pre-Service Teachers

Claire IsaBelle
University of Ottawa, Canada

Margot Kaszap
Laval University, Canada

ABSTRACT

Studies indicate that teachers are not effectively encouraging appropriate health and well-being strategies among their students (Turcotte, Gaudreau, & Otis, 2007). Because educational games offer many advantages in promoting health, motivation, and active participation in learning, (Sauvé, Power, IsaBelle, Samson, & St-Pierre, 2002), it is important to determine which types of games health education teachers can use best. Building on health education needs and social representation theory, this chapter presents a study of pre-service (student) teachers to identify social representations that pre-service teachers have about games, including whether they perceived games as supporting learning at home and in school, and which types and aspects of games they preferred. The answers to these questions helped the research team to create games to meet the needs of future teachers in enhancing their students' health education.

INTRODUCTION

Currently, few teachers use computerized games due to lack of resources appropriate to their education needs. As part of the Canada-wide *Simulation and Advanced Gaming Environments (SAGE) for Learning* project, a study was carried out of 300 pre-service (student) teachers and more than 150 other students on their perceptions of the relationship between the health of young people and games.

DOI: 10.4018/978-1-61520-731-2.ch007

In this chapter, we present the results of the first inquiry: student teachers' perceptions of whether games can support learning at home, the types of games that students like, and the aspects of games that they prefer. The answers to these questions provided input for creation of a game designed to meet the needs of future teachers in supporting health education for their students.

The following sections present background on the state of health among young people, the advantages of non-digital games for learning, social representations, survey methodology, and survey results.

HEALTH PROBLEMS AND YOUTH

Statistics show that young people have increasing health problems in their lives. Indeed, youth health concerns could be described as "nine Ss" (sedentary lifestyle, surplus weight, scrawniness, unhealthy sexuality, sleep (out of step with their biological clocks), stress, substances, $$ and suicide). Although we do not cover all these points here, we examine certain statistics and the connection between health and learning among the young as background for our study.

Sport and Physical Activity

During the school year, young people dedicate, on average, 30 hours per week to school, watch TV from 15 to 26 hours per week, and spend increasing numbers of hours playing electronic games and using the Internet (Clocksin, Watson, & Ransdell, 2002). In a study of 1,847 11-to-15-year-old students in Quebec, Pronovost (2007) found that greater consumption of multimedia corresponded to a lesser degree of physical and cultural activity (p. 125). In Nova Scotia, a 2002 study revealed that the majority of primary and secondary students in the province did not have the minimum exercise required to be healthy. In fact, of the 1,700 students participating in the study, only 10% of 16-year-olds met national exercise standards (Gagné, 2002). In Quebec, it seems that three out of five children failed to meet the minimum 60 minutes a day of activity recommended by the World Health Organization (WHO) (Allard, 2008). The Pronovost (2007) study also indicated that children who were active on sports teams expected to be more successful in their school years, and were more likely to believe in their capacities than those who were not part of a sports team.

Food and Young People

Between 1978 and 2004, the combined number of overweight and obese Canadian teenagers from 12 to 17 years old rose from 14% to 29% (Statistics Canada, 2005), with the prevalence varying by province. In 2004, the combined rate of overweight and obesity in young people between two and 17 years old in Newfoundland & Labrador, New Brunswick, Nova Scotia and Manitoba was significantly higher than the national average. In Newfoundland & Labrador and New Brunswick, the rate of obesity was sharply higher than the national average. However, combined rates in Quebec and Alberta were significantly lower than the national rate.

In addition, Statistics Canada data (2007) show that 70% of children from four to eight years old do not consume the recommended five daily servings of fruits and vegetables, and 71% of boys and 83% of girls from 10 to 16 years old do not consume the recommended three daily portions of dairy products. An Ontario study of 318 young people from 9 to 12 years old (Cohen, Evers, Manske, Bercovitz, & Edward, 2003), looking at possible links among smoking, physical activity, and missed breakfast, showed that only 48.8% of boys and 36.1% of girls had breakfast every morning. Generally, nutritionists recommend that a third of daily calories be consumed at breakfast; young people who skip breakfast risk health problems, decreased energy, and poorer cognitive performance (Bayne-Smith et al., 2004). Hospitalization rates for eating disorders in young women under 15 years old increased by 34% from 1987 to 1999 (STHC, 2007). Social pressure for an idealized physical appearance can cause severe problems of self-respect for a child, which can become an obsession. Skemp-Arlt (2006) found several consequences of eating disorders in young people, including fatigue, decreased academic performance, poor self-image, and a lack of necessary nutrients, including protein and vitamins, for growth.

Youth Suicide

It appears that every year, more than 20% of young Canadians between 13 and 18 years old live in such intense emotional distress that they consider self-mutilation or suicide (Instituts de recherche en santé du Canada, 2006). As part of a study in rural eastern Ontario schools comparing youth in cities and rural locations, Armstrong (2007) discovered that the incidence of suicidal thoughts and behavior is less prevalent among young people who report participating in extracurricular activities such as sports, music, theater, clubs, or religious groups. The researcher noted that for young people living in rural areas, the risks of suicide are particularly high, because "in rural communities, the farther young people live from school, the less they can participate in extracurricular activities and the more they risk feeling suicidal thoughts" (Instituts de recherche en santé du Canada, 2006, par. 6).

Despite health education and intervention programs that attempt to address health problems in youth, it seems that the outlook for young people's physical health is not so bright. In the face of these many issues, are their teachers prepared and well-equipped to teach these various health subjects?

The present study was aimed at identifying, for pre-service teachers, (1) how they perceive games for training, (2) which games they prefer, and (3) which aspects of the games they like most, in order to develop a game shell adapted to their preferences. The following section reviews health education, educational games, and generic game shells and their advantages.

CONTEXT FOR THE STUDY

Health Education

According to Harvey, Trudeau, Morency, and Bordeleau, (2007), health is a dynamic state which requires the individual to be both aware of his state of health and willing to take action to improve it. Health education is also associated with a relational, non-hierarchical process. Along with the ability to control factors that affect their health, individuals need the knowledge, attitudes and skills to act. "Consequently, education and learning are important aspects of health promotion. A first stage in the teaching and learning process is recognition of the knowledge, experience and skills existing in every person" (Hills & O'Neill, 2000, p. 10).

In 1992, Coppé and Schoonbroodt published their *Practical Guide for Health Education: Reflection, Experimentation, and 50 Index Cards to Help the Trainer.* This guide, still considered to be of major importance, proposes useful definitions:

Health education is a process of learning aimed at developing the capacities of people to adapt to their environment and at directing them in the transformation of this environment when its variations exceed their capacities. To educate for health consists in working with others to find together ways of living healthier. This work does not have to limit itself to a simple transmission of knowledge. The educator has to help the learner develop a more critical vision of reality and stimulate more effective behavior in the prevention of health problems. In other words, it is a question of helping people see more clearly the risks for their physical, mental and social health that exist around them, so that they can and want to choose the most effective and intelligent behavior to face these risks and avoid them, both as individuals and collectively (Castillo (1987), quoted in Coppé & Schoonbroodt, 1992, p. 178).

In turn, Cornillot (cited in Coppé & Schoonbroodt, 1992) states that health education is part of a wider educational process aimed at developing in the learner a set of knowledge, attitudes and behaviors that enables the learner to preserve, protect, or restore her health, or that of her friends or family. In brief, health education is empowering, and as such involves a socio-constructivist learning approach.

Teachers are capable of helping young people to be responsible for themselves, as mentioned by Turcotte, Gaudreau, & Otis (2007). Studies on health education in physical education show that teachers' intervention practices do not support learners in developing management skills for their health and well-being. Can games help teachers to reach this objective? The next sections explain key concepts about games, generic game shells and their advantages.

Advantages of Internet-Based Educational Games

With the rise of the Internet, we note an increasing interest in the use of educational games. At present, many educational games are available on the web, but their actual utility is not always evident, and their contents are not usually modifiable (Sauvé et al., 2002). However, researchers confirm that well-designed games have several advantages as learning tools. Games can accelerate and strengthen learning (Reuss & Gardulski, 2001) and can increase motivation, autonomy, and learner participation (Sauvé et al., 2005). Furthermore, they can enhance the development of interpersonal skills such as negotiation and cooperation (Ripp, 2001), cognitive skills such as memorization and learning procedures (Hourst & Thiagarajan, 2001), and mathematical coordination and problem-solving skills (Bricker, Tanimoto, Rothenberg, Hutama, & Wong, 1995).

Definition of a Computerized Frame Game (Generic Game Shell)

A frame game is built from elements of known games. It contains a structure that generates learning activities using various strategies. This structure determines the rules of the game, stages of game progress or player movement, the challenge that the players have to meet, and the strategies with which they can win. The structure can be easily adapted to a wide range of objectives and educational content (Sauvé & Chamberland, 2000; Stolovitch & Thiagarajan, 1980). A frame game is thus a generic shell emptied of its content. It allows a user to build a specific game by adding to it content from pre-established sources. This interchangeability of content makes frame games particularly practical for teachers. (see Section 4 for a detailed description of this topic.)

Essential Criteria for Frame Game Design

Prior to this project, five frame games had been created by the *SAVIE* (*Société d'Apprentissage à VIE*) (www.savie.qc.ca) research team for their *Carrefour virtuel de jeux educatifs/ Educational Games Central* site (http://egc.savie.ca). These frame games included *Snakes and Ladders, Concentration, Tic Tac Toe, Trivia, and Mother Goose.* The results of a survey of University of Moncton (New Brunswick) pre-service teachers who created educational games from these frame games for their future students, indicate that the generic shells were well-designed and easy to use. The response of these student teachers led us to believe that they are likely to use the frame games with their students in their future teaching (IsaBelle, Kaszap, Sauvé, & Samson, 2005).

Kaszap and Rail (2006) studied theoretical considerations for the design of a frame game using a socioconstructivist approach (see also Chapter 11 of this volume) and concluded that such games need several key features. For example, the game must stimulate motivation, since an important element of constructivist theory is to start from the student's experience, offering activities which motivate him, and give him a taste for learning. Therefore the game must take into account cultural characteristics and concerns of the target age group. The constructivist approach puts learners in complex situations in which they have to use their knowledge to solve problems, so an effective game must support knowledge transfer. In our frame game, players will be put into situations in which several solutions are possible, and they will be required to apply their knowledge to find the best solution. To enhance cognitive development during the game, participants will have to carry out different tasks to collect points, such as solving problems, finding information, organizing information, and making relationships that create meaning. They will also have to play in teams, since playing with others increases pleasure and competition (Kaszap & Rail, 2006, p. 6). Of course, the generic game will have to allow for the acquisition of knowledge, and especially the development of a positive attitude towards the different elements of health.

Social Representation

Social representation (SR) research is useful for understanding the social representations of educational games by student teachers. As a concept, SR is difficult to define: various authors from different fields give it different significance. For Moscovici (1961) in social psychology, inspired by the work of Jean Piaget, the notion of SR constitutes a process where "there is no gap between the external world and the internal world of the individual (or of the group)" (p. 9). In the same vein, Anadon (1990) describes SR as a "process of development, of appropriating and interpreting external reality and of internalizing models and social values" (p.16). Because individual thought is necessarily embedded in a matrix of social thought, SR becomes a creation of the individual, himself created by his environment. SR therefore has society as a matrix. It represents the interdependence of a subject and an object; it reflects neither the object itself, nor the concerned subject, but the complex, real and imaginary, objective and symbolic relations which the subject maintains with the object in a given milieu. Representation becomes a reconstruction of the object by the individual living in a social process, ipso facto, it becomes a cultural product. In the same way, Bertrand (1989) stipulates that the individual constructs social representations of an object "because it is useful or necessary for him in the conduct of his daily life to maintain connection with the world of which he is part. It is a social construction" (p.41).

In short, SR tends to support social identity and "sociocognitive balance." It provides a functional and normative vision of the world that allows the individual to give sense to her behaviors. In summary, SR is articulated around three interdependent elements: the subjectivity of the subject, the reality of the object, and the social and symbolic system in which the subject-object relationship appears. If a collective representation is common to all humans, SR proves to be linked to a social group. So, it becomes relevant to study SR on a comparative basis (Flament & Rouquette, 2003).

STUDY GOAL AND OBJECTIVES

The goal of our study was to identify social representations that pre-service teachers have about games, in order for us to make it easier for them to educate their students about health. More specifically, our objectives were to determine: first, which representations pre-service teachers have of games as training tools for their students; second, what non-computer games they prefer; and finally, what aspects of games they would most prefer in a newly-developed generic game shell on health education.

METHODOLOGY

Participants

Our survey was given to student teachers in New Brunswick (NB) and Quebec (QC). Participants in New Brunswick were registered in the course *Computers in the schools* (six groups) at the University of Moncton; participants in Quebec were registered in the course *Didactique de l'univers social pour les élèves de 4 à 7 ans* at Laval University (two groups) and from the University of Quebec at Rimouski (one group).

Data Collection Instruments

Data was collected using the questionnaire entitled *MOI, la santé des jeunes et les jeux* [Me, youth health, and games], developed to meet the needs of the study. Here we describe only the sections which relate to results discussed in this chapter. The first section concerns the identification of the respondent. The second part included seven questions on respondent perceptions of games, using a four-point Likert scale (1= strongly disagree to 4 = strongly agree). The third section concerned the non-computerized games they preferred, as well as which aspects of games they most liked. The student teachers were then asked to answer two open-ended questions.

Ethical Considerations

In a presentation by a member of the research team, the student teachers were informed about the research plan, and invited to complete the questionnaire anonymously after voluntarily signing consent forms.

Sample Size

In the autumn of 2004 and spring of 2005, the *MOI* questionnaire was given to 169 student teachers in New Brunswick and 168 in Quebec. All New Brunswick subjects completed the questionnaire; in Quebec, 95 out of 118 student teachers at Laval University and 43 of 46 at the University of Quebec at Rimouski completed the questionnaire, for a total of 138 responses.

Data Analysis

Quantitative data were coded and statistical analyses carried out with the aid of the *SPSS®* software package. Frequency distributions and averages were calculated, and t-test analyses were performed to establish comparisons according to location and sex. For qualitative data, the Glaser and Strauss (1967) qualitative and inductive analysis method for ethnographic research was used. We identified all possible categories so as not to lose detail and meaning. Categorization was accomplished by one research assistant, after which a second person re-coded 25% of responses. For all responses, inter-rater agreement was at least 85%.

SURVEY RESULTS

Profile of Respondents

The questionnaire was completed by 307 Canadian student teachers (169 In New Brunswick and 138 in Quebec). Of this number, 86.6% were women and 13.4% men (138 women and 31 men in New Brunswick and 128 women and 10 men in Quebec). In New Brunswick, 37.9% of the student teachers planned on working in primary schools and 45.5% in secondary education. In Quebec, all participants planned on working in primary schools. We divided respondents into four age groups; age distribution varied greatly between provinces. The majority of the Quebec student teachers (76.8%) and 31.9% of those in New Brunswick were aged 18 - 21 years. In New Brunswick we found a strong concentration (58.6%) of student teachers aged 22 - 25 years, while in Quebec only 18.8% were in this age group. Also, 9.4% of respondents in New Brunswick and 3.6% in Quebec were 26 or older. Two New Brunswick respondents and one in Quebec did not give their age.

Table 1. Number and percentage of student teachers who report playing games

How many times per week do you play computer or electronic games?	NB		QC	
	N	%	N	%
Never	77	45.6	91	**65.9**
1 time per week	46	27.2	24	174
3 times per week	19	11.2	11	8.0
5 times per week	9	5.3	3	2.2
Every day	10	5.9	4	2.9
No response	8	4.7	5	3.6
Total	169	100	138	100

Legend: N = number of respondents

Social Representation Applied to Games

To learn about the student teachers' game-related activities, we asked them how many times in a week they played computer or electronic games.

Although these results indicate that respondents in both provinces are not very involved with electronic games, 75% (NB) and 64% (QC) of student teachers reported agreeing or strongly agreeing with the statement "*Je peux apprendre des choses en jouant à des jeux.* (I can learn by playing games)." In addition, 88% (NB) and 9% (QC) of respondents reported agreeing or strongly agreeing with the statement "*Les élèves peuvent apprendre des choses en jouant à des jeux.* (Students can learn by playing games*)*." The data are shown in Table 2.

The t-test comparing provinces shows no significant difference; however, the t-test comparing females and males for each of the provinces taken separately shows that New Brunswick men are more in agreement than are the women of the same province with the statement: "*J'aime jouer à des jeux à l'ordinateur ou électroniques* (I like to play computer or electronic games)." Also, there was a significant difference between women and men in each province on the statements: "*J'aime jouer à des jeux à l'ordinateur ou électroniques avec des amies* (I like to play computer or electronic games with my friends)," "*J'aime jouer à toutes sortes de jeux* (I like to play all kinds of games)," and "*J'aime jouer à toutes sortes de jeux avec des amies* (I like to play all kinds of games with my friends)."

Preferred Types of Games

We asked the pre-service teachers what two non-computer games they preferred; Table 3 presents their responses. In order of preference, respondents in New Brunswick identified card games, *Cranium*®, and *Monopoly*®. In Quebec, respondents preferred *Monopoly*, card games, and *Cranium* in that order. 46 (New Brunswick) and 38 (Quebec) respondents did not identify a preferred game.

To identify which aspects of games the student teachers liked, we asked them "*Dans un jeu (toutes sortes de jeux: cartes, ballon, jeu à l'ordinateur), qu'est-ce que vous le PLUS?* (In a game (including all kinds of games, e.g., cards, ball games, computer games), what do you MOST like?" From all respondents, we obtained 231 (New Brunswick) and 201 (Quebec) answers. As shown in Table 4, we divided the aspects of games which respondents liked into nine groups. The New Brunswick respondents reported appreciating mainly the aspects of challenge and competition, social aspects, physical and sport aspects, and

Table 2. Numbers and percentages of student teachers agreeing with statements about games and learning

Statement	P	N	1	2	3	4	NR	Total %
a) *Je peux apprendre des choses en jouant à des jeux à l'ordinateur ou électroniques.* (I can learn by playing computer or electronic games). NB (p = 0.59) QC (p=0.079)	NB	169	6.5	11.2	42.0	32.5	7.7	100
	QC	138	5.8	26.1	40.6	21.7	5.8	100
b) *J'aime jouer à des jeux à l'ordinateur ou électroniques.* (I like to play computer or electronic games). NB (p < 0.001)* QC (p=0.11)	NB	169	18.9	26.0	27.2	21.3	6.5	100
	QC	138	35.5	31.9	19.6	8.0	5.1	100
c) *J'aime jouer aux jeux à l'ordinateur ou électroniques avec des amies.* (I like to play computer or electronic games with my friends). NB (p < 0.001)* QC (p=0.05)*	NB	169	21.3	29.6	23.1	19.5	6.5	100
	QC	138	42.0	29.0	14.5	9.4	5.1	100
d) *Je peux apprendre des choses en jouant à des jeux.* (I can learn by playing games). NB (p = 0.42) QC (p=0.17)	NB	169	3.6	4.1	43.2	42.6	6.5	100
	QC	138	1.4	10.9	40.6	42.0	5.1	100
e) *J'aime jouer à toutes sortes de jeux.* (I like to play all kinds of games). NB (p = 0.04)* QC (p=0.03)*	NB	169	4.1	17.8	32.5	39.1	6.5	100
	QC	138	2.9	14.5	40.6	37.0	5.1	100
f) *J'aime jouer à toutes sortes de jeux avec des amies.* (I like to play all kinds of games with my friends). NB (p = 0.007)* QC (p=0.03)*	NB	169	2.4	12.4	30.2	47.9	7.1	100
	QC	138	2.9	11.6	34.1	46.4	5.1	100
g) *Les élèves peuvent apprendre des choses en jouant à des jeux.* (Students can learn by playing games). NB(p = 0.67) QC (p=0.47)*	NB	169	1.2	3.6	25.4	62.7	7.1	100
	QC	138	0.7	2.9	23.2	68.1	5.1	100

Legend. P=province; N = no of responses; 1 = Strongly disagree; 2 = Disagree; 3 = Agree; 4 = Strongly agree; NR = no response; M = mean; * Difference is significant at 0.05.

entertainment and leisure aspects — fantasy, freedom and realism. Comparatively, the Quebec respondents reported preferring leisure first, then social aspects, challenge and competition, entertainment aspects, and physical and sport aspects. There was no answer from 28 (New Brunswick) and 21 (Quebec) respondents.

CONCLUSION

The data from our study indicate that 46% of New Brunswick student teacher respondents and 66% of Quebec student teacher respondents report that they never play computer or electronic games. However, 75% (NB) and 64% (QC) of respondents agree or strongly agree with the statement "I can learn by playing games." More than 85% of respondents from both provinces agree or strongly agree with "Students can learn by playing games." Therefore, we see that these student teachers believe that games can be efficient learning tools both for them and for students. This confirms the work of Reuss and Garaulski (2001), which maintains that games support learning.

Also, our results reveal that respondents' most preferred non-computer games are cards, *Cranium* and *Monopoly* and the aspects that they most like about playing these are challenge and competition, social, sport and physical activity, and entertainment. These conclusions agree with the Kaszap and Rail study (2006), which concluded that to be effective as a learning tool, a generic game must be designed to: support cognitive development; encourage the participant to carry out different tasks to collect points (e.g., solving problems, finding information); allow team play, because playing with others enhances pleasure and competitive character; and support the transfer of

Table 3. Responses to the question "What are your two PREFERRED non-computer games?"

Preferred non-computer games	NB			QC	
	1st	2nd		1st	2nd
	N	N		N	N
No response	46	73		38	49
Social games (cards, word games, puzzles)					
Social games (not specified), Chess, Jeopardy®, 200 (cards), Bingo, Blackjack, Cribbage, Poker, Crosswords, Scrabble®, Trivial Pursuit®, etc.	33	32		22	25
Cards	21	10		9	7
Cranium	17	6		9	7
Monopoly	6	10		12	8
Scattegories®	4	3		6	7
Sport and ball games					
Badminton, *balle molle, ballon prisonnier, ballon volant*, hockey, marche, natation, soccer, squash, tennis, volleyball, *se tirer une balle*, etc.	15	17		15	10
Arcade and electronic games					
Nintendo®, Zelda®, Donkey-Kong®, FFX (Final Fantasy)®, GameCube®-Hobbit®, Hallo 2, Lord of the Rings®, Sims®/PlayStation® games, Skip-bo®, Super Mario®, etc.	12	8		16	12
Simulation, strategy and action games					
Clue®, Destin, Grand Turismo™, LIFE, Malarky®, *Meurte et mystère, Chasse au trésor®*, Mortal Kombat®, Pay day, Risk®, etc.	6	5		5	8
Other					
Paddle games, *pieds de poule*, etc.	5	3		1	2
Non – I do not play games.	4	2		5	3
Total	169	169		138	138

Legend: 1st = first choice; 2nd = second choice.

knowledge. These attributes are consistent with a constructivist approach, which puts learners into complex situations in which they must use their knowledge to solve problems.

After further research (our field study and a literature search, described in Chapter 11) our team settled on a generic game form that reproduces some elements of the well-known game *Cranium*. The structure of *Cranium* is inspired by the game of *Parchees*[TMi], with modifications in terms of the number of cases and possible paths. Our choice takes into account our survey results and pedagogic requirements, particularly the need to be able to create a wide variety of learning activities that teach behaviors and attitudes (Sauvé et al., 2006).

To learn more about the design, development and evaluation of this frame game, we refer you to Chapter 11 and Section 4 of this volume.

Although the present study gives us important information on the social representations of games for student teachers in New Brunswick and Quebec, other research is needed to analyze which specific aspects of games are likely to facilitate health-related changes of attitude and behavior in students. Health education is a major issue, and schools have an important role to play in helping young people to become aware of their health, the importance of the health of their family, and the need to develop an interest in playing educational games about health education.

Table 4. Responses to the question: "In a game (including all kinds of games, e.g., cards, ball games, computer games), what do you MOST like?"

Game aspects	NB	QC
	N	N
None	28	21
Challenge and competition	68	37
Challenge; competition; winning; developing strategies; capacity to reason (logic); success; speed		
Social and individual aspects, with name of game	58	51
Social: participation in a team; social aspect; team games; being with friends; social games. **Solitaire**	1	1
Sport and physical activity (outdoors)	33	18
Do what I like; get fit; going outdoors; chasing the ball; being active		
Entertainment aspects – leisure, fantasy, freedom or realism	32	29
Pleasure –fantasy, having fun, when it is funny, entertainment, laughing **Realism**	5	0
Technology aspects	6	11
Computer games, computer graphics		
Learning aspects associated with a goal or mission	4	13
deepen my knowledge; use my knowledge; have a mission or purpose; learning		
Artistic aspects	3	1
Theatre; guitar; dance; odd jobs		
Violent aspects	2	2
Rigorous physical activity; fights; play outside (*jouer dehors à la lutte*), extreme games		
Names of specific games	19	36
Cranium™, cards, poker, bingo		
Other	0	2
Games that last for a long time		
TOTAL	259	222

REFERENCES

Allard, S. (2008, March 15). Moins de crayons, plus de ballons [Fewer pencils, more balls]. *La Presse*, 2-3.

Anadon, M. (1990). *Les rapports sciences/société et représentations scolaires* [Science and social reports and scholarly representations]. Québec, QC, Canada: Presses d'université du Québec.

Armstrong, L. (2007). *Le suicide chez les jeunes: le temps d'agir* [Youth suicide: The time to act]. *Le forum de l'Express.* Available at http://www.lexpress.to/forum/157/

Bayne-Smith, M., Fardy, P. S., Azzollini, A., Magel, J., Schmitz, K. H., & Agin, D. (2004). Improvements in heart health behaviors and reduction in coronary artery disease risk factors in urban teenaged girls through a school-based intervention: The PATH program. *American Journal of Public Health, 94*(9), 1538–1543. doi:10.2105/AJPH.94.9.1538

Bertrand, L. (1989). *Les effets de l'utilisation de la bureautique sur le développement des connaissances: Représentations discursives d'usagers* [The effects of the use of office automation on the development of knowledge: Discursive representations of users]. Unpublished doctoral dissertation, Laval University, Québec, QC, Canada.

Bricker, L., Tanimoto, S., Rothenberg, A., Hutama, D., & Wong, T. (1995). Multiplayer activities which develop mathematical coordination. In *Proceedings of CSCL'95* (pp. 32-39). New York: ACM Press.

Castillo, F. (1987). *Le chemin des écoliers: l'éducation à la santé en milieu scolaire* [The long way round: Health education in the schools]. Brussels, Belgium: De Boeck Université.

Clocksin, B. D., Watson, D. L., & Ransdell, L. (2002). Understanding youth obesity and media use: Implications for future intervention programs. *QUEST, 54*, 259–275.

Cohen, B., Evers, S., Manske, S., Bercovitz, K., & Edward, H. G. (2003). Smoking, physical activity and breakfast consumption among secondary school students in a southwestern Ontario community. *Canadian Journal of Public Health, 94*(1), 41–44.

Coppé, M., & Schoonbroodt, C. (1992). *Guide pratique d'éducation pour la santé: réflexion, expérimentation et 50 fiches à l'usage des formateurs* [Practical Guide for Health Education: Reflection, Experimentation, and 50 Index Cards to Help the Trainer]. Brussels, Belgium: De Boeck Université.

Flament, C., & Rouquette, M. L. (2003). *Anatomie des idées ordinaires: comment étudier les représentations sociales*[Anatomy of ordinary ideas: How to study social representations]. Paris: Armand Colin.

Gagné, S. (2002). *Bilan de santé des jeunes: exercice à la baisse et médication à la hausse* [Youth check-up: Exercise falls and medication increases]. *Passeportsanté.net.* Available at http://www.passeportsante.net/fr/Actualites/Nouvelles/Fiche.aspx?doc=2002112000

Glaser, B. G., & Strauss, A. (1967). *The discovery of grounded theory: Strategies for qualitative research.* Chicago: Aldine.

Harvey, G., Trudeau, F., Morency, L., & Bordeleau, C. (2007). *L'éducation à la santé* [Health education]. Retrieved January 15, 2008 from http://www.uquebec.ca/edusante/

Hills, M., & O'Neill, M. (2000, October). *Symposium à l'intention des enseignants en promotion de la santé et en santé Communautaire tenu durant la Conférence annuelle de l'Association canadienne de santé publique, Quebec.* [Symposium for teachers on health promotion and community health presented during the Annual Conference of the Canadian Association for Public Health] (Symposium report, J. Hills, translator). Available at http://www.utoronto.ca/chp/CCHPR/Ottawa_Symposium_fr_3.doc

Hourst, B., & Thiagarajan, S. (2001). *Les jeux-cadres de Thiagi: techniques d'animation à l'usage du formateur* [Frame games of Thiagi: Animation techniques for trainer use]. Paris: Les Éditions d'Organisation.

Instituts de recherche en santé du Canada (2006). *Le suicide chez les jeunes: Le temps d'agir* Youth suicide: The time to act]. Available at http://www.cihr-irsc.gc.ca/f/32154.html

IsaBelle. C., Kaszap, M., Sauvé, L., & Samson, D. (2005). Faciliter l'intégration des jeux éducatifs à l'aide de jeux-cadre [Facilitating the integration of educational games with the help of frame games]. In P. Tchounikine, M. Joab & L. Abrouk (eds.), *Environnements Informatiques pour l'Apprentissage Humain* (pp. 45-46). Montpellier, France: ATIEF, LIRMM Université de Montpellier CNRS.

Kaszap, M., & Rail, S. (2006, May). *Conception d'un jeu-cadre visant une socio construction des connaissances: Considérations théoriques et empiriques* [Conception of a frame game using a socio-constructivist approach to knowledge: Theoretical and empirical considerations. Paper presented at the 23e Congrès de l'AIPU, Association internationale de pédagogie universitaire, Monastir, Tunisia. Moscovici, S. (1961). *La psychanalyse, son image, son public* [Psychoanalysis, its image, its public]. Paris: PUF.

Pronovost, G. (2007). *L'univers du temps libre et des valeurs chez les jeunes* [The universe of free time and youth values]. Québec, QC, Canada: Presses de l'Université du Québec.

Reuss, R. L., & Gardulski, A. F. (2001). An interactive game approach to learning in historical geology and paleontology. *Journal of Geoscience Education, 49*(2), 120–129.

Ripp, K. (2001). *Bead game simulation lesson plan.* Davis, CA: Foundation for Teaching Economics.

Sauvé, L., & Chamberland, G. (2000). *Jeux, jeux de simulation et jeux de rôle: une analyse exploratoire et pédagogique* [Games, simulation games and role-playing games: An exploratory pedogical analysis. Cours TEC 1280: Environnement d'apprentissage multimédia sur l'inforoute. Québec, QC, Canada: Télé-université.

Sauvé, L., & Power, M. IsaBelle, C., Samson, D., & St-Pierre, C. (2002). *Rapport final - Jeux-cadres sur l'inforoute: Multiplicateurs de jeux pédagogiques francophones: Un projet de partenariat* [Final report – Frame games on the Internet: Multipliers of francophone educational games]. Québec, QC, Canada: Bureau des technologies d'apprentissage (SAVIE).

Sauvé, L., Renaud, L., & Kaszap, M. IsaBelle, C., Gauvin, M., & Simard, G. (2005). *Analyse de 40 jeux éducatifs* [Analysis of 40 Educational Games]. Québec, QC, Canada: SAGE and SAVIE.

Sauvé, L., Renaud, L., & Kaszap, M. IsaBelle, C., Gauvin, M., Rodriguez, A., & Simard, G. (2006) *Modélisation du jeu-cadre Parchesi* [Design of the frame game *Parcheesi*] (Research Report). Québec, QC, Canada: SAVIE and SAGE.

Skemp-Arlt, K. M. (2006). Body image dissatisfaction and eating disturbances among children and adolescents: Prevalence, risk factors, and prevention strategies. [JOPERD]. *Journal of Physical Education, Recreation & Dance, 77*(1), 45–51.

Statistics Canada. (2005). *Enquête sur la santé dans les collectivités canadiennes: Obésité chez les enfants et les adultes. In Le Quotidien* [Inquiry into the health of Canadian groups: Obesity in children and adults]. Retrieved October 17, 2006 from http://www.statcan.ca/Daily/Francais/050706/q050706a.htm

Statistics Canada. (2007). *Ressources éducatives journal annuel 2006-2007* [Annual education resources journal 2006-2007]. Retrieved November 7, 2007 from http://www.statcan.ca/francais/edu/lr2006/LR2006family_f.htm

STHC. (2007). *Quelques faits: Maladie mentale et toxicomanie au Canada* [Some facts: Mental Illness and drug dependency in Canada]. Guelph, ON, Canada: Société pour les troubles de l'humeur du Canada.

Stolovitch, H. D., & Thiagarajan, S. (1980). *Frame Games.* Englewood Cliffs, NJ: Educational Technology Publications.

Turcotte, S., Gaudreau, L., & Otis, J. (2007). Démarche de modélisation de l'intervention en éducation à la santé incluse en éducation physique [Steps in modeling an educational intervention for physical education]. *STAPS, 77*, 63–78. doi:10.3917/sta.077.0063

ADDITIONAL READING

Boudreau, P. (2009). Pour un modèle de supervision de type inductif en formation à la supervision de maîtres de stage en éducation physique [An inductive model of supervision for supervisory training by mentors of students in a physical education program]. *Éducation et francophonie, 37*(1), 121-139.

Cogerino, G. (2000). Curriculum en éducation physique et éducation à la santé: débats autour d'une difficile intégration [Curriculum in physical education and health education: discussions around the difficulty of integration] [STAPS]. *Revue Sciences et Techniques des Activités Physiques et Sportives, 53*, 79–90.

Godin, G. (2002). Le changement des comportements de santé [Changing health behaviors]. In G. F. Fisher (Éd.), *Traité de psychologie de la santé* (pp. 375-388). Paris: Dunod.

Institut national de la santé et de la recherche médicale (INSERM) (2001). *Éducation pour la santé des jeunes: démarches et méthodes* [Health education for youth: Steps and methods]. Paris: Éditions Inserm.

Mérini, C., Jourdan, D., Victor, P., Berger, D., & De Peretti, C. (2004). *Guide ressource pour une éducation à la santé à l'école élémentaire* [Resource guide for health education in the primary school]. Rennes, France: Éditions ENSP.

Turcotte, S. (2006). *L'inclusion de l'éducation à la santé en éducation physique: analyse des pratiques pédagogiques d'éducateurs physiques du primaire* [The inclusion of health education in physical education: Analysis of pedagogic practices of primary school physical educators]. Unpublished doctoral dissertation, Faculty of Sciences of Education, University of Quebec in Montreal, Montreal, QC, Canada.

KEY TERMS AND DEFINITIONS

Anorexia Nervosa: A condition in which the affected person fears gaining weight and is not able to maintain a normal minimum weight. To slim down excessively, the anorexic reduces food consumption, induces vomiting, uses purging medications, and exercises excessively. Serious medical consequences (malnutrition, dysfunction of kidneys, amenorrhea, somatic and psychological problems, etc.) are linked to this condition.

Appropriate Health Management: The development of an educational process for health and well-being that is centered on mediating the relationship between the personal health of the individual and the environment, with the intention of finding a collective way of living more healthily.

Bulimia: Characterised by the excessive ingestion of food in a short stretch of time, followed by a period of "repairing" (inappropriate behaviours including vomiting; fasting; excessive physical exercise; and the use of laxatives, diuretics or other medications) to avoid weight gain.

Educational Game: A fictitious, fantasy, or imaginary situation in which players, placed in conflict with others or assembled in a team against an external opponent, are governed by rules determining their actions, with a view to achieving learning objectives and a goal determined by the game, either to win or to seek revenge.

Obesity: An excess of fatty body mass with harmful consequences for health.

Chapter 8
Video Games and the Challenge of Engaging the 'Net' Generation

Anthony Gurr
Simon Fraser University, Canada

ABSTRACT

Video games are a popular form of entertainment for students in North America and around the world. They provide widely diverse experiences on a variety of platforms. Participants can engage in solo play, or in games that attract thousands of other players. The levels of player participation, skill mastery, and thought processes required by many video games attract and engage students because they are able to control and eventually master challenging virtual environments. The holding power of video games and their ability to engage players is the subject of much educational research as educators recognize that game technologies are highly sophisticated. Students are interacting with subject content in ways that differ greatly from established methods of classroom instruction. This chapter reviews the current discussion among educators, researchers, and professional game developers about using video games in the classroom.

INTRODUCTION

There has been much discussion in Canadian society about the possible benefits or negative effects of playing video games. Everyone has an opinion – academics, educators, the media, medical professionals, parents, and politicians. Many educators recognize that video games are highly sophisticated, developed with powerful hardware and software technologies that immerse players in challenging, engaging virtual experiences requiring high levels of participation, skill mastery, and thought. The current generation of students, born since 1990, views these technologies as a natural part of their lives. They interact with video games in ways that differ greatly from established methods of classroom instruction.

As a veteran video game developer with experience and formal training in education, I have often visited elementary and secondary schools

DOI: 10.4018/978-1-61520-731-2.ch008

in Canada and the United States to talk about video game design and what it was like to work in the game development industry. Parents and teachers frequently observe that students would gladly spend more time playing video games than doing schoolwork. Facer (2002) states "...computer games seem to motivate young people in a way that formal education doesn't" (p. 2). These comments confirm my own observations about the qualities shared by commercially-successful video game designers and outstanding educators. Both are passionate about their profession. They understand how to engage their audiences, immerse them in the content being presented, and help their audiences build on what is learned to master the next steps. Designing a unit of instruction and designing a video game are not dissimilar. Good video games clearly demonstrate how careful design and planning result in effective learning and application of knowledge (Squire, 2005). In this chapter, I argue that there are a number of compelling reasons for including video games at all levels of the curriculum.

THE "NET GENERATION" AND TECHNOLOGY

Canada's "Net Generation" at Play

Three decades ago, video games were perceived as little more than a child's toy and a nerd's hobby. The pixilated graphics were crude, the sound effects were minimal, and the game controls consisted mainly of moving a joystick and pressing one or two buttons. Many of them let two people play together by taking turns or participating at the same time. Today video games are considered a legitimate form of recreational entertainment around the world, competing with other established entertainment industries for the consumer's attention. According to the Entertainment Software Association of Canada (2008), nine out of ten Canadian households owned a personal computer in 2007. Four out of ten Canadian households owned a video game console. Canadian consumers spent (Cdn) $1.67 billion on video game hardware and software. They purchased 22.3 million units of video game software. People play video games across a wide variety of hardware platforms, including portable game systems, mobile and wireless devices, personal computers, and consoles. The availability of consumer broadband Internet technology in the last twelve years has provided a new opportunity for online game development and the creation of massively multiplayer online games. The current generation of video game consoles such as the Sony *PlayStation 3®* and the *Xbox 360®* are the technological equivalents of supercomputers; they use parallel processing cores, advanced three dimensional graphic capabilities, surround sound audio systems, and broadband Internet connections. The Nintendo *DS (i)®* portable game system incorporates a built-in camera, microphone, touch screen technology, and wireless connectivity. The Nintendo *Wii®* console uses motion sensors for its game controllers instead of a conventional button array. Video games of the 21st century offer players compelling, immersive, vivid, virtual entertainment experiences.

In November, 2003 the Canadian Broadcasting Corporation (CBC) aired a news story about the results of a large-scale media literacy survey commissioned by the Canadian Teacher's Federation and the Media Awareness Network (MNet) (Spears & Seydegart, 2003; 2004). The national survey, entitled *Kids' Take on Media*, was designed by Erin Research to examine the media viewing habits of 5,756 Canadian students from grades three to ten, across 122 public schools. The results were interesting, particularly when looking at video-game playing habits; 60% of boys in grades three to six reported that they played video games daily, and by grade ten, 30% of boys still played video games daily. 33% of girls in grade three played video games, but by grade ten the number was only 6%.

Figure 1. Teens, Video Games, and Civics: Summary of survey findings (adapted from Lenhart et al. (2008))

Teens, Video Games, and Civics: Summary of Findings at a Glance

- Almost all teens play games
- Gender and age are key factors in describing teen's video gaming.
- Youth play many different kinds of video games.
- The most popular games played by teens today span a wide variety of genres.
- Gaming is often a social experience for teens.
- Close to half of teens who play online games do so with people they know in their offline lives.
- Teens encounter both pro-social and anti-social behavior while gaming.
- The most popular game genres include games with both violent and non-violent content
- Parental monitoring of game play varies.

One noteworthy result from this survey was that the popular video game of choice for Anglophone boys from grades three to ten was the 'M' (Mature) rated title *Grand Theft Auto®*. (In Quebec, francophone boys from grades seven to ten selected hockey titles as their top video game of choice.) Children also reported little parental guidance about the types of video games they could play, or how long they could play. 75% of the grade seven boys reported that their parents never told them what computer or video games they could or could not play. These results raised some important questions. Why were young boys playing an 'M' rated video game title? Where were the parents when their children were playing games containing mature themes? Why were parents not paying attention to the types of games played by their children? Despite the Retail Council of Canada's partnership with the federal and provincial governments to promote the Entertainment Software Rating Board (ESRB) game rating system and prevent the sale of 'M' rated games to minors, the issue of children playing age-inappropriate video games continues to be a problem.

In 2005, MNet released the results of another large-scale survey entitled *Young Canadians in a Wired World* (Seydegart, Spears, & Zulinov, 2005). The survey examined the online activities of 5,272 students from grades four to eleven across 92 school districts in Canada. 94% of the respondents had home Internet access, with 61% indicating that their homes had high speed Internet access. 77% of the respondents reported that the main activity they engaged in at home during their free time was playing video games.

In September, 2008, the Pew Internet & American Life Project published the results of a national survey entitled *Teens, Video Games, and Civics* (Lenhart et al., 2008). The authors of this survey wanted to investigate the relationship between teenage video game play, teenage video gaming, and teenage civic engagement in the United States. It involved a nationally representative sample of 1,102 teenagers between the ages of 12 to 17 years old and a parent or guardian.

The findings showed that 99% of teenage boys and 94% of teenage girls between the ages of 12 and 17 played computer, web, portable, or console games; 86% of teenagers played video games on console platforms such as the Microsoft *Xbox®*, Sony *PlayStation®*, and the Nintendo *Wii*; 73% of teenagers played video games on a desktop or laptop computer; 60% of teenagers played video games on a portable gaming device such as the Sony *PlayStation Portable®* (PSP), *Nintendo DS*, or the Nintendo *Game Boy®*. 4% of teenagers played video games on a cell phone or hand-held organizer. Teenagers played a wide variety of video games. The top five popular titles they reported were *Guitar Hero®*, *Halo 3®*, *Madden NFL®*, *Solitaire*, and *Dance Dance Revolution®*. Contrary to the public perception of video game play as a solitary activity, the survey results showed that, for teenagers, video game play is often a social activity. 65% of teenagers played with other people in the same room, while 47% play with people they know in their offline lives. Another 27% play with people with whom they've connected through the Internet

The survey results about parental monitoring of teenage video game players were particularly interesting. 90% of parents surveyed said that they always or sometimes know what games their children play. 72% said that they always or sometimes check video game ratings before their children play are allowed to play a game, and 46% said they always or sometimes stop their children from playing a video game. According to survey results, 31% of parents say they always or sometimes play video games with their children.

The 'Digital Natives' Are a Restless Tribe

In the last five years, educational research literature has focused on how the generation born between 1980 and 1994 differ from their parents because they have grown up with computer technology as a natural part of their lives (Carlson, 2003). Children born in 1994 accept the Internet as a part of daily life in the same way their parents accept television. There are prominent educators and researchers who advocate that children and young adults born in the 1980s and 1990s perceive, process, and interpret the world differently from their parents and grandparents because of their relationship to computer and information technologies. Marc Prensky is a well known advocate of this position. In his book *Don't Bother Me Mom - I'm Learning!* (Prensky, 2006), he argues that there are 'digital natives' and 'digital immigrants.' Digital natives are individuals born in the last 25 years who grew up in an environment where they were continuously exposed to computer and information technology hardware and software. Prensky contends that digital natives act, behave, communicate, create, learn, organize, socialize, think, and understand in ways that are a result of their interactions with current information technologies. He argues that the challenges facing students are the pre-digital-age adults who do not understand the differences that the new technologies have created. Digital immigrants are individuals born before the introduction of personal computers in the late 1970s, and who subsequently experienced them later in life. These individuals retain an 'accent' of their previous life experiences before exposure to the knowledge and skills of the digital native's world (Prensky, 2006).

Prensky explains that "...the natives are used to receiving information far more quickly than the immigrants know how to dispense it" (Prensky, 2006, p.29). Carlson (2003) refers to this point of view as a pre-information society model: students who grow up in a digital environment at home attend schools that don't use these new technologies. Norton-Meir (2005) also identifies today's students as thinking and processing information differently from their parents. But is this perception true? Does the new technology really affect people's ability to interpret and process large amounts of information? Is today's generation significantly different from their parents because they grew up with computer technology? Downes (1988, cited by Facer, 2002, p.2) argues "While it would be fair to say that for many children today a computer is part of the furniture in their

Figure 2. Digital natives are different (adapted from Prensky, 2006)

Digital Natives are Different

Digital natives **analyze** differently	Digital natives **evolve** differently	Digital natives **evaluate** differently
Digital natives **buy and sell** differently	Digital natives **exchange** differently	Digital natives **meet** differently
Digital natives **communicate** differently	Digital natives **game** differently	Digital natives **program** differently
Digital natives **co-ordinate** differently	Digital natives **grow up** differently	Digital natives **report** differently
Digital natives **create** differently	Digital natives **learn** differently	Digital natives **socialize** differently

lives, for the vast majority of children, electronic games are a regular but not a central part of their lives…". Facer (2002) contends "To lump all children together as a new 'net' generation and to assume we can find a one size fits all answer, is to ignore the diversity that exists among young people as it does amongst adults" (p. 2).

Prensky's ideas about digital natives and their relationship to computers and information technology are based on the concept of using computers to develop ways of knowing and building an intellectual structure that helps to make sense of the world. Jean Piaget considered children as epistemologists who engaged in active, directed construction and assimilation of knowledge (Papert, 1980). Children find active engagement in meaningful activity. The books, movies, and video games of today's popular culture demand strategic thinking, technical language, and sophisticated problem solving skills (Schaffer, 2006). Modern technology exposes today's young people to learning processes outside of school that are deeper and richer than the ones that they are exposed to in school (Gee, 2007).

VIDEO GAMES AND LEARNING

The concept of teaching students with video games in the classroom has existed since personal computers were introduced into North American schools during the early 1980s. Their presence was controversial. Some parents were concerned that there was something unnatural about putting children and computers together (Turkle, 2005). Seymour Papert (1980) viewed personal computers as carriers of powerful ideas and seeds of cultural change. By writing computer programs in *LOGO* and developing procedural thinking skills, he believed that children could learn to use them in a masterful way that can change the way they learn everything else (Papert, 1980). In her book *The Second Self*, Sherry Turkle (2005, p. 12) used the metaphor of "the computer as Rorschach"; students projected personal and cultural differences through the computer programs they created. Turkle (1997, cited by Prensky, 2001, p.47) defines this condition as "agency"; "the satisfying power to take meaningful action and see the results of our decisions and choices." Experiences with computers become reference points for thinking and talking about other things (Turkle, 2005, p. 21).

The More You Play, the More You Know

Play is an inherent part of the human experience. The Dutch historian Johan Huizinga defined play as a form of free activity performed outside of ordinary life (Huizinga, 1955). Most psychologists agree that play is a crucial method for testing new ideas, developing new skills, and participating in new social roles (Piaget, 1962 and Vygotsky, 1978, cited by Squire, 2005). Games present players with imaginary or real situations that engage their attention and encourage them to test their abilities and skills. Schaffer (2006) contends that "...developmental psychologists have known for nearly a century that children learn from playing games" (p. 6). Piaget argued that the form of children's play mirrors the stages of their intellectual development. Vygotsky wrote about how play was critical to children's social and emotional development..." To play any game well, the player must learn to care about the kinds of things that matter in the game (Schaffer, 2006, p. 123). Koster (2005) explains "That's what games are, in the end. Teachers. Fun is just another word for learning" (p. 46).

Educators face the challenge of teaching students how to effectively master a body of knowledge. Traditional instruction methods use rote memorization, textbook readings, and examinations to deliver information to students and test their ability to recall information they learned. Schaffer (2006) argues that public education continues to follow a 19th-century industrial model of schooling that discourages innovative thinking, and values declarative knowledge, tested on exams, over procedural knowledge about how to apply what is learned. Schools teach facts and information but do not provide enough opportunities for students to apply what they learn to master the subject. John Dewey criticized the North American education system as suffering from a 'fact fetish' regarding "...any area of learning—whether physics, mathematics, or history—as a body of facts or information. The measure of good teaching and learning is the extent to which students can answer questions about these facts on tests" (Gee, 2004b, p.7). The issue is how to make learning what is taught in school an active process where the body of knowledge that is presented engages the student so it is viewed as more than an accumulation of facts and information.

Using video games to assist in classroom instruction can create meaningful learning experiences for students. Gros (2007, p. 23) maintains that "...video games are user-centered; they can promote challenges, co-operation, engagement, and the development of problem solving strategies." Squire (2005) points out that in the classroom, learners build representations of systems and examine their success or failure by passive observation. He explains that "...as learners play video games, they build a model of the game world based on experiences both within the game and outside of it" (p. 3). The best example of a commercially successful video game franchise that combines educational content with entertainment is *Where in the World is Carmen San Diego?®*, originally developed and published by Broderbund Software in 1985. Players took on the roles of investigators for the ACME Detective Agency and travelled the world searching for valuable cultural artifacts stolen by the international criminal mastermind Carmen San Diego and her underlings who worked for the evil organization known as VILE. The game play blended real world knowledge of subjects involving art, culture, geography, history, language, mathematics, music, and science, with the act of tracking down and arresting members of VILE. The series was a worldwide hit and generated spin-offs that included board games, books, and a long running television series on the American PBS television network.

There is more to the experience of playing a video game than the traditional view held by educators that they are a form of motivational reward for good behavior (Schrader, Young, & Zheng, 2006). Good video games allow the player to inhabit the game world, learn its rules, develop an identity, accomplish goals, develop a body of knowledge, and learn its language and syntax. A multiplayer video game offers the ability to develop effective social practices and communicate with a larger player community (Schaffer, Squire, Halverson, & Gee, 2005). Just as schools provide opportunities for developing social skills in the context of the school community, video games provide similar opportunities for social interaction within a player community. Crowley and Jacobs (2002) discuss the concept of 'islands of expertise,' which they define as "...any topic in which children happen to become interested and in which they develop relatively rich and deep knowledge" (p. 323). Schaffer (2005) believes that this development of knowledge creates practices and ways of 'knowing' that can be applied to situations in the world, creating an 'epistemic frame' that he explains "...are the organizing principles for practices..." (p. 228).

LEARNING IS EASY: MOTIVATION IS HARD

In the introduction to this chapter, I noted that commercially successful video game designers and outstanding educators share similar qualities. They also share the challenge of how to engage people and motivate them to learn content that is sometimes complex, difficult, and takes time to master (Gee, 2004b). Educators and video game designers work in two very different worlds. Most educators are civil servants employed by a local school district with publicly accountable trustees. Video game designers are generally self-employed or work for private sector businesses. Educators are mandated by legislation to teach subject content according to a particular curriculum. Video game designers are mandated to produce creative, profitable entertainment content according to consumer demand. The public education system evolves incrementally. The video game industry evolves at 'warp speed.' Both outstanding educators and video game designers are dedicated, passionate people who can overcome the challenges and difficulties placed in front of them.

The commercial video game industry is an intensely hit-driven business in which success is measured by the number of units sold globally. The pressure on video game development teams to create highly entertaining, immersive, profitable titles is immense. Most retail video games make the majority of their targeted sales in the first 90 days of their release date. Experienced video game developers acknowledge that 20% of the titles released each year generate approximately 80% of the revenues for video game publishers. As video game hardware and technologies evolve, consumer expectations go up at the same time. Consider the release of *Grand Theft Auto IV*® (*GTA IV*) in May, 2008. The game sold over three million units worldwide in the first 24 hours and earned USD $310 million. By the end of the first week, it sold six million units and earned $500 million. Compare the success of *GTA IV* in its first week to the movie *Iron Man* which was released on the same day. The movie earned USD $200 million in its first week of release and $500 million overall during the summer.

Seymour Papert (1998, pp. 1-2) compared the roles of game designers and curriculum designers, noting that "...game designers have a better take on the nature of learning than curriculum designers. They have to. Their livelihoods depend on millions of people being prepared to undertake the serious amount of learning needed to master a complex game." Halverson (2005) makes a distinction between education games and video games by using the definitions of 'exogenous' and 'endogenous' games developed by Malone and Lepper (1987). Exogenous games contain simple designs, adaptable content, and are widely used by curriculum designers and teachers as a supplement to classroom instruction. Popular quiz shows like *Jeopardy!*® and *Wheel of Fortune*® are examples of exogenous games that can be adapted to curricular content based on accepted standards for K-12 education. Endogenous games are different. Real time strategy (RTS) titles like *Civilization III*® or *Rise of Nations*® are examples of endogenous games. They use complex systems of building construction, diplomacy, governance, population control, resource management, and military strategy. Mastering the learning environment of the game is itself the learning outcome (Halverson, 2005). The learner builds a model of the game world based on experiences inside and outside the game (Squire, 2005). Integrating endogenous games into classroom instruction is a new area that requires more study. It can be argued that other commercial video game genres which let the player control multiple variables during the course of mastering the game's environment also meet the definition of an endogenous game. Massively multiplayer online games such as *Eve Online*® and *World of Warcraft*® qualify as endogenous games. Curriculum designers need to think about what players are learning from these games, and determine how to combine it with the requirements of the curriculum.

Good Video Games and Effective Learning Go Together

Some educators recognize the popularity of video games with their students (Barab, Arici, & Jackson, 2005). Parents and teachers often wonder why students do not apply the same amount of time to their studies as they do to playing video games. Paras and Bizzocchi (2005) explain that "... gaming environments are quite unlike any other environments we immerse ourselves in because they allow us to freely do as we please with little or no consequence..." (p. 1). Students like to play competitively against each other and compare their performance (Eglesz, Fekete, Kiss, & Izso, 2005). Playing video games offers an escape from everyday life and lets the player develop specific expertise (Gee, 2004a). Educational researchers recognize that well-designed video games provide engaging, challenging learning experiences that motivate players and provide them with the opportunity to master the knowledge that exists in the game world. Commercially successful video game designers understand intrinsically how to create an interactive learning experience that engages the audience, maintains their focus, teaches them the necessary skills, and ultimately lets them master the game's content. They understand how to introduce players to the basic game play mechanics required for interaction and navigation through the game world, and developing necessary advanced skill sets. They understand how to build a sense of pacing into the game so a new player won't feel frustrated and experienced players won't feel held back. They carefully plan how to graduate the level of difficulty and introduce the player to advanced levels of game play. People enjoy learning new things when they are presented in a way that engages them, holds their attention, and gives them a feeling of mastery.

Seeing Video Games Through 3D Rose-colored Glasses

The current literature about video games and learning acknowledges the potential value of using games in the classroom. However, not all educators regard them as beneficial to classroom instruction. Klopfer and Yoon (2005) explain "...video games and learning have had a tumultuous relationship because many perceive video games as taking away time from productive learning activities..." (p. 35). An adversarial relationship exists between the cultures of gaming and schooling; school leaders and teachers react negatively to video games and gaming culture (Halverson, 2005). Video games are portrayed as a distraction from education that prevents reflection by offering immersive, addictive experiences (Pelletier, 2005). De Freitas (2006) comments "...there has been a dominant perception of gaming as a leisure pursuit with no pedagogic value..." (p. 16). She suggests there are legitimate barriers affecting the use of video games for learning practices that include familiarity with game-based software, communities of practice for guidance and support, preparation time for learning, access to the required hardware, the cost of software, and the necessary technical support.

Although video games are recognized as a legitimate form of home entertainment, they are not perceived by educational stakeholders as necessarily having constructive learning value. There are a number of factors contributing to this situation. Part of the problem is generational; many administrators and teachers in today's public school system are middle-aged or older adults who possess little or no direct experience with video games. They do not understand the kinds of virtual experiences their students are encountering outside of school. Their knowledge is often based on sensational portrayals by the media that focus on a small number of controversial titles featuring sexually suggestive or violent themes played by a specific demographic of young adult males between the ages of 18 to 34 (ESA Canada, 2008, p.2). The video game industry complains that these reports are not always well-documented or researched, and show bias in their reporting. There is so much available information about the different ways video games affect society that anyone who seriously wants to understand the scope must take the necessary time and effort to filter and make sense of it all.

Historically, educational institutions make incremental changes when it comes to using new technologies. Over the last two decades, schools have dealt with the serious problems of integrating personal computers into classroom instruction, such as building and maintaining computer laboratories, evaluating educational software that matched curricular requirements, providing staff training and support, and regular technology upgrades. Video game hardware and software evolve quickly. The same issues affecting computer use in the schools also apply to using video games for instructional purposes. Educators must determine how to use video games with their students so that they support the curriculum. Imagine that a small group of dedicated secondary music teachers convinces the director of instruction for their school district that every secondary school should install a set of Microsoft *Xbox 360s* so they can teach music education using the hit video game *Guitar Hero*. The director of instruction submits the purchase order for several dozen video game consoles and all the requisite game copies and plastic guitar peripherals required for playing it. One can only imagine the reaction of elected school trustees, parents, and the general public when this request comes up for approval. Many parents would protest about their taxes being spent on video games that their children already play at home. They would certainly question the educational value and what exactly the students might learn from the experience. There is also the question of how the video game meets provincial music education curriculum requirements: what is the assessment method for evaluating student learning based on playing *Guitar Hero*? There would be a host of logistical issues to be addressed that include classroom and equipment setup, teacher training, scheduling, student assessment, and making sure every piece of hardware and software is accounted for at the end of class so that none of them mysteriously 'walk away.' Video game equipment is expensive.

Over the course of my long career as a video game developer, I can truthfully say that I spent several thousand hours evaluating and testing hundreds of commercial titles. I learned how to identify good video games from bad ones and provide specific details supporting my decision. My background and training as an educator helped me learn how to identify the inherent educational value contained in video games and how they might assist with classroom instruction. For many years, individual students and teachers took the initiative of bringing video games to school and using them in the classroom because they recognized their inherent educational value. An educator's personal attitude about using video game technology in the classroom is very important. Fear of looking technologically inadequate in front of students can get in the way of a productive lesson. A good solution to this often-encountered problem is to invite students to use their expert knowledge and get involved with the actual instruction. Students like to be recognized for their expertise, a point I raised earlier. The planning and implementation of video games into classroom instruction is not straightforward, and requires careful thought.

CONCLUSION

The science fiction writer Isaac Asimov once said "...kids like the computer because it plays back. It's a pal, a friend, but it doesn't get mad. It doesn't say 'I won't play,' and it doesn't break the rules..." (Poole, 2000, p. 172). The relationship between people and computer technology has evolved over the last quarter century; we've gone from viewing them as computational objects to being creative informational devices possessing minds and personalities of their own. Since the introduction of the Magnavox *Odyssey* home video game console in 1972, hardware and software developers have taken advantage of rapid technological advances to create more engaging, imaginative play experiences rivaling the concepts of cyberspace presented in William Gibson's book *Neuromancer* (1984) and avatars in virtual worlds described by Neal Stephenson in *Snowcrash* (1992). The mythical tales of JRR Tolkien were adapted by the late Gary Gygax into the classic role playing game *Dungeons & Dragons*® (created in 1984), and are now made manifest in the global legion of eleven million players adventuring in *World of Warcraft* (dating from 2004).

Schools are often described as miniature microcosms of society. Popular culture makes its way into the school by students sharing their artifacts, experiences and ideas. In the case of video games and education, students regularly participate in compelling, vivid, virtual learning environments designed as entertainment. This method has been employed for decades by the Walt Disney Imagineer Group. The current generation of video games available offer what James Gee calls deep learning experiences (Gee, 2007, p. 28). The player participates directly with the content and learns to master it at the same time. The most sophisticated video games force the player to think and use abstract thought. The best video games embody the practices and principles of learning and teaching that educators use in school. Video games are a dynamic form of learning experience (Poole, 2000).

The literature about the use of video games in education, particularly 'off the shelf' commercial video games purchased at retail online or in a store, shows that there is much interest about their potential, but also uncertainty about using them effectively in the context of the classroom and the curriculum. Video games offer a wide variety of game play experiences; there is something for everyone. There are educators who believe that the levels of learning offered in commercial video games, coupled with their multiplayer capability, can reach students who do not respond to traditional methods of instruction. This was what Kurt Squire considered when he wrote his case study about teaching history with *Civilization III* (Squire, 2005). Educational institutions and individual teachers are taking the initiative to use video games like *Guitar Hero*, *Myst* ®, and virtual worlds like *Second Life*® to teach curricular content. The commercial video game industry, educators, and educational researchers need to engage in more dialogue about how video games can best be used in the context of classroom instruction.

REFERENCES

Barab, S., Arici, A., & Jackson, C. (2005). Eat your vegetables & do your homework: A design-based investigation of enjoyment and meaning in learning. *Educational Technology Research and Development*, *65*(1), 15–21.

Carlson, S. (2003, August 15). Can Grand Theft Auto inspire professors? Educators say the virtual worlds of video games help students think more broadly. *Chronicle of Higher Education*, *49*(49), A31. Retrieved June 16, 2008 from http://chronicle.com/free/v49/i49/49a03101.htm

Crowley, K., & Jacobs, M. (2002). Islands of expertise and the development of family scientific literacy. In K. Crowley, K. Knutson & K. Leinhardt (Eds.), *Learning conversations in museums* (1st ed., pp. 289-325). Mahwah, NJ: Lawrence Erlbaum Associates Inc.

De Freitas, S. (2006). Learning in immersive worlds. A review of game based learning. London: JISC e-Learning Programme.

Downes, T. (1988). *Children's use of computers in their homes*. Unpublished Ph.D. dissertation, University of Western Sydney, Australia.

Eglesz, D., Fekete, I., Kiss, O. E., & Izso, L. (2005). Computer games are fun? On professional games and players' motivations. *Educational Media International, 42*(2), 117–124. doi:10.1080/09523980500060274

Entertainment Software Association of Canada. (2008). *Essential facts about the Canadian computer and video game industry 2008.* Montreal, QC, Canada: Ipsos Reid.

Facer, K. (2002). *Computer games and learning: Why do we think it's worth talking about computer games and learning in the same breath?* (Discussion paper). London, UK. Futurelab. Retrieved May 30, 2009 from http://www.futurelab.org.uk/resources/documents/discussion_papers/Computer_Games_and_Learning_discpaper.pdf

Gee, J. P. (2004a). Learning by design: Games as learning machines. *Interactive Educational Multimedia, 8*, 15–23.

Gee, J. P. (2004b). *Video games and the future of learning*. University of Wisconsin. Madison, WI: Academic Advanced Distributed Learning Co-Laboratory.

Gee, J. P. (2007). *Good video games and good learning. Collected essays on video games, learning, and literacy*. New York: Peter Lang.

Gibson, W. (1984) *Neuromancer*. New York: Ace Books.

Gros, B. (2007). Digital games in education: The design of games-based learning environments. *Journal of Research on Technology in Education, 40*(1), 23–38.

Halverson, R. (2005). What can K-12 school leaders learn from video games and gaming? *Innovate Online: Innovate Journal of Online Education, 1* (6). Available from http://www.innovateonline.info/index.php?view=article&id=81

Huizinga, J. (1955). *Homo Ludens, a study of the play element in culture*. Boston: Beacon Press.

Klopfer, E., & Yoon, S. (2005). Developing games and simulations for today and tomorrow's tech savvy youth. *TechTrends, 49*(3), 33–41. doi:10.1007/BF02763645

Koster, R. (2005). *A theory of fun*. Scottsdale, AZ: Paragylph Press.

Lenhart, A., Kahne, J., Middaugh, E., McGill, A. R., Evans, C., & Vitak, J. (2008). *Teens, video games, and civics: Teens' gaming experiences are diverse and include significant social interaction and civic engagement*. Washington, DC: Pew Internet & American Life Project. Available at http://www.pewinternet.org/Reports/2008/Teens-Video-Games-and-Civics.aspx

Malone, T., & Lepper, M. (1987). Making learning fun: A taxonomy of intrinsic motivations of learning. In R. E. Snow & M. J. Farr (Eds.), *Aptitude, learning, and instruction: Vol. 3. Conative and affective process analyses* (pp. 223-253). Hillsdale, NJ: Lawrence Erlbaum Associates Inc.

Murray, J. (1997). *Hamlet on the holodeck: The future of narrative in cyberspace*. Cambridge, MA: The MIT Press.

Norton-Meier, L. (2005). Joining the video-game literacy club: A reluctant mother tries to join the "flow." . *Journal of Adolescent & Adult Literacy, 48*(5), 428–432. doi:10.1598/JAAL.48.5.6

Papert, S. (1980). *Mind-storms: Children, computers, and powerful ideas*. New York: Basic Books Inc.

Papert, S. (1998, June). Does easy do it? Children, games, and learning. *Game Developer Magazine*, *4*, 88–91.

Paras, B. S., & Bizzocchi, J. (2005, June). *Game, motivation, and effective learning: An integrated model for educational game design*. Paper presented at the 2005 conference of the Digital Games Research Association (DiGRA), Changing Views: Worlds in Play. Vancouver, BC, Canada. Retrieved October 25,2007 from http://www.digra.org/dl/db/06276.18065.pdf

Pelletier, C. (2005, June). *Studying games in school: A framework for media education*. Paper presented at the 2005 conference of the Digital Games Research Association (DiGRA), Changing Views: Worlds in Play. Vancouver, BC, Canada.

Poole, S. (2000). *Trigger happy – Video games and the entertainment revolution*. New York: Arcade Publishing.

Prensky, M. (2001). *Digital game based learning*. St. Paul, MN: Paragon House.

Prensky, M. (2006). *Don't bother me mom! I'm learning! How computer and video games are preparing your kids for 21st century success*. St. Paul, MN: Paragon House.

Schaffer, D. W. (2005). Epistemic frames for epistemic games. *Computers & Education*, *46*(3), 223–234. doi:10.1016/j.compedu.2005.11.003

Schaffer, D. W. (2006). *How computer games help children learn*. New York: Palgrave Macmillan.

Schaffer, D. W., Squire, K. R., Halverson, R., & Gee, J. P. (2005). Video games and the future of learning. *Phi Delta Kappan*, *87*(2), 105–111.

Schrader, J., Young, M., & Zheng, D. (2006). Teacher's perceptions of video games: MMOGs and the future of preservice teacher education. *Innovate Journal of Online Education, 2* (3). Available from http://innovateonline.info/index.php?view=article&id=125

Seydegart, K., Spears, G., & Zulinov, P. (2005). *Young Canadians in a wired world, Phase II*. Erin, ON, Canada: Erin Research Inc. Available at http://www.media-awareness.ca/english/research/ycww/index.cfm

Spears, G., & Seydegart, K. (2003). *Kid's take on media survey: What 5700 Canadian kids say about TV, movies, video and computer games*. Toronto, ON, Canada: Canadian Teacher's Federation/Media Awareness Network.

Spears, G., & Seydegart, K. (2004). Kids' views on violence in the media. *Canadian Child and Adolescent Psychiatry Review*, *13*(1), 7–12.

Squire, K. (2005). Changing the game: What happens when video games enter the classroom? *Innovate Journal of Online Education, 1*(6). Available from http://innovateonline.info/index.php?view=article&id=82&highlight=Squire

Stephenson, N. (1992). *Snowcrash*. New York: Bantam Books.

Turkle, S. (2005). *The second self – Computers and the human spirit* (20th anniversary edition). Cambridge, MA: The MIT Press.

ADDITIONAL READING

Gee, J. P. (2007). *Good video games and good learning. Collected essays on video games, learning, and literacy*. New York. Peter Lang.

Poole, S. (2000). *Trigger happy – Video games and the entertainment revolution*. New York: Arcade Publishing.

Prensky, M. (2006). *Don't bother me mom! I'm learning! How computer and video games are preparing your kids for 21st century success.* St. Paul, MN: Paragon House.

Schaffer, D. W. (2006). *How computer games help children learn.* New York, NY: Palgrave Macmillan.

Turkle, S. (2005). *The second self – Computers and the human spirit. 20th anniversary edition.* Cambridge, MA: The MIT Press.

KEY TERMS AND DEFINITIONS

Commercial Video Game: Any game software developed for profit and made available for sale online through a website, or packaged and sold in a store. Also known as 'off the shelf' video games.

Educator: An individual who provides classroom instruction or instructional support in an educational institution.

Endogenous Game: A complex game design that lets the player interact with the game world and master its environment by learning to control multiple game variables that are related to each other and affect the final outcome. A real time strategy game (RTS) is an example of an endogenous game. A massively multiplayer online game (MMOG) is an example of an endogenous game.

Exogenous Game: A simple game design with one or two variables that can be adapted to use different content. This type of game design is often used in education to test student knowledge. *Snakes & Ladders* or a quiz show model like *Wheel of Fortune*® are examples of exogenous games.

Net Generation: People who were born in an industrialized country after the commercial introduction of personal computers in 1980, and grew up using information hardware and software technologiesin their lives. These are also known as 'digital natives' or 'millennials.'

Video Game: A game that can be played on an electronic device using computer hardware and software technology such as cellular phones, personal computers, personal digital assistants, portable video game systems, and video game consoles.

Video Game Designer: An individual who works on a game development team and is given the responsibility for conceptualizing the game world, how the player interacts with the game world, and who carries out the planning and implementation of how the player progresses through the game.

Virtual World: A computer-generated environment in which a person interacts and participates with the video game. The interaction is represented through a computer-created character known as an 'avatar' or by manipulating a computer-created object.

Section 2
Design and Prototyping

Chapter 9
Educational Games:
Moving from Theory to Practice

Suzanne de Castell
Simon Fraser University, Canada

Jennifer Jenson
York University, Canada

Nicholas Taylor
York University, Canada

ABSTRACT

This chapter describes and analyzes the design and development of an educational game, Contagion. In this account, we examine how knowledge is constructed through character selection, art, narrative, goals, and activity structures within the game, and attempt to show how those inter-related elements are mobilized to create an educational experience.

INTRODUCTION

In the spring of 2004, a small team of researchers, graduate students and college co-op students in Toronto and Vancouver[1] set to work developing an educationally-focused web-based game, *Contagion*. Not having many precedents for what a game about contagious disease might look like, we sought to create a game world "just real enough" in its invocations and analogies of what we witnessed first during the 2003 SARS crisis in Toronto, what we know already of the ongoing HIV/AIDS epidemic, and what we saw during the emergence of avian flu: fear and mistrust towards at risk populations, governments seemingly acting in the interests of their own self-preservation, and the tragic confluence of contagion and poverty.

This chapter charts our process of designing a game that, in attempting to engage players with these themes, departs from conventional approaches to deploying digital play for educative purposes. These varied approaches include articulating the ways classroom-based pedagogy can learn from commercial games (Gee, 2003), conceptualizing and building educational resources that play like commercial games but follow the disciplinary structures of formal schooling (Rieber, 1996; Woods et al., 2005), and framing commercial games as inherently educational, and arguing for their use in the classroom (Squire, 2004; Steinkuehler, 2004, 2006). After briefly sketching out these theoretical positions, we describe our own alternative, design-based approach

DOI: 10.4018/978-1-61520-731-2.ch009

to making and understanding digital play-based learning, one in which we have tried to mobilize our early theoretical work with educational gaming (de Castell & Jenson, 2003) to recover the classical connections between play and learning. We have done so through carefully tacking between educational and commercial game design traditions, while trying to avoid the pitfalls of both: on the one side, a conceptualization of learning as the delivery of quantifiable and testable content; and on the other, an over-reliance on formulaic violence and predictably misogynistic, racist, and homophobic representational modes.

The result is a bricolage of game mechanics, art styles, and environments in which content is both everywhere and nowhere, in so far as we have largely avoided framing the game's learning outcomes in propositional terms, but have instead tried to infuse educationally-valuable knowledge throughout all aspects of the game. We explore each of these aspects (character selection, art, narrative, goals, and activity structures) in turn to demonstrate how knowledge is constructed through these inter-related elements. The account we give is not intended as an exhaustive, or even particularly coherent, program for educational game development; rather, it should be read as a provisional coming to terms with sets of questions that have arisen for us in the very practical work of designing an educational game.

GAMES IN EDUCATION

Perhaps most prominent among educational theorists currently working on the educative possibilities of digital play is Jim Gee, whose approach is most fully available in his 2003 book, *What Videogames Have to Teach Us About Literacy and Learning* (Gee, 2003). Gee cites the great divide between the slow, painful, fragmented, decontextualized, and often unsuccessful, approaches to teaching reading and comprehension which define daily life in far too many schools and classrooms, and the pleasure-filled, engaged, and astonishingly sophisticated reading and comprehension of complex information which characterizes children's participation with videogames. Gee isn't asking how we can get games into classrooms, but rather what kinds of pedagogy can we extrapolate from studies of how videogames teach and players learn.

Gee's approach is very different from that initially articulated by Lloyd Rieber, in an article called "Seriously Considering Play" (1996), and enacted recently in educational game design projects by Kurt Squire (2004) and Henry Jenkins (2004). Their work, heading up the Education Arcade (http://www.educationarcade.org), as well as work by research teams at Carleton University (Woods et al., 2005) and the University of Minnesota (Berger, 2006), follows conventional disciplinary structures in designing and developing educational games, often by infusing modifiable commercial games (such as *Neverwinter Nights*®) with deliberately educative content. The results are games that look and play like commercial games, but cover the curriculum in traditional school subjects.

A third trajectory is one that seeks to identify educational value and significance in the (mostly commercial, mostly entertainment-oriented) games that children and young adults already play. Constance Steinkuehler (2004, 2005) looks primarily to the online, networked play of massively multiplayer online games (MMOGs), contending that the informal, apprenticeship-based and spontaneous learning opportunities that arise when playing MMOGs such as *World of Warcraft*® are more relevant to post-industrial workplaces and vocations than the didactic culture of schooling found in most classrooms (Steinkuehler, 2006). Commercial games, particularly those that allow for direct forms of player-to-player interaction, offer opportunities to learn, master, and in turn instruct other players in the complex social and cognitive skills required for successful play. From this perspective, the problem might be first to get teachers to allow games into labs and classrooms, then to help them to define activities and forms of de-briefing which enable learners to make good educational use of the knowledge and skills that these games depend upon and develop.

All of the above approaches represent greater and lesser departures from what has long been the hegemonic viewpoint: that the relationship between learning and play is an extrinsic one. Games and play are, by definition, fun; thus teachers can use games as motivational tools, whether directly as a reward for doing ones work well ("and now you get to play for 20 minutes"), or as a form, (actually more accurately as a disguise) to make learning more palatable: "the educational sugar coating" (Rieber, 1996) for the tough medicine of educational content. In this view school learning is structurally posited as unpleasant - the challenge is to determine what forms of sugar are both most effective for learning and most rewarding for learners. There is a preoccupation with ontology, asking questions such as: "What is a game? What is a simulation? What is a puzzle? What is a simulation game?" Then evaluation is pursued: "Which of these is best suited to this (or that) kind of learning/content, and how can we meaningfully measure and report relative effectiveness?" From this standpoint we are most likely to learn that games are good for teaching low-level content and skills, while puzzles are good for teaching mathematical reasoning, simulations are good for teaching social and communication skills, and strategic reasoning, and so on. Here disciplinary knowledge is again more or less held constant, reduced to fit the game frame, and the learning outcomes of its use are evaluated. Play is malleable; school is inviolable. Proponents of this view pay little attention to player volition: that we would and should require players to play games found to be educationally effective is not something over which we lose much sleep.

A dissenting view of educational game studies worries a good deal over volition and agency. The concern here is that just as we cannot be forced to be free, or punished until we cheer up, so we really cannot be compelled to play. According Johannes Huizinga, an early (1938) theoretician of play, it is no longer play if compulsion is part of the picture. "First and foremost...," he writes, "all play is a voluntary activity. Play to order is no longer play: it could at best be but a forcible imitation of it" (p. 7).

While much can be learned from all these approaches to educational game studies, it is in this last camp we ourselves are most at home (de Castell & Jenson, 2003). From this perspective, you can no more compel significant learning than you can compel serious play. Both, not just games but learning more generally, have a major, central, critically essential element of play; it is no add-on, no extrinsically motivating feature. Rather, education is where learning is seriously in play, and play is serious learning.

NOW ENTERING PYRAMIDEA

Contagion is a role-playing adventure game, set in a futuristic world, Pyramidea - an isolated and socially stratified city-state on the verge of a fearsome epidemic. As the name would suggest, Pyramidea is a large, vertically partitioned city divided into three segments, each of which serves as the home and starting point for one of the game's three main characters. The pyramid itself purposely invokes the metaphor of a socioeconomic hierarchy, setting the stage for the conflicts a player will encounter on their journey through the various layers of the city.

The Pyramidea Inoculation Network (PIN), a government-based organization which physically, as well as politically, separates Upper and Lower Pyramidea, at the start of the game is beginning to notice the rising tide of sickness sweeping through the socio-economically disadvantaged neighborhoods of the lower city. As a result of PIN's heavy-handed and misguided strategies of containment, quarantine, and removal, serious ill-

Figure 1. Pyramidea

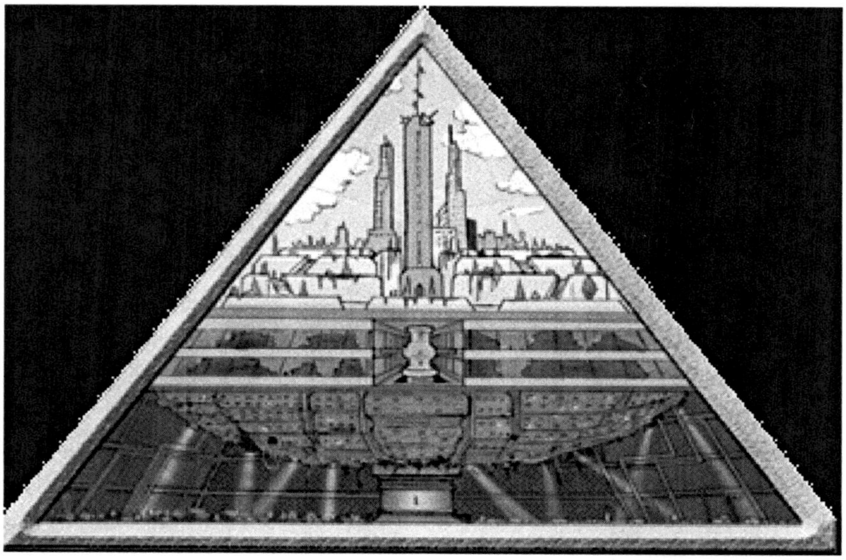

nesses are breaking out with increasing frequency. The game's introductory sequence sets the scene for playing in this socially stratified world by taking its viewers back to the time of the plague, recalling that problems of contagious disease are deeply historically rooted, and illustrating the historical continuities between the Middle Ages and our current medical crises; death carts, superstitions, and barricades have a different look, but ignorance has ever been and still remains the major hurdle in combating contagious disease.

Prototyped in Macromedia *Flash®* for players between the ages of 10 and 15, *Contagion's* goal is to develop, through "serious play" (Blanton, Moorman, Hayes, & Warner, 1997; Pillay, Brownlee, & Wilss, 1999; Rieber, 1996) the health-regarding knowledge, orientations and behaviours necessary for promoting individual and community well-being in the face of five quite different, but equally virulent diseases whose threats to public safety and economic security are currently affecting populations across the demographic spectrum, both locally and globally: severe acute respiratory syndrome (SARS), West Nile virus (WNV), avian flu, the H1N1 virus, and acquired immune deficiency syndrome (AIDS). At this time, these viruses can be combated effectively only through the consistent, comprehensive, mass-scale efforts of individuals for whom self-care becomes a permanent, habitual, behavioral change. For this reason, education with respect to these conditions and their prevention is urgent and critical.

From a school-based curriculum standpoint, *Contagion* pursues interdisciplinary subject matters that follow, complement, and extend prescribed learning goals for grades 7 to 9.[2] It emphasizes fields like technology, biology, and medical sciences as well as human and social sciences. Mobilizing gaming's established culture and commerce, *Contagion* plays on, and is indebted to, already-developed knowledge and expectations, including graphical conventions, character types, and game strategies, in order to benefit from, acknowledge, and exercise players' assumed cultural knowledge and gaming experience.

Production as Theory and Research

A shift in emphasis from reception-oriented to production-based approaches to educational games studies underlies *Contagion's* development.[3] Informed by design-based research in general, and more specifically, by the work of designer-researchers Mateas and Stern (2005) and colleagues, the *Contagion* project hopes to engineer innovative conditions for studying educational games, by moving intentionally outside the constraints of existing models for game design.[4] Methodologically, production-based approaches to inquiry in educational games studies are perhaps not fully an alternative to playing and studying existing games; however, building games outside these theories, concepts and models appears to play an indispensable role in advancing games research and scholarship: "building games… allows us to experiment with some of the more vexing questions in game studies…" (Mateas & Stern, 2005, pp. 299-300).[5]

Approaching our design of *Contagion* as central to our research about educational games has led to a very different kind of game than is currently available. This process has not been without tension, miscommunication, and misunderstandings, but over our development cycle, we have worked with eight undergraduate student artists, four undergraduate student programmers, and two graduate students who have all contributed significantly to the game. Literally, then, these students have been educated by working on the game, and we think it is not insignificant that this process has provided an educational context, support, and membership in a community that without this kind of funding and opportunity would not otherwise be available. In the following sections, we detail our design elements in relation to their contribution to, and representation of, knowledge within the game in an effort to show its interrelated and productive significance to what is recognized as educational content.

Narrative: A Framework for Meaningful Play

Upon first entering Pyramidea, players select one of three possible characters: a physician from Lower Pyramidea, a community health officer (PIN agent), and an eminent medical researcher specializing in infectious diseases, who works from the safe confines of Upper Pyramidea. The narrative begins with the report of another outbreak of a highly contagious life-threatening disease. The narrative progresses as the players interact within the game, and narrative paths vary with each player until she stops playing and/or reaches the end game. There, the player is confronted with her in-game choices, and the narrative arc is reached as things in Pyramidea go radically out of control – riots, outbreaks, and general mayhem have to be contained by the player and the consequences of her actions for the city and citizens of Pyramidea become either disastrous or transformational.

Embedded in the narrative, then, is the central conflict of the game which is sustained through simply playing within the game – viral, contagious diseases cannot ever fully be controlled. Ignorance, carelessness, state-based surveillance, self-interest and simply being in the wrong place at the wrong time contribute to the spread of disease. Narrative is in action in the game; it is not something that is added on or simply delivered, but is co-constructed with the player as the game progresses.

Programming

Contagion's gameplay space is built on an isometric engine, developed by student programmers entirely in Macromedia *Flash*® with artwork generated in *3DS Max*® and Adobe *Photoshop*®. Play involves navigating various environments (using either mouse or arrow keys) and interacting with Pyramidea's citizens through a point and click functionality, which brings up different interfaces and interaction options depending on the particular character/locale/objective. Using *Flash* means that players can access the game at school without having to download or install anything beyond an accessible and widely-used browser driver. School technological environments create significant barriers that have to be worked within; installing or downloading programs is frequently prohibited, and students and teachers are frequently unable to accomplish tasks on their computers as they wait for an authorized technician to provide necessary passwords or to install new software themselves. However, using *Flash* imposes serious programming restrictions which greatly affect, among other things, the size of explorable environments, the number of objects a character is able to interact with in a given space, and the actions and behaviours of non-player characters (NPCs). This means we are not free to take strategic advantage of the graphical, computational and architectural affordances of commercial gaming, but must instead limit ourselves to the domain of tactics.

Working within the constraints of *Flash's* limited computational and architectural vocabulary has meant authoring much of the game as a series of mini-games that deploy canonical game forms: navigating, *Pacman*®-like, around the streets of Lower Pyramidea in a driving mini-game, shooting bacteria with soap bubbles in a kind of remediated *Space Invaders*®, and matching microscopic images of diseases with their appropriate descriptions. These mini-games not only serve to advance the plot and provide breaks from the more involved play of the main game environments; they also work as a crash course in canonical game forms for players less game-literate, and as such add opportunities for the production of elementary gameplay competencies. This is not insignificant educationally, as it is most typically girls who, while they say they play, don't often have their hands on the controllers and are neither as confident nor as competent as their male counterparts with different types of gameplay (Jenson & de Castell, 2006).

Art and Architecture: Resisting Stereotypes

In her book, *Gender Inclusive Game Design: Expanding the Market* (2004), Sheri Graner Ray moves the discussion of gender and game design back to essentialized categories of difference. Her book's project, she asserts, is to "attempt to understand the difference between males and females, and then look at various ways to apply these differences to the traditional genres that make up the contemporary computer game industry" (p. xvii). What is disappointing is that this argument for gender inclusiveness centers around reductionist accounts of femininity and masculinity and attributes them to differences between sexes (Graner Ray, 2004). So often gender by design means video games in pink boxes (de Castell & Bryson, 1998).[6]

In *Contagion,* we leave behind Graner Ray's gender-inclusive design principles as well as any notion that we can build something just for girls, and instead approach the design of our game with gender as one of the game's central questions and problems. What this has meant is an ongoing contention with preconceived notions about narrative, content, plot, characterization, and learning as we attempted to script our game. In the development of concept artwork for "Dox," the game's resourceful community-based doctor, for example, we struggled in our conversations with student artists to achieve a character who was recognizably female, who appears strong and capable, and at the same time non-sexualized. Drafts ranged from the futuristic Barbie®-like character on the left in Figure 2, to the figure in the middle, which looks like a victim of disease herself. Appealing yet again for a strong engaging and non-stereotyped female street doctor, we got, finally (at the right), a young woman who is now more wary than terrified, and a bit more welcoming as a character. Note that in this draft she has a somewhat androgynous look.

Character Selection

For the characters they play in the game, we tried to move players away from the stereotypically radicalized and sexualized images found in standard role-playing games towards more

Figure 2. Drafts of "Dox" from "Barbie®," to victim, to someone you may want to be

cartoon-like representations that permit players a range of less orthodox choices to customize their in-game characters (Figure 3). Originally, we had wanted to create three androgynous characters and have the players assign gender attributes (or not) to their characters, but our own play testing and previous research suggests that the default presumption about androgynous characters was that they were male. As this was not a perception that we wanted to reinforce, we decided to give marked sex attributes to our characters, and allow the players to develop them as they will.

Because gender was very much central to our design process, not in terms of figuring out what

Figure 3. Character customization

Figure 4. Free Wattles!

girls want, but instead as an ongoing struggle with our own tendencies to reduce things to simple masculine and feminine binaries, one small achievement has been the re-assignment of roles and responsibilities to character-types that are outside the normative hegemonic patriarchal order. As players assume the role of one of three characters, each embodies and plays out a distinct approach to medical/humanitarian crises in dense human populations. Much of the learning that *Contagion* endeavors to facilitate comes through players' active exploration of their particular characters' capacities and roles in Pyramidean society, and from seeing the effects of their gameplay choices on individual non-player characters (NPCs) and on Pyramidea as a whole.

Content Development as Activity Structures

Like other would-be educational game designers, our *Contagion* team has spent considerable time mulling over the question of how best to embed content in a game that people would actually choose to play, without being coerced into using it, and we've been able to generate a few fun and playable sequences in the overall game, activities here and there that a player might freely choose and enjoy. None of these events, activities, and moments, however, appears to have much content to them. We have, for instance, a driving game, in which Dox, the street/community-based doctor, has been alerted via office computer of outbreaks of illness among citizens trying to get medical help while avoiding the evil PIN agents (who summarily pick up and dispose of anyone who shows signs of infection). Dox's mission involves driving through the streets of lower Pyramidea at night trying to locate patients identified as needing assistance, while avoiding the patrolling PIN vans, which could confiscate Dox's medical supplies. This is kind of fun, sure. But in the end, it's just another driving game. What's the content here? Then there's a turkey farm game, where poor Wattles, the infected wild turkey (Figure 4), gains access to the domestic turkey barn and in her mad dash to get as much food as possible manages to infect a number of domestic birds with avian flu. Did we want children to learn that to get rid of enemy turkeys you have to turn and face them, then hit the "z" key? Or that the way to eat is to walk over shining food pellets?

So: drive and avoid certain cars, peck at food pellets and fight off domestic turkeys. It begins to look as if the only parts of the game that look like fun are the parts with the least educational content. This way of seeing things suffers from the fatal flaw in most curriculum development, and in all instructional design driven by demands of testing and accountability: reductive conceptions of learning and knowledge. That learning consists in assimilating items of information capable of being expressed in discreet propositions, whether formulated in linguistic or any other form of codification, has now come very nearly to render all other kinds of learning unrecognizable as such. It will perhaps be one of the greater gifts that digital games studies has to offer to education that this model of content is proving grossly unworkable for game designers. Jumping ahead a bit, this is because it is grossly unworkable for education in most of its forms, game-based or not.

Contemporary schooling may have largely forgotten its roots in play (the Latin for school and play are the same). And yet, as anyone knows who has had the privilege of actually loving mathematics, or of becoming passionately involved in historical studies, or in ethnology, or in botanical classification, or in literary theory as much as in literature, there is every ounce as much immersion, engagement, exhilaration, flow, heart-pounding fear and anticipation, sweaty-palmed desire, in learning, in intellectual inquiry and production, as in the most spectacular laser battles, earth-exploding alien attacks, and bloody vampire wars. For some, educational game design offers the possibility to reclaim this traditional connection between work and play, largely lost within a discursive climate that often reads formal schooling as a political, rather than an educational matter, one in which administrators, teachers, and children themselves are held accountable to the taxpaying public for their performance. It might therefore be time to substitute nominalizations of play, the noun form in dismissives such as "It's just play" which references a waste of time, and revert in its place to interrogating the educational worth and significance of play as an active verb, as a reference to the rich kinds of active, inquisitive, and expressive doings that give educational knowledge a place to hang on to, beyond the words which we have for too long misconstrued as the knowledge which they always only incompletely represent.

It is not, then, that we need to fit lessons into games, or even that games contain good lessons. Rather, what we are trying to do in *Contagion* is to actively engage in a rhetorically-based and specifically Derridean project, a deconstructive reading and post-structuralist rewriting of education, a project which comprehends the mutually constitutive differences (Derrida, 1978) between learning and leisure, pleasure and penalty, immersion and engagement, structure and agency, work and play—and education and entertainment.

CONCLUSION

At the end of a long development cycle, we are beginning to articulate a metaphor for our deliberate, at times clumsy, design-based research, a metaphor that describes both the design process itself, as well as the kinds of play *Contagion* offers. "Slow gaming" borrows its name from the slow food movement (www.slowfood.com), which advocates food production and consumption practices that are sustainable and ethical, that work from and contribute to local networks of growers and retailers, and that, not insignificantly, encourage deeply pleasurable experiences. Much like slow food defines itself in opposition to a fast food industry that purchases efficiency and profit at the cost of our bodily, communal, and environmental well-being, our approach to slow gaming sets itself against a commercial games industry which, in its preoccupation with speed (from rapid development cycles, to the ever-increasing computational power required to run cutting-edge games, to play styles that celebrate time attacks and hair-trigger reactions), leaves behind any possibilities for reflection and deliberation, either on the part of designers or players). Applied to our production process, slow gaming emphasizes the *Contagion* team's close and intensive collaboration between project heads, programmers, and artists; recognizing that, when it comes to educational technologies, design considerations are at the same time pedagogical considerations (de Castell & Jenson, 2002), we have tried to weigh the pedagogical implications of our design decisions across each aspect of the game we discuss here. Slow gaming highlights as well the significance of our early choice to build a gaming engine, in *Flash,* from the ground up; like many ready-made food products which never quite tell you what you might be putting in your body, gaming engines like those offered by *Unreal Tournament*® and *Neverwinter Nights* certainly provide an expedient route to building polished and playable games – but would we really be aware of what we're putting in our game?

With regard to play, slow gaming means we have tried to enact experiences within the game that steer away not only from commercial gaming's reliance on formulaic violence and clichéd narratives, but also from formal education's emphasis on covering the curriculum as quickly as possible – a concern that arguably has more to do with administrative accountability than with sound pedagogy. To that end, we are beginning to see as shallow and unproductive the idea of embedding content, and are working instead with presumptions that to the extent that we can engage players' attention, we can also engage their intelligence. Our job is less to define and demonstrate facts and skills transmitted in the game, than to create a rich, sophisticated, complex, and nuanced attentional environment that opens up new horizons, introduces new questions, and explores new domains of epistemological and ethical significance, in ways that treat students as intelligent agents in the making of their own lives.

ACKNOWLEDGMENT

This chapter is based on a paper presentation entitled "Digital Games for Education: When Meanings Play", given at the Digital Games Research Association (DiGRA) Conference in Tokyo, Japan, in September, 2007. This earlier work can be accessed at http://www.digra.org/dl/db/07312.45210.pdf.

REFERENCES

Berger, A. (2006, January 31). 'Neverwinter Nights' in the classroom. *University of Minnesota News.* Retrieved June 16, 2008 from http://www1.umn.edu/umnnews/Feature_Stories/22Neverwinter_Nights22_in_the_classroom.html

Blanton, W. E., Moorman, G. B., Hayes, B. A., & Warner, M. L. (1997). Effects of participation in the Fifth Dimension on far transfer. *Journal of Educational Computing Research, 16,* 371–396.

Bryce, J., & Rutter, J. (2005). Gendered gaming in gendered space. In J. Raessens & J. Goldstein (Eds.), *Handbook of computer games studies* (pp. 301-310). Cambridge, MA: The MIT Press.

Butler, J. (1999). *Gender trouble: Feminism and the subversion of identity.* New York: Routledge.

de Castell, S., & Bryson, M. (1998). Re-tooling play: Dystopia, dysphoria, and difference. In J. Cassell & H. Jenkins (Eds.), *From Barbie to Mortal Kombat* (pp. 232-261). Cambridge, MA: The MIT Press.

de Castell, S., & Jenson, J. (2002, October). *Designing for interactivity in theory and practice.* Paper presented at the annual meeting of the American Association for Research in Education (AREA), New Orleans, LA.

de Castell, S., & Jenson, J. (2003). Serious play. *Journal of Curriculum Studies*, *35*(6), 649–655. doi:10.1080/0022027032000145552

de Castell, S., Jenson, J., & Taylor, N. (2007). Digital games for education: When meanings play. In *Proceedings, 2007 Conference of the Digital Games Research Association (DiGRA), Situated Play*, Tokyo, Japan. Available at http://www.digra.org/dl/db/07312.45210.pdf

Derrida, J. (1978). *Writing and difference* (A. Bass, Trans.). Chicago: University of Chicago Press.

Gee, J. P. (2003). *What video games have to teach us about learning and literacy.* New York: Palgrave Macmillan.

Giddings, S., & Kennedy, H. W. (2008). Little Jesuses and *@#?-off robots: On cybernetics, aesthetics and not being very good at *Lego Star Wars*. In M. Swallwell & J. Wilson (Eds.), *The pleasures of computer gaming* (pp. 13-32). Jefferson, NC: McFarland.

Graner Ray, S. (2004). *Gender inclusive game design: Expanding the market*. Hingham, MA: Charles River Media.

Huizinga, J. (1938). *Homo ludens: A study of the play element in culture.* Boston: Beacon Press.

Jenkins, H. (2004). Game design as narrative architecture. In N. Wardrip-Fruin & P. Harrigan (Eds.), *First Person: New Media as Story, Performance, and Game* (pp. 117-130). Cambridge, MA: The MIT Press.

Jenson, J., & de Castell, S. (2006). Keeping it real: Gender, equity & digital games. In J. Terkeurst & I. Paterson (Eds.), *Women & Games Conf. Proc. 2005* (pp. 106-115). Dundee, UK: Univ. of Abertay Press.

Katchabaw, J., Elliott, D., & Danton, S. (2005). Neomancer: An exercise in interdisciplinary academic game development. In S. de Castell & J. Jenson (Eds.), *Proceedings, 2005 Conference of the Digital Games Research Association (DiGRA), Changing Views: Worlds in Play.* Available at http://www.digra.org/dl/db/06275.08442.pdf

Koster, R. (2004). *A theory of fun for game design.* Scottsdale, AZ: Paraglyph Press.

Mateas, M., & Stern, A. (2005). Build it to understand it: Ludology meets narratology in game design space. In S. de Castell & J. Jenson (Eds.), *Proceedings, 2005 Conference of the Digital Games Research Association (DiGRA), Changing Views: Worlds in Play* (pp. 299-310). Burnaby, BC, Canada: Simon Fraser University.

Pillay, H., Brownlee, J., & Wilss, L. (1999). Cognition and recreational computer games: Implications for education technology. *Journal of Research on Computing in Education, 32*(1/2), 203–216.

Rieber, L. P. (1996). Seriously considering play: Designing interactive learning environments based on the blending of microworlds, simulations, and games. *Educational Technology Research and Development, 44*(2), 43–58. doi:10.1007/BF02300540

Rittel, H. W. J., & Webber, M., M. M. (1973). Dilemmas in a general theory of planning. *Policy Sciences*, *4*, 155–159. doi:10.1007/BF01405730

Squire, K. (2004). *Replaying history: Learning world history through playing Civilization III.* Unpublished PhD dissertation, Indiana University. Retrieved June 11, 2008 from http://website.education.wisc.edu/kdsquire/dissertation.html.

Steinkuehler, C. A. (2004). Learning in massively multiplayer online games. In Y. B. Kafai, W. A. Sandoval, N. Enyedy, A. S. Nixon, & F. Herrera (Eds.), *Proceedings of the 6th International Conference on Learning Sciences (ICLS 2004)* (pp. 521-528). Mahwah, NJ: Lawrence Erlbaum Associates Inc.

Steinkuehler, C. A. (2006). Massively multiplayer online videogames as participation in a discourse. *Mind, Culture, and Activity*, *3*(1), 38–52. doi:10.1207/s15327884mca1301_4

Woods, B., Whitworth, E., Hadziomerovic, A., Fiset, J., & Dormann, C. Caquard, et al., (2005). Repurposing a computer role playing game for engaging learning. In P. Kommers & G. Richards (Eds.), *Proceedings of World Conference on Educational Multimedia, Hypermedia and Telecommunications 2005* (pp. 4430-4435). Chesapeake, VA: AACE.

ADDITIONAL READING

de Castell, S., Bryson, M., & Jenson, J. (2001). Object lessons: towards an educational theory of technology. *First Monday*, *7*(1). Available at http://www.firstmonday.org/issues/issue7_1/castell/.

Giddings, S. (2007). Playing with non-humans: Digital games as technocultural form. In S. de Castell & J. Jenson (Eds.), *Worlds in play: International perspectives on digital games research* (pp. 115-128). New York: Peter Lang.

Jenson, J., de Castell, S., Taylor, N., & Droumeva, M. (2008). Baroque revolution: High culture gets game. In *Proceedings of the ACM FuturePlay 2008 International Academic Conference on the Future of Game Design and Technology* (pp. 105-112). Available at http://portal.acm.org/citation.cfm?doid=1496984.1497002

KEY TERMS AND DEFINITIONS

Activity Structure: A discrete game mechanic deployed in game design (i.e., rotating blocks in *Tetris®* or *Dr. Mario®*, jumping in *Super Mario Brothers®*, etc.). This is analogous to the notion of "ludemes," the basic unit in a grammar of game design, as developed by Raph Koster (2004).

Bricolage: Constructing texts (broadly understood as music, literature, art, clothing, games, etc.) by making use of whatever diverse range of materials and ideas might be available, i.e., .through the deployment of various and often disparate styles and conventions. For game design, this means borrowing game and conventions from existing games to create something new.

Digital Play: Movement and agency within a digitally-mediated space with predetermined rules, mechanics, and victory conditions.

Gameplay: The act of engaging in digital play: Seth Giddings and Helen Kennedy describe it as "a set of intimate circuits between human bodies and minds, computer hardware and the algorithms and affordances of the virtual worlds of video games" (Giddings & Kennedy, 2008, p. 19).

Gender: Sets of power asymmetries produced in and through localized, contingent contexts through the embodied performances of individuals (Bryce and Rutter, 2005). A category of difference preserved and naturalized through its conflation with physiological and biological differences between females and males (Butler, 1999).

Mini-Game: A small-scale game offering short durations of gameplay, and usually employing only one activity structure. The *Wario Ware®* franchise offers typical examples of games constructed from numerous discrete mini-games.

Slow Gaming: A way of theorizing and doing game design that looks to the slow food movement: slow gaming proposes deliberate, reflective, and holistic approaches to game production and resists quick fixes to design challenges.

ENDNOTES

1 The *Contagion* design team includes, besides the authors, Dawn Mercer and Caius Grozav (Seneca College), Nis Bojin (Simon Fraser University), Rita Baladi, and Dima Svetov.

2 Specific instances for the province of Ontario's curricular expectations include Grade 7 Science and Technology "Life Systems"; Grade 8 Geography "Patterns in Human Geography"; Grade 9 Canadian and World Studies "Social, Economic, and Political Structures"; and Grade 9 Health and Physical Education "Healthy Living." Specific curricular expectations in the province of British Columbia include Grade 7 Life Science "Ecosystems"; Grade 8 Science and Technology "Life Science"; Grade 8 and 9 Health and Career Education "Healthy Living"; and Grade 8 and 9 Information and Communications Technology "Foundations."

3 It is educationally significant that the actual work of production is being done by students at Seneca College and at York and Simon Fraser Universities, so that integral to this project is the fact that it has been working well as a vehicle for education, for skill development, and to enrich, direct, and extend the general curriculum these students receive within their different subject areas, from computing to humanities. For a related discussion, see Katchabaw, Elliot and Danton (2005).

4 Working in this way means engaging with what have been labeled "wicked problems" (Mateas & Stern, 2005; Rittel & Weber, 1973). Wicked problems are protean, changing their character as solutions are broached, so that "...you do not really understand what problem you were attempting to solve until you have a solution" (Mateas & Stern, 2005, p. 306).

5 Mateas and Stern's paper pays considerable attention to the foundational "ludology/narratology" debate in games studies, as an example of how design-based work might help "the field to avoid making taxonomic and prescriptive errors." Ours is similar: a longstanding feud between education and entertainment has impeded the development of educational technologies and has retarded for too long curricular and pedagogical practices in its schooled incarnation more generally. We are interested in ways to bring learning and play back together and in digital games as new tools for bridging the two.

6 For a more detailed account of the kinds of commercial approaches to gender inclusivity we tried to avoid in *Contagion*, please see de Castell, Jenson & Taylor (2007).

Chapter 10
Designing a Simulator for Teaching Ethical Decision-Making

Michael Power
Laval University, Canada

Lyse Langlois
Laval University, Canada

ABSTRACT

This chapter deals with a simulation-based learning environment called Ethical Advisor (EA). This case-based tool is aimed at immersing learners in a computer-generated, open learning environment in which they are challenged to identify relevant information using embedded clues and to analyze them in light of several theoretical models provided. Users resolve ethical dilemmas and moral problems related to everyday events as they learn how to manage information flow and select relevant items. The simulated environment reflects everyday situations drawn from a databank of over 200 case studies in educational administration. In our view, this learning environment is enabling development of a high level of competency in ethical decision-making and, as such, represents an excellent means of linking learning theory to technological advancement.

INTRODUCTION

The film *The Matrix* and its sequels introduced an old idea to a new crowd: what if life, as we know it, isn't? Of what can one be sure? Descartes was so preoccupied with this idea that his original thinking launched a scientific revolution (Burnham & Fieser, 2006). On the Internet you can listen to Oxford University philosopher Nick Bostrom (http://www.nickbostrom.com/) positing that we do indeed live in a matrix of sorts, but far less sexy than Neo and Trinity's (and did I mention Persephone's?). So, is there any sure way of knowing? Click on Hume, no, go back to Descartes...

So, thinking about reality and about whether we can know it is not new. Indeed, thinking about alternate realities and about simulating reality has become relatively commonplace, receiving huge twentieth- and twenty-first-century impetus from the entertainment world. In training and education, computer-generated simulation is entering its hey-day as a viable means of providing learners with

DOI: 10.4018/978-1-61520-731-2.ch010

new ways of interacting with real-world realities in a threat-free, error-leveraged environment. Indeed, in the military, you don't do it until you've simulated it, over and over again.

This chapter deals with a modest simulation-building initiative aimed at immersing learners in a computer-generated, open learning environment which prompts them to identify relevant information, analyze it in light of several theoretical models provided, and resolve ethical dilemmas and moral problems related to everyday events.

BACKGROUND

Simulations in Education and Training

Advances in educational technology in the fields of e-learning (Garrison & Anderson, 2003), blended learning environments (Garrison & Vaughan, 2008) and blended online learning (synchronous and asynchronous) environments (Power, 2008) as well as computer-based simulations (Lean, Moisier, Towler, & Abbey, 2006) result in the development of highly innovative teaching and learning tools (de Jong & van Joolingen, 1998). In their landmark study, Brown, Collins, and Duguid (1989) come to the conclusion that "learning methods that are embedded in authentic situations are not merely useful; they are essential" (p. 33). Simulations present students with just such authentic situations. Moreover, such tools, combined with problem-based learning strategies (Gredler, 1992; Kaufman & Schell, 2007), allow learners to experience situations that were formerly either too expensive, too complex or simply too difficult to emulate (Aldrich, 2004).

In this chapter, we go beyond the "computer-based simulations" definition presented by Lean et al. (2006, p. 230), preferring to situate the simulation described here as a "computer-simulated open learning environment." This emphasizes that: a) the simulation is computer-generated; b) it is used as part of an open learning environment involving more educational resources than simply the simulation in and by itself (the latter being a component of the overall learning environment); and c) "open" is used in the sense of relating to a socioconstructivist-inspired learning environment, which places the individual firmly in charge of managing available data and resources, identifying critical components and ultimately exercising personal judgment when making decisions. Furthermore, in reference to Lean et al.'s typology, which identifies three types of computer-based simulations (gaming, training, modeling), we would suggest a fourth type, "discovery" or "exploratory," to best describe the simulation in this chapter.

Professionals in widely varying fields such as business (Crichton, Flin, & Rattray, 2000), engineering (Ross, 2004), medicine and health care (Bergin & Fors, 2003), education (Gredler, 2004), and others increasingly have access to powerful and realistic simulators and simulated environments. Simulations, especially those which implement actual case study-based databases (Dobson, Ha, Ciavarro, & Mulligan, 2005), have proven to be highly motivating (Hertel & Millis, 2002) as well as cost-effective (Brandon–Hall, 2006) learning tools in providing both initial and ongoing training to students. For instance, in the field of management, Crichton et al. (2000) report evidence of "increased confidence, better understanding of the nature of the crisis management, less reliance on standard operating procedures, willingness to take risks and learn with colleagues" (p. 215). In a medical setting, it has been reported that "simulations provide optimal opportunities toward assessment and training in real-world-like medical task settings that never put a patient at risk" (Streufert, Satish, & Barach, 2001, p.165). (see Chapter 3 for a detailed discussion of simulation in medical settings.)

Yet, despite the advantages that simulations offer, prohibitive design- and development-related costs limit wide-scale implementation of such tools, especially in higher education (Lean et al., 2006). Moreover, closed-environment system simulators (Borges & Baranauskas, 1998) tend to be limited in their capacity to allow students to develop key higher-order reasoning and problem-solving skills (Darabi, Nelson, & Palanki, 2007). The simulator described in this chapter was designed to avoid just such limitations by offering an open-environment system in which students can move at their own pace, uncover information as they would in a real-life situation, and thereby construct their own understanding of phenomena encountered (Stover, 2007).

Finally, our development of a computer-simulated open learning environment was warranted by the need to address complex learning situations for which there were neither precise guidelines, nor any set precedents to follow (van Merriënboer & Kirschner, 2007). According to these authors: "Not surprisingly, students have difficulties combining all the things they learn into an integrated knowledge base and employing this knowledge base to perform real-life tasks and solve practical work-related problems once they have graduated" (p. 6). For such complex learning situations to be significant, learners need to be introduced to what we term an interrogative space in which they interact with fuzzy data as well as with one another, negotiating meaning, coming to a consensus, and making decisions based on the best information available (Fink, 2003). Despite the numerous and complex requirements of building such a system, we posit that an open environment simulation, as opposed to a closed-system environment, may be less taxing and expensive then is currently the view held in the simulation community.

Simulating Real-Life Experience

In his highly readable, even entertaining, *Simulations and the Future of Learning*, Aldrich (2004) states that "the validity of the simulation is based on how well it represents the real world" (p. 37). But obviously, a simulation cannot represent the entire real world. Hence, a basic and perennial problem involved in simulating reality is choosing what reality, or what part of reality, to simulate. As a result, simulations for education and training are generally focused on one specific aspect of reality, one given segment of reality or phenomenon, or even one episode in an unfolding event. Aldrich (2004) creates a content typology: linear content, cyclical content and open-ended content, stating that "in the traditional world of e-learning, most content is linear" (p. 25) and "most of the content that we have taught traditionally, especially history based, has no cyclical or open ended-content" (p. 29). Why so? Using existing linear content and developing new linear content are simply cheaper alternatives than creating cyclical or open-ended content which can get very involved, even tedious and is error-prone, not to mention very costly. Nonetheless Aldrich insists that "open-ended environments are very good for developing strategies, building up environments and taking ownership" (p. 28) and are hence highly desirable in a simulation.

Designers of simulations are caught between immovable objects — the need to create an environment in which deep, meaningful learning can occur (Aldrich, 2004), and the need to take resource availability and cost-effectiveness into account (Lombardi, 2007). Only a carefully-circumscribed yet context-rich reality can meet both requirements and be useful to learners intent on experiencing the unavailable, the inaccessible, the cost-prohibitive or the exceedingly dangerous (Plous, 1987).

In this light, an educational simulation is necessarily set within a framework that includes a sufficient number of real-life elements while observing limits imposed by cost factors. Limits must be set and hard choices made with regard to what to include and what to exclude, given the resources available. In educational and training circles, resource availability is, of course, a constant, unavoidable reality. As a result, design plays a major part in determining the parameters of a given simulation, its usefulness to learners, and the result it can achieve in enhancing their knowledge base or, as is our case, in familiarizing them with ethical decision-making and moral considerations in the workplace. It is within this simulation design context that we undertook the *Ethical Advisor* project.

CONCEPTUAL FRAMEWORK

Moral Dilemmas and Ethical Decision-Making: Context

Recent scandals involving unethical business practices (such as the ENRON and WorldCom fiascos) and in the civil service (the "sponsorships scandal" in Quebec, Canada) have led to calls for heightened sensitivity to ethical behaviour in business and government. This, in turn, has led to a need for specialized training in ethical awareness and values in various university programs (Langlois, 2004). However, teaching ethics is a daunting task, given the ill-defined problems, conflicting value systems and culturally sensitive issues that come into play (Loe, Ferrell, & Mansfield, 2000). Moreover, it has become clear that there is a gap between, on the one hand, one's ability to detect unethical activities and practices and, on the other, the ability to determine what actually constitutes ethical activities and practices as well as the integrity to act upon them (Bourgault, 2004). Applied ethics is an emerging field and has been little explored in a university setting. Moreover, the field is often limited to the deontological dimension, focusing on the rightness or wrongness of actions rather than their consequences (Kant), and little research and training exploit the group learning aspect. Case studies represent an excellent means of presenting real-world situations which, in turn, foster development of ethical competency, but few researchers are examining simulated ethical decision-making environments (Power, Langlois, & Gagnon, 2005).

We define "ethics" as an intellectual discipline which provides reflection-based tools to those who wish to understand human action. In our understanding, it is mainly a process by which the analysis of principles is activated when one is engaged in a decision deriving from a given act. Such an ethical reflection bears on ethical standards (prohibitions, possibilities) which guide human action, on values and practical rules which prompt us to act in one way or another, and on moral principles which we try to respect for ourselves and in dealings with others. Thus, simulating ethical behaviour, although a major challenge, is a worthy pursuit.

The Need for Simulation in Ethics Education

According to Kaufman (2005), a simulated environment provides students with the time necessary for thorough and deep learning, the security to make mistakes in order to learn, and the freedom from unwanted scrutiny of a superior or a peer during such a sensitive, experiential, learning phase. Le Boterf (2001) argues that traditional training approaches are not suited to developing complex competencies such as ethical skills in the workplace. Learning ethics calls upon complex skill sets such as using judgment, assuming critical distance, and evaluating consequences, as well as a good dose of moral imagination (Canto-Sperber, 2001). These skills require daily practice in order to face moral dilemmas in the workplace. Le Boterf (2001) also states that the most appropriate training method to develop competencies in the workplace is action-training:

Action-training is a training approach that brings one as close as possible to constructing competencies. In finalizing the treatment of real problems or projects, it constitutes an important opportunity to result in the combining and mobilization of relevant resources (knowledge, know-how...) to create and implement competencies." (p. 180)

Immersing students in a real situation via simulation technology represents, in our view, the most effective means for promoting ethical competency learning and development.

These reflections have led us to realise the potential of computer-simulated case studies. Solving real-world, workplace situations based on actual ethics-related problems requires a variety of high-level competencies and skills. Also, this project is original in that it sheds light on student ethical decision-making processes for which well-documented and freely-available resources are scarce. Problematic scenarios in the simulated environment prompt users to use their judgment and professional insight in finding ethically acceptable solutions. Incidents of values-related conflict bring to the fore ethical dilemmas, often juxtaposing organizational versus individual values.

Using Technology for Ethical Decision-Making

Several models of ethical decision-making have been developed in business ethics (Cooper, 2006), in psychology (Rest & Narvaez, 1994), in education (Legault, 1999) and in educational administration (Langlois, 2004; Starratt, 1997). Yet these empirically validated models are little used in training. *Ethical Advisor* presents three ethical analysis models, the first being that of ethical deliberation by Racine, Legault & Bégin (1991), whose work deals with the analysis of ethical dilemmas among engineers. The second model is that of Langlois (2005) whose work is based on Starratt (1997) and deals with ethical dilemmas in school administration. This model is founded on a reflexive process involving three ethical dimensions: caring, justice, and critique. It requires the learner to reflect on these dimensions when attempting to resolve actual ethical dilemmas, in order to develop a sense of responsibility, all the while remaining authentic to herself and others. This model requires that one deliberate on dilemmas using precise normative criteria. The third and final model proposed is that of Cooper (2006), whose main work was conducted among administrators in the American civil service. His model aims at developing a sense of organisational responsibility while encouraging the individual to develop a personal sense of moral imagination.

Few ethical management models currently exist. The choice of these three models seemed appropriate to us because they reflect the multiple realities of the workplace, such as private-sector engineers working in situations of potential high-level risk with regard to health and workplace safety, and public sector and school administrators experiencing various ethical dilemmas which affect society in general directly. The EA simulation presents these three models and leaves it up to the user to choose the one which best represents his or her moral stance.

Ethical decision-making (EDM) skills development is an incremental process that, in the past, usually required lengthy exposure to problematic situations that were rarely accessible outside the real-life workplace. As mentioned earlier, increasing interest in ethical decision-making has prompted researchers to investigate new ways and means of accelerating EDM skills development among university students, who are often confronted with problems requiring this skill set upon their entry into the workplace. Research conducted by Langlois (2001) has shown that training in ethical decision-making develops judgment, critical analysis, and awareness of one's ethical conscience. Currently, we are exploring the use of simulation-based learning environments in the development of ethical decision-making-related skills, attitudes and knowledge. In short, we are asking whether it is possible to learn how to be ethical and whether technology can enhance such learning.

Figure 1. The Ethical Advisor homepage

ETHICAL ADVISOR DESIGN

Currently, no computer-simulated open learning environment is available for teaching ethical decision-making which portrays actual, real-world, workplace moral dilemmas. Moreover, existing simulations, either from the military or business world, are both highly proprietary and costly or simply inappropriate. We have realized the wisdom of "build your own or buy into someone else's vision" (Aldrich, 2004, p. 126).

As a result, work has been ongoing since 2005 on the design and development of *Ethical Advisor*. EA is being developed for use with both undergraduate and graduate students enrolled in programs at the Department of Industrial Relations at Laval University in Quebec City, Canada. An educational technologist and an ethicist, working together with a senior instructional designer and a technical team, have developed a .php language-based simulated open environment integrating enhanced and augmented still photographic pictures with simulated and real video footage. The working EA prototype enables the individual to better define what constitutes a moral dilemma, to choose which ethical approach is most relevant to solve a given moral dilemma and, ultimately, to learn how to explain and justify ethically-based decisions. EA constitutes a highly motivating and innovative learning environment which allows learners to experience simulated, yet real-life, conflict-laden situations which have never been reproduced in a classroom setting.

EA users access theory-framed and evidence-based problem scenarios from a databank containing more than two hundred case studies of moral dilemmas. To date, one complex case study has been developed that allows users to experiment with EA. Pending post-test data analysis and interpretation (2008-09), more cases, ranging from simple to complex, will be developed.

Among the tools being developed, there are numerous sources of information such as technical reports, personnel files, memos, email and phone messages which require that the user access, analyze, and interpret them by applying theoretical principles to situations that often defy categorization. Users also encounter steps involved in solving ethical problems based on literature studied in class. The web-based walk-through interface presents the EA homepage interface and login interface, followed by access to learner-controlled resources and work sheets. We now present each component in the interface.

Homepage

Figure 1 depicts the EA homepage, highlighting its professional look and feel, and emphasizing the nature of the simulated office environment to come. The system is designed to allow registered users to access the environment. However, there is a demo site online where the public is provided with a narrated walk-through: (http://www.rlt.ulaval.ca/cev/). Currently, only the French-language version of the simulation is available online; plans are underway to make an English-language version available.

Models and Case Studies

Figure 2 provides users with the choice of the models presented earlier, which they can use to proceed with an analysis of the complex case study which has been elaborated. Note that at the present time only the "Commission scolaire les Mélèzes" (The Mélèzes School Board) case study is available for analysis. However, the databank from which it was developed contains more than 400 case studies. This project should thus be seen as the modest beginning of a rather long process which will likely occupy the researchers over many years to come.

Figure 2 presents the investigation homepage, where users can either initiate an investigation (*enquête*) or continue a running investigation. They can select one of the analytical models, access FAQs, print their current investigation, or delete it and start over.

The EA Office

When users initiate an investigation or review resources from a current investigation, they are ushered into the main simulation environment (Figure 3), which is based on a universal office metaphor. The choice of the office metaphor was prompted by a desire on the part of the design team to ensure the highest degree possible (given available resources) of closeness-to-reality for the

Figure 2. The Ethical Advisor Access-to-Investigations page

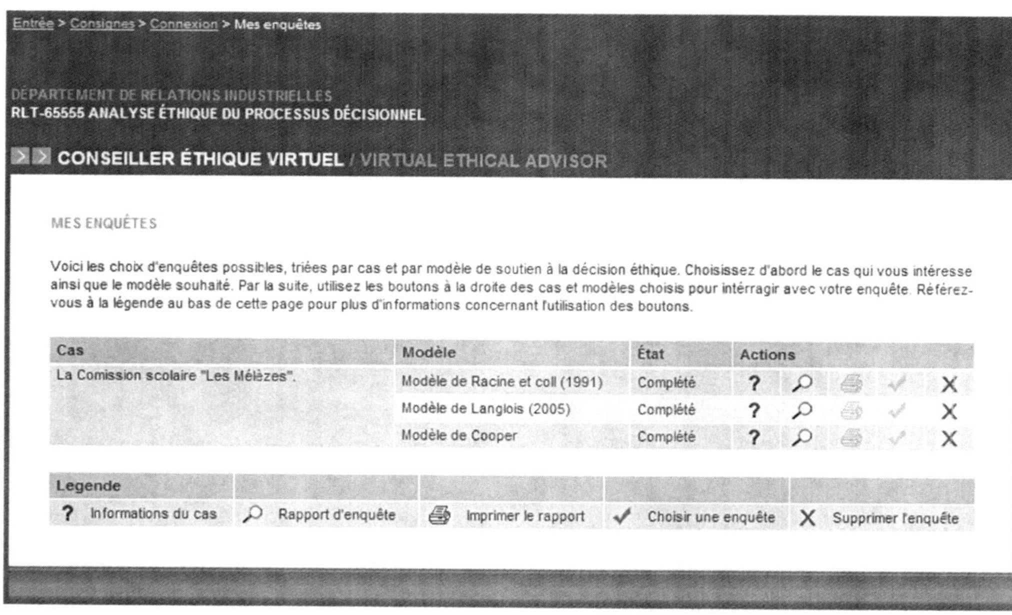

Figure 3. One of the two main interactive object-designed simulation pages

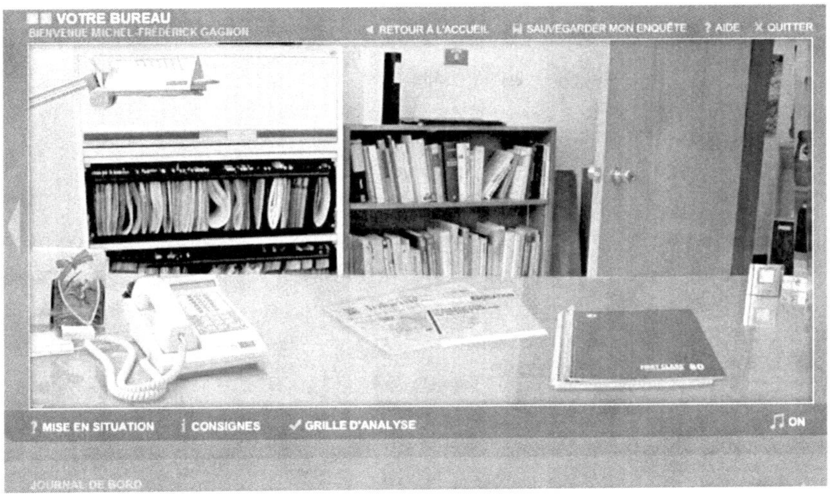

investigator-in-training. Standard office equipment and resources are clearly visible on-screen. These resources are all mouse-over, activated objects which are opened by a left double-click. For instance, the telephone provides users with pre-recorded vocal messages; the desk, the filing cabinet, and the bookshelves offer a variety of printed material, including reports, rules and regulations, even press releases. The door is also an activated object and provides the user with potentially useful information in the form of video clips of coworkers, supervisors, or "persons of interest."

Also in Figure 3, by clicking on the arrow in the middle left corner of the screen, the user swivels to the other side of the desk where a computer is located (Figure 4). In Figure 4, the computer, the main activated object, provides the user with timely information in the form of email messages and stored archives of various documents which may be helpful to the investigation. It should be noted that the emphasis is on an *open* learning environment which is, for the most part, non-directive, though certain parameters have been preset. The main limitation is that the user can only access available (pre-programmed) resources during the investigation. A further development of the simulation may eventually include real-time interaction with online tutors in the form of desktop synchronous conferencing, as well as a learning activity in which users will produce and add their own resources, thus adding to the overall complexity of the simulation.

The EA Simulation in Context

Figure 5 presents the simulation in context as part of an overall process of ethical competency development and assessment. The simulation is located at the beginning of the process, preceded only by a pre-test data-gathering questionnaire designed to provide faculty with initial user ethical competency profiles. The circular arrows indicate that users can go through the simulations as often as they like. After users individually conduct their investigation via the simulation, two outputs are recorded and archived: their individual investigation logbook and their individual results from a post-test questionnaire. This data is immediately accessible by authorized simulation administrators. Users then proceed to an online asynchronous forum in which they debrief, compare notes and discuss issues such as obstacles encountered and results obtained. This teamwork-generated data

Figure 4. The second main interactive object-designed simulation page

is also collected for analysis. Moreover, within an online learning context, real-time online exchanges allow teams to compare notes, and the faculty member to bring in new information in light of her analysis of previous individually- and team-gleaned data. Finally, the archived recording of real-time exchanges also provides a source of analyzable data. As testing continues and data is collected, results will be fed into a continuous improvement cycle of prototype development.

Figure 5. Design for assessing online ethical competency training

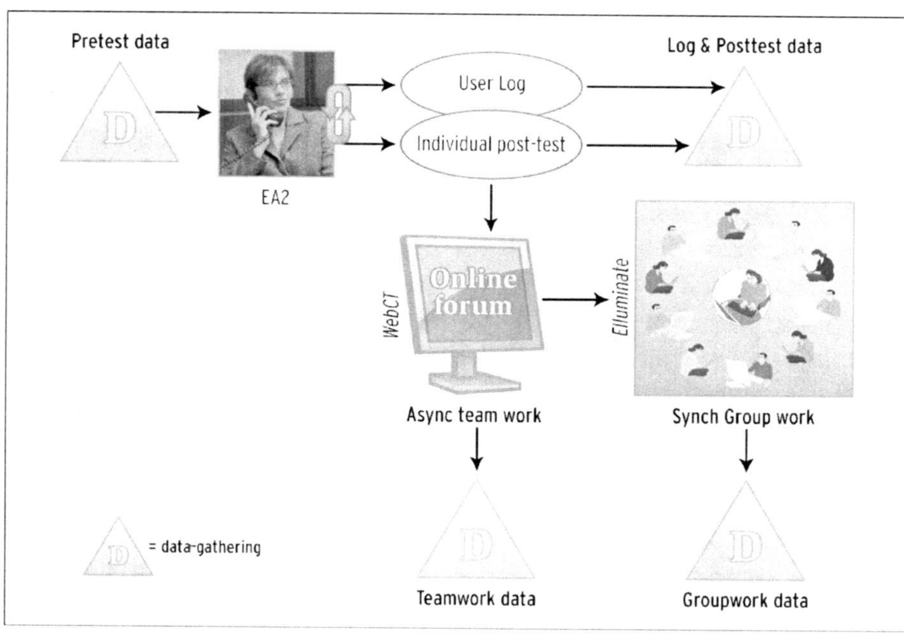

CONCLUSION

The impetus for this project was our realization that an in-depth experiential exploration by students of contemporary, complex ethical dilemmas would improve the quality of their learning. It was posited that this might be achieved through the use of a simulation as a component of an overall learning environment. Initial data analysis based on student usage of the *Ethical Advisor* simulation points to heightened levels of motivation and knowledge retention attributable to use of the ergonomically-designed educational tools integral to the EA environment. Moreover, students report that, by accessing realistic, case-based, ethical dilemma-related resources, their ethical decision-making capacity is enhanced. Finally, by using the EA simulation, students have access to both an asynchronous-based learning environment and a synchronous-based, virtual classroom environment where discussions and exchanges on their simulated experience can take place. Learners are able to evaluate their ethical and moral dilemma-solving skills as they evolve by means of comparison with their peers, negotiation of meaning, and repositioning of their decision-making process (Duffy & Cunningham, 1996; Duffy & Jonassen, 1992; Jonassen, 1999).

In our view, the learning environment that has been elaborated is enabling development of a high level of competency in ethical decision-making and, as such, represents an excellent means of linking learning theory to technological advancement. The technological development required will certainly be an aspect we will be studying intensively in the coming years. Next year, the scientific validity of the simulation will be analyzed to ascertain if it is effectively achieving ethical competency development and refinement. Development is currently underway with regard to assessment instrumentation and interview guides which will serve to validate the potential of this prototype learning environment.

REFERENCES

Aldrich, C. (2004). *Simulations and the future of learning*. San Francisco, CA: Pfeiffer.

Bergin, R. A., & Fors, U. G. H. (2003). Interactive simulated patient: An advanced tool for student-activated learning in medicine and healthcare. *Computers & Education*, *40*(4), 361–376. doi:10.1016/S0360-1315(02)00167-7

Borges, M. A. F., & Baranauskas, M. C. C. (1998). A user-centred approach to the design of an expert system for training. *British Journal of Educational Technology*, *29*(1), 25–34. doi:10.1111/1467-8535.00043

Bourgeault, G. (2004). *Éthiques, dit et non dit, contredit, interdit* [Ethics, said and not said, contradicted, forbidden]. Quebec, QC, Canada: Presses de l'Université du Québec.

Brandon-Hall. (2006). *Online simulations 2006*. Retrieved January 23rd, 2008 from http://www.brandon-hall.com/publications/simkb/simkb.shtml

Brown, J. S., Collins, A., & Duguid, P. (1989). Situated cognition and the culture of learning. *Educational Researcher*, *18*, 32–42.

Burnham, D., & Fieser, J. (2006). René Descartes (1596-1650). *In International Encyclopedia of Philosophy*. Retrieved June 12, 2008 from http://www.iep.utm.edu/d/descarte.htm

Canto-Sperber, M. (2001) *L'inquiétude morale et la vie humaine* [Moral unease and human life]. Paris: Presses universitaires de France.

Cooper, T. (2006). *The responsible administrator: An approach to ethics for the administrative role* (5th edition). San Francisco CA: Jossey-Bass.

Crichton, M. T., Flin, R., & Rattray, W. A. R. (2000). Training decision makers – Tactical decision games. *Journal of Contingencies and Crisis Management*, *8*(4), 208–217. doi:10.1111/1468-5973.00141

Darabi, A., Nelson, D. W., & Palanki, S. (2007). Acquisition of troubleshooting skills in a computer simulation: Worked example vs. conventional problem solving instructional strategies. *Computers in Human Behavior, 23*(4), 1809–1819. doi:10.1016/j.chb.2005.11.001

de Jong, T., & van Joolingen, W. R. (1998). Scientific discovery with computer simulations of conceptual domains. *Review of Educational Research, 68*(2), 179–210.

Dobson, M., Ha, D., Ciavarro, C., & Mulligan, D. (2005). From real-world data to game-world experience: A method for developing plausible and engaging learning games. In S. de Castell & J. Jenson (Eds.), *Proceedings of the Digital Games Research Association Conference (DIGRA 2005): Changing Views: Worlds in Play*, Vancouver, BC, Canada. Retrieved December 20th, 2007 from http://citeseer.ist.psu.edu/737505.html

Duffy, T., & Cunningham, D. (1996). Constructivism: Implications for the design and delivery of instruction. In D. H. Jonassen (Ed.), *Handbook of research for educational communications and technology* (pp. 170-198). New York: Simon and Schuster.

Duffy, T. M., & Jonassen, D. H. (1992) *Constructivism and the technology of instruction: A conversation.* Hillsdale, NJ: Lawrence Erlbaum Associates Inc.

Fink, L. D. (2003). *Creating significant learning experiences: An integrated approach to designing college courses.* San Francisco: Jossey-Bass.

Garrison, D. R., & Anderson, T. (2003). *E-Learning in the 21st century: A framework for research and practice*. London/New York: Routledge Falmer.

Garrison, D. R., & Vaughan, N. (2008). *Blended learning in higher education: Framework, principles, and guidelines.* San Francisco, CA: Jossey-Bass.

Gredler, M. E. (1992). *Designing and evaluating games and simulations: A process approach.* London: Kogan Page.

Gredler, M. E. (2004). Games and simulations and their relationships to learning. In D. H. Jonassen (Ed.), *Handbook of research on educational communications and technology* (2nd ed., pp. 571-581). Mahwah, NJ: Lawrence Erlbaum Associates Inc.

Hertel, J. P., & Millis, B. J. (2002). *Using simulations to promote learning in higher education: An introduction.* Sterling, VA: Stylus Publishing.

Jonassen, D. (1999). Designing constructivist learning environments. In C. Reigeluth (Ed.), *Instructional design theories and models: A new paradigm of instructional theory* (Vol. II, pp. 215-239). Mahwah, NJ: Lawrence Erlbaum Associates Inc.

Kaufman, D. (2005). Collaborative Online Multimedia Problem-based Simulations (COMPS). In *Proceedings, XXIIIrd International Council for Innovation in Higher Education*. Belfast, UK.

Kaufman, D., & Schell, R. (2007). Piloting a collaborative online multimedia PBL simulation. In C. Montgomerie & J. Seale (Eds.), *Proceedings of World Conference on Educational Multimedia, Hypermedia and Telecommunications 2007* (pp. 1834-1841). Chesapeake, VA: Association for the Advancement of Computing in Education (AACE).

Langlois, L. (2004). Responding ethically: Complex decision-making by school district superintendents. *International Studies in Educational Administration, 32*(2), 78–93.

Langlois, L. (2005). Comment instaurer un processus décisionnel éthique chez le gestionnaire? [How can we instill an ethical decision process in management?]In L. Langlois, R. Blouin, S. Montreuil, & J. Sexton (Eds.), *Éthique et dilemmes dans les organisations* [Ethics and dilemas in organizations] (pp. 13-26). Ste-Foy, QC, Canada: Presses de l'Université Laval.

Langlois, L., & Starratt, J. (2001). Identification of superintendents' and school commissioners' ethical perspective: Data talking to the model. In *Selected Papers presented at the 6th Annual Leadership & Ethics Conference,* Charlottesville, VA.

Le Boterf, G. (2001). *Construire les competences individuelles et collectives* [Building individual and collective competencies]. Paris: Editions d'organisation.

Lean, J., Moisier, J., Towler, M., & Abbey, C. (2006). Simulations and games: Use and barriers in higher education. *Active Learning in Higher Education*, *7*(3), 227–242. doi:10.1177/1469787406069056

Legault, G. (1999). *Professionnalisme et deliberation éthique* [Professionalism and ethical deliberation.]. Quebec, QC, Canada: Presses de l'Université du Québec.

Loe, T. W., Ferrell, L., & Mansfield, P. (2000). A review of empirical studies assessing ethical decision making in business. *Journal of Business Ethics*, *25*(3), 185–204. doi:10.1023/A:1006083612239

Lombardi, J. (2007). *Cost of simulations.* Weblog. Retrieved November 13th, 2007. http://jlombardi.blogspot.com/2007/10/cost-of-simulations.html

Plous, S. (1987). Perceptual illusions and military realities: Results from a computer-simulated arms race. *The Journal of Conflict Resolution, 31*(1), 5–33. doi:10.1177/0022002787031001002

Power, M. (2008, March). *Responsible outreach in higher education: The Blended Online Learning Environment.* Paper presented at the American Educational Research Association Instructional Design SIG, New York.

Power, M., Langlois, L., & Gagnon, M.-F. (2005). Ethical Advisor 1.0: Judge for yourself. In S. de Castell & J. Jenson (Eds.), *Proceedings of the Digital Games Research Association Conference (DIGRA 2005): Changing Views: Worlds in Play,* Vancouver, BC, Canada. CD-ROM.

Racine, L., Legault, G., & Bégin, L. (1991). *L'éthique et l'ingénierie* [Ethics and engineering]. Montréal, QC, Canada: McGraw Hill.

Rest, J., & Narvaez, D. (1994). *Moral development in the professions: Psychology and applied ethics.* Mahwah, NJ: Lawrence Erlbaum Associates Inc.

Ross, T. J. (2004). *Fuzzy logic with engineering applications*. Hoboken, NJ: Wiley.

Starratt, R. J. (1997). *Administrating meaning, administrating community, administrating excellence: The new fundamentals of educational administration.* New York: Merrill.

Stover, W. J. (2007). Simulating the Cuban Missile Crisis: Crossing time and space in virtual reality. *International Studies Perspectives, 8*(1), 111–120. doi:10.1111/j.1528-3585.2007.00272.x

Streufert, S., Satish, U., & Barach, P. (2001). Improving medical care: The use of simulation technology. *Simulation & Gaming, 32*(2), 164–174. doi:10.1177/104687810103200205

van Merriënboer, J. G., & Kirschner, P. A. (2007). *Ten steps to complex learning: A systematic approach to four-component instructional design.* London: Routledge.

Wikipedia (2008). Deontological ethics. Retrieved June 12, 2008 from http://en.wikipedia.org/wiki/Deontology

ADDITIONAL READING

Beauchamp, T. (2003). The nature of applied ethics. In R.G. Frey & C. Wellman (Eds.), *A companion to applied ethics* (pp. 1-16). Oxford, UK: Blackwell Publishing.

Blanchard, K., & Peale, N. V. (1998). *The power of ethical management.* New York: Fawcett Books.

Bransford, J. D., Brown, A. L., & Cocking, R. R. (Eds.). (1999). *How people learn: Brain, mind, experience and school.* Washington, D.C.: National Academy Press. Retrieved March 8, 2009, from http://books.nap.edu/html/howpeople1/

de Souza e Silva, A. (2009). Hybrid reality and location-based gaming: Redefining mobility and game spaces in urban environments. *Simulation & Gaming, 40*(3), 404–424. doi:10.1177/1046878108314643

Kitchener, K. S. (1985). Ethical principles and decisions in student affairs. In H. J. Canon & R.D. Brown (Eds.), *Applied ethics in student services.* San Francisco, CA: Jossey-Bass.

Langlois, L. (2008). *Anatomie d'un leadership éthique* [Anatomy of ethical leadership]. Québec, QC, Canada: Presses de l'Université Laval.

Legault, G. (1999). *Professionnalisme et délibération éthique, manuel d'aide à la prise de décision* [Professionalism and ethical deliberation: Manual to aid in decision-making]. Québec, QC, Canada: Presses de l'Université du Québec.

KEY TERMS AND DEFINITIONS

Applied Ethics: Field of study involving the practical applications of ethical principles namely in professional circles, especially medical ethics and business ethics.

Ethical Decision-Making: Requires development of ethical sensitivity allowing for the exploration of various facets of a problem from the standpoint of an ethical reflection. A decision-making process which requires a rigorous method based on specific benchmarks required to identify ethical issues in a given situation.

Ethics: Refers to manners and behaviors of a moral nature related to issues of responsibility and judgment.

Learning Environment: A concept present in constructivist literature; describes a learning context in which students interact with one another as well as with educational resources and supports.

Professional Ethics: Ethics including legal aspects aimed at insuring professionalism through the accomplishment of specific obligations in a given context. Associated with the term deontology indicating duty, an ethical approach is distinct from a legal approach insofar as the normative element is not obligatory.

Simulation: A technique which allows one to artificially recreate the main facets of a system, including aspects of structure, processes and outcomes.

Simulator: A device which is usually computer-driven, creating a threat-free, artificial learning environment suited for training purposes.

Chapter 11
Design of a Socioconstructivist Game for the Classroom:
Theoretical and Empirical Considerations

Margot Kaszap
Laval University, Canada

Claire IsaBelle
University of Ottawa, Canada

Sylvie Rail
Laval University, Canada

ABSTRACT

The overall goal of our research was to create a Web-based health education game that was compatible with new school requirements in Quebec, Ontario, and New Brunswick, Canada, covering the development of competencies including problem solving and critical thinking, while using a learning approach involving the collective construction of knowledge. This chapter introduces the theoretical and empirical studies which led us to choose the game framework and question types to achieve the desired learning objectives.

INTRODUCTION

Our overall research goal was to create a web-based health game within a game shell being developed in the *Carrefour virtuel de jeux éducatifs/ Educational Games Central* environment (http://egc.savie.ca).

While the game was intended for learners at all levels, we were specifically interested in the age group who are just completing elementary school, or starting secondary school. We began our work with a study of school programs in the Canadian provinces of Quebec, Ontario, and New Brunswick to identify the parameters which would guide our choices as well as the health subjects to be emphasized. (Parts of this study are described in Chapter 7.) We then based our development process on the work of Depover, Giardina, & Marton (1998), using their five-stage process for building a *Système d'Apprentissage Médiatisé Interactif* (*SAMI*, an interactive multimedia learning system). This chapter presents aspects of the first two stages: *data analysis* (theoretical and empirical), and *design* of the game shell and the health game. We first defined the crite-

DOI: 10.4018/978-1-61520-731-2.ch011

ria which drove the choice of the frame game we used and then determined the types of questions that would be consistent with a constructivist approach to game-based learning.

To start, we conducted a review of the the approaches to learning and health education recommended by new school programs in the provinces under study. We also analyzed a variety of educational games already offered on the Internet and on CD-ROM to highlight characteristics that would support learning according to the models prescribed in the school programs. We then studied the needs and preferences of the target audience for the types of educational games that would interest them. To do this, we used one questionnaire for students, and another for future teachers. We also held two focus groups with 5th and 6th year elementary school students in Quebec. The synthesis of these studies allowed us to define an optimal game framework, taking into account the constraints and preferences of both elementary school and university students (in their capacity as future teachers), and to outline possible health game subjects.

THE PROJECT: CONTEXT AND QUESTIONS

This project builds on several studies, game implementations, and development projects (five generic shells for multimedia educational games on the Internet in the *Carrefour virtuel des jeux éducatifs/ Educational Games Central* website (http://ecg.savie.ca) that were developed by the research team at *SAVIE* (Société d'apprentissage à vie), a partner in the Canadian *SAGE for Learning* research network. One of *SAVIE*'s aims is to provide teachers at all levels, in-house trainers, and community or non-profit organization workers with tools to develop educational games on the Internet and to use them with their students or clients by means of generic computer-based frame games. Some examples of frame games that have been programmed for online use are *Snakes and Ladders*, *Tic-Tac-Toe*, *Trivia*, and *Mother Goose*. A generic shell is a frame game which has had its original content removed and for which only the structure remains. Game authors can use the shell to build a new game by adding their own content. For example, a teacher who wishes to make a history game could input his own questions on the historic period that he wants to cover with his students. For this research, a new game shell was to be created to allow the construction of games in a new format. The specific game to be created was an educational game covering some aspect of health for young people between 10 and 12 years old.

Decisions related to the conception of the game shell and game were influenced by several constraints. The mandate was to build a game shell that met the strict definition of "game" as opposed to "simulation game" (see Chapter 1). The frame game had to allow the use of a socioconstructivist approach. We had to take into account the technological and ergonomic constraints found in schools. There was a limited budget. The game shell had to remain independent of any educational content and be reusable for various clientele. Finally, the learning environment had to allow for learning new content rather than serving only for testing student knowledge levels (Rail, 2005).

Several questions arose, such as,what frame game to choose? With what characteristics? How would we take into account new curricula for elementary and secondary education in Quebec, Ontario and New Brunswick? To answer these, we collected both theoretical and empirical data. The combination allowed us to choose a frame game adapted to the needs of future teachers and their students.

PROGRAM REQUIREMENTS

Because the target audience for our health game was young people from 10 to 12 years old, the elementary and secondary educational programs of Quebec, Ontario and New Brunswick were analyzed to determine both the approaches required for construction of new knowledge and the possible themes to be emphasized. These program requirements are outlined below.

The Quebec Elementary School Program

Health is one of five general learning domains defined by the Ministère de l'Éducation du Québec (2001). The five are: Health and Well-being, Leadership and Entrepreneurship, Environment and Consumption, Media, and Community Life and Citizenship. They are intended to move the curriculum closer to the knowledge needed for daily concerns of the student and to give them a greater understanding of real life (p. 42). We therefore expect to find health-related activities scattered throughout the school year. In addition, health coverage must be specifically included within the alloted time for physical education and health, the subject where students must develop the following three competencies: "Be active in various types of physical activity, interact in different types of physical activity and adopt a healthy and active way of life" (p. 257). The educational goal connected with the health and well-being domain is "to have the student adopt a reflective method in the development of good life habits from the perspective of health, well-being, sexuality and safety" (p. 44).

The proposed curriculum plans list all the important subjects and sub-subjects to be included:

- **Consciousness of oneself and one's fundamental needs:** Physical needs, the need for security, the need for acceptance and development as a boy or girl, the need for self-actualization
- **Consciousness of the consequences of personal choices on health and well-being:** Food, physical activity, sexuality, hygiene and safety, management of stress and emotions
- **Active lifestyle and personal security:** Physical activities integrated into class, at the school, in the family and in the other circles; behavior that protects personal security in all circumstances

These subjects must be approached in ways that help young people become aware of their fundamental needs and of the consequences of their personal choices on their health and well-being. However, this program contains only broad topics, without detailing all the concepts that must be included. It particularly emphasizes a competency-based approach, leaving the teacher latitude to allow the student to discover and work with information and knowledge through individual or team projects. In addition, it states that:

Some learning methods are inspired by behaviourist-centred practice, notably, memorization of knowledge through repeated exercises. However, many elements of the Program of learning, in particular those that concern the development of competence and the mastery of complex knowledge, rely on practices based on a constructivist conception of learning. In this perspective, learning is considered as a process, the first artisan of which is the student. He is supported in quite a particular way by situations which represent a real challenge, that is situations which entail a questioning of his knowledge and personal representations. (p. 5)

These two practices (behaviorist and constructivist) constitute the extremes within which we must design our new health games and, beforehand, choose the new frame game.

The Quebec Secondary School Program

As described in Kaszap, IsaBelle, and Rail (2005), the Quebec secondary school program (Ministère de l'Éducation du Québec, 2003) uses the same educational approaches, the same general learning domains, with the same subjects and educational intentions as the province's elementary school program. However, here health education not only includes physical education and health, but also moral education. The contents of the physical education and health curriculum cover the same essential knowledge as in the elementary school program, described in much the same way. However, the secondary program adds to it new knowledge such as: dietary needs according to type of activity; the benefits of sleep; dangerous habits; comparison of the beneficial and fatal effects of different substances including tobacco, drugs, alcohol, supplements, and food; and the effects of the excessive consumption of multimedia material.

The moral education curriculum approaches additional subjects related to the development of skills of moral and ethical judgment. This need had to be included in the design of the new frame game. Our approach was to have students discuss problems and choose the best solutions for various situations.

The Ontario Programs

The Ontario elementary school program (Ontario Ministry of Education, 1998) sets the following learning objectives:

1. To understand the importance of the physical condition, health and well-being, and recognize the factors contributing to them
2. To make a personal commitment to the practices of strong daily physical activity and the adoption of good dietary habits
3. To acquire motor skills allowing the student to participate with confidence in diverse physical activities throughout his life (p. 2)

The themes addressed are similar, for the most part, to those in the Quebec programs: physical condition, physical activity, personal and social skills, growth, food, safety and security, and the prevention of drug addiction. However, some very important subjects are not mentioned in the Quebec elementary school program, such as: male and female reproductive systems; healthy responses to certain situations, responsibilities of child-rearing, behavior in confrontational situations, the advantages of not consuming alcohol or tobacco, the harmful effects of illicit drugs, and community resources for obtaining information on drug addiction, and the available professional services for addiction problems (p. 30). The secondary school program includes all these subjects, with more clearly defined requirements.

The Program in New Brunswick

Health education in New Brunswick is taught in the Personal and Social Education curriculum (New Brunswick Ministry of Education, 2005). The guiding principles of the program state that students need an education which emphasizes meaning, interaction and collaboration; reflection rather than memorization; higher-order intellectual operations (e.g., critical thought and problem resolution strategies); interdisciplinarity and transdisciplinarity; the respect for varying paces and styles of learning; and the use of information and communication media (p. 9). One of the purposes of the program is to help students become aware of their lifestyle habits and their effects on health (p. 27). Health is presented as one of four dimensions of the person, along with consumption, citizenship, and interpersonal relations. These dimensions are interconnected, and the school framework does not have to separate them completely (p. 29). Contextualizing content and ensuring the transfer of knowledge are very important. Specific health subjects are the same as those found in the programs of the other two provinces in the 6th through 8th year and are listed and clearly detailed: satisfaction of needs, physical activity, sexuality, dietary habits, personal safety, consumption, drugs, physical transformtions and puberty, and identity.

The programs used in these three provinces all state the necessity of developing higher-level cognitive skills such as criticism, problem resolution, and clear decision-making. For students to build their own knowledge and to participate actively in learning, a constructivist approach is often recommended. We next briefly review this approach, which guided the choices of our new game's design characteristics.

THEORETICAL CONSIDERATIONS

Foundations of Constructivism

We based our game design decisions on the constructivist model of learning because it is recommended by the new school programs of Quebec, Ontario, and New Brunswick, and because it allows for new and transferable learning. Rail (2005) notes that in a literature review on constructivism, Minier (2000), summarizing the streams of thought, key ideas, and contributions by the originators of constructivism, states that Piaget (1896-1980) saw the individual as the heart of the process of developing intelligence in a process that assimilated new knowledge into the prior knowledge in the individual's cognitive structure. The individual is also capable of identifying the characteristics of his or her actions and cognitive processes (Goupil & Lusignan, 1993, pp.50-52). Minier also notes that for Vygotsky (1896-1934), children develop through contact with their social environment and through interaction with, and the help of, more experienced individuals who act as supports by questioning (sociocognitive conflict). In pursuit of learning in a "zone of proximal development," the individual thus builds his knowledge with the help of others (Goupil & Lusignan, 1993, pp.52-54). Bruner's (1990) theory echoes Piaget, with the idea of an active individual who constructs new concepts or ideas from stored knowledge. Bruner demonstrates the necessity of a coherent knowledge structure to promote the knowledge appropriation process by emphasizing the importance of psychological maturation, intrinsic motivation, and the participation of the student in the discovery process.

Rail (2005) also lists other theories influencing the constructivist approach. Giordan (1983), cited in Bertrand (1998), describes a dialectic process encompassing both continuation of prior knowledge and breaks with this same knowledge (Bertrand, 1998, pp.69-74; pp.76-79). He also explains that the prescientific culture of learning often puts obstacles in the way of a more effective and structured reorganization of their concepts. De Vecchi (1993) brings precision and distinctions to the concepts of representation and conception. Astolfi (1997) sheds light on the use of the error as a point around which learning can be solidified. Gagné (1976) and Tardif (1992), through cognitivism, as well as Bandura's (1986) social cognitive approach, also influenced the constructivist approach. Doise and Mugny (1981) integrate the role of multiple social interactions in the construction of knowledge and speak in terms of sociocognitive conflict. Brown and Campione (1995) emphasize the cultural aspect of knowledge and perceive culture as a sociocognitive filter that gives meaning to reality. Gilly (1988) is interested in competency development linked to problem sets and to the procedural perspective adopted in problem-solving. Inspired by work by Bruner and his colleagues, Brown and Campione (1995) offer a theory of learning which takes into account cultural and historical settings, learners' prior knowledge (which can create obstacles to the formation of new knowledge), cooperative work, tasking, and shared language as well as metacognition, which is linked to understanding one's own thinking and cognitive strategies.

In summary, it is necessary to be able to provide the learner with complex and rewarding activities that draw on problems from daily life, and that ask her to review her initial concepts and experiences before using a method that requires interaction with other students, and challenge her own assumptions. The new frame game must allow players to discuss, argue, and explore their points of view while allowing peers to express their opinions.

Pedagogical Applications of Constructivism

We now review how various approaches based on constructivism can influence educational practice, and especially educational multimedia game design. Meirieu (1990) described the characteristics of an effective learning device:

1. It engages the student's desire to learn
2. It has the student carry out a task in the form of problem to be solved
3. It provides set limits and instructions to be respected
4. It directs the student to build a mental process to support building the knowledge
5. It proposes the learning objective as an obstacle to be overcome
6. The structural limits of the task define set paths in knowledge construction, but they must also allow for strategy differentiation

He also suggests using differentiated organization, which consists in proposing multiple paths to pupils, to take into account such specifics as prior knowledge, educational profile, learning pace, culture and interests (Meirieu, 1997). Guilbert and Ouellet (1997) suggest the use of problem-based learning (PBL) as a way of applying the socioconstructivist model and of experiencing co-operative learning. The basic principles of PBL suggest that learners construct their own knowledge base, that they will learn better if they learn how to learn, and that social and environmental factors can be used to promote learning. PBL also allows for the integration of such notions as metacognition, multidisciplinary education, and the development of critical thinking. "The PBL case study, through the confrontation of varying points of view, makes learners aware of their own beliefs and of their egocentricity; they learn not to confuse their perceptions with reality" (Guilbert & Ouellet, 1997, p. 16). The same holds for reflexive pedagogy (RP), school of thought and "philosophy of the child" (Lipman, 1995), in which the student control over his learning processes helps him to become conscious of his use of learning skills, controlling his own activity and become aware of his use of the skills to be learned, and of his learning. Thus, we pose the question: how can we create a game that is educational and motivating, and that has the characteristics of constructivist learning?

Our challenge is to conceive a game which is not a simulation, can be placed in a game shell, can support multiple sorts of learning for various users, and which learners would find rewarding to play. According to Garris, Ahlers, and Driskell (2002), the main criteria that make learning rewarding are: significant learning (problem-solving, varied tasks which appear in a logical sequence), a task that is challenging to students, learning activities leading to actual results and requiring a cognitive commitment (students can make links with prior knowledge, use strategies, reorganize information, and formulate proposals), student empowerment (giving them opportunities to make choices), a collaborative atmosphere, interdisciplinary nature, and clear instructions. Motivation can come from the learning activities themselves, evaluations, rewards and penalties, passion for the subject, or the teacher's respect for the students (Kaszap, Rail, & Power, 2007).

Multimedia Design and the Constructivist Approach

Depover, Giardina, & Marton (1999) reviewed research over the last twenty years on multimedia learning design, proposing a new model that supports a constructivist approach to learning. Their complex intelligent system model:

> *...takes into account differences among learners, pace of learning, cognitive style, perception and treatment of information, characteristics of memory, cognitive ergonomics, motor and sensory reactions, and physical ergonomics. A model of the student is created from the strategies used by the learner; an intelligent advisor, using this information on the learner, can give advice, supplementary exercises, support and encouragement. The learner is placed in situations requiring the resolution of complex problems; the simulation of a real situation is important and should be as faithful as possible to reality, in a "dynamic manipulable situation." The learner must have the opportunity to make choices and decisions and to reflect on his actions and strategies. (Rail, 2005, p. 18)*

The complex intelligent system is a most interesting model. However, it does require a high level of expertise among designers and developers, and the costs of such a system are very high. Furthermore, the constraints inherent in our project would not allow us to apply such a model in any systematic way because (a) the frame game is not a simulation game; (b) the generic shell must allow teachers to design their own games quickly, without extensive programming skill; and (c) they must be able to do so on a limited budget and with a minimum of technological support. We can, however, use this model as an inspiration to design the new game shell and choose the new frame game.

Characteristics of an Educational Game

In their systematic review and analysis of the literature on the attributes of games and their educational impacts, *SAGE* project researchers (Sauvé et al., 2005a, b) identified the following authors as key contributors to the articulation of the characteristics of the *game*: Abt, (1968); Caillois, (1958); Chamberland, Lavoie, and Marquis, (1995); Coleman, (1968); Crawford, (1984), Cruickshank and Telfer, (1980), Garris et al., (2002); Gibbs, (1974); Hourst and Thiagarajan, (2007); Renaud and Sauvé, (1990); Stolovitch, (1983), and Thiagarajan, (1998).

From the study of these various definitions, we draw five attributes to define the concept of the game. As we are interested here in an educational game, we take the educational character of the game as the sixth attribute of this concept. The notion of educational game which we adopt thus concerns activities which have the following essential attributes: one or more players, interaction or conflict, rules, a predetermined goal, artificial character often described as fantasy, suspense, and the potential to support learning. (Sauvé et al., 2005b).

In summary, "the work of Sauvé et al., (2002) and Sauvé and Chamberland, (2003) define the game as a fictitious, fanciful or artificial situation in which one or several players, put into a position of conflict or challenge with regard to other players or together against other forces (teams), are governed by rules which structure their actions with the aim of achieving a predetermined goal, that is to win, to be victorious or to get revenge." (Sauvé et al., 2005b, p. 14). A game is different conceptually from a playful activity because the latter does not have all the essential attributes of the game. Our objective in this project is the creation of an educational game that will be neither a simulation nor a simulation game but rather a pure game in the format of a board game. (see Chapter 1 for a more complete discussion.)

EMPIRICAL CONSIDERATIONS

Because our objective was to choose a new frame game to be programmed to allow the creation of specific game instances, it is useful to review the main characteristics of the first five generic game shells (frame games) available online through SAVIE's *Carrefour Virtuel des Jeux Éducatifs/ Educational Games Central (EGC)* (http://egc.savie.ca). We then summarize the results of our study on game preferences of students and student teachers (also see Chapter 7). Finally we present results of the analysis of 40 Internet- and CD-ROM- based games (presented in more detail in Chapter 22).

Analysis of Five Existing Game Shells

By becoming members of the EGC, teachers and trainers can build or play with their learners games using any of five generic educational game shells. The first five game shells were based on the known games *Snakes and Ladders, Concentration, Tic-Tac-Toe, Trivial Pursuit*®, and the popular French-language game "*le jeu de l'oie*" (the *Mother Goose* game); a teacher can add a series of questions on any subject to one of these shells to create a specific game for students. Several observations can be made about the games created by teachers using these five game shells: players quickly understand the game rules because they are well known; the games are easy to create, taking only one hour on average; and previously-acquired knowledge can be tested and strengthened using these games while offering an entertaining experience to learners. With the exception of *Concentration*, these games are not designed to offer new learning experiences, but rather to review content that has already been taught, unless teachers decide to implement a trial-and-error approach. (However, if users have the chance to replay a game several times, they may learn something new.) Chance sometimes requires a player to answer only one or two questions during a game, while his opponent might have to answer several. Hence, these shells do not comply with a socioconstructivist approach, unless they are played in teams and are supplemented by other classroom activities. We therefore had to find or design a new and more suitable frame game in order to satisfy our criteria.

Analysis of Pre-Service Teacher Surveys

As described in Chapter 7, questionnaires were distributed to 307 Francophone pre-service student) teachers in New Brunswick (NB) and in Quebec (QC), Canada. Results indicated that between 45% (NB) and 65% (QC) of respondents never played games, between 17% (NB) and 27% (QC) played once a week and only between 2% (NB) and 6% (QC) played every day. However, over 80% of the student teachers polled believed that games promote learning. The games they preferred were: card games, *Cranium*®,, and *Monopoly*®, games which involve strategies, competition, challenges and which are fun to play (IsaBelle et al., 2005 and Chapter 7 of this volume).

Analysis of Surveys of Elementary School Students

Questionnaires were distributed to 204 youth in New Brunswick (NB) and 92 youth in Quebec (QC). We found that certain students wanted information about physical activity, health problems, nutrition, illicit substances, sexuality, body care and self image, while others did not want information on these subjects. The questionnaire also showed that respondents played a diverse set of computer and console games, that the most popular non-computer games were team games (hockey, basketball, soccer) and that they spent more time using email and chatting with their friends than they did playing games.

Analysis of Focus Group Data

In the spring of 2005, we met in 30-minute focus groups with four groups of 5th- and 6th-year students in the Chaudière-Appalaches Region of Quebec to discuss their preferences for games and for health subjects that they would like in an educational game. We met a total of 28 students aged between 10 and 12 years. They commented that they liked playing games; that they frequently played computer or console games; that some played every day and several hours a day, especially during the weekend; that boys, when they were not playing, preferred outdoor sports with their friends; that the girls often played games with their friends; and that they liked and knew such games as *Snakes and Ladders*, ,which they played occasionally with their families. Concerning health topics, the young people seemed well informed about the effects of cigarettes, alcohol, fast food and poor diet, and a sedentary lifestyle. On the other hand, they were not well informed about sexuality, sexually transmitted infections (STIs), drugs, or the infections and diseases which they or their peers might experience. They would be interested in discussing these subjects, especially if we presented them in overview form, or as case studies, or as problems to resolve.

Analysis of Games on the Internet or CD-ROM

We then conducted an analysis of various games of different types on the Internet or CD-ROM (Rail, 2005; Sauvé et al, 2005a; see also Chapter 22). The positive criteria identified in these games were: humour and fantasy in the questions and situations presented; positive and constructive feedback in response to wrong answers submitted; feedback including an explanation or a supplementary clue; interactivity and movement of clickable objects; as much variety as possible in player moves (cards, dice, points system, various movable objects); interacting with one or several players who might prevent one from advancing; answering faster that anyone else, accumulating more points; exercising control over others (rather than having two players who move at the same time, without mutual influence); exciting playing speed; a degree of pleasure in play; stimulating competition about winning the match or answering first to earn points (although it might be preferable, if speed is the issue, to offer more than one degree of difficulty); ubiquitous player choice; luck not unduly interfering with the game; and some degree of player risk-taking.

Elements to be avoided are: too small a game board; little player manipulation of objects, except with dice; the computer calculating everything so quickly that players do not see what has occurred; low or no competition (for instance, when players advance in parallel, or get to the end of the game at the same time); and disparity in effort exerted (e.g., when, by chance, some players rarely get to answer any questions).

While a single frame game cannot incorporate all these characteristics, we believe that it is necessary to keep them in mind when designing a game that will be rewarding, presents context-rich knowledge, and appeals not only to memory but to several cross-curricular competencies. Certain familiar games offer interesting degrees of complexity and could serve as a frame game, including *Monopoly, Career®, Payday®, Mille Bornes®,* and *Cranium.* These games share the following characteristics: the player can make choices (e.g., choosing a question theme); player choices affect the progress of the game; players can assess the consequences of their decisions, become aware of their strategies and revise them; and various types of interaction are possible, including confrontation, exchange, conflict, challenge, and deals. Each game is played in a given environment or social context.

Our choice settled on the board game *Parcheesi™*, which is the basis for *Cranium*, often mentioned by student teachers as being one of their favorite games. *Parcheesi* is very old, and not well known in its original form, but the updated version, with questions added, is very popular and easy to learn. We used the students' concerns as a basis for the questions in our adaptation of *Parcheesi.*.

GAME DESIGN ASPECTS AND HEALTH EXAMPLES

To illustrate our application of socioconstructivism in this game shell, we now return to each of the elements mentioned by Meirieu (1997) and Garris et al. (2002), explain how each is implemented in the new frame game, and give a health-related example consistent with elementary and secondary school programs.

Creating a Desire to Learn

An important element in constructivist theory is to base activities on a pupil's experience, thereby motivating him and kindling a fire for learning. The game thus takes into account cultural characteristics and concerns of the targeted age group. For example, before a question is asked, the player has to consult a learning segment which outlines the context of a situation to be investigated that is related to the concerns of young people. This segment can be presented in text, drawings, video, audio, graphs, diagrams, etc. It is important to add humorous events: for instance, a clumsy character, a funny situation or comical audio, humourous ways of asking questions, or visual cues for feedback purposes such as comments or winks of an eye.

Example 1: Indigestion. "You glutton! You took three big portions of chocolate cake with whipped cream. Result: you must spend the day inside. Match the names of these internal organs of the human body with their respective functions."

Motivation can also come from identification with a character. To allow this, players or game builders can choose or create their own game pieces or details. Although the text of questions and answers are written in international French, the characters can be customized to speak, move, or express attitudes that appeal to the target age group. The competitive aspect of the game increases pleasure, and motivates players to answer questions correctly. An element of chance balances intellectual skill, and gives a playful aspect to the game while preserving the self-respect of the losing players. Another interesting point is that players can learn as much by giving wrong answers as correct ones. Players can even make a game amusing in a different way by trying to accumulate the least possible points and see the consequences.

Presenting the Student with a Problem to Be Solved

The constructivist approach suggests putting students in a complex situation in which they must use their knowledge to solve problems, using reflection, research, and reasoning. In a frame game, players should be placed in situations where several solutions are available. To find the best solution, they must then appeal to their own knowledge and discuss their ideas with team-mates. During the game, they are confronted with other points of view and knowledge often tinged with prejudices or false concepts. Introductions accompanying the questions could also supply problems to be resolved; e.g., videos could be added to create case overviews, and responses could be explanations accompanied by arguments.

Example 2: Problem: You have decided to lose your small belly. Disaster! You skipped breakfast, ate a small salad for lunch, and soup for supper. In the evening, tired of this, you gobbled up three big sandwiches and a bag of chips. You now view a video on diets and reflect on the best choices to be made in the future. Present pros and cons for each of the three choices.

Setting Limits and Supplying Instructions

As in all board games, a set of rules governs the progress of the game. These can be seen at any time in context-sensitive help menus. The board game supplies a set of constraints for time limits and allowable moves. However, the frame game provides many types of questions and answers, including multiple choice (with one or several possible correct answers), matching questions, phrase completion, ordering, yes / no, true / false, short answer, narrative answer, questions requiring performance, or illustration with a drawing board.When a player chooses an answer, a short text confirms the correct choice or provides an explanation for an incorrect answer. The questions do not always have only one right answer. For certain questions, the opposing player or team must judge the quality of an answer given verbally and assign points to the player.

Example 3: This fruit prevents infections provoked by the bacterium E-coli. Possible answers: a. cornflower; b. tomato; c. kiwi; d. apple.

Example 4: What is the strongest muscle of the human body? Write a brief answer.

Building a Model for New Knowledge

The game's questions often push the learner to reapply what he has just learned in a new context. He then has to appeal to his judgment and reflection, not simply to memorization. To accomodate various cognitive styles, different discovery activities are available during the game, favoring students who are more visual, or auditory, or who need to manipulate objects, or prefer to read text.

Example 5: From the graph presented in the introduction, determine the quantity of syrup to give to a 9-month-old baby. Write a brief answer. (The student has to do a calculation because the physiology is given for a 12-month-old baby).

Presenting Learning Objectives as Obstacles

There can be various types of obstacles, as for example: approaching a little-known subject for which students often develop false ideas; investigating complex notions; presenting an ambiguous situation: or using complex reasoning to choose convincing arguments.

Example 6: Whew! Your girlfriend finally got her period. In the future, you will not take unnecessary risks. *Instructions*: What would you do if you woke up one morning to see that you had too much to drink and had had unprotected sex with a girl whom you hardly know? Click the letter which represents the best choice:

a. Have a bath in seaweed and sea salt
b. Consult an emergency service which will help diminish your risk of AIDS and other sexually transmitted infections
c. If your partner does not take the pill, quickly make an appointment for an abortion
d. Inform your partner of the necessity of taking emergency contraception (morning-after pill) if she does not take the pill regularly
e. The answers b. and d
f. The answers b and c
g. All these answers

Providing Tasks that Define Set Paths for Knowledge Construction while Allowing for Strategy Differentiation

During the game, the player has to carry out various tasks to accumulate the maximum points. The game tasks are designed to help the learner build a representation of declarative and procedural knowledge of the subjects addressed in the game. He is asked to relate and structure knowledge by manipulating images and words. Every knowledge segment is designed to use multiple skills: resolve problems; retrieve information; organize information; give structure to fragmented information; make meaningful links; or make complex decisions.

Example 7: You see a group of young people often bullying a classmate—laughing at him, knocking him down, taking his things. What do you do?:

a. I am going to tell a professor and a school official
b. I am going to tell the victim that I saw the scene and encourage him to tell an adult about it
c. I and my friends are going to speak to the leader of the gang to tell him that it is cowardly to do this
d. I think that it is safer to do nothing
e. The answers b. and c

Feedback: If the player chooses:

a. You are right to warn an adult. It is possible that this adult does not take the matter seriously. In this case, do not give up but talk about it to another adult who will take steps to solve the problem.
b. You help the victim by giving him your moral support. He might feel rejected by all, and the silence of witnesses can be worse to bear than the nasty gestures of a small group. It is possible that he is threatened and afraid of denouncing his aggressors. He may thus beg you not to speak about it. But if nobody encourages him to stop the bullying, things can continue to get worse for him.
c. Ah! You are nice. If all witnesses decided not to accept any more intimidation, these gestures would be much less frequent. If you are of the same age or older than the aggressors, what you say to them may make them reflect on what they are doing. On the other hand, if you are younger, you risk being threatened yourself. If things degenerate and they threaten you in turn, it is better to bring in adults. Don't forget that often the aggressors need help as much as the victims. Be careful not to provoke them pointlessly. We never settle violence with violence.
d. There is a proverb which says: "silence means consent", which means: if you say nothing, it means that you agree. If you know that a young person suffers and that he lives in fear, you have to take your courage in your hands and do something to denounce the violence.
e. You are brave! You are correct. These three gestures are important for stopping the intimidation.

Using Differentiated Organization

This board game has two versions (short and long), sometimes set according to the choice of the player, and sometimes as a consequence of a bad answer. The game uses a system of differential point accumulation according to the speed of the answer and the complexity of the questions. Activities are designed so that the learner can learn new knowledge during the game. Tasks require the learner to read information segments attentively, so that he can answer the questions that follow the segments. Some players will take time to read these segments carefully before answering the questions, while the others proceed by trial and error. After losing a piece or when landing on a special compartment, the player can choose the category of questions with which he feels most comfortable. Every category has to contain at least 20 questions so that the game is interesting. In every category, there must be at least two questions to be answered in teams, after discussion.

Example 8: The game *Young people and health* contains four categories: Diet, Problems and Diseases, Physical Activity, and Illicit Substances and Risky Behavior.

Summary

The objective of learning in our *Parcheesi* adaptation is not to memorize the contents of the game, but to learn to ask questions and to make informed decisions. During the game the player is called on to develop skills, and he receives a visual or audio message every time he has solved a problem, to encourage him and indicate that he can move ahead. Sometimes a problem can be resolved in several different ways. Points are not a formal indicator of success or failure in learning, given that chance plays an important part in the game. Errors here are opportunities to learn, and the player is invited to take risks.

CONCLUSION

Our new *Parcheesi* game shell extends the possibilities, limits, and learning strategies of games to be created by teachers and trainers in the future. The constraints which influenced our choice of a generic game shell were that it must be built from a game already known to the majority of the population, and it must be able to be played on the Internet. It was thus necessary to take into account the size of the application, in terms of memory needed. The breadth of the game in terms of educational content had to be set according to teachers' needs, so it was designed to handle more diverse content than in previously created shells, but not so much as to discourage future game builders. The interface had to be built with *Flash*®, to give the game more animation and interactivity possibilities. It also had to be possible to create context-sensitive windows during the game. The new game had to allow the addition of learning segments or capsules that had to be read to answer questions. These capsules would contain declarative knowledge or overviews, presented in various forms: text, images, graphs, photos, video, with or without sound. Capsules could also serve as data sources, reused in other contexts elsewhere in the game. The new game includes educational tasks for building new skills: memory, logic, reflection, attention, the capacity to apply new knowledge in other contexts, and to solve complex problems. The frame game allows the integration of various new types of questions: find elements in an image and move them or remove them; fill empty compartments in a missing paragraph; choose the assertion which is true; using an arrow, match statements which complement each other or which go together; crosswords, riddles; view a video or an audio extract, and answer a related question; choose or make a decision according to a text summary; infer from visual or sound information; assemble objects, reorder, sort out, match objects and words, complete sentences from a choice of words; make strategic choices during the game and see the consequences of the choices. Finally, one of the aspects that cannot be neglected during the design of an educational game is that the game must be rewarding to play. If there is no pleasure in the play, the game becomes just another disguised school task.

REFERENCES

Abt, C. (1968). Games for learning. In S.S. Boocock, & E. O. Schild (Eds.), *Simulation games in learning* (pp. 65-92). Beverly Hills, CA: Sage Publications.

Astolfi, J.-P. (1997). *L'erreur, un outil pour enseigner* [The error – a learning tool]. Paris: ESF.

Bandura, A. (1986). *L'apprentissage social* [Social learing theory]. Brussels, Belgium: Éditions Margada.

Bertrand, Y. (1998). *Théories contemporaines de l'éducation* [Contemporary theories of education] (4th ed.). Montréal & Lyon: Éditions Nouvelles et Chronique Sociale.

Brown, A. L., & Campione, J. C. (1995). Concevoir une communauté de jeunes élèves: leçons théoriques et pratiques [Designing a community for young students: Theoretical and practical lessons]. *Revue française de pédagogie, 111*(avril-mai-juin), 11-33.

Bruner, J. (1990). *Acts of meaning.* Cambridge, MA: Harvard University Press.

Caillois, R. (1958) *Les jeux et les hommes* [Games and men]. Paris: Gallimard.

Chamberland, G., Lavoie, L., & Marquis, D. (1995). *20 formules pédagogiques* [20 pedagogic templates]. Ste-Foy, QC, Canada: Les Presses de l'Université du Québec.

Coleman, J. S. (1968). Social processes and social simulation games. In S. S. Boocock, & E. O. Schild (Eds.), *Simulation games in learning* (pp. 29-51). Beverly Hills, CA: Sage Publications.

Crawford, C. (1984). *The art of computer game design.* Berkeley, CA: Osborne/McGraw-Hill.

Cruickshank, D. R., & Telfer, T. A. (1980). Classroom games and simulations. *Theory into Practice, 19*(1), 75–80. doi:10.1080/00405848009542875

De Vecchi, G. (1993). Des représentations, oui, pour en faire quoi ? [Representations, yes, for what?] *Cahiers pédagogiques, 312,* 55-57.

Depover, C., Giardina, M., & Marton, P. (1998). *Les environnements d'apprentissages multimédia - Analyse et conception* [Multimedia learning environments – Analysis and Design]. Paris: L'Harmatan.

Doise, W., & Mugny, G. (1981). *Le développement social de l'intelligence* [The social development of intelligence]. Paris: InterÉditions.

Gagné, R. M. (1976). *Les principes fondamentaux de l'apprentissage* [Fundamental principles of learning]. Montreal, QC, Canada: HRW.

Garris, R., Ahlers, R., & Driskell, J. E. (2002). Games, motivation, and learning: A research and practice model. *Simulation & Gaming, 33*(4), 441–467. doi:10.1177/1046878102238607

Gibbs, G. I. (1974). The use of simulations as achievement tests with programmed texts. *Programmed Learning and Educational Technology, 11*(4), 183–191.

Gilly, M. (1988). Interactions entre pairs et constructions cognitives [Interaction between peers and cognitive constructions]. In A. N. Perret-Clermond, & M. Nicolet (Eds.), *Interagir et connaître. Enjeux et régulations sociales dans le développement cognitif* (pp. 19-28). Cousset, Switzerland: DelVal.

Giordan, A. (1983). *L'élève et/ou les connaissances scientifiques: approche didactique de la construction des concepts scientifiques par les élèves* [Students and scientific knowledge: The didactic approach to the construction of scientific concepts by students]. Berne, Switzerland: Peter Lang.

Goupil, G., & Lusignan, G. (1993). *Apprentissage et enseignement en milieu scolaire* [Learning and teaching in the schools]. Montréal, QC, Canada: Gaëtan Morin.

Guilbert, L., & Ouellet, L. (1997). *Études de cas, apprentissage par problèmes* [Case studies: Problem-based learning]. Québec, QC, Canada: Presses de l'Université Laval.

Hourst, B., & Thiagarajan, S. (2007). *Modèles de jeu de formation – Les jeux-cadres de Thiagi* [Game models for training – the frame games of Thiagi] (3rd edition). Paris: Éditions Eyrolles.

IsaBelle. C., Kaszap, M., Sauvé, L., Renaud. L., Ngandu, M., & Leblanc, D. (2005). *Vision des élèves et des futurs enseignants du Québec et du Nouveau-Brunswick quant aux jeux et aux thèmes de la santé* [Vision of students and future teachers in Quebec and New Brunswick on games and health themes] (Research report). Ottawa, ON, Canada: University of Ottawa.

Kaszap, M. IsaBelle, C., & Rail, S., (2005) *Analyse des programmes scolaires -Québec, Ontario, Nouveau-Brunswick* [Analysis of school programs in Quebec, Ontario and New Brunswick]. Research report. Québec, QC, Canada: Laval University.

Kaszap, M., Rail, S., & Power, M. (2007). Web-based design for board games: Theoretical and empirical socioconstructivist considerations. *International Journal of Intelligent Games & Simulations*, *4*(2), 16–22.

Lipman, M. (1995). À l'école de la pensée [At the school of thought]. Brussels, Belgium: De Boeck University.

Meirieu, P. (1990). La pédagogie différenciée est-elle dépassée ? [Is differentiated pedagogy obsolete?]. *Cahiers pédagogiques, 286*(1), 48-53.

Meirieu, P. (1997). Plus que jamais la pédagogie différenciée [Differentiated pedagogy – more than ever?]. *Cahiers pédagogiques,* supplément no 3 (*Retours sur la pédagogie différenciée)*, 39 -40.

Minier, P. (2000). *Constructivisme* [Constructivism]. Available at http://wwwens.uqac.ca/~pminier/act1/constr.htm

Ministère de l'Éducation du Québec (2001). *Programme de formation de l'école québécoise. Éducation préscolaire. Enseignement Primaire* [Quebec elementary school curriculum]. Québec, QC, Canada: Government of Québec.

Ministère de l'Éducation du Québec (2003). *Programme de formation de l'école québécoise Enseignement secondaire, premier cycle* [Quebec secondary school curriculum, first level]. Québec, QC, Canada: Government of Québec.

New Brunswick Ministry of Education. (2005). *Programme d'étude. Éducation personnelle et sociale 6ème à 8ème année* [Program of study: Personal and social education, grades 6 – 8]. Frederickton, NB, Canada: Government of New Brunswick.

Ontario Ministry of Education. (1998). The Ontario curriculum for grades 1 through 8: Health and physical education. Available at http://www.edu.gov.on.ca

Rail, S. (2005). *Premières phases de conception d'un jeu éducatif sur la santé des jeune* [First stages in the design of an educational game on health in youth]. Unpublished master's thesis. Québec, QC, Canada: Université Laval.

Renaud, L., & Sauvé, L. (1990). *Simulation et jeu de simulation: outils éducatifs appliqués a la santé* [Simulations and simulation games: Educational tools applied to health]. Montreal, QC, Canada: Éditions Agence d'Arc, Inc.

Sauvé, L., & Chamberland, G. (2003). *Jeux, jeux de simulation et jeux de rôle: une analyse exploratoire et pédagogique* [Games, simulation games and role-playing games: An exploratory and pedagogical analysis]. Course TEC 1280: Environnement d'apprentissage multimédia sur l'inforoute. Québec, QC, Canada: Télé-université.

Sauvé, L., & Power, M. IsaBelle, C., Samson, D., & St-Pierre, C. (2002). *Rapport final - Jeux-cadres sur l'inforoute: Multiplicateurs de jeux pédagogiques francophones: Un projet de partenariat Bureau des technologies d'apprentissage* [Final report – Frame games on the Internet: Multipliers of francophone educational games: A partnership project of the Bureau des technologies d'apprentissage. Québec, QC, Canada: SAVIE.

Sauvé, L., Renaud, L., & Kaszap, M. IsaBelle, C, Samson, D., Doré-Bluteau, V.,et al. (2005b). *Revue systématique des écrits (1998-2004) sur les impacts du jeu, de la simulation et du jeu de simulation sur l'apprentissage* [Systematic review of the literature (1998-2004) on the impacts of games, simulations and simulation games on learning] (Research report). Québec, QC, Canada: SAGE and SAVIE.

Sauvé, L., Renaud, L., & Kazsap, M. IsaBelle, C., Gauvin, M., Simard, G. et al. (2005a). *Analyse de 40 jeux éducatifs (en ligne et cédérom)* [Analysis of 40 educational games (online and CD-ROM)] (Research report). Québec, QC, Canada: SAGE and SAVIE.

Stolovitch, H. D. (1983). *Notes de cours: jeux de simulation* [Course notes: Simulation games]. Montréal, QC, Canada: Université de Montréal.

Tardif, J. (1992). *Pour un enseignement stratégique: L'apport de la psychologie cognitive* [For a strategic education: The contribution of cognitive psychology]. Montréal, QC, Canada: Éditions Logiques.

Thiagarajan, S. (1998). The myths and realities of simulations in performance technology. *Educational Technology*, *38*(5), 35–40.

ADDITIONAL READING

De Grandmont, N. *Pédagogie du jeu...philosophie du ludique*.(En ligne). [Game pedagogy...philosophy of gaming] (Online). Available at http://cf.geocities.com/ndegrandmont/index.htm

Gardner, H. (1999). *Intelligence reframed: Multiple intelligences for the 21st century.* New York: Basic Books.

Gunter, B. (1998). *The effects of video games on children: The myth unmasked.* Sheffield, UK: Sheffield Academic Press.

Khan, M. M. (2002). Implementing an intelligent tutoring system for adventure learning . *The Electronic Library*, *20*(2), 134–142. doi:10.1108/02640470210424473

Lachance, B., Lapointe, J., & Marton, P. (1979). Le domaine de la technologie éducative [The learning technology domain]. *Bulletin de l'ADATE*, *2*(6), 10–15.

Meirieu, P. (1990). La pédagogie différenciée est-elle dépassée ? [Is differentiated pedagogy obsolete?]. *Cahiers pédagogiques, 286,* 48-53.

KEY TERMS AND DEFINITIONS

Competency: Know-how requiring knowledge and skills to accomplish a complex activity.

Frame Game: A basic board game structure such as *Snakes and Ladders*, *Mother Goose*, or *Parcheesi*, to which questions and supplementary rules can be added to make the game a learning activity.

Game: An activity requiring a player or multiple players, competition or conflict, rules, and a predetermined goal, carried out in an artificial environment often described as fantasy. An educational game must also include the potential to support learning.

Game Shell: A computerised empty game structure that allows any content to be inserted.

Health Education: An activity leading one to adopt a reflective practice in the development of healthy life habits in terms of health, wellness, of sexuality and safety.

Problem Solving: A process of thought for determining the best way to resolve a problem.

SAMI (système d'apprentissage médiatisé interactif): A learning system requiring a pedagogic scenario accompanied with technological support, through which the individual must participate and interact.

Simulation: An activity which imitates a real-life situation.

Simulation Game: An activity having the characteristics of a game while simulating some aspect of reality.

Socioconstructivist Approach: A learning approach involving collective construction of knowledge.

Chapter 12
Online Multiplayer Games:
A Powerful Tool for Learning Communication and Teamwork

Louise Sauvé
Télé-université, Canada

Louis Villardier
Télé-université, Canada

Wilfried Probst
University of Quebec in Montreal, Canada

ABSTRACT

*This chapter describes an online video teleconferencing tool the authors have created that allows learners to collaborate, negotiate, discuss, share ideas and emotions, and establish relationships while engaged in educational games and simulations. The ENJEUX-S (L'***En***vironnement multimédia évolué de* **JEUX** *éducatifs et de Simulations en ligne) multimedia environment relies on Web Services for the management and operation of online games and simulations and on real-time communication services (audio- and video-conferencing, chat) to support a collaborative working environment for players. The authors first describe the components of ENJEUX-S, their technological choices, and the environment's architecture. Then, they present the results of ENJEUX-S testing to correct problems and measure ease of use and functionality for target users. Finally, they outline the pedagogical contributions of such an environment in the context of online games and simulations, notably to development of interpersonal competencies including cooperation, communication, and teamwork.*

INTRODUCTION

Many recent studies have concluded that educational games and simulations develop a learner's capacity to establish relationships with others, negotiate, discuss, collaborate, share emotions and ideas, establish ties and friendships, and work in teams putting together ideas and resources (Sauvé, Renaud, Kaufman, & Sibomana, 2008b). The group becomes a place in which the learner identifies himself as belonging, where experience is shared, and learning is achieved.

At the same time, recent advances in synchronous technologies on the Internet now permit us to link

DOI: 10.4018/978-1-61520-731-2.ch012

together individuals, in real time, wherever they are and whatever the time zone. These technologies not only abolish the physical borders of space and time, but they create new realities (Probst, Villardier, & Sauvé, 2004) embodied in virtual worlds, where entire communities can communicate and exchange among themselves. This is a relatively new way of life (Villardier et al., 2006), spreading with the arrival of new direct communication technologies and taking an ever-larger place in our daily activities.

To achieve these communication dynamics, advanced educational game and virtual simulation environments must meet certain criteria; supporting direct communication and consultation, quick exchanges between team members, decision-making that incorporates the dynamics of interpersonal exchanges, spontaneous dialogue, instantaneous action, and, as far as possible, respect for confidentiality. The architecture of these environments must also conform to certain quality of service (QoS) requirements, including: flexibility, user friendliness, portability, interoperability, reliability and robustness.

It is in this context that an applied research project was financed by Canada's CANARIE Inc. (Canadian Advanced Network And Research for Industry and Education), with the objective of developing an environment based on a Web Services and telecommunications architecture, in order to support development and research activities related to generic game and simulation shells for the *Simulation and Advanced Gaming Environments (SAGE) for Learning* project and the *Carrefour de jeux éducatifs/ Educational Games Central* online portal (http://egc.savie.ca). This video teleconferencing environment was designed to support multi-user functions while offering transactional and interpersonal interactivity.

This chapter reports the results of this development effort. We first describe the components of *ENJEUX-S* (L'**En**vironnement multimédia évolué de **JEUX** éducatifs et de Simulations en ligne), a real-time multimedia environment for online games and simulations. We next explain the environment's architecture and technological choices. We then describe the *ENJEUX-S* testing, which allowed the detection and correction of bugs and technical problems as well as measurement of its user-friendliness and usefulness with a target group. Finally, we outline the contributions of such an environment in the context of online games and simulations to the development of interpersonal competencies, notably cooperation and collaboration, communication and teamwork.

AN ADVANCED ENVIRONMENT FOR EDUCATIONAL GAMES AND SIMULATIONS

ENJEUX-S is part of the continuing efforts of the Canadian *SAGE* research network (www.sageforlearning.ca or www.apprentissage-jes.ca). Its development has permitted the network to increase its real-time communication and interaction in online meetings and in the use of games and simulations. *ENJEUX-S* has integrated real-time communication components (audio, video, chat, white board, application sharing, and online access management) and multiple workstations into games developed with five generic educational game shells for the *Carrefour de jeu éducatifs/ Educational Game Central* online community (Sauvé, 2005) and two new shells, one for *Parcheesi*™ (Sauvé, 2006), and one for problem-based learning simulations (*COMPSoft*). (These shells are described in more detail in Section IV and Chapter 17 of this volume, respectively.) Introducing telepresence into the universe of educational games on the Internet, *ENJEUX-S* allows us to exploit enriched educational situations incorporating feedback, direct dialogue, immediate assistance, shared strategies, help, etc. (Sauvé et al., 2005). With *ENJEUX–S* the real world merges with the virtual world.

The user interface[1] of the *ENJEUX-S* environment consists of three spaces and a control panel (Figure 1). Each space comprises a series of action-specific functions accessible by menus. Let us look at them in greater detail.

Figure 1. The ENJEUX-S spaces and control panel

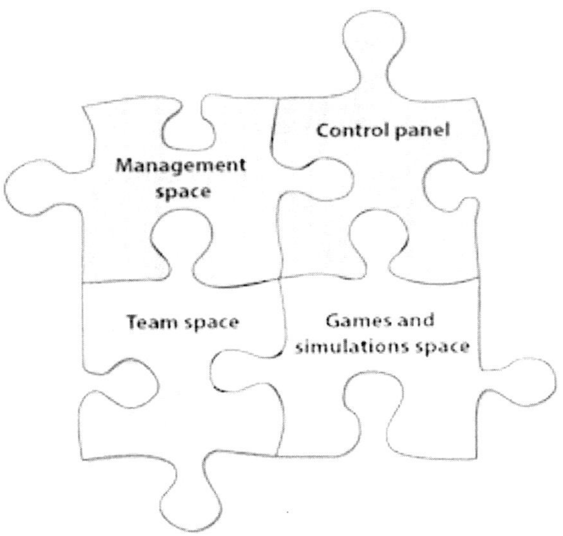

The *Management* Space

The *ENJEUX-SManagement* space includes four menus with different functions: (1) The *Create* menu, for the planning of a game or simulation meeting, (2) the *My Agenda* menu, for participation in meetings to which the participant has been invited, (3) the *My Profile* menu, for managing personal data, and (4) the *Join* menu, which enables participation at meetings without an invitation. Let us look at these different functions.

The *Create* menu is used to plan game activities that will be the subject of a meeting; a title; a brief description of the agenda or plan; and choice of time slot(s) using a calendar. One or several games and simulations can be chosen from a directory (Figure 2) and participants selected from a default list, a personal list of contacts, or a research tool. Passwords can be set up for private meetings, and invitations or reminder messages sent. The meeting coordinator or supervisor can also add complementary activities such as PowerPoint multimedia presentations, sharing of office applications or drawing software, video viewing,

Figure 2. Web page with directory for choosing a game

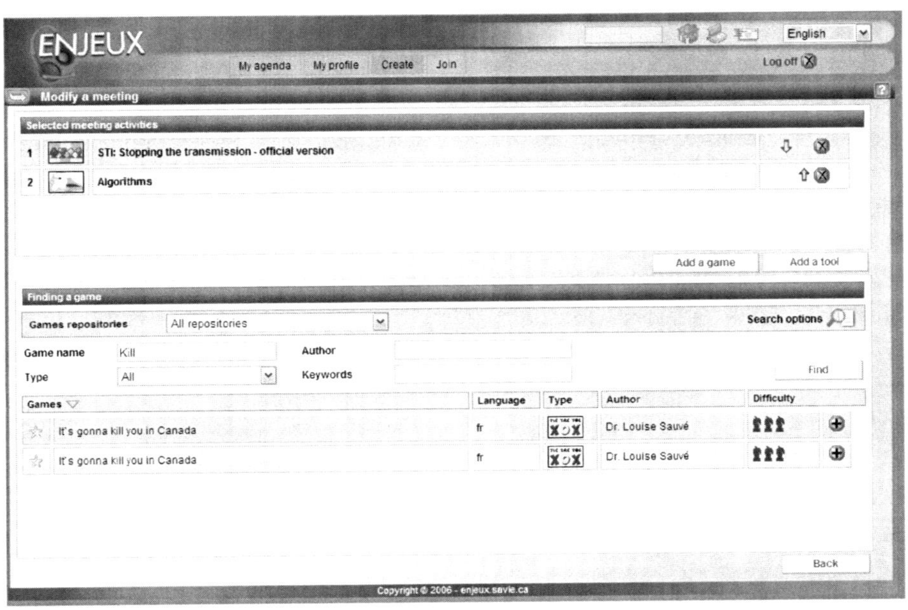

Figure 3. Agenda page showing meeting date and length

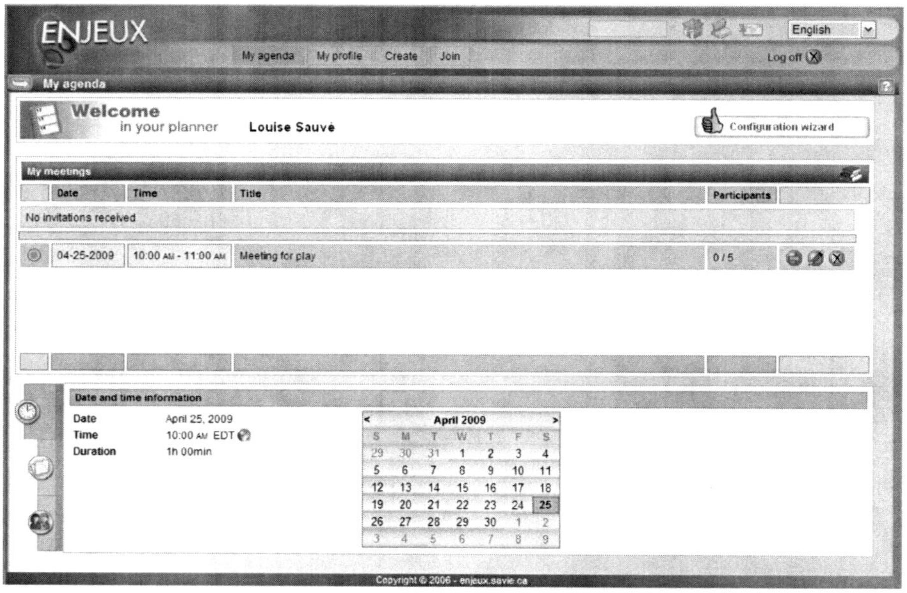

animation using a white board, or annotations on multimedia and video presentations.

The *My Agenda* menu displays invitations for games or simulations and the meetings for which the participant has accepted invitations. She can find here the description of each meeting: title of the session, date, duration, number of players (2-25), as well as the session description and proposed activities (Figure 3).

The *My Profile* menu manages the participant's personal data (last and first name, address, choice of avatar or photo), his archives (content of his private and public chats), and lists of activities (games, simulations, shared documents) for each meeting in which he participated. The participant can create a list of contacts (to facilitate the choice of participants when calling a meeting) and a personal list of games.

The *Join* menu allows all members of a given group to accept an invitation to participate at a game being validated when the participants have not received personal invitations via their agendas. This facilitates meetings that are scheduled by members of an organization but are accessible to all.

The *Team* Space

The *Team* space (Figure 4), also called the *Waiting Room*, is used to create teams in a game or simulation, by specifying the number of teams, the name of each team, designation of the team leaders and grouping of players in each team. When the teams have been created, all players are gathered in a Waiting Room in audio-conference mode. This room also allows the game supervisor or the coordinator of a simulation to select the communication mode of the exchanges (audio-conference or video-conference) and to communicate by audio or text with certain participants to ensure that all participants are present before activating the *Games and Simulations* space.

The *Games and Simulations* Space

The *Games and Simulations* space (Figure 5) handles all functions required for the animation of a game or a simulation. This space is divided into two zones. Zone A, common to all users who participate in real time in a game or a simulation, lets users consult the educational game rules or

Figure 4. Web page showing team management

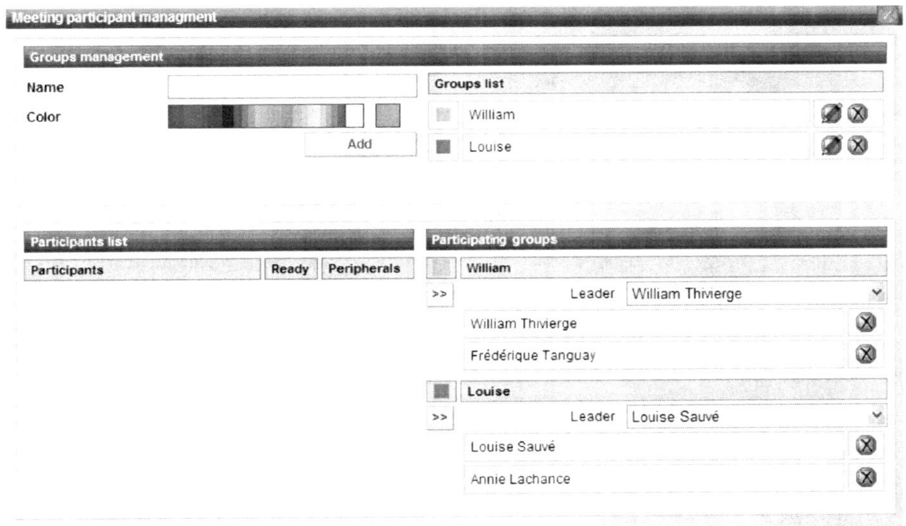

simulation instructions, answer questions or perform activities, display results (scores, successful or failed activities), and consult the online help. Zone B lets the coordinator and each player talk to (voice) and see (video image) the other players in his team (by private communication), talk to the players of the other teams (using public communication), and write private or public messages in a chat space. It also includes a control panel customized for a meeting coordinator, co-coordinator, or participant. We now examine it in greater detail.

Figure 5. Games and Simulations space

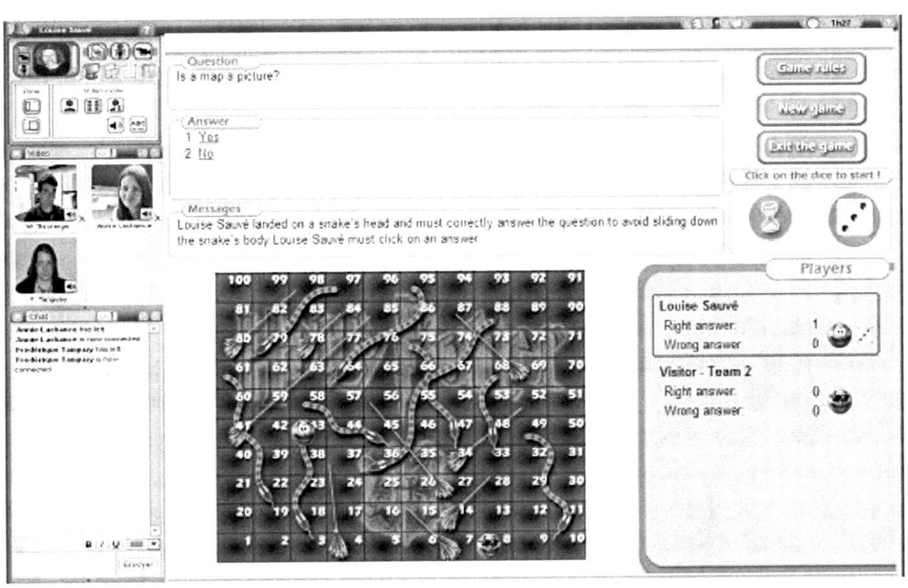

Figure 6. Control panel menus for the coordinator and co-coordinator

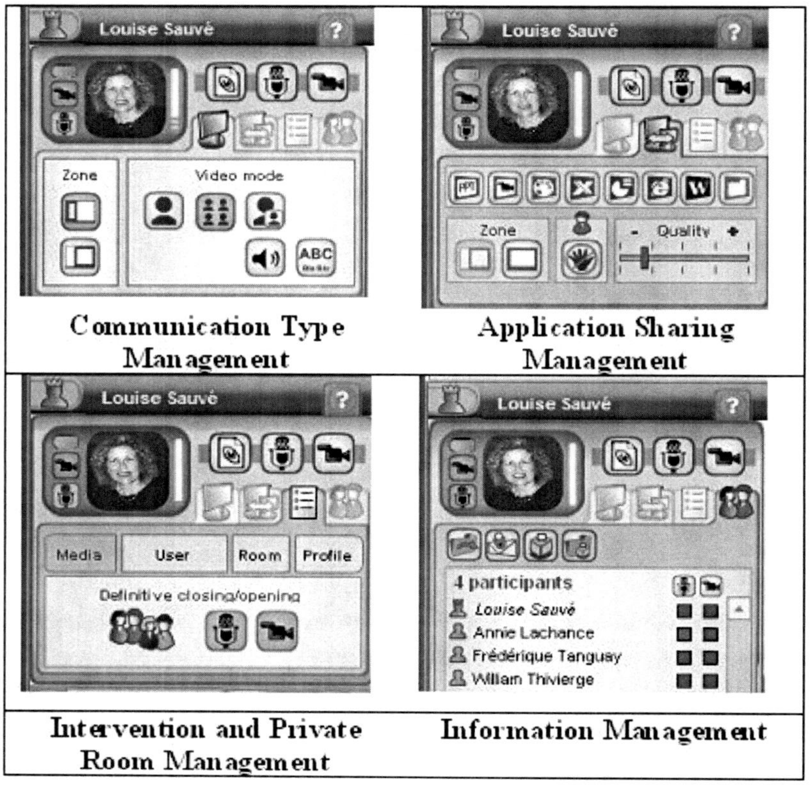

Coordinator and Co-Coordinator Control Panel

The coordinator and co-coordinator have access to a more sophisticated control panel than do participants (Figure 6). It offers four menus in the form of icons that provide access to all the options required for an efficient coordination of a game, as well as the activities preceding or following the game: (1) communications format, (2) application sharing, (3) management of interventions and private rooms, and (4) sound and visual management, sending of private messages and files, and participant polling.

The *Communication Type* menu offers three types of communication: audio-conference, video-conference, and text (chat). For video-conferencing two types of display are offered: (1) a small screen that groups up to twelve video screens in the green zone under the control panel, and (2) a large screen that moves the video screens into the blue zone, replacing the game or simulation. Also available at all times are four display modes: lecturer, group, alternating, random, and team (Figure 7).

The *Application Sharing* menu allows the coordinator to share a PowerPoint presentation, video viewing, the white board, an office application (word processing, spreadsheet, drawing software, etc.) or a web site with all participants. These tools facilitate activities that precede or follow a game, e.g., a PowerPoint presentation introducing the subject to be covered in the game, a demonstration video applying the subject that was covered in the game, or an exercise on a spreadsheet completed by the participants in real time at the end of the game so that the coordinator can check whether the desired knowledge has been acquired.

The *Intervention and Private Room Management* menu allows control over participant speaking order, as well as group meetings in private video break-out rooms with time controls. These private rooms facilitate teamwork on activities in a game or simulation.

The *Information Management* menu lets the coordinator exchange private messages with one, several or all participants, send them a file or verify their interest or comprehension by submitting a quiz prepared before or during the meeting.

The Participant's Control Panel

The control panel for participants offers three menus (Figure 8). The first, *Personal Data Management*, lets each of them manage his personal archives, agenda, contacts, and profile. The second, *Application Sharing*, permits the remote control of shared applications and the intervention on the current activity. The third, *Information Management*, offers the options of sending a private message, or a file, to one, several, or all participants, and answering a quiz.

Figure 7. Video-conferencing display formats

Figure 8. Participant's control panel

THE *ENJEUX-S* WEB SERVICES ARCHITECTURE

The *ENJEUX-S* architecture is characterized by *Web Services* development, based on a service-oriented architecture (SOA) model that ensures efficient management and operation of games and web simulations. We first examine the pedagogical and technological criteria underlying the choice of the architecture of our environment and of its programming languages. Then we describe its computer model, the development software, the standards and the programming languages selected, and the language adaptation of the environment.

ENJEUX-S Development Criteria

The choice of development technologies was based on both pedagogical and technological considerations. On the *pedagogical* level, the aim of the *ENJEUX-S* architecture was to be the least restrictive possible on the hardware side while being as flexible as possible in the integration of the Internet services, without requiring the downloading of any components onto the user's workstation. It was also to allow players transparent general access through a simple URL. For game playing or simulation, each supervisor (professor, game conductor, team leader) was to have the possibility of creating a more or less complex environment by using certain *ENJEUX-S* functions to adapt her game strategy to a particular learning situation.

On the *technological* level several considerations dictated our choices: (1) the robustness of the broadcasting environment, (2) a good potential for the evolution of the technologies to be used, and (3) the possibility of building components in the form of web objects that could be easily modified and parameterized by the supervisor and the participants, in order to create environments adapted to their needs.

These considerations led the research team to adopt a 100% Web Services architecture (SOA: *Service-Oriented Architecture*). This architecture employs *Flash*® technology for the video and audio components and Microsoft.Net technology for the application sharing components and the player management functions. The programming was done using Web 2.0 technology.

Figure 9. Model of the ENJEUX-S environment SOA architecture

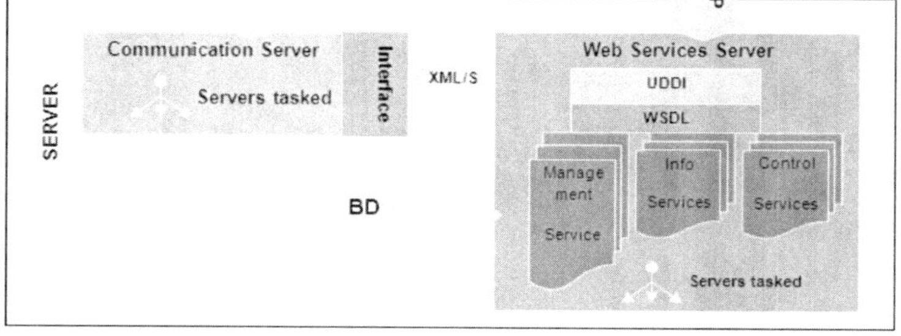

The *ENJEUX-S* Architecture

Figure 9 shows our SOA architectural model. This model is based on several layers: (1) a *client* layer, constituting the user interface. This layer comprises real-time communication components and functional game and simulation components; (2) a *network* layer which transfers data between the user interface and the servers; (3) a *server* layer consisting of a *communications server* for the management and the transmission of data flows in real time (video, audio, data) and a *data server* (*web services*) that executes database tasks or requests. The database contains data on players and game progress (profiles, player authentication, rules, etc.). Between the layers and the servers, the XML/ SOAP language permits encapsulation during information exchanges among distant and different systems when a data conversion into a universal language is required. Furthermore, this architectural model offers the possibility of calibrating and increasing the number of servers, depending on demand, an essential property to avoid service bottlenecks and slowdowns. Let us look at these architectural components in greater detail.

Client Layer Components

The real-time communication components (audio/videoconference and chat space) employ a basic architecture (*Component Framework*) that structures the functionalities of each communication component and links them with the core components (*Core Object Model*). These core components manage the peripherals (microphone, camera, screen capture, etc.) and the fundamental classes of the operating system.

The functional game and simulation components constitute the central part of the user interface. They comprise three types of elements: (1) games already existing on the web and usable in *ENJEUX-S*, the integration of which is transparent independently of their development platform, (2) games developed by the *Societe d'apprentissage a vie* (SAVIE) for *Carrefour de jeux éducatifs/ Educational Games Central*, and (3) games and simulations developed in the *SAGE* project.

Network Layer

The *network* layer uses the CA*net-4 communication protocols and services of CANARIE. This layer offers the possibility of combining a high bandwidth with an excellent quality of real-time multimedia and multipoint services, all while ensuring the management, the reliability, and the security of the network. It permits instant and simultaneous exchanges of data, and greatly facilitates transactional and interpersonal interactivity among a large number of users. Moreover, it enables interoperability with high-speed international networks.

Server Layer

The communications server is based on the Adobe *Flash Media Server 2®*. It manages communications between the real-time communication components developed in the project and the users. An access interface enables the communications server to be linked to the data server in order to execute the management tasks or requests.

The data server is the intermediary between client requests and the *ENJEUX-S* database. It provides *management services* by executing requests related to group management, user profiles and identification. The *information services* deal with requests by different components of the architecture. A group of *control services* make it possible to control certain user actions in games or simulations. These services, however, can only control games and simulations developed by SAVIE and by the *SAGE* project, and those that take into account our architecture.

The Development Software

Three development packages were used to develop objects for the *ENJEUX-S* environment, discussed here.

.Net Web Services

The *.Net Web Services* software was chosen to develop the web services of *ENJEUX-S*. This choice takes into account that it was already used for the creation of the user interface (Figure 9) and that it is preferable to maintain the greatest homogeneity between the different interfaces of the environment. This software has been used for developing large scale web services. It is also the basis for most *ENJEUX-S* management functions:

- participant management (registration, getting information, etc.)
- group management (reservation, invitation, etc.)
- tool management (getting available tools);
- game management (getting available games)

These web services carry out all the requests in the database as well as more complex operations, such as sending invitation emails or obtaining the connection availabilities of the communications server.

Macromedia Flash

Flash software is used for its performance in real-time communications. A zone has been set aside in the user interface to display the communication tools and another for the games and simulations designed for the web. Tools interfacing with the database are also available in the Adobe *Flash Media Server 2* platform. The Flash Remoting function allows the database to display the required information in the user interface, and to manage the proper operation of the system.

ASP.Net Environment

The integration of different technologies (*Web Services* and *Flash*) was done in the *ASP.Net* environment for the benefit of the most recent functions to be added to this environment.

Standards and Programming Languages

The use of standards defined by W3C (XML, SOAP, WSDL and UDDI) has permitted the development of objects meeting the norms and standards of accessibility, interoperability, reusability, durability and adaptability. These norms meet those of the Canadian computer industry. They ensure a ubiquity of services in order to make them accessible and transparent to most users. To participate in a game, the players are no longer required to download software and its components. All they have to do is access the *ENJEUX-S* web site.

The use of the *Web Services* architecture requires that all *Web Service* functions be converted so that these functionalities can be implemented in other environments, other sites or other applications.

The use of a client-server technology added to *Flash 9.x* avoids using a download technology such as Java applets that requires the installation of certain components on the client stations. Finally, to simplify installation of an *ENJEUX-S* server, the development team limited the technologies used to a *Flash* and *.Net*.

Two languages were dominant in the development of the project: *Action Script 2.0* (*Flash*) and *Microsoft ASP.Net*.

Language Adaptation

To quickly translate the user interfaces and allow multilingual displays, a translation matrix managed by a database was programmed and integrated into the organizational management interface, available directly on the web. By allowing an easy translation and adaptation of all texts of the environment, *ENJEUX-S* offers a user-friendly linguistic adaptation. With a simple selection in a scroll-down menu, it is possible to switch instantly to the environment in the chosen language. At present French, English, and Spanish are available. One user's choice of language is not binding on the other participants: each is free to select his own interface language in the same meeting.

ENJEUX-S TESTING

Testing the *ENJEUX-S* user interfaces focused on the development and quality assurance of the product. Its objectives were:

- to test *ENJEUX-S* in-house with the technical team and project researchers, and externally with the partners and collaborators
- to test *ENJEUX-S* on different types of computers and Internet connections
- to test specific functions of *ENJEUX-S* intensively to correct technical problems that might be encountered later
- to perfect the *ENJEUX-S* access and user guides

The *Learner Verification and Revision* (LVR) formative evaluation procedure was adopted. This method permits the improvement of a system while it is still being developed (Perron & Bordeleau, 1994; validated by Sauvé, Power, IsaBelle, Samson, & St-Pierre, 2002 and Sauvé & Samson, 2004 in the context of an online product). Our procedure consisted in validating the prototype with a limited sample of users in order to measure its performance.

Three groups of respondents participated: 18 members of the project's technical team and other SAVIE personnel for in-house testing, seven project researchers for both internal and external testing, and 77 partners and collaborators from the education, public, and private sectors (computer technicians, professionals, teachers, trainers, community educators, and others) for external testing.

Three data collection tools were used: (1) a test grid permitting us to execute, at a minimum, a predetermined series of tests and gather data on anomalies and technical problems. This grid was used by the technical team, SAVIE personnel and researchers of the project; (2) an evaluation and global opinion questionnaire completed after testing by the researchers, the partners, and the external collaborators of the project; and (3) an open question period between 10 and 15 minutes allowing for feedback on the use of *ENJEUX-S* during a meeting with 12 people. The data gathered concerned the user-friendliness, usefulness, technical difficulties, and anomalies encountered during meetings.

In-House Testing Results

The experiments took place between September 2006 and January 2007. 14 online meetings took place with the technical team and the researchers of the project in order to validate the system aspects and to correct errors. The first four testing sessions uncovered the majority of flaws and technical problems. The fifth and sixth sessions were used to re-test and validate the corrections made, in addition to investigating some rather specific technical difficulties. Sessions 7 to 11 permitted us to achieve some stability in the environment and to fix more specific bugs. At the three last sessions, we verified the corrections to previously-detected problems and noted no further operational problems.

Communication Modes

The *ENJEUX-S* communication modes (video- and audio-conference) were operational and seamless. The choice of the *Flash Media Server* technology for the management of video images during video-conferencing offered a high quality video display, but required a lot of computing power and network bandwidth from the server for managing the digital data flow. The different tests let us establish upper video fluidity bounds for a system with limited equipment and connectivity, that is, the display of a dozen participants. However, having the computer handle the data flow by alternating the display of participants in pairs allowed us to noticeably increase their number in video mode and to ensure its use within minimal limitations of hardware and connectivity.

Moving from one mode of communication to another during a meeting revealed some instability problems. To facilitate data flow management, *ENJEUX-S* had given the coordinator the option of switching from video to audio mode and vice-versa during a session. This option, while perfectly stable when switching from video to audio, showed some instability when switching from audio to video. This problem was solved by having the coordinator choose the mode, audio or video, at the start of the meeting.

Games and Simulations

Two types of delivery for games and simulations were developed in *ENJEUX-S*: single-station for those existing on the web, and multi-station for those developed with the generic game and simulation shells of the *Educational Games Central* and *SAGE*.

Single-station coordination of games with *ENJEUX-S* is done by web sharing. The display quality and fluidity of a game in application sharing is directly related to the display quality of the web site in which it is run, no loss having been detected with any number of players. The sharing control request function permits all the players of the game to participate in turn. The actions and movements in the game are also followed in real-time by all players.

As far as multi-station games are concerned, two types of participation were programmed: individual mode and team mode. No problems were detected in individual mode, the actions and the movements in the game being seamless and in real time. In team mode, however, several anomalies were identified with games developed by means of generic shells that did not contain Flash programming; only the (newer) *Parcheesi* game shell operated smoothly in the tested version. Furthermore, when players were grouped in teams, some of them were unable to participate in, or to view the game. This problem was linked to the number of players as determined by the game or simulation. Thus, if a game allowed a maximum of eight players divided into four teams, and there were 13 participants, five of them had a blank screen instead of the game. To solve this problem, a *Spectator* function was programmed, allowing the extra players to watch the game;

Application Sharing

Sharing of office or web applications was operational and the screen display instantaneous. During tests it was discovered that the handling of shared applications was more or less user-friendly but required a higher level of training of both supervisor and participants than other functions in general.

The Presentation Viewer

The quality and the fluidity of slide presentations are very high thanks to the conversion of files into Flash. Only one problem was identified: the conversion of Microsoft PowerPoint presentations into Flash files deleted certain slide animation options when displaying them in *ENJEUX-S*. In spite of a software revision of the converter, this problem has not been fixed. The solution to reduce the impact of this difficulty for the supervisor was to insert a warning when converting the file into Flash and to offer instructions in the contextual help of the work tool to create animations with Microsoft files before conversion.

Table 1. Degree of user-friendliness of the ENJEUX-S tools

Respondents (n=84)	User-friendliness	Required training
Microphone and camera controls	97.6%	Minimal
Display and videoconferencing modes	97.6%	Minimal
PowerPoint presentation and video viewer	95.2%	Minimal
Games in multi-station mode (*Parcheesi*)	95.2%	Minimal
Agenda	89.3%	Minimal
Private video and audio rooms	84.5%	Medium
Meeting control by the coordinator (console)	84.5%	Minimal
Application sharing (office and web applications)	81.0%	High
Creation of meetings	81.0%	Minimal
Communications in the team space (Waiting room)	81.0%	Minimal
Team management	81.0%	Medium
User Guide	81.0%	None

External Tests

Following internal testing and bug-fixing on *ENJEUX-S*, sixteen meetings with project researchers and partners were held in order to validate the environment's user friendliness. These sessions were held with groups varying from three to eighteen people and different objectives: work meetings of the research team, administrative meetings, and training and demonstration meetings. 84 respondents completed a questionnaire.

The majority of respondents considered the functions offered by *ENJEUX-S* to be simple to use without much training, except for application

Table 2. Usefulness of the functions of the three ENJEUX-S spaces

Respondents (n=84)	Very useful	Useful	Little usefulness	No usefulness	Total of Respondents
The Game and Simulation Space					
Microphone and camera controls	97.6%	2.4%			100.0%
Display and video-conferencing modes	89.3%	9.5%	1.2%		100.0%
PowerPoint presentation and video viewer	71.4%	23.8%	4.8%		100.0%
Games in multi-station mode (*Parcheesi*)	59.5%	35.7%	4.8%		100.0%
Private video and audio rooms	65.5%	29.8%	4.8%		100.0%
Meeting control by the coordinator (console)	100.0%				100.0%
Application sharing (office and web applications)	71.4%	23.8%	4.8%		100.0%
The Management Space					
Creation of meetings	89.3%	9.5%	1.2%		100.0%
Agenda	89.3%	9.5%	1.2%		100.0%
The Team Space	97.6%	2.4%			100.0%
Team management	81.0%	9.5%	9.5%		100.0%
Communications	54.8%	35.7%	9.5%		100.0%
User Guide	71.4%	20.2%	4.8%	3.6%	100.0%

Figure 10. The Configuration Assistant

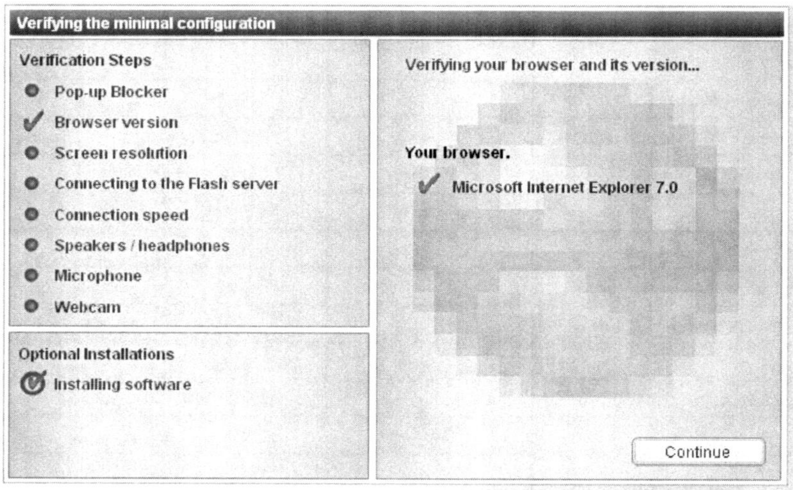

sharing (Table 1). Their degree of satisfaction was very high for microphone and camera controls, video-conferencing display modes, PowerPoint, and video viewing, as well as multi-station games.

The majority of respondents found the *ENJEUX-S* functions to be very useful or useful during their session, as shown in Table 2. It should be noted that the meeting control by the coordinator was considered the most useful function by the participants as a whole. Very few (1.2% to 9.5%) deemed the functions to be of little usefulness. The User's Guide was thought to be useless by 3.6% (n=3) of the participants, who preferred to use contextual help when needed rather than consult a guide with a table of contents.

Two problems also emerged during testing: running on obsolete computer equipment, and the level of network security.

Issues with User Equipment and Software

As stated earlier, *ENJEUX-S* is entirely a web-based environment that doesn't require downloading software onto the user's workstation. Still, some certain technical problems linked to the hardware and software components of outside equipment arose during testing:

- Client computers that were not powerful enough to receive audio and video simultaneously
- Absence of the *Macromedia Flash Player* software
- Presence of pop-up blocking software in web browsers
- Technical difficulties with web cameras or headphones
- Too-slow Internet connections

These problems were taken care of by creating an *ENJEUX-S* Access Guide that lists the minimal hardware and software configuration needed to use the environment efficiently, and by including a Configuration Assistant (Figure 10), which reduces to a minimum the technical difficulties encountered by a participant during his first use of *ENJEUX-S*.

Access Blocking by User Networks

An Internet address allows users to access *ENJEUX-S*. To open a microphone or camera, the

Flash Media server requires the remote control of the equipment via the port 1935. During testing, we noted that large organizations often had strict access limitations that blocked port access to *ENJEUX-S*. To overcome this difficulty, users had to contact the person responsible for network security in their organization to accept the *ENJEUX-S* Internet address. Likewise, the computer networks implemented in Quebec schools employ the NAT (Network Address Translation) principle and for safety reasons they close all ports except the HTTP port 80. Given this situation, the team developed a dedicated "tunneling" channel in order to ensure that the *ENJEUX-S* Flash server can establish a connection via port 80, without having to contact network security administrators.

ENJEUX-S PEDAGOGICAL CONTRIBUTIONS

ENJEUX-S's innovation is to make real the concept of "proximity" in the domain of online educational games by offering players:

- *Technological* proximity that provides: (1) ease of access and simplicity of use of the technical environment by the users as shown in the test results, and (2) a variety of tools and communication modes: video, voice and textual communications, display formats (individual display screens of up to 12 players, alternating with a larger number, or fixed with only the coordinator), private and public communication channels, as well as the following work tools: PowerPoint and video viewing, office and web application sharing, games and simulations, white board, etc. These functions offer a diverse communications environment that allows each player to communicate with other players in real time.
- *Spatial* proximity, synonymous with distance zero, which is linked to the *ENJEUX-S* attributes of bi-directionality, directness, and real time that draw players closer and interconnects them in a multi-player and multi-station environment. It also introduces a dimension of flexibility with its mechanisms of game, scheduling, and team management.
- *Social* proximity that introduces collective enrichment by adding to *ENJEUX-S* mechanisms of learning among equals, group affiliation, team work, and telepresence in online games. These mechanisms enhance and reinforce the team spirit, the sense of belonging, working together, collegiality, healthy and stimulating competition among teams, and group participation.
- *Cognitive* proximity in which the transparent integration in *ENJEUX-S* of games and simulations with learning content, in generic shells, allows the quick and simple development of online educational games adapted to learning needs at different levels of teaching. With the availability of these tools, teachers have new means of introducing methods of active pedagogy in online education.

Thus, the aspects of teamwork and real-time exchange in *ENJEUX-S* let teachers explore online new pedagogical directions that employ dynamic learning situations where learner participation is at the core of the process. In addition to strategy games, role-playing games, and interactive simulations, *ENJEUX-S* also facilitates the set-up of case studies, brainstorming sessions, and group discussions.

Furthermore, the integration of real-time communication tools and teamwork in the world of games and simulations contributes to reinforce the models of pedagogy based on joint acquisition of knowledge, sharing of experiences, cooperation between individuals, and collective enrichment in a group. We now consider how *ENJEUX-S* can contribute to mastering interpersonal competencies such as cooperation, teamwork, and communication.

Cooperation

Cooperation in games is often defined as the capacity to establish a relationship with others, to negotiate, discuss, collaborate, share emotions and ideas, develop bonds and friendships, or build a team spirit. It manifests itself in games when players join each other to reach a common goal. In team games the degree of cooperation and competition varies, and must consequently be balanced by rules to ensure that all the team members master the content. For example, in the game *Earth Ball* (Brand, 1968) the players face certain obstacles that can only be overcome by pooling their resources. This pooling requires group tasks (Gray, Topping & Carcary, 1998) that are governed by rules in a game or instructions in a simulation.

The learning of social interdependence, of empathy, listening and trusting others, leads players to become conscious that they cannot solve the problems presented to them by themselves, and that they must collaborate in order to succeed (Cioffi, Purcal, &Arundell, 2005; Hamalainen, Manninem, Jarvela, & Hakkinan, 2006). With the dynamics of online games, the cooperation between players in a team requires the addition of web communication tools – textual (*chat*), audio or video. These forms of communication, depending on the quality and speed of real-time exchanges, facilitate to a lesser (chat) or greater (videoconference) degree the participation of each team member in reaching the common goal.

Moreover, the mechanisms for assembling players into teams and the possibility of forming group strategies in audio or video without letting the other teams listen or see, support group cooperation and discussion – conditions that improve players' involvement, contribution to exchanges, reflection on the viewpoints of others, and decision making based on consensus.

Communication and Teamwork

The integration of real-time communication modes in online games or simulations provides them with dynamic face to face exchanges. Studies on team games have concluded that "the pleasure expressed by emotions awakened during an authentic exchange via the emotional complicity created by the game allows players to weave a bond and to enrich future exchanges" (Guillot, 2004, pp. 57-58). Others have emphasized that teamwork in simulation develops tolerance in a participant: he becomes more lenient or shows more understanding towards those with whom he lives in reality, since he has already lived the situation in a modeled environment (Klein, Stagl, Salas, Parker, & Van Eynde, 2007; Witteveen & Enserink, 2007). Some add to this that real-time exchanges, coupled with the mechanisms of a game that foster mutual assistance, for example encouraging team members to help their mate who can't answer a question or to complete a task that would allow the team to win some points (Sauvé, Renaud, & Hanca, 2008a). The actions of all these mechanisms encourage collaboration, mutual motivation, and acquiring joint knowledge. Peters and Vissers (2004) refer to this as "distributed cognition," "collective learning," or "organizational learning," underlining the impact of team collaboration which *ENJEUX-S* can facilitate so extensively. In most cases the introduction of conditions for real-time exchanges improves the communication abilities (empathy and listening) of participants while they master teamwork techniques and cooperative learning (Kiegaldie & White, 2006; Ramirez, 2001).

SUMMARY AND CONCLUSION

ENJEUX-S development required more than two working years for a multi-disciplinary team of specialists in educational technology, communications, and computer science. Its trials helped to make it robust, user-friendly, and accessible to non-specialists, while reducing, as much as possible, the technical issues that are inherent in a project this complex. The *ENJEUX-S* environment is composed of three spaces. Its *Individual Management* space, which allows the creation and modification of game and simulation sessions, is user-friendly, simple and flexible. The *Team* space makes it easy to group players and to exchange in text and audio modes before the start of a game. The *Games and Simulations* space exhibits an excellent display quality, stability, and fluidity in the audio and video exchanges and offers several video screen display modes (up to 12 participants individually, fixed for the coordinator or in alternation). In addition to providing the coordinator with ancillary work tools that facilitate his teaching (PowerPoint and video viewer, application sharing, white board, polling), the *Games and Simulations* space enables supervision by means of a control panel that allows the coordinator to direct all aspects of communication among participants. Finally, collaborative learning is enhanced with the creation of private audio and video rooms where participants can work or communicate in parallel for a length of time, predetermined or not by the supervisor.

In addition to enabling interactive games and of simulations, the *ENJEUX-S* environment permits an increased use of collaborative work by instructors. Both inexpensive and accessible on the Internet, the environment can also help learners develop life-long competencies by offering them a new, dynamic and interactive way of studying. It can also be used for leisure by diversifying the choice of games offered, that is, by offering educational games in which the entire family can interact, regardless of their location. Finally, the possibility of communicating in real time will help in bringing together and enabling exchanges among cultural communities dispersed across the country and the world.

Access to *ENJEUX-S* in libraries, schools, municipalities, aid centers or community support organizations will offer the most deprived members of society the means of communicating with others, thus assisting their social integration and reducing the digital chasm. Thanks to *ENJEUX-S*, it is no longer necessary to resort to downloads that might reduce access or usage, or even present a potential danger such as viruses.

The *ENJEUX-S* communication and collaboration environment is a powerful tool for supporting synchronous online learning, and reducing the isolation of distance students by facilitating their communication with other students (teamwork, socialization), teachers, and learning support staff. It is also an efficient management tool for geographically disbursed staff who need to meet regularly. Finally, it is a useful tool for research networks or communities of practice, supporting their collaborative actions and promoting the achievement of their objectives through knowledge sharing and new practices.

To use *ENJEUX-S*, each player must have a computer with a web camera, a headset and a high-speed Internet connection. *ENJEUX-S* is available in three languages: French, English and Spanish, and can be accessed at http://enjeux.savie.ca.

ACKNOWLEDGMENT

We would like to thank the researchers Víctor Sánchez Arias, Laboratorio Nacional de Informática Avanzada A.C. (LANIA); Thomas Michael Power, Laval University; David Kaufman, Simon Fraser University; and Gary Boyd, Concordia University, who came together to support the development of *ENJEUX-S* with their ideas and feedback. We also thank the staff of SAVIE (Societé d'Apprentissage à VIE), who brought the software to life with their excellent technical work and support: Pascal Boutin, Jérémie Charest, Gilles Simard, David Samson, Andréa Rodriguez Nava, Jean-Simon Marquis, Louis Poulette, Sylvain St-Pierre, Simon Gingras, Marc-André Girard, Jean-François Paré, Jean-Philippe Bessette, Raphaël T. Riel, Simon Vallières, Maxime Tremblay, Frédéric Dion, and Annie Lachance.

REFERENCES

Brand, S. (1968). *Whole Earth Catalog*. Menlo Park, CA: Portola Institute.

Cioffi, J., Purcal, N., & Arundell, F. (2005). A pilot study to investigate the effect of a simulation strategy on the clinical decision making of midwifery students. *The Journal of Nursing Education*, *44*(3), 131–134.

Gray, A. R., Topping, K. J., & Carcary, W. B. (1998). Individual and group learning of the Highway Code: Comparing board game and traditional methods. *Educational Research*, *40*(1), 45–53.

Guillot, B. (2004). La psychothérapie assistée par ordinateur: PsyaO [Computer-assisted psychotherapy: PsyaO]. *Adolescence*, *22*(1), 53–58.

Hamalainen, R., Manninen, T., Jarvela, S., & Hakkinen, P. (2006). Learning to collaborate: Designing collaboration in a 3-D game environment. *The Internet and Higher Education*, *9*(1), 47–61. doi:10.1016/j.iheduc.2005.12.004

Kiegaldie, D., & White, G. (2006). The virtual patient: Development, implementation and evaluation of an innovative computer simulation for postgraduate nursing students. *Journal of Educational Multimedia and Hypermedia*, *15*(1), 31–47.

Klein, C., Stagl, K. C., Salas, E., Parker, C., & Van Eynde, D. F. (2007). Returning to flight: Simulation-based training for the US National Aeronautics and Space Administration's Space Shuttle Mission Management Team. *International Journal of Training and Development*, *11*(2), 132–138. doi:10.1111/j.1468-2419.2007.00274.x

Perron, L., & Bordeleau, P. (1994). Modèle de développement d'ensembles didactiques d'intégration pédagogique de l'ordinateur [Development model for integrating pedogogy and the computer]. In P. Bordeleau (Ed.), *Des outils pour apprendre avec l'ordinateur* (pp. 513-553). Montréal, QC, Canada: Les Éditions Logiques.

Peters, V., & Vissers, G. (2004). A simple classification model for debriefing simulation games. *Simulation & Gaming*, *35*(1), 70–84. doi:10.1177/1046878103253719

Probst, W., Villardier, L., & Sauvé, L. (2004). A real-time configurable web-based tool for teleconferencing and telelearning. In C. Crawford et al. (Eds.), *Proceedings of Society for Information Technology and Teacher Education International Conference 2004* (pp. 644-651). Chesapeake, VA: AACE.

Ramirez, L. L. (2001). They're taking me to Marrakesh! A seventh grade French class's fantasy trip to Morocco. *The French Review*, *74*(3), 552–560.

Sauvé, L. (2005). Open and distance educational gaming: Using generic frame games to accelerate game design. In A. Lionarakis (Ed.), *Applications of Pedagogy and Technology, Proceedings of 3rd International Conference on Open and Distance Learning (ICODL 2005)* (pp. 393-398). Patras, Greece: ICODL.

Sauvé, L. (2006). *Rapport de modélisation du jeu-cadre Parchési* [Report on modelling the frame-game Parcheesi] (Research report). Québec, QC, Canada: *SAGE* and SAVIE.

Sauvé, L., & Power, M. IsaBelle, C., Samson, D., & St-Pierre, C. (2002). *Rapport final - Jeux-cadres sur l'inforoute: Multiplicateurs de jeux pédagogiques francophones* [Final report – Frame games on the Internet: Multipliers of francophone learning games.] Report for partnership, Bureau des technologies d'apprentissage. Québec, QC, Canada: SAVIE.

Sauvé, L., Renaud, L., & Hanca, G. (2008a). *Étude de cas du projet: Apprendre par les jeux* [Case study: Learning with games] (Research report). Québec, QC, Canada: *SAGE* and SAVIE.

Sauvé, L., Renaud, L., Kaufman, D., & Sibomana, F. (2008b). *Revue systématique des écrits (1998-2008) sur les impacts du jeu, de la simulation et du jeu de simulation sur l'apprentissage: rapport final*. [Systematic review on the impact of games, simulations, and simulation games on learning: Final report] (Research report). Québec, QC, Canada: *SAGE* and SAVIE.

Sauvé, L., & Samson, D. (2004). *Rapport d'évaluation de la coquille générique du Jeu de l'oie du projet* [Evaluation report for the generic game shell Mother Goose]. Report for the project Jeux génériques: multiplicateurs de contenu multimédia éducatif canadien sur l'inforoute. Québec, QC, Canada: SAVIE and Fonds Inukshuk inc.

Sauvé, L., Villardier, L., Probst, W., Boyd, G., Kaufman, D., & Sanchez Arias, V. G. (2005). Playing and learning without borders: A real-time online play environment. In S. de Castell & J. Jenson (Eds.), *Online Proceedings, Digital Games Research Association (DiGRA) 2005 Conference, Changing Views: Worlds in Play.* Vancouver. Retrieved December 15, 2005 from www.digra.org/dl/.

Villardier, L., Sauvé, L., Probst, W., Kaufman, D., Boyd, G., Sanchez-Arias, V., et al. (2006, May). *ENJEUX-S: Un environment d'enseignement synchrone au service de la formation à distance* [*ENJEUX-S*: A synchronous learning envrionment for distance education]. Paper presented at the ACED/AMTEC Symposium, Montreal, QC, Canada.

Witteveen, L., & Enserink, B. (2007). Visual problem appraisal - Kerala's Coast: A simulation for social learning about integrated coastal zone management. *Simulation & Gaming*, *38*(2), 278–295. doi:10.1177/1046878107300667

ADDITIONAL READING

Bello, A., Knowlton, E., & Chaffin, J. (2007). Interactive videoconferencing as a medium for special education: Knowledge acquisition in pre-service teacher education. *Intervention in School and Clinic*, *43*(1), 38–46. doi:10.1177/10534512070430010501

Chomienne, M. (2007). *The video teleconference: A valuable academic tool.* Quebec, QC, Canada: profweb. Available at http://www.profweb.qc.ca/en/reports/the-video-teleconference-a-valuable-academic-tool/the-issue/dossier/32/index.html

Dahl, A. (2009). Visioconférence en éducation: Exploite-t-on son potentiel pédagogique? [Videoconferencing in education: Are we exploiting its learning potential?]. *Revue DistanceS*, *11*(1), 1–16.

Robinet, J.-M. (2003). Visioconférence: Perspectives scientifiques. [Visioconferencing: Scientific perspectives] (Web bibliography). Retrieved May 24, 2009 from http://users.belgacom.net/bn580601/visioconference.htm

KEY TERMS AND DEFINITIONS

Application Sharing: A generic tool that allows multiple users to use applications that are either on one computer or on an Internet site concurrently.. For example, several users can work on a document at the same time and see their modifications included in the document.

Chat: A synchronous text communication between two users (private chat) or several (public chat) using a keyboard and software for instantaneous message forwarding.

Cooperation: In games, the capacity to establish a relationship with others, negotiate, discuss, collaborate, share emotions and ideas, develop bonds and friendships, or build a team spirit.

Educational Game: A fictitious, fantasy or imaginary situation in which players, placed in conflict with others or assembled in a team against an external opponent, are governed by rules determining their actions with a view to achieving learning objectives and a goal determined by the game, either to win or to seek revenge.

Simulation: A simplified, dynamic, and accurate representation of a reality represented as a system.

Video Teleconference (Visioconference): A point-to-point or multipoint conference that allow geographically-distributed participants to see each other by video and talk in real time via Internet networks (web conferencing) or by telephone (videophone), or with a mixture of both technologies (VoIP). A video teleconference differs from a videoconference. Videoconferencing requires sophisticated and specialized equipment resembling a television console, to be able to receive and broadcast pictures; broadcasting takes place across specially-equipped rooms. Video teleconferencing requires a web camera and a headset with integrated microphone.

White Board: A collaborative space shared by several users for sharing text and annotations, drawings, images, graphs, etc. Each user sees the shared items, and has tools to modify them.

ENDNOTE

1 The *ENJEUX-S* environment offers two interfaces: the user interface and the administrator interface. In this chapter we cover only the user interface.

Chapter 13
Advancing the Study of Educational Gaming: A New Tool for Researchers

Herbert H. Wideman
York University, Canada

Ronald Owston
York University, Canada

Christine Brown
Ryerson University, Canada

ABSTRACT

Most of the published research in educational gaming has had methodological limitations. Process data critical to understanding under what conditions games can promote learning are typically not collected, and unreliable student and teacher self-reports are often the primary data source used when assessing the educational efficacy of many games. To address these and other methodological issues, the authors have developed a research software tool, OpenVULab[1], which can record screen activity during game[2] play in classroom settings remotely and unobtrusively, together with a synchronized audio track of player discussion. This chapter describes the structure, operation, and affordances of the tool and reports on the results of a field trial designed to evaluate its utility. In this trial, 42 college students were studied using OpenVULab as they played a coursework-related web-based learning game. The chapter concludes with an analysis of the trial outcomes, showing how they concretely demonstrate the methodological advantages that the use of OpenVULab offers researchers.

INTRODUCTION

Researchers investigating advanced digital games[3] and gameplay as a medium for learning face a number of methodological challenges that, while not unique to this domain of study, are heightened by the technical and pedagogical complexities of the games themselves and the wide range of potential gameplay practices, strategies, and outcomes possible when they are used by diverse learners in differing contexts. Successful gameplay in genres such as role-playing games, simulation games, and real-time strategy games necessitates the application

DOI: 10.4018/978-1-61520-731-2.ch013

of a range of cognitive and metacognitive skills in the service of learning and problem-solving. In addition, where students play collaboratively, they need to apply social learning skills in support of collective problem solving, social negotiation, and distributed learning (Gee, 2003). The majority of game studies have used teacher and student self-reports as their primary data source, which places serious constraints on their utility. Even when quantitative, experimental, or quasi-experimental designs have been applied to the investigation of educational gaming, it has typically been in studies that address only a narrow set of achievement outcomes that can be readily quantified, that make little attempt to understand critical contextual factors, and that typically do not inquire into the mediating processes of player experience and interpretation or the development of player gameplay strategies.

More recently, game and simulation investigators have begun to make use of richer multi-method research designs that offer greater insight into the differential impacts of specific interface and pedagogical design choices made in a game or simulation and that further our understanding of the player's experiences, play strategies, and learning. However most of these studies still bypass important data sources, as gathering complete data on all aspects of gameplay has traditionally been very labor intensive, requiring the presence of obtrusive video cameras to capture player and screen activity. The associated cost and logistics issues have meant that such studies are typically run over a short time, often out of the students' normal classroom milieu, in specially-equipped labs. To address these limitations, we have developed the Open Virtual Usability Laboratory (*OpenVULab*), a software tool specifically designed to enable researchers to collect a rich set of process and outcome data in such studies, remotely and unobtrusively, in a readily usable form at relatively low cost.

In the following section of this chapter, we further develop the rationale for *OpenVULab*'s development through a closer examination of the constraints that traditional data collection strategies impose on gaming and simulation studies, and the affordances and limitations of extant software tools (developed primarily for usability studies) which can be used to capture play process data. We then provide an overview of the data collecting, retrieval, and analysis functionalities of *OpenVULab*, discussing the advantages these offer the researcher over other tools and approaches. A more detailed description of *OpenVULab*'s structure and functionality is followed by a summary report on the outcomes of a pilot trial of the tool, in which it was used to study the deployment of a simple learning game in a university freshman course. *OpenVULab*'s utility is then discussed in light of the pilot study experience. The chapter concludes with a brief overview of plans for the further development of the software.

METHODOLOGICAL ISSUES IN GAMING RESEARCH

Historically, the majority of studies of digital educational gaming have relied on teacher and student self-reports of attitudes and perceptions as their sole or primary source of data. Some have used open-ended surveys or interview schedules to probe perceptions about the game and its efficacy as a learning tool, whereas others have collected more quantitative data using Likert-type rating scales. A few have employed standardized evaluation forms for user assessments (e.g., Becta, 2001). Although data of this type is of value in uncovering certain usability issues and in determining attitudes and perceptions, it cannot provide an adequate measure of learning outcomes or gameplay strategies.

Self-reports of all types are known to be subject to halo effects—when participants enjoy an experience, they are more likely to report having learned from it regardless of actual learning (Gosen & Washbush, 2004). In a validation study conducted on an undergraduate level business simulation game, no correlations at all were found between self-perceived and objectively measured learning from the game for any of ten different types of learning investigated (Gosen & Washbush, 1999). Questionnaire responses completed following any treatment intervention are also subject to demand characteristics, in that a respondent's unconscious biases to respond in a positive (or negative) manner based on their interpretation of the researcher's aims can distort the responses (Orne, 1969).

Software usability researchers have shown that when questionnaire data alone are analyzed, the analysis is less likely to reveal severe usability problems with applications when compared to either data from direct observation of users' screens only, or from the viewing of user screens supplemented by the audio from testers who were instructed to verbalize their thoughts and decisions as they worked through tasks with the software (i.e., instructed to use the think-aloud protocol) (Lesaigel & Biers, 2000).

A number of studies have either replaced or supplemented learning and attitudinal self-report data collection with the use of quantitative learning outcome measures, using an experimental or quasi-experimental design in which the control group learns the same curriculum without the aid of the game or simulation being tested, or varying game attributes to discern their relative impact on outcomes (e.g., Cordova & Lepper, 1996; Sherer, 1998). To the extent that the outcome measures used are reliable and valid, the use of control groups and pre- and post-game testing makes possible stronger causal claims about the impact of games and game attributes. However, many of the potential learning benefits of advanced educational gameplay touted by gaming advocates are not readily amenable to paper-and-pencil measurement. Quantifying the assessment of such outcomes as the development of students' self-management skills and meta-cognitive strategies, their ability to collaborate effectively, or their capacity to abstract and transfer new problem-solving strategies has continued to be problematic. And as these studies have typically included no observation component, they have not been able to capture any changes in student practice that might provide process evidence for these desired developments.

The development of an empirically grounded theory of educational gameplay and its varied impacts will require a thorough understanding of the interrelationships between game design features, player practices, and a range of learning outcomes. But, as several scholars have noted, very few studies have attempted to collect the requisite data on gameplay processes and experiences needed to inform and substantiate current theoretical speculations regarding the educational benefits of game use (Pelletier & Oliver, 2006; Squire, 2002). What has been missing are adequate methods for collecting data that can be used to illuminate the relationships between game design, play practices, the contextual dimensions such as the social interactions and pedagogical interventions in which play is embedded, and learning outcomes (Pelletier & Oliver, 2006). As Pelletier and Oliver note, "...learning is not understood to flow unproblematically from the game as a text to the player, but to emerge from the interaction between various elements in the socio-cultural system" (p. 339). The importance of a range of contextual and mediating factors is suggested both by the few studies of digital gaming that have addressed some of these factors and by the broader literature of technology-augmented learning. In a recent meta-analysis of digital educational games and simulations, Vogel and colleagues found that contextual factors such as levels of learner control and student groupings were important determinants of learning (Vogel et al., 2006). The degree of self-regulated learning has been shown to influence outcomes in computer-based learning environments which have the high levels of user control common to advanced games and simulations. Winters notes in a review of relevant literature that in these environments the students demonstrating more self-regulated learning were more successful; their use of more active learning strategies led to greater achievement (Winters, Greene, & Costich 2008). Reviews of integrated learning systems research have made clear that the learning impacts of these systems are heavily mediated by the teaching practices surrounding their use (Wood, Underwood, & Avis, 1999; see also Becker, 1992).

Understanding the effects of game design attributes, including the user interface, is critical to the correct interpretation of game study outcomes. Software usability and human-computer interaction researchers have demonstrated that poorly-designed or hard-to-master interfaces impose so large a cognitive load that they distract from the software's true purpose, make it difficult for users to accomplish desired tasks, and quickly lower user motivation (Jacko & Sears, 2003). Without gathering data that assess ease of use, any lack of success may be incorrectly attributed to the underlying game design model or associated pedagogical theory, when in fact the model or theory was never properly investigated due to the confound imposed by the poor user interface. A large design study of a major package of educational science simulations clearly demonstrated how collecting detailed player process data can avoid such a confound, and how such data can contribute to greatly improving student learning from complex, open-ended educational software (Adams et al., 2008a, 2008b).

Adams and her colleagues had students think aloud as they investigated the simulations, sometimes pursuing tasks assigned by the researchers. Individual student sessions were videotaped and analyzed for usability "pain points" and conceptual misunderstandings. The research team discovered that testing with a relatively small group of four to six students was sufficient to find nearly all significant usability issues in a given simulation. On retesting, following the implementation of interface revisions suggested by the initial tests of these problematic simulations, students demonstrated substantially greater mastery, with no change in the fundamental design of the simulation being required. (The study's large-scale testing program led the researchers to develop a set of empirically-grounded guidelines for simulation interface design that have direct applicability to educational game design).

Two other technology-based learning environments, adaptive learning systems and intelligent tutoring systems, include automated data collection subsystems that capture data related to learner competencies, learning styles, and progress through the learning system to tailor instructional delivery. This data can be mined by researchers to trace learner paths through the system, looking at both individual and aggregate data on the resources used, learning paths chosen, time spent at various points, learning aids and scaffolds employed, and automated assessment results (Butler & Lumpe, 2008; Kelly, 2008; Schaiffino, Garcia, & Amandi, 2008). Mistakes and misconceptions can be traced and reported on (Merceron & Yacef, 2004). Some of these learning systems can automatically conduct associational analyses to uncover any covariance of factors such as learning style and mastery level (Lee, 2007). However these data streams, while relatively easy to collect and access unobtrusively, provide no insight into the learner's thinking and they will not capture spoken utterances, attentional focus, drafting processes or any forms of collaborative learning that learners might engage in while using these systems (O'Rourke, 2008). More generally, these techniques fail to take into account offline contextual events that invariably mediate learning. Different data mining metrics can also generate divergent pictures of user engagement (Feldon & Kafai, 2008).

A few case studies of educational gaming have incorporated observation of the gameplay process, either directly or indirectly (through audio and video recordings), in naturalistic settings such as classrooms and school computer labs (e.g., Henderson, Lemes, & Eshet, 2000;

Squire, 2005). This approach has a number of strengths. It allows the close study of the effects of a range of advanced gaming attributes (the provision of authentic learning challenges, powerful narratives, the assumption of new identities and roles, immersion in high-resolution virtual environments, etc.) and interface features on user behavior and learning. Observational studies of games can document any shift away from novice understanding to the development of expertise by mapping changes in knowledge acquisition and application, pattern recognition, strategy deployment, and metacognitive functioning. Individual differences in game experience and performance can be examined in detail. The impact of game players' social and educational worlds on their gaming experiences and outcomes can be explored in a way not possible with other designs, including critical factors such as cooperation or competition with peers, interactions with the teacher, the curricular and instructional frames in which the game is presented, and the game-related pedagogical supports and learning opportunities (such as debriefing) provided by the teacher. But the extremely high personnel costs for such studies (for both the direct observation time and the equally lengthy periods required for analyzing the resultant field notes and/or video) mean that researchers tend to use a small player sample (typically no more than one class of students) and to run the studies for intermittent periods over several weeks at best. This makes it difficult to make any supportable inferences about longer term, ongoing gameplay, or to generalize findings to other educational contexts, as it has been well established that the impact and outcomes of any pedagogical innovation are very dependent on the nature and quality of a specific implementation, including the teacher practices employed and a range of other contextual variables (Bransford, Brown, & Cocking, 2000).

More recently, game researchers have begun to employ multi-method research designs to gather the full range of data needed to understand how playing certain educational and simulation games affect learning (e.g., Eslinger, White, Fredrickson, & Brobst, 2008; Feldon & Kafai, 2008; Hamalainen, 2008; Pelletier & Oliver, 2006; Tuzun, 2007). Various strategies have been used in combination to gather the requisite data for detailed qualitative gameplay analysis, including in-person observation and/or audio/video recording of gameplay, direct screen capture and storage in real time for later playback and analysis, the recording of think-aloud protocols as part of gameplay videos or synchronized to screen recordings, keystroke and mouse movement logging, and the archiving of any online chatting during gameplay. In one of these studies, a prompted recall technique was used to elicit player understandings of critical play moments. Video of these moments was played back to users and their thinking and decision-making at the time probed (Hamalainen, 2008). Eslinger and colleagues investigated the use of a general purpose software framework and shell for inquiry-based science that incorporated simulations (Eslinger et al., 2008). The software environment itself incorporated many tools for the collection of process data, including keystroke logging and the tracking of the use of software features such as self-assessment rating sliders and the help system, and also captured audio and video recordings during simulation use through the computer's built-in hardware. Custom-written software allowed the researchers to visualize and filter the data logs and synchronize them with the audio-video record. Playback of key incidents could then be done using a timeline style interface, with video fully coordinated with the keystrokes and mouse clicks generated. This system made it possible for the researchers to conduct a highly detailed analysis of student activities, including teacher-student and student-student interactions, helping them clarify the process by which students built up their inquiry skills.

Even with the employment of powerful data collection tools, however, ecologically valid data cannot be collected if the study setting is not embedded in the typical contexts-of-use for which the game or simulation is designed. Clark has long contended that there is a heightened requirement for external validity with respect to instructional technology research due to the extremely context-sensitive nature of this technology's effects (e.g., Clark, 1989). Of relevance here are the findings of Tuzun (2007), who conducted a study in which educational game use was embedded in the ongoing curriculum of one class. It was, he noted, a "real" class in which teachers were constrained in the time they could make available for gameplay by their schedules and curriculum coverage expectations, and students interacted in normal fashion. Observational data clearly showed the central role of the teacher in mediating how and what students learned from the game. The study also highlighted a number of constraints around game usage in everyday classroom settings that the author contends would not necessarily come to light in other contexts.

The practice of having observers and/or obtrusive recording equipment present at a research site can introduce distortions in participant behaviors and outcomes in a number of ways: by creating demand characteristics in students, by increasing the likelihood of generating Hawthorne and novelty effects that distort process and outcome findings, and/or by inhibiting students' everyday patterns of behavior and learning. It is certainly true that conducting unobtrusive research in naturalistic classroom settings can be very challenging, and introducing any learning technology component into the test milieu heightens the complexities involved. But as we have seen, technology can also offer affordances for the collection of detailed process data that has considerable analytic value. A few commercially available software tools allow the dynamic capture of screen activity, and one, *Morae*®, (www.techsmith.com/morae) can capture synchronized audio and video from computer hardware as well, eliminating the need for an obtrusive audio/video recording system that might reduce the internal and ecological validity of the data. *Morae* can also automatically trigger the presentation of custom-developed questionnaires before and after application use, and observation notes can be indexed into the screen recording timeline for synchronous playback when analyzing data. It does, however, have one major disadvantage as a research tool (beyond its high licensing costs): it cannot be used for remote Internet-based testing, which means that it must be installed, configured, and started up at each test station (as in, for example a school computer lab), and any data files generated during a recorded session must be manually moved off the local system.

The capacity for conducting remote testing offers a number of methodological advantages and cost efficiencies. By eliminating the obtrusiveness associated with researcher presence and/or the use of video recording equipment, it reduces the threats to internal validity arising from the resultant demand characteristics and Hawthorne effects. And by significantly reducing the costs associated with data collection, as well as the burdens placed on participating school staff, it can make possible longer-term studies, which provide useful data on student learning trajectories over periods of extended use, and reduces the potential for novelty effects to distort study findings. Remote testing also permits testing in a much wider range of naturalistic contexts, such as in schools that are dispersed widely in geographical location, vary in their levels of technology infusion and teacher expertise, and differ in student population characteristics.

While a few commercial and freeware tools are available for remote screen recording, such as *Userview*® (http://www.techsmith.com/uservue), none offer the capacity to record synchronized audio along with the screen activity. This is a major deficiency from a research perspective, as the use of the think-aloud protocol has been proven to be a powerful method both for uncovering limitations in interface design during user testing (Dumas, 2003), and for eliciting thought processes in studies of situated cognition and decision-making (Gordon & Gill, 1997). In game research it can serve ends, unmasking interface issues and illuminating player misconceptions, learning strategies, and decision-making processes. Research suggests that the use of the think-aloud protocol does not inhibit performance or increase task difficulty for the user (Dumas, 2003). The capacity to record audio also makes it possible to archive the student-student and student-teacher dialogs that can be critical to the learning process. One of the primary functional objectives for the development of *OpenVULab* was to meet the need for a remote dynamic screen capture tool that could also record synchronous audio data.

THE OPEN VIRTUAL USABILITY LABORATORY

To address many of the methodological limitations of the game study designs and data collection tools discussed above, we developed *OpenVULab* to collect the kinds of rich and "thick" game-play process data we have argued is needed to answer some of the most important research questions about advanced educational gaming. *OpenVULab* evolved from a tool developed by Kushniruk & Patel (2004) for evaluating the usability of health care information systems. It has since been redesigned as an open source application and extended for use in researching and evaluating educational gaming environments. More specifically, *OpenVULab* is designed to work with any computer game, provided the computer is simultaneously connected to the Internet. The game or other application being tested does not have to run in a web browser window. The tool makes it possible to remotely capture process data in the everyday classroom context or other settings using unobtrusive techniques that do not require researcher presence or the use of extra devices such as video cameras or specially modified computers. This capability makes possible the remote administration of naturalistic field trials or experiments in situ, maintaining a study's ecological validity.

OpenVULab can collect data from game players before, during, and after gameplay without any researcher intervention. Before and after gameplay, users are presented with an online questionnaire designed by the researcher. The pre-session questionnaire could be used to query users' demographic information, previous gaming experience, or pre-game expectations, for example, and the post-session questionnaire might elicit users' perceptions about their game playing experience or suggestions for improving the game. During gameplay *OpenVULab* creates on its server a virtual videotape of all on-screen interactions. If a microphone is connected to the computer, player verbalizations are also recorded and synchronized with the video. This makes possible the recording of think-aloud protocols during gaming. The microphone also records student–student and student–teacher interactions, provided the people are within the microphone's pickup range.

OpenVULab Components

OpenVULab has a web-based interface and resides on a central server. It does not require any special software to be installed on the remote game player's computer, nor does it require any modifications to the programming code of the game. The tool is made up of four interacting system components: a *user presentation* component, a *researcher* component, a *relational database* component, and a *recording* component.

A testing session begins with the user logging into the web-based *user presentation* component shown in Figure 1 below. At this point the user is presented with a list of one or more studies that have been assigned by the researcher. A study consists of a specific task set by the researcher for the user to carry out, pre- and post-session questionnaires, and a URL if it is a web-based game. A task might be to play an entire game if it can

Figure 1. Screenshot of user presentation component

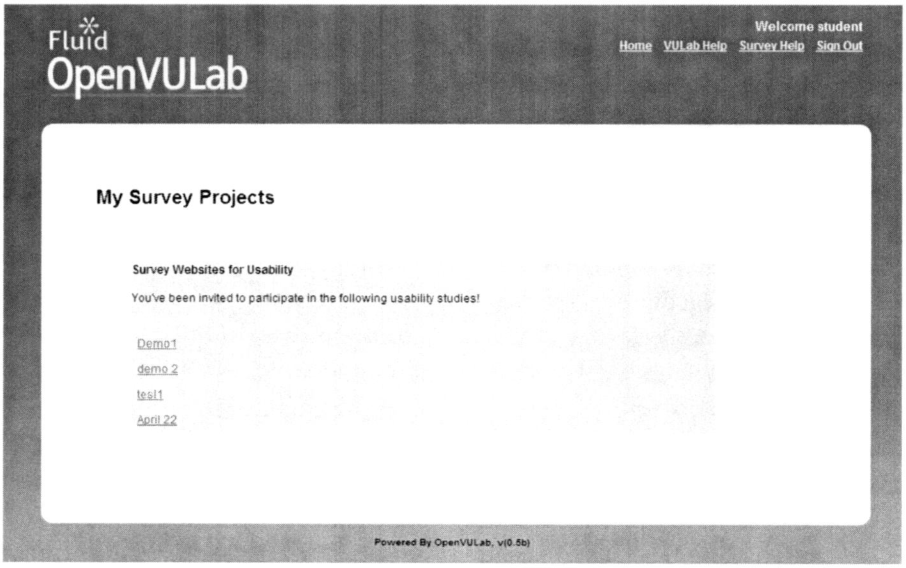

be done in one sitting, or to do only one component of a game such as design a character. Once a study is selected, the pre-session questionnaire for that study appears. After the questionnaire is completed, the user is redirected to either a website determined by the researcher, if the game is web-based, or to their desktop, if it is a standalone game, and the audio and screen recording begins. When the testing task is finished, the user is directed back to the *OpenVULab* site, recording is terminated, and the post session questionnaire is presented. At that point the study is complete and the user may log out or take part in another study if one is assigned.

The *researcher* component allows the researcher to design a study, assign users to a study, and retrieve study data. Figure 2 illustrates four options available to the researcher upon login to this component: *create a project, edit a draft project, review an active project,* and *view results of a completed project.*

To create a project, the researcher follows a template for creating pre- and post-session user questions. The questions asked can be in any combination of yes/no, true/false, short answer, rating scale, or multiple choice formats. Currently, this template is based on the open source survey tool *phpESP* (www.butterfat.net/wiki/Projects/phpESP/). The researcher also needs to define a task for the user and enter the URL of the site to be tested if applicable. During the creation process, the researcher can save a draft of the project and return to work on it later. Once the researcher is satisfied with all aspects of the project, it is activated and users are assigned. An automatically generated email message is sent to users inviting them to participate in the project. Once a project is activated it cannot be modified, although more users can be added to an active project at any point afterwards. This is done by clicking on the active projects list and following the menus. Once a project is completed, the researcher can de-activate it and it will appear in the list of completed projects. Completed projects cannot be reactivated; however, they can be copied and converted into new projects.

Project results can be viewed from within the researcher component while the study is still active or after it is completed. The results consist of user questionnaire responses and the associated

Figure 2. Screenshot of project management page

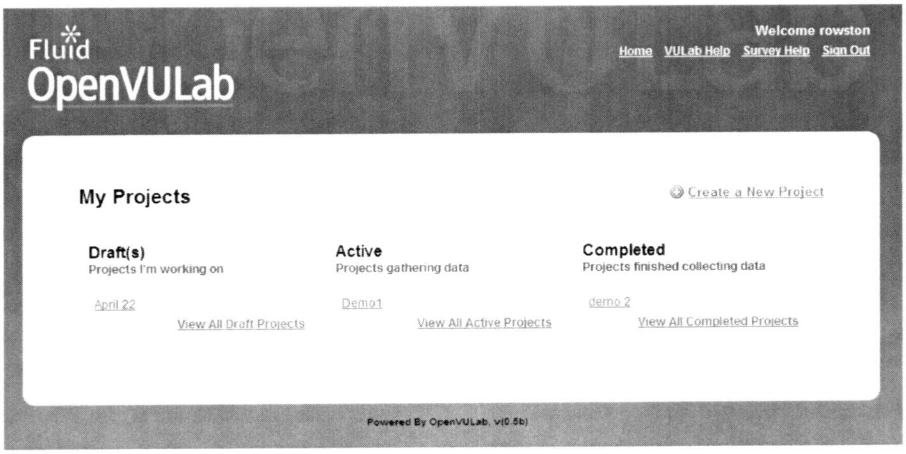

video. Data are stored in a *MySQL* open source relational database, which is the third component of *OpenVULab*. Currently, the researcher can view any individual user's pre- and post-session questionnaire responses and video by selecting the person from a list of users. Aggregate summaries of all questionnaire responses can also be viewed. A future version of *OpenVULab* will allow the researcher to query the database using predefined or custom Structured Query Language (SQL) commands. This feature will allow the researcher to retrieve the videos of users based on their responses to any combination of answers on the questionnaires. For example, to conduct an analysis of gender differences in game-play patterns, the researcher could query the database to retrieve all of the videos for females and then all of the videos for males (assuming the researcher asked players to identify their gender in a questionnaire). Or one could query the database to retrieve the videos of all users who answered particular postgame questions incorrectly. *OpenVULab* does not do any analysis for the researcher. Instead, the application provides the researcher with a raw data set that can be exported for subsequent analysis with external tools. The videos can be analyzed with qualitative data analysis software such as *Transana*® (http://transana.org) or *Atlas.ti*® (www.atlasti.com). These tools allow the researcher to add time-based codes to the video, labeling, and categories of events of interest for the data analysis using standard qualitative research coding techniques (see, e.g., Bogdan & Biklen, 1998). For example, a researcher might assign a "peer reinforce" code to all observed instances of peer reinforcement (as when one student compliments another's solution of a game-presented problem). Qualitative coding of open-ended questionnaire responses can also be developed. Quantitative questionnaire responses can be analyzed using any common statistical package such as *SPSS*®.

The fourth component of *OpenVULab*, called *RASCAL*, does the audio and video recording. *RASCAL* consists of a JAR file (or Java ARchive) and a server module. The JAR file runs in the background of the user's web browser after submitting the pre-session questionnaire and ends when the user is ready to complete the post-session questionnaire. This file invokes rapid snapshots of the user's screen, compresses them, and uploads them to the server. It also uploads microphone audio to the server. The RASCAL server module synchronizes the screen snapshots with the audio file and assembles a video file. Links to this file are then placed in the relational database.

OpenVULab Research Affordances: A Recap

OpenVULab offers a number of powerful affordances to the researcher. Its capacity for remote deployment and administration makes it much more feasible to evaluate game use outside of major urban centers and in remote areas where travel costs may be prohibitive, greatly expanding the repertoire of naturalistic settings available for unobtrusive study and (potentially) the capability to generalize study findings. In addition, by not requiring the researcher's presence on-site during data collection, it greatly reduces the cost per site of collecting rich data, making it possible for more sites to be researched within a given budget—also potentially increasing study generalizations. The detailed process data *OpenVULab* provides is another advantage as it makes it possible to uncover unanticipated game practices and outcomes. This will be of great value in understanding the relationship of gaming processes and practices to outcomes that are assessed either via *OpenVULab* itself or using additional measures. Finally, because *OpenVULab* is an open source application, it can be downloaded at no cost and customized to suit a particular researcher's needs. At the same time, the development community can contribute computer code that fixes bugs and enhances its features.[4]

OPENVULAB FIELD TESTING

Tests of *OpenVULab* were conducted in a computer laboratory of a university in a large Canadian city. The computers used for the test were PCs with a hardware configuration that was standard throughout all of the university's labs. Students were asked to play a simple game, similar to *Trivial Pursuit®*, during their regularly scheduled 50 minute class period. The web-based game shell package was chosen because it did not require substantial changes to the hardware or software available in the lab, and it did not require 3D video functionality. The only requirement to play the game was that the computers had Internet connectivity and sound capability and the only modification made to the computers was that the pop-up blocker security feature was temporarily disabled. This was necessary for the games to run. The game shell allowed the teacher to enter content specific to the course, thereby enabling the students to use the game as a review of materials in preparation for writing their mid-term exam. This provided the researchers with a realistic educational context to test *OpenVULab*'s functionality, usability, and potential for gathering data that would be of value to game developers and researchers.

Procedure

Two separate testing sessions were run, using two classes from the university's School of Business. The students were all enrolled in an introductory level course called Introduction to Business Systems, which is a required course for students in the Information Technology, Accounting, and Business Administration degree programs. Of the 80 students enrolled in the course, 42 volunteered to participate in the field test. The two classes regularly attended classes in the laboratory used and so ecological validity was ensured for the field study. The students had all attended a minimum of six classes in the laboratory prior to the field test, where they had received instructions related to the logon procedures used in the lab, and completed exercises requiring them to navigate around the Internet and use basic software packages. Students were provided with written instructions on navigating to the *OpenVULab* website, but no additional information was presented.

A single game could be played in less than 30 minutes, allowing the students to complete at least one full game in the 50 minute period available. The students played the game in teams of two to four people, with each team using a single

Figure 3. Screenshot of TRIVIA game

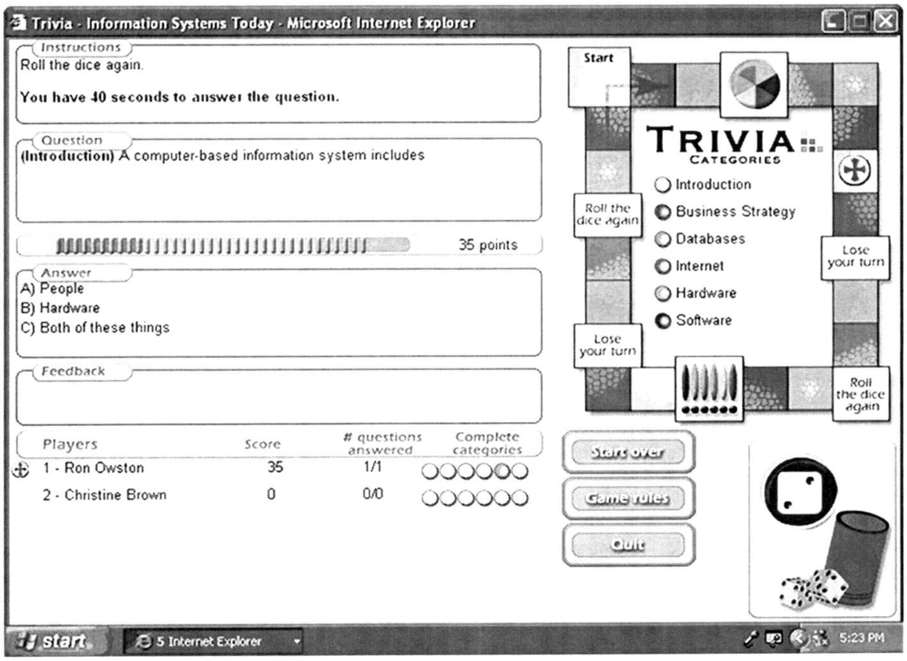

computer. In the first trial 10 game playing sessions were recorded using *OpenVULab*, however technical issues with the microphone resulted in very faint audio recordings. A second test was conducted, and clear audio and video data were captured from the eight game sessions.

The students engaged in game playing using a shell called *Trivia* (see Figure 3). This game, modeled after the board game *Trivial Pursuit,* is one of several game shells available online at *Educational Games Central* (http://egc.savie.ca). The game shell allowed the researchers and teacher to modify all of the instructions: the board design, the number of players allowed on a team, length of time the game would run, the questions and feedback presented to the players, and other administrative aspects of the game. One of the researchers, who had previously taught the course, created and entered 60 multiple choice questions for the students to answer based on the textbook material that was to be included in the students' midterm exam. The questions were organized into six categories based on the textbook chapters, and were ranked as being "easy," "intermediate," or "hard." Initially, students were presented with questions ranked as being "easy," however as they progressed through the game the questions presented were from the "intermediate" and then "hard" categories. Students were instructed not to refer to their textbook or any other documents during gameplay.

On entering the *OpenVULab* environment, students were presented with a short pre-game questionnaire developed specifically for this study. Data, including demographic information such as gender, age, and computer experience, were gathered from the players. Upon completion of the questionnaire, *OpenVULab* redirected them to the *Trivia* website so that they could begin playing the game.

Students selected the order in which they would play the game by selecting a name from a list prior to play. The game was loaded by clicking on the "Start" button. Players then commenced gameplay by clicking on the picture of dice, thereby "rolling the dice." The game automatically moved a player's game token around the board, and then selected and displayed a multiple choice question based on the category that the token landed on. The question was presented to the student with four possible answers, and the student had 40 seconds to answer. If they answered the question correctly they were awarded a token corresponding to that category. If the student answered the question incorrectly, feedback was presented on screen, and the next player was prompted to roll the dice. The first student to gather tokens for all six categories was deemed to be the winner, and received a congratulatory message prior to the game ending. Throughout their game playing, students were encouraged to use a "think aloud" protocol, verbalizing their experience with and reaction to the game. Audio data were captured via a small microphone connected to each PC.

Upon completing a game, the players returned to the *OpenVULab* environment where they were presented with a series of open-ended post-game questions. Questions such as "Did you enjoy playing this game?" and "Did you experience any difficulties playing this game?" allowed the players to describe their experiences with the game.

Data Analysis

The audio and visual data gathered was entered into *Atlas.ti*, where it was analyzed using procedures described by Pandit (1996) for a grounded theory approach. Grounded theory is described by Strauss and Corbin (1998) as "inductively derived from the study of the phenomenon. . . . That is, [they are] discovered, developed, and provisionally verified through systematic data collection and analysis of data pertaining to that phenomenon" (p. 23). An initial case was coded, with three broad dimensions of user experience emerging: usability issues, technical issues, and play patterns. The remaining cases were then analyzed and, as a result, codes were added and existing codes were modified. Finally, the data from the pre- and post-game questionnaires were used to explore different dimensions of gameplay discovered from the audio and visual data analysis.

Results

Overall, the students reported that they enjoyed playing the games, and they felt that the game provided an interesting way to review the course material in preparation for their upcoming midterm exam. However, analysis of the recordings and questionnaires revealed that there were several aspects of the game that were confusing and/or frustrating for the students, discussed below.

Usability Issues

Students had difficulty at three specific points throughout the gameplay, namely accessing instructions while playing the game, loading the game, and starting the game. Each of these is noted below.

1. **Accessing game instructions**. On entering the game environment, players were presented with the option of reviewing game instructions via a link on the initial screen. These instructions provided users with information on how to start and play the game. Only one of the 18 teams read these instructions, and none of the teams made any attempt to return to these instructions, even when they experienced difficulties loading and starting the game.
2. **Loading the game**. When users entered the game environment, they were required to identify the players' names. Once the players had been identified, they had to scroll down to locate the button that loaded the game. Some users did not realize that they had to scroll down, and therefore were unsure about how to start the game. The audio recordings confirmed that users were confused and/or frustrated when they experienced this difficulty.

3. **Starting the game**. Once the game had been loaded, the players were instructed to "select the Start button." However, the game board itself had a square labeled "Start," and the actual button was labeled "Click to Start." A review of the video data revealed that some teams clicked on the board game square, and the audio data confirmed that users were confused about how to start the game.

Technical Issues

Three teams had technical issues when playing the game. After successfully gathering all six colored tokens, the winning player was required to answer one additional question in a category of her choice. Three of the teams experienced the game freezing before the final question was displayed. Analysis of the video tapes revealed that they encountered a "Script Error" resulting from an incompatibility between an earlier version of Internet Explorer, which was installed on the three failing computers, and the version required for the game. The problem was shown to the game developers using the *OpenVULab* video recordings, allowing them to identify and fix the problem. None of the teams in the second test experienced this problem.

Play Patterns

The audio and video data gave researchers the ability to recreate and examine game playing activities and provided insight into the players' experiences using the game system. The game players enjoyed using the games to review their course materials; however the usability and technical issues discussed above negatively affected their perception of the game. When reviewing the *OpenVULab* data, we found two unexpected playing patterns related to player identification and cooperative playing in a competitive game environment:

1. **Player identification**: Prior to starting the game, players were required to select a name from the list of registered players. As an early version of the game, the list of names presented to the players included only the developers who had worked on the game shell. The students studied the list of names, and carefully selected a name which they then assumed during the gameplay. They often referred to their team mates using these assumed names and it appeared that using different names enhanced their experience with the game, a finding that was unanticipated by the game developers and the researchers.
2. **Cooperative playing patterns**: *Trivia* was intended to be a competitive game environment, where the players were competing to answer more questions correctly in order to beat their teammates. The audio and video recordings revealed that the players worked cooperatively, helping each other to correctly answer the questions. It was noted, though, that the person who won the game was congratulated by their teammates as the winner, and individually claimed ownership of the win.

CONCLUSION

The field test results clearly demonstrate the feasibility and value of *OpenVULab* for the unobtrusive capture of data central to understanding many of the key elements of educational gaming without requiring that gameplay be artificially isolated from the educational context for which it is designed and in which it is normally used—the lived social world of the classroom. The well-documented importance of a range of contextual factors in determining educational outcomes (e.g., Bransford et al., 2000) and the evidence for their significance in educational gaming (e.g., Becta, 2001; Tuzun, 2007) highlight the critical importance of being able to research and evaluate educational games in conditions with high ecological validity. In the case of more advanced games that students might use for several weeks, *OpenVULab* makes it possible to study the entire arc of gameplay as it unfolds and is integrated into classroom life.

The field trial showed that *OpenVULab* can operate unobtrusively. After startup, the screen and audio recording functions were transparent to the user and did not change the appearance or functionality of the game in any way. No interactions with the tool were required of players during gameplay beyond those needed to respond to questionnaires. Neither the presence of a small table microphone, nor the request that students verbalize their thinking as they played their game, appeared to inhibit play in any way, and the synchronized audio recordings generated valuable insights into obstacles players encountered and their patterns of competitive and cooperative play. The remote, unobtrusive, and transparent nature of *OpenVULab*'s operation seems in practice to deliver on its promise of making possible the collection of extremely "thick" data without significant risk of triggering Hawthorne effects or other methodological artifacts that threaten the validity of more obtrusive techniques.

The field trial also demonstrated the value of *OpenVULab* for documenting unintended or unanticipated processes and outcomes during gameplay. The audio recordings revealed the surprising meaningfulness of assumed identity and role in a game where role playing was not a design element, a finding that is in accord with Cordova and Lepper's (1996) discoveries about the positive impact of opportunities for personalization on children's attitudes toward and success with computer puzzle games. They also showed the unanticipated predominance of a cooperative ethos during what was intended to be competitive gameplay. Findings of this type are crucial to research examining the basic processes of gameplay in different educational contexts, and to usability studies and formative evaluations focused on determining how a game's design, architecture, and rules will be interpreted and appropriated by players. The tool's capacity to record the conversations of a small group of players makes it possible for the researcher to capture much of the social discourse around gameplay that is central to situated learning and the functioning of communities of practice (Kirshner & Whitson, 1997; Lave & Wenger, 1991) and the collaborative nature of collective knowledge building (Scardamalia & Bereiter, 1992). Social interaction around gaming is often substantial (Mitchell & Savill-Smith, 2004), and its role in mediating learning from educational games cannot be ignored.

Through its relational database, *OpenVULab* facilitated the triangulation of audio and screen recording data with survey and questionnaire data. The value of this capability was highlighted in the trial: students did not mention encountering any problems when asked about difficulties on the response forms presented at the end of the gameplay period and made no suggestions for improvements, and yet our analysis of the screen and audio recordings revealed that they had encountered several operational difficulties in the initial stages of game use. *OpenVULab*'s capacity to capture real-time play data makes it possible for the researcher to transcend the well-known limitations of relying strictly on post-use surveys for illuminating user experiences and perspectives (Dumas, 2003; Shneiderman & Plaisant, 2004).

OpenVULab offers researchers and evaluators several other potential affordances that this pilot trial did not attempt to assess. By collecting rich process data, it makes feasible a more thorough exploration of the causal relationships between specific game design attributes, gameplay processes and practices and game-learning outcomes. An understanding of these relationships is crucial to improving the efficacy of educational gaming. In addition, it makes it far easier to assess the practicality and utility of a game or simulation across a range of real-world educational settings. Games that foster extensive learning in atypical demonstration sites or laboratory schools may not necessarily be practical or robust enough to produce the same exemplary outcomes in typical school cultures, due to differing student backgrounds and prior experiences, weaker school computing technologies, or a lack of sufficient pedagogical support in the classroom. Cultural differences can also affect the interpretation of game content, design, and images (Asakawa & Gilbert, 2003). With *OpenVULab* it should be possible to closely study game use at reasonable expense in widely dispersed locations and highly divergent contexts.

Finally, when it is more fully developed, *OpenVULab* has the potential to facilitate student learning in a more direct fashion. If made available to teachers, it could be used to deliver supplementary learning materials of any type before, during, or after gameplay, providing a channel for scaffolding and support at key points during the game. Students could be encouraged to externalize their reasoning and problem-solving steps at critical decision points in the game, having them respond to pop-up game journal questions. Similar techniques used in other learning contexts have proved effective in developing domain expertise (Bransford et al., 2000). Teachers could access a potentially rich source of formative data on student knowledge and strategies in real time through the *OpenVULab* database, making it possible to quickly and precisely determine which students need support to correct important misconceptions or advance their learning strategies.

Further in-house development of *OpenVULab* is being undertaken to extend its data collecting capabilities to a variety of other educational computing applications, to improve the functionality of the researcher component, and to increase the upload speed of sound and images from the remote PC to the server. Moreover, we hope to engage the game development community and other developers to contribute bug fixes, code, and design enhancements.

REFERENCES

Adams, W. K., Reid, S., LeMaster, R., McKagan, S. B., Perkins, K. K., & Dubson, M. (2008a). A study of educational simulations part I – Engagement and learning. *Journal of Interactive Learning Research, 19*(3), 397–419.

Adams, W. K., Reid, S., LeMaster, R., McKagan, S. B., Perkins, K. K., & Dubson, M. (2008b). A study of educational simulations part II – Interface design. *Journal of Interactive Learning Research, 19*(4), 551–557.

Asakawa, T., & Gilbert, N. (2003). Synthesizing experiences: Lessons to be learned in Internet-mediated simulation games. *Simulation & Gaming, 34*(1), 10–22. doi:10.1177/1046878102250455

Becker, H. J. (1992). Computer-based integrated learning systems in the elementary and middle grades: A critical review and synthesis of evaluation reports. *Journal of Educational Computing Research, 8*(1), 1–41. doi:10.2190/23BC-ME1W-V37U-5TMJ

Becta. (2001). *Computer games in education project*. Retrieved May 20, 2009 from http://partners.becta.org.uk/index.php?section=rh&&catcode=&rid=13595

Bogdan, R., & Biklen, S. K. (1998). *Qualitative research for education: An introduction to theory and methods*. Boston, MA: Allyn & Bacon.

Bransford, J. D., Brown, A. L., & Cocking, R. R. (2000). *How people learn: Brain, mind, experience, and school* (expanded edition) Washington, DC: National Academy Press.

Butler, K. A., & Lumpe, A. (2008). Student use of scaffolding software: Relationships with motivation and conceptual understanding. *Journal of Science Education and Technology, 17*(5), 427–436. doi:10.1007/s10956-008-9111-9

Clark, R. (1989). Current progress and future directions for research in instructional technology. *Educational Technology Research and Development, 37*(1), 57–66. doi:10.1007/BF02299046

Cordova, D. I., & Lepper, M. R. (1996). Intrinsic motivation and the process of learning: Beneficial effects of contextualization, personalization, and choice. *Journal of Educational Psychology, 88*(4), 715–730. doi:10.1037/0022-0663.88.4.715

Dempsey, J. V., Haynes, L. L., Lucassen, B. A., & Casey, M. S. (2002). Forty simple computer games and what they could mean to educators. *Simulation & Gaming, 33*(2), 157–168. doi:10.1177/1046878102332003

Dumas, J. S. (2003). User-based evaluations. In J. A. Jacko & A. Sears (Eds.), *The human-computer interaction handbook: Fundamentals, evolving technologies, and emerging applications* (pp. 1093-117). Mahwah, NJ: Lawrence Erlbaum Associates Inc.

Eslinger, E., White, B., Frederiksen, J., & Brobst, J. (2008). Supporting inquiry processes with an interactive learning environment: Inquiry Island. *Journal of Science Education and Technology, 17*(6), 610–617. doi:10.1007/s10956-008-9130-6

Feldon, D. F., & Kafai, Y. B. (2008). Mixed methods for mixed reality: Understanding users' avatar activities in virtual worlds. *Educational Technology Research and Development, 56*(5-6), 575–593. doi:10.1007/s11423-007-9081-2

Gee, J. P. (2003). *What video games have to teach us about learning and literacy*. New York: Palgrave Macmillan.

Gordon, S., & Gill, R. (1997). Cognitive task analysis. In C. Zsambok & G. Klein (Eds.), *Naturalistic decision making* (pp. 131-140). Mahwah, NJ: Lawrence Erlbaum Associates Inc.

Gosen, J., & Washbush, J. (1999). As teachers and researchers, where do we go from here? *Simulation & Gaming, 30*(3), 292–303. doi:10.1177/104687819903000305

Gosen, J., & Washbush, J. (2004). A review of scholarship on assessing experiential learning effectiveness. *Simulation & Gaming, 35*(2), 270–293. doi:10.1177/1046878104263544

Hamalainen, R. (2008). Designing and evaluating collaboration in a virtual game environment for vocational learning. *Computers & Education, 50*(1), 98–109. doi:10.1016/j.compedu.2006.04.001

Henderson, L., Lemes, J., & Eshet, Y. (2000). Just playing a game? Education simulation software and cognitive outcomes. *Journal of Educational Computing Research, 22*(1), 105–130. doi:10.2190/EPJT-AHYQ-1LAJ-U8WK

Jacko, J. A., & Sears, A. (Eds.). (2003). *The human-computer interaction handbook: Fundamentals, evolving technologies, and emerging applications.* Mahweh, NJ: Lawrence Erlbaum Associates Inc.

Kelly, D. (2008). Adaptive versus learner control in a multiple intelligence learning environment. *Journal of Educational Multimedia and Hypermedia, 17*(3), 307–336.

Kirshner, D., & Whitson, J. A. (Eds.). (1997). *Situated cognition: Social, semiotic, and psychological perspectives*. Mahwah, NJ: Lawrence Erlbaum Associates Inc.

Kushniruk, A. W., & Patel, V. L. (2004). Cognitive and usability engineering methods for the evaluation of clinical information systems. *Journal of Biomedical Informatics, 37*(1), 56–76. doi:10.1016/j.jbi.2004.01.003

Lave, J., & Wenger, E. (1991). *Situated cognition: Legitimate peripheral participation*. Cambridge, UK: Cambridge University Press.

Lee, C. (2007). Diagnostic, predictive and compositional modeling with data mining in integrated learning environments. *Computers & Education, 49*(3), 562–580. doi:10.1016/j.compedu.2005.10.010

Lesaigle, E. M., & Biers, D. W. (2000). Effect of type of information on real-time usability evaluation: Implications for remote usability testing. In *Proceedings of the IEA 2000/HFES 2000 Congress* (pp. 585-588). Santa Monica, CA: Human Factors and Ergonomics Society.

Merceron, A., & Yacef, K. (2004). Mining student data captured from a web-based tutoring tool: Initial exploration and results. *Journal of Interactive Learning Research, 15*(4), 319–346.

Mitchell, A., & Savill-Smith, C. (2004). *The use of computer and video games for learning: A review of the literature.* Learning and Skills Development Agency. Retrieved May 20, 2009 from http://www.lsda.org.uk/files/PDF/1529.pdf

O'Rourke, B. (2008). The other C in CMC: What alternative data sources can tell us about text-based synchronous computer mediated communication and language learning. *Computer Assisted Language Learning, 21*(3), 227–251. doi:10.1080/09588220802090253

Orne, M. (1969). Demand characteristics and the concept of quasi-controls. In R. Rosenthal & R. Rosnow (Eds.), *Artifact in behavioral research* (pp. 143-179). New York: Academic Press.

Pandit, N. (1996). *The creation of theory: A recent application of the grounded theory method.* Retrieved May 20, 2009 from http://www.nova.edu/ssss/QR/QR2-4/pandit.html

Pelletier, C., & Oliver, M. (2006). Learning to play in digital games. *Learning, Media and Technology, 31*(4), 329–342. doi:10.1080/17439880601021942

Scardamalia, M., & Bereiter, C. (1992). Text-based and knowledge-based questioning by children. *Cognition and Instruction, 9*(3), 177–199. doi:10.1207/s1532690xci0903_1

Schiaffino, S., Garcia, P., & Amandi, A. (2008). eTeacher: Providing personalized assistance to E-learning students. *Computers & Education, 51*(4), 1744–1754. doi:10.1016/j.compedu.2008.05.008

Sherer, M. (1998). The effect of computerized simulation games on the moral development of junior and senior high-school students. *Computers in Human Behavior, 14*(2), 375–386. doi:10.1016/S0747-5632(98)00013-2

Shneiderman, B., & Plaisant, C. (2004). *Designing the user interface: Strategies for effective human-computer interaction* (4th ed.). Boston, MA: Addison-Wesley.

Squire, K. (2002). Cultural framing of computer/video games. *Game Studies, 2*(1). Available from http://www.gamestudies.org/0102/squire

Squire, K. (2005). Changing the game: What happens when video games enter the classroom? *Innovate, 1* (6). Avail. from http://www.innovateonline.info/index.php?view=article&id=82&action=synopsis

Strauss, A. L., & Corbin, J. (1998). *Basics of qualitative research: Techniques and procedures for developing grounded theory* (2nd edition). Thousand Oaks, CA: Sage Publications.

Tuzun, H. (2007). Blending video games with learning: Issues and challenges with classroom implementations in the Turkish context. *British Journal of Educational Technology, 38*(3), 465–477. doi:10.1111/j.1467-8535.2007.00710.x

Vogel, J. J., Vogel, D. S., Cannon-Bowers, J., Bowers, C. A., Muse, K., & Wright, M. (2006). Computer gaming and interactive simulations for learning: A meta-analysis. *Journal of Educational Computing Research, 34*(3), 229–243. doi:10.2190/FLHV-K4WA-WPVQ-H0YM

Winters, F. I., Greene, J. A., & Costich, C. M. (2008). Self-regulation of learning within computer-based learning environments: A critical analysis. *Educational Psychology Review*, *20*(4), 429–444. doi:10.1007/s10648-008-9080-9

Wood, D., Underwood, J., & Avis, P. (1999). Integrated learning systems in the classroom. *Computers & Education*, *33*(2-3), 91–108. doi:10.1016/S0360-1315(99)00027-5

ADDITIONAL READING

Federation of American Scientists. (2006). *Summit on educational games: Harnessing the power of video games for learning*. Available at http://fas.org/gamesummit/

Gee, J. P. (2007). *Good video games + good learning: Collected essays on video games, learning, and literacy*. New York: Peter Lang.

Isbister, K., & Schaffer, N. (2008). *Game usability: Advancing the player experience*. San Francisco, CA: Morgan Kauffman.

KEY TERMS AND DEFINITIONS

Ecological Validity: The degree to which a study's methods, materials and setting approximate the real-life situation that is under investigation.

External Validity: The degree to which a research study's findings can be generalized to real life settings.

Hawthorne Effect: A confounding bias introduced into a research study when the research participant's awareness of being studied affects the behavior and performance under study.

Intelligent Tutoring Systems: Tutoring software that incorporates internal models of user characteristics and ongoing performance, and uses these models to recommend educational activities to the learner and deliver individual feedback.

Internal Validity: The degree to which a research design controls variables so as to allow accurate inferences to be drawn from the findings.

Novelty Effect: A confounding bias introduced into an educational research study when participants perform better temporarily because of heightened interest stimulated by the introduction of new technology and/or teaching strategies.

Triangulation: The use of several sources and/or methods to gather research data. It is typically undertaken as a means of broadening the evidentiary base for theorizing and cross-checking suppositions.

ENDNOTES

1. *OpenVuLab* can be downloaded from http://wiki.fluidproject.org/.
2. Following Dempsey et al. (2002), a game is defined here as a rule-guided set of activities involving one or more players, which has goals, constraints, payoffs, and consequences; is artificial in some respects; and involves some aspect of competition (with self or others).
3. The term *digital gaming* is used in this article to refer to the playing of computer and video console (e.g., Xbox®) video games. For the sake of brevity and clarity of writing, the broader terms *game* and *gaming* are used here to refer only to computer games and gaming (unless otherwise specified).
4. More information on OpenVULab can be found at http://wiki.fluidproject.org/display/fluid/Open+Virtual+Usability+Lab. The source code can be downloaded from http://wiki.fluidproject.org/display/fluid/Source+Code.

Chapter 14
Designing Socially Expressive Character Agents to Facilitate Learning

Steve DiPaola
Simon Fraser University, Canada

ABSTRACT

This chapter discusses the design and implementation issues around creating an expressive but easy-to-author 3D character-based system. It then describes several application spaces, including simulated face-to-face collaboration, adaptive socially-based presentations in informal learning settings such as public aquariums and science museums, and multi-user, avatar-based distance education scenarios.

INTRODUCTION

Most computer-based communication and learning systems, such as web sites, information kiosks, or e-books, are informational in nature rather than socially-based. However, many educators prefer socially-based techniques to convey their message – they rely on narrative techniques, detailed lesson plans, flexible content, eye contact, humor, and voice modulation. Socially-based techniques, using a communicative face-based computer character system, can open up more engaging and human-centric applications in many formal and informal technology-supported learning areas.

DOI: 10.4018/978-1-61520-731-2.ch014

This chapter first discusses the design and implementation issues around creating an expressive but easy-to-author character-based system, then provides details for several application spaces including simulated face-to-face collaboration, adaptive socially-based presentations in informal learning settings, and multi-user, avatar-based distance education scenarios.

BACKGROUND

The last decade of the twentieth century experienced the merging of traditionally separate forms of audio-visual art and entertainment-based media. Boundaries separating media types such as live-action feature films, animation, simulations and games have begun to disappear, as these media overlap in many areas and coalesce. The key to the newly-forming comprehensive medium is interactivity. Advances in computer hardware and software have introduced the interactive multimedia presentation as a common base for a variety of audio-visual applications, including learning systems, with computer-generated facial and character simulation as a rapidly growing part of such presentations. For instance, current computer games make limited use of facial expressions, but next-generation computer platforms will provide hardware that is capable of delineating more complex characters.

One of the main objectives of designers is to introduce more realistic characters who can change expressions more frequently, demonstrate personality traits more clearly, and behave more interactively. With such innovation, typical gaming systems open up to wider, more socially-based application spaces. Besides more dramatically engaging gaming and conversational applications, socially expressive character agents are starting to show up in learning situations, including informal learning kiosks in zoos, museums, and aquariums as well as in online and computer-based traditional learning systems.

Some of the issues facing content and application developers developing face-based socially expressive character agents are:

- **Behavior:** Designing different facial actions, expressions, and personality traits is usually a painstaking and time-consuming process, where artists create the related animation using conventional 3D software and defining key frames for the movement of each facial feature. This is one of the major difficulties of increasing the number of moveable features (and also the visual and social realism).
- **Re-usability:** Designs for one head model are not generally usable on another model. As a result, even a similar action on a new head requires the design process to be repeated.
- **Interaction:** The need for a detailed design process limits the amount of interactivity and dynamic behavior a character can have at run-time. The characters cannot be completely autonomous.
- **Programmability:** There are few programmable components that can be re-used in new applications to provide facial animation capabilities. Each application has to be developed by implementing such functionality from scratch.
- **Level of detail:** Developers, especially when using conventional graphics software, have to deal with all the details of a head model to perform actions. Intelligent software that is aware of head regions and their functions can hide the details unless necessary, by performing group actions on all the points that are functionally related. For example, averting the gaze direction is a simple action that should involve only a single input as new direction. The rest, such as rotating eyeball points, should be taken care of by the software. This feature is missing in most design and runtime environments because they are not customized for face animation.

In the next part of this chapter, we will discuss **the design and implementation issues** of our *FaceSpace* system, which provides solutions to these problems in a unified face animation and simulation framework. *FaceSpace* parameter spaces allow designer to effectively control facial geometry, perform MPEG-4 compatible facial actions (Battista, Cassalino, & Lande, 1999), show expressions, and display behaviors based on definable personality types. All of these are encapsulated within a face multimedia object (FMO) that can be used in several different kinds of learning applications through programming interfaces. We

Figure 1. An online 3D virtual world with integrated voice avatars, virtual website displays and video walls (left); the real-life CoLab (right)

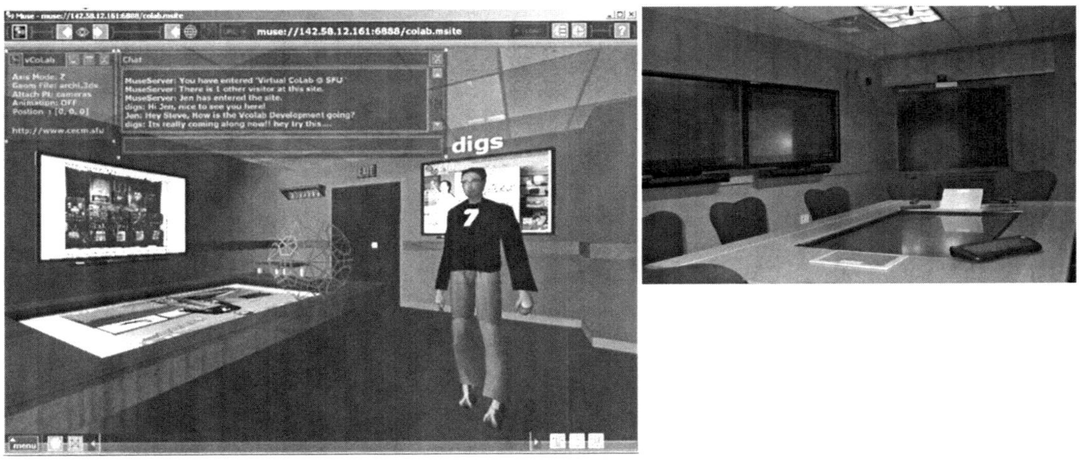

then will detail several *FaceSpace*learning application spaces. Before specifically focusing on facially-based expression agents, we will quickly review our non-facial (i.e., full character)-based research efforts, which have many of the same development issues as face-based systems.

NON FACE-BASED SOCIALLY EXPRESSIVE AGENTS

While this chapter specifically focuses on *facial* expressive agents as a newly evolving area in character systems, socially expressive character agents that use next generation techniques like artificial intelligence and real-time 3D online communication typically manifest as full bodied humanoid avatars or as other realistic or non-realistic creatures. This section will quickly review two research efforts in this area.

Our *Virtual CoLab Project* (http://www.colab.sfu.ca/Muse/) is researching how mathematicians, as well as other scientists and professionals, can use 3D virtual environments to collaborate and communicate with each other from different locations. It uses 3D environments with in-world rich media objects (e.g., browsers, video, 3D models, animation), avatar embodiments and spatial user interface constructs to create a shared experience that gives the remote participants a sense of telepresence, that is, a feeling that they are "there" in the same place with others. We are experimenting with virtual social and information environments (DiPaola & Collins, 2003; DiPaola, Dorash & Brandt, 2004) connected among themselves (all multi-user virtual spaces) as well as existing alongside and in connection with a physical collaborative laboratory, as seen in Figure 1, where our online 3D avatar chat application has been modeled after the CoLab laboratory at Simon Fraser University. Note that this system allows Java-based and web-based sites to exist on physical monitors in the *CoLab*, as well as on fully interactive texture mapped displays in the virtual world.

While the math *CoLab* uses 3D server-based communication and display technologies, our *Virtual Beluga Interactive* (DiPaola, Akai, & Kraus, 2007) is being prototyped as a location-based virtual reality learning exhibit at the Vancouver Aquarium in Vancouver, Canada. The goal in this project is to use socially expressive technology to better immerse and engage the visitors in complicated educational concepts about the life of wild belugas. We were interested in encouraging deeper exploration of the content

Figure 2. Screen shot from Virtual Beluga interactive prototype

than what is typically possible via wall signage or a video display (DiPaola & Akai, 2007). The beluga simulation uses extremely realistic graphics with a sophisticated artificial intelligence system that allows the virtual belugas to learn and alter their behavior based on the visitor interaction. It was informed by research data from the live belugas, (e.g., voice recordings tied to mother/calf behavior) obtained from interviews with the marine mammal scientists and education staff. Observation and visitor studies determined that visitors rarely visit alone, so the interface was designed to encourage collaboration. It allows visitors and their companions, via a tabletop setup, to engage in "what-if" scenarios of wild beluga emergent behavior, as seen by a large projection of a real-time 3D whale pod simulation (Figure 2) that uses artificial intelligence, physically-based animation, and real-time graphics. The program can be linked to the aquarium website to allow for an extension of the visitor experience.

The *Virtual Beluga* system takes advantage of high-end consumer 3D graphics hardware allowing it to be run on desktop computers without the need for expensive, specialized hardware or costly IT maintenance. It allows for:

- real-time interaction among organisms as well as between organisms and the viewer
- lifelike organic movement through the use of actuators ("virtual bones and muscles") and a virtual physics model
- intelligent behavior, in which some animals have the ability to learn from experience
- a true 3D environment with collision detection, realistic objects, lighting and shadows, as well as directional sound

The system, through its modular structure and intelligent object design, has several benefits that fit our design goals, including:

- support for variable content. Individual organisms can grow and change over time, and new organisms can be added and removed
- easily-updated simulation. Changes in scientific thinking can be reflected easily with non-deterministic simulations. No two simulations are alike
- interactive simulations. The viewer can perform "what if" scenarios
- full scalability. The number and complexity of organisms is limited only by the speed

Figure 3. Sample animated heads showing expressions, talking, and moving

and memory of the computer on which the system runs

FACE-BASED SOCIALLY EXPRESSIVE AGENTS

FaceSpace is our socially expressive agent authoring environment for creating, animating and communicating with computer-generated faces in many interdisciplinary applications such as gaming, interactive web systems, informal learning kiosks, and CD-ROMs, as well as in more formal computer-based entertainment and learning areas (Figure 3). This research toolkit is based on a hierarchical parametric approach that allows for an additive real-time language of expressions, emotions and lip-sync sequences. *FaceSpace* uses a parameterized model for authoring and analyzing facial communication. We consider face authoring as an expressive endeavor, and so the *FaceSpace* model includes the following groups of parameters:

- **Geometry:** A hierarchy of modules on top of 2D or 3D data, providing different levels of abstraction such as *Point*, *Feature*, and *Component*, allowing for image-based, line rendered, or 3D facial output (Figure 4)
- **Knowledge:** Including stimulus-response rules of interaction
- **Personality:** Long term individual characteristics
- **Mood:** Short-term emotions and sensations)

Animated heads are created from one synergistic system with the goal of communicating any (knowledge) stream using any head with any behavior.

One major contribution of this framework is the inclusion of temporal and spatial parameters (e.g., expressions over time), intuitive parameter spaces (e.g., personality space), and hierarchical parameters with different levels of abstraction (e.g., heroicness built on top of simpler behavior types). Besides the face-centric knowledge approach, and weighing towards communication and behavior of faces, another goal of the *FaceSpace* framework has been to decouple output details from the face-centric core, allowing for intuitive face oriented authoring which can be applied at any level, to any model, with any emotion. For instance, we could add an expressive audio sequence to a chosen cartoon face type, but add more goofiness with a little heroicness to the personality as it animates through the given sequence, outputting it as a 3D-rendered movie. Then we could take that same knowledge sequence and try it on a realistic face with a more angry tone, outputting it as an interactive sequence. Because the multidimensional parameters are aligned in a face-centric way, it is also possible to affect a face from another knowledge or expression data stream. For example, one application of *FaceSpace* has been to remap emotional channels of music to emotional aspects of the face.

In the following sections, we briefly review some related works, describe the basic concepts of *FaceSpace*, and introduce some *FaceSpace*-based applications which begin to work with our stated goals of a face-centric expression/communication-based system.

Related Facial Work

One of the earliest works on computerized head models for graphics and animation was done by Parke (1972; Parke & Water, 2000). It can be considered as the first parameterized head model, which was extended by other researchers (DiPaola, 1991, 2002; Valentine, 1999; Waters, 1987) to include more facial features and add more flexibility. Different methods for initializing such generic models based on individual (3D or 2D) data have been proposed and successfully implemented (Lee, Terzopoulos, & Waters, 1995). Parameters are usually grouped into conformation and expression categories, the former for building a particular head and the latter for animating it. The *Facial Action Coding System* (FACS) (Ekman & Friesen, 1978) was an early (and still valid) study of possible facial actions related to such feature points. Although not originally a computer graphics technique, FACS has been widely used by researchers in parameterized models and others. This approach has been formalized in MPEG-4 standard.

The behavioral modeling of animated characters has been studied by some researchers (Cassell et al., 1994; Funge, Tu, & Terzopolous, 1999). Funge et al. define a hierarchy of parameters. At the base of their pyramid is the geometric group, on top of which are kinematic, physical, behavioral, and cognitive parameters and models. Although very important in introducing behavioral and cognitive modeling concepts, this pyramid may not be suitable for face animation purposes because of the interaction of the groups and the need for emotional parameters as opposed to physically-based ones. Cassell et al. (1994) and Cassell, Vilhjlmsson, and Bickmore (2001) define behavioral rules to be used in creating character actions but do not propose a general head model that integrates geometrical and behavioral aspects. This will be discussed in more detail in the next section.

Face Parameter Spaces

The essence of the *FaceSpace* environment is a set of numerical parameters, each of which controls some aspect of a character's face and expression. Parameters are typically unitized vectors, each representing a sub-routine, which performs some low-level complex transformations on the part of the face it controls. Because parameters are abstracted from their low-level techniques, they have mathematically rigorous properties, such as the ability to be combined, subtracted, and added together, while still maintaining controllable and repeatable effects to their face model. Therefore, they can be used in any possible way with an application or authoring tool while still maintaining face naturalness. In this way, parameters can be built up to create complex emotions or personalities, or to allow any face to accept animation from any other face, or remap streams from other conceptual sources such as drumming or music, and still work on the face in an appropriate way.

Parameters can be varied independently to modify specific features of the face (e.g., cheekbone prominence, forehead height, and jaw width). The entire set of parameters can be exposed individually for full low-level authoring control, or a sub-set of these parameters with constraints can be presented to a novice user for customization and personalization. Higher-level constructs can be imposed on the basic parameter scheme by combining low-level parameters to create application-specific descriptive elements. For example, a user could modify the character's appearance from sophisticated to silly with a single control that simultaneously modifies eye separation, forehead height, nose scale, etc.

Groups of high-level parameters can act on the face simultaneously, creating lip-sync speech with one channel while specifying an astonished look for the whole face on another independent

Figure 4. FaceSpace parameter spaces

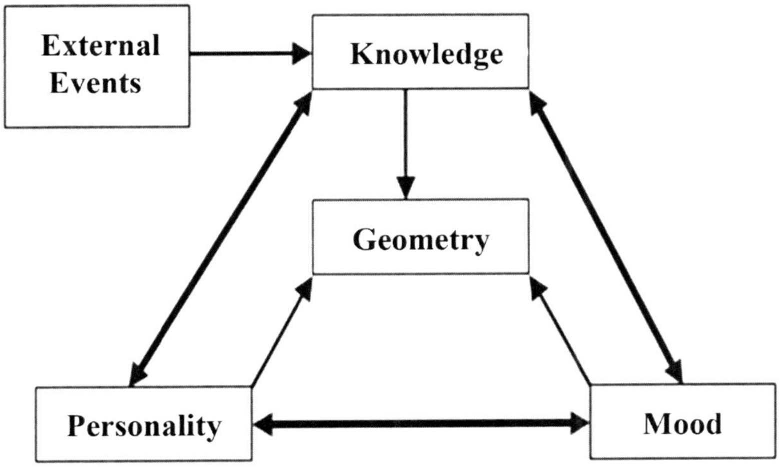

Figure 5. Neutral, talking, and frowning facial states (left to right) applied to four different characters

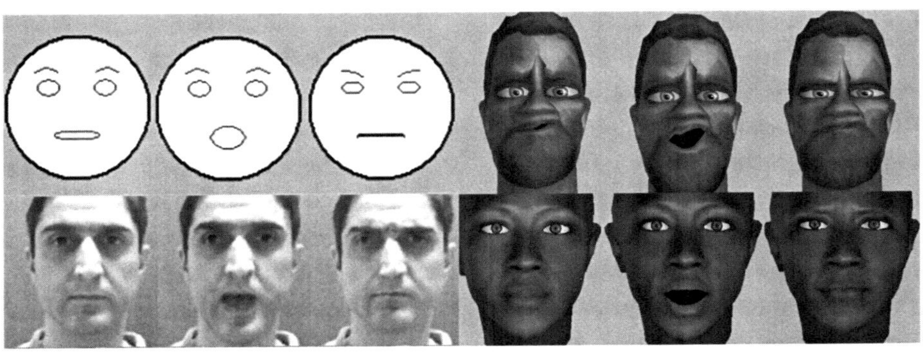

channel. Because of their associative properties and their abstraction from the actual face topology, results typically look natural, as noted in the example of Figure 5, although naturalness can be arbitrary as you move away from realistic. In fact, one of the driving forces behind our system is the ability to explore different dimensions of face spaces, to begin to understand faces as a language, just like the language of cinema, or painting, or modern jazz. *FaceSpace* allows the concept of faces and face expressions to be explored at an intuitive level.

Communicative Face

A communicative face focuses on those aspects of facial actions and features that express a message or feeling. Typically, this requires the animator or real-time performance actor (in the case of motion capture) to work within the non-facial specific technical tools of their craft (key-framing, 3D motion paths, point cluster manipulation, motion capture processes) while maintaining the expressions, personality, implicit message, and mode of the facial character in their head and using their craft tools to realize their internal narrative. Since face communication is ubiquitous, we have sought to make these communicative face-centric concepts part of the system with the efficient use of parameters and their structural patterns.

Rousseau and Hayes-Roth (1997) consider personality traits, moods, and attitudes as major parameters in their social-psychological avatar model. In a similar but revised way, we believe that the communicative behavior of a face can be considered to be determined by the following factors as shown in Figure 4:

- **Geometry:** This forms the underlying physical appearance of the face. Creating and animating different faces and face-types is done by manipulating the geometry that can be defined using 2D and/or 3D data (i.e., pixels and vertices). This geometry is based on a hierarchy of facial regions and sub-regions as illustrated in Figure 3. Our system decouples final output from the expressive content allowing a number of realizations.
- **Knowledge:** Behavioral rules, stimulus-response association, and required actions are encapsulated in knowledge. In the simplest case, this can be the sequence of actions that a face-animation character has to follow. In more complicated cases, knowledge can be all the behavioral rules that an interactive character learns and uses. See the work of Funge et al. (1999) on cognitive modeling.
- **Personality:** Different characters can have the same knowledge, but their actions will be different, depending on individual interests, priorities, and characteristics. Personality encapsulates all the long-term modes of behavior and characteristics of an individual
- **Mood:** Certain individual characteristics are transient results of external events and physical situation and needs. These emotions (e.g., happiness and sadness) and sensations (e.g., fatigue) may not last for a long time, but will have a considerable effect on the behavior. The mood of a person can even overcome his/her personality for a short time

Face Types, Geometry Space, and the Hierarchical Head Model

Head geometry is the basis for the proposed multi-dimensional model. Figure 6 shows our modular head model designed as a hierarchy of objects. Each one of these objects exposes its own functionality and parameters, and can be activated only when necessary. The level of details is locally controlled by advancing down the tree structure. As illustrated in Figure 3, this allows the model to work with different amount of details, from a simplistic cartoon to complicated 3D heads. Also, dependence on the type of data (2D or 3D) only exists at the lower levels of the hierarchy, so the model exposes the same interface to users regardless of data type and details

Face regions are small areas that usually move together and are controlled by feature points. *FaceSpace* components (e.g., eye area), are related groups of these regions. The effect of different facial regions (Figure 7) on each other during facial actions is a major issue when defining hierarchical and regional models for face. As we will see later, this is dealt with by allowing transform groups and also the control of higher-level objects on multiple child regions. Considering the communicative objectives, the head model, as shown in Figure 5, is tested with a variety of geometry types, including simple 2D cartoons, 3D cartoon heads, photo-realistic images, and 3D realistic heads. Note how this parameterized approach retains face characteristics while adding expression states, as in the 3D cartoon character's asymmetrical mouth.

Behavioral Parameter Spaces

Knowledge, personality, and mood are behavioral parameter spaces. The best way to describe these

Figure 6. Head object aggregation model

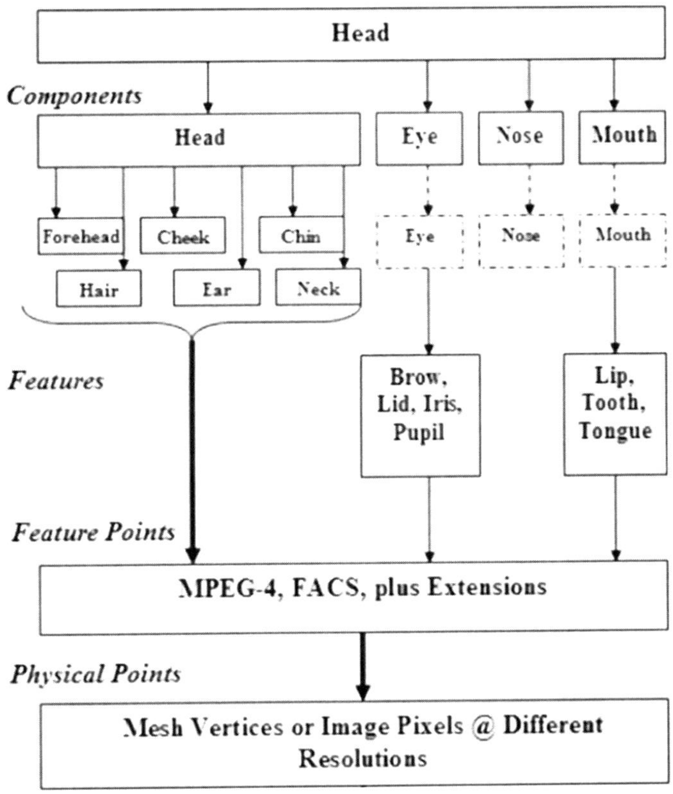

Figure 7. Face regions

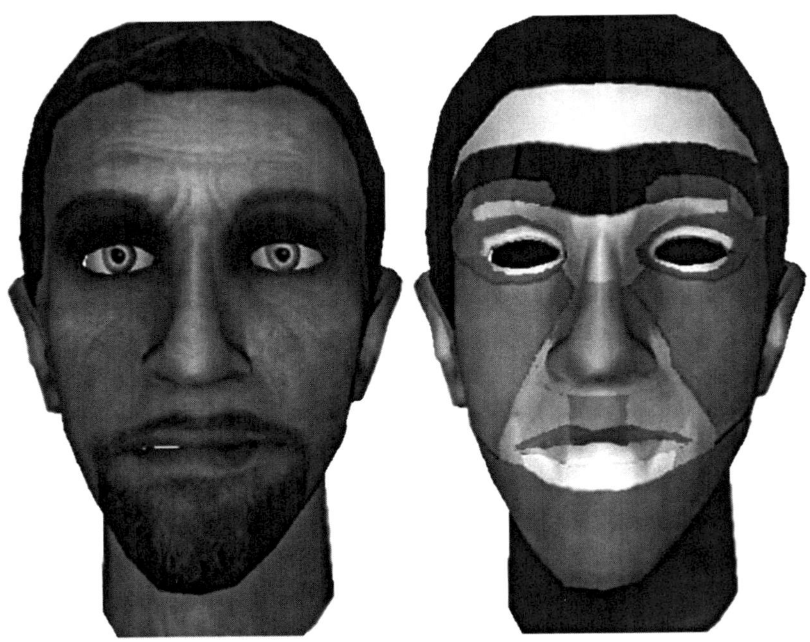

high-level personality meta-parameters (referred to as "behavior" controls within *FaceSpace*) is with an example. Let us suppose that a game or interactive film developer wants to use *FaceSpace* to create an interactive spy character for an adventure game or film. The designer can create the face and head for the spy in *FaceSpace* by adjusting low level parameters until the character has a slim, gaunt face with a shifty slant to the eyes. Alternatively, he can browse *FaceSpace* and find the character he wants. The designer can then save this set of parameters as a character library entry called "Spy."

The spy character must deliver various pieces of dialog, some of which must be delivered nervously, and others slyly. The designer can create a sly mood (with solid eye-contact and smooth, shifty gestures) and a nervous mood (with darting glances, rapid blinking, and jerky motions), also saving each mood as expression library entries. A voice talent can record the speeches and the *FaceSpace* system will analyze them for lip-synching and inflection. The spy character can then be made to play back any of the speeches with either the sly or nervous mood, as determined by the programmed logic of the interactive film or game. The spy's face will lip-sync the words and respond to the inflections, using whatever mood is specified at run-time. If a new spy character is introduced into the story line, with different speeches and voice talent, the same sly and nervous moods can be used to accent the new character's performances. Individual facial expressions (smiles, frowns, ticks, etc.,) can be created, stored as libraries and overlaid on top of the speeches at run-time, under program control. For example, a player may perform some action in the middle of a spy's speech, causing him to be displeased and frown, or to be surprised and look startled. In short, the player's interaction with the spy characters can be varied, subtle, and life-like to whatever extent the designer desires.

We have worked with a major game company as well as educational staff in the museum, zoo and aquaria fields on research in this area, where more dramatically sophisticated facial characters can be authored in games or interactives with a new production path that is economical and efficient, yet yields emotional character sequences at the quality of movies, and can be dynamically controlled interactively or under real-time program control. In this way we have begun to build up a hierarchical library of behaviors, expressions and character types that can be combined and changed in any number of ways. These then become a large continuous domain of facial expression space.

Just as we have described exploring or browsing a space of facial types, we now can begin to explore a space of facial expressions and emotions. According to Russell's circumplex model (1980), *arousal* and *valence* are two independent parameters that can control and create different moods and emotions (see Figure 8a). These two are main mod parameters in the *FaceSpace* model. Various emotions can be generated by activating *arousal* and *valence* at different levels. The corresponding facial expression is determined by associating simple units of facial action such as eyebrow-raise and stretch-lips to these parameters and emotions. See FACS (Ekman & Friesen, 1978).

Similarly, a 2D space can be defined for different personality types. *FaceSpace* uses these two dimensions (*affiliation* and *dominance*) as major parameters for creating personality types. Facial actions such as head movements and their frequency and speed are associated to observers' perception of personality, and to different personality types and parameters. For example, raising a single eyebrow quickly and frequently seems to cause the perception of high dominance, so it will be used in animation when a high-dominance personality has been selected. Using a research application of *FaceSpace*, we have begun working with physiologists in this area to better understand personality and mood models (those mentioned above and in future models) (Arya, Enns, Jefferies, & DiPaola, 2006). This gives another example of the range of uses of a face-centric system by, in this

Figure 8. Two-dimensional model for moods (Wiggins, Trapnell, & Phillips, 1988) (left); Two-dimension model for personality (Russell, 1980) (right)

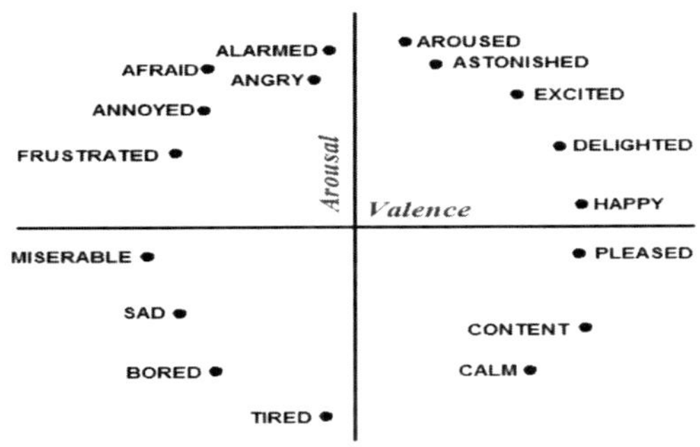

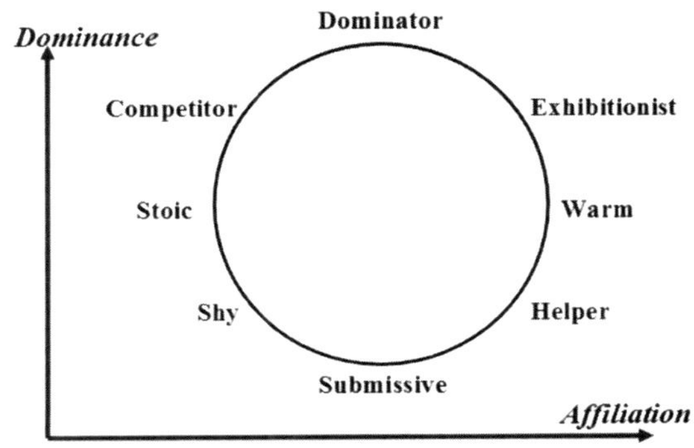

case, non-animation experts such as psychologists working with personality models. We also have an application in health education (DiPaola, Arya, & Chan, 2005) and are in discussions to create an application that would benefit autism research.

SOCIALLY EXPRESSIVE CHARACTER APPLICATIONS

Once a believable, controllable, and communicative face environment is available to application developers, we believe that a new range of socially-based applications is possible. As noted earlier, most computer-based communication systems are informational in nature rather than social. However, people use more socially-based techniques to convey their message. We believe that socially-based techniques using a communicative face system can open up more human-centric applications in many areas, such as:

- video games that can convey subtle dramatic nuances more common to cinema, thereby extending games to a wider audience and into the educational and adult realms
- chat systems that use voice and facial expression for better, deeper communication
- education systems that bring the passion of a teacher into distance education

In the remainder of this chapter, we will concentrate on applications that support more engaging art and science educational systems. We will discuss, in particular, three ongoing applications where expressive agents can engage the viewer with the deeper or complicated back-story of an artifact or science concept.

Most art or science museums (including zoos and aquariums) often use static displays of text and graphics to explain the deeper historical or scientific concepts about the nearby artifact (i.e., a portrait, a model of a planet), and often the display is not read. The situation is very different when a human guide gives a presentation about that same artifact, engrossing the viewers in the subject as they use narrative, real-time, and socially-based deliveries. Can this experience be mimicked with interactive systems, allowing students, who do not have geographically or financial access to a science facility, a similar level of engagement and educational experience? Can a facility create a better level of engagement when a human guide is not available? We will now describe two active prototypes that address these questions.

Storytelling Masks

Museums of anthropology, especially in North America, display a variety of First Nations artifacts. Among the most attractive of these are masks and head figures presented on objects such as totem poles. Songs, myths, and stories relate these figures to the history of the people who made them. Computer-generated characters with those figure-forms, who tell their stories and sing their songs, are appealing and informative for viewers, and provide First Nations artists with a new means of creativity and expression. Combinations of *FaceSpace* design and scripting tools provide such a creative environment.

We have begun working with the Parks Department of British Columbia, Canada, and the First Nations communities to create a museum display in which a virtual version of an artist appears, and, telling the story of his work, can virtually turn into the artwork—a native mask—and have a virtual version of the art tell its own story. This is shown in Figure 9, where a real artist's voice first introduces himself, his passion, stories, and expression. As he speaks, his work (a), begins to transform into his artwork; (b), has his work tells its back story with full voice and expression; (c, d), and can return to his persona to interactively answer questions or give other educational content (a).

Because all of this is under computer control, it is possible to create many of the perceptual and educational techniques that a live human guide/ artist could achieve, including:

- **Introduction:** The ability to announce and bring the audience to the work
- **Narrative style:** Conveying the back-story, passion, timing, and expressiveness
- **Multiple contexts:** Via interactive control, the material can be tailored to different age levels, different perspectives and focus areas, and can be readily updated
- **Presentation:** The exhibit can feel like a live presentation. For example, in the interplay between artist and artifact, the mask is not displayed until the artist gives sufficient context, and afterwards the mask returns to the artist/guide for additional commentary
- **Q&A:** At end of the session, the viewers can select question topics for a more tailored commentary

Evolving Faces

With goals and techniques similar to those of the storytelling mask project, *Evolving Faces* attempts to use facial agents to better engage viewers with the content. In this case the agents are used to describe complicated scientific details, and also act as an integral part of the content, evolving in their appearance to tell the story of man's migration out of Africa, based on new DNA techniques. *FaceSpace* allows a designer to create head models that correspond to various stages of human evolution, and assign different types of behavior (e.g., coarse or fine) to them to be expressed during talking or interaction. Such

Figure 9. Frames from "Storytelling Mask" interactive

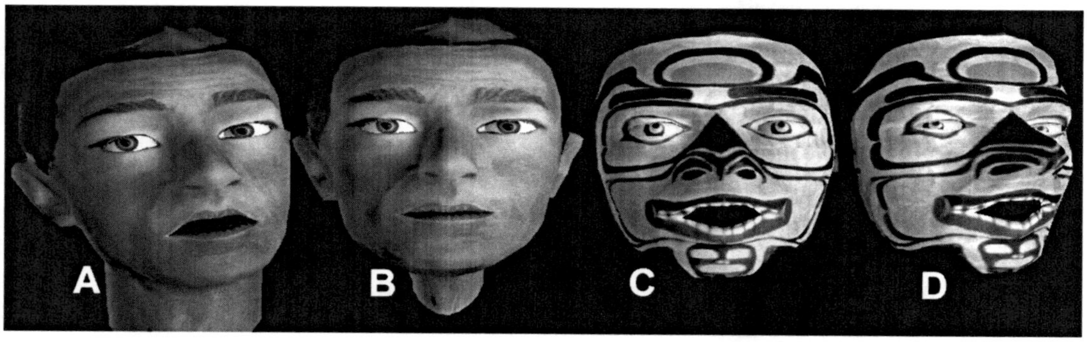

Figure 10. Screenshot of "Evolving Faces"

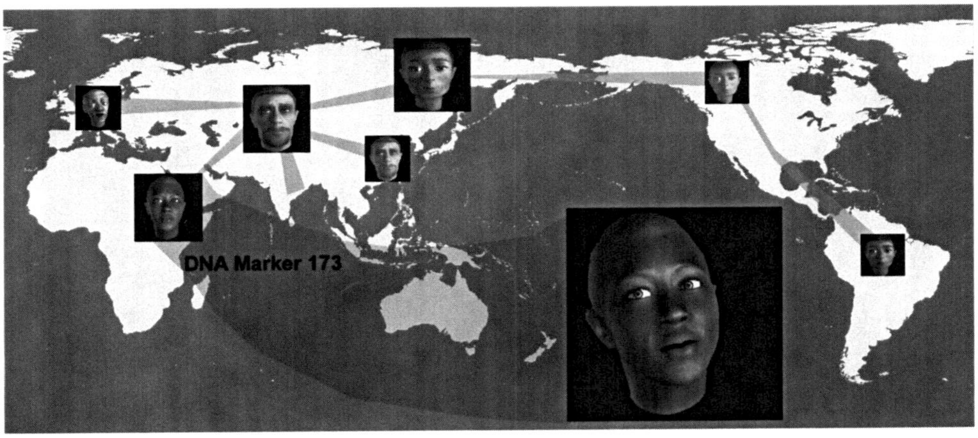

characters are ideal for science booths or online learning. Adding simple or complex artificial intelligence can improve the behavioral capability of the characters for real-time interaction. The display uses voices, change, and expressive faces and maps rather than charts and text.

The screen shot from the *Human Migration* interactive is shown in Figure 10. It shows how complex subject matter, such as how we migrated from Africa some 50-100,000 years ago, with evidence drawn from DNA markers and facial types, can be put forth engagingly. Viewers can click on a specific face/area and have it tell the story of that DNA marker, or click on a migratory path, and have an evolving face explain the journey of man.

Figure 11. The problem-based learning process

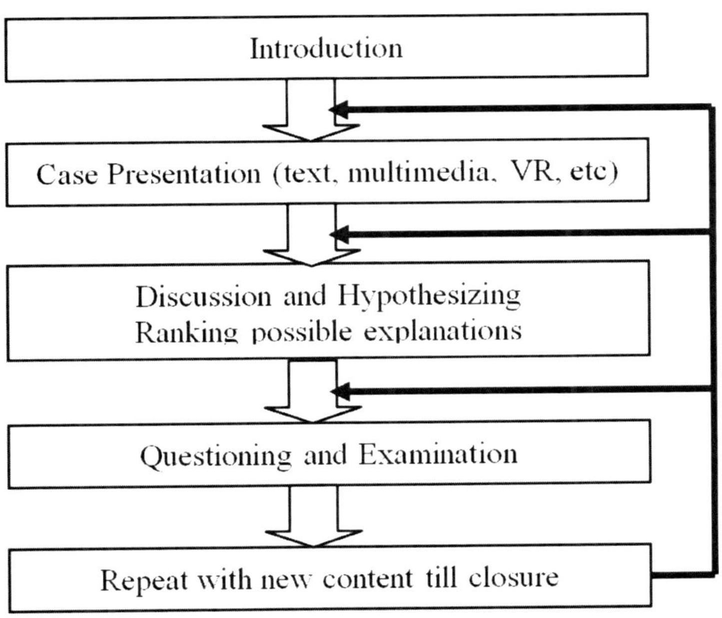

Figure 12. Instructor delivering COMPS content through the FaceSpace face agent

FaceSpace COMPS Case Study

The *Simulation and Advanced Gaming Environment* (*SAGE*) (Kaufman & Sauve, 2004) initiative is a joint project among Simon Fraser University and other Canadian universities. Among the areas of research in *SAGE* are e-learning tools in general, and problem-based learning (PBL) (Barrows, 2000) in particular. *Collaborative Online Multimedia Problem-based Simulation Software* (*COMPS*) (described in more detail in Chapter 17), is a system being developed in the *SAGE* project to support online PBL for medical students. PBL works by introducing students to a case (problem), giving them some facts, and taking them through cycles of discussion and hypothesizing until the

Figure 13. Screenshot of COMPS User Interface with a Simulated Patient

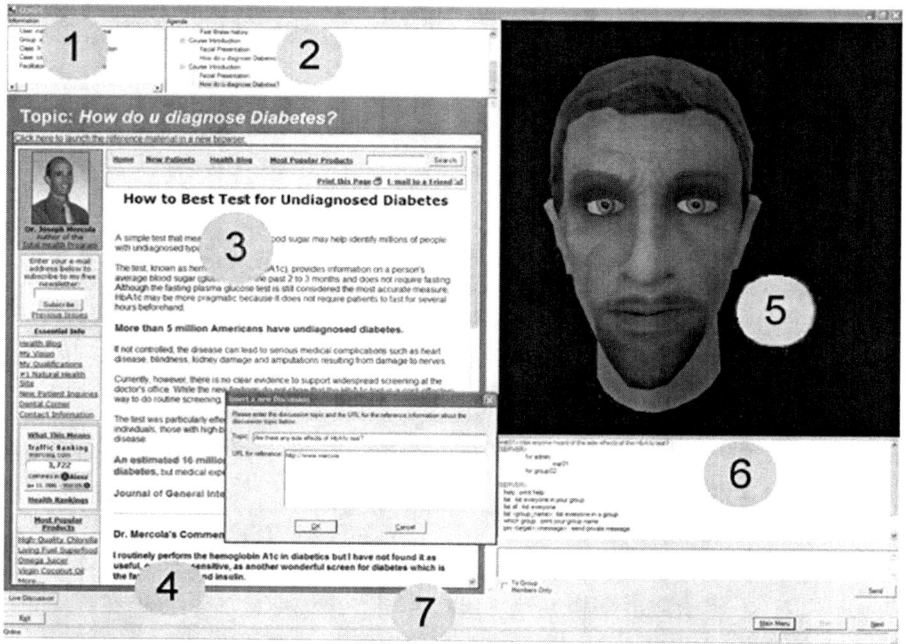

learning objectives have been met. A typical flow of a PBL scenario is shown in Figure 11.

A major part of a PBL-based approach for medical students is to interact with patients, especially listening to them as they describe their symptoms. Bringing patients to a classroom or examination room is difficult, and in some cases impossible. Using actors for this purpose is a common but expensive alternative. A social conversational agent (SCA) is an ideal replacement. The SCA can also be an automated instructor, or represent a remote instructor (or patient). Transmitting real-time video is not possible, but the SCA can be animated, based on real audio data (Figure 12). Here, we briefly review two examples of simulated patient and remote instructor as typical applications of *FaceSpace* in *COMPS*:

Simulated Patient

An FML script file (*Face Modeling Language* - Arya & DiPaola, 2004, 2007) is the primary animation control file for *FaceSpace*. Using *FaceSpaceStudio* authoring tools, a set of keyframe animations are created to represent typical head movements of the patient. These are then associated with a new personality type. The script selects the type and then gives the face object a text or audio file to speak. During the speech, the typical behaviors (head movements) are selected randomly and performed by the animated head. The presentation can be more complex, using event-processing and decision-making capabilities of FML. Events can be associated with user selections (e.g., from a pre-defined set of questions), and the animation can go through different branches.

Remote Instructor

A simpler mechanism for controlling *FaceSpace* animation is to provide only the audio data as input. Data can come from a local file or a network stream. As seen in Figure 12, a remote instructor can use *FaceSpace* recording capability to send his/her voice data to one or more remote *FaceSpace* objects, which in turn use the data to drive the animation. Again, proper personality and mood can be selected.

The face's outlook and emotional status can be changed from activity to activity. How the face changes is determined by the case script. When the instructor authors the case script, all the resources, including the face, meshes and behavioral specifications, are assigned an ID at the script's global section (Figure 13). At each activity specification, parameters for *FaceSpace* are specified by referencing the ID. As the user logs in, all the necessary resources will be downloaded to the user's machine. *COMPS* will then instruct *FaceSpace* to use specific parameters when it starts a new activity.

CONCLUSION

In this chapter, we describe the issues associated with using socially expressive character agents in a variety of informal and formal educational situations, especially as they relate to higher end simulation and gaming techniques. One of the most expressive surfaces available to humans, either for communication or reception of meaning, is the human face. We have presented our main research system, *FaceSpace*, a framework for socially expressive character agents. *FaceSpace* encapsulates all the functionality required for face animation and simulation into a single object with proper application programming interface, scripting language, and authoring tools to facilitate simple authoring of complex, expressive, face-based, interactive and linear social agent scenarios.

Future research on *FaceSpace* will involve a comprehensive association of all facial actions and expressions to the most likely personality type to be perceived, exploring the possibility of higher level parameters in face personality (on top of affiliation and dominance) in order to define practical character types (such as nervous, or heroic), and realistic combinations of current mood and facial actions by using non-linear functions. Future learning application spaces include our new work on understanding face-to-face autism communication, as well as remote expert agents systems that allow (in one of our projects) teachers and scientists from all over the world to be virtually situated next to an aquarium or science museum exhibit, where their passion and story-telling abilities (recorded or live over the Internet) can communicate, in a socially exciting way, deep information to local visitors via simple voice-based input.

ACKNOWLEDGMENT

Ali Arya was the co-researcher on much of the 3D facial animation work, along with J. Enns, J. Jefferies and V. Zammitto for the facial personality work. Caitlin Akai was the graduate co-researcher for the 3D whale pod simulation using artificial intelligence along with B. Kraus.

REFERENCES

Arya, A., & DiPaola, S. (2004, April). *Face as a multimedia object.* Paper presented at the 5th International Workshop on Image Analysis for Multimedia Interactive Services (WIAMIS 2004), Lisbon, Portugal.

Arya, A., & DiPaola, S. (2007). Face modeling and animation language for the MPEG-4 XMT Framework . *IEEE Transactions on Multimedia, 9*(6), 1137–1146. doi:10.1109/TMM.2007.902862

Arya, A., Enns, J., Jefferies, L., & DiPaola, S. (2006). Facial actions as visual cues for personality. *Computer Animation and Virtual Worlds (CAVW) . Journal, 17*(3-4), 371–382.

Barrows, H. (2000). *Problem-based learning applied to medical education.* Springfield, IL: Southern Illinois University School of Medicine.

Battista, S., Cassalino, F., & Lande, C. (1999). MPEG-4: A multimedia standard for the third millennium. *Multimedia, 6*(4), 74–83. doi:. doi:10.1109/93.809236

Cassell, J., Pelachaud, C., Badler, N., Steedman, M., Achorn, B., Becket, T., et al. (1994). Animated conversation: Rule-based generation of facial expression, gesture and spoken intonation for multiple conversational agents. In *Proceedings of ACMSIGGRAPH '94.* Available at http://citeseer.ist.psu.edu/cassell94animated.html

Cassell, J., Vilhjlmsson, H., & Bickmore, T. (2001). BEAT: The Behavior Expression Animation Toolkit. In *Proceedings of ACM SIGGRAPH 2001.* Available at http://citeseer.ist.psu.edu/cassell01beat.html.

DiPaola, S. (1991). Extending the range of facial types. *Visualization and Computer Animation, 2*(4), 129–131. doi:10.1002/vis.4340020406

DiPaola, S. (2002). *FaceSpace*: A facial spatial-domain toolkit. In *Proceedings of the IEEE Symposium on Information Visualization 2002 (InfoViz 2002)* (pp. 49-55).

DiPaola, S., & Akai, C. (2007). Blending science knowledge and AI gaming techniques for experiential learning, *Loading... - . Journal of the Canadian Games Studies Association, 1*(1), 40–45.

DiPaola, S., Akai, C., & Kraus, B. (2007). Experiencing belugas: Developing an action selection-based aquarium interactive. [Special Issue on Action Selection]. *Journal of Adaptive Behavior, 15*(1), 99–113. doi:10.1177/1059712306076251

DiPaola, S., Chan, J., & Arya, A. (2005). Simulating face to face collaboration for interactive learning systems. In G. Richards (Ed.), *Proceedings of World Conference on E-Learning in Corporate, Government, Healthcare, and Higher Education 2005* (pp. 1998-2003). Chesapeake, VA: Association for the Advancement of Computing in Education (AACE).

DiPaola, S., & Collins, C. (2003). A social metaphor-based 3D virtual environment. In *Proceedings, International Conference on Computer Graphics and Interactive Techniques: ACM SIGGRAPH 2003 Educators' Program.* doi 10.1145/965106.965134.

DiPaola, S., Dorash, D., & Brandt, G. (2004). Ratava's Line: Emergent learning and design using collaborative virtual worlds. In *Proceedings, International Conference on Computer Graphics and Interactive Techniques: ACM SIGGRAPH 2004 Educators' Program.* doi 10.1145/1186107.1186136.

Ekman, P., & Friesen, W. V. (1978). *Facial Action Coding System: A technique for the animation of facial movement.* Palo Alto, CA: Consulting Psychologists Press Inc.

Funge, J. Tu, X., & Terzopolous, D. (1999). Cognitive Modeling: Knowledge, reasoning, and planning for intelligent characters. In *Proceedings of ACM SIGGRAPH 1999* (pp. 29-38).

Kaufman, D., & Sauvé, L. (2004). Simulation and Advanced Gaming Environments (SAGE) for Learning; A Pan-Canadian research project. In L. Cantoni & C. McLoughlin (Eds.), *Proceedings, ED-MEDIA 2004: World Conference on Educational Multimedia, Hypermedia & Telecommunications* (pp. 4568-4573). Norfolk, VA: Association for the Advancement of Computing in Education (AACE).

Lee, Y., Terzopoulos, D., & Waters, K. (1995). Realistic modeling for facial animation. *Computer Graphics, 29*, 55–62. doi:10.1145/204362.204374

Parke, F. I. (1972). Computer generated animation of faces. In *Proceedings of the ACM Annual Conference*, volume 1 (pp. 451-457). doi 10.1145/800193.569955.

Parke, F. I., & Waters, K. (2000). *Computer facial animation.* Natick, MA: A. K. Peters Ltd.

Rousseau, D., & Hayes-Roth, B. (1997). *Interacting with personality-rich characters.* Knowledge Systems Laboratory Report No. KSL 97-06, Stanford University, Palo Alto, CA.

Russell, J. A. (1980). A circumplex model of affect. *Journal of Personality and Social Psychology, 39*, 1161–1178. doi:10.1037/h0077714

Valentine, T. (1999). Face-space models of face recognition. In M. J. Wenger, & J. T. Townsend (Eds.), *Computational, geometric, and process perspectives on facial cognition: Contexts and challenges* (pp. 83-113). Mahwah, NJ: Lawrence Erlbaum Associates Inc.

Waters, K. (1987). A muscle model for animating 3D facial expression. *Computer Graphics, 21*(4), 17–24. doi:10.1145/37402.37405

Wiggins, J. S., Trapnell, P., & Phillips, N. (1988). Psychometric and geometric characteristics of the revised Interpersonal Adjective Scale. *Multivariate Behavioral Research, 23*, 517–530. doi:10.1207/s15327906mbr2304_8

ADDITIONAL READING

Bates, J. (1994). The role of emotion in believable characters. *Communications of the ACM, 37*(7), 122–125. doi:10.1145/176789.176803

Magerko, B., Wray, R., Holt, L., & Stensrud, B. (2005). Customizing interactive training through individualized content and increased engagement. In *Proceedings of the Interservice/Industry Training, Simulation and Education Conference.* Arlington, VA: I/ITSEC. Available at http://ntsa.metapress.com/app/home/contribution.asp?referrer=parent&backto=issue,53,153;journal,4,12;homemainpublications,1,1

McQuiggan, S., & Lester, J. (2007). Modeling and evaluating empathy in embodied companion agents. *International Journal of Human-Computer Studies, 65*(4), 348–360. doi:10.1016/j.ijhcs.2006.11.015

Reilly, W. S. (1996). Believable social and emotional agents. Unpublished Ph.D. dissertation, Department of Computer Science, Carnegie Mellon University, Pittsburgh, PA.

Riedl, M., & Stern, A. (2006). Believable agents and intelligent scenario direction for social and cultural leadership training. In *Proceedings of the 15th Conference on Behavior Representation in Modeling and Simulation* (CD-ROM). Orlando, FL: Simulation Interoperability Standards Organization (SISO).

KEY TERMS AND DEFINITIONS

3D Avatar: A computer user's representation of himself/herself, in an embodied three-dimensional form (usually a character). Typically a real person can chat, talk and express themselves through their avatar to other users over a network. Avatars typically have a real person controlling them, while agents are computer software simulating a person or entity.

3D Facial Animation: A three-dimensional computer graphics technique that is capable of modeling and animating a model of the human face/head.

Artificial Intelligence: A branch of computer science in which software can perform functions that are normally associated with human intelligence, such as reasoning and optimization through experience.

Character Agents: Software entities that help or communicate with the computer user. Character agents take on a (simulated) embodied character form and narrative.

Expressive Agents: Software that helps or communicates with the computer user. Expressive agents can emote and express themselves in human-like ways.

Social Agents: Software that helps, or communicates with the computer user. Social agents use and/or understand human social conventions.

Chapter 15
The Use of Virtual Reality in Clinical Psychology Research:
Focusing on Approach and Avoidance Behaviors

Patrice Renaud
University of Quebec in Outaouais / Institut Philippe-Pinel de Montréal, Canada

Sylvain Chartier
University of Ottawa, Canada

Paul Fedoroff
University of Ottawa, Canada

John Bradford
University of Ottawa, Canada

Joanne L. Rouleau
University of Montreal, Canada

Jean Proulx
University of Montreal, Canada

Stéphane Bouchard
University of Quebec in Outaouais, Canada

ABSTRACT

This chapter presents research that is laying a foundation for new simulation applications that promise learning-oriented treatments for mental health conditions. After presenting background on their technologies and measurement techniques, the authors describe experimental applications of this approach. Analysis of negative and positive responses to virtual reality (VR) stimuli, as well as their complex composites, can lead to a better understanding of patient responses, including fundamental perceptual and cognitive causal relationships. Measuring patients' dynamic parameters in VR simulations can possibly lead to new treatment approaches for psychopathologies The biological and behavioral feedback obtained by virtual mediation, based on parameters of the perceptivo-motor dynamics such those described in this chapter, represents a promising avenue for future investigation.

DOI: 10.4018/978-1-61520-731-2.ch015

INTRODUCTION

This chapter presents research that, while outside the domains of most *SAGE* research presented in this volume, is laying a foundation for new simulation applications that promise learning-oriented treatments for mental health conditions. Using virtual reality (VR) immersive technologies with tracking of ocular and physical movements, this work makes possible more in-depth recording, analysis, and understanding of patient responses, eventually leading to more successful simulation-based treatments. After presenting background on our technologies and measurement techniques, we describe experimental applications of this approach.

BACKGROUND AND TECHNOLOGY

Capturing Perceptual-Motor Dynamics in the Virtual Reality's Loop of Data

Since the first prototypes proposed by Morton Heilig, Myron Krueger and especially Ivan Sutherland in the 1950s and 1960s, the essentials of understanding technological assembly required by VR have hardly changed (Ellis, 1995; Rheingold, 1991; Stanney & Zyda, 2002). Starting from to the simulator machine, we can arbitrarily identify VR's technical assembly according to both the *inputs* transmitted to the computer through reactions recorded from the human operator, and the *outputs* transmitted to the human operator' different sensory channels.

Inputs are produced via a series of sensors and transducers that transform behavioral and physiological variables into physical ones, which are in turn stored in the computer's register. Motor displacements in particular are recorded by a tracking system (generally magnetic, using infrared and/or ultrasound) that isolates the coordinates specific to where the sensors are found on the human operator's body (Ellis, 1995; Foxlin, 2002). The operator is localized within a defined sensory space and his movements are registered across a series of orientational and positional changes. As the operator moves and orients himself in a simulated area, he can perform hand, head, eye, or full body movements. Physiological measures that characterize the state of the human operator in virtual immersion can also be transmitted to the computer (Palsson & Pope, 2002; Wiederhold, Jang, Kim, & Wiederhold, 2002; Wiederhold & Rizzo, 2005). In most cases, the inputs' main function is to vary the parameters that control the state of the virtual environment (VE), i.e., the multimedia arrangement of stimuli oriented towards the human subject.[1] Furthermore, they can help analyze the behavioral dynamics that contribute to interactions with simulated objects in virtual reality for experimental or clinical purposes (Foxlin, 2002; Renaud, Bouchard, & Proulx, 2002a; Renaud et al., 2002b; Renaud, Singer, & Proulx, 2001).

After the fashion of chronophotography— a technique developed by Étienne-Jules Marey (1830-1904) during the 19th century and described in Paul Virilio's *The Aesthetics of Disappearance* (1980) —virtual reality's technical assembly enables a systematic analysis of motor sequences. This assembly allows for an unusual incursion into the motor activities that support kinematic variations of the subjective viewpoint in virtual immersion, i.e., an analysis of the human subject's first-person experience while interacting with the simulated content. In VR, the field of vision that is developed by the subject varies simultaneously in terms of displacement and orientation following the movements that are recorded directly or indirectly using a head-mounted display or stereoscopic glasses. Variations in Cartesian coordinates (*x*, *y* and *z*) and in Eulerian coordinates (yaw, pitch and roll) modify in a coherent way the subject's visual experience. Registering these coordinates allows us to establish an index concerning the spatial relationship between this viewpoint and the geometric properties of virtual objects. As a result, different contexts of approach and avoidance motor actions can be measured in subjects moving from one place to another in virtual immersion (Renaud et al., 2001, 2002a, 2002b). Accounting for the oculomotor activity observed in immersion (which will be discussed later) enables us to complete this analysis by accurately determining the portion of the virtual environment (VE) to which the subject pays his overt visual attention (Duchowski, Medlin, & Cournia, 2002; Renaud et al., 2002a; Renaud, Decarie, Gourd, Paquin, & Bouchard, 2003; Wilder, Hung, Tremaine, & Kaur, 2002).

As for the outputs, the computer produces a number of stimulations for different sensory segments that make up the human subject's sensorium. This particular event occurs following an analysis of the inputs, which are transmitted by the transduction of the human operator's voluntary and involuntary behaviors. Sound, touch, olfactory and proprioceptive stimuli may join visual stimuli to reinforce the effect of realism in virtual immersion.

The human-computer interface that is unique to the assembly used in VR favors a continuous and coherent perceptual-motor loop in the human subject (Biocca, 1995; Ellis, 1995). Through a feedback mechanism, the outputs become a source of information for the human operator regarding his spatial position in the virtual environment. These outputs then drive the motor behaviors to adjust the virtual environment's resulting state. Through this perceptual-motor relay, immersive VR becomes possible and the illusion effect (i.e. the feeling of presence) occurs (ISPR, 2000; Renaud 2006a; Renaud et al., 2002a, 2002b, 2006b; Slater, Steed, & McCarthy, 1998; Witmer & Singer, 1998).

Immersion and Presence

Slater and Wilbur (1997) define immersion as the measure in which a computer system can offer illusions of reality that are: inclusive (eliminating the inputs outside of the virtual environment); demanding (mobilizing sensory modalities); panoramic (covering the visual field); and vivid (offering a good resolution of the image). Immersive potential is measured by "the feeling of presence", a theoretical concept characterized principally as a psychological state or subjective perception that causes an individual to surrender to the illusion created by an immersive technical assembly. This illusion consists in forgetting both the exterior environment and immersive technology in favor of the virtual environment (ISPR, 2000; Witmer & Singer, 1998). The feeling of presence is considered a product of many factors, mainly the level of immersion, the subject's level of attention and the degree of interaction (Renaud et al., 2007; Schubert, Friedmann, & Regenbrecht, 2001; Slater, Steel, & McCarthy, 1998). Acting as a kind of perception, presence must have perceptual-motor determinants that tie the subjective perspective to a limited set of possible viewpoints. These perceptual processes that create the illusion of presence are most likely mediated by oculomotor behaviors, since they form the main entry to visual perception (Renaud et al., 2006b, 2007).

The Scientific Advantages of VR in Psychology

A literature review performed by Riva (2005) deals with the use of VR in psychology and identifies 996 published scientific articles accessed in an April, 2005 *PSYCINFO* quick search. The author notes that more than one third of these articles (371) were written over the last three years, suggesting a strong growth, as well as an increasing interest for VR research, which began around 1992.[2]

According to Riva (2005), most controlled scientific studies have clinical samples of more than 10 subjects and show efficiency in VR systems resulting from the integration of cognitive-behavioral or strictly cognitive approaches. These treatment methods are known in psychology for their adherence to principles of the scientific method.[3]

In fact, VR favors the scientific method in clinical research for multiple reasons; one being that virtual reality noticeably improves the external validity (also called ecological validity) of the results that it generates. When compared to oversimplified stimuli found in certain laboratory studies, those that come from VR are much closer to exterior reality, and thus may lead to a better generalization of the results.

Contrary to what usually occurs in scientific research, this gain in external validity is not achieved to the detriment of a rigorous control of the experimental variables. Even though stimuli presentation in a virtual environment may be closer to exterior reality, it is rigorously and faithfully the same experimental condition that occurs in each trial. As a result, valid causative inferences based on the variables involved are favored, more specifically the effects of simulated conditions on behavior and the subjective reactions of human subjects (Brewer, 2000).

Virtual reality may even strengthen the internal validity of collected laboratory measures by providing recording and quantitative control of the first-person visual content experienced by a human subject in virtual immersion (Duchowski, Medlin, & Cournia, 2002; Renaud et al., 2002b, 2003; Wilder et al., 2002). By analyzing in more detail the contingencies that unite subjective experience in virtual immersion with the human subject's responses (i.e., responses obtained by means of a questionnaire, as well as behavioral and physiological responses), less ambiguous causative links can be established between psychological subjectivity and its quantifiable manifestations. The possibility of examining subjective experience and its attentional content via VR's mediation may significantly improve the value of other measures that are obtained simultaneously. In general, when coupled with VR, the use of psychophysiological measurement techniques such as electrocardiography and electroencephalography greatly increases validity (Bullinger et al., 2001; Mager, Bullinger, Mueller-Spahn, Kuntze, & Stoermer, 2001).

Clinical Advantages of VR for Treatment

From a clinical viewpoint, the use of VR in mental health leads to a number of therapeutic benefits:

1. simulating treatment contexts that are not easily accessible or are practically impossible to reproduce in reality (e.g., simulating an airplane take-off, locomotion in high-altitude places or potential victims for a sexual aggressor)
2. the possibility of repeating on demand a given context in virtual immersion. This controlled repetition allows clinicians to better target a debilitating symptom and to accurately treat it in a patient
3. the implementation of a clinical treatment protocol, which is both automated and controlled, ensuring a better adherence to its various procedures. This benefit becomes extremely useful when struggling with dimensions of non-compliance or even malingering in some patients
4. the recording and storage of immersive sessions, facilitating records management and clinical follow-up and helping to bridge the gap between clinical practice and scientific research in psychology
5. increased self-motivation in patients using VR treatments compared with the use of more standard methods (Garcia-Palacios, Hoffman, & See, 2001; Rothbaum, Hodges, Smith, Lee, & Price, 2000)

The Assessment of Avoidance and Approach Behaviors in Virtual Immersion

Any clinical process unique to mental health requires a diagnostic evaluation and an appropriate treatment that can correct a given pathological state. The evaluation process is generally applied before and after treatment in order to verify the efficacy of the therapeutic procedure. Research studies that are attempting to use VR for diagnostic evaluation purposes are less numerous than those focusing on treatment, but studies on attention deficit and hyperactivity disorder (Rizzo et al., 1999; Wann, Rushton, Smyth, & Jones, 1997), anxiety disorders (Renaud et al., 2002a; Wiederhold & Wiederhold, 2004), autistic disorders (Trepagnier, Sebrechts, & Peterson, 2002), addictive behaviors (Baumann & Sayette, 2006) and deviant sexual preferences (Renaud, 2004; Renaud et al., 2005; Renaud, Rouleau, Granger, Barsetti, & Bouchard, 2002c) have been conducted so far. The following two studies show the relevance of assessing perceptual-motor dynamics in phobic avoidance as well as in deviant sexual attraction from the use of virtual stimuli.

STUDY 1: ASSESSING PHOBIC AVOIDANCE IN VIRTUAL IMMERSION

Arachnophobia is a specific animal-type phobia that is classified among the most common phobias today. According to a study conducted in England, 32 percent of women and 18 percent of men showed anxiety or great fear in the presence of a spider (Davey, 1994). Although it can appear insignificant at first, this fear gives rise to major debilitating effects in people who are affected by its pathological form. It is characterized by extreme and irrational fear resulting from the presence or anticipation of a spider. The fear is also accompanied by an active avoidance of this animal (APA, 1994).

To expand our knowledge of the mechanisms at work in treating phobic disorders with VRE, we have developed a diagnostic evaluation procedure regarding motor behaviors that are necessary for movement and for the orientation of overt visual attention in arachnophobic patients. In our study, arachnophobic patients were placed in immersion and were exposed to phobogenic stimuli in order to better understand the dynamics of behavioral avoidance and the information processing associated with it (Renaud et al., 2002a). The diagnostic evaluation procedure regarding phobic avoidance behavior is a computerized behavioral avoidance test (BAT) that can capture the nature of a patient's subjective experience by witnessing events through his visual perspective. We present here preliminary results on these developments.

Methods and Apparatus

Subjects

We tested a small sample of five women between 24 and 49 years of age (mean = 35.6, sd = 11.5) who were all diagnosed with arachnophobia according to the Diagnostic and Statistical Manual of Mental Disorders criteria (APA, 1994). These subjects entered treatment for their condition after the experimental trial.

Immersive Virtual Reality

A CAVE-type immersive vault (Cruz-Neira, Sandin, DeFanti, Kenyon, & Hart, 1992) at the University of Quebec in Outaouais was used in this study. This immersive system consists of a cluster of four computers that generate the VE and one computer that records ocular measures. One of the four computer clusters acts as the master, while the other three are slaves connected to a projector displayed on one of the walls of the immersive vault. All computers communicate through a network using a CISCO 100 Mbps switch. The master computer gathers the inputs provided by a human subject (keyboard, mouse, motion sensors, ocular measures) and distributes them to the slaves so that all cluster machines can calculate the changes made in the VE and also generate a report.

The graphic cards are interconnected, allowing them to be frame locked. The positional and ori-

Figure 1. Subject wearing stereoscopic glasses coupled with an oculomotor tracking device 1) IS-900™ motion tracker from InterSense 2) active Nuvision 60GX™ stereoscopic glasses 3) oculomotor tracking system (ASL model H6™) 4) a virtual spider in wired frame 5) a virtual measurement point (VMP) 6) a gaze radial angular deviation (GRAD) from the VMP.

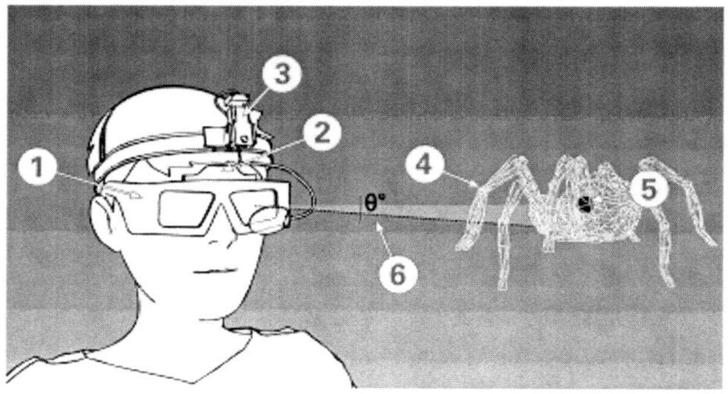

entational coordinates are provided by an IS-900 motion tracker from InterSense Inc. The *Virtools 3.5* middleware is responsible for creating the appropriate environment and ensuring communication between the computer clusters. Finally, *OpenGL 2.0* plays a role in the rasterization process to benefit from active stereoscopy.

Immersive Video-Oculography

Our method performs gaze analysis by way of virtual measurement points (VMPs) placed over virtual objects. The gaze radial angular deviation (GRAD) from VMPs is obtained by combining the six degrees of freedom (DOF) resulting from head movements and the two DOF (x and y coordinates) resulting from the eye-tracking system (Duchowski et al., 2002; Renaud, Chartier, & Albert, 2008; Renaud et al., 2002b). While variations in the six DOF developed by head movements define momentary changes in the global scene experienced in the immersive vault, the two DOF generated by the eye-tracking device allow line-of-sight computation relative to VMPs. The

Figure 2. A five-second sample of GRAD fluctuations from a virtual spider (pink) and a virtual neutral object (blue) for one representative subject. The closer the data approach zero, the closer the gaze is to the centre of the moving target.

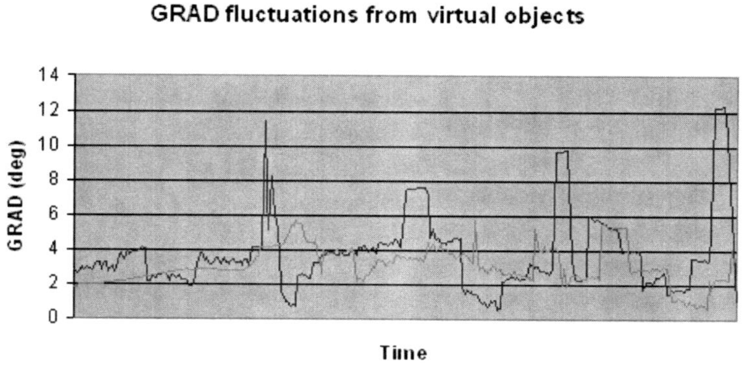

Figure 3. A three-minute sample showing distance fluctuations from the spider (dark line) and the neutral object (light line) for one representative subject. This person was getting closer to the target in the presence of the neutral object than when she was exposed to a phobogenic stimulus (dark line).

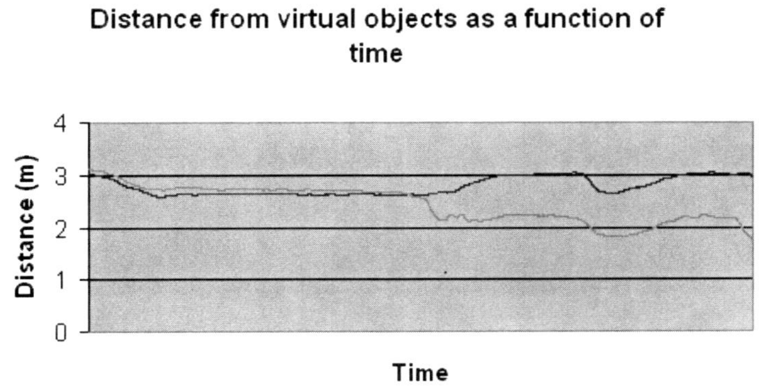

more this measure approaches zero, the closer the gaze dwells in the immediate vicinity of the selected VMP. Moreover, VMPs are locked onto and therefore move jointly with virtual objects, making it possible to examine the visual pursuit of dynamic virtual objects. Therefore, this method allows us to measure the visual response from GRAD patterns relative to VMPs (see Figures 1 and 2). Average GRAD and GRAD standard deviation were taken as dependent variables in the present study.

Computerized Behavioral Avoidance Test (BAT) Applied in Virtual Immersion

Avoidance behavior is measured by calculating the distance separating the patient from the VMP placed on virtual objects that will be approached by the patient (Renaud et al., 2002a). The coordinates obtained at a frequency of 60 Hz through the motion tracker are fed into a trigonometric function that calculates the distance between the patient and the virtual object. From this calculation, we can get an accurate picture of the temporal evolution associated with phobic avoidance (see Figure 3). The average distance from virtual objects was taken as dependent variable in the present experiment.

Experimental Task and Protocol

The subjects were standing at the centre of an immersive vault and were asked to move as much as possible towards a virtual tarantula (condition 1; Figure 4a) or a virtual sphere acting as a neutral stimulus (condition 2; Figure 4b). The following instructions were given to the participants: "Try not to lose sight of the spider (or sphere) while moving as much as possible towards it. You can also move backwards if fear overcomes you, and then proceed forward shortly after by approaching the spider (or sphere) as close as possible until the end of the session. Although this exercise will last three minutes, do not preoccupy yourself with the time. We will notify you when the session is over." The exercise was held in a virtual room that simulated a kitchen, with a counter on which the spider or sphere was moving. The targets (spider or sphere) in both experimental conditions shared exactly the same kinematic properties, moving according to variable speeds and trajectories that were similar to those that a real spider would trace.

Figure 4. (a) The virtual spider and (b) the neutral target; crosshairs depict the immersed subject's momentary point of regard in the VE.

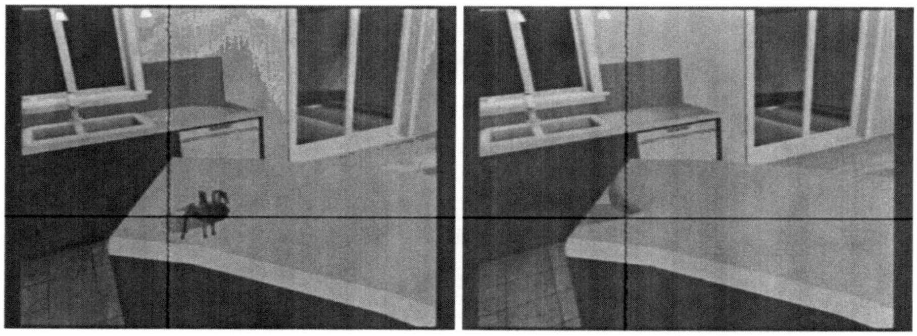

Results

Raw data are displayed in Table 2. Repeated analyses of variance were done to compare the subjects' responses to the neutral target (sphere) and to the phobogenic target (spider). Consequently, we observed that the subjects were on average further away from the phobogenic stimulus ($F(1,4) = 8.344$, $p<0.05$). This result fits our usual observations during BATs involving phobic patients. As seen in Figure 3, however, the computerized BAT applied in immersion provides more accurate information on the temporal evolution of avoidance in phobic patients, which depends on where they are spatially located with respect to the phobogenic object.

Next, the subjects were shown to have their attention more precisely centered on the phobogenic target when compared to the neutral one, ($F(1,4) = 9.134$, $p<0.05$). As measured by the GRAD, the phobic subjects seemed to be more easily attentive to the stimulus associated with their fears. Finally, the patients' lability of visual pursuit behavior, measured by the GRAD's standard deviation, was significantly lower when tracking the phobogenic stimulus than it was when tracking the neutral one ($F(1,4)=8.475$, $p<0.05$). The greatest mobilization of attention towards the phobogenic stimulus is therefore characterized by a tighter control of the motor processes that maintain critical information processing. (Table 1)

Discussion

Although this first study contained preliminary data from a very small clinical sample, it was able to demonstrate VR's potential in the detailed analysis of motor behavior when coupled with analytical

Table 1. Case Summaries

Subjects	Average GRAD with neutral target (deg)	Average GRAD with phobogenic target (deg)	GRAD SD with neutral target	GRAD SD with phobogenic target	Average distance from neutral target (m)	Average distance from phobogenic target (m)
1	8.79	8.93	6.11	4.87	.66	.77
2	11.69	4.37	6.69	2.62	1.30	2.24
3	9.12	5.35	7.96	2.87	1.84	2.67
4	9.74	3.44	12.22	2.29	2.42	2.78
5	9.25	6.49	6.61	4.64	1.06	1.24
Mean	9.72	5.72	7.92	3.46	1.45	1.94

instruments of attentional activity. The VR system allows us to measure the patients' attentional engagement in immersion, both qualitatively and quantitatively. In the qualitative sense, researchers or clinicians can witness events through the subject's visual first-person perspective in immersion. They can also better understand how patients occupy the VE and manage their visual attention in relation to critical simulated zones. As for the quantitative aspect, statistical data that are similar to those obtained in the previous section may accurately illustrate the perceptual-motor parameters reflecting the phobic patients' attentional organization, while also monitoring their progress during VRE. Taking advantage of this important clinical advantage, diagnostic evaluation is no longer performed exclusively before and after treatment, but over the course of the entire VRE. As a result, the patients' clinical evolution may be described more accurately, allowing us to more easily show the individual differences that lie in the expression of a given pathology, particularly patterns of motor avoidance and attentional bias. Adjusting the application of clinical protocols to the subjects' idiosyncrasies may therefore be greatly facilitated.

Table 2. Means and standard deviations.

	Groups		Statistics
Penile response neutral	non deviants	Mean	1.2073
		Std. deviation	1.70547
	pedophile	Mean	1.1484
		Std. deviation	.67992
Penile response 6-yr-old female	non deviants	Mean	.5120
		Std. deviation	.56609
	pedophile	Mean	2.8523
		Std. deviation	3.81430
GRAD neutral	non deviants	Mean	8.9235
		Std. deviation	5.10516
	pedophile	Mean	9.0917
		Std. deviation	2.28015
GRAD 6-yr-old female	non deviants	Mean	10.3379
		Std. deviation	4.20964
	pedophile	Mean	9.1237
		Std. deviation	2.07773
GRAD SD neutral	non deviants	Mean	4.1402
		Std. deviation	1.47011
	pedophile	Mean	5.3579
		Std. deviation	1.78830
GRAD SD 6-yr-old female	non deviants	Mean	3.1494
		Std. deviation	1.47214
	pedophile	Mean	3.5130
		Std. deviation	1.80997
D2 neutral	non deviants	Mean	1.8081
		Std. deviation	.30819
	pedophile	Mean	1.5764
		Std. deviation	.19322
D2 6-yr-old female	non deviants	Mean	1.8831
		Std. deviation	.36155
	pedophile	Mean	1.6309
		Std. deviation	.26549

STUDY 2: ASSESSING PERCEPTUAL-MOTOR NONLINEAR DYNAMICS IN VIRTUAL IMMERSION AS A DIAGNOSTIC INDEX OF SEXUAL ATTRACTION IN PEDOPHILES

Aside from the clinical interview, the use of questionnaires and the examination of collateral records, which are essential yet clearly incomplete sources of information, there exist to this day primarily two methods meant to be objective that are used in both research into and the clinical assessment of sex offenders: penile plethysmography (PPG) and approaches based on viewing time (VT) (Laws & Gress, 2004). However, these methods present certain methodological shortcomings in terms of reliability and validity.

Since its introduction by Freund (1963), the measurement of penile tumescence by means of a plethysmograph (a device to measure variations in the blood volume of a sexual organ) has been the target of much criticism on both ethical and methodological grounds (Kalmus & Beech, 2005; Laws, 2003; Laws & Gress, 2004; Laws & Marshall, 2003; Marshall & Fernandez, 2003). In particular, it has been attacked for demonstrating weak test-retest reliability and questionable discriminating validity with respect to distinguishing sexual deviants from non-deviants and to correctly differentiating the categories of sexual deviants among themselves (Kalmus & Beech, 2005; Looman & Marshall, 2001; Marshall & Fernandez, 2000; McConaghy, 1999; Simon & Schouten, 1991). However, a large part of the method's test-retest reliability and discriminating validity problems have arisen from PPG's proneness to strategies used by sex offenders to voluntarily control their penile response in order to fake their sexual arousal response and thus present a non-deviant preference profile (Quinsey & Chaplin, 1988; Seto & Barbaree, 1996). This is where the heaviest criticism has been leveled. Indeed, the use of mental distraction strategies is widespread. In this regard, it has been reported that up to 80% of subjects who were asked to voluntarily control their erectile response succeed in doing so (Farkas, Sine, & Evans, 1979; Howes, 1998; Kalmus & Beech, 2005). They generally manage to lower their scores through the use of aversive or anxiogenic (anxiety-inducing) thoughts and images, that is, by diverting their attention from the sexual stimuli that they are exposed to. These distraction strategies are reputed to be difficult or impossible to detect, and attempts to control this factor have yielded mixed results (Golde, Strassberg, & Turner, 2000; Proulx, Cote, & Achille, 1993; Quinsey & Chaplin, 1988).

VT-based methods of addressing pedophilia have grown out of the work of Rosenzweig (1942) and Zamansky (1956), who demonstrated a positive correlation between VT and sexual interest. On the strength of these findings, teams led by Abel (*Abel Assessment for Sexual Interest*) (Abel, Jordan, Hand, Holland, & Phipps, 2001), Glasgow (Affinity) (Glasgow, Osbourne, & Croxen, 2003), and Laws (Psychological Assessment Corporation) (Laws & Gress, 2004) developed sexual interest assessment protocols based on VT on photographs of real models (Abel et al., 2001; Glasgow et al., 2003) or on static images of synthetic characters generated by modifying photographs of real models (Laws & Gress, 2004).

As pointed out by Fischer and Smith (1999; Smith & Fischer, 1999) regarding the *Abel Assessment for Sexual Interest*, the use of VT to assess sexual interest presents major problems in terms of test-retest reliability and external validity. Moreover, as is the case with PPG, VT-based measures can have their internal validity affected by the use of result-faking strategies (Fischer & Smith, 1999; Kalmus & Beech, 2005). Although it is not divulged at the time of testing, it is easy enough to identify VT as the dependent variable and, once its significance becomes widely known, subjects have little difficulty "cheating."

Furthermore, both PPG and VT-based methods make it possible to evaluate only a small portion of the sexual interest and preference response. This comprises at least three components: aesthetic interest, sexual attraction, and sexual arousal (Kalmus & Beech, 2005; Laws & Gress, 2004; Singer, 1984). PPG serves to evaluate the response process's physiological dimension of arousal, whereas VT-based methods discern the aesthetic interest response only in part (Fischer & Smith, 1999). What's more, the aesthetic interest response itself can be broken down into a series of perceptual and cognitive processes whose opaqueness transforms into important assets in the assessment of sexual interest and preference, as we will see later. Finally, as Laws and Gress (2004) pointed out, the victimization of children is another major shortcoming of assessment procedures that use pictures of real models to arouse either physiologic sexual responses or deviant interest as indexed by PPG or VT.

Virtual Reality and Attention Control Technologies as an Alternative

The use of fully synthetic characters obviously precludes the above mentioned ethical problems. If those characters could be presented in virtual immersion, coupled with attention control technologies such as eye-trackers, the other methodological shortcomings explained previously could likely also be circumvented. Moreover, data generated by tracking gaze behavior could possibly also be diagnostically indicative in themselves (Renaud, 2004; Renaud et al., 2002c, 2005, 2006b).

The following experimental study is based on these theoretical and methodological rationales. It aims first at demonstrating that it is technically feasible to take the patients' point of view into account while presenting them with clinically relevant virtual stimuli. It also aims at bearing out that gaze behavior, and especially gaze behavior dynamics, is a potential source of diagnostic information about deviant sexual preferences.

Methods and Apparatus

Subjects

Eight male pedophile patients and eight male non-deviant control subjects were recruited for the present study. Patients were attending treatment at the Forensic program of the Royal Ottawa Hospital. Control subjects were recruited via newspapers. Subjects of both groups were matched according to their age and socioeconomic status.

Immersive Virtual Reality and Video-Oculography

The CAVE system and video-oculography technique described above were also used in this study. Our method performs gaze analysis by way of virtual measurement points (VMPs) placed over virtual objects or over features of virtual objects (ex.: sexual organs of the virtual characters; see Figure 5). A gaze radial angular deviation (GRAD) from VMPs is obtained by combining the six degrees of freedom (DOF) resulting from head movements and the two DOF (x and y coordinates) resulting from eye movements tracked by the eye-tracking system (Duchowski et al, 2002; Renaud, 2006a; Renaud et al., 2008; see Figure 5). While variations in the six DOF developed by head movements define momentary changes in the global scene experienced in the immersive system, the two DOF generated by the eye-tracking device allow line-of-sight computation relative to VMPs. The closer this measure approaches zero, the closer the gaze dwells in the immediate vicinity of the selected VMP. In the present study, one VMP is used, the latter being installed at the virtual characters' genitalia level.

Virtual Sexual Stimuli

The sexual stimuli that we use are 3D virtual characters presented in virtual immersion. They depict realistic human male and female characters (see Figure 6). Two stimuli are used in the present study, one depicting a six-year-old girl, and the other one a neutral stimulus, i.e., a textureless virtual character. Both stimuli are animated and each one is presented in virtual immersion for a 120-second duration. Subjects are seated in front of the virtual character that is presented in life-size. In this study, the three-wall immersive

Figure 5. Example (Component 4) of a virtual character in wire mesh. (See Figure 1 for component descriptions)

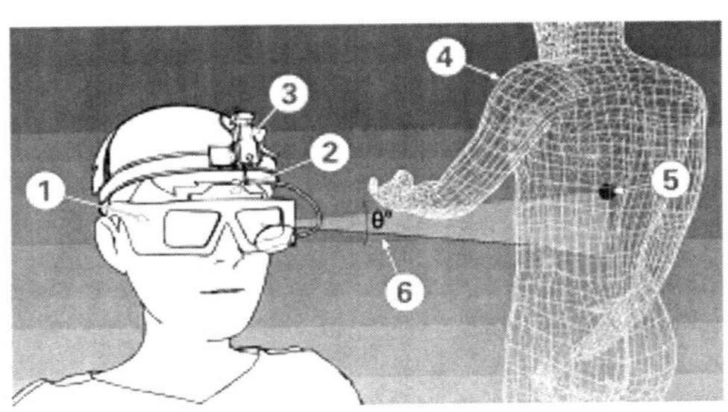

system was used to simulate a room into which the virtual characters were standing in front of the seated subjects. These characters were animated to mimic a neutral attitude; these animations were developed using a motion capture system and the movements of actors wearing data suits. Life-size 3D virtual characters were chosen to increase realism and thus get a better ecological validity.

Sexual Plethysmography

Sexual (penile) plethysmography measures variations in sexual organs' blood volume; it is used particularly to assess sexual arousal. Penile plethysmography requires the wearing of a thin mercury-in-rubber-strain-gauge around the shaft of the penis. This gauge is simply a small rubber tube filled with mercury forming a ring. During an erectile response, the gauge stretches and changes in the mercury column produces variations in electric conductibility, expressed as a voltage gradient.

The sexual response is recorded while subjects are immersed with one of the virtual characters. The maximum erectile value recorded in a trial is taken as the response.

Figure 6. Left: A censored image of the animated 3D virtual character used as a sexual stimulus depicting a 6-yr old female. Right: A neutral textureless virtual character.

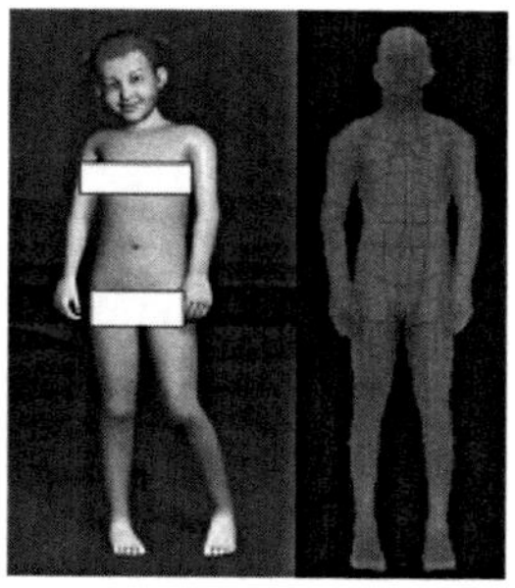

Procedure

Subjects were briefed and given a five-minute training period during which they were immersed in a realistic apartment furnished with various pieces of furniture. They were then simply asked to pay attention to the 3D animations they were about to be immersed with for two 120-second periods.

Data Analyses

Correlation Dimension (D_2)

In order to grasp the dynamic side of the visual scanning response, we analyzed the nonlinear

Figure 7. Typical GRAD signal obtained from a 120-second recording made at 60 hz with one control subject, in one experimental condition; the closer the GRAD value gets to zero, the closer the gaze dwells in the vicinity of the associated VMP.

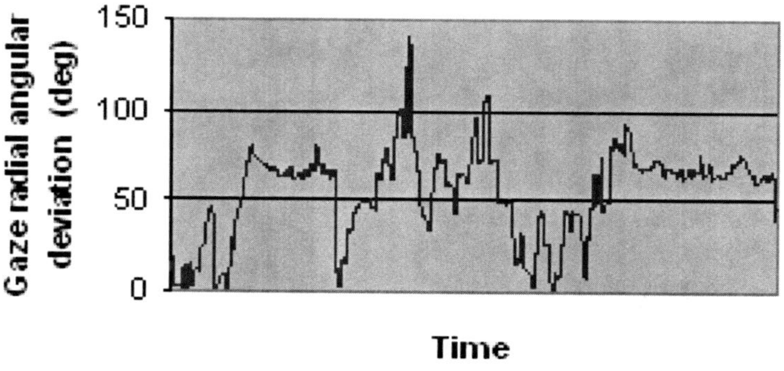

properties of the GRAD signals for each subject, in each condition. To do so, we relied upon a well known fractal index, i.e., the correlation dimension (D_2).

D_2 is a measure of the complexity of the geometric structure of an attractor in the phase space of a dynamic process (Sprott, 2003). The invariant topological properties of the attractor – those that do not vary under the continuous and differential transformations of the system's coordinates – may be extracted by calculating D_2 (Renaud et al., 2008). This measurement is consistent with a non-fractal object: lines have a dimension of 1, while a plane has a dimension of 2, etc. Calculation of D_2 is obtained from the Grassberger-Procaccia algorithm (Grassberger & Procaccia, 1983; Grassberger, Schrieber, & Schaffrath, 1991). The idea is to take a given embedded time series x_n and for a given point x_i count the number of other points x_j that are within a distance of ε. Then repeat this process for all the points and for various distances of ε. This correlation sum is expressed as:

$$C(\varepsilon) = \frac{2}{N(N-1)} \sum_{i=1}^{N} \sum_{j=i+1}^{N} \Theta\left(\varepsilon - \left\|\mathbf{x}_i - \mathbf{x}_j\right\|\right) \quad (1)$$

where N is the number of points in the time series, ||x|| is the Euclidian norm and Θ(x) is the Heaviside function expressed by

$$\Theta(x) = \begin{cases} 0 \text{ for } x < 0 \\ 1 \text{ for } x \geq 0 \end{cases}$$

Consequently, the double sum expressed in Equation 1 counts only the pairs (xi, x_j) whose distance is smaller than ε. The sum C(ε) is expected to scale like a power law for small ε and large N. Therefore, a plot of log C(ε) versus log ε should give an approximate straight line.

$$D_2 = \lim_{\varepsilon \to 0} \lim_{N \to \infty} \frac{d \log C(\varepsilon)}{d \log \varepsilon} \quad (2)$$

The correlation sum in various embeddings can serve as a measure of determinism in a time series. For pure random noise, the correlation sum satisfies $C(m, \varepsilon) = C(1, \varepsilon)^m$. In other words, if the data are random, they will fill any given embedding dimension. On the other hand, determinism will be shown by asymptotical convergence of D_2 as the embeddings increase. All D_{2s} obtained from the GRAD time series recorded in the present study show this asymptotic stabilization.

Surrogate Data Tests

To make sure that D_2 exponents are significantly distinct from exponents coming from correlated noise processes, a surrogate data method introduced by Theiler, Eubank, Longtin, Galdrikian, and Farmer (1992) was used to statistically differentiate each computed D_2 from a sample of D_2s coming from quasi-random processes (McSharry, 2005). For each GRAD time series, we generated twenty surrogate time series by doing a Fourier transform of the original data (the phase of each Fourier component was set to a random value between 0 and 2π) while preserving their power spectrum and correlation function (Sprott, 2003). These surrogate data correspond to a quasi-random trajectory of exploratory visual behavior (GRAD). Using a one-sample T test, we were able to establish that D_{2s} calculated from the original data differ significantly from the mean of the 20 D_2 correlation dimensions based on surrogate data (AVG=5.67, SD=0.21; $p < .0001$).

This means that the gaze behavior recorded in virtual immersion using GRAD data is a highly structured and well-organized perceptual-motor process that appears to be significantly distinct from a quasi-random phenomenon. It also implies that the gaze behavior dynamics are probably identifiable by a fractal signature present at multiple scales of the visual scanning behavior (Renaud et al., 2008).

Statistical Analyses

A series of eight ANCOVAs with groups (pedophile vs. non-deviant subjects) as an independent variable were conducted. The erectile response, the average GRAD response, the GRAD standard deviation and the D_2 fractal indices obtained with the neutral and the six-year-old female virtual characters were submitted to analyses as dependent variables. GRAD acceleration was used as a covariate.

Results

See Table 2 for means and standard deviations. Pedophile and non-deviant subjects did not differ on their sexual responses toward neither the control ($F(1,13) = 0.698$, *N.S.*) nor the female child character ($F(1,13)= 4.12$, *N.S.*), even though it was quite close with the latter ($p=0.064$). Pedophile subjects were clearly more inclined towards having a greater sexual response when looking at the child female character, with an average penile gauge stretching of 2.9 mm compared to 0.5 mm for the non-deviant subjects.

Subjects did not differ significantly on their average GRAD response, either with the control stimulus ($F(1,13)= 0.006$, *N.S.*) or with the sexual one ($F(1,13)=0.103$, *N.S.*). The same was obtained with the GRAD standard deviation ($F(1,13)=3.28$, *N.S.*); $F(1,13)= 2.50$, *N.S.*)).

However, subjects did differ significantly on their gaze behavior dynamics as expressed by the D_2 fractal index. They did so only when facing the sexual virtual stimulus ($F(1,13)= 5.1$, $p < .05$), not with the neutral one ($F(1,13)= 1.71$, *N.S.*). These last results mean that pedophile and non-deviant subjects appear to display distinct perceptual-motor dynamics when facing a simulated encounter with a 3D naked female child. The D_2 average value of the pedophile subjects is of a lesser complexity, which means that their gaze behavior dynamic is most probably more readily and steadily attracted to the virtual character depicting a 6-yr old female child (i.e. to where the VMP was tagged on the virtual objects).

Contrary to the average GRAD response, the calculation D_2 allows us to extend our understanding of the perceptual-motor invariance extraction dynamics by more clearly qualifying the processes at work as they unfold over time. The latter information appears to be richer and more able to grasp the impinging influences of psychological factors such as sexual preferences can be.

Discussion

First, the method put forward in this second study is about controlling the attentional content of the assessee through the minute examination of his observational behavior. Knowing if the assessee's eyes are open or not is the very first requisite that our method accomplishes in order to ensure a valid forensic assessment of sexual preferences based upon visual stimuli.

Pinpointing the gaze location relative to the layout of virtual sexual stimuli is a second crucial aspect of the method that can significantly increase the internal validity of the sexual preference assessment procedure based on penile plethysmography. Knowing how and when the assessee scans specific parts of the sexual stimuli clearly opens up new vistas on perceptual and motor processes involved in the control of sexual response.

Finally, this method is also about the possibility of developing an original index of sexual preferences whose basis would be the inherently dynamic properties of the oculomotor behavior as it probes sexual virtual stimuli. The latter possibility is probably the most interesting avenue, since it taps into aspects of the deviant behavior that are not as obvious and overt, and therefore less subject to voluntary control and faking strategies. Further studies are obviously required to clearly disentangle which factors contribute specifically to these distinguishing organized complexities. In particular, the special role of the inhibiting processes used to alter erectile responses has to be experimentally controlled and linked to dynamic patterns.

CONCLUSION

More and more, VR is considered an important therapeutic addition because of its scientific and clinical advantages. This technology will, of course, not replace the therapist's human input into the treatment process, but it can definitely allow patients that benefit from it to expand and develop a range of important experiences that can lead them to a more adaptive lifestyle. Consideration of the perceptual-motor measures associated with the immersive experience is certainly a tool to advance this purpose.

Analysis of negative and positive responses to stimuli, as well as their complex composites, can lead to a better understanding of the manifestations of psychopathologies. By clarifying and deepening our understanding of patient responses, it becomes possible to better understand fundamental perceptual and cognitive causal relationships while revealing the dynamic character of the psychopathology.

Finally, measuring patients' dynamic parameters in VR simulations can possibly lead to new treatment approaches for psychopathologies. The biological and behavioral feedback obtained by virtual mediation, based on parameters of the perceptivo-motor dynamics, such those described in this chapter, represents a promising avenue for future investigation (Renaud et al., 2006c).

REFERENCES

Abel, G. G., Jordan, A., Hand, C. G., Holland, L. A., & Phipps, A. (2001). Classification models of child molesters utilizing the Abel Assessment for Sexual Interest. *Child Abuse & Neglect*, *25*(1), 703–718. doi:10.1016/S0145-2134(01)00227-7

Allanson, J., & Mariani, J. (1999). Mind over virtual matter: Using virtual environments for neurofeedback training. In *Proceedings, IEEE Virtual Reality 1999* (pp. 270-273). New York: IEEE. doi 10.1109/VR.1999.756961.

American Psychiatric Association (APA). (1994). *Diagnostic and statistical manual of mental disorders* (4th edition). Washington, DC: APA.

Baumann, S. B., & Sayette, S. A. (2006). Smoking cues in a virtual world provoke craving in cigarette smokers. *Psychology of Addictive Behaviors*, *20*(4), 484–489. doi:10.1037/0893-164X.20.4.484

Biocca, F. (1995). *Communication in the age of virtual reality*. Mahwah, NJ: Lawrence Erlbaum Associates Inc.

Brewer, M. (2000). Research design and issues of validity. In H. Reis & C. Judd (Eds.), *Handbook of research methods in social and personality psychology*. Cambridge, UK: Cambridge University Press.

Bullinger, A. H., Mueller-Spahn, F., Mager, R., Stoermer, R., Kuntze, M. F., & Wurst, F. (2001). Virtual reality in future diagnoses and treatment. *The World Journal of Biological Psychiatry*, (Suppl. 1), 194S.

Cruz-Neira, C., Sandin, D. J., DeFanti, T. A., Kenyon, R., & Hart, J. C. (1992). The CAVE, Audio Visual Experience Automatic Virtual Environment. *Communications of the ACM*, *35*(6), 64–72. doi:10.1145/129888.129892

Davey, G. C. L. (1994). Self-reported fears to common indigenous animals in an adult U.K. population: The role of disgust sensitivity. *The British Journal of Psychology*, *85*(4), 541–554.

Duchowski, A., Medlin, E., & Cournia, N. (2002). 3-D eye movement analysis. *Behavior Research Methods, Instruments, & Computers*, *34*(4), 573–591.

Ellis, S. R. (1995). Virtual environments and environmental instruments. In K. Carr & R. England (Eds.), *Simulated and virtual realities: Elements of perception* (pp. 11-51). London: Taylor & Francis.

Farkas, G. M., Sine, L. F., & Evans, I. M. (1979). The effects of distraction, performance demand, stimulus explicitness and personality on objective and subjective measures of male sexual arousal. *Behaviour Research and Therapy*, *17*, 25–32. doi:10.1016/0005-7967(79)90047-0

Fischer, L., & Smith, G. M. (1999). Statistical adequacy of The Abel Assessment for interest in paraphilias. *Sexual Abuse*, *11*(1), 195–205. doi:10.1177/107906329901100303

Foxlin, E. (2002). Motion tracking requirements and technologies. In K. Stanney (Ed.) *Handbook of virtual environments: Design, implementation, and applications* (pp.163-210). Mahwah, NJ: Lawrence Erlbaum Associates Inc.

Freund, K. (1963). A laboratory method for diagnosing predominance of homo- and hetero-erotic interest in the male. *Behaviour Research and Therapy*, *1*, 85–93. doi:10.1016/0005-7967(63)90012-3

Garcia-Palacios, A., Hoffman, H. G., & See, S. K. (2001). Redefining therapeutic success with virtual reality exposure therapy. *Cyberpsychology & Behavior*, *4*(3), 341–348. doi:10.1089/109493101300210231

Glasgow, D. V., Osbourne, A., & Croxen, J. (2003). An assessment tool for investigating paedophile sexual interest using viewing time: An application of single case research methodology. *British Journal of Learning Disabilities*, *31*(2), 96–102. doi:10.1046/j.1468-3156.2003.00180.x

Golde, J. A., Strassberg, D. S., & Turner, C. M. (2000). Psychophysiologic assessment of erectile response and its suppression as a function of stimulus media and previous experience with plethysmography. *Journal of Sex Research*, *37*(1), 53–59.

Grassberger, P., & Procaccia, I. (1983). Characterization of strange attractors. *Physical Review Letters*, *50*(5), 346–349. doi:10.1103/PhysRevLett.50.346

Grassberger, P., Schreiber, T., & Schaffrath, C. (1991). Nonlinear time sequence analysis. *International Journal of Bifurcation and Chaos in Applied Sciences and Engineering*, *1*(3), 521–547. doi:10.1142/S0218127491000403

Howes, R. J. (1998). Plethysmographic assessment of incarcerated nonsexual offenders: A comparison with rapists. *Sexual Abuse: Journal of Research and Treatment*, *10*(3), 183–194.

International Society for Presence Resarch (ISPR). (2000). *The Concept of Presence: Explication Statement.* Available at http://www.temple.edu/ispr/frame_explicat.htm

Kalmus, E., & Beech, A. R. (2005). Forensic assessment of sexual interest: A review. *Aggression and Violent Behavior*, *10*(2), 193–217. doi:10.1016/j.avb.2003.12.002

Laws, D. R. (2003). Penile plethysmography. Will we ever get it right? In T. Ward, D. R.Laws, & S. M. Hudson (Eds.), *Sexual deviance: Issues and controversies* (pp. 82-102). Thousand Oaks, CA: Sage Publications.

Laws, D. R., & Gress, C. L. Z. (2004). Seeing things differently: The viewing time alternative to penile plethysmography. *Legal and Criminological Psychology*, *9*(2), 183–196. doi:10.1348/1355325041719338

Laws, D. R., & Marshall, W. L. (2003). A brief history of behavioral and cognitive-behavioral approaches to sexual offenders, Part 1, Early developments. *Sexual Abuse*, *15*(2), 75–92. doi:10.1177/107906320301500201

Looman, J., & Marshall, W. L. (2001). Phallometric assessments designed to detect arousal to children: The responses of rapists and child molesters. *Sexual Abuse*, *13*(1), 3–13. doi:10.1177/107906320101300102

Mager, R., Bullinger, A. H., Mueller-Spahn, F., Kuntze, M. F., & Stoermer, R. (2001). Real-time monitoring of brain activity in patients with specific phobia during exposure therapy, employing a stereoscopic virtual environment. *Cyberpsychology & Behavior*, *4*(4), 465–469. doi:10.1089/109493101750527024

Marshall, W. L., & Fernandez, Y. M. (2000). Phallometric testing with sexual offenders: Limits to its value. *Clinical Psychology Review*, *20*(7), 807–822. doi:10.1016/S0272-7358(99)00013-6

Marshall, W. L., & Fernandez, Y. M. (2003). Sexual preferences: Are they useful in the assessment and treatment of sexual offenders? *Aggression and Violent Behavior*, *8*(2), 131–143. doi:10.1016/S1359-1789(01)00056-8

McConaghy, N. (1999). Unresolved issues in scientific sexology. *Archives of Sexual Behavior*, *28*(4), 285–318. doi:10.1023/A:1018744628161

McSharry, P. E. (2005). The danger of wishing for chaos. *Nonlinear Dynamics Psychology and Life Sciences*, *9*(4), 375–397.

Norcross, J. C., Hedges, M., & Prochaska, J. O. (2002). The face of 2010: A Delphi poll on the future of psychotherapy. *Professional Psychology, Research and Practice*, *33*(3), 316–322. doi:10.1037/0735-7028.33.3.316

North, M. M., North, S. M., & Coble, J. R. (2002). Virtual reality therapy: An effective treatment for psychological disorders. In K. M. Stanney (Ed.), *Handbook of virtual environments: Design, implementation, and applications* (pp. 1065-1078). Mahwah, NJ: Lawrence Erlbaum Associates Inc.

Palsson, O. S., & Pope, A. T. (2002). Morphing beyond recognition: The future of biofeedback technologies. *Biofeedback*, *30*(1), 14–18.

Proulx, J., Cote, G., & Achille, P. A. (1993). Prevention of voluntary control of penile response in homosexual pedophiles during phallometric testing. *Journal of Sex Research*, *30*(2), 140–147.

Quinsey, V. L., & Chaplin, T. C. (1988). Preventing faking in phallometric assessments of sexual preference. *Annals of the New York Acad. of Sciences*, *528*, 49–58. doi:10.1111/j.1749-6632.1988.tb50849.x

Renaud, P. (2004, October). *Moving assessment of sexual interest into the 21st century: the potential of new information technology.* Invited presentation at the 23rd Annual Research and Treatment Conference (ATSA), Albuquerque, NM.

Renaud, P. (2006a). *Method for providing data to be used by a therapist for analyzing a patient behavior in a virtual environment.* US patent 7128577.

Renaud, P., Bouchard, S., & Proulx, R. (2002a). Behavioral avoidance dynamics in the presence of a virtual spider. *IEEE (Institute of Electrical and Electronics Engineers). Transactions in Information Technology and Biomedicine*, *6*, 235–243. doi:10.1109/TITB.2002.802381

Renaud, P., Chartier, S., & Albert, G. (2008, accepted). Embodied and embedded: The dynamics of extracting perceptual visual invariants. In S. Guastello, M. Koopman, & D. Pincus (Eds.), *Chaos and complexity: Recent advances and future directions in the theory of nonlinear dynamical systems psychology*. Cambridge, UK: Cambridge University Press.

Renaud, P., Chartier, S., Albert, G., Cournoyer, L.-G., Proulx, J., & Bouchard, S. (2006b). Sexual presence as determined by fractal oculomotor dynamics. *Annual Review of Cybertherapy and Telemedicine*, *4*, 87–94.

Renaud, P., Chartier, S., Albert, G., Décarie, J., Cournoyer, L.-G., & Bouchard, S. (2007). Presence as determined by fractal perceptual-motor dynamics. *Cyberpsychology & Behavior*, *10*(1), 122–130. doi:10.1089/cpb.2006.9983

Renaud, P., Cusson, J.-F., Bernier, S., Décarie, J., Gourd, S.-P., & Bouchard, S. (2002b). Extracting perceptual and motor invariants using eye-tracking technologies in virtual immersions. In Proceedings of *HAVE'2002-IEEE (Institute of Electrical and Electronics Engineers) International Workshop on Haptic Virtual Environments and their Applications* (pp. 73-78). doi 10.1109/HAVE.2002.1106917.

Renaud, P., Decarie, J., Gourd, S. P., Paquin, L. C., & Bouchard, S. (2003). Eye-tracking in immersive environments: A general methodology to analyze affordance-based interactions from oculomotor dynamics. *Cyberpsychology & Behavior*, *6*(5), 519–526. doi:10.1089/109493103769710541

Renaud, P., Proulx, J., Rouleau, J.-L., Bouchard, S., Bradford, J., Fedoroff, P., et al. (2006c, November). *Sexual and oculomotor biofeedback mediated by sexual stimuli presented in virtual reality*. Paper presented at the 49th annual meeting of the Society for the Scientific Study of Sexuality, Las Vegas.

Renaud, P., Proulx, J., Rouleau, J.-L., Bouchard, S., Madrigrano, G., & Bradford, J. (2005). The recording of observational behaviors in virtual immersion: A new clinical tool to address the problem of sexual preferences with paraphiliacs. *Annual Review of Cybertherapy and Telemedicine*, *3*, 85–92.

Renaud, P., Rouleau, J.-L., Granger, L., Barsetti, I., & Bouchard, S. (2002c). Measuring sexual preferences in virtual reality: A pilot study. *Cyberpsychology & Behavior*, *5*(1), 1–10. doi:10.1089/109493102753685836

Renaud, P., Singer, G., & Proulx, R. (2001). Head-tracking fractal dynamics in visually pursuing virtual objects. In W. Sulis, & I. Trofimova (Eds), *Nonlinear dynamics in life and social sciences* (pp. 333-346). Amsterdam: IOS Press NATO Science Series.

Rheingold, H. (1991). *Virtual reality: The revolutionary technology of computer-generated artificial worlds - and how it promises and threatens to transform business and society*. New York: Summit Books.

Riva, G. (2005). Virtual reality in psychotherapy [review]. *Cyberpsychology & Behavior*, *8*(3), 220–230. doi:10.1089/cpb.2005.8.220

Rizzo, A., Buckwalter, J. G., Neumann, U., Chua, C., Van Rooyen, A., & Larson, P. (1999). Virtual environments for targeting cognitive processes: An overview of projects at the University of Southern California Integrated Media Systems. *Cyberpsychology & Behavior*, *2*(2), 89–100. doi:10.1089/cpb.1999.2.89

Rosenzweig, S. (1942). The photoscope as an objective device for evaluating sexual interest. *Psychosomatic Medicine*, *4*, 150–158.

Rothbaum, B. O., Hodges, L. F., Smith, S., Lee, J. H., & Price, L. (2000). A controlled study of virtual reality exposure therapy for the fear of flying. *Journal of Consulting and Clinical Psychology*, *68*(6), 1020–1026. doi:10.1037/0022-006X.68.6.1020

Schubert, T., Friedmann, F., & Regenbrecht, H. (2001). The experience of presence: Factor analytic insights. *Presence (Cambridge, Mass.)*, *10*(3), 266–281. doi:10.1162/105474601300343603

Seto, M. C., & Barbaree, H. E. (1996). Sexual aggression as antisocial behavior: A developmental model. In D. Stoff, J. Brieling, & J. D. Maser (Eds.), *Handbook of antisocial behavior* (pp. 524-533). New York: Wiley.

Simon, W. T., & Schouten, P. G. (1991). Plethysmography in the assessment and treatment of sexual deviance: An overview. *Archives of Sexual Behavior*, *20*, 75–91. doi:10.1007/BF01543009

Singer, B. (1984). Conceptualizing sexual arousal and attraction. *Journal of Sex Research*, *20*(3), 230–240.

Slater, M., Steed, A., & McCarthy, J. (1998). The influence of body movement on subjective presence in virtual environments. *Human Factors*, *40*(3), 469–477. doi:10.1518/001872098779591368

Slater, M., & Wilbur, S. (1997). A framework for immersive virtual environments (FIVE): Speculations on the role of presence in virtual environments. *Presence (Cambridge, Mass.)*, *6*(6), 603–616.

Smith, G. M., & Fischer, L. (1999). Assessment of juvenile sex offenders: Reliability and validity of The Abel Assessment for interest in paraphilias. *Sexual Abuse*, *11*(3), 207–216. doi:10.1177/107906329901100304

Sprott, J. C. (2003). *Chaos and time-series analysis*. Oxford, UK: Oxford University Press.

Stanney, K. M., & Zyda, M. (2002). Virtual environments in the 21st century. In K.M. Stanney (Ed.), *Handbook of virtual environments: Design, implementation, and applications* (pp. 1-14). Mahwah, NJ: Lawrence Erlbaum Associates Inc.

Theiler, J., Eubank, S., Longtin, A., Galdrikian, B., & Farmer, J. D. (1992). Testing for nonlinearity in time series: The method of surrogate data. *Physica D. Nonlinear Phenomena*, *58*(1-4), 77–94. doi:10.1016/0167-2789(92)90102-S

Trepagnier, S., Sebrechts, M. M., & Peterson, R. (2002). Atypical face gaze in autism. *Cyberpsychology & Behavior*, *5*(3), 213–217. doi:10.1089/109493102760147204

Virilio, P. (1980). *Esthétique de la disparition*. Paris: Balland.

Wann, J. P., Rushton, S. K., Smyth, M., & Jones, D. (1997). Virtual environments for the rehabilitation of disorders of attention and movement. *Studies in Health Technology and Informatics*, *44*, 157–164.

Wiederhold, B. K., Jang, D. P., Kim, S. I., & Wiederhold, M. D. (2002). Physiological monitoring as an objective tool in Virtual Reality therapy. *Cyberpsychology & Behavior*, *5*(1), 77–82. doi:10.1089/109493102753685908

Wiederhold, B. K., & Rizzo, A. (2005). Virtual Reality and applied psychophysiology. *Applied Psychophysiology and Biofeedback*, *30*(3), 183–187. doi:10.1007/s10484-005-6375-1

Wiederhold, B. K., & Wiederhold, M. D. (2004). *Virtual Reality therapy for anxiety disorders*. Washington D.C: American Psychological Association Press.

Wilder, J., Hung, G., Tremaine, M., & Kaur, M. (2002). Eye tracking in virtual environments. In K. M. Stanney (Ed.), *Handbook of virtual environments: Design, implementation, and applications* (pp. 211-222). Mahwah, NJ: Lawrence Erlbaum Associates Inc.

Witmer, B. G., & Singer, M. J. (1998). Measuring presence in virtual environments: A Presence Questionnaire. *Presence (Cambridge, Mass.)*, *7*(3), 225–240. doi:10.1162/105474698565686

Zamansky, H. S. (1956). A technique for measuring homosexual tendencies. *Journal of Personality*, *24*(4), 436–448. doi:10.1111/j.1467-6494.1956.tb01280.x

ADDITIONAL READING

Guastello, S., Koopman, M., & Pincus, D. (2008). *Chaos and complexity: Recent advances and future directions in the theory of nonlinear dynamical systems psychology.* Cambridge, UK: Cambridge University Press.

International Society for Presence Resarch (ISPR). (2000). *The concept of presence: Explication statement.* Available at http://www.temple.edu/ispr/frame_explicat.htm.

North, M. M., North, S. M., & Coble, J. R. (2002). Virtual reality therapy: An effective treatment for psychological disorders. In K. M. Stanney (Ed.), *Handbook of virtual environments: Design, implementation, and applications* (pp. 1065-1078). Mahwah, NJ: Lawrence Erlbaum Associates Inc.

KEY TERMS AND DEFINITIONS

Approach Behavior: Tropism toward a source, usually expressed in the presence of an appetitive source.

Arachnophobia: A psychiatric disorder characterized by a pathological fear of spider.

Avoidance Behavior: Tropism away from a source, usually expressed in the presence of an aversive source.

Feeling of Presence: A psychological state or subjective perception while using technology such as virtual reality, in which an individual does not maintain full awareness of the role of the technology but perceives partly or fully as though the technology-filtered experience is "real."

Immersive Video-Oculography: Eye-tracking performed in virtual immersion.

Nonlinear Dynamics: The study of systems governed by equations in which a small change in one variable can induce large systematic fluctuations. Nonlinear dynamics may lead to chaotic behaviors and generate fractal patterns.

Paraphilia: A psychiatric disorder characterized by deviant sexual behaviours.

Virtual Reality: An artificially simulated reality that may induce a feeling of presence, generally a 3D environment generated by computer.

ENDNOTES

1 Recent studies aiming to use electroencephalographic signals for biofeedback purposes in VR have been reported. This biofeedback, mediated by the virtual environment's intermediate, is also called "neurofeedback" (Allanson & Mariani, 1999). We have developed the first biofeedback prototype of male and female sexual responses mediated by VR (Renaud et al., 2006c).

2 VR in clinical psychology dates back to 1992. It was introduced by the Human-Computer Interaction Group at Clark University (North, North, & Coble, 2002).

3 Based on studies conducted by Norcross, Hedges, and Prochaska (2002), these approaches are among some of the most promising ones.

Section 3
Learning Efficacy

Chapter 16
The Efficacy of Games and Simulations for Learning

Louise Sauvé
Télé-université, Canada

Lise Renaud
University of Quebec in Montreal, Canada

David Kaufman
Simon Fraser University, Canada

ABSTRACT

This chapter presents a synthesis of the literature (1998-2008) on the efficacy of games and simulations for learning. Based on definitions and sets of essential attributes for games and for simulations, the authors examine the contributions of each to knowledge structuring and the development of problem solving skills. Noting that games and simulations have positive learning outcomes in various situations, the authors present variables to measure the knowledge and skills developed by learners who use games and simulations. This work is intended to contribute to the development of an analytical framework for future studies on the efficacy of games and simulations for learning.

INTRODUCTION

Game and simulation research on learning has been characterized by a large variety of approaches, as well as discrepancies in the presentation and interpretation of results. These have led to contradictory and confusing results on their educational efficacy. To begin to address these issues, we undertook a literature review based on a validated analytical framework to gauge the efficacy of educational games and simulations on learning (Sauvé, Renaud, Kaufman, & Sibomana, 2008). This review identified 2,244 articles on games, simulations and simulation games published during the period 1998 – 2008 and analyzed in detail 806 relevant English and French articles to reach our conclusions.

To ensure that the activities in the reviewed literature were truly "games" and "simulations," we initially determined the essential attributes of these concepts, as presented in Chapter 1. This work enabled us to identify specific impacts as arising from games, simulations, or simulation games, based on descriptions or definitions of the learning activities as written by the article authors. Based

DOI: 10.4018/978-1-61520-731-2.ch016

on our definitions, some of the activities studied were rejected (if the learning activity was neither a game nor a simulation); if they were labeled as games but fit our definition of simulations, they were reviewed as such.

This chapter introduces a synthesis of the publications (1998-2008) that treat the most significant contributions of games and simulations on learning. Additional results can be found in an extensive research report (Sauvé et al., 2008). In this chapter, we first discuss the main motivation for the systematic review. Next, we describe the methodology underlying our study, including the analytical framework, database searches, data collection and organization, and analysis. We then outline the efficacy of games on learning in the areas of knowledge structuring and problem solving. Finally, we discuss the most prominent learning efficacy of simulations that emerged from the review. We hope that this chapter will contribute to establishing a frame of reference for future research on the efficacy of games and simulations for learning.

THE PROBLEM

Because authors seldom distinguish among games, simulations and simulation games, the debate on the efficacy of (broadly-defined) "games" for learning, as well as their impact on other aspects of life (e.g., health, sedentary lifestyle, violence), draws many confusing comments on what games and simulations can achieve, not only for learning, but also as a societal phenomenon. Feinstein, Mann, and Corsun (2002) comment on their reaction to this amalgamation of terms:

This article arises from frustration, the frustration from reading a wide variety of papers each using words like simulation, games, role playing, gaming, and symbolic modeling either without definition or inconsistency from one work to another. (p. 732)

Some studies have shown that games and simulations provide favorable learning conditions, in particular through feedback, interaction and active learner participation; for examples, see Baranowski et al. (2003), Becker (2007), Egenfeldt-Nielsen (2005), and Jones (1998). Others (e.g., Bottino, Ferlino, Ott, & Tavella, 2006; Facer et al., 2004; and Garris, Ahlers, & Driskell, 2002) have demonstrated that games and simulations have an unquestionable efficacy for cognitive and emotional learning as well as motor skills.

In contrast, other authors[1] claim that it is difficult to gather strong evidence on the effectiveness of games and simulations on learning because of certain research obstacles:

- factors related to the research, such as weakness of studies' theoretical framework, defective or overly varied methodology, and lack of a continuum between theory and practice
- factors related to learner characteristics: for example, his/her past experiences—school, social, cultural and economic, age, and gender
- procedural factors: for example, the way in which the teacher/instructor introduces the game or simulation, the involvement of the teacher/instructor during the course of the game or simulation (before, during, and after), and the way in which the teacher/instructor hosts the wrap-up discussion (face-to-face or at distance)
- factors relating to game and simulation characteristics and the learning context, including: pedagogical aspects (feedback, motivation, interaction, quality, authenticity, adequacy of the contents in light of the learning goals, etc.), organizational factors (class time limits, lack of verification, lack of support materials, lack of time to learn a game, curriculum unsuitability, etc.) and technical aspects (consistency, appearance, simplicity, adaptability, etc)

In general, the goal of research is to advance a discipline by outlining theories as well as practices and by evaluating or modifying them as needed (Gauthier, 2005). With this intent, it is essential to note the factors that have been received special attention from other researchers and that have led to well-established conclusions. In order to establish a theoretical foundation for effective analysis of the efficacy of games and simulations for learning, our systematic analysis of the literature from 1998 to 2008 addressed the question "Does the use of the essential attributes, identified in the research literature as criteria for the classification of games and of simulations, lead to a different interpretation from existing results? If yes, what type of learning do educational games and simulations support? "

METHODOLOGY

In this study we used the Aktouf (1987) method, described as establishing the current "state of knowledge." This involves a review that is, if possible, complete, exhaustive, and critical, of the specific work that has been done on a problem which one would like to address; it is, in effect, a review of all principal research on the subject (p. 55). We began with an exhaustive search for articles on games and simulations, followed by a detailed examination of the results of select articles discussing their learning impacts (contributions to learning).

Patton (1980, p.163) emphasizes the importance of undertaking a literature review prior to conducting a study in order to be informed when determining the questions to be investigated and to know which approaches have been used by other researchers in this field. As Quivy and Campenhoudt (1988) note:

Any research work takes place in a continuum and can be located in or in comparison with the currents of thought which precede it and influence it. It is therefore normal that a researcher acquaints himself with previous work concerning comparable objects and is explicit about what is close to what differentiates his own work from these trains of thought.. (pp. 40-41)

The Analytical Framework

To conduct the literature review, we designed and validated an analytical grid for articles and research reports on the efficacy of games and simulations on learning. The design of the grid (see Sauvé et al., 2008 for details) was based on the research hypotheses, and the grid was validated by inter-rater agreement (Lincoln & Guba, 1985) to ensure data coding reliability. Four researchers who were not involved in the original coding process coded the articles separately according to the grid categories and subcategories. When coding was not identical among researchers, a discussion led to mutual understanding regarding the points of difficulty and to an adjustment of certain elements in the grid, if necessary. This operation, applied to many articles, led to an eventual agreement of greater than 80% and made it possible to confirm the relevance of the categories in the grid. Once the grid was validated, the agreed codes and interpretations were transferred to an Internet-accessible database. This database presently contains the analysis of 806 articles and research reports on games, simulations and simulation games. (Note that some analyses concluded that the articles were not relevant for the purposes of the "definitions" or "impact" aspects of the study).

Databases

To locate relevant articles and research reports, 21 databases, of which 18 were in English and three in French (Appendix 1), were consulted, as well as the proceedings of the last four years' *ED-MEDIA*, *E-Learn*, and *SITE* conferences. Bibliographical database searches were done with the terms *jeu, simulation, jeu de simulation*, game, serious game, simulation and game, simulation, gaming, simulation, impact, effects, *éducation*, education, *apprentissage*, learning, educational game, learning game, and game & experimental.

Articles, theses and reports published from 1998 (the date of our original funding proposal for this work) to 2008 were identified and integrated into the bibliographical (*EndNote®*) and grid databases. These were developed in two stages:

- location, and sorting of references: 2,244 articles were examined, 806 of which were selected for our study
- reading and detailed analysis of the 806 selected texts and completion of a record for each in the online database

Summaries of the Literature Review

Since the systematic analysis of texts was carried out over five years and involved more than twelve research assistants, five annual reports on the literature review were written. The final report (Sauvé et al., 2008) is available online at www.sageforlearning.ca.

Concepts Used in the Analysis

To answer the research question, we adopted the following definitions for the concepts being studied:

- **(Educational) game** is a fictitious, fantasy or imaginary situation in which players, placed in conflict with others or assembled in a team against an external opponent, are governed by rules determining their actions with a view to achieving learning objectives and a goal determined by the game, either to win or to seek revenge. The majority of the articles analyzed reported on studies of paper or board-based games or digital games on a computer or online.
- **Simulation** is a simplified, dynamic, and accurate representation of a reality, represented as a system.
- **(Educational) efficacy** is central to analyses in education research, referring to discussion of the consequences of practices, methods, structures, changes, or innovations (Gayet, 2006). Our conceptual approach in this study is normative: identification of positive or negative consequences for learning. In our analysis, educational efficacy is defined by positive consequences from the use of a game on participant knowledge, attitudes, or psychomotor skills. It takes into account the relationship between the learning results of game or simulation use and the initial objectives (Blouin & Bergeron, 1997).
- **Learning** is the acquisition of knowledge or skills with the help of experience, practice or study. Learning results include knowledge, attitudes and skills acquired by students.
- **Knowledge structuring** refers to the construction and organization of knowledge, schemas (mental models), or representations by the learner in order to understand a concept, principal, procedure to be followed, or a given situation. To give us a frame of reference for the variables of analysis that measure knowledge structuring with games or simulations, we used six types of links that an activity must create, according to Andrieu and Borgeois (2003), to develop knowledge structuring capacities in the learner:
  1. **Sequential**: Link between two elements of chronological order among information, concepts and propositions.
  2. **Discriminating**: Link based on the principle of contradiction, involving the operations of differentiation, selection, sorting and classification. It invites the learner to put concepts into methodological or conceptual order.

3. **Conditional**: Link corresponding to a hypothetical relationship between two logical elements. It invites the learner to use her knowledge to explore a hypothesis.
4. **Causal:** Link of cause and effect between two ideas, pieces of knowledge, or concepts. It can also work in reverse, asking the learner to discover or establish a cause.
5. **Transfer**: Link requiring the use of knowledge apart from its initial validation domain. It applies to new concepts and knowledge and is a question of transferring acquired knowledge.
6. **Problem**: Link connecting an element of knowledge with problems to be solved by the learner. It is a higher level link than the others and is often proposed for the formal aspects of organization or implementation.

- **Problem solving skills** cover several aspects of cognition such as schemas (recognition of familiar problem elements), transfer (skill required to establish a link to similar problems), creativity (development of new solutions), and critical thought (reflection). The goal of learning through problem solving is to help learners apply abstract or theoretical concepts to concrete situations or practical cases.

We now examine what the literature says about the efficacy of games and simulations for certain aspects of learning.

THE CONTRIBUTIONS OF GAMES TO LEARNING

While opinions vary, games are increasingly seen as effective resources for learning (DeMaria, 2007; Galloway, 2006; Gee, 2007; Moline, 2008; Shaffer, 2006). Their effectiveness is such that the *Federation of American Scientists* (FAS) uses educational games to teach academic content, to improve a learner's critical thinking and to evaluate their learning (FAS, 2006). Academic journals have dedicated special issues exploring how and why computer games can be efficacious for learning, in particular *Tech Trends* (Squire, 2005) and the *Journal of Educational Multimedia and Hypermedia* (Ferdig, 2007). However, other studies (e.g. Baldaro et al., 2004; Barab, Thomas, Dodge, Carteaux, & Tuzun, 2005; Kelly, 2005) note negative or non-significant results of games on cognitive and affective learning. Shreve (2005) is an enthusiast when it comes to the introduction of educational computer games in the classroom but emphasizes the difficulties associated with their use. For example, it is difficult to follow multiple learners' progress in a game while they are all using one assigned computer (the teacher then has difficulty controlling the group), and the games used do not always respond adequately to the educational objectives determined by teachers. Virvou, Katsionis and Manos (2005), who have developed educational software, have noted that many digital educational games created in the past were either not particularly fun or not very educational.

Cuban (2001) echoes this prudence with respect to the introduction of digital games in teaching. He notes, based on varied research sources, that specialists in the domain of child development do not agree with the use of information and communication technologies (ICTs) and consequently on the use of educational computer games. Their agreement on the use of these technologies is highly conditional, including several "ifs" and many precautions. Finally, Fournier, Vincent, and Brougere (2004) note that the evidence of the educational value of the games in scientific research is insufficient, but they believe that it is possible to learn while playing.

In light of these mixed viewpoints, our analysis focused on two specific learning impacts: *knowledge structuring* and *problem solving*.

The selection of these two areas is based on past studies carried out on this subject with generally positive results.

The following sections summarize our results; as noted above, our full report with detailed analyses and a full bibliography is available online at www.sageforlearning.ca.

Knowledge Structuring

Our review of the literature concluded that games (digital, video, and traditional) have a positive result on knowledge structuring, and it identified variables used by researchers to measure efficacy. Some studies mentioned specifically that the participation of learners in the game improved or reinforced their knowledge of the subject matter being studied. Others[i] confirmed this conclusion based on comparative experimentation using pre-tests and post-tests on the subject matter taught by the game, which shows significant positive results of games for knowledge structuring. For example, Shaftel, Pass, and Schnabel (2005) obtained positive results in tests of mathematics games. Ravenscroft (2007), in teaching reasoning at the secondary level, noted that trying out an educational game allowed the learners to improve their understanding of key concepts. The majority of cases reported in the reviewed articles stated that the games tested by learners facilitated assimilation of key information.

Seven studies [i] showed that games develop in learners the capacity to build schemas, which in turn enables them to better solve a problem, visualize a concept, establish links among concepts, etc. A game can make it possible for the learner to integrate new subject matter and new concepts in a more intuitive way, in addition to allowing prior knowledge to be reorganized to facilitate understanding. Regarding the structuring of mathematical knowledge, Shaftel et al. (2005) emphasized that games can provide an environment in which incorrect solutions are not errors, but help in assembling mathematical knowledge. Tommelein, Riley and Howell (1998, p. 13) concluded that "...the game does not require many resources to be played but it does allow the players to develop a better, intuitive understanding of several fundamental production concepts, including variability and throughput." Finally, four authors mentioned that games support the structuring of knowledge, without defining this concept or providing results from experiments.

Some authors[i] have examined how games allow learners to develop their capacity to establish links, intuitively or not, showing that games support development of the capacity to transfer knowledge acquired in other contexts. Other authors [i] have considered the notions of assimilation, knowledge strengthening through statistical analysis, or learner results following the use of a game in a school context or for a particular subject (e.g., mathematics, French, or medicine). Finally, Wissman and Tankel (2001) mentioned the capacity for appropriation as being an element of knowledge sructuring.

In short, studies have shown that games support learning through the development of many of the capacities involved in knowledge structuring:

- the capacity to call upon prior knowledge, or establish a link (sequential or chronological) between prior knowledge and information acquired during the learning process (sequential link)
- the capacity to observe, organize and gather the data elements in order to integrate them (discriminatory link)
- an increased awareness of the differences and similarities between the various elements of the subject being studied, establishing a link based on the principle of contradiction. This discriminatory link comes into play in the operations of distinction, selection, sorting and classification
- the capacity to establish an analogy or comparison between two additional pieces of information, either contradictory or

complementary, in order to gain understanding (discriminatory link)

- the capacity to locate key elements of the subject under study, as in identifying theoretical or declaratory knowledge of a given subject, and to put it in logical order. This conditional link corresponds to a hypothetical relationship between several elements of the same content
- the capacity to explain ideas and to consolidate comprehension of the principles implied in the game (conditional link)
- the capacity to establish links across concepts, as in developing a cause-and-effect link between two or more ideas or concepts, or starting with the result and discovering and establishing the cause
- The capacity to transfer knowledge into other contexts (transfer link)

The game studies that we reviewed did not consider development of the capacity to establish cognitive links.

Problem-Solving Skills

Our analysis showed that 40 articles[i] described the efficacy of games for learning in a similar manner. Most see it as a learner's development of strategies and capacities to make decisions, to understand a problem, to develop hypothetical solutions, and to solve a given problem. Games allow the learner to develop the logic needed to solve a problem and to test it in an entertaining, relaxed learning environment. Shi (2000) and Squire (2005) consider that problem-solving is one of the important contributions of game-based learning.

In their study of computer games, Bottino et al. (2006) showed that the games *PappaLOTTO, Hexip, Studio 5* and *Magic Bass* allowed elementary-level students in Italy to develop aptitudes for reasoning and the use of cognitive strategies. More precisely, the students noted that leaving things to luck did not pay off, and it was more advantageous to establish a work strategy to solve the problems encountered during the game in order to win. Similarly, Ko (2002) concluded that students at the elementary education level who played *Find Flamingo* learned how to build hypotheses (differentiating the cards) and find the answer (finding the "Flamingo" card hidden in a deck of 25 cards).

Six authors[i] mentioned the educational efficacy of computer games for solving problems, without always defining the type of game used. Shreve (2005) discussed video games (*serious games*) without differentiating between types of games, nor between games, simulations and simulation games, but stated their educational advantages.

Randel, Morris, Wetzel, and Whitehill (1992) carried out a literature review for the period 1963 to 1991 on educational games and simulations. They noted that games have a beneficial effect on learning when they concentrate on clearly defined contents and require many exercises, such as solving problems in mathematics. Shaftel et al. (2005), citing Holton, Ahmed, Williams, and Hill (2001) and Quinn, Koca, and Weening (1992), also emphasized the increased potential of (mathematical) games to encourage new strategies and the use of logical reasoning.

Generally, the studies we reviewed clearly identified variables used to analyze the efficacy of games for developing problem-solving skills. The variables include:

- the capacity to recognize familiar elements in a problem in the form of a diagram
- the capacity to draw a link between similar problems
- the capacity to formulate hypothetical answers
- the capacity to formulate and apply strategies to develop a solution
- the capacity to develop new solutions
- the capacity to explain the problem (comprehension) and the solution (evaluation)

- the capacity to reflect and distance oneself from the results obtained

THE CONTRIBUTIONS OF SIMULATIONS TO LEARNING

Simulations, as distinguished from games and simulation games (see Chapter 1), offer learners an ideal context for exploration, discovery, communication, practice, and creation of their own understanding of complex phenomenon (Boethel & Dimock, 1999; Gradler, 2004). Simulation models allow the learner to practice successful experiences, which helps to develop self-confidence and other positive attitudes (Bandura, 1986; Kaufman, Mann, & Jennett, 2000). Reflection in practice and reflection on practice are considered indispensible elements in the development of metacognitive abilities and for the development of expertise (Dobson et al., 2002; Schön, 1987). Simulations allow the development of multiple abilities through their interactivity, immersion and sustained motivation, degree of control, practice, feedback, and authentic experimental learning that would be impossible in a real-life situation because of cost and the need for personnel (Johne, 2002; Ruben, 1999; St-Germain & Laveault, 1997).

Our review of articles on the impacts of simulations was based on the work of Sauvé (1985) and Kaufman and Sauvé (2003). The articles we analyzed came primarily from five fields: businesses, health, organizational management, second language learning, and manual skills training where the actual experience is difficult, dangerous or expensive to acquire, such as learning to fly a fighter plane. Clearly certain educational advantages make simulations practically indispensible. For example, it would be too dangerous to ask a doctor in training to "practice" on a patient, and unreasonable to create a combat situation so that a fighter plane pilot could practice. We now examine the most significant impacts of simulation raised in the analysis of the articles.

Knowledge Structuring

Van Houcke, Vereecke and Gemmel (2005, p. 563) defined knowledge structuring in reference to the process of organizing knowledge in a context of active learning and constant feedback. They emphasized that simulations offer a favorable context, allowing students to learn at their own pace, and argue that this is an important component in the knowledge structuring process. More precisely, Kokol, Kokol, and Dinevski (2005) noted that students learn more effectively when they are in control of the pace of their learning, when they are actively involved, and when feedback is regularly provided. More precisely, knowledge structuring comes from the concrete experience given by simulation, called the "experiential base" (Apkan, 2002). Learners acquire new information (Olsen, 2000), build their own understanding and interpretation (Repine & Hemler, 1999; Windschitl & Andre, 1998), and develop more sophisticated and full comprehension (Moseley, 2001; Pei, 1998) that can be generalized (Mechling, Gast, & Langone, 2002). They increase their comprehension of the principles which they apply during simulation. Bridge, Appleyard, Ward, Philips, and Beavis (2007) meant something similar when they confirmed that students in radiotherapy developed better comprehension of their participation in treatment following simulation.

Apkan (2002) concluded that simulation based on "guided discovery" contributes to the integration of information. For Schmidt (2003), students who must explain their ideas in a simulation consolidate their understanding of the principles involved. Other authors[i] added that simulations allow leaners to repeat or vary actions to ensure acquisition and understanding of all concepts. The more the situation requires the learner to use knowledge, the more the knowledge becomes concrete.

Schnotz and Rasch (2005, p. 47) described the process of knowledge structuring as the way in which the learner assimilates information and masters various possible representations in order to integrate it into a coherent "big picture." Certain learning environments, for example simulations, encourage learners to develop their research competencies and information evaluation in complex informational spaces so that they learn how to structure their knowledge coherently. Feinstein, Mann, and Corsun (2002) reiterate that: "... authors have contended that an effective learning environment is one that allows learners to explore and learn independently. Simulation seems to fall into this category in particular, because of its inherent ability to allow learners to evaluate and manipulate an object system" (p. 735). Alberto, Cihak and Gama (2005) noted that simulation allows the student to react in the event of an error and to carry out necessary adjustments, consolidating knowledge and maximizing learner understanding of the concepts to be mastered. In the health field, Alinier, Hunt, Gordon, and Harwood (2006) concluded that medical simulations are an effective way to practice new procedures and to learn the effects of new drugs.

Goldenberg, Andrusyszyn and Iwasiw (2005, p. 311) noted that simulation helps improve certain capacities, particularly the observation, organization and integration of information. Shellman and Turan (2006) explained that simulation requires participants to continually link their theoretical knowledge to their actions. Olsen (2000) noted that in a simulation, learners "reconcile" their theories with reality.

Finally, other authors stressed the importance of discussion (debriefing) while learning with simulations in order to ensure that the process of knowledge structuring is adequate. According to Medley and Horne (2005, p 32) "the debriefing seminar is essential and must not be omitted because most of the learning occurs at this time." During these discussions, learners can discuss their simulation experience. They can enrich their learning by listening to the experiences of other learners. They can also find the answers to their questions while talking with the other learners and teachers involved in the simulation. These discussions make it possible to link the process related to the structuring of knowledge by offering the learner the opportunity to challenge his/her new knowledge and to validate it. Bos, Shami and Naab (2006) emphasized the importance of discussions among learners at the end of a simulation; exchanges among peers allow the resolution of ethical dilemmas in a field of studies as well as learning through the discussion. Also, Van Houcke et al. (2005) stated that:

In the discussion following the game, performance of the teams is compared and participants are asked to describe the strategies they have followed. This leads them to a clear understanding of the meaning of the critical path and the impact of activities on the critical path. (p. 55)

The studies analyzed in this area reached positive conclusions with regards to developing learners' capacity to refer to concepts, definitions, and theories acquired beforehand and to apply them to concrete situations during a simulation. Some added that consolidating knowledge through repetition and variation of actions will ensure that learners acquire and understand new concepts. Briefly, the studies showed that simulations support the development of capacities involved in knowledge structuring:

- the capacity to consolidate prior knowledge (sequential link)
- the capacity to observe, organize and gather information (discriminatory link)
- the capacity to assimilate information and to master the different possible representations in order to integrate them into a coherent ensemble (conditional link)
- the capacity to apply adequate behaviors, in the event of an error during the sequence of operations and carry out necessary adjustments (causal link)

- the capacity to explain their ideas and consolidate understanding of the principles involved in the simulation (conditional link), to interpret them and to generalize (problem link)
- the capacity to refer to concepts, definitions and theories previously acquired, and apply them to concrete and individual situations (transfe link)
- the capacity to challenge one's knowledge and validate it (problem link)

This review of studies on simulation shows that simulation supports the development of all the capacities that structure knowledge. However, some studies attributed the development of the capacity to establish problem links to the use of debriefing at the end of the simulation. We hypothesize that a debriefing discussion at the end of an educational game would support the development of this capacity.

Problem-Solving Skills

Twenty-two authors[i] agreed that the purpose of learning through problem solving is to help students apply a learned theory to a concrete situation in which the learner develops mental models, transfers the learning and displays creativity. These authors stated that the capacity to solve problems is, among other things, the result of greater understanding of the problem domain. For Jones (1997), this demonstrates Piaget's theory of accommodation, in which the solution to a simulation problem is not obvious but requires accumulation and assimilation of information, then linking this information to schemas (knowledge) that the learner already has.

Simulation makes it possible to define a desirable situation and to find solutions to reach it (Barnaud, Promburom, Trebuit, & Bousquet, 2007). It supports decision making and faster resolution of problem situations than more traditional education or training (Cioffi, Purcal & Arundell, 2005; Feinstein, Mann, & Corsun, 2002). It causes learners to analyze, and encourages them to develop coherent potential explanations (Goldenberg et al., 2005). Lastly, it exercises learners' cognitive skills through role-playing (Gradler, 2004) without explicitly defining the types of skill. Gradler noted that the learner who examines a problem situation with a point of view that is not necessarily his/her own widens his/her spectrum of possible solutions by adapting to situations or new perspectives:

Simulations require participants to apply their cognitive and metacognitive capabilities in the execution of a particular role. Thus, an important advantage of simulations from the perspective of learning, is that they provide opportunities for students to solve ill-defined problems. (p. 573)

Simulation is appropriate for teaching decision making and teamwork. It offers similar situations to those of real organizations, which makes it possible for the learner to experience and understand decision-making errors and inaccuracies resulting from the interaction of people and their personalities, without the inherent risks (Dong & Kwonki, 2008; Pittaway & Cope, 2007). However, these authors did not say whether participation in team simulations develops any cognitive aspects of problem solving.

In the health field, simulations provide alternative and autonomous learning environments where knowledge is acquired and applied, thus allowing the development of professional experience (Kiegaldi & White, 2006). Rosenbaum, Klopfer, and Perry (2007) studied an infection-transmission simulation in secondary level science in which the participants learned how to collect and evaluate the necessary information to solve a given problem, allowing them to contain the spread of an epidemic by finding the toxin responsible. Goldenberg et al. (2005) noted that simulation can help nursing students broaden their knowledge of the teaching-learning process, identify common experiences, generate explanations and analyses, and address a number of issues important to their practice experiences.

Several authors highlighted simulation mechanisms that support problem solving: the use of graphs (Rodriguez, 1998), the visual aspect of simulations compared to reading-based teaching (Zhu, Zhou, & Yin, 2001), rotation through tasks by each learner for better understanding of the decision-making process (Jacobs et al., 2003), learning with peers or in a group (Schmidt, 2003), and repetition (Cioffi et al., 2005). Brozik and Zapalska (1999) and Gaba, Howard, Fish, Smith, and Sowb (2001) mentioned the active participation of a learner during a simulation. Cherry, Williams, and Ali (2007) agreed, based on a study in which students in the medical emergency field, involved in a simulation relating to the process of diagnosis of trauma and the prescription of treatment, developed their skills in problem solving. Under these study conditions, it appears that simulation is an effective means for learning problem solving methods.

For the majority of the authors reviewed, simulation supported the development of the following problem solving skills:

- the capacity to accumulate and assimilate information and to build schemas
- the capacity to collect the necessary information to solve the problem presented
- the capacity to identify common experiences
- the capacity to analyze and identify a certain number of applicable questions in their practices
- the capacity to analyse and create coherent potential explanations or hypotheses
- the capacity to make decisions
- the capacity to transfer knowledge into practice

CONCLUSION

In light of assertions by researchers on the difficulties of showing the learning efficacy of games and

Table1. Summary of indicators used to measure the educational efficacy of games and simulations for knowledge structuring

Game	Simulation
• the capacity to call upon prior knowledge, or establishing a link (sequential or chronological) between prior knowledge and information acquired during the learning process; • the capacity to observe, organize and gather data elements in order to integrate them. (discriminatory link); • an increased awareness of the differences and similarities between the various elements of the subject being studied, establishing a link based on the principle of contradiction. This discriminatory link comes into play in the operations of distinction, selection, sorting and classification; • the capacity to establish an analogy or comparison between two additional pieces of information, either contradictory or complementary, in order to gain understanding (discriminatory link); • the capacity to locate key elements of the subject under study, as in identifying theoretical or declaratory knowledge of a given subject and to put it in logical order. This conditional link corresponds to a hypothetical relationship between several elements of the same contents; • the capacity to explain ideas and to consolidate comprehension of the principles implied in the game (conditional link); • the capacity to establish links across concepts, as in developing a cause-and-effect link between two or more ideas or concepts. This can also work in the other direction, starting with the result and discovering and establishing the cause; • the capacity to transfer new knowledge into other contexts (transfer link).	• the capacity to call upon prior knowledge to consolidate new knowledge (sequential link); • the capacity to observe, organize and gather information (discriminatory link); • the capacity to assimilate information and to master the different possible representations in order to integrate them into a coherent ensemble of knowledge (conditional link); • the capacity to apply adequate behaviors in the event of an error during the sequence of operations and carry out necessary adjustments (causal link); • the capacity to explain ideas and consolidate understanding of the principles involved in the simulation (conditional link), to interpret and generalize them (problem link); • the capacity to refer to concepts, definitions, and theories previously acquired, and apply them to concrete and individual situations (transfer link); • the capacity to challenge and validate one's knowledge (problem link).

Table 2. Summary of indicators used to measure the educational efficacy of games and simulations for problem-solving

Game	Simulation
• the capacity to recognize familiar elements in a problem in the form of a diagram; • the capacity to draw a link between similar problems; • the capacity to formulate hypothetical answers; • the capacity to formulate and apply strategies to develop a solution; • the capacity to develop new solutions; • the capacity to explain the problem (comprehension) and the solution (evaluation) in different words; • the capacity to reflect and distance oneself from results obtained.	• the capacity to accumulate and assimilate information to build schemas; • the capacity to collect the necessary information to solve the problem presented; • the capacity to identify common experiences; • the capacity to analyze and identify a certain number of applicable questions in their practices; • the capacity to analyze and conceive of coherent potential explanations or solution hypotheses; • the capacity to make decisions; • the capacity to transfer knowledge into practice.

simulations, we undertook a systematic review of the literature (1998-2008) on games and simulations for learning (Sauvé et al., 2008).

To answer our first research question, we reviewed 806 articles that included definitions and attributes describing one or several games or simulations. Of these articles, 504 mentioned the contribution of games and simulations to knowledge structuring and/or the development of problem-solving skills. The great majority of articles analyzed showed positive learning results, allowing us to hypothesize that any research analysis should take into account a clear definition of 'game' and 'simulation' as well as their attributes. This is not the case for many studies in this domain.

For our second research question, regarding the types of learning supported by games and simulations, the review allowed us to list indicators measuring the educational efficacy of games and simulations in terms of knowledge structuring (Table 1) and the development of problem solving skills (Table 2).

Table 1 shows that studies of the efficacy of games and simulations for learning knowledge structuring show positive results on similar measurement variables, if we exclude the capacity to establish problem links.

Table 2 shows that studies of both games and simulations for the development of problem-solving skills show positive results on similar variables. These results, together with those outlined above, allow us to recommend to teachers who want support their learners in developing knowledge structuring and problem solving capacities the use of both games and simulations.

This study was limited in that we did not conduct an exhaustive examination of the variables that support learning. However, we believe that those variables identified in this analysis can act as a frame of reference for future systematic analyses of the literature. This study can also provide variables for analysis in experimental studies of the educational efficacy of games and simulations.

In closing, it would be interesting to refine our analytical framework to better describe the educational efficacy of games and simulations by examining whether there are differences in capacities developed in learners if we take into account the variables of learning content, educational level, sex, and age.

ACKNOWLEDGMENT

We would like to thank the students who performed the analysis of the many articles reviewed for this study, including Mahboubeh Asgari, Shaoleh Bigdeli, Julie Bourbonnière, Pascal Bujold, Catherine

Dumais, Mathieu Gauvin, Jean-Simon Marquis, Andrea Rodríguez, Frédéric Sibomana, Gilles Simard, Amélie Trépanier, and David Samson.

REFERENCES[1]

Aktouf, O. (1987). *Méthodologie des sciences sociales et approche qualitative des organisations* [A qualitative approach to social science and organizational research]. Québec, QC, Canada: Presses de l'Université du Québec.

Alberto, P. A., Cihak, D. F., & Gama, R. I. (2005). Use of static picture prompts versus video modeling during simulation instruction. *Research in Developmental Disabilities, 26*(4), 327–339. doi:10.1016/j.ridd.2004.11.002

Alinier, G., Hunt, B., Gordon, R., & Harwood, C. (2006). Effectiveness of intermediate-fidelity simulation training technology in undergraduate nursing education. *Journal of Advanced Nursing, 54*(3), 359–369. doi:10.1111/j.1365-2648.2006.03810.x

Andrieu, B., & Bourgeois, I. (2003). Interaction enseignant-élèves au cours des TPE, les dynamiques du processus de structuration des connaissances [Teacher-student interaction during independent study projects: Dynamics in the process of structuring knowledge]. In C. Larcher & A. Crindal (Eds.), *Structuration des connaissances et nouveaux dispositifs d'enseignement* (pp. 40-45). Paris: Institut national de recherche pédagogique.

Apkan, J. P. (2002). Which comes first: Computer simulation of dissection or a traditional laboratory practical method of dissection? *Electronic Journal of Science Education, 6*(4), 1–20.

Baldaro, B., Tuozzi, G., Codispoti, M., & Montebarocci, O. (2004). Aggressive and non-violent videogames: short-term psychological and cardiovascular effects on habitual players. *Stress and Health, 20*(4), 203–208. doi:10.1002/smi.1015

Bandura, A. (1986). *Social foundations of thought and action: A social cognitive theory*. Englewood Cliffs, NJ: Prentice Hall.

Barab, S., Thomas, M., Dodge, T., Carteaux, R., & Tuzun, H. (2005). Making learning fun: Quest Atlantis, a game without guns. *Educational Technology Research and Development, 53*(1), 86–107. doi:10.1007/BF02504859

Baranowski, T., Baranowski, J., Cullen, K. W., Marsh, T., Islam, N., & Zakeri, I. (2003). Squire's Quest! Dietary outcome evaluation of a multimedia game. *American Journal of Preventive Medicine, 24*(1), 52–61. doi:10.1016/S0749-3797(02)00570-6

Barnaud, C., Promburom, T., Trebuil, G., & Bousquet, F. (2007). An evolving simulation/gaming process to facilitate adaptive watershed management in northern mountainous Thailand. *Simulation & Gaming, 38*(3), 398–420. doi:10.1177/1046878107300670

Becker, K. (2007). Battle of the titans: Mario vs. MathBlaster. In C. Montgomerie & J. Seale (Eds.), *Proceedings of World Conference on Educational Multimedia, Hypermedia and Telecommunications 2007* (pp. 2707-2716). Chesapeake, VA: AACE.

Blouin, M., & Bergeron, C. (1997). *Dictionnaire de la réadaptation, tome 2: termes d'intervention et d'aides techniques* [Dictionary of rehabilitation, volume 2: Terms of intervention and technical help] (p. 32). Québec, QC, Canada: Les Publications du Québec.

Boethel, M., & Dimock, V. (1999). *Constructing knowledge with technology: A review of the literature*. Austin, TX: Southwest Educational Development Laboratory.

Bos, N., Shami, N. S., & Naab, S. (2006). A globalization simulation to teach corporate social responsibility: Design features and analysis of student reasoning. *Simulation & Gaming, 37*(1), 56–72. doi:10.1177/1046878106286187

Bottino, R. M., Ferlino, L., Ott, M., & Tavella, M. (2006). Developing strategic and reasoning abilities with computer games at primary school level. *Computers & Education, 49*(4), 1272–1286. doi:10.1016/j.compedu.2006.02.003

Bridge, P., Appleyard, R. M., Ward, J. W., Philips, R., & Beavis, A. W. (2007). The development and evaluation of a virtual radiotherapy treatment machine using an immersive visualisation environment. *Computers & Education, 49*(2), 481–494. doi:10.1016/j.compedu.2005.10.006

Brozik, D., & Zapalska, A. (1999). Interactive classroom economics: The market game. *Social Studies, 90*(6), 278–282. doi:10.1080/00377999909602431

Cherry, R. A., Williams, J., George, J., & Ali, J. (2007). The effectiveness of a human patient simulator in the ATLS Shock Skills Station. *The Journal of Surgical Research, 139*(2), 229–235. doi:10.1016/j.jss.2006.08.010

Cioffi, J., Purcal, N., & Arundell, F. (2005). A pilot study to investigate the effect of a simulation strategy on the clinical decision making of midwifery students. *The Journal of Nursing Education, 44*(3), 131–134.

Cuban, L. (2001). *Oversold and overused: Computers in the classroom*. Cambridge, MA: Harvard University Press.

DeMaria, R. (2007). *Reset: Changing the way we look at video games*. San Francisco: Berrett-Koehler Publishers, Inc.

Dobson, M., Pengelly, M., Sime, J.-A., Albaladejo, S., Garcia, E., Gonzales, F., et al. (2002). Situated learning with co-operative agent simulations in team training. In M. Dobson (Ed.), *Computers in Human Behavior (*special issue) (pp. 457-573). Amsterdam, The Netherlands: Elsevier Science.

Dong, U. C., & Kwonki, Y. (2008). Validating a simulation for improving teacher's motivating skills. In K. McFerrin, R. Weber, R. Carlsen, & D. A. Willis (Eds), *Proceedings of 19th International Conference Annual of Society for Information Technology & Teacher Education* (pp. 1640-1645). Chesapeake, VA; AACE.

Egenfeldt-Nielsen, S. (2005). *Beyond edutainment: Exploring the educational potential of computer games*. Unpublished PhD dissertation, IT University Copenhagen, Denmark.

Facer, K., Stanton, D., Joiner, R., Reid, J., Hull, R., & Kirk, D. (2004). Savannah: Mobile gaming and learning? *Journal of Computer Assisted Learning, 20*(6), 399–409. doi:10.1111/j.1365-2729.2004.00105.x

Federation of American Scientists (FAS). (2006). *Harnessing the power of video games for learning: Final report on the Summit on Educational Games*. Available at http://www.fas.org/gamesummit/Resources/Summit%20on%20Educational%20Games.pdf

Feinstein, A. H., Mann, S., & Corsun, D. L. (2002). Charting the experiential territory: Clarifying definitions and uses of computer simulation, games, and role play. *Journal of Management Development, 21*(10), 732–744. doi:10.1108/02621710210448011

Ferdig, R. E. (2007). Preface: Learning and teaching with electronic games. *Journal of Educational Multimedia and Hypermedia, 16*(3), 217–223.

Fournier, M., Vincent, S. & Brougère, G.(2004). À quoi sert le jeu ? [What use are games?] *Sciences humaines, 152 (August-September),* 19-45.

Gaba, D. M., Howard, S. K., Fish, K. J., Smith, B. E., & Sowb, Y. A. (2001). Simulation-based training in anesthesia crisis resource management (ACRM): A decade of experience. *Simulation & Gaming, 32*(2), 175–193. doi:10.1177/104687810103200206

Galloway, A. R. (2006). *Gaming: Essays on algorithmic culture.* Minneapolis, MN: University of Minnesota Press.

Garris, R., Ahlers, R., & Driskell, J. E. (2002). Games, motivation, and learning: A research and practice model. *Simulation & Gaming, 33*(4), 441–467. doi:10.1177/1046878102238607

Gauthier, B. (2005). *Recherche sociale de la problématique à la collecte de données* [Social research and the problem of data collection]. Québec, QC, Canada: Presses de l'Université du Québec.

Gayet, D. (2006). *Pédagogie et éducation familiale. Concepts et perspectives en sciences humaines* [Pedagogy and family education: Concepts and perspectives in the human sciences]. Paris:L'harmattan.

Gee, J. P. (2007). *Good video games + good learning: Collected essays on video games, learning and literacy.* New York: Peter Lang.

Goldenberg, D., Andrusyszyn, M.-A., & Iwasiw, C. (2005). The effect of classroom simulation on nursing students' self-efficacy related to health teaching. *The Journal of Nursing Education, 44*(7), 310–314.

Gradler, M. E. (2004). Games and simulations and their relationships to learning. In D. H. Jonassen (Ed.), *Handbook of research for educational communications and technology* (2nd ed, pp. 571-581). Mahwah, NJ: Lawrence Erlbaum Associates Inc.

Holton, D., Ahmed, A., Williams, H., & Hill, C. (2001). On the importance of mathematical play. *International Journal of Mathematical Education in Science and Technology, 32*(3), 401–415. doi:10.1080/00207390010022158

Jacobs, J., Caudell, T., Wilks, D., Keep, M. F., Mitchell, S., Buchanan, H., et al. (2003) Integration of advanced technologies to enhance problem-based learning over distance: Project TOUCH. *The Anatomical Record (Part B: New Anatomy), 270B*, 16-22.

Johne, M. (2002, September 27). On-line simulations put e-learners into action. *The Globe and Mail*, B16.

Jones, K. (1998). Hidden damage to facilitators and participants. *Simulation & Gaming, 29*(2), 165–172. doi:10.1177/1046878198292003

Jones, M. G. (1997). *Learning to play, playing to learn: Lessons learned from computer games.* Paper presented at the annual conference of the Association for Educational Communications and Technology. Retrieved January 7, 2005 from http://www.gsu.edu/~wwwitr/docs/mjgames/

Kaufman, D., & Sauvé, L. (2003). *Literature review for an SSHRC grant proposal.* Vancouver, BC, Canada, and Quebec, QC, Canada: SAGE Project.

Kaufman, D. M., Mann, K. V., & Jennett, P. A. (2000). *Teaching and learning in medical education: How theory can inform practice.* Edinburgh, UK: Association for the Study of Medical Education.

Kelly, H. (2005). Games, cookies, and the future of education. *Issues in Science and Technology, 21*(4), 33–41.

Kiegaldie, D., & White, G. (2006). The virtual patient: Development, implementation and evaluation of an innovative computer simulation for postgraduate nursing students. *Journal of Educational Multimedia and Hypermedia, 15*(1), 31–47.

Ko, S. (2002). An empirical analysis of children's thinking and learning in a computer game context. *Educational Psychology, 22*(2), 219–233. doi:10.1080/01443410120115274

Kokol, P., Kokol, M., & Dinevski, D. (2005). Teaching evolution using visual simulations. *British Journal of Educational Technology, 36*(3), 563–566. doi:10.1111/j.1467-8535.2005.00483.x

Lincoln, Y. S., & Guba, E. G. (1985). *Naturalistic inquiry.* Beverly Hills, CA: Sage Publications.

Mechling, L. C., Gast, D. L., & Langone, J. (2002). Computer-based video instruction to teach persons with moderate intellectual disabilities to read grocery aisle signs and locate items. *The Journal of Special Education, 35*(4), 224–240. doi:10.1177/00224669020350040 4

Medley, C. F., & Horne, C. (2005). Using simulation technology for undergraduate nursing education. *The Journal of Nursing Education, 44*(1), 31–34.

Moline, T. (2008). "I get competent pretty quickly": How adolescents play their way to cognitive self-efficacy. In K. McFerrin, R. Weber, R. Carlsen, & D. A. Willis, (eds)., *Proceedings of 19th International Conference Annual of Society for Information Technology & Teacher Education* (pp. 1213-1219). Chesapeake, VA: AACE.

Moseley, W. G. (2001). Computer assisted comprehension of distant worlds: understanding hunger dynamics in Africa. *The Journal of Geography, 100*(1), 32–45. doi:10.1080/00221340108978415

Olsen, F. (2000). Computer models teach scientists what experiments can't. *The Chronicle of Higher Education, 46*(49), A49.

Patton, M. Q. (1980). *Qualitative evaluation and research methods*. Beverly Hills, CA: Sage Publications.

Pei, X.-S. (1998). Using interactive physics in planetary motion. *The Physics Teacher, 36*(1), 42–43. doi:10.1119/1.879975

Pittaway, L., & Cope, J. (2007). Simulating entrepreneurial learning: Integrating experiential and collaborative approaches to learning. *Management Learning, 38*(2), 211–219. doi:10.1177/1350507607075776

Quivy, R., & Campenhoudt, L. V. (1988). *Manuel de recherche en sciences sociales* [Manual on research in the social sciences]. Paris: Dunod.

Randel, J., Morris, B. A., Wetzel, C. D., & Whitehill, B. V. (1992). The effectiveness of games for educational purposes: A review of recent research. *Simulation & Gaming, 23*(3), 261–276. doi:10.1177/1046878192233001

Ravenscroft, A. (2007). Promoting thinking and conceptual change with digital dialogue games. *Journal of Computer Assisted Learning, 23*(6), 453–465. doi:10.1111/j.1365-2729.2007.00232.x

Repine, T., & Hemler, D. (1999). Outcrops in the classroom. *Science Teacher (Normal, Ill.), 66*(8), 29–33.

Rodriguez, E. E. (1998). A proposal for experimental homework. *The Physics Teacher, 36*(7), 435–437. doi:10.1119/1.879915

Rosenbaum, E., Klopfer, E., & Perry, J. (2007). On location learning: Authentic applied science with networked augmented realities. *Journal of Science Education and Technology, 16*(1), 31–45. doi:10.1007/s10956-006-9036-0

Ruben, B. D. (1999). Simulation, games, and experience-based learning: The quest for a new paradigm for teaching and learning. *Simulation & Gaming, 30*(4), 498–505. doi:10.1177/104687819903000409

Sauvé, L. (1985). *Simulation et transfert d'apprentissage. Une étude sur les niveaux de fidélité pour le transfert d'apprentissage* [Simulation and the transfer of learning: A study of levels of fidelity for the transfer of learning. Unpublished Ph.D. dissertation, University of Montreal, Montreal, QC, Canada.

Sauvé, L., Renaud, L., Kaufman, D., & Sibomana, F. (2008). *Revue systématique des écrits (1998-2008) sur les impacts du jeu, de la simulation et du jeu de simulation sur l'apprentissage:rapport final*. [Systematic review on the impact of games, simulations, and simulation games on learning: Final report] (Research report). Québec, QC, Canada: SAGE and SAVIE.

Schmidt, S. J. (2003). Active and cooperative learning using web-based simulations. *The Journal of Economic Education*, *34*(2), 151–167. doi:10.1080/00220480309595209

Schnotz, W., & Rasch, T. (2005). Enabling, facilitating, and inhibiting effects of animations in multimedia learning: Why reduction of cognitive load can have negative results on learning. *Educational Technology Research and Development*, *53*(3), 47–58. doi:10.1007/BF02504797

Schön, D. A. (1987). *Educating the reflective practitioner*. San Francisco: Jossey-Bass.

Shaffer, D. W. (2006). *How computer games help children learn*. New York: Palgrave Macmillan.

Shaftel, J., Pass, L., & Schnabel, S. (2005). Math games for adolescents. *Teaching Exceptional Children*, *37*(3), 27–33.

Shellman, S., & Turan, K. (2006). Confronting global issues: A multipurpose IR simulation. *Simulation & Gaming*, *37*(1), 98–123. doi:10.1177/1046878105278924

Shi, Y. (2000). The game PIG: Making decisions based on mathematical thinking . *Teaching Mathematics and Its Applications*, *19*(1), 30–34. doi:10.1093/teamat/19.1.30

Shreve, J. (2005, April). Let the games begin. Video games, once confiscated in class, are now a key teaching tool if they're done right. *Edutopia*, 29-31.

Squire, K. (2005), *Game-based learning: An X-learn perspective paper*. Sarasota Springs, NY: MASIE center: e-Learning Consortium.

St-Germain, M., & Laveault, D. (1997). Factors of success of simulations and games: A systemic approach to the evaluation of an organization's impact on the user. *Simulation & Gaming*, *28*(3), 317–336. doi:10.1177/1046878197283006

Tommelein, I. D., Riley, D., & Howell, G. A. (1998). Parade Game: Impact of work flow variability on succeeding trade performance. In *Proceedings, Sixth Annual Conference of the International Group for Lean Construction, IGLC-6*, Guaruja, Brazil.

Van Houcke, M., Vereecke, A., & Gemmel, P. (2005). The Project Scheduling Game (PSG): Simulating time/cost trade-offs in projects. *Project Management Journal*, *36*(1), 51–59.

Virvou, M., Katsionis, G., & Manos, K. (2005). Combining software games with education: Evaluation of its educational effectiveness. *Educational Technology & Society*, *8*(2), 54–65.

Windschitl, M., & Andre, T. (1998). Using computer simulations to enhance conceptual change: The roles of constructivist instruction and student epistemological beliefs. *Journal of Research in Science Teaching*, *35*(2), 145–160. doi:10.1002/(SICI)1098-2736(199802)35:2<145::AID-TEA5>3.0.CO;2-S

Wissmann, J. L., & Tankel, K. (2001). Nursing student's use of a psychopharmacology game for client empowerment. *Journal of Professional Nursing*, *17*(2), 101–106. doi:10.1053/jpnu.2001.22274

Zhu, H., Zhou, X., & Yin, B. (2001). Visible simulation in medical education: Notes and discussion. *Simulation & Gaming*, *3*(3), 362–369. doi:10.1177/104687810103200306

ADDITIONAL READING

Sauvé, L., Renaud, L., Kaufman, D., & Sibomana, F. (2008). *Revue systématique des écrits (1998-2008) sur les impacts du jeu, de la simulation et du jeu de simulation sur l'apprentissage:rapport final*. [Systematic review on the impact of games, simulations, and simulation games on learning: Final report] (Research report). Québec, QC, Canada: SAGE and SAVIE.

KEY TERMS AND DEFINITIONS

Educational Efficacy (the positive consequences on knowledge): attitudes, and skills of the participant resulting from the use of a game or other learning activity.

Educational Game: A fictitious, fantasy or imaginary situation in which players, placed in conflict with others or assembled in a team against an external opponent, are governed by rules determining their actions with a view to achieving learning objectives and a goal determined by the game, either to win or to seek revenge.

Knowledge Structuring: Refers to the construction and organization of knowledge, schemas (mental models), or representations by the learner in order to understand a concept, principle, procedure, or a given situation.

Learning: The acquisition of knowledge or skills with the help of experience, practice or study.

Problem Solving Skills: Covers several aspects of cognition such as schemas (recognition of familiar problem elements), transfer (skill required to establish a link to similar problems), creativity (development of new solutions) and critical thought (reflection). The goal of learning through problem solving is to help learners apply abstract or theoretical concepts to concrete situations or practical cases.

Simulation: A simplified, dynamic, and accurate representation of a reality, represented as a system.

State of Knowledge: A review that is, as far as possible, complete, exhaustive, and critical, of the specific work that has been done on a problem. In effect, it is a review of all principal research on the subject.

ENDNOTE

1 The reference list for this chapter contains only references cited in the text. For full details of articles consulted for literature review topics, see Sauvé et al. (2008), available at www.sageforlearning.ca.

APPENDIX 1

Databases Consulted

Database Title	Reference
Eric	http://www.eric.ed.gov/
Francis	http://webspirs.bibl.ulaval.ca:8590/
First search education	http://newfirstsearch.oclc.org/dbname=EducationAbs;autho=100195256;FSIP
Ariane Thesis collection, Laval University*	http://ariane.ulaval.ca/web2/tramp2.exe/log_in?setting_key=french
Tecnedoc	http://bdd.inrp.fr:8080/Tecne/TecneWelcome.html
Emile	http://www.inrp.fr:8080/Emile1/EmiWelcome.html
Current Contents*	http://www.ovid.com/site/catalog/DataBase/45.jsp
Repère	http://repere.sdm.qc.ca/
MedLine*	http://medline.cos.com/
Academic search premier*	http://www.ebscohost.com/thisTopic.php?topicID=1&marketID=1
Religion and philosophy collection*	http://www.ebscohost.com/thisTopic.php?marketID=1&topicID=131
Scholar Google	http://scholar.google.com/
SAGE Full-text collections*	http://www.csa.com/
Ingenta*	http://www.ingentaconnect.com/
Emerald*	http://www.emeraldinsight.com/
Web of Science*	http://portal.isiknowledge.com/
Springerlink*	http://www.springerlink.com/home/main.mpx
Science direct*	http://www.sciencedirect.com/
Social Science*	http://portal.isiknowledge.com/portal.cgi/
Health Science*	http://www-md1.csa.com
Google (advanced search)	http://www.google.ca/advanced_search

Chapter 17
Collaborative Online Multimedia Problem-Based Learning Simulations (COMPS)

Robyn Schell
Simon Fraser University, Canada

David Kaufman
Simon Fraser University, Canada

ABSTRACT

This chapter describes the development, implementation and evaluation of a Collaborative Online Multimedia Problem-based Learning Simulation (COMPS) instructional model designed to help students and practitioners in the health professions develop clinical reasoning and diagnostic skills. Both students and instructors are searching for effective learning platforms and pedagogical models that enable them to collaborate, study, and work at a distance. In order to address this need, COMPS was developed to support a case-based tutorial model where learners can work together online to solve authentic problems no matter where they are located. The model aims to bring together the strongest features of simulations, namely engagement and immersiveness, with one of the strongest features of face-to-face learning—social interaction. The COMPS model combines these strengths to create a new learning system for health education and examines how students learn in this online environment. This chapter also discusses the next steps in our research and development, investigating the use of a COMPS model on a dedicated platform.

INTRODUCTION

Changes in the health care system have transformed the delivery of medical education. Traditional venues for practice and experience have disappeared due to a higher ratio of acutely ill patients and shorter hospital stays (Issenberg, Mcgaghie, Petrusa, Gordon, & Scalese, 2005). There are now fewer opportunities for face-to-face encounters with patients, and the students may not see the range of diseases and conditions they saw in the past. Consequently, medical students find it increasingly

DOI: 10.4018/978-1-61520-731-2.ch017

difficult to practice and gain experience in hospital settings. This trend has converged with the growth of distance education (Cook & Dupras, 2004), creating a need to standardize learning and teaching experience for medical students no matter where they live or study.

Our research study involved transferring a well-known medical education approach, problem-based learning (PBL), to an online environment. Our goal was to push the boundaries of PBL and transform it into a kind of simulation that would allow medical students to practice their skills together in a risk-free setting. In our pilot study we created and tested an online case-based tutorial in which learners could work together in a distributed environment to address authentic problems and situations, a process thought to be essential for professional development (Albanese, 1993). Our design included the following key features:

a repository of narrative-based case studies created by the instructors and accessible by the students; (2) asynchronous and synchronous tools where students can collaborate with one another; (3) a repository of multimedia resources that students can access as they work through a case study; (4) an archive of group sessions that can be reviewed at a later date; (5) a database that includes information on the client's present illness and medical history, the results of lab tests performed on the client, and medical management information; and (6) lab results and medical records such as x-rays, MRI, and nuclear imaging.

This chapter describes the various design elements of our prototype, as well as the implementation and evaluation of the online tutorial conducted in this model. Our evaluation examined the ability of an online environment to support a collaborative problem-solving approach in health education in two ways: (1) by asking the students to assess the tutorial, and (2) through an analysis of the level of critical thinking that took place. Finally we discuss how this research may inform the development and testing of *COMPSoft*, our new online dedicated *COMPS* platform.

BACKGROUND

Problem-Based Learning in Medical Education

For more than three decades, problem-based learning (PBL) has had a major impact on thinking and practice in medical education (Colliver, 2000). PBL is defined as a method of instruction that uses patient problems as a context for developing students' problem-solving skills, and gaining knowledge about basic and clinical sciences (Albanese, 1993). Case studies provide the structure for problem-based learning and offer an ideal practice environment for social negotiation and reflection – two of the activities that promote high-quality thinking (Orrill, 2002).

PBL's student-centred approach is thought to develop competencies in reasoning critically, adapting to change, dealing with problems, developing self-directed learning skills (Barrows, 1984), adapting a holistic approach, appreciating other points of view, and self-assessment (Kamin, Deterding, Wilson, Armacost, & Breedon, 1999). PBL also seems to be a challenging, motivating, and enjoyable way to learn (Kaufman & Mann, 1997). Lastly, when compared to more traditional methods, PBL appears to lead to equivalent levels of performance on professional licensing exams, which tend to emphasize knowledge acquisition, application, and analysis (Mann & Kaufman, 1999).

PBL is usually carried out in groups of six to eight students with a faculty tutor who offers appropriate feedback and guidance (Wilkerson & Feletti, 1989). The facilitator reveals the case study to the students in stages; at each stage, students discuss the issues of the case, what they already know, and what they need to find out in order to resolve the case. The students then research the learning issues identified in the process of case study and present this new information to the group in order to move the case forward. More specifically, the PBL process uses the following steps (Barrows, 1985):

1. encountering the problem
2. solving the problem using clinical reasoning skills
3. identifying what information is needed through an interactive collaborative process and self-study
4. applying the new information to the problem and summarizing what has been learned

The process may conclude with an evaluation of the session and the resources used.

PBL and Critical Thinking

At every stage of the medical diagnostic cycle, health professionals make decisions: what questions to ask, what information to consider, what treatment would be appropriate, etc. Medical education often discusses teaching methods that encourage deep processing, a characteristic of critical thinking necessary to derive clinical inferences from available data, recognize unstated assumptions by weighing evidence, and distinguishing between weak and strong arguments (Miller, 1992).

To assess the learning impact of our online PBL tutorial, we focused on the relationship between critical thinking and problem-based learning. Looking at the concept of critical thinking in discourse, Garrison (1991) integrated earlier work (Brookfield, 1987; Dewey, 1910) to create five stages of critical thinking: problem identification, problem definition, exploration, applicability, and integration. This model was further developed by applying codes to analyze discourse (Newman, Webb, & Cochrane, 1995). These codes contained deep or shallow thinking codes at each stage of Garrison's model.

Later these codes were refined to measure critical thinking in PBL in a medical education context, in order to compare the differences between text, video, and online modalities (Kamin, O'Sullivan, Deterding, & Younger, 2003). In this study, four groups met in face-to-face group to discuss a text case, four groups met face-to-face with a video case, and five groups worked virtually with digital video. The virtual group participated in web-based asynchronous discussions but posted their facts about the case and their hypothesis before reading what other students wrote. The researchers discovered significant differences at each stage, with the virtual groups showing the highest ratio of critical thinking. The ratio of critical thinking of the video groups was higher than the text groups except in the problem identification stage. Both video groups recorded a high level of rapport building, with the video groups producing more explanations and commitment than the text group.

We adapted and applied Kamin's coding system to our analysis of PBL tutorial transcripts to measure the level of critical thinking in our online sessions.

Collaborative Learning in PBL

The ability to communicate as a group and refer to shared documents is important in helping students gain an understanding of the problem as social negotiation, and collaborative work is at the center of PBL (Orrill, 2002). Technology can provide a useful platform for students to work together to solve problems (Taradi, Taradi, Kresimir, & Pokrajac, 2005), especially through the integration of collaborative learning models such as computer-supported problem-based learning and distributed problem-based learning (Naidu, 2003). Both asynchronous and synchronous text chat have been used to support interaction in web-based PBL models; examples include *Asynchronous Conferencing Tool (ACT)* (Duffy, Dueber, & Hawley, 1998), *CSC-PBL* (Naidu & Oliver, 1996) and *Project LIVE* (Kamin et al., 1999). Synchronous web conferencing was selected as a communications option for our model, as it has shown the ability to support meaningful learning that engages and enhances multiple forms of thinking (Jonassen & Jonassen, 2000).

We used web conferencing (audiographic) software as a communications tool. We believe this technology shows promise because of its ability to support sessions that resemble traditional face-to-face PBL tutorials. For example, this software supports conversation in real time, and the ability to display multimedia to the group. Students can also record and modify key points, learning issues, and hypotheses that can be seen by all the participants.

Multimedia Resources

Multimedia software can be a powerful tool in enhancing learning by helping learners to create a deeper understanding than from words or pictures alone (Mayer, 2001). The use of visualization enhances learning and recall, in part because images and words are processed in different parts of the brain (Paivio, 1991). Furthermore, the addition of multimedia can create a more complex authentic case that provides students with the opportunity to interpret a variety of visual, auditory, and nonverbal cues, preparing them to deal with a variety of real problems (Hoffman & Ritchie, 1997).

In our study we developed video scenarios for the case study, and offered multimedia PBL resources to help students resolve the case. Also, VoIP (voice over Internet protocol) video conferencing allowed participants to discuss the case in audio and text chat and to use a whiteboard for activities such as recording notes and presenting graphics.

The Narrative-Driven Case Study

Traditional PBL relies on short text-based cases that briefly describe the patient's medical problem. The case is disclosed in stages, and at each stage students identify information they can apply to the case, as well identify what they need to know in order to move toward a resolution (Barrrows & Tamblyn, 1980).

Our model integrated narrative by presenting the case study as videotaped scenarios that included details about the patient's personal situation as well as medical information. Designing a problem as a story or an open-ended narrative is a new way to think about developing problem-based learning (PBL) scenarios that few have explored. Presenting a problem as a story may help to create a more holistic approach to medical education by engaging learners in more authentic, patient-centered problems (Kenny & Beagan, 2004). Studies have shown that in professional and everyday contexts, narrative is the primary medium for problem solving. It seems feasible that case studies built around a story or narrative or "thick" cases, described as richly detailed cases portraying patients as multi-dimensional persons (Hunter, 1991), could facilitate the development of problem-solving ability over a range of problems and situations not possible in a short text-based case study. (For a deeper discussion of the role of narrative in our project, see Chapter 4 of this volume.)

Simulation and Learning

The *COMPS* design meets some of the criteria for a basic role-playing simulation. Early references to role-play and simulations can be traced to the work of Kurt Lewin, who argued that effective learning takes place when there is interaction between the learner and the environment, and an opportunity exists for social interaction that facilitates the student's reflections on the experiences in that environment (Lewin, 1951). Learning occurs when an action takes place, and the participant can see the consequence of that action, and can choose either to continue or take a new and different action (Lewin, 1951). Participation and reflection allows us to learn from the simulation.

David Kolb, whose work in experiential learning began with experiments in games, simulations, and case studies, described simulations and games as presenting learners with a broad experiential learning environment that offers learners support for active experimentation (Kolb, 1984). He describes learning as a four-step process: (1) watching, (2) thinking, (3) feeling (emotion), and (4) doing. Each experience allows us to reflect and generalize, to form new principles to guide us in future situations. Active participation allows us to test these theories.

Studies in educational technology show that learning is enhanced in an environment that simulates the actual one in which the activity takes place, as in, for example, work completed on goal-based scenarios (GBS) and story-based curricula (Schank, 2002; Schank & Cleary, 1995). This research supports the idea that role-playing in an authentic situation can help learners to practice skills in a memorable context where they can be recalled and transferred to the workplace.

Other researchers echo Schank's words when they talk about the value that experience and stories play in the construction of memory and reasoning, and the ways they help us to understand and operate in the world (Ip & Naidu, 2001). Although role-play is commonly used as a strategy in conventional educational settings, it is less widely used in distributed online learning environments. These studies claim that the essential ingredients of the online role-playing simulation are: dynamic goal-based learning, a role-play simulation, and online communication and collaboration.

Although there has been little work done on effective design of online simulation environments, design criteria based on a constructivist or situated framework suggests problem-solving skills can be promoted in several ways (Hawley & Duffy, 1998):

- building around authentic problems
- producing authentic cognitive demands in learning
- building scaffolding that supports a focused effort relevant to the learning goals
- promoting learning by coaching rather than directing or correcting performance
- supporting, abstracting, synthesizing, and extending the learning through reflection
- creating engaging environments

Providing guidelines, conducting a debriefing, creating an authentic environment, and implementing a strategy for assessment and role assignment are all considered important criteria when creating role playing simulations (Freeman & Capper, 1999). Providing students with background material on the topic to be discussed, their role, and the context, helps them to reflect on what happens in the simulation and associate it with the problem being simulated. Asking the students to evaluate the simulation is also considered valuable for reflection, understanding, and improving a simulation.

Prior instruction should model and teach the expected research skills such as planning, testing, collecting data, and evaluating (Gredler, 2004). In this way, students can develop the competencies to create conceptual models of an element of a domain, and test them in a systematic way.

There seem to be many good reasons to use simulations for learning and teaching that offer opportunities that may be impossible to achieve in more conventional settings. Next we describe some of the techniques we used to build a simulation that allows students to practice in an authentic environment in an online collaborative PBL setting.

TUTORIAL PILOT STUDY

Our PBL tutorial was designed in a web-based environment using *WebCT®* as a repository for course resources. Students accessed *elive Elluminate®* by clicking the Classroom icon (see Figure 1) and used this tool for collaborating in real-time audio discussions, tutorial activities, and presenting case study videos.

Figure 1. Screenshot of COMPS home page

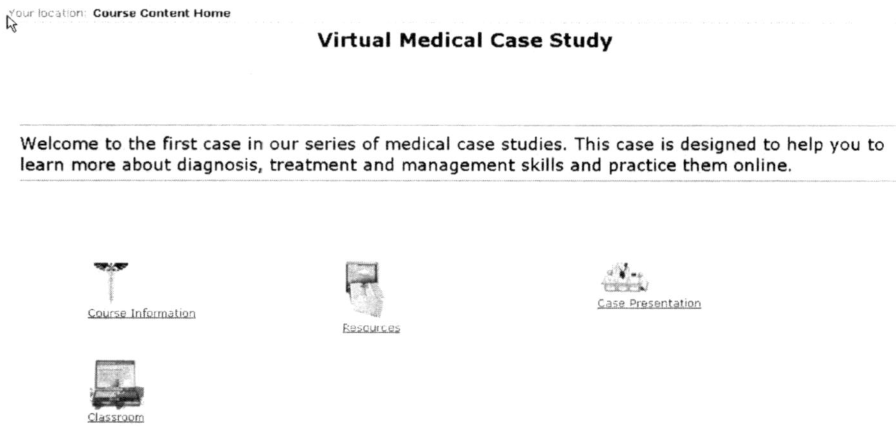

In the tutorial, two groups of three students joined their facilitator in a web conference. The facilitator released information about the case incrementally in a series of videos. Throughout the discussion, students identified relevant information, tracked topics that needed further research, and documented hypotheses that might account for the patient's medical problem (Figure 2).

Later, when conducting research, students accessed the multimedia resources stored in *WebCT*. Resources included multimedia such as scanned medical images and illustrations, photos of the patient, a 3D model of the neck and throat area, scan of test results, videos of procedures, articles, and web sites links (Figure 3).

Participant Profile

Although our future goal is to create a dedicated online PBL platform for medical and nursing stu-

Figure 2. Screenshot of hypotheses list in web conferencing tool

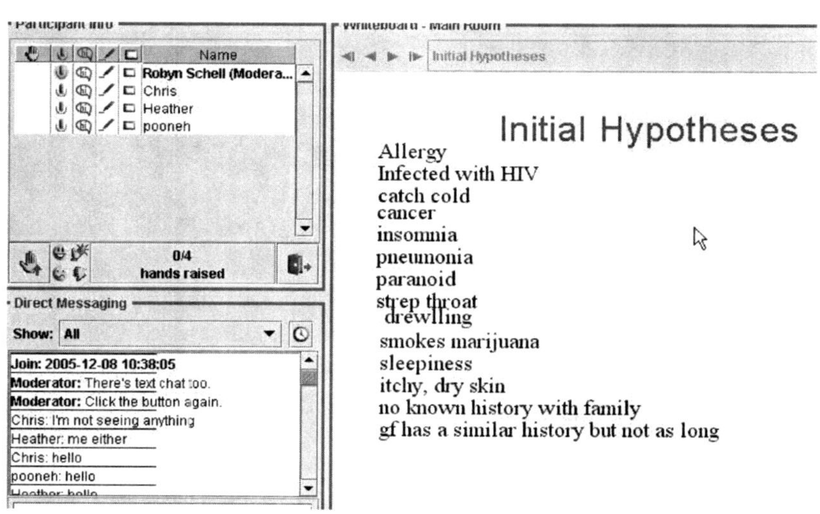

dents, there is no medical or nursing school at our university. We recruited undergraduate kinesiology students because they are studying to become health professionals, and had some background in anatomy and patient assessment. The student participants were in their mid-twenties, had computer experience and used the Internet for research. They were not familiar with the PBL process but had had some experience with the medical diagnoses process (interview, exam, history) in a kinesiology context.

Tutorial Goal and Objectives

The overall goal of the case study tutorial was to learn to how to use clinical reasoning to diagnose and form a treatment management plan. More specifically, the objectives were to improve learner's clinical reasoning skills, to improve their ability to collect information that provides a more in-depth, holistic profile of the patient, and to practice skills such as history taking, exam, record keeping, and interpersonal communications.

Data Collection Tools and Methods

We collected the case study data during two online tutorial sessions using three methods: pre- and post-test surveys, post-test focus group interviews, and analysis of the tutorial transcripts.

The pre-test survey included questions about the students' academic background as well as their experience with the Internet and computers. After the tutorial, the students completed a survey rating the tutorial experience, and participated in a focus group where we gathered information about their perceptions of the tutorial experience in a more informal setting. This conversation was recorded and transcribed. The tutorial was also recorded, and captured the audio of the conversation as well as the activities, such as text chat and whiteboard activities. Transcription included dialogue, whiteboard, text messaging, and notes about activities, for example, "Second video shown." Analysis of the post-tutorial survey and focus group transcripts was oriented to the student's assessment and discussion of some of the tutorial design features.

Student Evaluation

When asked in the survey about their overall experience, students rated how helpful the audio web conferencing was to their learning experience on a scale of 1 "Not helpful at all" to 5 "Extremely helpful". Their rating averaged at a high level of 4.7, with four students rating it a 5 and two others a 4. They recorded an identical rating for class activities and exercises. They also rated the discussions as very helpful to their learning, with an average score of 4.3.

Figure 3. Case resources page

Your location: Course Content Home › **Resources**

Case Resources: Use these resources for your research assignment.

Image: Mononucleuosis Rash	Image: Mononucleosis rash in face
Image: Tonsils with infectious Mononucleosis	An Example of Mono Test Results
3D Model: Neck and throat	Video: How to palpate the cervical node: Part 1
Epstein Barr: Recent Advances	Article: Evaluation of 12 Commercial Tests for Detection of Epstein-Barr Virus-Specific and Heterophile Antibodies
Article: Infectious Mononucleosis web sites	Pharyngitis, Tonsillitis, and other Throat Problems: Web Sites

Interestingly, the students were critical of some of the whiteboard and audio chat features. For instance, they found writing on the whiteboard awkward, as sometimes students' notes could overlap. They also were a little frustrated with *eLive's* 'push to talk' button, which enabled the participants to talk to one another but could only be used by one participant at a time. However, they agreed that one person speaking at a time might be a positive feature and, in any case, text chat was an option. Several students commented on how engaging they found their options for communication and their ability to collaborate with one another in the tutorial.

When asked to rate the case presentation videos and the patient's story as a format for the case study, the students rated both as very helpful to their learning. For example, they found the narrative helped them know more about the patient and the complexity of the situation. The story also engaged them and they found themselves wanting to know more about what would happen next. Four of the students rated the multimedia resources highly, while two students found them less useful. One student felt too many resources focused on mononucleosis, and another suggested that more in-depth resources, such as more academic papers, might have been helpful.

Several of the students commented on how realistic and interactive they found certain aspects of the tutorial and indicated that they found the tutorial a place where they could have more hands-on practice.

Evaluating the Tutorial Transcripts

In our search for instruments that would help us evaluate the online tutorial, we turned to studies (see our earlier discussion) that examined the relationship between problem-based learning and critical thinking. To measure the level of critical thinking in the tutorial, we adapted Kamin, O'Sullivan, Younger, & Deterding's (2001) coding system, used originally to measure critical thinking in a PBL medical video case study tutorial. This system uses 35 indicators of five critical thinking stages and four group process issues. Indicators occur by stages, and each stage includes indicators of both shallow (s) and deep (d) thinking.

When we first began to apply the codes for deep and shallow thinking, we found the shallow thinking codes very similar and difficult to apply to a specific stage. For example, we felt the code labelled (NPs) *Repeating information that has already been said* (example: "Yeah, he's fussy") could be applied at any stage, rather than just at stage 1, as an example of shallow thinking. Overall, the shallow thinking codes referred to statements that had little or no connection to the case or did little to move the case towards a resolution. As a result, we simplified the shallow thinking codes by collapsing them into one category that could be applied at any stage.

We also added another code for technology (T). Technology codes applied to statements that included comments and questions about the technology (Example: Delegates took turns to type on the whiteboard. One commented that "you should be able to write – you just click on the whiteboard and click ctrl V – it should paste whatever you have copied, on the clip board.") We also used Kamin's group process statements. Technology and Group Process codes were considered neither critical nor non-critical statements.

Raters and Inter-Rater Reliability

Two researchers were involved in the inter-rater reliability trials. The senior supervisor led the training session by having the researchers discuss how the codes would be interpreted, and practice applying them. Based on the training, the definitions of the codes were revised as described in the previous section. Since the transcript contained about 300 lines, we coded 30 statements, or about 10% of the entire number of statements in the transcript.

To determine the starting point, a random number between one and 10 (generated by the website random.com) was selected. To code at least 10% of the statements available, we coded every eighth statement. After three trials, we achieved an inter-rater agreement ratio of 77.4%, based on the percentage of statements we coded identically to the total number of statements coded.

Results

The discussion was broken down into units of information that represented a single element of case information. Units included both phrases and sentences. The length was determined by a single unit of meaning, and each unit was assigned to an existing code. Only one code could be applied to each statement, and every statement in the transcript was coded.

Tables 1 and 2 show the number of critical thinking and non-critical statements, group process statements, and technology statements. The total number of coded statements for November 18 (Group 1) and December 8 (Group 2) tutorials were 250 and 273 respectively.

Table 1. Number of critical thinking statements per code (CT)

Stage	Code	Group 1	Group 2
Identification	NP	22	22
	NI	13	19
CT codes/stage		35	41
Problem description	A	3	3
	AI	25	13
	OE	2	0
CT codes/stage		30	13
Problem exploration	L	9	3
	LT	0	0
	LV	0	4
	LG	7	3
Justification	JH	9	6
	JS	31	10
CT codes/stage		56	26
Applicability	P	5	3
Integration	LI	22	19
Total CT codes	CT	148	102
Total NCT Codes	NCT	44	71

Analysis and Discussion of Transcript Coding Results

Table 3 summarizes the coding results. When comparing the ratio of critical thinking statements to non-critical thinking statements in Group 1, 77% were coded as critical thinking and 23% were coded as non-critical thinking; in Group 2, 58% of the statements were coded critical thinking and 42% were coded as non-critical thinking.

The ratio of critical thinking was higher than for non-critical thinking in both groups of participants. The number of types of critical thinking statements per stage was fairly even, except in three instances: stages 2 AI (*Asking for information not provided yet*), and 3 JS (*Justifying hypotheses or orders*), and *Rapport building* in the Group Process category.

When we looked more closely at transcripts to account for the discrepancy between the two groups, we discovered that Group 1 asked more questions about what they needed to know, while Group 2 went directly to developing a list of their hypotheses. Through exploring what they needed to know, Group 1 showed a tendency for more collaborative discussion, particularly in the earlier stages where their level of critical thinking was

Table 2. Number of group process statements and technology codes

Process	Code	Group 1	Group 2
Rapport	R	29	74
Explaining Process	E	16	15
Dividing	D	5	1
Volunteering	V	3	1
Total Group Process Codes		53	91
Technology Codes	T	5	6

Table 3. Summary of code numbers

Code	Group 1	Group 2
CT codes	148	102
NCT codes	44	71
Group Process Codes	53	91
Technology	5	6
Total Coded Statements	250	270

higher, contributing to their overall higher ratio of critical thinking.

Group 1 also had more instances of justifying their hypotheses, while Group 2 suggested hypotheses but was less able to show why these hypotheses were credible. Group 1 statements also contained fewer instances of simple group rapport statements such as "OK," "Yes," and "I agree." After viewing all the videos in the case presentation, Group 1 talked at length about how to prioritize their list of hypotheses. Group 2 chose not to review their hypotheses at this stage but decided they were fine with them as they were. The higher number of critical thinking statements at the justification (JS) stage does not appear to reflect Group 1's interview with a physician, who appeared only in the first session, as the statements focused on what they had seen in the case presentation videos.

Although Kamin did not consider the ratio of critical or noncritical thinking to all statements, it is interesting to note that 59% of the items of the total statements were coded as critical thinking and 18% as noncritical thinking in Group 1, with the balance of the other codes relating to group process or technology. In Group 2, 38% of the total statements were coded as critical thinking and 26% were coded as noncritical thinking, again with the balance of coded statements relating to group process or technology. From this perspective, the difference in each group's level of critical thinking is more dramatic.

We also compared our results with Kamin's study. Kamin used $(xd - xs)/(xd+xs)$, where xd = number of critical thinking statements and xs = number of non-critical statements, as a formula for measuring the level of critical thinking. This formula was considered independent of the quantity of participation, reflecting only the quality of the discussion. In Kamin's study a critical thinking ratio between -1 and +1 was calculated for each of the five critical thinking stages (Kamin et al., 2003).

We found that our participants showed a lower level of critical thinking, especially in Group 2. This may be explained by the differences in our participants. Our group included six undergraduate kinesiology students with little or no experience with clinical reasoning, while Kamin's participants included 128 third-year medical students.

Discussion of Research Results and Limitations of the Study

We now review the students' perceptions of the tutorial, the analysis of the transcript, and limitations of the study in light of our original concern: Can an online environment support a collaborative problem-solving approach in health education?

The student participants in our study found the technology easy to use and the case study content and format engaging and lifelike. They agreed that the tutorial provided an environment that allowed them to practice online. They also enjoyed the ability to collaborate in a web conference environment and believed that this was helpful when working remotely.

When assessing the multimedia resources, two students suggested the inclusion of more diverse resources. We agree that it is a challenge to create the right balance of multimedia while not divulging too much information. It is also important to consider that our participants were working in a compressed timeframe and did not have the opportunity to conduct extensive independent research. It also might be helpful to have students add items that they found helpful to the repository.

Figure 4. COMPSoft home page

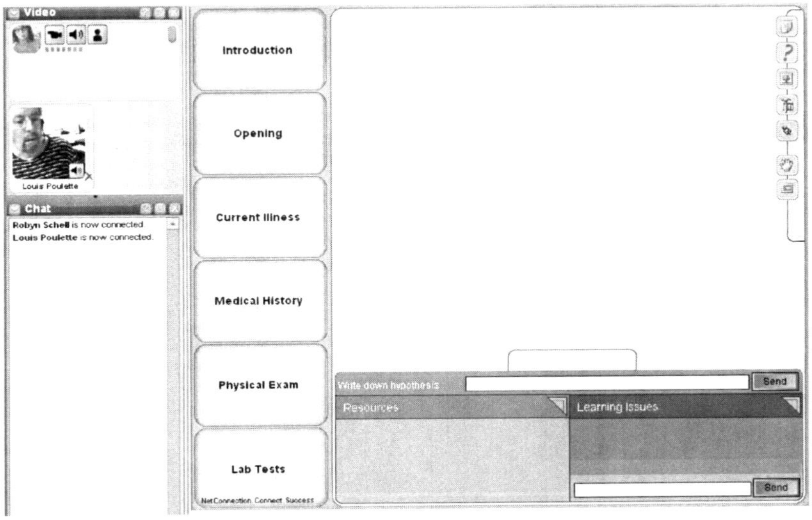

Turning to the results of the transcript analysis, we concluded that this online PBL system could have several advantages. By studying the transcripts in relation to the level of critical thinking, we could analyze why the students were more or less effective in developing critical thinking skills. For example, the facilitator found that one group of students appeared to work more collaboratively than the other group, especially when analyzing available information, backing up their hypotheses, and narrowing down pertinent research topics. With this type of knowledge, it might be possible to help the students develop better critical thinking strategies in future tutorials. Our coding system could also prove useful for measuring the effects of different variables in *COMPS*, for example, comparing the level of critical thinking in tutorials that included text-based case studies versus video case studies or as a way to compare the usefulness of different combinations of multimedia resources.

Although the findings of this study suggest a number of design implications, they must be viewed within the limitations of the study. Our small group of students were not the intended audience of the prototype design. We also suggest this tutorial could be more successful if it were situated in an actual medical curriculum and responded to the goals of the students enrolled in a specific medical education program (Issenberg et al., 2005). It may be reasonable to believe that critical thinking levels would be higher if students had more experience with the clinical reasoning process.

Next Steps: *COMPSoft*

Building on what we have learned in the study, we have designed a dedicated collaborative online multimedia PBL platform we call *COMPSoft* (Figure 4). *COMPSoft* offers similar capabilities as our current model, but also allows participants to use a web cam to see and communicate with other tutorial members. Multimedia can be displayed in the centre screen by either the case study facilitator or by students who wish to share multimedia with the group.

Using *COMPSoft*, instructors can create their own cases using a template system (Figure 5). Cases can be customized by adding text and slides as well as multimedia such as images, sounds, animation, and videos. Multimedia resources can

Figure 5. COMPSoft template for creating a case

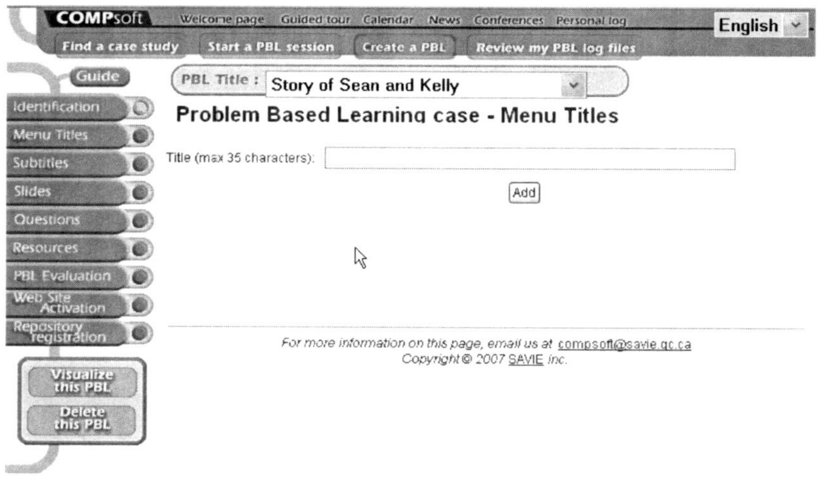

also be added to support the case. Using various tools, learning issues and hypotheses can be prioritized, modified, and archived and learning issues can be assigned to group members. *COMPSoft* is described in more detail in Chapter 3.

The next stage in our research is to run a series of tutorials on the *COMPSoft* platform using the evaluation model described in this chapter.

CONCLUSION

The results of this study showed that critical thinking can be enhanced through an online PBL environment. *COMPS* and *COMPSoft* are tools for bringing such environments to medical and health professional education; future research should further refine their utility, range, and ease of application

REFERENCES

Albanese, M. A. (1993). Problem-based learning: A review of literature on its outcomes and implementation issues. *Academic Medicine*, *68*(1), 52–81. doi:10.1097/00001888-199301000-00012

Barrows, H. S. (1984). A specific problem-based, self-directed learning method designed to teach medical problem-solving skills, and enhance knowledge retention and recall. In H. G. Schmidt, & M. L. De Volder (Eds.), *Tutorials in problem-based learning: A new direction in teaching the health professional.* Maastricht, The Netherlands: Vaan Gorcum.

Barrows, H. S. (1985). *How to design a problem-based curriculum for the preclinical years.* New York: Springer Publishing Company.

Barrrows, H., & Tamblyn, R. (1980). *Problem-based learning: An approach to medical education.* New York: Springer Publishing Company.

Brookfield, S. (1987). Developing critical thinkers: *Challenging adults to explore alternative ways of thinking and acting* (1st edition). San Francisco, CA.: Jossey-Bass.

Colliver, J. A. (2000). Effectiveness of problem-based learning curricula: Research and theory. *Academic Medicine*, *75*(3), 259–266. doi:10.1097/00001888-200003000-00017

Cook, D. A., & Dupras, D. M. (2004). A practical guide to developing effective web-based learning. *Journal of General Internal Medicine: Official Journal of the Society for Research and Education in Primary Care Internal Medicine*, *19*(6), 698–707.

Dewey, J. (1910). *How we think.* Boston: D.C. Heath & Co.

Duffy, T. M., Dueber, B., & Hawley, C. L. (1998). Critical thinking in a distributed environment: A pedagogical base for the design of conferencing systems. In C. J. Bonk & K. S. King (Eds.), *Electronic collaborators: Learner-centered technologies for literacy, apprenticeship, and discourse* (pp. 51-78). Mahwah, NJ: Lawrence Erlbaum Associates Inc.

Freeman, M. A., & Capper, J. M. (1999). Exploiting the web for education: An anonymous asynchronous role simulation. *Australian Journal of Educational Technology*, *15*(1), 95–116.

Garrison, D. R. (1991). Critical thinking and adult education: A conceptual model for developing critical thinking in adult learners. *International Journal of Lifelong Education*, *10*(4), 287–303. doi:10.1080/0260137910100403

Gredler, M. (2004). Games and simulations and their relationships to learning. In D. H. Jonassen (Ed.), *Handbook of research on educational communications and technology* (2nd ed., pp. 571-582). Mahwah, NJ: Lawrence Erlbaum Associates Inc.

Hawley, C. L., & Duffy, T. M. (1998). Design model for learner-centered, computer-based simulations. (ERIC Document Reproduction Service No. ED423838). Retrieved from ERIC database.

Hoffman, B., & Ritchie, D. (1997). Using multimedia to overcome the problems with problem-based learning. *Instructional Science*, *25*(2), 97–115. doi:10.1023/A:1002967414942

Hunter, M. K. (1991). *Doctors' stories: The narrative structure of medical knowledge*. Princeton, NJ: Princeton University Press.

Ip, A., & Naidu, S. (2001). Experience-based pedagogical designs for E-learning. *Educational Technology*, *41*(5), 53–58.

Issenberg, S. B., Mcgaghie, W. C., Petrusa, E. R., Gordon, D. L., & Scalese, R. J. (2005). Features and uses of high-fidelity medical simulations that lead to effective learning: A BEME systematic review. *Medical Teacher*, *27*(1), 10–28. Available at http://www.bemecollaboration.org/beme/pages/reviews/issenberg.html. doi:10.1080/01421590500046924

Jonassen, D. H., & Jonassen, D. H. (2000). *Computers as mindtools for schools: Engaging critical thinking* (2nd ed.). Upper Saddle River, NJ: Merrill.

Kamin, C., O'Sullivan, P., Deterding, R., & Younger, M. (2003). A comparison of critical thinking in groups of third-year medical students in text, video, and virtual PBL case modalities. *Academic Medicine*, *78*(2), 204–211. doi:10.1097/00001888-200302000-00018

Kamin, C. S., Deterding, R. D., Wilson, B., Armacost, M., & Breedon, T. (1999). The development of a collaborative distance learning program to facilitate pediatric problem-based learning. *Medical Education Online, 4*(2). Available at http://www.Med-Ed-Online.org

Kamin, C. S., O'Sullivan, P. S., Younger, M., & Deterding, R. (2001). Measuring critical thinking in problem-based learning discourse. *Teaching and Learning in Medicine*, *13*(1), 27–35. doi:10.1207/S15328015TLM1301_6

Kaufman, D. M., & Mann, K. V. (1997). Basic sciences in problem-based learning and conventional curricula: Students' attitudes. *Medical Education*, *31*(3), 177–180. doi:10.1111/j.1365-2923.1997.tb02562.x

Kenny, N. P., & Beagan, B. L. (2004). The patient as text: A challenge for problem-based learning. *Medical Education, 38*(10), 1071–1079. doi:10.1111/j.1365-2929.2004.01956.x

Kolb, D. A. (1984). *Experiential learning: Experience as the source of learning and development.* Englewood Cliffs, NJ: Prentice-Hall.

Lewin, K. (1951). *Field theory in social science: Selected theoretical papers.* New York: Harper.

Mann, K. V., & Kaufman, D. M. (1999). A comparative study of problem-based and conventional undergraduate curricula in preparing students for graduate medical education. *Academic Medicine: Journal of the Association of American Medical Colleges, 74*(10Suppl), S4–S6.

Mayer, R. E. (2001). *Multimedia learning.* New York: Cambridge University Press.

Miller, M. A. (1992). Outcomes evaluation: Measuring critical thinking. *Journal of Advanced Nursing, 17*(12), 1401–1407. doi:10.1111/j.1365-2648.1992.tb02810.x

Naidu, S. (2003). *Learning and teaching with technology: Principles and practices.* London: Kogan Page.

Naidu, S., & Oliver, M. (1996). Computer-supported collaborative problem-based learning: An instructional design architecture for virtual learning in nursing education. *Journal of Distance Education, 11*(2), 1–22.

Newman, D. R., Webb, B., & Cochrane, C. (1995). A content analysis method to measure critical thinking in face-to-face and computer supported group learning. *Interpersonal Computing and Technology, 3*(2), 56–77.

Orrill, C. H. (2002). Supporting online PBL: Design considerations for supporting distributed problem solving. *Distance Education, 23*(1), 41–57. doi:10.1080/01587910220123973

Paivio, A. (1991). Dual coding theory: Retrospect and current status. *Canadian Journal of Psychology, 45*(3), 255–287. doi:10.1037/h0084295

Schank, R. C. (2002). Every curriculum tells a story. *Tech Directions, 62*(2), 25–29.

Schank, R. C., & Cleary, C. (1995). *Engines for education.* Hillsdale, NJ: Lawrence Erlbaum Associates Inc.

Taradi, K., Taradi, M., Kresimir, R., & Pokrajac, N. (2005). Blending problem-based learning with web technology positively impacts student learning outcomes in acid-base physiology. *Advances in Physiology Education, 29*(1), 35–39. doi:10.1152/advan.00026.2004

Wilkerson, L., & Feletti, G. (1989). Problem-based learning: One approach to increasing student participation. *New Directions for Teaching and Learning, 37*, 51–60. doi:10.1002/tl.37219893707

ADDITIONAL READING

Issenberg, S. B., Mcgaghie, W. C., Petrusa, E. R., Gordon, D. L., & Scalese, R. J. (2005). Features and uses of high-fidelity medical simulations that lead to effective learning: A BEME systematic review. *Medical Teacher, 27*(1), 10–28. Available at http://www.bemecollaboration.org/beme/pages/reviews/issenberg.html. doi:10.1080/01421590500046924

Issenberg, S. B., & Scalese, R. J. (2008). Simulation in health care education. *Perspectives in Biology and Medicine, 51*(1), 31–46. doi:10.1353/pbm.2008.0004

Kamin, C., O'Sullivan, P., Deterding, R., & Younger, M. (2003). A comparison of critical thinking in groups of third-year medical students in text, video, and virtual PBL case modalities. *Academic Medicine, 78*(2), 204–211. doi:10.1097/00001888-200302000-00018

Kamin, C. S., O'Sullivan, P. S., Younger, M., & Deterding, R. (2001). Measuring critical thinking in problem-based learning discourse. *Teaching and Learning in Medicine*, *13*(1), 27–35. doi:10.1207/S15328015TLM1301_6

Kenny, N. P., & Beagan, B. L. (2004). The patient as text: A challenge for problem-based learning. *Medical Education*, *38*(10), 1071–1079. doi:10.1111/j.1365-2929.2004.01956.x

Ker, J., & Bradley, P. (2007). *Simulation in medical education*. Edinburgh, UK: Association for the Study of Medical Education (ASME).

KEY TERMS AND DEFINITIONS

Collaborative Learning: The ability to communicate as a group and refer to shared documents in a group.

Critical Thinking: A style of cognitive processing comprising five stages: problem identification, problem definition, exploration, applicability, and integration.

Experiential Learning: The process of making meaning from direct experience. It involves learning through reflection on doing. Experiential learning requires no teacher and involves the individual in making meaning through direct experience. However, Kolb asserts that in order to gain genuine knowledge from an experience, the learner must: (1) be willing to be actively involved in the experience; (2) be able to reflect on the experience; (3) possess and use analytical skills to conceptualize the experience; and (4) possess decision making and problem solving skills in order to use the new ideas gained from the experience.

Multimedia Software: In this context, it is the combined use of media, such as video, audio (speech, music, sound), graphics, and text for education or entertainment.

Narrative-Based PBL: Presenting a problem as a story may help to create a more holistic approach to medical education by engaging learners in more authentic, patient-centered problems

Problem-Based Learning (PBL): A learner-centred, small group method of instruction that uses patient problems as a context for developing students' problem-solving skills, and gaining knowledge about basic and clinical sciences. Case studies provide the structure for problem-based learning.

Web Conferencing: This is used to conduct live meetings or presentations through the Internet. In a web conference, participants work at a computer and are connected to other participants via the Internet. This can be either a downloaded application on the attendees' computers or a web-based application where the attendees can enter a website address to participate in the conference.

Chapter 18
Games for Children with Long-Term Health Problems

Carolyn Watters
Dalhousie University, Canada

Sageev Oore
Saint Mary's University, Canada

Hadi Kharrazi
Dalhousie University, Canada

ABSTRACT

Games are designed to generate a high level of motivation and engagement in their players. Game players often display intensity in their interaction with and devotion (compulsion) to a game and play the game over and over. In this chapter, the authors present a framework of motivational constructs found in games that are applicable to the design of interactive health software. The framework includes four dimensions of constructs: control, competency, context, and engagement. The authors developed a platform supporting a variety of games that include these constructs, and through two focus groups we examined the impact of these interactions with children with long-term health disorders. The goal is to determine if games developed with health-related goals provide an opportunity to engage children over time with some responsibility for their own condition; that is, can we build games that function like personalized coaches?

INTRODUCTION

Digital games provide both personal engagement and social interaction for children and adults alike. In this chapter we explore issues related to the use of games and game-like interactions specifically for children with long-term health disorders. These children have to make and sustain a commitment to ownership of their own treatment, typically by some type of behavioral modification or adaptation of lifestyle that may include taking medication, pain control, exercise, food choices, and daily journaling.

We began this work with a literature review of the theoretical constructs of motivation from the psychological literature to form a basis for design choices in the development of appropriate games. An

DOI: 10.4018/978-1-61520-731-2.ch018

initial survey of university students allowed us to test the relevance of designated motivational constructs extracted from the review to game playing specifically. Using these results, a framework and architecture were designed within which specific games could be developed and tested. A focus group study examined the relevance of these features using prototype games with health-related themes targeted for pre-teen children in a health context. One of the games, chosen from the prototypes based on feedback from the focus group, was then developed further and tested in a second focus group setting. This game targeted young girls with inflammatory bowel disease (IBD). The goal of the game is to increase their motivation in maintaining their treatment regimes and to increase and maintain a positive attitude to this treatment.

BACKGROUND

Games have become very popular and have been shown to be effective in capturing the attention of children in the promotion of healthy lifestyles to help them learn about a variety of health conditions and treatments (Fishman, 1999; Games for Health, 2005).

Our goal in this work, however, has been to explore a new generation of health-related games that move beyond the educational phase to the longer-term support of children with chronic conditions. These children have individual treatment regimes, often on a daily basis, that stretch over extended periods of time. Can games be used to motivate these children to satisfy the treatment requirements and to maintain positive outlooks? For example, can games reinforce healthy choices, remind the child of treatment specifics, distract their attention, and at the same time maintain individual health status and treatment records? The success of digital games across a broad demographic has led researchers to speculate that game interaction can be used to advantage in health contexts. This is based on an observation made by Turkle (1995, p. 69) that users of *SimCity®* liked it because "even though it is not a video game, it plays like one." Supporting high levels of motivation in the players is crucial for young patients facing months and years of treatment. Games, whether single-player or collaborative, provide players with the autonomy to practice, use the computer as a coach, and yes, zone out.

While the focus of game play is largely entertainment, it is entertainment that includes challenges, skills, self-motivation, and simulation. Consequently, the use of game structures in other contexts has appeal where the goals of the context include as core values self motivation, learning, the practice of skills, and successful meeting of challenges. Chapman (1999) suggests that there should be increasing emphasis on learners "situating" themselves in the world of study, in order to explore possibilities from other perspectives. Games do this.

Most health-related games to date target the initial period after diagnosis, when the primary goal is learning. That is, the child and the family need to learn a great deal about the disorder, the treatment, and the effects of treatments. The long-term treatment phase, however, is not so much about education as it is about dealing with the reality of the disorder. This phase, which may span considerable time, has not really benefited from the use of games. The design of games for this extended period is, in some ways more challenging than the short-term engagement needed for the interactive learning of the diagnostic phase. Their focus is more on the child who would be expected to return to the game frequently over longer periods of time, during which the child may mature or simply get bored. As children mature, they may become eager for more sophisticated game interactions. Furthermore, over time the particular treatment and characteristics of the disorder may change. Consequently, the goals of games targeted for the treatment phase may be closer to goals of strictly entertainment games than to the goals of educational games in several key ways. Treatment games must reinforce new skills in the context of changing challenges that reflect actual behaviour of the participant and patterns of data related to that behaviour. Critically, games in this context demand the engagement and commitment of the player to continue playing over multiple sessions.

Why Games?

One of the most significant factors in good health outcomes for children with long-term or chronic disorders is consistent adherence to the treatment regime, even when they are not experiencing direct effects. Our working hypothesis is that the ubiquitous digital game (Woolf, 2001) can be exploited to achieve this health objective. That is, the factors that make digital games so engaging can be applied usefully in health contexts where motivation and engagement are important factors in the successful management of chronic conditions.

Games differ from most applications we use in their use of visual, textual, and auditory channels for feedback, scaffolding challenges, visible goal indicators, overviews and schematics, and ease of learning (Dyck, Pinelle, Brown, & Gutwin, 2003). The process of learning how to play, how to improve skills, and how to succeed is much more natural in most games than in other software applications. Games may use sample play, hints or avatars for learning by watching. Few games rely on formal instruction or courses to get the player involved. Most games support scaffolded challenges with easier levels used to develop the skills needed at more advanced levels. One of the appeals of games is the ease with which the user can personalize and customize a game in ways that are easily reversible and riskless for the user. Game interfaces have brought a level of fluidity and contextual grounding that is largely missing from most other application interfaces.

Games in Health

There are many health-related games targeted for children with a wide variety of goals, including education, distraction, data recording, and reminding. The use of games related to a long-term treatment strategy for children with chronic disorders has not, however, been pursued to the same degree as those for the initial learning phase. There is evidence that children are quite willing to use electronic devices for health-related purposes.

Games for Learning

The use of games to encourage the learning of health content has become very popular in the last five years. Studies have shown that children who know more about their disorder have better health outcomes. The premise, then, is that game scenarios and game interactions will increase children's engagement and interaction to foster better mastery of the educational content. A good example is *Bronkie the Bronchiosaurus*, a game that helps children learn about asthma and about managing their own asthma (Super Nintendo Classics, n.d.). A study using that game showed that the children who had completed the game understood the impact of decisions they made, and overall made better choices than the children who did not have the game. Furthermore, those children who used the game to learn about asthma treatments were found to have 40 percent fewer hospital emergency room visits (Lieberman, 2001).

Operation IBD was a game developed earlier by our research team, working with researchers at the Izaak Walton Killam (IWK) Children's Hospital in Halifax, to reinforce a learning component for 6-to-10-year-old children diagnosed with IBD. The game was included as part of a web site (Family Help, 2005) of material to help children learn how to manage the symptoms of their condition (www.bringinghealthhome.com). The goal of this game was to reinforce the material given in web-based interactive lessons.

The material was related mainly to making good food choices. Several lessons were learned from this first work about making games specifically for the health context. First, making standalone games is very expensive, but good graphics and audio are essential, and worth the cost. Second, if children understand the lesson after playing the game once, they do not really learn much new by playing it again. Third, and related to the second, the game challenges must require skill building so that repeat play has an element of novelty.

Games as Distraction

Games have also been used successfully in pain treatment as a distraction (Das, Grimmer, Sparnon, McRae, & Thomas, 2005), and *Game Boys®* have been used pre-surgery to reduce anxiety. In Patel's 2005 study of 26 children, 4 to 12 years old, the *Game Boy* outperformed the use of tranquilizers in the reduction of anxiety (Patel et al., 2006).

Games as Journals

Particularly for children with long-term treatment regimes, the daily journaling of health status and health-related activities (e.g., food intake, exercise, medication) offers an opportunity for games and game-like interfaces to motivate this activity, especially when the child is not feeling adverse affects. Palermo, Valenzuela, & Stork (2004) used PDAs for children with headaches or juvenile arthritis to keep their daily journals. In a study with 60 children (ages 8 to 16), they found that that children with a PDA electronic diary completed the diary on more days (6.6 days) than children using a paper journal (3.8 days). Furthermore, the children using the PDA made fewer errors. We extended this concept for a study at the IWK Children's Hospital, examining the relationship of adolescent girls to pain and stress, designing a game-like PDA interface for the girls to use to record data four times a day that was successfully used for a four-month trial.

Games as Coach

The use of games beyond learning, distraction, and recording of data – that is, games that provide feedback to the participant based on their health-related activities or health status in the real world, much as a coach might – has not had the same profile. An early example is *Glucoboy* (Diabetes in Control, 2003), which was a personal device using a plug-in to a *Game Boy* to help children with diabetes monitor their blood levels.

In this research, we explore games that are meant to be used by children over longer periods as they cope with treatment regimes and potential social isolation. We are not designing an encompassing one-off game, but rather developing a framework that supports a variety of game genres and game choices. This is not to downplay the importance of games that make the initial and ongoing education for the patient and the family more engaging, but to explore a framework for the support of games designed more specifically for distraction, journaling, and coaching. That is, how can we use and design games that support the child: reinforce information gained in the learning phase, use distraction as coping strategy, act as a reminder system, encourage skill practice, encourage the recording of treatment and status data, provide appropriate health-related feedback, and provide social support. Long-term engagement means that participants need games that they want to continue to play as the treatment progresses, the child ages, and behaviour improves or regresses.

Health games in this context, then, need to satisfy the following criteria: be adaptive to the player, allow direct input of data, provide social support, provide variety and novelty over time, and provide player choice.

RELATING GAME DESIGN FACTORS TO MOTIVATION

Games engage users in a way that traditional educational material, including web sites, do not. The underlying premise of the use of games for more than entertainment is that we can capitalize on the motivation exhibited in playing games to develop engaging interaction in other areas. In particular, we theorize that games and game-like activities will enhance motivation for the learning of complex skills and in persistence in desirable activity. The question remains: what can we learn about motivation factors from games and game play that we can use to build interactions in a health context that are more engaging, more challenging, and foster social connections? There is a similarity in the goals of health treatment and digital games in that both depend on the motivation of the participant to meet challenges, be responsible for their own success, be persistent in applying their skills, and develop strategies to cope with difficult situations.

Meta-Level Analysis

To develop a framework for design and exploration, we first conducted a meta-level analysis of motivational factors in educational contexts and for which there was empirical evidence in the psychological literature (Watters & Duffy, 2005).

The meta-level analysis focused on empirically supported research on motivation in three main areas: intrinsic motivation, expectation of success, and incentives. Intrinsic motivation theories, such as self-determination (Deci, Schwartz, Sheinman, & Ryan, 1981), flow (Csikszentmihalyi, 1990), and goal theories (Eccles & Wigfield, 2002) focus on the reasons for participation. In general, the individual is completing a task largely for the personal enjoyment in doing the task. Self-efficacy (Bandura, 1977; 1986) and control theories are based on expectations of success, self-beliefs of competence, and feelings of control over outcomes have been shown to be relevant to the motivation of children in school achievement (Eccles & Wigfield, 2002). Attribution (Weiner, 1985) and expectancy-value (Read, MacFarlane, & Casey, 2002) theories integrate competence beliefs and expectancies of success with incentives and rewards to foster engagement in accomplishing tasks.

Design Factors

From this meta-level analysis, a framework of design factors for educational games was proposed based on the following motivational factors, with both positive and negative aspects, in the educational context: control, context, competency, and engagement. Control factors support self-regulation or autonomy, such as interaction, encouragement of innovation, providing rationales, providing relevant goals, choice and managed guidance. Context includes rationales, feedback and storyline. Competency factors include scaffolding of tasks, appropriate feedback, attainable challenges, and models of successful strategies. Engagementfactors include personalization, rewards, role-playing, challenge, personal notes, collaboration and communication. These factors are not necessarily discrete sets, and aspects may be associated with multiple factors.

Motivation Survey

This was followed by a survey (Kellar, Watters, & Duffy, 2005) in which we examined the role of the motivational factors identified in the framework in two game-playing populations: computer science students and business students. Group I consisted of 111 Masters of Business Administration (MBA) students (43% female) recruited from the Faculty of Business at Dalhousie University; the median age of these participants was 26. Group II consisted of 59 Computer Science (CS) students (17%

female) recruited from the Faculty of Computer Science at Dalhousie University; their median age was 22.

The survey questions were designed to probe game playing habits related specifically to the four motivation factors of interest: control, context, competency, and engagement. The first section of the questionnaire was related to preferred game types (single versus multiplayer games) and factors that influence which games participants seek out, keep playing, and stop playing. The second section of the questionnaire asked participants to choose a favorite electronic game and answer the questions in that section using their chosen game as a reference point.

General user profiles were constructed for both groups highlighting similarities and differences. The MBA students did not see game playing as a prime entertainment activity, playing on average only two different games typically once a week when they were bored or needed a break. The CS students, who were younger and more technically oriented, ranked playing electronic games as their second most favorite activity (out of seven). As outlined below, the survey results validated generally the framework developed from the meta-level analysis of the literature and allowed us an opportunity to refine it before beginning the development phase.

Control factors, related to self-regulation or autonomy, are obvious in participants' game choices and in game play. The two groups shared similar strong preferences for games which allowed them some control. Both groups reported playing games that allowed them to make choices and to develop skills related to control, for example, increasing the speed of action, managing multiple views, time limits, and the difficulty of the challenge. Students reported that they would often replay previously played levels and almost always finished one level before moving on to the next.

Context factors include rationales, personalization, and storyline. There were very few significant differences between the groups. The importance of a complex storyline and character development were not as important as we expected, especially among the business students, whose favorite games were puzzle and card games, such *Tetris®*, *Snood* and *Solitaire*. Immediate feedback, particularly using animation and high quality graphics, and personalization, however, were rated as important for both groups in choosing games to play.

Competency factors include establishing an appropriate level of challenge. This was important to both groups, and they reported a preference for games that were difficult to master. When learning how to play new games, both groups reported that they learned by a combination of exploration, help from friends and using game instructions. Difficult levels, when encountered, were conquered mainly through persistence and help from friends, and occasionally online hints.

Engagement factors focus on enhancing the commitment of the participant during play. The two groups of students differed in this area the most, based at least partially on how game playing met their social expectations. While both groups reported that they liked multiplayer games, the business students preferred playing with players they knew while the computer science students often played online in gaming communities. When engagement was measured as the voluntary commitment of time to the activity, the average length of session for both groups was not significantly different; computer science students played on average for 96 minutes and business students played on average for 87 minutes.

We conducted a validation of the survey with seventeen high school students and their responses were consistent with respect to the motivational factors noted in the older students.

GAME DESIGN

Our goal in designing individual games for use in the health context for children then drew on the framework of motivational factors, shown to be effective in educational contexts and relevant to game players, and applied these to developing games for children with long-term health problems. According to the framework and survey results, our games had to: (1) afford the participant control over choices; (2) use high quality animation and graphics; (3) be useful in a health setting; (4) exhibit appropriate levels of challenge; and (5) be fun, in and of themselves, particularly through a sense of social interaction.

Plug'n Play Architecture

Games designed as part of a long-term treatment strategy are different from games meant for learning about a newly-diagnosed disorder (Watters et al., 2006). The learning phase is relatively short-term, and once the participant has completed the learning program he or she is unlikely to return. On the other hand, games that one expects a participant to return to over a period of weeks or months must be personalized and adaptable over time. This means that novelty and interest must be maintained over the time period, perhaps with new games or substantial rewards.

To support these expectations, the game framework was developed based on the following design guidelines:

1. A platform with individualized game components that can be accessed through that scenario. The platform provides the continuity over time and is responsible for personalizing individual game components and collecting health data from all games as used.
2. Plug'n play game components so that individual games can be added and removed from the scenario by the player in a very simple manner.
3. Customizable individual games for inclusion in the framework, including non-health-related games chosen by the child.
4. Dynamically tailored game components for different disorders and treatments.
5. Databases at the server managed by the common platform to provide customized game instances dynamically and to capture user actions and health-related input.

Overall Scenario

The platform was designed as a web-based interactive cityscape of nine city blocks, in *Flash®*, through which the player navigates to choose specific game activities. Figure 1 shows an opening scene in the Halifax version of the cityscape. The player returns to the street level between

Figure 1. Two blocks of the Halifax cityscape

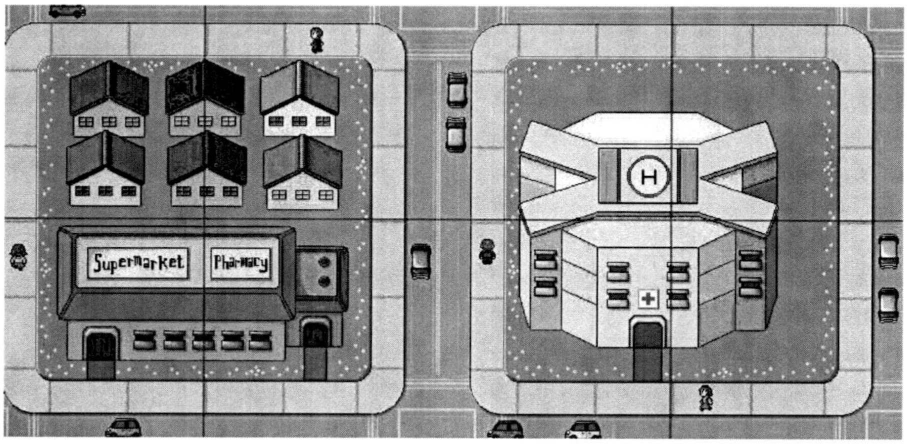

Figure 2. Character in backpack, not feeling well, and in a game, feeling better

activities, and at the street level the player has access to global health information, reminder boards, a clock, and a backpack of tools. Each game component communicates directly to the databases at the server to instantiate games, provide personalized information to the games as requested, and to record game interactions in the database. Within this framework we can then plug in a wide variety of games.

The only game elements permanently connected to the cityscape are the player's backpack and personal pet. If the player neglects to tend to his or her health needs, such as good food, taking medication, or practicing relaxation techniques at appropriate times during the day, the pet begins to look ill, as shown in Figure 2. The backpack also contains supporting materials for all health-related interactions including charts of progress, health information, schedules, etc.

Database Layer

The data layer has two main databases, the user database and the game database. The user database contains user profiles and use data while the game database contains rules and content for each game available. The player profile includes treatment parameters, user characteristics, user preferences, game scores, and game interactions and monitoring information. This data is used not only to drive the individual game instances, but by coaches and clinicians to be apprised of treatment compliance and difficulties experienced by the child during the course of the treatment phase.

The game database contains parameters about the runtime environment of each game, including parameters that are needed from a user profile, disorder-specific content, and multilingual information.

The design of games as components in a common framework means that core games are built content-free and context-specific information is loaded only at runtime. This not only reduces the time and effort to build new games for new disorders or other languages, but makes the addition or changing of content much more efficient. Building games as components in a common framework also supports cross-game consistent monitoring of activities and data as well as analysis for both longitudinal studies and clinical trials.

Plug'n Play Games

Within the context of the overall scenario, individual players make activity choices either by entering a building or opening their backpack. For example, entering the library might result in access to the IBD web site, entering their house could start a text-based role-playing game, or entering the Children's Hospital might start up one of the user's own games. The actual activities at any site are individualized and driven by the user profile so that the activity that results from entering a given building can be different for different players. All of the component games are designed or wrapped to comply with a simple set of http- and xml-based protocols so that new games can be easily added and games can be easily removed. This provides individualized experiences and allows for scenario renewal over time and as interests change. The participant can repopulate the specific games as they like, including bringing in games of their own.

Not all of the games are health-related. Other games can be included by the player as a distraction for coping with pain or treatments, to reduce anxiety, to cope with boredom, or as reward for achieving health goals.

Game Adaptation

We have been successful in adapting games for health purposes from entertainment games, making variations of games that are readily available, such as airplane shooters or quest-like games. This approach has several advantages, including cost savings, higher quality games, more complex games, and customization. Instances of the adapted game are generated at runtime to incorporate the specific health context from the database with the user's profile. This means that the play of the game remains consistent across its use for different health conditions but that the content reflects specific conditions (e.g., IBD, asthma, or diabetes) and a specific user (e.g., by language, age, or skill level).

By way of example, we have adapted for more general use a widely available *Flash* game, *AirFox®* (*PCman*, 2005), by inserting a "streamer" object that attaches itself to one class of attack ships. This object also reports related activities to the central database. One of the properties of the inserted object is to insert a short text string, drawn from the database, to individual ships. As the game is played, text from the database is bound dynamically to these objects and the player uses this information to pick which ships to shoot. In Figure 3 we see the streamers used to reinforce healthy eating; in another version of the game, we use the same streamers for relaxation treatments. The results of user actions are stored in the database and the user profile is updated after each episode of play. The manner and sequence of play is not altered from its original form, but the insertion of health-specific content has been used to support a treatment agenda, in this case by reinforcing choices, presenting treatment options, providing timely reminders of treatment, or recording of treatment specifics. Furthermore, the design allows the dynamic composition of versions of the game for a range of conditions, such as asthma or diabetes, and a range of languages, such as English, French, or Chinese.

Figure 3. Airfox variation, shown using food choices, and in French

Figure 4. Leopardy Q&A prototype, shown using IBD questions in English

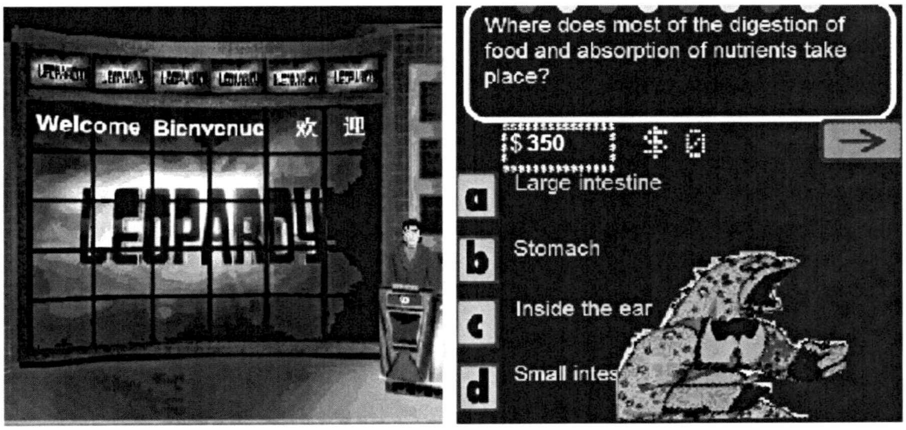

New Games

While it was not our intent to design large-scale new games, we introduced several smaller games that could be used for multiple disorders and multiple languages, be easily updated, and be connected to a central database at the server. In this chapter we describe three of these prototypes: a Q&A game, a text interaction game, and a dressup game.

Q&A Game

As a Q&A game example, we developed a simple multilingual, multiuse game as a prototype. Written in *Flash*, the question-answer style game *Leopardy*, shown in Figure 5, provides a context for health-related Q&A interaction where the questions and answers are drawn in real time from a database. Since the questions and response choices are stored in a database at the server, the databank of questions can be quite extensive, easily updated, and furthermore can contain question sets for several specific disorders. The use of Unicode text supports multilingual versions, including Chinese. Although the basis of the game is traditional Q&A, the design specifically included features for motivating children, such as increasing challenge, immediate feedback, rewards, autonomy, and personalization of the character. The children in our focus groups (see below) enjoyed this game more than we had anticipated, especially when played in small groups.

Figure 5. Dressup game, showing a happy and unhappy Gobi.

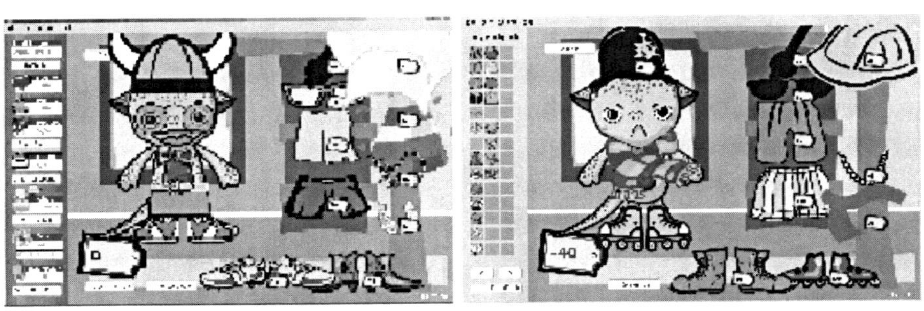

Text Adventure Game

We also developed an interactive text adventure game using the *Inform Z-machine* (2005) for both parents and children coping with chronic pain. The goal of this game is for parents or children to practice making the decision on whether the child should go to school that particular day. The scenario takes place in a simple kitchen with a window to the street and a clock that starts at 8 am. The child character comes down the stairs and the parent initiates a dialog which the Inform engine parses to create appropriate responses. The decision on whether the child goes to school that day must be made before the bus appears in the window at 8:15.

Dressup Game

One of our most popular games was a dressup game, shown in Figure 5, using the character in the backpack, called the Gobi, as the model. The children could dress up the Gobi from a store of fanciful clothes and other articles (e.g., fans, masks) using "money" they earned by following their medical treatment carefully. That is, the reward for real life behaviour was points (money) they could use in the game. Their personal health status, based on their own health-related behaviour, is reflected on the colour and expression on their personal Gobi.

EVALUATION

Two focus group studies, one year apart, were conducted at the IWK Children's Hospital in Halifax. In the first focus group we asked a mixed-gender group of children to play with the full set of games built for the plug'n play architecture. A grounded-theory analysis of this data led to insights into gender-specific and motivation factors in the context of health-based games for children. The first focus group clearly demonstrated that the children were—to their own surprise—not turned off by the health content, but in fact appreciated it. The results of this focus group were used to refine one of the games specifically for young girls, which was the target of interest in the second focus group. The results of the second focus group indicated that the single gender game as revised was ready for use in clinical trials.

Focus Group 1

The goal of the first focus group was to engage children (Morgan, Gibbs, Maxwell, & Britten, 2002) in discussions about the potential use of games in their treatment, to get their feedback on the games and game prototypes we had developed, and to gain general information about their likes and dislikes related to games and gameplay. The focus group ran for 1.5 hours with eight participants ages 7 to 11. All of the children either had IBD or had a sibling with IBD. The focus group was managed by a team that included a nurse and a pediatric gastroenterologist, and two researchers. Eight different games were installed in three stations. The children formed three groups (three boys, three girls, two girls) that rotated through the stations. At the first station a researcher showed how the games were played; at the second station each child played one or more games and the others watched; at the third station the children played a game collaboratively. As is typical with qualitative methods, questions were asked to encourage discussion and comments were recorded at each station. A total of 159 comments were recorded and partitioned into nine sets corresponding to the three stations by three groups.

Grounded theory analysis (Glaser, 1992) was used to explore categories based on the data rather than trying to fit the data into predefined categories. After the focus group activities, an independent observer (a psychologist) developed the following twelve categories to account for all 159 comments using a transcript of the children's comments (Table 1):

Table 1. Children's comment categories and definitions

Code	Definition	Description
C1	**Caretaker role**	acting as doctor, nurse, or other type of caregiver
C2	**Control over character/situation**	choosing aspects of the character, his or her health problems, and the game scenario
C3	**Interaction**	like to type in guesses and see if they are right; like to enter information about themselves and get feedback; like to chat online with other (real) kids who are sick
C4	**Visually exciting and text related**	fast, colorful visuals, and have mixed opinions on text
C5	**Points for health/ incentives**	incentives or points for healthy choices and actions along with progression through levels; comparing points and scores
C6	**"Cool & fun"**	non-specific positive reactions.
C7	**Relating to the game**	general ideas of how aspects of their lives as patients could fit into the game
C8	**How to?**	how to operate or improve the game.
C9	**Aggression/anger elements**	shooting things and crashes
C10	**Purpose & complexity to game environment**	connection between game "city" and theme of each game; more complex games
C11	**Unsure what is healthy**	expressions of uncertainty
C12	**Miscellaneous**	all other comments.

The data was normalized by gender as the girls made many more (i.e., 2.7 times more) comments per person than did the boys.

Some key effects that were noted included:

1. The girls enjoyed playing doctor, having control, interaction and seeing connections between real life and the game. For example, one girl reported "*If a game character has the same thing as you it makes you feel better about it.*" For categories C1, C2, C3, C7, however, there were **no** comments made by boys.
2. The boys liked speed and preferred sparse text. Over 30% of the boys' comments pertained to C4. Although both boys and girls liked action and visual interest, only the boys complained about too much reading.
3. An analysis of C5 indicated that the boys were more interested in winning points than the girls and the girls were more interested in health-incentives than the boys. It was the girls who connected points with good health, for example: "*If you are late for your blood work your health points should decrease.*"; "*If you get 100% in a health category you should go to the next level.*"

The results of the first focus group supported our premise that children would be motivated by games with a health context in ways similar to their interactions with non-health-related games. That is, that they would look for characteristics of control, competency, content, and engagement. The strength of the difference in specific preferences by gender was not surprising as this difference was also found in the older populations. Nonetheless, this difference led us to narrow our scope in the design of a game for possible use in a clinical trial to a game for young girls, rather than attempt to build a game for both genders.

New Game and Focus Group 2

Based on the evident gender differences and the predominance of girls with IBD, we focused on improving the online dressup game, which was particularly popular with the young girls. We incorporated many of the suggestions made by the children in the first focus group, including

Figure 6. Dressup game showing the chat window including the player's character.

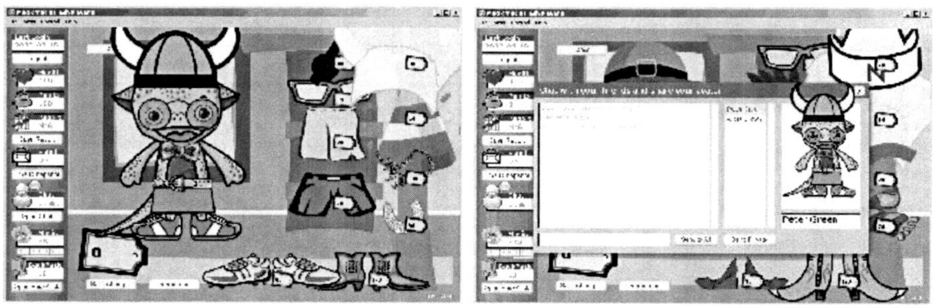

many more clothes, clothes with more fun in their design, sharing with friends, dynamic selection of clothes, a closet to save clothes, points gained by good health behavior, and a reflection of their health behaviour on the character in the game.

In the second version of the game (Figure 6), more specific attention was made to enhancing the game characteristics related to the motivation factors identified earlier. For example, the character was more personalized, with options of dancing to a selection of music; social perspective was provided with a chat and email feature; and a more challenging and sophisticated dressup play was developed. The health connection of the child to her own treatment was improved so that the character accumulates health and money points based on the participation of the child in her own health care regime outside the game. That is, points for use in the game are earned by taking medicine on time, eating the right food, and exercising. The health points earned by the child are not only used as value in the game, but also directly reflect the behavior of the player as reflected in the expression and color of the character. So that even though a player may have stockpiled points, and they continue to play, their character may become sad and greenish if no new points are earned by the player. The characters play a dominant role in the chat module where each person is represented by the current state of their character.

We validated this game with a second focus group of six girls aged 8-11, led by the same team. This study allowed the kids to play for approximately 30 minutes and then answer individual surveys followed by a group discussion. When asked what they like about the game, and what they would like to change about the game, responses included: *"[I'd like to be able to] change the character"; "[I like] earning the money"; "I like getting points and buying clothes"; "[I like] that it is easy to get money and to change the outfit screen. Also that it could remind people to take their medication."*

The girls spent a lot of time showing and talking about what to get, and interestingly, the girls wanted to earn their points rather than just be given them. They asked if other games could be included so they would not get bored, which we were able to do based on reusing the plug'n play concept from the full version cityscape game. The system is thus ready to be fine-tuned, based on the second group feedback, and given to the medical team as part of a larger clinical trial.

CONCLUSION

From a practical design perspective, designing reusable classes of smaller specific health games significantly reduces the time and cost of development, and accommodates the wide range of motivating factors for girls and boys. Comments indicated the children liked having a variety of games so they could replace them as desired, but they wanted connections maintained between the games. Our plug'n play framework connected to a central database is ideally suited for these considerations.

The focus group results support our underlying hypothesis that health care applications for children can be designed that leverage on the same motivational constructs in existing games. Very importantly, our work showed that the health context and social interaction were highly relevant to these children.

Our design process was successful in working within the constraints of the health-based applications, where opportunities are limited to do field studies of the tools with children with chronic illness before participating in a clinical trial. Having built games on a flexible platform, conducting an exploratory focus group with open-ended conversation with children was critical, and grounded theory was an effective method for analyzing the resulting unstructured data. We were able to incorporate most of the suggestions, and a second focus group validated the motivational potential in this game—at least as much as could be done at this stage.

Returning to our question: What if the child can tell that the game has an "ulterior" educational motive; will this trump any interest she or he might have otherwise had in the game? We answer with two children's' comments: *"These games are actually really cool!"; "I never thought it would be fun, but it's really fun."*

REFERENCES

Bandura, A. (1977). Self-efficacy: Toward a unifying theory of behavioral change. *Psychological Review, 84*, 191–215. doi:10.1037/0033-295X.84.2.191

Bandura, A. (1986). *Social foundations of thought and action: A social-cognitive theory*. Upper Saddle River, NJ: Prentice-Hall.

Chapman, M. L. (1999). Situated, social, active: Rewriting genre in the elementary classroom. *Written Communication, 16*(4), 469–490. doi:10.1177/0741088399016004003

Csikszentmihalyi, M. (1990). *Flow: The psychology of optimal experience*. New York: Harper and Row.

Das, D. A., Grimmer, K. A., Sparnon, A. L., McRae, S. E., & Thomas, B. H. (2005). The efficacy of playing a virtual reality game in modulating pain for children with acute burn injuries: A randomized controlled trial. *BMC Pediatrics, 4*(27). doi:.doi:10.1186/1471-2431-5-1

Deci, E., Schwartz, A. J., Sheinman, L., & Ryan, R. M. (1981). An instrument to assess adults' orientations toward control versus autonomy with children: Reflections on intrinsic motivation and perceived competence. *Journal of Educational Psychology, 73*(5), 642–650. doi:10.1037/0022-0663.73.5.642

Diabetes in Control. (2003). *Glucoboy moves closer to reality*. Retrieved May 20, 2009 from www.diabetesincontrol.com/issue173/np.shtml

Dyck, J., Pinelle, D., Brown, B., & Gutwin, C. (2003). Learning from games: HCI design innovations in entertainment software. In *Proceedings of the Conference on Human-Computer Interaction and Computer Graphics (GI'03), Halifax, Canada* (pp. 237-246). San Francisco, CA: Morgan Kaufmann.

Eccles, J., & Wigfield, A. (2002). Motivational beliefs, values, and goals. *Annual Review of Psychology, 53*, 109–132. doi:10.1146/annurev.psych.53.100901.135153

Fishman, M. (1999). Evaluating the effects of a virtual environment (STARBRIGHT World) with hospitalized children. *Research on Social Work Practice, 9*(3), 365–382. doi:10.1177/104973159900900310

Games for Health. (2005). *Games for health blog.* Available at www.gamesforhealth.org

Glaser, B. (1992). *Basics of grounded theory analysis: Emergence vs. forcing.* Mill Valley, CA: Sociology Press.

Inform Z-machine. (2005). *Inform Z-machine* (software program). Available at http://www.inform-fiction.org/zmachine/

Kellar, M., Watters, C., & Duffy, J. (2005, June). *A comparison of motivational factors between game players*. Paper presented at the 2005 conference of the Digital Games Research Association (DiGRA), Vancouver, BC, Canada.

Lieberman, D. A. (2001). Management of chronic pediatric diseases with interactive health games: Theory and research findings. *The Journal of Ambulatory Care Management, 24*(1), 26–38.

Morgan, M., Gibbs, S., Maxwell, K., & Britten, N. (2002). Hearing children's voices: methodological issues in conducting focus groups with children aged 7-11 years. *Qualitative Research, 2*(1), 5–20. doi:10.1177/1468794102002001636

Palermo, T. M., Valenzuela, D., & Stork, P. P. (2004). A randomized trial of electronic versus paper pain diaries in children: Impact on compliance, accuracy, and acceptability. *Pain, 107*(3), 213–219. doi:10.1016/j.pain.2003.10.005

Patel, A., Schieble, T., Davidson, M., Tran, M. C. J., & Schoenberg, C., Delphin, E.et al. (2006). Distraction with a hand-held video game reduces pediatric preoperative anxiety. *Paediatric Anaesthesia, 16*(10), 1019–1027. doi:. doi:10.1111/j.1460-9592.2006.01914.x

PCman. (2005). *Free Airfox destroyer game.* Available at http://www.thepcmanwebsite.com/media/air_fox/airfox.shtml.

Read, J. C., MacFarlane, S. J., & Casey, C. (2002). Endurability, engagement and expectations: Measuring children's fun. In *Proceedings, Interaction Design and Children 2002* (pp. 189-198). Eindhoven, The Netherlands: Shaker Publishing. Super Nintendo Classics (n.d.). *Bronkie the Bronchiasaurus.* Retrieved July 2, 2009 from http://www.snesclassics.com/snes-archive/bronkie.php

Turkle, S. 1995. *Life on the screen.* New York: Simon and Shuster.

Watters, C., & Duffy, J. (2005). Metalevel analysis of motivational factors for interface design. In K. Fisher & S. Erdelex (Eds.), *Theories of information behavior: A researcher's guide* (pp. 242-246). Medford, NJ: Information Today Press.

Watters, C., Oore, S., Shepherd, M., & Abouzied, A. Cox, A., Kellar, M., et al. (2006). Extending the use of games in health care. In *Proceedings of the 39th Annual Hawaii International Conference on the System Sciences (HICSS39) - volume 05* (p. 88.2). Washington, DC; IEEE Computer Society. doi: 10.1109/HICSS.2006.179.

Weiner, B. (1985). An attributional theory of achievement motivation and emotion. *Psychological Review, 92*(4), 548–573. doi:10.1037/0033-295X.92.4.548

Woolf, M. J. P. (Ed.). (2001). *The medium of the video game.* Austin, TX: University of Austin Press.

ADDITIONAL READING

D'Alessandro, D. M., & Dosa, N. P. (2001). Empowering children and families with information technology. *Archives of Pediatrics & Adolescent Medicine, 155*(10), 1131–1136.

Dyck, J., Pinelle, D., Brown, B., & Gutwin, C. (2003). Learning from games: HCI design innovations in entertainment software. In T. Möller & C. Ware (Eds.), *Graphics Interface Proceedings 2003* (pp. 237-246). Mississauga, ON, Canada: Canadian Information Processing Society and A. K. Peters Ltd.

Jorgensen, A. H. (2004). Marrying HCI/ usability and computer games: A preliminary look. In R. Raisamo (Ed.), *Proceedings of the Third Nordic Conference on Human-Computer Interaction 2004* (pp. 393-396). New York: ACM Press.

KEY TERMS AND DEFINITIONS

Architecture: In this chapter, refers to the underlying information framework that is implemented in software to support the game activities and research agenda.

Extrinsic Motivation: Related to rewards that occur as an outcome of a task or activity, for example, getting money or a prize. Research indicates that while extrinsic motivation may produce results, it may reduce motivation of the player to engage in the process.

Health Games: Refers to games or game-like interactions that have a game context based on good health information, provide interactions that are engaging for the player, and can be used to affect the player's behavior outside the game playing.

Intrinsic Motivation: Related to rewards that are derived from engagement in the doing of a task or activity rather than the outcome, for example playing a game for enjoyment, rather than to win a prize or conquer an opponent. Research indicates that intrinsic motivation is an important factor in achieving goals.

Plug 'n Play: A style of design in the middle layer of a three-level architecture in which each component, games in this case, are built independently and may be added or taken away as needed.

Three-Level Architecture: A commonly used design in which the lowest level refers to the databases, the middle level refers to the software manipulating the data from and into the databases, and the upper level refers to the software with which the user interacts directly.

Chapter 19
Handheld Games:
Can Virtual Pets Make a Difference?

Yueh-Feng Lily Tsai
Simon Fraser University, Canada

David Kaufman
Simon Fraser University, Canada

ABSTRACT

Children who care for real pet animals have shown higher levels of empathy and positive attitudes toward the humane treatment of animals. However, only a limited number of studies have examined whether caring for a virtual pet would have similar associations. This study investigated the question of whether a handheld virtual pet videogame can improve children's empathy and humane attitudes. The results showed that after playing Nintendogs® for three weeks, participants showed higher levels of empathy on the Bryant Empathy Index, and had higher levels of humane attitudes on the Intermediate Attitude Scale, compared to their scores before they played.

INTRODUCTION

With the growing popularity and sophistication of computer-based games including handheld portable units, it now becomes increasingly important to determine the socio-emotional effects of computer game play, including whether children can develop empathy and positive humane attitudes toward animals through interacting with, and responding to, virtual pets.

Building on evidence in the literature to suggest that empathy and humane attitudes can be enhanced through caring for pets, this research study investigated the potential of a handheld virtual pet video game to improve children's empathy and their humane attitudes toward real animals. For this research, the game software *Nintendogs®* was used as the object of study. The *Nintendogs* game cartridges and *Nintendo DS®* systems were bought at retail cost without corporate sponsorship from Nintendo. We hope that the understanding gained through this study about children's interaction with virtual pets may be applied to developing new technology to facilitate social and emotional development.

DOI: 10.4018/978-1-61520-731-2.ch019

LITERATURE REVIEW

Empathy encompasses a broad range of concepts. The Canadian Oxford Dictionary states that empathy is "the power of identifying oneself mentally with and so fully comprehending a person or object of contemplation" (Barber, 1998). In general, the process of empathy includes the empathizer and the empathized. The empathized often refers to another human being, but it can also refer to other objects such as art (Lipps in Goldstein & Michaels, 1985) and animals (Buber, 1948).

Cognitive and Emotional Influences of Empathy

Since 1897, when the German philosopher Theodor Lipps first introduced the idea of empathy, the concept has gone through various constructs as scholars and philosophers have defined it in different ways (Goldstein & Michaels, 1985). Recent theories of children's empathic development have generally supported a definition of empathy that includes both cognitive empathy and emotional empathy. Two important models, one from Hoffman (1982, 1987, 2000) and another from Feshbach (1982) have provided important explanations about how emotional and cognitive elements may be interrelated and influence children's empathic development.

According to Hoffman, children's empathic development is influenced by their cognitive and emotional development, and empathic distress (i.e., affective response to another person's distress) may be the key factor which joins the two domains (Hoffman, 1987). Based on the concept of empathic distress, Hoffman introduced five modes of empathic arousal: primary circular reaction, mimicry, conditioning, direct association, language-mediated association, and role-taking (Hoffman, 1987). The first three modes are emotional responses, and the last two require greater cognitive engagement. Language-mediated association, for example, requires the empathizer to connect his own experience with the empathized person's distress cues cognitively, through language. In role-taking, the empathizer is required to put himself in another's situation cognitively, and imagine what those circumstances might feel like. Hoffman further suggested that empathy can be encouraged and enhanced through training and guidance including encouraging children to experience a range of emotional experiences by engaging in different situations such as through pretend play and games. He further added that children's role-taking abilities should be enhanced by providing them with opportunities to share life experiences and improve their language and communication abilities (Hoffman, 2000).

Feshbach (1978), like Hoffman, believed that emotional and cognitive factors influenced children's development of empathy, and that empathy consists of three components. The first two components require cognitive abilities to receive emotional cues, identify others' emotions, and take the role or perspective of others. The last component is emotional responsiveness, which is the capability to experience emotion. Feshbach (1982) stated that, "the observing child must be able to experience the emotion that is being witnessed in order to be able to share that emotion" (p.320). She also indicated that empathy can be developed through training. Feshbach's (1979) empathy training addressed two important aspects: affective-cognitive training and cognitive training. Affective-cognitive training focuses on training children's ability in affect identification, perspective-taking, and emotional responsiveness; its purpose is to encourage children to explore different emotional experiences as well as freely express and discuss emotions. Cognitive training is focused on "non-emotional aspects of social interaction, discrimination of social cues that contain information about the thoughts, intentions, and probable future behavior of others" (p.240). Unlike affective-cognitive training, discussion "centers on intentionality, motivation, and problem solving rather than on emotion" (p. 240). Therefore, by learning about social cues, it is believed that one can gain greater understanding of others, including their emotional states and disposition to further enhance empathy.

In summary, both Hoffman and Feshbach emphasize the importance of cognitive and emotional factors in children's empathic development and recommend that children's empathy be enhanced through training and guidance. They suggest providing children with various life and emotional experiences using methods such as role-playing, taking other perspectives, and greater use of language. They also recommend providing opportunities for children to freely explore and express their emotions and to exercise their perception and understanding of emotions and non-emotional cues in a social context.

Animals and Empathy

Several research studies have suggested that animals may be able to enhance children's empathic development or abilities that relate to empathic development (Ascione, 1992; George, 1999; Levinson, 1972, 1978) and humane attitudes toward animals (Ascione & Weber, 1996). Levinson (1978) wrote that "communicating with a nonverbal creature—be it infant or animal—requires empathy, an ability to imagine how another thinks and feels, a capacity for mentally stepping into the other's place and to some extent experiencing what he is experiencing" (p.1036) and posited that animals can play effectual roles in enhancing children's empathic development. Myers (1998) stated that animals represent a potential medium to encourage children to play different roles that they seldom engage in in their real lives. For example, in pretend play, a child might assume the role of a caregiver or imitate animal behaviors. These interactions may provide children with opportunities to develop their role-taking and perspective taking abilities. George (1999) also advocated the importance of interacting with animals in children's empathic development, writing that:

> *...animals can teach children behaviors not easily acquired by usual learning techniques, such as the capacity to communicate nonverbally and social behaviors such as sharing and responsibility for others. Animals can also help children to develop self-esteem, a sense of achievement, nurturing, cooperation, and socialization, all of which contribute to the building of empathy. (p.382)*

The positive influence of pets on empathy development was also supported by Paul (2000), who concluded that there are "significant correlations between level and intensity of childhood pet relationships, concerns for the welfare of animals, and empathy with humans" (p.174). In summary, the individual studies of George, Levinson, Myers, as well as Paul, all theorized that interacting with animals can provide children with opportunities to practice role-taking and perspective-taking abilities. To communicate with animals, children also gain opportunities to practice language and learn how to perceive cues through interaction. These cognitive and emotional abilities are important elements that Hoffman and Feshbach consider necessary for empathic development.

Virtual Characters and Children's Empathy Development

If real pets can have potential benefits for children's empathic development, will virtual pets have the same effects? Although research on virtual pets is limited, there are some studies which indicate that virtual characters can influence children's emotional and empathic development. Research based on the anti-bullying software program *FearNot* found that the computer-simulated characters were able to evoke empathic responses such as distress and sympathy for the virtual victim character (Dias, et al., 2006). Another study examined the impact of a research-designed robot called Sparky that simulated expressions when interacting with people, and found that Sparky's simulations of sadness and fear were able to stir emotion among children (Scheef, Pinto, Rahardja, Snibbe, & Tow,

2002), further supporting the idea that virtual characters can evoke empathic response.

Studies investigating the influence of commercial virtual pets have also reported that users were aroused to display emotion and felt inclined to recognize virtual pets as life-like agents and engage in social interactions, including relationship building with them, despite knowing that the virtual pets were non-living creatures. One research study about preschoolers' reasoning and interaction with a robot pet dog called *AIBO®* found that, despite recognizing AIBO as a non-living robot, young children still believed that AIBO could feel pain (Kahn, Friedman, Perez-Granados, & Freier, 2006). This belief discouraged them from treating the robot dog in ways they thought would be hurtful. The research also found that a majority of children believed that they could build a social relationship with AIBO, including the giving and receiving of mutual love. Another research study compared children's attitude and interaction toward a real pet dog versus that shown to AIBO (Melson et al., 2005). It asked children whether they thought AIBO was a computer or live dog, and found that although children actually recognized that AIBO was a robot dog, a majority of them believed that AIBO had emotional states, morality, and the ability to socialize. The study concluded that children can perceive a non-living robot dog to have emotion, morals and the capacity to establish social relationships similar to real pet animals (Melson, et al 2005).

In summary, research has indicated that children's empathic development may be enhanced through training and guidance. Factors that can promote children's development of empathy include providing different emotional and life experiences, enhancing language ability, encouraging children to engage in role-taking as well as freely exploring and expressing their emotions and feelings. Furthermore, children should be encouraged to look for emotional and non-emotional cues from empathized objects. Studies that examined the relationship between animals and children's development of empathy have theorized that animals may be used as a medium in providing children with a catalyst to learn and enhance important empathic-related abilities. Studies on virtual pets that were designed to imitate real animal behaviors to encourage interaction with users have found that children can have an emotional and social connection to their virtual pets. Therefore, it is important to examine whether virtual pets can enhance children's empathic development. As Melson (2001, p.14) posited, "If we learn more about children's interaction with real pets and other real animals, as well as children's use of animal symbols... we then may have the tools to influence the development of this technology in directions that benefit children."

DESCRIPTION OF *NINTENDOGS*

Nintendogs is a computer-simulated virtual pet game that operates on the handheld *Nintendo DS* videogame console. The game was first released in Japan on April 21, 2005 by Nintendo (Jenkins, 2005, April 28). There are many different types of simulation pets in the game market, and *Nintendogs* is one of the best sellers. In Japan, 180,974 units of *Nintendogs* were sold in the first week it was released (Jenkins, 2005, April 28). In Europe about one million units were sold in the first two months (Nintendo World Report, 2005, November, 28). In North America, almost a quarter million units were sold in the first week of release (Carless, 2005, September 1). *Nintendogs* are sold in five different versions in the North American market. Each edition consists of six different breeds of dogs, including Dalmatian, golden retriever, Yorkshire terrier, beagle, boxer and German shepherd. *Nintendogs* has won several major awards, including overall Game of the Year and Handheld Game of the Year at the 9th Annual Interactive Achievement Awards (AIAS, 2006, February 9). *Nintendogs* also won the category of Best Technology Prize and Innovation at 2006 Game Developers Choice Awards (Game Developers Conference, 2006). The animal rights organization PETA gave *Nintendogs* the award for Best Animal-Friendly Videogame in 2006 (PETA, 2006).

Playing *Nintendogs* consists of caring for and training a computer-simulated virtual pet dog, and competing with other players and their virtual pets. Players are able to play, feed, touch, brush, wash, train, and join competitions with their virtual dogs by using the game's stylus to contact the unit's screen, as well as by speaking into a built-in microphone. The dog has basic needs such as hunger and thirst, which the player should meet by feeding and watering. A player's success in taking care of the dog is shown as higher training scores and the winning of competition prizes. There are several competitions that players can enter, including disc competitions, agility trials, and obedience trials. Players usually need to train their dog and do some practice before prizes can be won.

Through competitions, players are able to win virtual money, which they can use to buy food, accessories, or even a new house for the dog. Training for competitions can encourage players to better understand their dog. For example, in disc training, the dog may refuse to play if it is tired. Therefore players need to understand their dogs and learn when to stop training or when to provide food and water. Obedience trials often require time for the dog to learn a trick. Also the dogs tend to forget their old tricks if players do not repeat them regularly. However, once a new trick has been learned, the dog can obey the players' verbal commands, transmitted through the game unit's microphone. *Nintendogs* has a function called Bark mode in which two players can enable their dogs to play together. It should be noted, however, that once a dog has been imported onto the screen, play between the two dogs is associative rather than cooperative. Although the players' dogs will show up in the other's screen, each player experiences different events, and the two screens do not simultaneously show the same interaction.

RESEARCH QUESTIONS

This study addressed the following questions:

1. Can playing and interacting with, and responding to, a virtual pet dog game help to promote children's development of empathy?
2. Can playing and interacting with, and responding to, a virtual pet dog game help to promote children's development of positive humane attitudes toward animals?

RESEARCH METHODOLOGY

This research study used a quasi-experimental repeated measures design with pretest and post-test, as well as checklist and interview. The participants consisted of 52 children (27 boys and 25 girls) ages 9 to 11 years, in grades 4 or 5 from an elementary school in Surrey, a suburb of Vancouver, Canada. Participants had permission from their parents, had not previously played *Nintendogs*, and did not own a real pet dog.

Fifteen participants, who formed the pilot, received one set of empathy and attitudes pretests prior to the experimental treatment of interacting with a virtual pet dog. The other 37 participants used repeated measures with two identical sets of pretests, separated by three weeks, to determine reliability of control and measure any changes in children's empathy and humane attitude without the experimental treatment. The first set was termed "original" and the second set "pretest." After the pretest, the participants were introduced to the features and functions of *Nintendogs*. They then borrowed the game cartridge and Nintendo DS system for three weeks. Although the participants were asked to play with the game at least once each day if possible, they could decide the amount of time (i.e., duration) and how to play (i.e., interaction) with it. Once each week for three weeks, the researcher met with the participants to collect and confirm the weekly log. At the

Table 1. Research design

	O1		O2	X	O3
Duration		3 weeks		3 weeks	
Test	Original Measure	No intervention	Pre-test Measure	Intervention	Post-test Measure
No. of Students	N=37		N=37 Plus 15 (pilot)		N=36 Plus 15 (pilot)

end of three weeks, the participants completed the empathy and attitudes post-tests, and were interviewed regarding their feelings and ideas about interacting with their virtual pet dogs. The interview included a questionnaire regarding the companionship bond. The data from the pre- and post-tests, checklists, questionnaire, and interviews were used to examine the effect of taking care of a virtual pet dog on children's development of empathy as well as attitudes concerning the humane treatment of animals. Table 1 illustrates the research design.

The following instruments were used:

1. **Bryant Index of Empathy for Children and Adolescents** (Bryant 1982). This 22-item index was designed to assess human empathic tendencies in children and has been used in other companion animal studies with children (Bryant, 1982; Malcarne, 1986 cited in Ascione, 1992). Both convergent and discriminate validity have been demonstrated for this index; its reported coefficient alphas range from .54 to .79 (Bryant, 1982). The range of possible scores is from 0 to 22 with higher scores reflecting greater empathy. Bryant's Index was chosen for the research because the index had been used in other relevant research studies, and was designed for the age group of the children in this study. An example question from the Bryant's Index is "It's silly to treat dogs and cats as though they have feelings like people."
2. **Intermediate Attitude Scale** (Ascione, 1988). The original 36-item scale was designed for use with third, fourth, fifth and sixth grade students in companion animal studies. It contains statements with which a child can strongly agree, agree, disagree, or strongly disagree. For each item, the most humane choice is worth four points and the least humane choice is worth one point. The range of possible scores is from 36 to 144. The scale's reported coefficient alpha is .70, and its validity has been demonstrated (Ascione & Weber, 1996). Since the original Intermediate Attitude Scale does not contain a neutral opinion selection, we added "undecided" to this study. Participants who chose more than one answer or did not choose any answer were included in this calculation. After the change, the range of possible scores is from 36 to 180. An example question from the Intermediate Attitude Scale is "A cat might feel lonely if it had no one to care for it over a weekend."

DISCUSSION OF FINDINGS

Paired sample statistical analysis of the Bryant Empathy Index - Original (BIorgTOT) and the Bryant Empathy Index - Pretest (BIpreTOT) showed that mean scores remained relatively stable (Table 2). Based on a sample size of $N = 37$, the mean score for BIorg was ($M = 13.65$, $SD = 3.58$) and for BIpre ($M = 13.81$, $SD = 3.79$). The paired T-test was not statistically significant ($t = 40$; $p = .69$). Test-retest reliability showed the Pearson Correlation Coefficient between BIorgTOT and BIpreTOT to be 0.78.

Analysis of the Intermediate Attitude Scale-Original (IASorgTOT) and the Intermediate Attitude Scale (IASpreTOT) showed that the mean for the two tests was also quite stable (Table 2). The score for IASorg was (M = 121.05, SD = 11.54) and the score for IASpre was (M=120.81, SD= 11.95). The paired T-test was not statistically significant (t =.16; p =.87), and the Pearson Correlation Coefficient between IASorg and IASpre was found to be .71. Therefore, it can be assumed that both instruments, the Bryant Empathy Index and the Intermediate Attitude Scale, are relatively stable and may not be subject to fluctuation when no intervening factor such as the experimental treatment of this research study is introduced.

After playing with the virtual pet for three weeks, paired sample statistical analysis showed that the post-test empathy score (M= 15.78, SD = 3.56) on the Bryant Empathy Index for 51 participants increased an average of (M= 1.86) from the pretest score (M = 13.92, SD = 3.66) (Table 3). This was statistically significant (t = 4.53; p = .00).

On the Intermediate Attitude Scale, analysis of 51 participants also showed a significant (t = 4.62; p = .00) increase in post-test scores (M= 128.57, SD = 12.27) from the pretest score (M= 121.92, SD= 11.85) with a two-tailed significance of .00 (t = 4.62; p = .00) (Table 3).

As noted above, animal research studies have suggested that direct interaction with pets or farm animals can have positive influences on children's humane attitudes (George, 1999), and animals could also play effective roles in enhancing children's empathic development or abilities that relate to empathic development (Ascione & Weber, 1996; George, 1999; Levinson, 1972, 1978; Myers, 1998). Also, some virtual pet studies have also showed that preschoolers believe robot dogs can feel pain (Kahn, et al., 2006) and that children aged 7 to 15 believe that AIBO has mental states, sociality and moral standing (Melson et al., 2005). However, the previous researchers did not prove that interacting with virtual pet dogs can enhance children's humane attitudes and empathic development. In this research, quantitative analysis directly showed that the participants had significantly higher average scores on post-test levels of empathy on both the Bryant Empathy Scale and the Intermediate Attitude Scale. Therefore it can be concluded that playing/ interacting with a virtual pet over three

Table 2. Paired sample t-test of empathy, original vs. pretest and pretest vs. post-test

	Scale	Mean	N	SD	T	P
Pair 1	**BIorgTOT**	**13.65**	**37**	**3.58**		
	BIpreTOT	**13.81**	**37**	**3.79**	**0.40**	**0.69**
Pair 2	BIpreTOT	13.92	51	3.66		
	BIpstTOT	15.78	51	3.56	4.53	0.00

Table 3. Paired sample t-test of humane attitude, original vs. pretest and pretest vs. post-test

	Scale	Mean	N	SD	t	P
Pair 1	IASorgTOT	121.05	37	11.54		
	IASpreTOT	120.81	37	11.95	0.16	0.87
Pair 2	IASpreTOT	121.92	51	11.85		
	IASpstTOT	128.57	51	12.27	4.62	0.00

weeks has a statistical association with children's development of empathy and improvement in humane attitude towards animals.

CONCLUSION

Children's empathic development can be influenced by many different developmental factors, such as their level of cognitive and emotional development and their life experiences (Feshbach, 1978, 1979, 1982; Hoffman, 1982, 1987, 2000). The possibility that animals may have the potential to contribute to children's development of empathy has been suggested by research including George (1999), Levinson (1972, 1978), Myers (1998), and Paul (2000). Other research (Dias et al., 2006; Scheeff et al., 2002) has found that virtual characters can elicit emotional and empathic responses from children. In this study using the *Nintendogs* handheld computer game, we attempted to answer the question of whether a virtual pet dog can enhance children's empathic and humane attitude development. Our results found that after playing with *Nintendogs* for three weeks, study participants on average showed higher scores of empathy on the Bryant Empathy Index, and higher scores of humane attitude on the Intermediate Attitude Scale, compared to their pretest scores before they played with the virtual pet. Thus there is a statistical association between playing with a virtual pet and improved scores in empathy and humane attitude toward animals.

Due to practical difficulties, this study used repeated measures as the research design. We suggest that further studies should use an independent control group and enlarge the participant group size. Also, this research was conducted in an elementary school with an experimental duration of three weeks; it was anticipated that a longer period might disrupt the school's curriculum and students' routines. Furthermore, it was anticipated that the participants might lose interest in continuing with the research. Although this research has initially showed a positive relationship between playing with virtual pets with higher empathic and humane attitude scores, it is important to conduct further studies that involve a longer duration with more participants in order to explore the long term influence of a handheld virtual pet game on children's empathic development and other pro-social behaviors.

REFERENCES

Academy of Interactive Arts & Sciences (AIAS). (2006, February 9). *9th Annual Interactive Achievement Awards.* Retrieved February 14, 2008, from http://www.interactive.org/awards.php?winners&year=2006&cat=200625#200625

Ascione, F. R. (1988). *Intermediate Attitude Scale: Assessment of third through sixth graders' attitudes toward the treatment of animals.* Logan, UT: Wasatch Institute for Research Evaluation.

Ascione, F. R. (1992). Enhancing children's attitudes about the humane treatment of animals: Generalization to human-directed empathy. *Anthrozoo, 5*(3), 176–191.

Ascione, F. R., & Weber, C. V. (1996). Children's attitudes about the humane treatment of animals and empathy: One-year follow up of a school-based intervention. *Anthrozoo, 9*(4), 188–195.

Barber, K. (1998). *Canadian Oxford dictionary.* Toronto, ON, Canada: Oxford University Press.

Bryant, B. (1982). An index of empathy for children and adolescents. *Child Development, 53*, 413–425. doi:10.2307/1128984

Buber, M. (1948). *Between man and man.* New York: Macmillan.

Carless, S. (2005, September 1). Nintendo reveals impressive U.S. Nintendogs™ figures. *Gamasutra.* Retrieved February 14, 2008, from http://www.gamasutra.com/php-bin/news_index.php?story=6393

Dias, J., Paiva, A., Vala, M., Aylett, R., Woods, S., Zoll, C., & Hall, L. (2006). Empathic characters in computer-based personal and social education. In M. Pivec (Ed.), *Affective and emotional aspects of human-computer interaction.* Amsterdam, Netherlands: IOS Press.

Feshbach, N. D. (1978). Studies on empathic behavior in children. In B. A. Maher (Ed.), *Progress in experimental personality research 8* (pp. 1-47). New York: Academic Press.

Feshbach, N. D. (1979). Empathy training: A field study in affective education. In S. Feshbach & A. Fraczek (Eds.), *Aggression and behavior change* (pp. 234-249). New York: Praeger Publishers.

Feshbach, N. D. (1982). Sex differences in empathy. In N. Eisenberg (Ed.), *The development of prosocial behavior* (pp. 315-338). New York: Academic Press.

Game Developers Conference (2006). *6th Annual game developers' choice awards.* Retrieved February 16, 2008, from http://www.gamechoiceawards.com/archive/gdca_6th.htm

George, M. H. (1999). The role of animals in the emotional and moral development of children. In F. R. Ascione & P. Arkow (Eds.), *Child abuse, domestic violence, and animal abuse* (pp. 380-392). West Lafayette, IN: Purdue University Press.

Goldstein, A. P., & Michaels, G. Y. (1985). *Empathy: Development, training, and consequences.* Hillsdale, NJ: Lawrence Erlbaum Association Inc.

Hoffman, M. L. (1982). The development of prosocial motivation: Empathy and guilt. In N. Eisenberg (Ed.), *The development of prosocial behavior* (pp. 281-313). New York: Academic Press.

Hoffman, M. L. (1987). The contribution of empathy to justice and moral judgment. In N. Eisenberg & J. Strayer (Eds.), *Empathy and its development* (pp. 47-80). Cambridge, UK: Cambridge University Press.

Hoffman, M. L. (2000). *Empathy and moral development.* Cambridge, UK: Cambridge University Press.

Jenkins, D. (2005, April 28). Japanese sales charts, week ending April 24th. *Gamasutra.* Retrieved February 14, 2008, from http://www.gamasutra.com/php-bin/news_index.php?story=5386

Kahn, P. H., Friedman, B., Perez-Granados, D. R., & Freier, N. G. (2006). Robotic pets in the lives of preschool children. *Interaction Studies: Social Behaviour and Communication in Biological and Artificial Systems,* 7(3), 405–436. doi:10.1075/is.7.3.13kah

Levinson, B. M. (1972). *Pets and human development.* Springfield, IL: Charles C Thomas.

Levinson, B. M. (1978). Pets and personality development. *Psychological Reports, 42,* 1031–1038.

Melson, G. F. (2001). *Why the wild things are: Animals in the lives of children.* Cambridge, MA: Harvard University Press.

Melson, G. F., Kahn, P. H., Beck, A. M., Friedman, B., Roberts, T., & Garret, E. (2005). Robots as dogs? Children's interactions with the robotic dog AIBO and a live Australian shepherd. In G. C. van der Veer & C. Gale (Eds.), *Extended Abstracts Proceedings of the 2005 Conference on Human Factors in Computing Systems, CHI 2005,* (pp.,1649-1652). Retrieved from http://faculty.washington.edu/pkahn/articles/Robots_as_Dogs.pdf.

Myers, G. (1998). *Children and animals: Social development and our connections to other species.* Boulder, CO: Westview Press.

Nintendo World Report. (2005, November 28). *Europe loves Nintendogs.* Retrieved February 14. 2008, from http://www.nintendoworldreport.com/newsArt.cfm?artid=10961.

Nintendo.com. (2008, February). *Game guide.* Retrieved February 17, 2008, from http://www.nintendo.com/games/guide#qhardware=DS.

Paul, E. S. (2000). Love of pets and love of people. In A. L. Podberscek., E. S. Paul & J. Serpell (Eds.), *Companion animals and us: Exploring the relationships between people and pets* (pp. 168-188). Cambridge, UK: Cambridge University Press.

People for the Ethical Treatment of Animals (PETA), (2006). *2006 PETA Proggy award.*

Retrieved February 10, 2008, from http://www.peta.org.uk/feat/proggy/2006/index.html

Scheef, M., Pinto, J., Rahardja, K., Snibbe, S., & Tow, R. (2002). Experiences with Sparky, a Social Robot. In K. Dautenhahn, A.H. Bond, L. Canamero, & B. Edmonds (Eds.). *Socially intelligent agents: Creating relationships with computers and robots* (pp. 173-180). Norwell, MA: Kluwer Academic Publishers.

ADDITIONAL READING

Ascione, F. R. (2005). *Children and Animals: Exploring the roots of kindness and cruelty.* West Lafayette, IN: Purdue University Press.

Davis, M. H. (1994). *Empathy: A social psychological approach.* Dubuque, IA: Wm. C. Brown.

Trappl, R., Petta, P., & Payr, S. (Eds.). (2002). *Emotions in human and artifacts.* Cambridge, MA: The MIT Press.

Turkle, S. (2005). *The second self: Computers and the human spirit.* Cambridge, MA: The MIT Press.

KEY TERMS AND DEFINITIONS

Cognitive Empathy: The ability to understand others' emotions and thoughts.

Emotional Empathy: An emotional reaction or response to another's emotion.

Empathic-Related Abilities: Abilities which relate to children's empathic development, such as affect and social cue identification, perspective-taking, and emotional responsiveness.

Empathy: A cognitive and emotional process that is involved in perceiving and responding to others' emotional states and dispositions.

Humane Attitude: The demonstration of kind, caring behavior and attitude toward animals.

Nintendogs®: A virtual pet game that operates on the handheld *Nintendo DS®* videogame console, first released by Nintendo in 2005.

Virtual Pet: A computerized electronic toy that simulates a character which elicits the need to be cared through the display of physical features, actions and characteristics of life.

Chapter 20
The Learning Impact of Violent Video Games

Alice Ireland
Simon Fraser University, Canada

Nathaniel Payne
Simon Fraser University, Canada

ABSTRACT

There is strong research evidence to suggest that exposure to violent video games is related to an increase in aggressive behaviors in children. Violent video games trigger short-term bursts of aggression, but more importantly they can actually change the user's thinking processes over time. However, there is also strong evidence to the contrary. This chapter presents an overview of recent evidence for and against the argument on violent games and aggression, together with suggestions for ways that parents can help to mitigate negative effects.

INTRODUCTION

"Should I worry about my kids playing violent video games?" is a question concerned parents often ask video game researchers. Faced with ever-higher gameplay statistics and more frequent incidents of school violence, parents are concerned about the impact of video game violence on children, adolescents, and adults—often putting themselves at odds with industry spokespeople. To help researchers respond to these questions, this chapter gives an overview of concerns, controversy, and research evidence surrounding possible relationships between video games and violent behavior. We start by outlining why video games are potentially more influential than other forms of electronic entertainment, and we outline theories that attempt to explain connections between violent video gameplay, aggression, and violent behavior. We then present evidence from both sides of the debate, discuss issues that complicate research in this area, and conclude with recommendations for parents to monitor and mitigate the effects of violent video game content in their children more effectively.

DOI: 10.4018/978-1-61520-731-2.ch020

CAUSES FOR CONCERN

The video game industry has experienced staggering growth over the past two decades. In 2007, total US game industry sales jumped to $US18.8 billion, a 40% increase over 2006 (NPD Group Inc., 2008). In the US, video game sales overtook music sales in 2008, and the worldwide video gaming market, excluding hardware and accessories, is projected to reach US$48.9 billion by 2011 (Reuters, 2007). It has been estimated that nearly 80% of US children between the ages of 6 and 11 play online games (Mediamark Research and Intelligence, 2007), and youth aged 12 to 17 play for an average of 10 hours each week (NPD Group Inc., 2007).

As video games have evolved over time, aggression and violence have become dominant game themes; for example, Haninger and Thompson (2004) found that 98% of a random sample of 81 games contained violence, and 90% either rewarded players who injured characters, or required them to do so. Public concern with video game violence has grown with school shootings such as the 1999 Columbine High School shooting in Colorado, in which the student killers were players of Doom®, a game licensed as a US military training tool. As a result, parents, advocacy groups and media organizations press researchers to accelerate their study and understanding of the relationships between violent video games and violent behavior.

Video game researchers commonly define aggression as "behavior (verbal or physical) that: (a) is intended to harm another individual; (b) is expected by the perpetrator to have some chance of actually harming that individual; and (c) is believed by the perpetrator to be something that the target individual wishes to avoid" (Gentile & Anderson, 2006, p. 226). Physical aggression takes place on a continuum from mild to very severe, and violence happens at the severe end of that continuum. Researchers apply these definitions to behavior in both video games and physical reality.

Why might violent video games (VVGs) lead to aggression and violence? VVGs typically require players to perform simulated aggressive and violent acts, including repeated killing, in highly realistic virtual "worlds." Many features of these simulation games embody the best practices used in learning environments and advertising, both of which are consciously designed to change knowledge, attitudes, and behaviors. Specific violent video game features that appear to make them effective learning tools, particularly for adolescents who are still developing attitudes, beliefs, judgment, and moral control, (summarized from Anderson, 2004; Dill & Dill, 1998; Eron, 2001; and Funk, Baldacci, Pasold, & Baumgardner, 2004) include:

- rewards for violent and anti-social behavior
- player identification with violent aggressors through characters or avatars
- extreme simulated violence in realistic situations
- active, intense player involvement compared to passive media forms such as television and film, potentially leading to stronger effects on the player's cognition and emotion
- continuous stimulation and a highly interactive entertainment environment, possibly creating addiction
- frequent exposure, modelling, practice, and, as noted above, rewards for violent behavior
- desensitization to violence after frequent exposure, which has been found to be associated with both lower empathy and stronger pro-violence attitudes

In a conceptual analysis, Gentile and Gentile (2008, p. 128) identify seven ways in which video games "systematically and effectively use educational principles" to engage players and teach them the skills they need for violent gameplay. These are:

- clear objectives, often set at multiple difficulty levels, that match objectives and pace to the capabilities of learners
- active learning with practice, feedback, and more practice to the point of mastery
- "overlearning" of knowledge and skills so that they become automatic, freeing the player to focus on new information
- reinforcement of mastery, both extrinsic (through points, better weapons, more money, or health) and intrinsic (through higher game levels and self-esteem)
- sequencing of games into increasingly difficult and complex levels, often (in newer games) adapting controls to user skills
- embodiment of a spiral curriculum in which mastery of a learning objective becomes the beginning of a new learning phase within a long and complex path
- massed (intense) practice to build initial mastery, followed by distributed (interspersed) practice later in the game to prevent forgetting – an approach found to be optimal for the development of automatized structures of knowledge or schemas
- knowledge and skills practice on several problems or in multiple contexts, helping the learner to transfer underlying concepts to new situations

They conclude that "it should be no surprise that video games are excellent teachers… of violent content" (Gentile & Gentile, 2008, p. 139) and present correlational research evidence for two of their initial hypotheses.

THEORETICAL CONNECTIONS

Theoretical models, arising from generic work on violence from several domains, guide research into the VVG/ violent behavior question by hypothesizing connecting mechanisms and causal relationships to be tested. Models relating social, cognitive, emotional, environmental, behavioral, and other factors have so far proved useful in this research. Examples (summarized from Anderson & Bushman, 2002 and Kirsh, 2003) include:

Social Learning Theory and Social Cognitive Theory

Social Learning Theory (Bandura 1977) argues that children, and to a lesser degree adults, continually learn both desirable and undesirable behaviors from direct experience and observation in their environments, even when their models are not trying to teach those behaviors. Social Cognitive Theory (Bandura, 2001) focuses on the cognitive processes that mediate observation and behavior, proposing that individuals witnessing actions that are rewarded tend to interpret these actions positively and adopt them to achieve their own goals. In the context of violent video games, this suggests that VVG players learn that violence and killing are acceptable and rewarded, possibly choosing to adopt those behaviors when in a situation of anger or similar emotion (e.g., see Browne & Hamilton-Giachritsis, 2005).

Cognitive Neo-Association Aggression Model

Berkowitz's (1990) Cognitive Neo-Association Model (CN) proposes that media or video game violence works to prime, create, and activate networks of aggressive thoughts, feelings, memories, and beliefs that result in aggressive action, anger, or hostile thought. When people are repeatedly exposed to aggression, they create in their minds more detailed and interconnected aggressive thought networks that then trigger related feelings, cloud judgment and increase the tendency of an individual to act aggressively.

Script Theory

Scripts are "sets of particularly well-rehearsed, highly associated concepts in memory, often involving causal links, goals, and action plans"

(Anderson & Bushman 2002, p. 31, summarizing Abelson, 1981). Once learned and practiced, scripts guide behavior. They become more accessible with repeated exposure and practice, as happens with violence in video games.

Excitation Transfer Theory

This theory suggests that physiological arousal dissipates slowly and can be misattributed to a later event (Zillmann, 1988). This means that an angry response to an event can be made more intense by lingering physiological arousal from an earlier event; for example, lingering physiological arousal from playing a violent video game could intensify a later aggressive response to frustrating driving conditions.

Automaticity Theory

Todorov and Bargh (2001) argue that, based on a literature review and experimental evidence, "priming, including subliminal priming, of mental constructs related to aggression leads to reliable effects on perceptions, judgments, and behavior. Specifically, after such priming, people perceive ambiguous behaviors as more aggressive and tend to act more aggressively; prolonged exposure to violence can result in the development of chronic accessibility of aggressive constructs that affect how the social environment is interpreted; and even goal-directed behavior can be automatically triggered by situational features if this behavior is consistently and frequently enacted in the same situation" (p. 53).

Desensitization and Moral Evaluation

Based on evidence that desensitization to violence is an effect of exposure to violent media, Funk, Buchman, Jenks, and Bechtoldt (2003) describe the evolution of moral evaluation processes in children. They hypothesize that video games desensitize children to violence by rewarding simulated violent acts and dehumanizing victims, thereby lessening the development of empathy and affective cues that would support automatic moral evaluation against violence.

Biological Age Theory and Physiological Development

Spear (2000) notes that early adolescence brings increases in hormones which are positively correlated to aggression, as well as excessive synapse connections that may limit the prefrontal cortex's ability to efficiently process and evaluate situations, in turn reducing early adolescents' ability to make sound judgments. Thus, it is possible that higher levels of aggressive behavior during early adolescence are in part due to biologically driven limitations in rational thought and evaluation of consequences. Focusing on physiological arousal, Anderson and Bushman (2001) argue, based on a meta-analysis, that increases in heart rate and blood pressure have been seen to accompany violent video game play in all age categories and especially within the adolescent age brackets. This research supports the hypothesis that VVG gameplay does result in an increase in physiological arousal, with this arousal increasing the tendency of adolescents to respond aggressively in the short term.

General Aggression Model (GAM)

The General Aggression Model (GAM) (e.g., Anderson & Carnagey, 2004) has been developed, tested and expanded since 1995 in an effort to combine causal theories of aggression from social, developmental, and personality psychology into a validated, coherent framework. The GAM focuses on the "person in the situation" in a systems model that includes (a) person and situation inputs, (b) highly interrelated cognitive, affective, and arousal routes through which these input variables have their impact; and (c) outcomes of the underlying appraisal and decision processes. Person factors include traits, sex, beliefs, attitudes, values, long-term goals, and scripts. Situational factors include aggressive cues, provocation, frustration, drugs, and incentives that can increase aggression. Routes include cognition (hostile thoughts, scripts), affect (mood, emotion, expressive motor responses), and arousal (physiological and psychological). Outcomes result from automatic "appraisal" processes which lead to impulsive action, and from more controlled "reappraisal" leading to thoughtful action (Anderson & Bushman, 2002).

The GAM argues that five different types of knowledge structures are influenced or altered from violent and aggressive video games and media, and these knowledge structures affect perception, interpretation, decision making and action (Anderson & Carnagey, 2004). The model suggests that long-term exposure to media violence results from the development, overlearning, and reinforcement of that violence in the brain's aggression-related knowledge structures. Each time people play a violent video game, they rehearse aggressive scripts that teach and reinforce vigilance for enemies (i.e., hostile perception bias), aggressive action against others, expectations that others will behave aggressively, positive attitudes toward use of violence, and beliefs that violent solutions are effective and appropriate.

This repeated exposure works with desensitization theory to desensitize the individual to the graphic nature of the violent scenes, as well as desensitizing their moral value system. This desensitization is dangerous because it can significantly change the individual's personality over the long run. As a result, long-term violent video game players can become much more aggressive in outlook, perceptual biases, attitudes, beliefs, and behavior than they were before the repeated exposure, or would have become without such exposure (Anderson & Dill, 2000).

EVIDENCE FOR THE CONNECTION

A number of research studies suggest links between VVG exposure and several specific indicators or manifestations of aggression and violence. Significant conclusions associate playing VVGs with the outcomes described below.

Increases in Aggressive Behavior

Early studies often focused on demonstrating a strong correlation between violent video games and both short-term and long-term aggressive behavior. For example, observational field studies were conducted by Irwin and Gross (1995); Schutte, Malouff, Post-Gorden, and Rodasta (1988); and others, using children up to 11 years old. Measuring children's responses to violent video games using observation during free play and other indicators such as parental and teacher surveys, they found both short- and long-term increases in aggression in subjects who had played aggressive video games. Silvern and Williamson (1987) tested children aged 4 to 6 and found that all subjects, regardless of sex, became significantly more aggressive after playing aggressive video games.

Increases in Aggressive Cognition

Rushbrook (1986) found through self-report questionnaires that a strong correlation existed between the amount of video game play and attitudes that were more favourable to war in a group of 5th - to 11th-grade males. This evidence was reinforced by Anderson and Dill's (2000) comprehensive GAM study, which randomly assigned young adults to play a violent or a non-violent video game and measured the time it took them to recognize and begin pronouncing aggressive words. They concluded that even brief exposure to violent video games (a situational input), could prime aggressive thoughts and act as a major cause of short-term increases in aggressive behavior.

Uhlmann and Swanson (2004), in a study of 121 university students, discovered that while most video game enthusiasts insist that the games they play have no effect on them, their exposure to scenes of virtual violence influenced them automatically and unintentionally and had a definite impact on their subjects' cognitions. Additionally, they found that participants who had played the bloody and violent video game Doom for 10 minutes subsequently associated the self more with aggressive traits and actions on an IAT (Implicit Association Test), but did not associate self with aggressive traits on a variety of self-report measures.

INCREASES IN AGGRESSIVE FEELINGS, EMOTIONS, AND DESENSITIZATION

Anderson and Ford (1986) found that playing aggressive video games had a defined, short-term negative effect on undergraduate players' emotional state. In addition, players of a highly aggressive video game showed increased hostility and anxiety. Funk et al. (2004) found that long-term exposure to violent video games in 5-to-12-year-olds was associated with significantly lower empathy in some children, providing evidence of desensitization. Their data also showed that playing violent video games negatively affected the children's moral decision-making. In another example, Carnagey, Anderson, and Bushman (2007) reported evidence of physiological desensitization to violence resulting from VVG gameplay.

Decreases in Pro-Social Behavior

Other studies have linked violent video games with decreased pro-social behavior and increased short-term aggression. Sheese and Graziano (2005), for example, found that playing violent video games undermined pro-social and altruistic motivation, promoted competitive behavior in deliberate decision making, and appeared to contribute directly to participants' willingness to exploit their interaction partners. They found that violent video game players were more likely than others to exploit existing trust, leading to more aggressive behavior over the short term.

Increases in Physiological Arousal

Increases in physiological arousal have been strongly linked to increases in short-term aggressive behavior in individuals by various theoretical models. For example, Mathews et al. (2006) found that teenagers who had played violent video games had more activity going on in the amygdala than did teenagers in their study who played non-violent games. Those playing the violent games also had lower activity in prefrontal areas of the brain associated with self control, inhibition and focus (concentration), compared to the non-violent game players. The researchers said further studies are needed to determine whether these physiological changes make individuals behave more violently.

Studies Based on the General Aggression Model

The general aggression model (GAM), integrating concepts from social learning theory, cognitive psychology, script theory, development, and biology, has given researchers a more comprehensive picture of how video game violence increases aggression in both short- and long-term contexts (e.g., see Anderson & Bushman, 2002; Anderson & Carnagey, 2004; Carnagey et al., 2007). Anderson and Bushman's 2001 meta-analytical review of GAM-related research studies argued that playing violent video games increases aggressive behavior, aggressive cognitions, hostile aggressive affect, and physiological arousal, which lead to short-term increases in aggressive behavior. Similarly, they were able to demonstrate that video game violence influenced long-term aggressive behavior by promoting aggressive beliefs and attitudes and creating aggressive schemas, behavioral scripts, and expectations, as well as desensitizing individuals to aggression. This results in biasing the individual's personality toward aggression in the long term, which resulted in more frequent episodes of aggressive activity. Anderson (2004) updated this meta-analysis, concluding that:

...exposure to violent video games is significantly linked to increases in aggressive behavior, aggressive cognition, aggressive affect, and cardiovascular arousal, and studies reveal a linkage to serious, real-world types of aggression. Methodologically weaker studies yielded smaller effect sizes than methodologically stronger studies, suggesting that previous meta-analytic studies of violent video games underestimate the true magnitude of observed deleterious effects on behavior, cognition, and affect. (p. 113)

Gentile, Lynch, Linder, and Walsh (2004) conducted a study using GAM in an attempt to prove that a strong link existed between video game violence and violent behavior. The study, covering 607 8th- and 9th-grade students, concluded that adolescents who exposed themselves to greater amounts of video game violence were more hostile, reported getting into arguments with teachers more frequently, were more likely to be involved in physical fights, and performed less well in school. As well, the researchers were able to confirm that exposure to video game violence was positively correlated with trait hostility (aggressive or hostile outlook, perceptual biases, attitudes, beliefs, and behavior), thought to be the mediating factor between VVG exposure and violent behavior. Similarly, they found that students who played more violent video games were more likely to have been involved in physical fights and get into arguments with teachers more frequently, in both the short and long term. On the whole, their study was able to validate much of the work done on previous research studies using the GAM model, and showed that violence in video games was strongly correlated to increases in short-term and long-term behavior because of the influence of the violent video game on the individual's arousal, cognitions, affect, and trait hostility.

EVIDENCE AGAINST: THE VIDEO GAME CONTROVERSY

As with issues of media violence, the violent video game question has generated strong arguments on the negative as well as the positive side. The catharsis theory has provided one of the primary counter-arguments against the link between video games and violent behavior. This predicts that violent video gameplay leads to decreases in aggression because violent video games can provide a safe outlet for aggressive thoughts and feelings; highly stressed or frustrated individuals may play violent video games to re-establish emotional equilibrium through arousal or relaxation, and thus realize a reduction in the levels of physical arousal and aggressive behavior following gameplay through a "venting off" of aggressive energy or aggressive desires (Dill & Dill, 1998).

Graybill, Kirsch, and Esselman (1985) and Graybill, Strawniak, Hunter, and O'Leary (1987), in comprehensive mixed-methodology studies, concluded that video games may have a short-term beneficial effects for children, rather than exacerbating their aggressive tendencies. The authors studied aggression using a projective test, and concluded that their results were consistent with catharsis theory, and that violent video games discharge aggressive impulses in a socially acceptable way. More recently, Unsworth, Devilly, and Ward (2007) found evidence suggesting that individuals with more introverted personality measures might play video games to channel and control their aggression.

Other individual studies have produced negative or insignificant results that conflict with the conclusions reported in Section 1 above. For example, an early self-report study (Gibb, Bailey, Lambirth, & Wilson, 1983) found no relationship between the amount of video game play, hostility, and self esteem. Gardner (1991) concluded that the use of video games in his psychotherapy sessions provided common ground between himself and his client, and provided excellent behavioral observational opportunities, although this has been criticised as anecdotal evidence. Scott (1995) found that university students exhibited no changes in aggressive affect while playing video games across varying levels of video game violence, as measured by hostility and personality assessment scores. Funk et al. (2003) found that a brief period of playing either a violent or non-violent game did not affect children's tendencies to respond in an empathic or aggressive manner to vignettes, which was contrary to their predictions. The authors noted that the violent games used in the test did include a pro-social element of rescuing, which might have complicated the interpretation of the child's responses. Kutner and Olson (2008) surveyed 1,300 children and concluded that most boys play video games to test boundaries and to experiment safely with risky behavior rather than to practice violence; many use games to develop social skills, release stress and relax.

COMPLICATING ISSUE: THE QUESTION OF METHODOLOGY

A primary criticism of VVG research is that it is impossible, for ethical and practical reasons, to conduct experiments that directly measure causality. As Freedman (2001) notes:

To determine whether exposure to violent video games causes aggression, the ideal experiment would randomly assign children to play or not playing video games containing violence. Some would play violent video games for a great many hours, some would play such games for less time or would play games with less violence, others would play no video games, and so on. They would continue to do this for many years, and during and after that time one would obtain measures of their aggressive behavior. If those who played violent video games engaged in more aggressive or violent behavior, it would indicate that the video games caused aggression; and if this difference did not emerge, it would provide evidence that playing violent video games did not cause aggression. (p. 2)

Instead, experiments are shorter-term, use inconsistent designs and indirect measures for violent behavior, and may ignore mediating factors that could change the interpretation of the data.

Hypothesized relationships between VVGs and aggressive and violent cognition, affect, and behavior, including specific aspects of GAM, have been tested using three approaches: experimental, correlational, and longitudinal. Each of these has strengths and weaknesses that should be recognized in evaluating the evidence that they provide (Gentile & Anderson, 2006):

- Experimental studies, either in laboratories or in the field, use random assignment of subjects to different groups (e.g., playing non-violent or violent games) and, if well done, control for confounding factors such as sex, personality traits, and prior attitudes and beliefs. These can provide strong evidence for causal connections. However, they cannot, for ethical reasons, use real-world measures of aggressive or violent behavior (such as hitting), so proxy measures must be used and shown to predict real-world outcomes.
- Correlational studies, often using observation or self-reporting, and collecting data collection through survey instruments, can document real-world behavior but are limited to showing association among factors and cannot show true causal relationships.

Longitudinal studies document changes over a longer period, providing evidence of changes over time. However they are more difficult and costly to carry out than are other study types.

Literature reviews and meta-analyses have attempted to explain the contradictions in research evidence. A literature review by Griffiths (1999) concluded that at that time, published studies all had methodological problems and only included possible short-term measures of aggressive consequences. Anderson (2004) argued that weak results have often been caused by weak methodology, but stronger results have been produced by studies using identified "best practices." Unsworth et al. (2007) argued that differing conclusions need not be mutually exclusive because studies to date have generally not taken into account temperament and player feelings immediately prior to gameplay, which mediate post-play anger ratings. Sternheimer (2007) states that we cannot draw sound conclusions from current research, but instead need a broader perspective that considers the influence of the broader social context, including "the roles that guns, poverty, families and the organization of schools may play in youth violence in general" (pp. 14-15). Kutner and Olson (2008) argue that violent video games affect different children differently, so that some are more at risk for violent behavior than others; also, "... violent video game play is extremely common, and violent crime is extremely rare. This makes it tough to document whether and how violent video and computer games contribute to serious violence... Criminals are also much more likely to have past exposure to other factors, such as poverty, alcoholism, family violence or parental neglect, that are know contributors to violent behavior" (p. 66).

Huesmann (2007) argues that because aggressive behavior in a child is the best predictor of violent behavior when the child becomes an adult, studies that statistically link VVGs with aggressive behavior in children indicate risk factors for adult behavior. Methodology-based criticisms of current research have also arisen from industry groups and broader public organizations (e.g., see ESA, 2006). In a final example, Ferguson (2007) presents statistical evidence of publication bias in the violent video game literature that magnifies the apparent strength of conclusions so far available to the public. He argues for improvements in research approaches including (a) standardization, empirical validation, and consistent use of measurement tools; (b) research on individuals who actually commit violent crimes; (c) reporting of inter-reliabilities when multiple aggression measures are used; and (d) improved inclusion of third variables, such as violence in the family, gender, and trait aggression.

CONCLUSION: DISCRETION IS ADVISED

We see, therefore, that there are strong arguments from both sides about the hypothesis that violence in video games increases aggressive and violent behavior. Video games appear to provide a very effective learning environment for violence, and to lead to a number of indicators of aggressive and possibly violent behavior. However, because testing the links is so difficult, research results so far show conflicting evidence and generate much criticism. What, then, can we say to parents concerned about the possible impact of VVGs on their still-developing children and youth?

Gentile and Anderson (2006) argue that parents: (a) need to educate themselves about video game ratings, (b) learn why it is important to pay attention to the ratings and descriptors (which show content), and (c) act on their knowledge to stay involved and informed about their children's video game play. Parental involvement in video game habits appears to act as a protective factor in several ways. For example, Gentile et al. (2004) found that parental limits to violent video game play were negatively correlated with arguments with teachers and physical fights, and positively correlated with school performance. However, sceptics argue that these and similar results may simply be due to the broader pattern of more involved parenting styles and increased attention, rather than simply the parent's media monitoring behavior.

Perhaps due to ignorance on the subject, parents do not seem to spend the time monitoring and playing an active role in the selection of video game content for their children. A (US) nationally representative parent-focused study (Gentile & Walsh, 2002) found that 55% of parents say they "always" or "often" put limits on the amount of time their children may play computer and video games, and 40% say they "always" or "often" check the video game rating before allowing their children to buy or rent computer or video games, but other studies (e.g. Walsh & Gentile, 2001) have concluded that parents are not as actively involved as they should be when it comes to violent video games and their children. Anderson and Bushman (2001) suggest that parents take steps such as removing the TV, the video game console, and the computer from the child's room to an area that is more easily monitored by the parent, and scheduling limited time when the child or adolescent can use the video games. Parents could also monitor and control the computer games loaded onto the child's computer and restrict the websites that the computer can access while in use by the child. When parents place restrictions on media, parents should actively try to teach their children the reasons behind the restrictions they place on certain types of media, such as why the media might be bad for them. This teaching will enable them to become much more media savvy individually. Kutner and Olson (2008) state that it is important for parents to interact with their children, learn about the games they play, and be alert for many behavioral issues in addition to violent gameplay that could indicate problems.

When parents are monitoring the violent video game content of their children, Anderson (2004) notes that there are a number of key questions parents should ask, as well as things they should look for in terms of content. Parents need to be on the alert for any game that encourages or allows the player to harm another creature, human or nonhuman. Such games are very likely teaching the game player subtle but harmful aggression lessons, regardless of how cute the game characters are, or how unrealistic the violence appears. More specifically, parents should work through six questions for every game they evaluate. These are:

1. Does the game involve some characters trying to harm others?
2. Does this happen frequently, more than once or twice in 30 minutes?
3. Is the harm rewarded in any way?
4. Is the harm portrayed as humorous?
5. Are non-violent solutions absent, or less fun than the violent ones?
6. Are realistic consequences of violence absent from the game?

If the answers for two or more of these questions are "yes," parents should think very carefully about the lessons being learned from the game, as well as the impact the game is having on their children.

REFERENCES

Abelson, R. P. (1981). Psychological status of the script concept. *The American Psychologist*, *36*(7), 715–729. doi:10.1037/0003-066X.36.7.715

Anderson, C. A. (2004). An update on the effects of playing violent video games. *Journal of Adolescence*, *27*(1), 113–122. doi:10.1016/j.adolescence.2003.10.009

Anderson, C. A., & Bushman, B. J. (2001). Effects of violent video games on aggressive behavior, aggressive cognition, aggressive affect, physiological arousal, and prosocial behavior: A meta-analytic review of the scientific literature. *Psychological Science*, *12*(5), 353–359. doi:10.1111/1467-9280.00366

Anderson, C. A., & Bushman, B. J. (2002). Human aggression. *Annual Review of Psychology*, *53*(1), 27–51. doi:10.1146/annurev.psych.53.100901.135231

Anderson, C. A., & Carnagey, N. L. (2004). Violent evil and the general aggression model. In A. Miller (Ed.), The social psychology of good and evil (pp. 168-192). New York: Guilford Publications.

Anderson, C. A., & Dill, K. E. (2000). Video games and aggressive thoughts, feelings, and behavior in the laboratory and in life. *Journal of Personality and Social Psychology*, *78*(4), 772–790. doi:10.1037/0022-3514.78.4.772

Anderson, C. A., & Ford, C. M. (1986). Affect of the video game player: Short-term effects of highly and mildly aggressive video games. *Personality and Social Psychology Bulletin*, *12*(4), 390–402. doi:10.1177/0146167286124002

Bandura, A. (1977). Social learning theory. New York: Prentice Hall.

Bandura, A. (2001). Social Cognitive Theory: An agentic perspective. *Annual Review of Psychology*, *52*(1), 1–26. doi:10.1146/annurev.psych.52.1.1

Berkowitz, L. (1990). On the formation and regulation of anger and aggression: A cognitive neoassociationistic analysis. *The American Psychologist*, *45*(4), 494–503. doi:10.1037/0003-066X.45.4.494

Browne, K. D., & Hamilton-Giachritsis, C. (2005). The influence of violent media on children and adolescents: A public-health approach. *Lancet*, *365*(9460), 702–710.

Carnagey, N. L., Anderson, C. A., & Bushman, B. J. (2007). The effect of video game violence on physiological desensitization to real-life violence. *Journal of Experimental Social Psychology*, *43*(3), 489–496. doi:10.1016/j.jesp.2006.05.003

Dill, K. E., & Dill, J. C. (1998). Video game violence: A review of the empirical literature. *Aggression and Violent Behavior*, *3*(4), 407–428. doi:10.1016/S1359-1789(97)00001-3

Entertainment Software Association (ESA). (2006). Essential facts about games and youth violence. Washington, DC: Entertainment Software Association. Retrieved March 4, 2008 from http://www.theesa.com/archives/2006EF%20Youth%20Violence.pdf

Eron, L. D. (2001). Seeing is believing: How viewing violence alters attitudes and aggressive behavior. In A. C. Bohart & D. J. Stipek (Eds.), Constructive and destructive behavior: Implications for family, school, and society (pp. 49-60). Washington, DC: American Psychological Association.

Ferguson, C. J. (2007). Evidence for publication bias in video game violence affects literature: A meta-analytic review. *Aggression and Violent Behavior*, *12*(4), 470–482. doi:10.1016/j.avb.2007.01.001

Freedman, J. L. (2001, October). Evaluating the research on violent video games. Paper presented at the Playing by the Rules conference, University of Chicago Cultural Policy Center. Retrieved March 4, 2008 from http://culturalpolicy.uchicago.edu/conf2001/papers/freedman.html

Funk, J. B., Baldacci, H. B., Pasold, T., & Baumgardner, J. (2004). Violence exposure in real life, video games, television, movies, and the Internet: Is there desensitization? *Journal of Adolescence*, *27*(1), 23–39. doi:10.1016/j.adolescence.2003.10.005

Funk, J. B., Buchman, D. D., Jenks, J., & Bechtoldt, H. (2003). Playing violent video games, desensitization, and moral evaluation in children. *Journal of Applied Developmental Psychology, 24*(4), 413–436. doi:10.1016/S0193-3973(03)00073-X

Gardner, J. E. (1991). Can the Mario Bros. help? Nintendo games as an adjunct in psychotherapy with children. Psychotherapy: Theory, Research, Practice . *Training (New York, N.Y.), 28*(4), 667–670.

Gentile, D. A., & Anderson, C. A. (2006). Violent video games: The effects on youth, and public policy implications. In N. Dowd, D. G. Singer, & R. F. Wilson (Eds.), Handbook of children, culture, and violence (pp. 225-246). Thousand Oaks, CA: Sage Publications.

Gentile, D. A., & Gentile, J. R. (2008). Violent video games as exemplary teachers: A conceptual analysis. *Journal of Youth and Adolescence, 37*(2), 127–141. doi:10.1007/s10964-007-9206-2

Gentile, D. A., Lynch, P. J., Linder, J. R., & Walsh, D. A. (2004). The effects of violent video game habits on adolescent hostility, aggressive behaviors, and school performance. *Journal of Adolescence, 27*(1), 5–22. doi:10.1016/j.adolescence.2003.10.002

Gentile, D. A., & Walsh, D. A. (2002). A normative study of family media habits. *Journal of Applied Developmental Psychology, 23*(2), 157–178. doi:10.1016/S0193-3973(02)00102-8

Gibb, G. D., Bailey, J. R., Lambirth, T. T., & Wilson, W. P. (1983). Personality differences in high and low electronic video game users. *The Journal of Psychology, 114*(2), 159–165.

Graybill, D., Kirsch, J. R., & Esselman, E. D. (1985). Effects of playing violent versus nonviolent video games on the aggressive ideation of aggressive and nonaggressive children. *Child Study Journal, 15*(3), 199–205.

Graybill, D., Strawniak, M., Hunter, T., & O'Leary, M. (1987). Effects of playing versus observing violent versus nonviolent video games on children's aggression. Psychology: A Journal of Human Behavior, 24(3), 1-8.

Griffiths, M. (1999). Violent video games and aggression: A review of the literature. *Aggression and Violent Behavior, 4*(2), 203–212. doi:10.1016/S1359-1789(97)00055-4

Group, N. P. D. Inc. (2007). Press release: Amount of time kids spend playing video games is on the rise. Retrieved February 19, 2008 from http://www.npd.com/press/releases/press_071016a.html

Haninger, K., & Thompson, K. M. (2004). Content and ratings of teen-rated video games. *Journal of the American Medical Association, 291*(7), 856–865. doi:10.1001/jama.291.7.856

Huesmann, L. R. (2007). The impact of electronic media violence: Scientific theory and research. *The Journal of Adolescent Health, 41*(6Supplement 1), S6–S13. doi:10.1016/j.jadohealth.2007.09.005

Irwin, A. R., & Gross, A. M. (1995). Cognitive tempo, violent video games, and aggressive behavior in young boys. *Journal of Family Violence, 10*(3), 337–350. doi:10.1007/BF02110997

Kirsh, S. J. (2003). The effects of violent video games on adolescents: The overlooked influence of development. *Aggression and Violent Behavior, 8*(4), 377–389. doi:10.1016/S1359-1789(02)00056-3

Kutner, L., & Olson, C. (2008). Grand Theft Childhood: The surprising truth about violent video games and what parents can do. New York: Simon & Schuster.

Mathews, V., Wang, Y., Kalnin, A. J., Mosier, K. M., Dunn, D. W., & Kronenberger, W. G. (2006, November). Short-term effects of violent video game playing: An fMRI study. Paper presented at the Annual Meeting of the Radiological Society of North America, Chicago, IL.

Mediamark Research and Intelligence (MRI). (2007, December 19). Gaming nearly ubiquitous among kids online, one-third have email address. Press release on the 2007 American Kids Survey. Retrieved March 4, 2008 from http://www.marketingcharts.com/direct/gaming-nearly-ubiquitous-among-kids-online-one-third-have-email-address-2839/

Reuters (2007). Video-game sales overtaking music. Retrieved February 14, 2008 from http://articles.moneycentral.msn.com/Investing/Extra/VideoGameSalesOvertakingMusic.aspx

Rushbrook, S. (1986). "Messages" of video games: Social implications. Unpublished Ph.D. dissertation, University of California, Los Angeles.

Schutte, N. S., Malouff, J. M., Post-Gorden, J. C., & Rodasta, A. L. (1988). Effects of playing videogames on children's aggressive and other behaviors. *Journal of Applied Social Psychology*, *18*(5), 454–460. doi:10.1111/j.1559-1816.1988.tb00028.x

Scott, D. (1995). The effect of video games on feelings of aggression. *Journal of Psychology: Interdisciplinary & Applied*, *129*(2), 121–132.

Sheese, B. E., & Graziano, W. G. (2005). Deciding to defect: The effects of video game violence on co-operative behavior. *Psychological Science*, *16*(5), 354–357. doi:10.1111/j.0956-7976.2005.01539.x

Silvern, S. B., & Williamson, P. A. (1987). The effects of video game play on young children's aggression, fantasy, and prosocial behavior. *Journal of Applied Developmental Psychology*, *8*(4), 453–462. doi:10.1016/0193-3973(87)90033-5

Spear, L. P. (2000). The adolescent brain and age-related behavioral manifestations. *Neuroscience and Biobehavioral Reviews*, *24*(4), 417–463. doi:10.1016/S0149-7634(00)00014-2

Sternheimer, K. (2007). Do video games kill? *Contexts*, *6*(1), 13–17. doi:10.1525/ctx.2007.6.1.13

Todorov, A., & Bargh, J. A. (2001). Automatic sources of aggression. *Aggression and Violent Behavior*, *7*(1), 53–68. doi:10.1016/S1359-1789(00)00036-7

Uhlmann, E., & Swanson, J. (2004). Exposure to violent video games increases automatic aggressiveness. *Journal of Adolescence*, *27*(1), 41–52. doi:10.1016/j.adolescence.2003.10.004

Unsworth, G., Devilly, G. J., & Ward, T. (2007). The effect of playing violent video games on adolescents: Should parents be quaking in their boots? *Psychology, Crime & Law*, *13*(4), 383–394. doi:10.1080/10683160601060655

Walsh, D. A., & Gentile, D. A. (2001). A validity test of movie, television, and videogame ratings. *Pediatrics*, *107*(6), 1302–1308. doi:10.1542/peds.107.6.1302

Zillmann, D. (1988). Cognition- excitation dependencies in aggressive behavior. *Aggressive Behavior*, *14*(1), 51–64. doi:10.1002/1098-2337(1988)14:1<51::AID-AB2480140107>3.0.CO;2-C

ADDITIONAL READING

Anderson, C. A., Gentile, D. A., & Buckley, K. E. (2006). Violent video game effects on children and adolescents: Theory, research, and public policy. Oxford, UK: Oxford University Press.

Kierkegaard, P. (2008). Video games and aggression. *International Journal of Liability and Scientific Enquiry*, *1*(4), 411–417. doi:10.1504/IJLSE.2008.018288

Kutner, L., & Olson, C. (2008). Grand Theft Childhood: The surprising truth about violent video games and what parents can do. New York: Simon & Schuster.

KEY TERMS AND DEFINITIONS

Aggression: Verbal or physical behavior that is intended to cause physical or psychological harm to another and that the target individual wishes to avoid.

Catharsis: Relief from tension and anxiety through the discharge of pent-up emotions and repressed feelings

Desensitization: To end a reaction of fear, anxiety, etc. in response to a specific stimulus

Violence: Physical or psychological force intended to violate, damage, or abuse.

Chapter 21
A Study of Biofeedback in a Gaming Environment

Xin Du
Simon Fraser University, Canada

Stephen R. Campbell
Simon Fraser University, Canada

David Kaufman
Simon Fraser University, Canada

ABSTRACT

This chapter reports on a study of biofeedback in a gaming environment incorporating the acquisition and analysis of physiological data sets in tandem with other behavioral and self-report data sets. Preliminary results presented here provide some groundwork toward subsequent study in this area, as more comprehensive and detailed treatments will require further research. The main contribution and focus of this chapter concerns our experiences in applying methods not typically available to educational researchers. Our results are promising, though they cannot be taken to be definitive. Further developments and applications of these methods will lead to more detailed investigations as to what people may learn or gain from biofeedback in gaming environments, along with interdependencies of biofeedback and gaming pertaining to affect, motivation, behavior and cognition, and perhaps especially, to learning anxiety.

INTRODUCTION

This chapter reports on a collaboration between the *SAGE for Learning* project and *ENGRAM/ME*. *ENGRAM/ME* (Educational Neuroscience Group for Research into Affect and Mentation / in Mathematics Education, www.engrammetron.net) is a diverse collection of researchers with a special but not restricted emphasis in mathematics education, concerned with augmenting educational research with methods and results from psychophysiology and cognitive neuroscience (Campbell, with the ENL Group, 2007). The central hub for *ENGRAM/ME* activities is the *ENGRAMMETRON*, the second author's state-of-the-art educational neuroscience laboratory in the Faculty of Education at Simon Fraser University, where the research reported herein was conducted.

DOI: 10.4018/978-1-61520-731-2.ch021

This study observed, recorded, and analyzed participants' experiences playing a biofeedback-based video game called *Journey to Wild Divine*®. The virtual nature of this game invites players into an interactive realm of seemingly endless possibilities. This interactive gaming environment, consisting of graphics and music, entices and affects changes in players' energy levels by encouraging alterations in their breathing rates and levels of relaxation, thereby determining their progression through the game. We hope that this preliminary study will inform future research that can unveil novel educational implications leading to interesting new ways to improve teaching and learning.

BACKGROUND

Biofeedback has been studied for more than 40 years, and has well-established utility. Many of its clinical applications have been identified for quite some time. Biofeedback training has been broadly used as a treatment for addiction, attention-deficit hyperactivity disorder (ADHD), autism, and epilepsy. At present, there are more than 1,500 professionals practicing biofeedback training in hundreds of mental fitness centers in North America. According to the Biofeedback Certification Institute of America (BCIA) (www.bcia.org), there are currently more than 1,000 practitioners with BCIA certification in the U.S. and about 33 in Canada.

Why Learn Biofeedback?

Biofeedback is based on direct, immediate feedback to the person about the state of some aspect of his/her body, such as heart rate, respiration rate, or temperature. According to Whitehouse and Turner (2007), biofeedback typically involves the use of electronic equipment to monitor peoples' internal physiological states and provide them with feedback that consequently helps them learn to influence those states, "to activate, balance, release or recover from them" (para. 2). Biofeedback presenting some aspect of an individual's brain behavior to that individual in real time, using methods such as electroencephalography (EEG), is commonly referred to as neurofeedback. (Note that although we recorded participants' EEG, neurofeedback was not a part of this study because they were not presented with these data).

Biofeedback training has been proven to have a powerful, positive effect on one's emotional and physical condition through many medical interventions and educational training programs (e.g., see Larsen, 2006). A noted example is the "New York Program," which demonstrated that a biofeedback program can have a significant positive effect on school and community. This effect has been referred to as "The Ripple Effect" (Biofeedback Consultants, 2008; see also, Imel, Baldwin, Bonus, & MacCoon, 2008).

Research has also shown that biofeedback training can be an appropriate and efficacious treatment for children with ADHD (Fuchs, Birbaumer, Lutzenberger, Gruzelier & Kaiser, 2003; Lubar, Swartwood, Swartwood, & O'Donnell, 1995; Warnes & Allen, 2005). Some researchers have further confirmed that biofeedback is an effective way to control anxiety and panic (Plotkin & Rice, 1981; Rice, Blanchard, & Purcell, 1993; Townsend, House, & Addario, 1975) because biofeedback can often be helpful "in stabilizing a nervous system so that it no longer makes excursions into panic" (EEG Spectrum International Inc., 2007, para. 3). Research also suggests that skills people have developed through biofeedback training can be transferred to daily life after they have developed habitual behaviors, and that they feel comfortable with their new response patterns.

So, why learn biofeedback? Research and accepted practice in this area have shown that biofeedback can provide advantages for people in improving self-control and performance in daily life. Measuring effectiveness is a non-trivial matter, however (Tinius, 2006). General questions of interest to us concern the ways and extent to which biofeedback can be learned through a gaming environment.

Why Study Biofeedback in a Gaming Environment?

Although biofeedback as typically practiced has been successful for a variety of populations in a variety of areas, the practice has not proven to be universally effective. Othmer and Othmer (1994) noticed that there was a lower success rate among adults than children in their EEG bio(neuro)feedback training program. They suggested that one reason was because the adults were much more difficult to retain in the program than children. Several other explanations may help to account for this finding. First, a large number of people consider that biofeedback training is used for people with special needs, not for the general populace. Secondly, trainees typically found that the training sessions were iterative and dull, with little interactivity, and many found the training too boring to be completed. Finally, the biofeedback training program was expensive for many individuals. The literature indicates that the necessary training period to obtain good results was 10 sessions, 45 minutes per session (Vernon, 2005); usually, in a clinical or consulting company, 20 to 40 sessions with 30 minutes for each session are found to be the most effective for training. The price ranged from $100 to $150 per session in different areas. The cost to finish the entire program was at least $3000 to $6000. Overall, though, an alternative explanation might be that children simply have fewer distractions to deal with than do adults.

There are many areas associated with access, interest, and cost that undermine the potential utility of biofeedback as currently practiced. It seems clear that learning biofeedback through a video game would be potentially more accessible and engaging and less expensive. This could be a preferred option for many, especially if it were to prove equal to, or more effective than, current clinical approaches.

It has been well established that more and more people around the world are playing video games. According to PIALP (2008), 92% of people aged 18-29 and 85% of people aged 30-49 use the Internet. The survey also indicates that 75% of American adults use the Internet and 35% of the Internet users reported that they play online games. 72% of American adults who use the Internet use it daily, and 9% of them reported that they play online games daily. Other studies have shown that virtually all college students play video, computer, or Internet games, as do 73% of teens (Rainey, 2006). According to the International Telecommunication Union (Internet World Stats, 2008), 84.3% of Canadians use the Internet; Statistics Canada (2005) reported that 27.9% of households used the Internet for playing games.

Although games are usually considered as a recreational activity, a number of research studies have shown that games have great potential advantages for educational purposes. For example, neuroscientists Green and Bavelier (2003) suggested that playing action video and computer games has positive effects on student's visual selective attention. Prensky (2001) stated that "video games are not the enemy, but the best opportunity we have to engage our kids in real learning" (p.1), and Beck and Wade (2006) asserted that "videogames have replaced television as kid's babysitter. But they are much more insidious. They (videogames) get into our brains. TV is about watching; games are about doing. And doing is where we learn" (p. xi).

Furthermore, younger people, who are considered "digital natives" today, have a generational advantage compared to their "digital immigrant" elders (Prensky, 2003). They are video gamers, and that gives them different expectations about how to learn, work, and pursue careers (Rainey,

2006). Beck and Wade (2004) argued that their research shows that this new generation is indeed very different from older people in many ways:

> *... [The new generation] have a systematically different way of working. They choose systematically different skills to learn, and different ways to learn them. They desire systematically different goals in life ... How hard this huge new cohort works, how they try to compete, how they fit into teams, how they take risks – all are different in statistically verifiable ways. And those differences are driven by one central factor: growing up with video games. (p. 2)*

Beck and Wade (2004) also argued that games are the "training programs" for young workers that help to form their attitudes about the way the work-world operates – a world full of data streams, where analysis and decisions come at speed, where failure at first is the norm, where the game player is the hero, and where learning takes place informally (Rainey, 2006, summarizing Beck & Wade, 2004).

In summary, research on games conducted within the past 20 years or so has shown that gaming is an engaging and effective approach to assisting teaching and learning, especially for the new generation. Digital natives are more used to playing video games and being engaged by the computer than are digital immigrants. Therefore, they might be more open to learning in gaming environments. We have also glimpsed some of the utility of biofeedback and identified some current limitations. It appears as though these limitations dovetail well with the strengths of gaming. What would it be like, then, to bring these two areas together and study biofeedback in gaming environments?

RESEARCH METHODS AND TECHNIQUES

Research Questions

The general purpose of this preliminary study was to investigate the ways and extent to which people can learn biofeedback in a gaming environment. The biofeedback game we use is called *Journey to Wild Divine* (www.wilddivine.com), henceforth referred to as the *Wild Divine*. We chose this game because throughout the time of this study, it has been the most popular game of its kind; and it has the qualities of being accessible, engaging, and affordable, if not just plain fun.

The aim of this study is to better understand what is experienced and learned by players of *Wild Divine* by closely observing the effect of the game on its players as they interact with it. Exploring these issues may enable educators and biofeedback practitioners to provide more effective and enjoyable experiences and support to learners. The research questions guiding this study of biofeedback in a gaming environment variously concerned: 1) effects; 2) performance; 3) learning; and 4) process. Due to space limitations, we focus mainly in this chapter on the first two questions, but we list all four questions guiding this study here:

1. What are the effects of *Wild Divine* on players, including: (a) How enjoyable and engaging do they find this game? and (b) What are the effects of this game on players' physiological states and psychological states?
2. How well do players perform when encountering this game for the first time?
3. What is being learned by playing *Wild Divine*?
4. How might subsequent experimental designs be improved?

However, using players' physiological and psychological data to study biofeedback in a gaming environment involved many factors, and this is brand-new research in this area using new research methods and techniques. This chapter's main purpose is to investigate the strengths and limitations of these new methods and techniques to provide groundwork for further research, which may eventually enable such questions to be addressed in more detail.

The instrumentation we used in this study enabled us to acquire what we will refer to as *behavioral* and *reflective* data sets. Behavioral data consist of audiovisual, eye-tracking, and psychophysiological data sets, whereas reflective data sets consist of data from questionnaires and self-reports.

Behavioral Data Sets

Traditionally, behavioral instrumentation in educational research has been restricted to audiovisual observations of overt behavior. Conducting this study in the *ENGRAMMETRON*, however, enabled psychophysiological observations capturing some aspects of more covert embodied behaviors simultaneously with audiovisual data sets (Campbell with the ENL Group, 2007).

Audiovisual and Keystroke Capture Data

Participants' vocal and facial expressions and body movements were recorded through three cameras and a highly sensitive microphone. In addition, all keystrokes made by both experimenter and participants were captured and recorded as they occurred.

Eye-Tracking and Screen Capture Data

An eye-tracking system was used to present stimuli to our participants. This system consisted of a 17" monitor equipped with low-level infrared emitters and detectors used for tracking eye movements. The screen stimuli were captured and recorded simultaneously, and the eye-tracking data was overlaid upon the screen capture recording and rendered as a video file for subsequent analysis.

Psychophysiological Data

Electrical transducers and conductors (electrodes) were used to collect psychophysiological data sets from participants during the course of this study. Data collected included:Saliva samples may also be collected for measuring cortisol, a hormone involved in response to electroencephalograms (EEG), which measure bioelectrical activity manifested on the scalp that is generated through neuronal activity within the brain; electrocardiograms (EKG or ECG), which detects and records bioelectrical activity generated by the beating of the heart; electromyograms (EMG), which record bioelectrical activity generated by muscle movements; and electrooculograms (EOG), which record bioelectrical activity generated via eye-movements (Shipulina, Campbell, & Cimen, 2009). All of these psychophysiological data sets were recorded from on-going changes in voltage potentials from various locations on the surface of the skin. Respiration, blood pressure, and heart rate (calculated from the EKG data) were also measured.

Reflective Data Sets

Beyond recording behavior, data in educational research also comes from traditional questionnaires and other forms of self-reports, referred to here as reflective data sets. We do not mean for behavioral and reflective data sets to be considered independently. We have evidence to suggest that reflective and behavioral data sets are not always consistent (e.g., Sha, Winne, & Campbell, 2009). What the subject does, thinks, or feels, is not always what he or she may articulate.

Pre-Screening Questionnaire and Demographic Questionnaire

Paper pre-screening and demographic questionnaires were used to ensure that participants were able to safely take part in minimal risk education research, which involves the use of minimal risk eye-tracking and electrophysiological instrumentation described above. As part of the pre-screening process, we also inquired in confidence about the participants' medical history, such as stigmatisms, epilepsy, and recent concussions, before clearing them for the experiment.

State-Trait Anxiety Inventory (STAI)

The State-Trait Anxiety Inventory form (STAI Y-1; Y-2) was used to measure anxiety levels associated with the research process. The form was first developed by Spielberger in the 1960s and revised in 1983. It provides a reliable measure of both temporary and dispositional anxiety in adults through self-report, which includes separate measures of state and trait anxiety (Maria & Lynne, 2006).

The S-Anxiety scale (STAI Y-1) consists of 20 statements that evaluate how respondents feel "right now, at this moment." Responses are recorded using a four-point Likert-type scale that ranges from *Not At All, Somewhat,* and *Moderately so,* to *Very Much So*.

In contrast, the T-Anxiety scale (STAI Y-2) consists of 20 statements that assess how respondents feel generally. Responses are recorded using a four-point Likert-type scale that ranges from *Almost Never, Sometimes,* and *Often*, to *Almost Always*.

Post-Test Questionnaire

A post-test questionnaire was designed to collect background information about participants' experience with biofeedback and video games. There were ten self-report questions, four of which described participant history with biofeedback, meditation, and playing video games. Three sets of Likert scale questions pertained to previous gaming experience, how it compared with their experience with *Wild Divine*, and their ability to apply biofeedback to their daily life both before and after the experiment. The last three questions asked participants for their opinions and ideas on the utility of *Wild Divine* for learning biofeedback, and for improving the experiment.

Sample

28 graduate and undergraduate students enrolled in Simon Fraser University programs participated in the study; their mean age was 24.6 years. All participants were novice gamers who had never participated in biofeedback training before. A novice gamer is defined here as having played at least one video game before, but who plays video games less than once a month. All participants were also required to be nineteen years of age or older, to ensure adult consent in British Columbia.

Ethics Approvals

Prior to data acquisition, ethics approvals were obtained from the Simon Fraser University (SFU) Research Ethics Board, in compliance with guidelines outlined in the Canadian Tri-Council Policy Statement (http://www.sfu.ca/~palys/TriCncl.htm) pertaining to informed consent and ethical conduct for research involving humans. This research was deemed "minimal risk," and ethics approval to use data for academic purposes was obtained from participants prior to data acquisition. Participants were assigned and referred to by anonymous numbers to ensure privacy, and permissions to use their anonymous likeness were obtained. All data sets were securely maintained in the *ENGRAMMETRON*.

Figure 1. A participant after being wired up

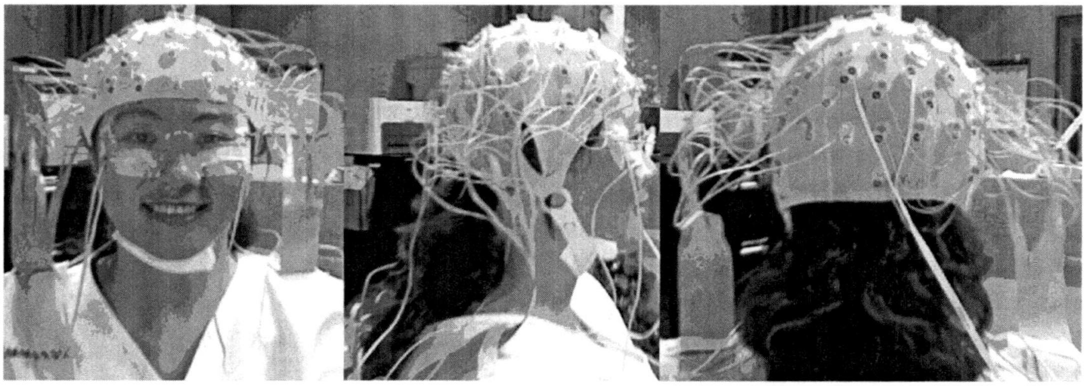

Procedures

Here, we outline our procedures in four basic parts: preparation of our participants, the experiment, recording of observations, and analysis of results.

Preparation

Participants were wired up for EEG, EKG, EMG, EOG, and respiration (Figure 1). After being wired up, participants were led into the observation room, especially constructed to attenuate acoustic and electromagnetic noise, where their eyes were calibrated to a *Tobii 1750®* eye-tracking system, and the various electrodes were connected to a *BioSemi ActiveTwo®* biopotential measurement system. Once a participant was wired up and plugged in, the instrumentation was turned on in the adjacent control room, through which stimuli were presented to the participant, connections were tested and adjusted as required, the experiment was initiated and the data collected and recorded. As this entire process is quite involved, participants were asked to review videos (online at http://engrammetron.net/participate/what-s-involved/) that demonstrated these procedures as part of the informed consent process

The Experiment

Ten pre-selected episodes, or activities, were chosen from *Wild Divine*. These fell into four categories, based on different kinds of breathing. The four categories consisted of "peaceful breath" (three activities); "raise energy" (two activities); "lower energy" (two activities); and "heart breath" (three activities). The first activity for each category usually included a short instruction period, which let players know the aim of the activities and taught them how to successfully accomplish them. Participants were invited to engage in the activities in category order. Not all activities were presented to all participants for various reasons. Usually, the activities assigned to and completed by a given participant were based mainly on factors such as the time limitation and the participant's performance. Some participants did not complete or got stuck with some activities and usually, depending on time, were given a choice to continue with a given activity or move on to the next activity.

Recording of Observations

Once participants were pre-screened and informed consent obtained, their heart rate and blood pressure were measured and recorded. After being wired up, heart rate and blood pressure were measured again. Once participants were plugged in, all necessary adjustments made, and recording of the observation began, they were invited to relax with eyes closed in order to obtain the first of at least three baseline recordings of their resting physiological state. These recordings typically took from three to five minutes. After this, the State-Trait Anxiety Inventory questionnaire was presented to participants. The Trait-Anxiety questionnaire, which evaluates how the participants feel "*in general,*" was presented to the participants first, followed by the State-Anxiety Questionnaire, to evaluate how respondents felt "*right now, at this moment*." Here, we recorded how the participants felt *before* playing the game episodes. This State-Trait anxiety component of the observation was followed by the second baseline reading.

We then invited the participants to start to play the pre-selected game episodes. We recorded the entire process of what they played and how they performed, collecting the behavioral data sets noted above. A third baseline reading was then recorded and we used the State-Anxiety questionnaire again to evaluate how the participants felt *after* playing the game episodes. The observation was concluded with participants filling out the post-experiment questionnaire, entering their responses into SFU's secure Academic Computing Services online survey system. Audiovisual data, along with the physiological data, were monitored and captured in real time using TechSmith's *Camtasia Studio*®. Screen capture video with eye-tracking overlay (the blue dot and trace) were also recorded in the control room. A two-way glass window separated the participant from the experimenters to ensure that participants would not feel uncomfortable being alone in such an enclosed dark space. Once the observation was complete, blood pressure and heart rate were measured one last time.

Observation times typically ranged from 45 minutes to 60 minutes in total. Data were transferred to and stored on Network Accessible Storage (NAS) units, with data volumes typically ranging from 20 GB to 30 GB per observation. Once the observations were complete, the Camtasia files were rendered into .avi movie files, and the eye-tracking data was integrated with the stimuli screen capture data and also were rendered into an .avi movie file for subsequent analysis.

Analysis

Data from SFU's secure Academic Computing Services online survey system were downloaded into an *Excel*® spreadsheet. Combined with these data were data obtained from the demographic questionnaires. The most difficult challenge in using so many instruments for recording behavioral data was to effectively and efficiently integrate them in a time-synchronous manner, as described below. This was accomplished using Noldus's *Observer XT 7.0*®. The .avi (movie) files were stored and accessed by the Observer via the NAS units, and time synchronized for each observation.

Data presented here include both behavioral and reflective data sets. After these data sets were synchronized for each participant, various aspects of each observation were coded. For example, we coded activities into three different groups: baseline, training, and biofeedback activities. There were a total of 10 activities in the biofeedback activities group, two activities in the training activities group, and four activities in the baseline group. The two activities in the training activities group were sessions provided to participants before they engaged in the "raise energy" activities and "lower energy" activities described above. After these data were coded for activity time, they were entered into a spreadsheet, which allowed for inter-participant comparisons (reported on in the Results section below). The STAI data, blood pressure, and heart rate readings were also input into an Excel data file and exported to *SPSS*® for further analysis.

Synchronizing these data sets in time enabled us to navigate through them in an integrated fashion.

Figure 2. An integrated and time-synchronized data set

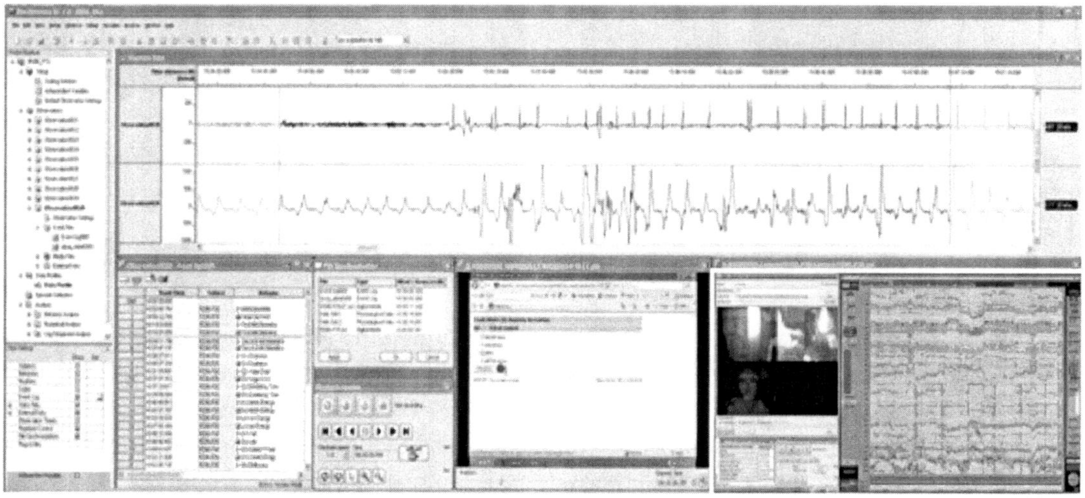

For instance, in moving to a certain point for one data set, the rest of the data sets are automatically reset to that point as well. Our preliminary approach to the behavioral data was to analyze them using the Observer XT. Figure 2 illustrates this, with the control room screen capture Camtasia file and the stimulus eye-tracking screen capture data incorporated in the lower right panes of the window. The lower left panes include data coding, time synchronization, and control panels. The two time series data sets running across the upper part of the window are eye-blinks (top), and breathing (bottom). The first few seconds of these data in Figure 2 indicate that this participant was in a resting baseline mode, breathing gently with eyes closed, just prior to filling out one of our online questionnaires. Once these data sets were integrated and time-synchronized, we determined and coded the time durations of the various activities for each participant, recorded these in an Excel spreadsheet, and then compared them to the average time taken by participants who successfully completed the various activities.

RESULTS AND DISCUSSION

For this study we acquired reflective data from 28 of the 30 participants we had anticipated; two participants were "no shows." Behavioral data for one participant were inadvertently erased, and behavioral data for another were lost due to insufficient disk space. We were also limited in collecting behavioral data from a fifth participant due to other technical problems with data acquisition.

General Points of Interest

According to their reported background, 89% of participants (25/28) had no previous experience with biofeedback, and 78.5% of participants (22/28) had no experience with meditation before the experiment. 93% of participants (26/28), however, did have previous experience with computer/video games. Post-experiment questionnaire results indicated that 93% of our participants (26/28) were of the opinion that biofeedback could be learned from this game. Of the remaining two participants, one found the game episodes stressful, and the other was not interested in this game at all because he strongly preferred the action video

Figure 3. Effect of age on anxiety

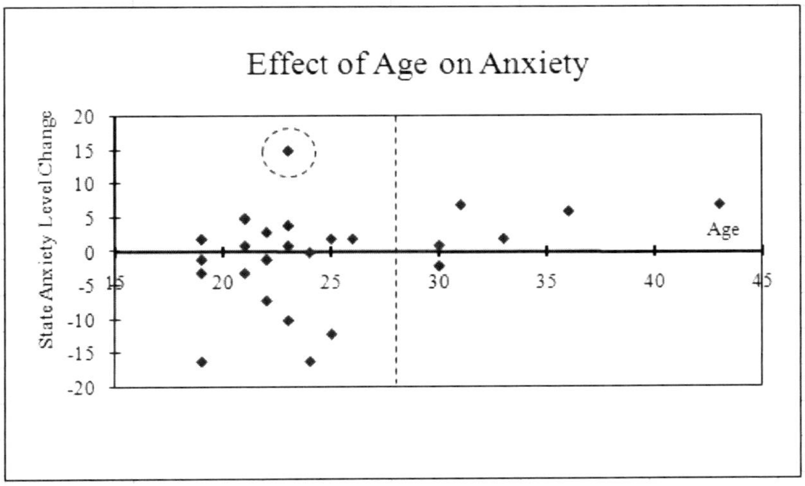

games he was familiar with. Also, our post-test questionnaire showed that participants' opinions on their ability to apply biofeedback to daily life improved on average from 2.14 before the experiment to 3.36 after the experiment. Again, due to space limitations, we only report data and results pertaining to our first two research questions: 1) What are the effects of this game on players, including: a) how enjoyable and engaging is the game? b) What are the effects of the game on players' physiological states and psychological states?; and, 2) How well do players perform when encountering this game for first time?

Results and Discussion Pertaining to Research Question #1

We first report some results that relate to our research question on effects on participants' physiological/ mental states. More specifically, these results describe anxiety effects of age, gender, and language or culture. We also summarize the physiological results from our repeated measurements of participant blood pressure and heart rate.

Result 1

The *Wild Divine* game appears to have had a disproportionate effect on our participants who were younger than 27 years old (Figure 3). The figure shows that nine of 22 participants younger than 27 years of age reported reduced state anxiety levels after having played the game, whereas only one of the six older participants reported a reduced state anxiety level. Of course, the sample size is too small to draw general conclusions. However, this result is perhaps indicative of a more general phenomenon, i.e., that younger participants are more likely to be "digital natives" (Rainey, 2006), and hence may be more relaxed with gaming environments.

Result 2

About half of our participants (16/28, six female, ten male) had changes in pre-game and post-game state anxiety levels. Among them, female participant changes were considerably larger than male participant changes (Figure 4). The mean of the six female participants with changes greater than ± 2 on their state anxiety level is 10.83, which is larger than 6.10, the mean of the 10 male partici-

Figure 4. Effect of gender on anxiety

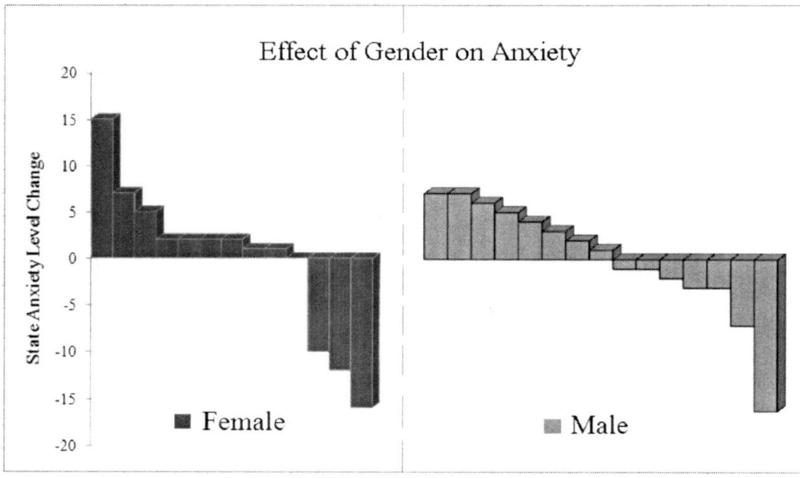

pants with changes greater than ± 2 on their state anxiety level. This result could indicate that this game has greater change in state anxiety level effect on female participants.

This result could indicate, in part, that some female participants have a higher tolerance for discomfort. Some of the male participants complained about the chair and desk in the observation room, and the contrast of the computer screen with the darkness of the room affected their performance. However, not one female participant voiced any complaints of this nature. Also, perhaps males, as opposed to females, are more interested in action games than in biofeedback-based games.

Result 3

The effects of this game on participants also appear somewhat related to their language or cultural background. For example, for five of six participants whose native language was Mandarin, their state anxiety level increased rather than decreased. Participants showing largest decreases in state anxiety appear to have had greater exposures to English.

Potential reasons for such a linguistic/cultural effect may simply be that *Wild Divine* is rendered in English, and thus it is possible that accents of the game interlocutors, or guides, constituted a language barrier. Alternatively, or in addition, these non-English native speaking participants may have experienced difficulties understanding what the task was for some activities.

Result 4

There was no notable change in participants' blood pressure over the three times these data were acquired (viz., after the consent forms; after being wired up; and after the game episodes). These ambivalent results are consistent with previous literature. Bali (1979), for instance, found no statistical relationship between reductions in blood pressure and anxiety. Other researchers have also found that relaxation was not significantly associated with changes in blood pressure (McGrady, Yonker, Tan, Fine, & Woerner, 1981).

Result 5

On the other hand, the cumulative averaged heart rate of our participants progressively decreased, in beats per minute (bpm), from after the consent form (74.8 bpm), to after being wired up (71.4

Figure 5. Total times of successful and unsuccessful task engagement

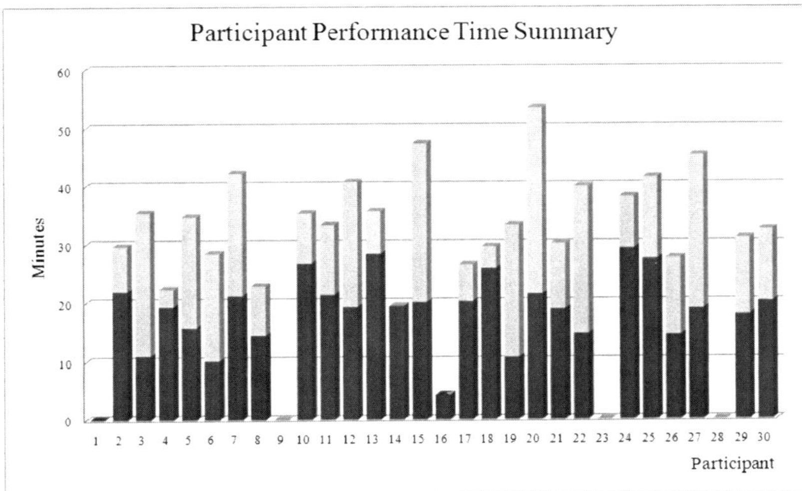

bpm), and then further (69.3 bpm), after all of the activities were completed. The first average cumulative reduction of 3.4 bpm may reflect the effectiveness of our prepping procedures, as we attempted to make participants as comfortable as possible given the circumstances. Such a decrease in heart rate indicates that participants were fairly relaxed after being prepped and prior to beginning the experiment. When considering the effect of the game itself, the average cumulative reduction was 2.1 bpm. Thus, even though the cumulative averaged decrease in heart rates of our participants was less during this second interval while they were playing the game, these data indicate that overall, the effect of the game experience had a positive effect on their level of relaxation, at least in so far as a decrease in heart rate can serve as an indicator in this regard.

Results and Discussion Regarding Research Question #2

We now report on some results that emerged that relate to our research question about effects on participants' performance from playing *Wild Divine*. As alluded to above, participants 23 and 28 were "no shows," we did not obtain behavioral data pertaining to performance for participants 1 and 9, and we only obtained a limited data set from participant 16. We first consider the overall performance of all of the participants from whom we obtained behavioral performance data, and then we focus in more detail on the performance of participants 18 and 20.

An obvious measure of performance is the amount of time our participants took to complete the activities in which they engaged. Figure 5 summarizes these data for all of our designated participants. For each participant, the bar indicates total time of task engagement. As can be seen, each bar consists of two tones. The dark tone indicates the total time of task engagement that eventuated in *successful* task completions, whereas the light tone indicates the total time of task engagement that eventuated in *unsuccessful* task completions.

Not all participants engaged in the same number of tasks, however. Figure 6 complements Figure 5 in summarizing the total number of tasks in which each participant engaged. Again, each bar in this figure also consists of two tones. The dark tone indicates the total number of tasks that each participant *successfully* engaged, and the light tone indicates the total number of tasks *unsuccessfully* engaged.

Figure 6. Total activities in which participants successfully and unsuccessfully engaged

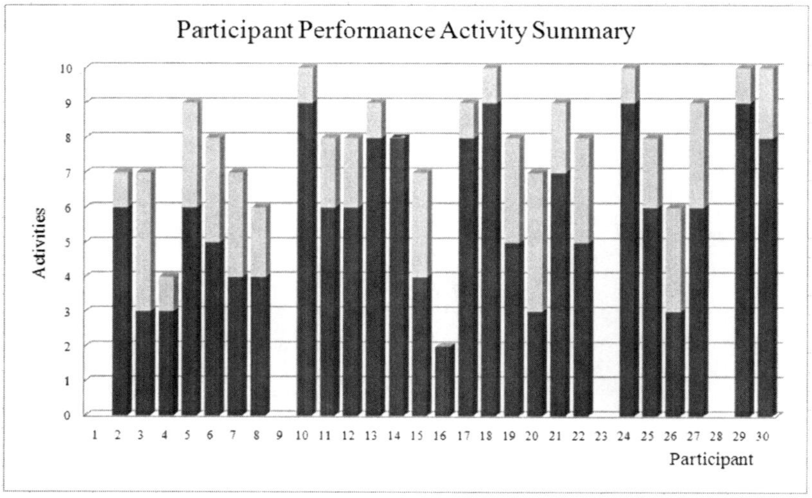

For instance, these two figures collectively illustrate that Participant 18 was engaged for about 29 minutes (see Figure 5) with all 10 activities (see Figure 6). They further indicate that Participant 18 spent most of that time successfully engaging in 9 of those 10 activities. In contrast, Participant 20 spent over 53 minutes successfully engaging in only 3 of 7 activities.

A cursory glance at Figures 5 and 6 shows that, cumulatively speaking, a disproportionate amount of time was spent by our participants engaged in activities that they were not successful at completing. This result could have been even more disproportionate, had the experimenters not invited participants to move on to the next task. In some cases, some participants obstinately persevered, and in others, the experimenter eventually intervened.

Looking at Participants 18 and 20 in greater detail, Figures 7 and 8 illustrate respectively, us-

Figure 7. Successful and unsuccessful task engagement with respect to average time spent (Participant 18)

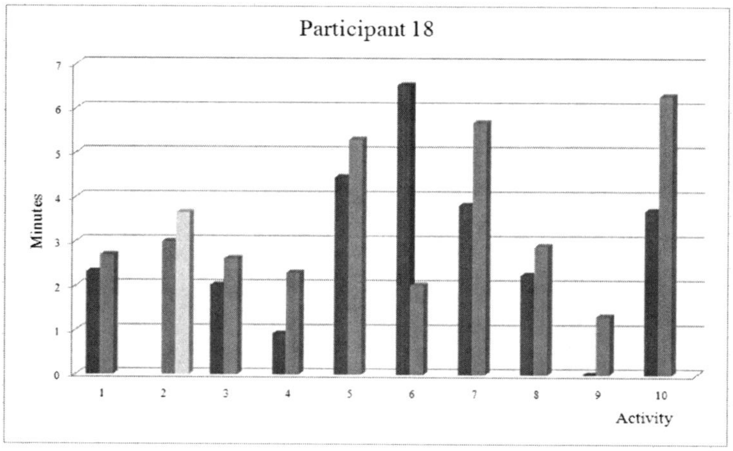

Figure 8. Successful and unsuccessful task engagement with respect to average time spent (Participant 20)

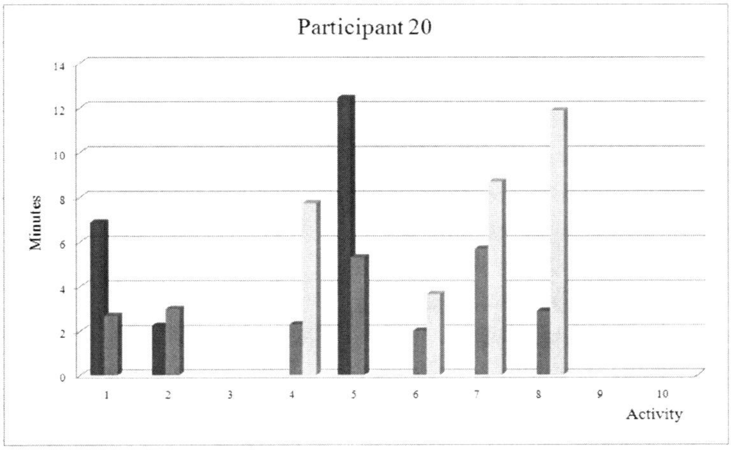

ing dark and light tones, exactly which activities they successfully and unsuccessfully engaged in with respect to the amount of time they were engaged in each of these tasks. The intermediate tone (following the dark tones and preceding the light tones) compares their performance with the average engagement time of all the participants that engaged in that particular task.

For instance, Figure 7 illustrates that Participant 18 engaged in the second activity for almost four minutes, about one minute more than the average engagement time of participants engaging in this activity, and did not successfully complete it. This participant successfully completed all the other activities s/he engaged in, and with the exception of activity 6, did so in less time relative to the norm. In contrast, Figure 8 illustrates that Participant 20 did not fare nearly as well.

With the analysis completed thus far, it would be fairly straightforward to rank participant performance based on some weighting formulae based on the number of activities successfully completed with respect to the amount of time taken to complete them. We are not convinced that such an approach would be particularly informative, however. These behavioral results were based solely on coding the screen capture data, by simply observing how long participants were engaged in which activities, and which of those activities were completed successfully. As such, these results do not give us any insight into what was happening for our participants at a physiological level. Our analysis of these data are on-going, but we have found our analysis of the screen capture data to be an invaluable guide to which aspects of these physiological data sets to focus on, and which participants to compare and contrast. For instance, we are particularly interested in investigating if some common physiological states or processes are to be found among participants who successfully completed the same task. We are not so interested in doing this kind of analysis among participants who unsuccessfully completed the same task, as there are likely too many factors or reasons that could account for an unsuccessful result. By focusing on successful results, we hypothesize that common factors for success are more likely to be identified. We also wish to compare and contrast baseline physiological responses that we obtained from our participants before and after the experiment, between the least and most successful participants. We hope that such an analysis can provide us with some insight into what physiological factors might predict that a given participant will be successful in engaging in these kinds of activities.

SUMMARY OF FINDINGS

This preliminary study was limited by a number of factors. The sample size was not large enough, there were too many variables, and we had no control group. We had planned to have 30 participants in this study. However, for reasons including conflicting schedules and technical problems such as running short of disk space and low battery power, we only collected data from 28 individuals. Of those 28 data sets, not all were complete. Only five participants completed all 10 activities with *Wild Divine*; however, a total of 22 participants completed at least seven of those 10 activities. Another factor that may have influenced the data collection was the higher-than-usual level of stress the subjects were facing at that time, because the data was mainly collected from October until Christmas, the midterm and final exam period for most students. Busy schedules, lack of sleep, and limited time made it difficult for them to finish the experiment. There was also a lack of an objective measure to show the extent to which their performance improved as they progressed through the activities.

Another factor that may have influenced the results was that all subjects participating in this study were enrolled in Simon Fraser University's programs, and all of them were volunteers. This limited the scope of the results to those individuals who were capable of attending university-level courses. All the subjects were novice gamers who had played video games for less than one month previously and had never participated in biofeedback training before. As volunteers, however, they may have been more motivated to play the game and more concerned with performing well than participants selected from a random population. Furthermore, we limited the subjects to being at least 19 years of age or older, to avoid the necessity of obtaining parental consent.

As for our remaining two research questions with regard to *learning* biofeedback in a gaming environment and improving our experimental design, we will need to refine what we mean by learning, and gain insight into how physiological responses predict successful completion of an activity. Clearly, these two questions are not unrelated. Successfully addressing the later may shed light on the former. We anticipate that to do so will require further progress in addressing our first two questions.

CONCLUSION

Can biofeedback be learned through a gaming environment? Overall, in this study we encountered great variety in individual differences, and no general claims regarding learning biofeedback in a gaming environment can be made beyond that from the results to date. That is to say, results here cannot be reliably generalized to a greater population. Having said that, this preliminary report helps to identify some of the complexities that can be anticipated and encountered in pursuing future research in this area.

This chapter should be taken as a preliminary report on a detailed pilot study. The study of biofeedback in a gaming environment reported here also introduces new methods for educational research. The preliminary results are promising, but cannot be taken in any way to be definitive. Further developments and applications of these methods opens a door to more detailed investigations as to whether, and the extent to which, people can learn biofeedback in a gaming environment, along with interdependencies of biofeedback and gaming regarding various aspects of affect, motivation, behavior and cognition, and especially learning anxiety.

Can biofeedback be learned through a gaming environment? As noted above, that depends on what one takes "learning" to mean. Results to date provide some indications that some participants may be successful in learning biofeedback in a gaming environment. Some interesting effects were detected on reducing participants' state anxiety level through playing the game episodes, especially for younger participants. However, this conclusion was mostly based on the reflective data sets, especially the participants' self-report data such as the STAT and post-questionnaire. This self-reported data heavily related to people's personal feelings. As such, this result may not accurately reflect objective reality.

However, it may be that physiological data will prove to be more valid and reliable than self-reports. In subsequent analyses, using the performance analysis from the screen capture data as a guide, these and subsequent data sets like them can be investigated in more detail in future research. Both baseline data and data obtained while participants were engaged in biofeedback activities may prove to be a more reliable approach to accurately determining patterns and changes in participants' psychological states and processes. If so, it can decrease the traditional dependence on reflective self-report data, and at the same time, complement and expand on the use of audiovisual behavioral data sets. Our work continues with the physiological data to analyze whether people can learn biofeedback in a gaming environment.

Can biofeedback be learned through a gaming environment? The tentative and qualified answer to this question is, in some cases, 'yes.' Further analyses of data we have already acquired, and subsequent studies will be required to be more definitive that this. Our work to date has been more of an exploratory pilot study that has served to provide some insights into the effectiveness and limitations of the methods and toward improving the experimental designs for future studies in this area. With these methods, however, we believe the field is wide open for furthering this research, not only in the area of video games, but with all media forms.

REFERENCES

Bali, L. R. (1979). Long-term effect of relaxation on blood pressure and anxiety levels of essential hypertensive males: A controlled study. *Psychosomatic Medicine, 41*(8), 637-646. Retrieved from http://www.psychosomaticmedicine.org/cgi/reprint/41/8/637.pdf

Beck, J. C., & Wade, M. (2004). *Got game: How a new generation of gamers is reshaping business forever.* Boston, MA: Harvard Business School Press.

Beck, J. C., & Wade, M. (2006). *The kids are alright: How the gamer generation is changing the workplace.* Boston, MA: Harvard Business School Press.

Biofeedback Consultants. (2008). *EEG biofeedback: New York ripple effect.* Retrieved May 8, 2008, from http://www.therippleeffect.org/biofeedback_new_york.html#yonkers

Campbell, S. R. with the ENL Group. (2007). The ENGRAMMETRON: Establishing an educational neuroscience laboratory. *Simon Fraser University Educational Review*, *1*, 17–29.

EEG Spectrum International Inc. (2007). *Biofeedback for anxiety and panic.* Retrieved June 26, 2008, from: http://www.eegspectrum.com/Applications/Intro/UltimateSelf-Help/SpecificApplications/

Fuchs, T., Birbaumer, N., Lutzenberger, W., Gruzelier, J. H., & Kaiser, J. (2003). Neurofeedback treatment for attention-deficit/hyperactivity disorder in children: A comparison with methylphenidate. *Applied Psychophysiology and Biofeedback*, *28*(1), 1–12. doi:10.1023/A:1022353731579

Green, C., & Bavelier, D. (2003, May 29). Action video game modifies visual selective attention. *Nature*, *423*, 534–537. doi:10.1038/nature01647

Imel, Z., Baldwin, S., Bonus, K., & MacCoon, D. (2008). Beyond the individual: Group effects in mindfulness-based stress reduction. *Psychotherapy Research*, *18*(6), 735–742. doi:10.1080/10503300802326038

Internet World Stats. (2008). Canada Internet usage, broadband and telecommunications report. Retrieved April 19, 2009 from: http://www.internetworldstats.com/am/ca.htm

Kaufman, D., Sauve, L., & Ireland, A. (2005). Simulation and advanced gaming environments: Exploring their learning impacts. Keynote paper in Q. Medhi, N. Gough & S. Natkin (Eds.), *Proceedings, CGAMES05 (7th International Conference on Computer Games)* (pp. 16-25). Wolverhampton, UK: School of Computing and Information Technology, University of Wolverhampton.

Larsen, S. (2006). *The healing power of neurofeedback, the revolutionary LENS technique for restoring optimal brain function.* Rochester, VT: Healing Arts Press.

Lubar, J. F., Swartwood, M. O., Swartwood, J. N., & O'Donnell, P. H. (1995). Evaluation of the effectiveness of EEG neurofeedback training for ADHD in a clinical setting as measured by changes in T.O.V.A. scores, behavioral ratings, and WISC-R performance. *Biofeedback and Self-Regulation*, *20*(1), 83–99. doi:10.1007/BF01712768

Maria, J., & Lynne, A. (2006). Measurement of anxiety for patients with cardiac disease: A critical review and analysis. *The Journal of Cardiovascular Nursing*, *21*(5), 412–419.

McGrady, A. V., Yonker, R., Tan, S. Y., Fine, T., & Woerner, M. (1981). The effect of biofeedback-assisted relaxation training on blood pressure and selected biochemical parameters in patients with essential hypertension. *Biofeedback and Self-Regulation*, *5*, 25–44.

Othmer, S. F., & Othmer, S. (1994). *EEG biofeedback training for PMS.* Retrieved February 5, 2008, from: http://members.aol.com/eegspectrm/articles/pms94.htm

Pew Internet & American Life Project (PIALP). (2008). *Demographics of Internet users.* Washington, DC: Pew Research Center. Retrieved June 11, 2008 from http://www.pewinternet.org/trends/User_Demo_2.15.08.htm

Plotkin, W. B., & Rice, K. M. (1981). Biofeedback as a placebo: Anxiety reduction facilitated by training in either suppression or enhancement of alpha brainwaves. *Journal of Consulting and Clinical Psychology*, *49*(4), 590–596. doi:10.1037/0022-006X.49.4.590

Prensky, M. (2001). *Digital game-based learning.* New York: McGraw-Hill.

Prensky, M. (2003). Escape from Planet Jar-Gon: Or what video games have to teach academics about teaching and writing. A review of *What Video Games Have To Teach Us About Learning and Literacy* by James Paul Gee. *On The Horizon*, *11*(3). Retrieved July 15, 2009 from http://www.marcprensky.com/writing/Prensky%20-%20Review%20of%20James%20Paul%20Gee%20Book.pdf

Rainey, L. (2006). *Digital 'natives' invade the workplace.* Washington, DC: Pew Research Center. Retrieved June 11, 2008, from http://www.pewinternet.org/ppt/New%20Workers%20--%20pewresearch.org%20version%20_final_.pdf

Rice, K. M., Blanchard, E. B., & Purcell, M. (1993). Biofeedback treatments of generalized anxiety disorder: Preliminary results. *Biofeedback and Self-Regulation*, *18*(2), 93–105. doi:10.1007/BF01848110

Sauvé, L., Renaud, L., Kaufman, D., & Marquis, J. S. (2007). Distinguishing between games and simulations: A systematic review. *Journal of Educational Technology & Society*, *10*(3), 244–256.

Sha, L., Winne, P., & Campbell, S. R. (2009, April). *Personal factors underlying the relations between metacognitive judgments and control in self-regulated learning*. Paper presented at the annual meeting of the American Educational Research Association, San Diego, CA.

Shipulina, O. V., Campbell, S. R., & Cimen, O. A. (2009, April). *Electrooculography: Connecting mind, brain, and behavior in mathematics education research*. Paper presented at the annual meeting of the American Educational Research Association, San Diego, CA.

Statistics Canada. (2005). *Household Internet use at home by Internet activity*. Retrieved on April 19, 2009 from: http://www40.statcan.gc.ca/l01/cst01/comm09a-eng.htm

Tinius, T. (2006). Measuring the effectiveness of neurotherapy. *Journal of Neurotherapy*, *10*(1), 1–3. doi:10.1300/J184v10n01_01

Townsend, R. E., House, J. F., & Addario, D. (1975). A comparison of biofeedback-mediated relaxation and group therapy in the treatment of chronic anxiety. *The American Journal of Psychiatry*, *132*, 598–601.

Vernon, D. J. (2005). Can neurofeedback training enhance performance? An evaluation of the evidence with implications for future research. *Applied Psychophysiology and Biofeedback*, *30*(4), 347–364. doi:10.1007/s10484-005-8421-4

Warnes, E., & Allen, K. D. (2005). Biofeedback treatment of paradoxical vocal fold motion and respiratory distress in an adolescent girl. *Journal of Applied Behavior Analysis*, *38*(4), 529–532. doi:10.1901/jaba.2005.26-05

Whitehouse, B., & Turner, S. (2007). *Biofeedback technology in the Journey to Wild Divine*. Retrieved June 26, 2008 from http://www.alivematrix.info/html/scienceofbiofeedback.html

ADDITIONAL READING

Hammond, D. C. (2006). What is neurofeedback? *Journal of Neurotherapy*, *10*(4), 25–36. doi:10.1300/J184v10n04_04

Vernon, D., & Gruzelier, J. (2008). Electroencephalographic biofeedback as a mechanism to alter mood, creativity and artistic performance. In B. N. DeLuca (Ed.), *Mind-body and relaxation research focus* (pp. 149-164). New York: Nova Biomedical Books

Wiederhold, B. K., & Rizzo, A. (2005). Virtual reality and applied psychophysiology. *Applied Psychophysiology and Biofeedback*, *30*(3), 183–185. doi:10.1007/s10484-005-6375-1

KEY TERMS AND DEFINITIONS

Biofeedback: Conveying information regarding some aspect of one's physiological state, such as blood pressure, heart rate, and so on, in real time so that one may use that awareness to maintain or alter that aspect of one's physiological state accordingly.

Educational Neuroscience: A new transdisciplinary area of educational research that seeks to reconcile mind-body dualisms and integrate psychology and physiology using methods of educational psychology, cognitive psychology, psychophysiology, and cognitive neuroscience.

Gaming: Participation in some kind of game, typically a structured activity in accordance to some predetermined or evolving set of rules, commonly presented within a computer graphics environment.

Journey to Wild Divine®: A biofeedback video game that promotes stress management and overall wellness through the use of breathing, meditation, and relaxation exercises.

ENDNOTE

i Two 19-year olds had a change of 2, two 21-year olds had a change of 5, and two 25-year olds had a change of 2. The circled outlier indicated a history of migraines following stress or extended computer usage.

Section 4

Special In–Depth Section on Game Shell and Game Creation

Chapter 22
Initial Analysis for Creating a Generic Online Educational Game Shell

Louise Sauvé
Télé-université, Canada

Lise Renaud
University of Quebec in Montreal, Canada

Mathieu Gauvin
Laval University, Canada

ABSTRACT

As the first of five chapters describing the development process for a generic educational game shell, this chapter discusses how the authors analyzed 40 computerized educational games to determine the main characteristics built into digital educational games. The analysis allowed comparison of game attributes with the pedagogic and technical needs of target populations (i.e., primary and secondary school teachers and students) and their learning contexts.

INTRODUCTION: DEFINITIONS AND DEVELOPMENT PROCESS

This and the next four chapters describe in detail the development process used by the research team at SAVIE (*Société d'apprentissage à vie* – www.savie.qc.ca) at Télé-université in Québec, Canada, to develop a generic educational game shell (GEGS) based on *Parcheesi* for the *Carrefour virtuel de jeux éducatifs/ Educational Games Central* online community (http://egc.savie.ca).

DOI: 10.4018/978-1-61520-731-2.ch022

Before defining a GEGS, we note that any game can be broken down into two components:

- The game's *structure* determines the way the game is played: rules, the stages of the game and player moves, challenges that the players face, and strategies which they can use to win. In the context of a game, we say that we "empty" the game of its content to uncover its unique underlying structure. This structure, once clearly defined and analysed, becomes a "frame," or a "generic game shell," when it is programmed and put online.

- The game's *content* consists of the information employed in the game: this content is generally found (for non-computerized games) in cards and on game boards. In the case of educational games, it also includes stated learning goals and competencies to be developed by playing the game. Once a frame game is fully defined, it is enough to insert new content, accompanied by predetermined learning objectives, to generate an up-to-date educational game adapted to a particular target group.

Based on this division, a *frame game* is an existing game, e.g., *Parcheesi™*, with its content emptied and only the structure retained (Hourst & Thiagarajan, 2007; Stolovitch & Thiagarajan, 1980).

Board games are the easiest to adapt into frame games because they have simple structures with few rules, which makes adaptation easier, and they are likely to fit the definition of a game as distinguished from simulation, because they take place in an imaginary environment rather than a simulated "real" environment (Sauvé, Renaud, Kaufman, & Marquis, 2007; see also Chapter 1 of this volume). They are often well-known; who has not played *Snakes and Ladders*, *Tic Tac Toe* or *Parcheesi?*

When used for online learning, a frame game becomes a generic educational game shell (GEGS). A GEGS is an online design environment that facilitates game creation by teachers and trainers, providing them with the tools they need to: (1) set technical and pedagogical parameters for the game; (2) create strategies and rules that direct players' actions; (3) create learning materials; (4) set criteria to define the end of the game and determine the winner; and (5) expand on the tools required for game review and evaluation, ensuring that the game is regularly updated and strengthening its learning impact.

The SAVIE development process for an online GEGS was adapted by Sauvé (2002) from learning design models that generally include five stages (Brien, 1981; Dick & Carey, 1996; Grafinger, 1988; McGriff, 2000). The process, validated by Sauvé et al. (2002, 2004) during the creation of four online GEGS, consists of the following five stages:

- **Preliminary analysis and planning:** analysis of the target learner group(s) and the learning context; specification of the shell's pedagogical and technological requirements; review of existing frame games; and selection of the structure of the game to be adapted.
- **Design:** description of the structural components and content elements of the existing game to be saved, modified, or added to create the shell; creation of a design model in the form of screen pages and reference documents describing the GEGS components.
- **Media development:** development of technical specifications for the online shell's graphic and multimedia components; programming of different elements and their functions in the shell; and functional integration testing of the shell.
- **Validation:** specification of the formative evaluation framework; development of evaluation instruments for the target population; target population trials; and making any necessary revisions.
- **Formative evaluation of games created with the GEGS**: development of an educational game using the shell; specification of the experimental framework; development of measurement instruments to be used by experts and the target population; validation of the game by experts, and revisions if necessary; game trial by the target

population, and revision of the game and the shell if necessary.

This chapter presents the initial analyses done in developing a GEGS based on *Parcheesi.* In the planning stage for developing a digital learning application, preliminary analyses provide the developers with a clear idea of the dimensions of the project, the development steps, a schedule of due dates, and budget forecasts for carrying out the plan (Marton, 1994).

Analysis of existing game shells and games provides valuable input to the process of choosing a game from which to create a new shell. In our process, one or more designers first analyzes the target learners and the context(s) of game use, setting out the pedagogic needs the GEGS will address. They also examine existing game shells for strengths and weaknesses and conduct an analysis of existing digital educational games used by the target learners to learn about similarities and differences with their game structure and learning content. The synthesis of this accumulated information guides the designers in their choice of a frame game on which to base their GEGS.

In our project, the target users of the GEGS were elementary and secondary school teachers. The learning content determining the objectives of the educational games to be generated by GEGS was primarily related to the health education of their students. We examined the pedagogical requirements for GEGS structure and content of both students and teachers. Finally, we analyzed 40 existing computerized educational games to help the designers better understand the variety of games available, and to identify elements likely to guide us in the creation of the future GEGS (Sauvé et al, 2005a).

The first part of this chapter presents the results of our analysis of 40 computerized educational games, while the second part summarizes the pedagogic and technical requirements defined for the GEGS by a panel of teachers and experts. In the third part of the chapter, the results of our educational game analysis are related to the pedagogic and technical needs of the target users and experts. Finally, we present the criteria used for the choice of *Parcheesi* as a model for the new GEGS.

METHODOLOGY FOR THE GAME ANALYSIS

Following definition of the target public and pedagogic context for our new GEGS, we analyzed existing computerized educational games (on CD-ROM or the Internet) in order to establish design parameters for the new shell. Here we first explain our process for selecting games for review. We then present an analysis of their characteristics—format, support, length, goal, number of players, rules, presence of conflict and cooperation, technical requirements, and the need for motor skills.

Game Selection and Data Collection

Our search and data collection for existing educational games involved four steps:

Step 1. Identification of search criteria for choosing games matching our research objectives: Our search criteria were the following:

1. The educational games had to vary in terms of frame game, content, and teaching objectives
2. Ideally, each game had to have the essential attributes identified by Sauvé et al., (2005b)
    - Have a minimum of one player
    - Involve conflict (competition, struggle) and/or co-operation
    - Be structured by rules
    - Include a predetermined goal leading to reward and victory
    - Involve an imaginary environment (e.g., fantasy, mystery, curiosity, or

- chance elements that distinguish the game from a simulation)
- Include learning objectives

3. The games had to serve at least one of the two populations being studied (primary- or secondary-school students)
4. The games had to be available in French or in English

More specific criteria in our research were used to reduce the number of games to be analyzed:

1. Use of a "winner / loser" format
2. Time constraints
3. Scoring
4. Rewards (part of feedback)
5. Complete and sufficient feedback
6. Free access, whether through the Internet or through an institution

In researching educational games, our primary sources were the Internet and the *Didacthèque de l'Université Laval* (Laval University's teaching resource center). Forty computer games, chosen after an initial analysis, satisfied the essential overall game attributes.

Step 2. Development and validation of a game analysis grid: In order to standardize data collection by three research assistants, a game analysis grid was developed and validated for inter-rater reliability (see Step 4, below) (Lincoln & Guba, 1985). This grid contained descriptions of the fields to be completed and comments on information to be inserted into these fields (Sauvé, 2005). The grid was discussed and agreed on by the researchers as they carried out a detailed examination of each field and its contents. (See Appendix A for the grid variables and their definitions.)

Step 3. Game search: Locating educational games which met our criteria was challenging. We used several search approaches in order to ensure covering maximum ground. Most of the research was carried out using Internet search engines; in addition to keyword searches, additional searches targeted companies, non-profit organizations, and governments, which sometimes invest in the creation of educational computer games intended for the general public.

The work of identifying games proved to be difficult because of potentially misleading vocabulary in the domain of education and because of certain budget constraints. Despite these challenges, we believe that our bank of forty educational computer games represents the variety as well as the average quality of digital educational games available in North American and European markets at the time of the search (March and April, 2005).

Step 4: Data collection using the game analysis grid: For each game selected during the search process, each research assistant played the game and then completed a game analysis grid using *Excel*®. To ensure data consistency, the results of the three research assistants' data for the first five games were discussed and adjusted under the supervision of a researcher.

Analysis of Pedagogical Variables

Once the data were collated in the grids, a comparative quantitative analysis was carried out.

Variables used to analyze the pedagogical aspects of the games included the environments for which the games are suitable, the nature of the games, content discussed, learning objectives, the degrees of difficulty of the game, associated evaluation instruments, and the language of the games.

Target Population

18 games (45%) were intended for children 11 years old or younger, and 9 games (30%) targeted students 12 to 16 years old. Ten games (25%) were aimed at any age from 7 to 77 years old. In other words, 70% of the games analyzed could be used with elementary school students and 55% with those in secondary school.

Context of Use

39 games (97.5% of the sample) were created with learning goals specifically for elementary and secondary school students and one game (2.5%) was intended for general learning. In the publicity for these games, 37 (92.5%) were also described as for use in the family, while 13 (32.5%) were intended for use in a community milieu and one game was to be used in hospitals.

Pedagogical Function

The pedagogical function of the game refers to the use of the game as intended by its creators. Games can be used to motivate, sensitize, teach basic notions (or progressively complex ones), develop psychometric abilities, review, diagnose or evaluate. Among the indexed games, 28 (70%) were intended to teach concepts, 18 (45%) were for review, 18 (45%) were motivational, 11 (27.5%) were centered around creation of awareness, and one game focused on developing psychometric abilities. Results showed that certain games had more than one use. For example, six games (15%) dealt with concepts and were also for review, seven games (17.5%) were intended for both teaching concepts and motivation, five games (12.5%) taught concepts and created awareness, and four games (10%) were for both review and motivation. Moreover, seven games (17.5%) fit into other possible combination categories.

Learning Content

The classification of games by content mainly concerned various school subjects: mathematics (9 games), geography (9 games) and languages (French or English) (8 games), sciences (7), health (5), nutrition (3), and music (1). The language games are primarily concerned with vocabulary and spelling.

Learning Objectives

To understand the degree of complexity of the knowledge and intellectual skills the indexed games involved, we classified them according to Bloom's (1956) cognitive pedagogical objectives. The majority of the games (26 out of 40, or 65%) involved knowledge acquisition, nine (22.5%) required comprehension, three (7.5%) required application, and two games (5%) required analysis. Note that the games that required application all dealt with mathematics. Moreover, one game on the analysis level also dealt with mathematics, while the other was a game of logic. For affective objectives, we classified the games based on Nadeau (1981), cited in Renaud and Sauvé (1990). The analysis showed that 11 games (27.5%) were designed for raising consciousness and that all were in the first emotional category (reception) presented by Nadeau (1981). Eight games (20%) encouraged learners to be involved in the action (motivation) and to respond to the challenges proposed by the game. Finally, 21 games (53.5%) did not intend, or minimally intended, to achieve affective goals. Even if they provide some feedback to the players, these were insufficient to include these games in the affective category.

Player Ability to Select the Degree of Difficulty

Some games could vary in difficulty depending on the player's choice at the start of gameplay. Some games offered only one level, while others offered several. 21 games (52.5%) offered one level of difficulty, versus 19 (47.5%) that offered several levels. Among the games that offered several difficulty levels, nine (22.5%) provided a choice of two or three levels, seven (17.5%) provided more than three levels, and three (7.5%) gave players the option of setting the difficulty level according to selected characteristics.

Feedback Provided

Feedback supports learning, and it is preferable that an educational game include some form of feedback. Two forms of feedback were examined: feedback related to learning, which examines learning errors made by the players and provides explanations, and motivational feedback, which uses rewards, interesting visuals, etc., to keep the player sufficiently engaged to finish the game. Only the *Deviens Sécuri-Prêt* game included learning feedback, although two games included elements close to feedback, e.g., providing hints in the case of a wrong answer or action without explaining the actual error. The majority of the games (29 out of 40 or 72.5%) included motivational feedback; however, eight games offered no feedback.

Evaluation Tools

Since the games were identified as educational, we examined whether they included evaluation tools (e.g., criterion-based tests, norm-based tests, evaluation comments) for teachers and learners. None of the games provided evaluation questionnaires in the game itself or on the Internet site where the game was found. Two games offered a form for game evaluation by teachers, and five games (12.5%) were accompanied by an evaluation form for learners. In general, designers did not provide evaluation mechanisms.

Game Language

Out of a total of 40 games analyzed, 18 games (45%) were unilingual French, nine games (22.5%) were unilingual English, ten (25%) were bilingual (English and French), and three games (7.5%) were offered in three or more languages (including French and English). Translation into a second language did not change the game or culture context. Only textual elements were translated; images remained in the original language.

Analysis of Technical Variables

In addition to the pedagogical aspects, we examined the technical aspects of the games: the title, frame used if any, support, duration, goal, number of players, rules, conflict and co-operation, and, finally, technical and motor skills requirements.

Table 1. Classification of game titles according to identification criteria

Name Refers to:	No. of games	Game ID* and Name
Subject /learning contents	24	(1, Océan) (2, Trésors de la Martinique) (4, Word rotation) (5, Happy Note! Clé de Sol et Clé de Fa) (6, World Slinger) (7, Matchlt Math!) (8, GéoJeu 2004) (9, Clop Attaque) (10, 2K40) (11, Sur la piste des dangers) (13, Quelques mots) (15, Les Aventures de Globe Trotteur) (18, L'escalade du mont Humain) (21, In yer pants) (22, Turbo mots) (23, Bon appétit) (25, 20 / 20 en calcul) (26, CosmoLogique) (28, Envol Mathématique) (30, MindTwister Math) (31, Le laboratoire du professeur XYZ, Mission Savotron) (32, Le laboratoire du professeur XYZ, Mission 3,2,1 Feu!) (38, 103 Découvertes) (40, Deviens Sécuri-prêt)
Actions or movement in the game or their character-istics	9	(3, Défi +) (12, Comment est-ce rangé?) (17, L'étrange disparition du professeur Scientifix) (20, Typer Shark) (27, Mia. Juste à temps!) (29, Mais où se cache Carmen Sandiego?) (35, Rallye X 5) (36, Lâchez prise) (39, Feed the monster)
Game materials	4	(14, Les jetons) (16, Les Netoons et Buurkis) (24, ScholarCards) (37, Mango dans l'espace)
Game frame-work	2	(33, EuropaGO Jeu de mémoire) (34, EuropaGO Puzzle de l'Europe)
Learning results	1	(19, Les Motivés)
Legend: The number preceding each game title corresponds to the game ID number used in Appendix 1, which lists game sources.		

Game Title

All of the games analyzed had clearly identifiable titles (Table 1). They were named according to topic or learning contents (24), actions carried out by the players (9), game materials (4), frame game (2), and expected learning results (1).

Game Frames

The game structure is a combination of rules, stages in gameplay or player actions, challenges which players must face and the strategies they can call upon to win. This structure, once clearly defined and analyzed independent of content, becomes a frame. To identify the frames of the games analyzed, we used the game classification used in (Sauvé & Chamberland, 2006). 38 games used ten different frames, while two were difficult to classify (Table 2).

Based on their frequency of occurrence, the three most common frames in our analysis were pathway games with tests (n=9), discovery games such as *Clue®* (n=6) and board games (n=5). Note that the games were selected with a view to including as many different frames or formats as possible.

Game Support

All of the games analyzed were played on a computer and did not require non-technological accessories such as dice, charts or video-cassettes.33 of them (82.5%) were tested on the Internet by downloading the game or by playing online. Seven games (17.5%) were found through the Laval's

Table 2. Classification of games by frame or format

Frame or format	No. of games	Game
Puzzle	1	EuropaGO Puzzle de l'Europe (34)
Pathway games	2	Défi + (3) ; 20 / 20 en calcul (25)
Board games –Static version	5	Océan (1) ; Trésors de la Martinique (2) ; GéoJeu 2004 (8); Les Aventures de Globe Trotteur (15); Rallye X 5 (35)
Games using clues and deduction	6	Comment est-ce rangé? (12) ; CosmoLogique (26) ; Mais où se cache Carmen Sandiego? (29) ; Les Netoons et Buurkis (17) ; L'étrange disparition du professeur Scientifix (23) ; Lâchez prise (36)
Pathway games with challenges such as PacMan / Mario Bros*	9	L'escalade du mont Humain (18) ; Envol Mathématique (28) ; Clop Attaque (9) ; Mia. Juste à temps! (27) ; 2K40 (10) ; Typer Shark (20) ; In yer pants (21) ; Mango dans l'espace (37) ; 103 Découvertes (38)
Word games Scrabble / Crossword	2	Word rotation (4) ; World Slinger (6)
Memory games Memory / Concentration	4	Matchlt Math! (7) ; Quelques mots (13) ; EuropaGO Jeu de mémoire (33) ; ScholarCards (24)
Quiz (television type)	3	Turbo mots (22) ; MindTwister Math (30) ; Deviens Sécuri-prêt (40)
Arcade games: "Shoot them all" (hitting a target)	4	Happy Note! Clé de Sol et Clé de Fa (5) ; Les Motivés (19) Feed the monster (39) ; Le laboratoire du professeur XYZ, Mission Savotron (31) ; Le laboratoire du professeur XYZ, Mission 3, 2,1 Feu! (32)
Construction games (Hangman)	1	Les jetons (16)
Other	2	Sur la piste des dangers (11) ; Bon appétit (14)

* Here we included the games in which the player accumulates energy, wins challenges and avoids mistakes in order to survive. These games are very different from each other. Note also that two of the games (Le laboratoire du professeur XYZ, Mission Savotron et Le laboratoire du professeur XYZ, Mission 3, 2,1 Feu!) are levels of a more global game.

University's teaching resource centre and are available on CD-ROM only. None of the games tested online offered additional multimedia options. Note that Internet game load times caused some installation and operational problems that were taken into account when we later chose a framework for our game shell.

Game Duration

The duration of the game refers to playing time from start to finish. Only two games specified a time limit. We estimated the duration of the remaining games by playing them. (Note that these estimates are influenced by the skill and knowledge of the testers.) 21 games (52.5%) lasted up to 30 minutes, eight (20%) lasted up to 60 minutes, and 11 (27.5%) took longer than one hour (sometimes several hours) to play. Many of the longer games included stages which made it possible to play the game in several sessions. Thus, all the games could be played in one or more school periods.

Predetermined Game Goal

The goal of a game refers to the end result as defined by the rules and determined by designation one or more winners and often by one or more losers. Players make choices in order to reach the game goal. All games had a predetermined goal; however the way to attain it differed. 32 games (80%) determined the winner by highest number of points, while eight games (20%) required the winner to be the first to solve one or more puzzles or mysteries. 22 games (55%) did not reward winners, ten games (25%) games displayed the winning results in an honor roll, and eight games (20%) gave external rewards, e.g., prizes, "diplomas," electronic rewards allowing access to other games. Eight games (20%) pitted players against a virtual adversary who must be thwarted throughout the game or a human adversary who is overcome by either accumulating more points or by solving a mystery being the first to complete a test.

Number of Players

25 of the games tested (62.5%) involved solo players, who played against the computer, while 11 games (27.5%) could be played with one or more players. Three games (7.5%) required at least two players. Out of the 11 games which provided for one or more players, seven ran on CD-ROM, and four (notably the pathway and board games) allowed users to play in teams.

The Rules

Rules specify the extent and nature of legitimate player actions, and determine the sequence and structure in which player actions unfold. Only one game did not have clear rules. Neither did it include enough hints to give players a clear idea of what to do.

Conflict and Co-Operation

As specified in the methodology, we wanted to index and analyze games corresponding to both conflict and co-operation, essential attributes of games established in our research (see Chapter 1). Our analysis tested the games for competition, against either the computer or other human players, and for co-operation. Conflict is demonstrated by four characteristics: competition, confrontation, challenge, and chance. Among the 40 games analyzed, 35 (87.5%) included a conflict between players or a confrontation with the computer. Five of the games analyzed did not meet our competition criterion, despite being described as such.

Cooperation is present when the game can be played as a team with the objective of a team victory. Three games (7.5%) offered cooperative elements; the games with cooperative elements also had elements of conflict.

Technical and Motor Skill Requirements

All the games required the use of a mouse, a keyboard, or both to interact with the computer. No other possible way (for example using the player's voice) was noted. 30 games (75%) required the use of the mouse alone, versus five (12.5%) that used a keyboard and five (12.5%) that used both keyboard and mouse. Only 13 games (32.5%) required motor skills (reaction speed using a keyboard, precision with the mouse, etc.); 27 (67.5%) did not require any of these skills.

PEDAGOGIC AND TECHNICAL NEEDS OF TEACHERS AND EXPERTS

To establish pedagogic and technical requirements for the GEGS, we used a collaborative approach (Desgagné, 1997; Miles & Huberman, 2003) with a participative process (Floch'lay, 1997; Mayer, Ouellet, Saint-Jacques, & Turcotte, 2000). Fundamentally, this approach is based on collaboration among designers, domain experts and potential users. This approach also uses the evaluation protocol to link the construction and validation of the computer product, and it primarily values the user's viewpoint.

Data Collection

To identify pedagogic requirements of the target users for educational games, a questionnaire was given to approximately 30 elementary and secondary school teachers. The questionnaires listed eight requirements generally associated with online educational games: interactivity, friendliness, accessibility, adaptability of the game and the resulting impact on learning, motivation, appropriateness of the game for student characteristics (knowledge, level of language), aesthetic design, and the modernity of the game.

To identify pedagogic and computer requirements for the GEGS, we asked eight pedagogic experts and game experts to analyze five generic educational game shells already developed for the *Carrefour virtuel de jeux éducatifs/ Educational Games Central* (http://egc.savie.ca) with respect to the types of game which they could build with the shells. Afterward, they participated in a discussion group to suggest improvements in terms of game structure and learning content.

Identification of Pedagogic Requirements

The teachers reported that the GEGS must:

1. be reliable, convenient and complete
2. be flexible so that it can be easily used in different learning situations. This means, among other things, that teachers can adapt the game to their students' needs and class schedules
3. be straightforward and easy to use so that teachers can easily find all the necessary elements for a given context or situation
4. allow changes to game content at any time to ensure that it is accurate and directly linked to the teaching programs
5. support activities that support attaining cognitive and affective objectives from simple to complex
6. integrate different types of learning activities through closed or open-ended questions with varying degrees of difficulty
7. provide activities which allow a player to complete a learning goal (with the help of an information module) before responding to a question (e.g. demonstrations, situational role-plays)

The game and domain experts listed a number of pedagogic needs for the GEGS. It should:

1. produce games that can adapt to a class's technological context by being playable on one computer or on multiple computers according to available equipment
2. allow the insertion of video scenarios for work on behavior or to support other types of learning
3. allow the formulation of text, visual, audio or audiovisual based questions
4. allow the formulation of different types of answers, including intermediary choices (neither yes nor no, grey zones)
5. allow text, audio, or audiovisual feedback
6. allow prompt, just-in-time feedback linked to learning
7. insert motivational feedback as text, audio, or icons
8. support reflection on the material learned (metacognition) following the game, with the help of a debriefing questionnaire
9. save each player's results in a personal folder, viewable by the player
10. allow each player to measure her learning during the game and at the end of the game, with real time feedback
11. allow the teacher to provide complementary pedagogical material or to suggest activities once the players have completed the game
12. offer mechanisms that facilitate adaptation of a game into another language (French or English)

Finally, teachers and experts agreed that the frame game had to be well-known and very popular among the target audience, to reduce the time it takes to learn game rules and how the game board works. They suggested conducting a study to identify the game preferences of elementary and secondary school teachers. (Chapter 7 describes a study with pre-service teachers to address this suggestion.)

Planning the Structure of the GEGS

The group of experts argued that the GEGS's structure should be adaptable enough to:

1. allow players to cooperate by forming groups or teams to work together to win the game
2. create competition among players and provide them with a challenge that would maintain their interest and involvement during their in-game learning
3. include a point system as a formal indicator of success or failure in learning the material
4. offer different paths on the game board to increase the uncertainty of a player's chances of winning
5. support real-time exchange between players
6. play solo against oneself (by creating a fictitious opponent), in teams (with collaboration mechanisms), and against other players or in teams (using conflict mechanisms)

THE CHOICE OF A FRAME GAME

To identify the frame game to serve as the basis for a new GEGS, we first linked the results of the pedagogic analysis with learning content needs. Then we examined the results of the technical analysis of 40 games relative to needs for the structure of the game, as well as the required technical features.

Game Characteristics vs. Pedagogical Needs

Once the analysis was completed of the 40 computerized educational games and requirements were gathered from teachers and experts, we examined how the pedagogic characteristics of the games matched the requirements identified by the teachers and experts.

1. The analyzed games were developed for use in schools, particularly for primary and secondary students. Most of the games were inspired by known parlor games, such as pathway games with tests, discovery games, and board games. Our analysis led us to recommend the choice of a frame game based on a parlor game familiar to elementary and secondary school teachers and students.
2. The analyzed games focused on attaining cognitive objectives, from simple to complex, including knowledge, comprehension, application, and analysis. In spite of the varied choice of educational games on the market, none of the games under examination allowed learners to attain synthesis or evaluation objectives. Since our teachers and experts specified these types of objectives, it was necessary to examine how the new GEGS would support these types of learning.
3. Fewer than half of the analyzed games (19) supported the attainment of affective objectives such as sensitization and motivation. As these are also included in the teachers' and experts' needs, it became necessary to examine how the new GEGS would include content that supports these objectives.
4. The frames of the analyzed games allowed users to develop educational games having four types of pedagogic functions: conceptual, review, motivational and sensitization. These types are therefore candidates for use in the development of the new GEGS.
5. Regarding content, the majority of the analyzed games taught elementary and secondary school subjects, notably geography, mathematics, French and English language (vocabulary and grammar), natural science, health, nutrition, and music. For analyzed games in health education (the first planned GEGS application), designers drew inspiration from the structure of the *Mario Bros®* game, arcade games, and *Pac-Man®*.
6. Although fewer than half of games provided varying levels of game difficulty at the player's choice (before or during the game), this option was requested by our panel and would have to be available in the chosen frame game and GEGS. The teachers, in particular, viewed the option to choose the degree of learning difficulty as supporting the motivation of their students.
7. Only one game provided feedback on learning, and 29 games provided motivational feedback. It was therefore necessary to examine if the chosen frame game would give these two types of feedback throughout the game (as part of the existing game structure) or whether a new feedback mechanism would have to be built into the GEGS.
8. Seven games provided evaluation instruments within the game rather than post-game summaries for teachers and students. Although frame games do not generally have this mechanism, it was recommended for inclusion in the GEGS so that game builders could include it in their educational games.

Our analysis of existing games showed that certain pedagogic aspects were not offered in the analyzed games:

1. None of the games recorded player results in a personal database accessible by players
2. None of the games allowed players to measure his learning during or after the game with the help of real-time feedback
3. None of the games allowed the learner to offer complementary learning materials or to propose activities during or after the game
4. None of the games proposed reflection on learning (metacognition) after the game with the help of a questionnaire and synthesis of its results

5. No games offered a way of adapting the game into another language

Game Characteristics vs. GEGS Technical Requirements

Since the GEGS was to be a tool for constructing educational games online, we compared the technical parameters of existing digital educational games with those required by our experts.

More and more educational games are being offered online, and 33 out of the 40 games analyzed were played on the Internet. Given the difficulties encountered when downloading certain games, it was recommended that the GEGS ensure that the games developed do not require downloading or the installation of a plug-in.

1. 37 of the 40 educational games analyzed were based on known games, reducing the time needed to learn the game rules and play process. Three game frameworks were drawn from our analysis: pathway games with tests, discovery games such as *Clue*, and board games.
2. All the games had a clear and identifiable title. 24 game titles referred to the learning content 9 referred to the actions carried out by the player, and 4 to the game material. The generic game shell must instruct teachers to title their game according to one of these three aspects. This helps guide the teacher when choosing an educational game.
3. All games studied were single-station games, whether played as a team or alone. The generic game shell must offer this condition in order to ensure the broadest possible distribution in schools of the games eventually developed using the shell.
4. All the games had a predetermined objective to win, whether the game was won by accumulating the most points (in 32 games) or solving one or more mysteries (in eight games). Some games also gave rewards, for example giving a prize, or displaying the best results in an honor roll. The GEGS must have at least one of these rewards.
5. 25 games were played against the computer only, and 15 included a multiplayer option. The GEGS structure must allow a variable number of players and teams. Almost all the games (39) had clear and explicit rules which the players can read at any time. The framework must have clear, precise rules, and the GEGS must allow them to be accessible at any time during the game.
6. 35 of the games included an element of competition or conflict between players and only three involved cooperation. Five games did not include conflict or cooperation. To include the critical attributes of a game as defined in our research protocol, the frame game must include elements of competition and conflict between players and provide rules allowing cooperation between players or the selection of teams.
7. 30 games required only the use of a mouse. 27 did not require any motor skills to win, facilitating their use. The educational games built with the aid of the GEGS must not require high levels of motor skill in using the computer.
8. Only 13 games were available in both French and English. Their linguistic adaptation consisted of a translation of the textual elements without real cultural adaptation. Considering the context of experimentation of our study (in both official languages of Canada), it was important to pay particular attention to the GEGS's degree of linguistic adaptation, allowing both a visual and a textual adaptation.
9. Finally, none of analyzed games had mechanisms to support real-time communication among the players. To provide this, a search of web-based communication tools is needed.

Frame Game Requirements

Our examination of computerized educational games showed that the frame games most used are pathway games with tests, discovery games, and board games. The frame games that are most preferred by our target GEGS users, primary and secondary-school teachers, are the board games *Cranium®* and *Monopoly®*.

Since *Monopoly* is considered in general to be a simulation game (see Chapter 1) and we wanted to test an educational game, our choice was the game *Cranium.* Examining its structure, we noted that this game was a modification of the board game *Parcheesi.* Since the structure of this activity has all critical attributes of a game (players, competition, rules, winning / losing) and is easily adaptable to include learning goals, *Parcheesi* was chosen for the development of the new GEGS. Figure 1 gives a brief description of the original American version of the game.

CONCLUSION

The first stage in the process of creating a GEGS is to perform preliminary analyses to better understand one or several target user groups as well as their pedagogic and technical needs. These analyses can be supplemented with the help of expert teachers and educational computer game specialists. It is also helpful to examine existing digital educational games to identify their characteristics and technical features.

Figure 1. Original American structure of the game Parcheesi

Purpose of the game: be the first player to arrive with all four pawns into the final zone.

Number of players: 2 to 4

Length of game: 30 to 45 minutes

Game play:

1. Four pawns are then automatically placed into each team's personal space.
2. To get to the starting square of your personal square, a player must roll a six. A player that rolls a 6 is rewarded by another roll of the die.
3. The pawn advances along the arm of the cross in a clockwise fashion (in a counter clockwise fashion for the Indian version). A pawn that stops on a square already occupied by a pawn from another player forces that player to remove his pawn and place it back in his personal space. The pawn that was removed can only be placed back in the game if the player rolls a six at his turn in the game.
4. A pawn can only enter the end zone of the game by an exact die result. For example, if a pawn is five squares away from the end zone and the player rolls a six, the player must wait for his next turn to try and roll a five. But since the player rolled a 6, the player can move any other pawn or he can also liberate one pawn from the personal space.
5. Different throws of the die can be made to move different pawns. A throw of the die cannot be split in two; for example, a result of 6 cannot be separated to move one pawn forward 4 squares and another pawn moved forward by 2 squares.
6. A pawn that enters the end zone is removed from the board. The first player to remove all his pawns wins the game.

Our project carried out an analysis of 40 educational games, together with focus groups of experts and members of the new game shell's target user population. Synthesizing the information collected provided the criteria for the choice *Parcheesi* to serve as the basis for a new generic educational game shell. However, it is clear that the structure and content of this frame game requires adaptation to meet the pedagogic and technical requirements of our research and our target users. These modifications are reviewed in the following chapters.

ACKNOWLEDGMENT

We would like to thank Sylvie Rail, Gilles Simard, and Mathieu Gauvin for their work on the game analysis.

REFERENCES

Bloom, B. S. (1956) *Taxonomy of educational objectives: The classification of educational goals. Handbook 1: Cognitive domain.* New York: David McKay Company Inc.

Brien, R. (1981). *Design pédagogique* [Pedagogic design]. Ste-Foy, QC, Canada: Les Éditions St-Yves.

Desgagné, S. (1997). Le concept de recherche collaborative: idée d'un rapprochement entre chercheurs universitaires et practiciens enseignants [The concept of collaborative research: The idea of a rapprochement between university researchers and practicing teachers]. *Revue des Sciences de l'Education, 23*(2), 371–394.

Dick, W., & Carey, L. (1996). *The systematic design of instruction* (4th edition). New York: Harper Collins College Publishers.

Foch'lay, B. (1997, July). *L'évaluation participative: une mise en œuvre du modèle de rationalité procédurale au service de la modernisation de l'action publique* [Participative evaluation: A process modelled on procedural rationality in the service of modernizing public action]. Paper presented at the conference of the Society for the Advancement of Socioeconomics (SASE), Montréal.

Grafinger, D. J. (1988). *Basics of instructional systems development.* INFO_LINE Issue 8803. Alexandria, VA: American Society for Training and Development.

Hourst, B., & Thiagarajan, S. (2007). *Les modèles de jeux en formation* [Game models for training] (3rd ed.). Paris: Éditions d'Organisation.

Lincoln, Y. S., & Guba, E. G. (1985). *Naturalistic inquiry.* Beverly Hills, CA: Sage Publications.

Marton, P. (1994). *La conception pédagogique de systèmes d'apprentissage multimédia interactif: fondements, méthodologie et problématique* [The pedagogic design of interactive multimedia learning systems: Fundamentals, methodology, and problems]. *Educatechnologiques, 1* (3). Available at http://www.sites.fse.ulaval.ca/reveduc/html/vol1/no3/concept.html

Mayer, R., Ouellet, F., Saint-Jacques, M.-C., & Turcotte, D. (Eds.). (2000). *Méthodes de recherche en intervention sociale.* Boucherville, QC, Canada: Gaëtan Morin.

McGriff, S. J. (2000). *Instructional system design (ISD): Using the ADDIE model.* Retrieved May 26, 2009 from http://ehopac.org/Transformation-Reports/ISD-ADDIEmodel.pdf

Miles, M. B., &t Huberman, M. A. (2003). *Analyse des données qualitatives* [Analysis of quantitative data] (2nd ed.). Paris: Deboeck.

Nadeau, M. A. (1981) *L'évaluation des programmes d'études* [Evaluation of study programs]. Québec, QC, Canada: Presses de l'Université Laval.

Renaud, L., & Sauvé, L. (1990). *Simulation et jeu de simulation: outils éducatifs appliqués à la santé* [Simulation and simulation games: Educational tools applied to health]. Montreal, QC, Canada: Éditions Agence d'Arc Inc.

Sauvé, L. (2002, May). *Jeux-cadres en ligne: un outil d'aide pour le concepteur d'environnement d'apprentissage* [Frame games online: A tool to help the learning environment designer]. Paper presented at Nouveau centenaire - nouveaux modèles: Colloque de l'ACDE/ICDE.

Sauvé, L. (2005). *La grille d'analyse de base des jeux numériques éducatifs* [Analysis grid for digital educational games] (Research report). Québec, QC, Canada: SAGE and SAVIE.

Sauvé, L., & Chamberland, G. (2006). TEC 1280: *Jeux, simulations, jeux de simulation et jeux de rôle: exploration et analyse pédagogique* [Games, simulations, simulation games, and role-playing games: Exploration and pedagogical analysis Course notes, revised 2006 from original version 2003. Québec, QC, Canada: Télé-université.

Sauvé, L., Renaud, L., Kaufman, D., & Marquis, J.-S. (2007). Distinguishing between games and simulations: A systematic review of the literature. *Journal of Educational Technology & Society, 10*(3), 244–256.

Sauvé, L., Renaud, L., Kaufman, D., Samson, D., Doré-Bluteau, V., Bourbonnière, J., et al. (2005b). *Revue systématique des écrits (1998-2004) sur les fondements conceptuels du jeu, de la simulation et du jeu de simulation* [Systematic review of the literature (1998-2004) on the conceptual foundations of games, simulations, and simulation games] (Interim Research Report I). Québec: SAGE and SAVIE.

Sauvé, L., Renaud, L., & Kazsap, M. IsaBelle, C., Gauvin, M., Simard, G. et al.(2005a). *Analyse de 40 jeux éducatifs (en ligne et cédérom)* [Analysis of 40 educational games (online and CD-ROM] (Research Report). Québec, QC, Canada: SAGE and SAVIE.

Stolovitch, H. D., & Thiagarajan, S. (1980). *Frame games*. Englewood Cliffs, NJ: Educational Technology Publications.

ADDITIONAL READING

Sauvé, L., Renaud, L., & Kazsap, M. IsaBelle, C., Gauvin, M., Simard, G., et al. (2005a). *Analyse de 40 jeux éducatifs (en ligne et cédérom)* [Analysis of 40 educational games (online and CD-ROM] (Research Report). Québec, QC, Canada: SAGE and SAVIE.

KEY TERMS AND DEFINITIONS

Content: The information conveyed in the game. In a pedagogical game, "content" also refers to the objectives being pursued, and the abilities that will be developed by playing the game.

Educational Game: A fictitious, fantasy or imaginary situation in which players, placed in conflict with others, or assembled in a team against an external opponent, are governed by rules determining their actions with a view to achieving learning objectives and a goal determined by the game, either to win or to seek revenge.

Frame Game: A digital game structure that generates learning activities, supports diverse strategies, and imposes rules and criteria that end the game by declaring a winner.

Generic Educational Game Shell (GEGS): An online environment that allows teachers and trainers to create games by providing the tools needed to set the game parameters, direct player actions, create pedagogical content, and determine the game winner. The tools required for revision and evaluation ensure that the game can be updated regularly.

Structure: Determines how the game is played. The game is "emptied" of its contents so that its unique structure can be laid bare. This structure, once clearly defined and analyzed, becomes a "frame," or for the purposes of our research, a generic game shell.

APPENDIX A

Game Analysis Variables and Definitions

Variable	Definition/Instructions
Information About the Game	**This section contains information on the game analyzed.**
Name of the game	Indicate the name of the game
Author(s) / designer(s)	Indicate the family name and the first name of all the game's authors and creators. If there are many authors or creators, identify the main creator or head creator by name.
Year	Indicate the game's year of production or its last update.
Producer	Indicate the name of the game producer (the editor or producer), address, telephone number and Web address.
Complete reference	Indicate a thorough game reference which conforms with APA standards.
Support	Indicate the tool which supports the game, e.g., Internet, intranet, CD-ROM
Web address	Indicate the game's URL. If the game has no Internet address and you have to refer to the home page which hosts the game, specify the steps necessary for finding the game.
Purchase and cost	Indicate whether the game is free or has a cost (for use or for purchase), the location where this game can be purchased (provider) if different from the producer, the mailing address, the Web address, or telephone number.
ISBN or ISSN	Indicate whether there are author's rights attached to this game or specify any references to author's rights, for example, the © (copyright) of the author's rights.
Language(s)	Indicate the languages in which the game is offered.
Min. system requirements	Indicate, if possible, the game's ideal platform, the type of computer, virtual memory and disk space, graphics card, and sound card required.
Game Description	**This section describes the game analyzed.**
Game framework	Indicate whether the game reminds you of another game. For example: *Tic-Tac-Toe, Mother Goose, Memory, Monopoly, Snakes and Ladders, Bingo, Dominos*, common card games (*Crazy Eights, Dame de cœur,* etc.), *Milles bornes, Parcheesi, Chinese Checkers, Backgammon, La course des grenouille (Frogger)*. There may be game chains which include different frameworks played consecutively. The results from the first game are imported into the next ones. If there is no recognizable framework, leave this field blank.
Predetermined goal	All games have an end (determined by the rules), have a winner or winners and often a loser or losers. The will to win determines player choices during the game. Indicate whether the aim is to win by point accumulation, by defeating opponents, obtaining a reward (a prize), by luck, or by completing a challenge. For example, the winner is determined by the highest score.
Length	Indicate the game duration in light of the level(s) of difficulty offered by the game. The duration is often determined by the designer or the research assistant during the course of her/his game.
Learning objectives targeted	Indicate the educational objectives included in the game. For example, the cognitive aspect: to know, understand, analyze, apply, synthesize, transfer. The affective aspects: raise awareness, feelings of self-worth, etc. The motor skills involved: new habits and behaviors, motor skills acquisition, etc.
Target population	Indicate all the populations who can play the game using the following categories: Age, sex, language, education level, etc.
Possible context for use	Indicate the context in which the game can be used: training teacher candidates, training students (primary and secondary), training community workers or clients of community workers.
Environment	Indicate the environments specified by the author: community environment, family environment, school environment, hospital environment. If the author does not specify an environment, indicate that this field was your interpretation.
Game contents	Indicate the game's contents. For example, a game on smoking tobacco: health risks, second hand smoke, impact of smoking on the school environment, etc.
Difficulty levels available	Indicate if the game offers different levels of learning: Beginner, Intermediate, Expert.

Function of the game	Indicate the function(s) of the game: raising awareness, motivational, learning of a concept, revisional, evaluative, etc.
Materials	Indicate the game materials in the following manner: number of dice, number of tokens, description of cards and game board, chance cards, characters, avatars, etc.
Players and numbers	Indicate if the game involves one person or a group of people. The number of players is usually limited or variable within given limitations. Do you play alone, with others, or against others?
Use of a single station or multiple stations	Indicate if all the players use the same station or if each uses a different station (multi-player).
Rules	Indicate the number of rules and the contents of the main rules as well as the point at which the rules are presented: before the game, during the game or after a level has been completed. Rules are defined as a combination of instructions, simple or complex, describing the relation between players and the game environment. The rules specify the nature and limitations to the actions a player can commit and they also define a structure for the players to play the game.
Conflict (battle, confrontation, cooperation)	Indicate whether the game includes cooperation, confrontation, battle, challenges or threats that motivate the player to fill her/his role in the game and to make game decisions.
How the game was adapted from the framework	Indicate the game elements that distinguish it from the original framework: new elements, missing elements.
Game Evaluation	**This section contains the evaluation of the game analyzed.**
Difficulties encountered during use by the assistant	Indicate all the problems encountered during the game installation process, or while accessing the game, or while playing the game, etc.
Evaluation questionnaire	Include the questionnaire (taken from the web site, CD-ROM or intranet) used for the evaluation of the game in the appendix.
Evaluation by the trainers	Indicate if the game has been evaluated by a trainer on the web site. Note the comments made by the trainers on the pedagogical and technical problems. Note also whether the comments are positive or negative (with the total number of evaluators if possible). Note if there is a formal evaluation (use of a questionnaire) or an informal one (chat or open-ended answers).
Evaluation by the learners	Indicate whether the game was evaluated on the web site by learners. Note any comments made by learners on pedagogical or technical issues encountered. Note also whether the majority of the users left comments that were positive or negative (if this information is accessible). Note also whether there has been a formal evaluation (using a questionnaire) or an informal evaluation (chat or open ended answers).
What you most enjoyed	Indicate the principal elements in the game that motivated you and interested you. What made the game interesting and what surprised you? If you have nothing to say for this field leave it blank.
Technological aspects	**This section concerns the technological aspects analyzed in the games.**
Ergonomics	Indicate whether the game causes visual strain, poses potential health risks such as tendinitis.
User-friendliness	Indicate the game's ease of navigation, the content's pedagogical readability, ease of installation.
Presentation	Indicate the game's visual and textual quality as well as uniformity, etc.
Feedback	Indicate whether the game offers feedback corresponding to player actions, right or wrong answers linked to learning, etc.
Other	Indicate all other comments concerning the game's technological aspects that you could not fit into previous categories.
Comments	**This section contains comments on the analyzed game.**
Comments	Indicate the difficulties faced during the game analysis.
To do	Indicate whether the author used a game creation system or a tool which was used to create the game, for example *Explorer* or *Klik & Play*. Indicate whether there are other games to evaluate on the site. Indicate whether there is a new version of the game on its way. Send the author an email to obtain additional information.

Appendix B

Games by ID Number and Source

1 Cizaire, P. (2001). *Océan*. Retrieved February 18, 2005 from http://www.jeuxeducatifs.fr.st.
2 Lange, J.-P. (no date). *Trésors de la Martinique*. Retrieved February 21, 2005 from http://www.tresor-martinique.com.
3 Cizaire, P. (2003). *Défi +*. Retrieved February 21, 2005 from www.jeuxeducatifs.fr.st.
4 Kprobe Inc. (2004). *FreeWord Rotation*. Retrieved February 25, 2005 from http://www.kprobe.com/kprobe/index.htm.
5 Riben, P. (1999). *HappyNote!* Retrieved February 25, 2005 from www.happynote.com.
6 GameHouse. (no date). *WordSlinger*. Retrieved March 3, 2005 from http://www.gamehouse.com.
7 Soft One Inc. (2001). *MatchIt! Math*. Retrieved March 1, 2005 from http://store.yahoo.com/softoneonline.
8 Fortrye, H. (2004). *GéoJeu2004*. Retrieved March 3, 2005 from http://geojeu2004.chez-alice.fr/.
9 Conseil québécois sur le tabac et la santé (2003). *Clop attaque*. Retrieved February 17, 2005 from http://www.multimage.qc.ca/clop/
10 Julien, C. (2004). *2K40*. Retrieved April 4, 2005 from http://www.2k40.com/index_en.htm
11 Internence (no date). *Sur la piste des dangers*. Retrieved March 23, 2005 from http://www.castokids.com.
12 Les jeux de Lulu (1999-2005). *Comment est-ce rangé?* Retrieved March 4, 2005 from http://perso.wanadoo.fr/jeux.lulu.
13 Les jeux de Lulu. (1999-2005). *Quelques mots*. Retrieved March 4, 2005 from http://perso.wanadoo.fr/jeux.lulu.
14 Les jeux de Lulu. (1999-2005). *Les jetons*. Retrieved March 4, 2005 from http://perso.wanadoo.fr/jeux.lulu.
15 Roustan, I. (no date). *Les aventures de Globe Trotteur*. Retrieved March 9, 2005 from http://www.ia05.ac-aix-marseille.fr/ecoles/globe/.
16 L'institut Pasteur in collaboration with Procter & Gamble (no date). *Le jeu des Netoons et des Buurkis*. Retrieved March 14, 2005 from http://www.hygiene-educ.com.
17 CREO Inc. (2004). *L'étrange disparition du professeur scientifix*. Retrieved March 15, 2005 from http://debrouillards.creo.ca/.
18 Landry, I. (1996). *L'escalade du mont humain*. Retrieved March 15, 2005 from http://www.lescale.net.
19 Clepsydre Communication (no date). *Les motivés*. Retrieved March 22, 2005 from http://www.motives.be.
20 PopCap Games (2003). *Typer shark*. Retrieved March 21, 2005 from www.popcap.com.
21 RU Thinking (no date). *In yer pants*. Retrieved March 29, 2005 from http://www.bbc.co.uk/radio1/onelife/fun/health/pants/pantman.html.
22 L'école d'Hénouville. (no date). *Turbo mots*. Retrieved March 29, 2005 from http://ecoles.henouville.org/flash/index.php3.
23 FunSchool. (2001). *Bon appétit*. Retrieved March 9, 2005 from http://www.funschool.com.
24 KnowledgeProbe Inc. (2004). *ScholarCards*. Retrieved March 4, 2005 from www.kprobe.com.

25 Devaux, M. (2003). *20/20 en calcul*. Retrieved March 31, 2005 from la didactèque de l'Université Laval.

26 Novelli, B. (2000). *CosmoLogique*. Retrieved March 31, 2005 from la didactèque de l'Université Laval.

27 Vincent, R., Hausen, U., & Aubry, M. (2001). *Mia. Juste à temps!*. CD-ROM. Retrieved April 1, 2005 from la didactèque de l'Université Laval.

28 Macouin, C., Deminier, J.-Y., & Dousset, M. (1999). *Envol Mathématique*. CD-ROM. Retrieved April 1, 2005 from la didactèque de l'Université Laval.

29 Everson, B. (1999). *Mais où se cache Carmen Sandiego*? Version 2. CD-ROM. Retrieved April 2, 2005 from la didacthèque de l'Université Laval.

30 Riverdeep Inc. (no date). *MindTwister Math*. Retrieved April 4, 2005 from www.learningco.com.

31 Studio Animation et Jeunesse, Programme Français, Office National du Film du Canada (2001). *Savotron*. Retrieved April 1, 2005 from http://onfjeunesse.ca/jeunesse/.

32 Studio Animation et Jeunesse, Programme Français, Office National du Film du Canada. (2001). *Mission "3,2,1... Feu! Le jeu"*. Retrieved April 1, 2005 from http://onfjeunesse.ca/jeunesse/.

33 Commission européenne (Union européenne) (2004). *EuropaGO-Jeu de mémoire*. Retrieved April 5, 2005 from http://europa.eu.int/europago/.

34 Commission européenne (Union européenne) (2004). *EuropaGO-Puzzle de l'Europe*. Retrieved April 11, 2005 from http://europa.eu.int/europago/.

35 Sarbakan.(2004). *Rallye X 5*. Retrieved April 11, 2005 from www.telequebec.qc.ca/jeunesse/.

36 Centre des sciences de Montréal - Lâchez prise (Hydro-Québec) (no date). *Lâchez prise*. Retrieved April 5, 2005 from http://www.centredessciencesdemontreal.com/.

37 Fortin, C., & Podesto, M. (2001). *Mango dans l'espace*. Retrieved April 1, 2005 from la didacthèque de l'Université Laval.

38 Moiley, J., Macdonald, F., & Salarieja, D. (1998). *103 Découvertes*. Retrieved April 1, 2005 from la dicdacthèque de l'Université Laval.

39 National Dairy Council (2002). *Feed the monster*. Retrieved April 18, 2005 from http://www.nutritionexplorations.org.

40 Sarbakan (2002). *Deviens Sécuri-prêt*. Retrieved April 18, 2005 from www.msp.gouv.qc.ca/jeunesse/.

Chapter 23
Designing a Generic Educational Game Shell

Louise Sauvé
Télé-université, Canada

ABSTRACT

This chapter describes the design phase of the creation of a generic educational game shell (GEGS) for the frame game Parcheesi™. The frame game structure was adapted through modifications to the game board, materials, and game scenario, and navigation aids were added to guide players. Learning content was integrated into the game, and pedagogical aspects of the game (i.e., objectives, target learners, school learning material) were specified. Mechanisms were added to create various question types and to provide for feedback, debriefing, and game evaluation. Finally, these modifications and additions were summarized into a design plan for the technical/ media development team. Screen and form layouts were used to communicate the plan in non-technical terms for feedback and to further guide the developers. Finally, the Web pages of the GEGS were designed in the form of a model. The chapter closes with suggestions for avoiding common errors in the design of online educational games.

INTRODUCTION

Designing a generic educational game shell (GEGS) based on a frame game involves first defining the elements of the game structure that are to be supported, added or modified, and describing the mechanisms for inserting learning content into the game. Subsequently, a design prototype showing screen and form layouts is posted online to show how game builders will use the GEGS to create educational games. This becomes the basic reference for the developers of GEGS interface and media elements. Finally, elaboration of the models of the principal components of the GEGS are worked out and validated by the design team.

In this chapter, we illustrate stages in the design of the *Parcheesi*™GEGS (Sauvé, 2006; Sauvé et al., 2006). We first explain our adaptations of the frame game board, accessories, scenario (gameplay), rules, and instructions. We then describe our changes to

DOI: 10.4018/978-1-61520-731-2.ch023

Figure 1. (a) The original Parcheesi game board;(b) Adapted Parcheesi board.

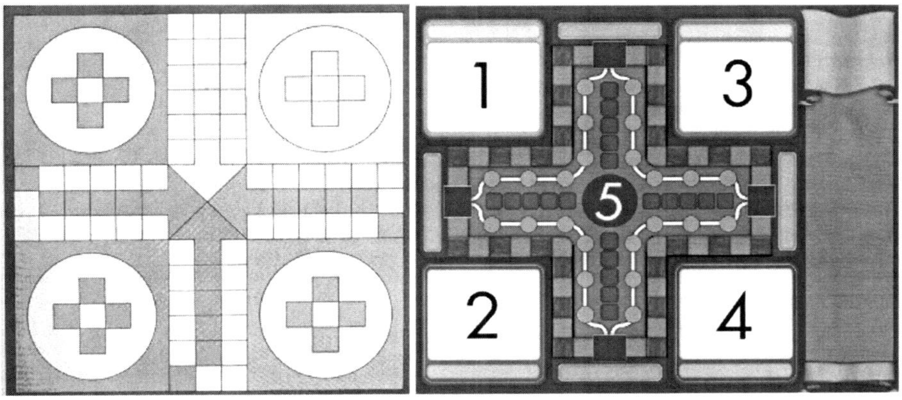

Figure 2. Parcheesi game tokens

the frame game content, including its description, learning questions, and pedagogic features. In the third part of the chapter, we describe two evaluation mechanisms that were missing in the original frame game but were included in the GEGS in response to feedback and evaluation of the game by its users. In the fourth part of the chapter, we show an example of the design prototype based on GEGS screens. Finally, we note errors to be avoided when a frame game is adapted to become an online GEGS.

ADAPTING THE STRUCTURE OF A FRAME GAME

In creating a GEGS, the structure of a frame game must generally be altered to include pedagogic and technical aspects while taking into account the requirements of its target users. We now examine the steps in adapting a game frame, accessories, and scenario (gameplay), including its rules and instructions.

The Game Board

Generally, the game board is not modified when it is reproduced in GEGS. The number of paths in the initial itinerary of a player's position marker ("token") should be maintained to sustain interest in the game, which was the case for our GEGS: 56 squares in the regular path (Figure 1a) were maintained on the GEGS board. However, to meet our pedagogical requirements, we added a second fast track to the original board, while maintaining the original number of squares and the square board shape. The second track allows a player's token to reach the center of the board with half as many squares as in the original track (Figure 1b). We also replaced the pluses in the four corners with slots for photos or images to illustrate learning content.

Game Accessories

Parcheesi accessories include dice, tokens, needles or spinners, playing cards – all objects which can potentially be manipulated and changed. For a GEGS, all additions of new elements must be

Table 1.

Event 1: Interaction with materials
Action: Each player places four tokens of the same color in her personal space, located in each corner of the game board. *Reaction:* The four tokens must leave the start square, the player-selected personal space. *Consequences:* No player can leave from another player's personal space and start square.
Event 4: Relations among players
Action: A token stops on a square already occupied by an adversary's token. *Reaction:* The token already present on the square is removed and placed once again in the player's personal space. *Consequences:* Once the token has been removed, it cannot come back into the game unless the player rolls a six on the dice. This reduces her chances of reaching the end of the track first, and consequently her chances of winning.

explained and rules to regulate them added to the game. In the *Parcheesi* GEGS, the number of tokens per player or team (4) was maintained although we added the ability to change their appearance (Figure 2).

In our adaptation, players click (roll) two dice rather than just one. We added the second die to speed up token movement.

Although the original game did not have cards, we added game cards containing closed or open questions that must be correctly answered for a player to move a token or receive rewards or setbacks. Three types of cards were added to introduce learning content and the element of luck:

- *Learning cards*, which have thirteen different types of questions to integrate simple and complex learning content.
- *Team cards* to stimulate competition among players while they are displayed. The first player to respond correctly to the learning activity displayed on a card wins additional points.
- *Good luck/bad luck cards,* which introduce an element of luck and add suspense by increasing the uncertainty of a player's chances of winning.

These cards support learning objectives and help maintain motivation. These additions also affected the game rules and instructions, as explained below.

The Game Scenario

During gameplay, players must react to different events according to precise instructions or rules (Dickey, 2005). By game events, we mean player actions and reactions to situations in the game, as well as the resulting consequences; in other words, it is necessary to determine within the game's framework, who does what, when do they do it, and how. The combination of events creates the game scenario (Sauvé & Chamberland, 2006).

Frame Game Events

To create a GEGS, we must specify all possible events within the game's framework. Determining these events is done using the game's rules and instructions as given in the game manual. For each of the events, the action and reaction of the players towards other players, to materials and rules which guide them, are isolated and the consequences are identified. The original American version of the *Parcheesi* game, the basis for our modifications, included nine events. Two examples are shown here: one shows the game materials, and the other illustrates management of player actions (see Table 1)

Of the nine events in the original *Parcheesi,* three were kept, two eliminated, and four modified, as shown in Appendix A (left column).

Adding Events to Support the Generic Shell's Objectives

Once the events have been recorded, the designer must consider whether it is necessary to add elements or make modifications to existing events in reaction to the number of players, game materials, and to learning objectives they wish to attain in the game framework. Guiding questions to do this include:

In what situation does the player(s) interact with the materials in the game framework? Is it the same for the Parcheesi shell?

For each situation, the designer must describe the player action that begins the event, the reaction, and the consequences for the game's progress.

In our example, Event 2 in the original game specifies that the player must roll a die and can retry if she gets a six. In the generic shell, it was decided that the player must click on the two dice to accelerate the rate at which tokens move along the tracks towards completion of the game and to remove the reward for obtaining a six.. The addition of a second die does not change the movement of tokens, but it does alter the consequences linked to the number six. This change involves a modification to the consequences of Event 2 in the GEGS. (See Table 2)

What are the choices offered to a player? What type of interaction is created when a player encounters another player (conflict or cooperation)? With which resources and equipment does the player interact? When? What is the reaction (action or decision) of another player to the action or decision made? With which resources and equipment does the second player interact? When? What are the consequences of the reaction of other players for the environment, resources and equipment?

In each situation, the player must chose from a certain number of options relating to the action or decision which she will make. This decision, made when presented with a situation, can determine which player plays next and the options this player will have available during her turn. These choices, made by a player (strategy) can be known or unknown to other players. In chess, all the choices are known, while in card games, luck is a factor and masks the choices of other players.

In our example, Event 8 in the original game does not require any questions to advance a token. Introduction of learning content into the game framework involves a modification of Event 9 in the GEGS for aspects such as the reaction of players and the resulting consequences. (See Table 3)

What Are the Rules Governing Each Situation?

The GEGS must take into account control and procedural rules that govern situations, as well as the rewards or punishments to be given for ac-

Table 2.

Event 2 in the original version: Interaction with materials	**Event 2 in the GEGS: Interaction with materials**
Action: The player rolls the die to obtain a six. **Reaction**: If the player gets a six, she advances her token to the Start square. **Consequences**: The player rolling a six is awarded a second roll, which increases her chances of reaching the end of the track and winning the game.	**Action**: The player clicks the two dice to roll them and to obtain a double (1-1, 2-2, 3-3, 4-4, 5-5, 6-6). **Reaction**: The player obtains a double; she moves one of her four tokens to the Start square. **Consequences**: If the player has no token already on the Start square, her chances of winning are increased. If one of her tokens is already on the Start square, she reduces her chances of winning, since a player can not have two tokens in the same square.

Table 3.

Event 8 in the original version: Interaction with materials	**Event 9 of the GEGS change: Interaction with materials**
Action: A player obtains a number that is higher than the number needed to reach the center of the board; for example, a token is five squares from the finish, and the player rolls a six. **Reaction**: The player has two options: (1) she must wait for the following turn to advance a token; (2) she can advance one of the other tokens she has in play, one of the tokens freed from the personal space. **Consequences**: Choosing the first option will reduce her chances of reaching the finish first, and therefore of winning the game.	**Action**: The player obtains a number higher than the number of squares left before reaching the finish at the center of the board. **Reaction:** The player has two options: (1) she succeeds in the learning activity, or (2) she does not succeed. **Consequences:** If the player succeeds in the activity, there are two possible consequences: (1) if the player has no more than one token in play, she wins points and moves her token back and forth on the central path according to the number obtained by the dice roll; (2) if she has more than one token in play, she wins points and moves another token along the track and therefore increases her chances of winning the game. If she does not succeed in the activity, she does not win any points, her token stays in the same square and she waits for the next turn to succeed in a learning activity.

Table 4.

Original *Parcheesi*	*Parcheesi* **GEGS**
Rule 5. A token can only enter the final zone by rolling the exact number needed. For example, if a token is five squares from the finish and the player rolls a six, the player must wait until the next turn to move this token. The player may however move another token if she currently has one active (freed from the personal space).	**Rule 10.** A token can land in the center of the board only if the exact number of squares between it and the finish is the number obtained in the roll. The center counts as one square. Once the token has arrived in the center, the token is taken off the board and that team is awarded 200 points.
	Rule 11. When a team has rolled the dice and obtained a number greater than the number of squares between a token and the final square, there are three options: • Leave the token where it is until the exact number needed is obtained, and click another token to move it along the track according to the number obtained. • Move the token ahead to the center and then back the remaining number of squares according to the number obtained in the roll. For example: if a player's token is two squares from the center and the team rolls a five, this token moves forward three squares, and then back two. • The token that moves back along the central track cannot go back further than the first square of the central track. If the token lands on this square while moving backwards and is still required to move further, it begins to move back to towards the center of the board again.

tions performed. (Appendix A shows the original *Parcheesi* rules.)

In our example, GEGS Event 9 results in a modification of Rule 6 of the original version of the *Parcheesi* game (now Rule 10), and the addition of one new rule (Rule 11) (see Table 4)

What Is the Frequency of a Situation During Gameplay?

In any game, situations repeat. This repetition can be predetermined or can be a matter of chance. It can also be determined by a player's movements, or take place only once. Procedural rules are used to control repeating situations.

In our example, Event 4 stays the same in the game shell. It occurs as many times as the four players roll the dice and land on the same square as another player as shown in Event 7. In the GEGS, if the Start square is already occupied by a token, this token is sent back to the personal space. This is a modification from the original version of the game. (See Table 5)

Adjusting the Scenario

Once the players' movements have been revised, the designer must adjust the shell's scenario, asking "How are these events connected? Do they differ from the original version? In order to facilitate the scenario creation process, here are some questions to ask to revise event connections:

Table 5.

Event 4 of the original version: Relations among players	**Event 7 of the GEGS: Relations among players**
Action: A token lands on a square already occupied by an adversary. **Reaction:** The token which was already on the square is removed and sent back to the player's personal space. **Consequences:** The token that was sent back cannot come back into play until the player rolls a six. This reduces her chances of reaching the end of the track and winning the game.	**Action**: A player's token lands in a square already occupied by another player's token. **Reaction:** The token which was already on the square is sent back to the Start square. **Consequences:** If the Start square is already occupied by a token, that token is sent back the personal space, reducing this player's chances of winning the game.

Table 6.

Original *Parcheesi*	*Parcheesi* **GEGS**
	Event 1. Interaction with the system and materials **Action:** Every player clicks on the dice in turn. **Reaction:** Every player obtains a number between one and six. **Consequences:** The player who obtains the highest number begins the game and increases her chances of winning the game.
Event 2: Interaction with materials **Action:** The player rolls the dice to obtain a six. **Reaction:** If the player obtains a 6, she moves her token to the Start square in the personal space. **Consequences:** Once the player has obtained a six, she is rewarded with a second roll of the die. This increases her chances of reaching the end first, and winning the game.	**Event 2: Interaction with materials** **Action**: The player clicks the two dice in turn to obtain a double (1-1, 2-2, 3-3, 4-4, 5-5, or 6-6). **Reaction:** The player obtains a double and advances one of the four tokens to the Start square. **Consequences:** If the player does not have a token in the Start square, her chances of winning are increased. If one of her tokens are already on the Start square, the player's chances of winning are reduced because a player cannot have two tokens on the same square.

Is the event which begins the original game the same in the game shell? Is the choice predetermined (a question for the facilitator) or chosen at random (e.g., with dice, cards, or rotation of a spinner needle)?

The events are similar in the original version and in the GEGS. Luck determines whether a token is moved to the Start square, because the player first has to roll a six or a double. It is not necessary in the original game to specify who begins the game, because rolling a six determines it. In the GEGS, the system begins the game by identifying the player who will be the first to roll the dice. This task, completed by the computer, integrates an additional event into the game to begin, as displayed in Event 1. (See Table 6)

Is the sequence of events the same in the game frame as in the generic game shell? Have new events been added? Do the new events follow the same order (linear or predetermined, according to players' strategies, etc.,) as in the game frame?

Most of the time, learning content is added in the form of cards or accessories needed for new events. Here, nine new events were integrated into the GEGS to take into account the modifications made to the game materials and contents (see Appendix A).

Does the GEGS generic game shell end in the same way and at the same time as the original game?

Generally, the frame game describes how the rules play out among players, how the winner or loser is determined and how players score points

Table 7.

Original *Parcheesi*	*Parcheesi* **GEGS**
Event 9: Interaction with materials and other players *Action:* The first player to get all her tokens into the final square on the game board. *Reaction:* She removes the last token from the final square in the game. *Consequences:* She wins the game.	**Event 15 - Interaction with game materials** *Action:* One of the players removes her fourth token from the board. *Reaction:* The game ends. *Consequences:* The player with the highest score wins the game.
	Event 16 - Interaction with game materials *Action:* The allotted time runs out. *Reaction:* The game ends. *Consequences:* The player with the highest score wins.

and the payoff: e.g., winning money, honors, and distinctions. In our example, the addition of a new ending to that already envisaged in original game (Event 9) was necessary to integrate the educational content for which GEGS was developed. A choice of game ending allows players to respect the class timetable or the time allocated by the teacher for the game. This addition required Event 16 (see Table 7)

Once any new endings have been identified and the relationship among the different events has been examined and revised, the scenario must be reviewed to include rules and instructions (see the following points), provide an overview of information presented to and by participants, their options, etc. Also, the amount of time required to play the game must be determined. Table 8 illustrates the changes we made to the information presented to the players.

Rules

The frame game is structured by rules that are essential for managing the player actions and the game process. These rules usually refer to the equipment needed, rules of behaviour, and

Table 8. Changes made to the information provided to players

Original *Parcheesi*	*Parcheesi* **GEGS**
The goal: Be the first player to get all her tokens to the final square.	**Goal of the game**: There are two ways to win the game: • Be The first player or the first team to get all four tokens into the central square in the the game and to succeed in the final challenge wins. • Be The player or team with the highest score at the end of play wins.
Game materials **The game board** is made up of four personal spaces (one in each corner) and a 56 square cruciform game space with a game center. The personal space, the central column of the arms of the cross and the final zone of each player are all the same color. **Accessories:** Sixteen tokens are available for a maximum of four tokens per player and one die.	**Game materials** **The game board** is made up of a series of squares with two levels, consists of four zones, each referring to a different question. The two levels or tracks are made up of 56 steps for the regular track (squares) and 28 steps for the fast track (circles). On the board, each team has a personal space, a scorecard, and team identification. **Accessories:** Four sets of four tokens, different in color and appearance (for example, sets of four horses, four cats, four monkeys, and four dogs). Each token corresponds by color to a series of questions. For example, if a team has four dog-shaped tokens, one is red, one is green, one is blue and one is yellow). Four packs of cards or a set of questions to correspond with each color (at least eight learning activity cards, two *Team* cards and two *Chance* cards, for a total of 12 cards per pack), one chronometer, and a pair of dice.
Number of players: two to four.	**Number of players or teams:** Minimum: two players or two teams of two players. Maximum: four players or four teams of four players.
Duration of game: undetermined	**Game duration:** While players are in the process of creating teams, they can determine the exact duration of the game (30 or 45 minutes, for example). They can also decide not to set a time limit, and in this case the game will continue until one team has moved all its tokens into the center of the board and completed the final challenge.

scoring methods (Salen & Zimmerman, 2003). The rules must be known, accepted and adhered to by all players. During the creation of our game shell, certain rules were improved or added in order to respond to pedagogical needs. These rules are linked to new and adapted events in the GEGS definition.

In the *Parcheesi* GEGS, we added seven rules as shown in Appendix B (right column):

- *Procedural* rules describe the elements that comprise the game: the number of participants (players) or the number of teams (addition to Rule 1), the role of each participant, player activities, their available movements, how the game starts, how the players proceed through the game, the scoring, and the duration of the game. In our adaptation, we modified rules 5, 6, 9 and 10 and added rules 7, 8, 11, 12 and 13 to guide player actions during the learning activities and the movement of tokens between the regular track and the fast track.
- *Closing* rules explain how the winner is decided or how the game ends. Generally, the end of the game determines a winner; however, there are certain games where there is a possibility of a tie. In GEGS *Parcheesi*, the end of the game occurs once a player or a team reaches the end of a track. We added a second way to end the game in order to respect the allotted time (a class period) as shown in rules 2 and 14 of the adapted version.
- *Control* rules describe the consequences for a player who performs an action that does not respect the previously mentioned rules and instructions. In the *Parcheesi* shell, we did not set any control rules linked to the original structure, but we added token movement constraints to rules 5 through 7 while a team has not successfully completed the questions.

After revising the rules, the designer had to organize them as follows:

- Regroup the rules based on the game framework
- Simplify the rules by using short and concise phrases and simple language
- Place the rules in order according to how the game unfolds, sequence by sequence
- Number the rules
- Use the images to illustrate the rules when possible
- For each rule, create an example
- Have the revised rules read by experts and target users to verify their comprehensiveness

Instructions

In table games, unlike digital games, there is no distinction between rules and instructions. It is the players who carry out actions such as moving the tokens, identifying the player who will begin the game, and the next player to play. In a computerized game, the one goal of instructions, as distinguished from rules, is to help the player understand the constraints imposed by the game's mechanisms. For example, instructions show the name of the player who must click on the dice or complete a learning situation to obtain points. No other player can act until the identified player has completed her action. According to Millerand and Martial (2001), instructions function to make navigation easier in a site, allowing players to concentrate on game's content, rather than the navigation mechanisms involved.

In the *Parcheesi* GEGS, seventeen instructions were developed, to be displayed as the game progresses. For example:

- The game is starting. Please wait for all players (or teams) to be ready before beginning (network instructions).

- To determine the player (or team) who will begin the game, click the dice in turn. The player (or team) with the highest number begins the game.
- Your four tokens have been removed from the board. You must complete the following final learning activity to win the game.
- You did not complete the final activity successfully; wait for your next turn to try again.
- The game is now over. **[Player Name/ Team]** has won the game.

ADAPTATION AND SPECIFICATION OF *PARCHEESI* FRAME GAME CONTENT

Generally, the content of the game is completely modifiable. In the majority of social games, the content, aside from the numbers provided by the die or dice to advance a token, takes the form of a detailed game description and learning content. We now look at how these elements were introduced into the *Parcheesi* GEGS.

Game Description

To more easily locate and identify the content of educational games constructed from a GEGS, it is necessary that the shell describe each game in terms of both its presentation and its pedagogic aspects (learning objectives, audience, domain material covered, education level, etc.). In general, it is necessary to build an identification form into the GEGS to collect these parameters.

In the *Parcheesi* GEGS, the identification form includes the following items and instructions:

- **Game title:** Indicate the new game title, taking into account the subject, the material and the actions completed by players
- **Name of author(s):** Indicate the author(s) name(s), their position and, if applicable, the team who created the game
- **Goal of the game:** Indicate how the game will end and how to win. The goal is different from the learning objectives
- **Learning objectives:** Indicate the learning objectives that are promoted by your game to make it clear to the player what the function and contents of the game are. These objectives can be cognitive, affective, and motor-skill-based
- **Target audience:** Describe the target audience who will benefit from this game. Describe the main characteristics: age, cultural milieu, prior knowledge and competencies needed for this game. Certain games require prior knowledge, particularly complex games or games that aim to review subject matter
- **Game theme:** Describe the subject, the object or the foundational elements of the game in order to inform the players; for example, sexually transmitted infections are the theme for the game *STI's: Stop the Transmission*
- **Game subject:** Identify the domain of study for which the game was developed: for example, mathematics, languages, administration, health education, etc.
- **Level of studies:** Identify the level or levels of study for which the game was developed: from preschool to university, as well as community and continuing education.
- **Game materials:** Describe the game board and the different accessories necessary for the game (tokens, game cards, die, etc.)
- **Number of players:** Indicate the minimum and maximum number of players required by the game
- **Game duration:** Inform the player of the time required to play the game. The allotted time is an important constraint during scenario development, especially in the classroom context. The duration of the class and the proportion of time that is reasonable to spend on the objectives being sought are

Figure 3. Question form for the generic Parcheesi game shell.

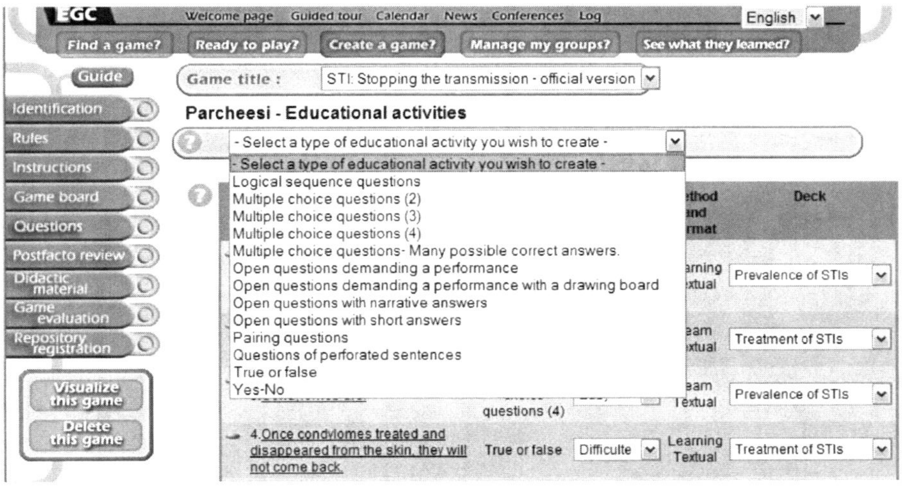

limitations that must be taken into account. Certain games are very precise in terms of time management, while others give players plenty of leeway in this aspect. The time factor must not, therefore, be underestimated because it is a fundamental element to the game's success, especially as it relates to player motivation.

Question Cards

To ensure that a game's learning content is made available to the target learners, mechanisms must be built to allow it to be entered. Learning content items are typically put on cards in the form of questions or units of text. To create these cards, the GEGS must offer predefined forms (Figure 3). In the case of the *Parcheesi* GEGS, content can be entered as closed questions (fill-in-the-blank, matching, multiple choice with one or more correct answers, logical sequencing, true or false, yes or no) and open-ended questions (short answer, long answer, answers requiring a physical action, answers requiring an action with a drawing board) as well as illustrated, audio or video scenarios and situations to analyze.

The thirteen types of questions include a correction mechanism and feedback associated with learning in real time. Some of these develop simple or complex knowledge (Dessaint, 1995; Prégent, 1990; True/false questions, multiple choice with one response, fill-in-the-blank, sentence completion are most effective for the development of knowledge and understanding. Short-answer questions and questions with several answer choices better support the application of knowledge. Finally, long-answer questions better support analysis, synthesis, and evaluation of knowledge. They also provoke reflection and work on behaviors and attitudes. Every question, open or closed, allows the insertion of video clips, images and sounds either in the question or in the answer(s) or feedback. Moreover, each question is displayed in the game with an iconic motivational message.

Throughout the game, it is strongly suggested that the designer include reviewable personal folders to collect game performance data for each player. This feature was integrated into the GEGS, as shown in Figure 4.

To meet the needs of teachers who want to insert learning materials into a game before or after gameplay, a form was included in the GEGS so that a game builder can upload learning content in visual, audio, or text format. The builder can also suggest web links in the school material included

Figure 4. Player results in the game STIs: Stopping the Transmission.

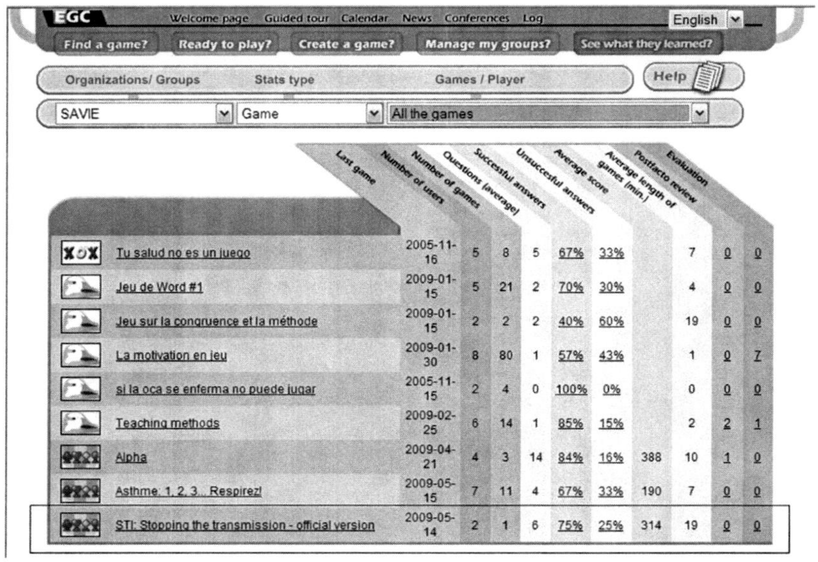

in a game. Instructions can be added to guide the student in reading, listening, or watching tasks.

FEEDBACK AND GAME EVALUATION

In light of the educational aims of games developed with the aid of a GEGS, it was important to create mechanisms to allow game builders to assess the efficacy and efficiency of their games. Therefore, a debriefing outline was included to facilitate peer evaluation at the end of a game session, and a game evaluation questionnaire outline was provided to help game builders specify their evaluation questions.

Debriefing

Game researchers point out that feedback, in the form of debriefing, is an important stage in using an educational game; it supports the integration of knowledge and the processing of feelings and attitudes developed during the game (Asakawa & Gilbert, 2003; Coco et al., 2001; Saliés, 2002; Vandeventer & While, 2002). Debriefing must be done immediately after gameplay. If done well, debriefing strengthens the process of knowledge structuring by giving the learner an opportunity to confront and validate his new knowledge. It is important that player or team performances are compared, and that players are invited to describe their strategies.

To ensure that debriefing takes place, it is necessary for the GEGS to include a form for defining a debriefing process. The designer can activate it if he wishes the players to give feedback about the game.To simplify the job of writing debriefing guidelines, the form offers questions with wording that can be adapted to the learning content of a game. In the GEGS, it is suggested that the game builder include at least fourteen questions grouped into four categories: catharsis, description, analysis, and generalization (Sauvé & Chamberland, 2006).

Catharsis

Catharsis, used mainly in role-playing games, is meant to release tension, strong emotions, perceptions, attitudes, and reactions of the participants towards their experience. During this step, participants freely express their feelings, reacting emotionally. No one should be forced to do this, but everyone must be given the opportunity. Some possible catharsis questions are:

- How did you feel when you lost?
- How did you feel when you won?
- Did you enjoy playing this game?

Description

This type of debriefing invites participants to describe their experiences during the game, including such elements as their initial perception of the game and their progress; the results obtained, the acquisition of knowledge and competencies, a factual, psychological, and symbolic description of what happened in the game, the problems they faced, and the relationship between cause and effect. Here are a few examples of descriptive questions:

- Can you give a report on the situation you just experienced?
- Were the resources or methods available to you sufficient?
- What impact did these resources or methods have on your results?
- Identify the reasons and reasoning that you used to win. Are you satisfied with them?
- What did you do or say when your opponent won?
- What did you do or say when you won?

Analysis

Analysis links the events of an educational game and completed learning, allowing conclusions to be drawn. Here are a few examples of analytical questions:

- What was the objective or the goal of the educational game?
- What was the best strategy/decision/action in the educational game?
- What factors explain your gains or losses in the game?

Generalization

The questions in this final category allow some general conclusions to be drawn from the experience, reveal players' reflections, and help them to better integrate their learning into their own contexts. Some generalization question examples are:

- What were the important elements that you have retained from the game?
- What did you learn about the subject matter being taught?

Finally, when debriefing is activated in a game, it is displayed when the players end the game. Players are invited to complete the debriefing in order to obtain their points. It is not necessary for all questions to be answered to complete the debriefing.

Evaluation of the Game

Although the games we originally analyzed did not have evaluation tools, it is important that each educational game developed using the GEGS be evaluated to verify that it meets the pedagogical and technological expectations of designers, and also to measure its effectiveness with the target audience. To evaluate games made with the *Parcheesi* GEGS, we developed a two-part questionnaire (Table 9). The first part includes questions on the structure of the game; these cannot be modified. The second part includes modifiable default questions about the game, its learning content, the target audience, motivation, and the learning in general.

Table 9. The game evaluation questionnaire available in the Parcheesi game shell.

Mandatory Questions	Adaptable Questions
• I find that the game board is appropriate for the game content. • I had no trouble following the instructions guiding me through the game. • I had no trouble understanding the activities, items, or questions included in the game.	• This game helped me apply my knowledge about sexually transmitted infections (STIs) to practical situations. • This game increased my awareness of my attitudes and behaviors about STIs. • I felt that I participated actively in my learning with this game.

Figure 5. Instructions for creating written pages

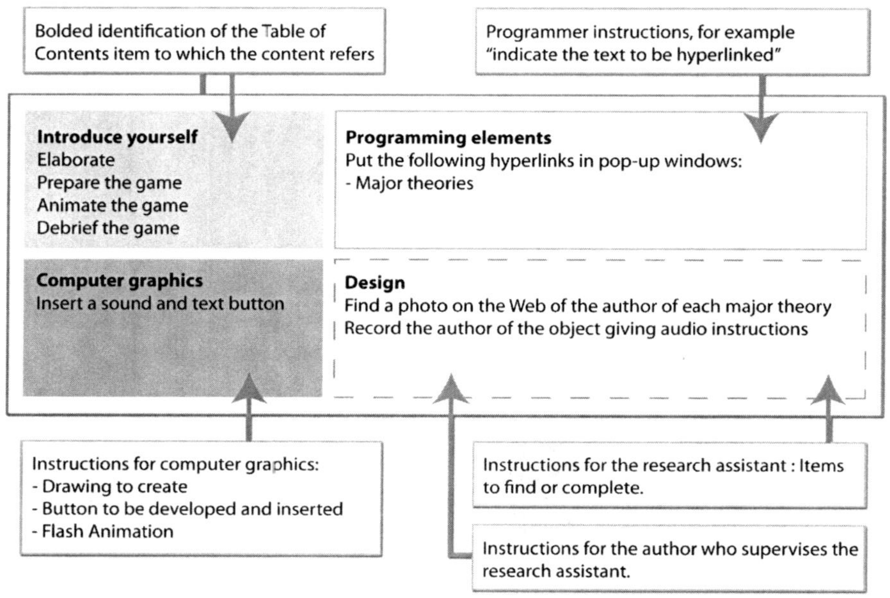

THE DESIGN SPECIFICATION

The design specification consolidates all modifications and additions to the structure and content of a frame game into screen layouts. To organize the contents of the web pages of the GEGS, the user's perspective on the information was taken into account. According to Millerand and Martial (2001), the organization and ranking of content in a web site must rely on a process of consultation with the user, making the most important, or most frequently used information accessible from the first interface level. In view of the types of users of the GEGS, all of the web pages are to be displayed as forms to be completed. The use of forms is particularly well adapted to the web because it explicitly guides data capture into specific fields. In addition, the form as style of interaction is suitable for all types of users, from beginners to those who are more experienced (Bastien & Rubio, 2001).

As shown in Figure 5, each GEGS screen page contains five sections that must be completed. Four of these sections provide direction for the GEGS' technical, media design, and development team. These areas include content, programming, graphics, and design. The fifth section contains the content of the page as it will be displayed. The 'content' section lists pages to be displayed online and their titles. The programming section gives instructions for the technical development team. The graphics section gives instructions for finding or creating images, animations, video clips, and sound recordings to include in the shell. The design section lists tasks to be finalized by the design team before building the tool's content. The content section includes text to be shown on the screen, to be used in video or in another way, and a model of its presentation.

Figure 6 gives an example of a design page for the *Parcheesi* GEGS. In this form, the designer adapts the game board in two different ways and chooses the form of the tokens.

Once the design specifications are complete, they are discussed with the graphics design team and page models defined. Figure 7 shows a model for the modifiable game board to be shown by the *Parcheesi GEGS*.

Figure 6. Example of a specification page for the Parcheesi GEGS: The game board

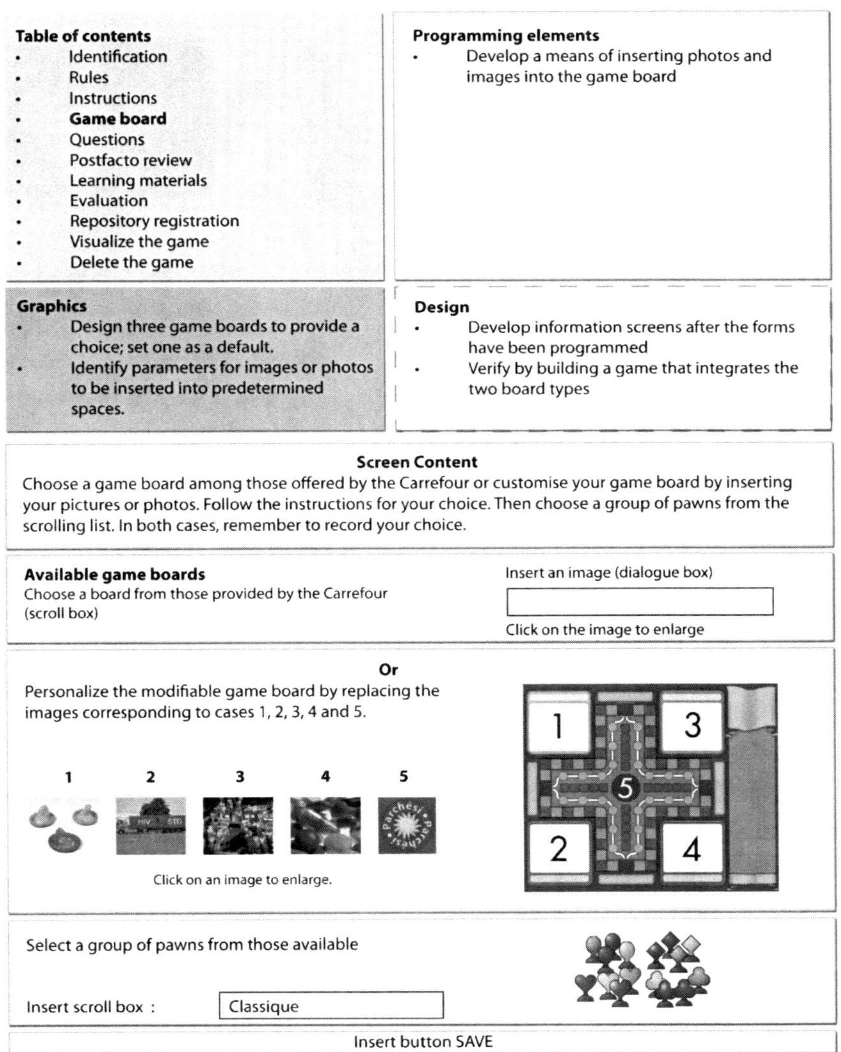

Table of contents
- Identification
- Rules
- Instructions
- **Game board**
- Questions
- Postfacto review
- Learning materials
- Evaluation
- Repository registration
- Visualize the game
- Delete the game

Programming elements
- Develop a means of inserting photos and images into the game board

Graphics
- Design three game boards to provide a choice; set one as a default.
- Identify parameters for images or photos to be inserted into predetermined spaces.

Design
- Develop information screens after the forms have been programmed
- Verify by building a game that integrates the two board types

Screen Content

Choose a game board among those offered by the Carrefour or customise your game board by inserting your pictures or photos. Follow the instructions for your choice. Then choose a group of pawns from the scrolling list. In both cases, remember to record your choice.

Available game boards
Choose a board from those provided by the Carrefour (scroll box)

Insert an image (dialogue box)

Click on the image to enlarge

Or

Personalize the modifiable game board by replacing the images corresponding to cases 1, 2, 3, 4 and 5.

1 2 3 4 5

Click on an image to enlarge.

Select a group of pawns from those available

Insert scroll box : Classique

Insert button SAVE

Figure 7. Model of a game board

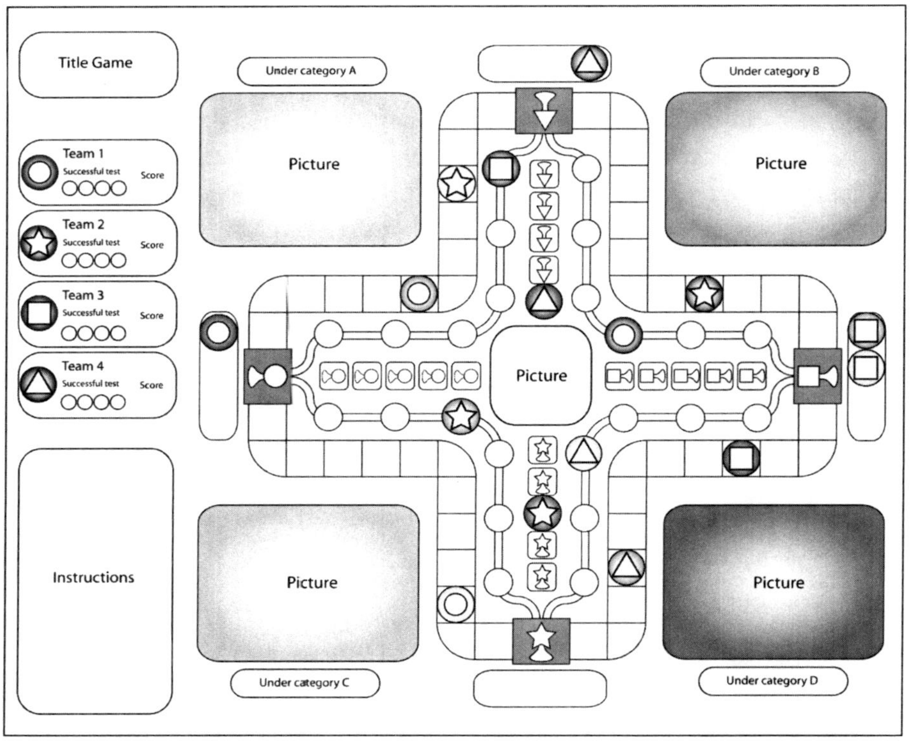

GEGS Design Errors

In order to aid game designers, we will conclude this chapter with a list of errors to avoid in designing a GEGS:

- **Choosing a frame game that uses only limited objectives or learning content that is too easy for the target population.** The designer must establish from the start the objectives and characteristics of the target population and examine the most pertinent frame. The designer can also foresee, if applicable, a GEGS hierarchy, from simple to complex, relying on the same principles but accommodating various limitations, objectives, and target audiences.
- **Using chance and luck inappropriately**. The designer must use luck in situations involving chance. It is common for designers to use chance (e.g., rolling the dice, picking a card) when they do not know how to establish a game situation or to determine a player's actions.
- **Having an incomplete game.** The game developer must avoid the need for a facilitator to lead, explain or adjust the game. All rules must be described so that players can play a game without the intervention of a facilitator. The GEGS must collect all necessary parameters and information so that the builder develops a complete game.
- **Failing to ensure that all information present in the game material is learned.** According to research, no educational tool has 100 percent coverage for the content to be learned. The GEGS must allow the designer to develop tools and complementary content for the game if he wishes all the information to be learned.

- **Adapting a frame game in which the methods of winning contradict the learning objectives.** The designer must verify the game with the target audience, by running a trial to ensure that winning strategies for the new game are in accord with the learning objectives.
- **Including useless elements or stimuli in the tasks or the learning content in the GEGS.** The designer must analyze the essential elements that the GEGS must contain according to the desired type of learning. He must ask whether secondary elements are justified, and keep in mind the costs associated with additional elements.
- **Giving the game an inappropriate point system.** The designer must ensure that the rewards and penalties are not arbitrary, and that they conform to the degree of difficulty of the questions presented and to the objectives to be reached.

CONCLUSION

This chapter has described, with extensive examples, the steps in designing a GEGS to ensure that the GEGS offers game builders all the necessary tools to define game parameters (i.e., board, tokens, questions), generate instructions and rules and to establish criteria to end the game by declaring a winner.

In terms of content, the GEGS offers an identification form to specify the items such as target learners, pedagogic objectives, subject matter, educational level, and type of learning. It then offers 13 types of closed and open questions with real-time correction and feedback mechanisms. This variety gives flexibility to use games developed with the GEGS for various types of learning, including development of simple to complex knowledge and modification of behaviors and attitudes. Each question type can include video clips, images, sound, one or several answers, and feedback.

With regard to evaluation, ddebriefing and game evaluation, mechanisms integrated into the GEGS ensure the efficacy and efficiency of the educational games developed using the GEGS. A process of creating screen pages to facilitate the GEGS design was described and illustrated. Finally, some advice on avoiding common design mistakes was provided.

REFERENCES

Asakawa, T., & Gilbert, N. (2003). Synthesizing experiences: Lessons to be learned from *Internet*-mediated simulation games. *Simulation & Gaming*, *34*(1), 10–12. doi:10.1177/1046878102250455

Bastien, C., & Rubio, R. (2001). *La conception de formulaires en ligne* [Design of online forms]. Retrieved March 15, 2005 from http://www.ler-gonome.org/dev/pages/article_5.asp

Coco, A., Woodward, I., Shaw, K., Cody, A., Lupton, G., & Peake, A. (2001). Bingo for beginners: A game strategy for facilitating active learning. *Teaching Sociology*, *29*(4), 492–503. doi:10.2307/1318950

Dessaint, M. P. (1995). Évaluer*:* de la mesure avant toute chose. [Evaluation: Measure above all] In M.P. Dessaint (Ed.). *La conception de cours. Guide de planification et de rédaction* [Course design: Guide to planning and writing] (pp. 207-247). Québec, QC, Canada: Les presses de l'Université du Québec.

Dickey, M. D. (2005). Engaging by design: How engagement strategies in popular computer and video games can inform instructional design. *Educational Technology Research and Development*, *53*(2), 67–83. doi:10.1007/BF02504866

Millerand, F., & Martial, O. (2001). *Guide pratique de conception et d'évaluation ergonomique de sites Web* [Practical guide to the design and ergonomic evaluation of web sites], Montreal, QC, Canada: Centre de recherche informatique de Montréal. Retrieved May 28, 2009 from http://www.crim.ca/files/documents/services/rd/GuideErgonomique.PDF

Prégent, R. (1990). *La préparation d'un cours* [Preparation of a course]. Montreal, QC, Canada: Éditions de l'École Polytechnique de Montréal.

Saliés, T. G. (2002). Simulation/gaming in the EAP writing class: Benefits and drawbacks. *Simulation & Gaming*, *33*(3), 316–329. doi:10.1177/104687810203300306

Sauvé, L. (2006). *La scénarisation et la production du jeu éducatif* [Design and production of an educational game]. Québec, QC, Canada: Télé-université.

Sauvé, L., & Chamberland, G. (2006). *Jeux, jeux de simulation et jeux de rôle: une analyse exploratoire et pédagogique* [Games, simulation games and role-playing games: An exploratory pedogical analysis. Cours TEC 1280: Environnement d'apprentissage multimédia sur l'inforoute. Québec, QC, Canada: Télé-université. Salen, K., & Zimmerman, E. (2003). *Rules of play: Game design fundamentals*. Cambridge, MA: The MIT Press.

Sauvé, L., Renaud, L., & Kaszap, M. IsaBelle, C., Gauvin, M., Rodriguez, A. et al., (2006) *Modélisation du jeu-cadre Parchési* [Designing the frame game *Parcheesi*]. Québec, QC, Canada: SAVIE and SAGE.

Vandeventer, S. S., & While, J. A. (2002). Expert behavior in children's video game play. *Simulation & Gaming*, *33*(1), 28–49. doi:10.1177/1046878102033001002

ADDITIONAL READING

Hourst, B., & Thiagarajan, S. (2007). *Les modèles de jeux en formation: Les jeux-cadres de Thiagi* [Models of games for training: The frame games of Thiagi]. Paris: Éditions d'Organisation.

Rollings, A., & Morris, D. (2005). *Conception et architecture des jeux vidéo*. Paris: éditions Vuibert.

KEY TERMS AND DEFINITIONS

(Educational) Game: A fictitious, fantasy or imaginary situation in which players, placed in conflict with others or assembled in a team against an external opponent, are governed by rules determining their actions with a view to achieving learning objectives and a goal determined by the game, either to win or to seek revenge.

Frame Game: A means of teaching which comprises a structure that generates learning activities supporting the use of diverse strategies, implying a conflict and a set of rules for the movement of players, and criteria that ends the game by declaring a winner. This structure can easily be adapted to many different objectives and pedagogical content. Any game can be broken down into two main parts: (1) The structure, which determines the way in which you play: the rules, the steps for the course of the game, the movements of the players, the challenges the players must face, and the strategies they must employ to win. The game is emptied of its contents, leaving its structure bare, so that, once clearly defined and analyzed, it becomes a frame, or for the purposes of our research, a generic educational game shell (GEGS). The content is the information conveyed in the game. In the case of a pedagogical game, it is also the objectives being pursued and the abilities that will be developed by playing the game.

Generic Educational Game Shell (GEGS): An online environment that allows teachers and trainers to create games by providing all the tools needed to: (1) set the game parameters, (2) create instructions and rules that direct player actions, (3) create pedagogical materials, (4) set the criteria that determine the end of the game and the winner, and (5) customize the tools required for revision and evaluation of the game to ensure that the game can be updated regularly and that learning is maximized.

Debriefing (or Postfacto Review): A discussion at the end of a game that supports feedback. It allows participants to see whether they have attained the learning objectives, to assess their experience in the game and their acquired knowledge, to become aware of their feelings and attitudes, and to relate the game experience with reality or their personal context.

APPENDIX A

List of Events in the GEGS

Original *Parcheesi* game	*Parcheesi* GEGS
Event 1: Interaction with game materials *Action:* Each player places four tokens of the same color in her personal space, located in each corner of the game board. *Reaction:* The four tokens must leave the start square, the player-selected personal space. *Consequences:* No player can leave from another player's personal space and start square.	This event is started automatically by the game engine. The actions do not require players' actions but are controlled by the game. **Event 1 – Interaction with game materials** *Action:* Each player clicks the dice on their turn. *Reaction:* Each player obtains a number between 1 and 6. *Consequences:* The player who obtains the highest number begins the game and increases her likelihood of winning.
Event 2: Interaction with game materials *Action:* The player rolls the dice to obtain a 6. *Reaction:* If the player obtains a 6, her token moves to the start square at the beginning of her personal space. *Consequences:* A player obtaining a 6 is rewarded by the opportunity to roll the dice once again, which raises her chances of reaching the end of the game more quickly and, consequently, winning.	**Event 2 - Interaction with game materials** *Action:* The player clicks the two dice in turn to get a double (1-1, 2-2, 3-3, 4-4, 5-5, 6-6). Reaction: The player obtains a double and moves one of her tokens to the Start square. *Consequences:* If no token is currently in the Start square, the player increases her chances of winning. If one of her tokens is already on the Start square, the player reduces her chances of winning because two tokens from the same player cannot occupy the same square at once.
	Event 3 - Interaction with game materials *Action:* The player responds to the learning activity that corresponds to the color of the token she places on the Start square. *Reaction:* If a player successfully completes the activity on the first try, she wins points and is sent to the fast track. If the player does not successfully complete the learning activity on the first try, she does not gain any points and must follow the regular track. This token remains where it is until the next turn, after the player has successfully completed a learning activity in this same category. *Consequences:* In the first situation, the player increases her chances of winning the game. This is not the case in the second situation.
	Event 4 - Interaction with game materials *Action:* A player responds to a learning activity when her token passes a Start square as it moves along the track. *Reaction:* If the player completes the activity successfully, she wins points and the token of her choice moves along the fast track. If the player fails the learning activity, she does not win any points and the token of her choice moves along the regular track. *Consequences:* In the first situation, the player increases her chances of winning the game. This is not the case in the second situation.
	Event 5 - Interaction with game materials *Action:* The player completes a learning activity when one of her tokens crosses the *Start* square below the central track that leads to the center of the game. *Reaction:* If the player succeeds in the activity, she wins points and the token moves along the center track. If the player fails the learning activity, she does not win any points and the token stays in place, waiting for the next turn where the player will attempt another learning activity to move along the center track. *Consequences:* In the first situation, the player increases her chances of winning the game. This is not the case in the second situation.

Event 3: Interaction with game materials *Action*: Players take turns rolling the dice. *Reaction:* The players advance their tokens along the squares corresponding to the number obtained in their roll. The tokens advance clockwise along the cross-shaped pathways. *Consequences:* They advance along the squares, reacting to the different events which can occur. These events can augment or diminish players' chances of reaching the end of the game more rapidly.	**Event 6 - Interaction with game materials** *Action:* Each player rolls the dice in turn. *Reaction:* Each player advances a token along the squares along the arms of the cross in a clockwise direction according to the number obtained in the roll. *Consequences:* The player advances along the squares and reacts to the different events that can occur. These events can increase or decrease her chances of reaching the center first and winning the game.
Event 4: Relations among players *Action:* A token stops on a square already occupied by an adversary's token. *Reaction:* The token already present on the square is removed and placed once again in the player's personal space. *Consequences:* Once the token has been removed, it cannot come back into the game unless the player rolls a 6; this reduces her chances of reaching the end of the track quickest and consequently her chances of winning.	**Event 7 – Relations among players** *Action:* A player's token lands on a square already occupied by another token. *Reaction:* The token, which was on the square, is sent back to the *Start* square. *Consequences:* If the *Start* square is already occupied by a token, this token is sent back to the personal space, decreasing the player's chances of winning the game.
Event 7: Interaction with game materials *Action:* The player obtains the exact number needed to land in the center of the board. *Reaction:* The player can move her token all the way to the middle of the board. *Consequences:* The token, entering the final zone, is removed from the board. The player thus increases her chances of reaching the end of the game and winning.	**Event 8 - Relations among players** *Action:* The player rolls the dice and obtains an exact number (the number of squares between a token and the final central square) needed to move the token into the center of the game board. *Reaction:* The player succeeds or fails in the learning activity. *Consequences:* If she succeeds in the activity, the player receives 200 points, removes that token and increase her chances of winning the game. If she fails, the token stays in place until the next turn, decreasing this player's chances of winning the game.
Event 7: Interaction with game materials *Action:* The player obtains the exact number needed to land in the center of the board. *Reaction:* The player can move her token all the way to the middle of the board. *Consequences:* The token, entering the final zone, is removed from the board. The player thus increases her chances of reaching the end of the game and winning.	**Event 9 - Interaction with game materials** *Action:* The player obtains a number higher than the number needed for the token to arrive directly in the center of the game board. *Reaction:* The player has two options: (1) she succeeds or (2) fails the learning activity. *Consequences:* If the player succeeds in the activity, two consequences are possible: (1) if she only has one active token, the player wins points and moves her token along the central track the appropriate number for the number obtained in the last roll and (2) if the player has more than one token in play, she wins points and moves another token along the path, increasing her chances of winning the game. If she does not succeed the activity, the player wins no points, her token stays in its place and waits for the next turn to successfully complete a learning activity.
Event 5: Interaction with game materials *Action:* Once a player has more than one token on the game board, she can choose to advance any of these tokens at every roll of the dice. *Reaction:* The player can move any of her tokens along the squares according to the numbers obtained in the roll. The tokens move clockwise along the cross-shaped pathways. *Consequences:* The strategic movement of tokens on the game board increases a player's chances of reaching the end of the game quickly and consequently of winning the game.	
Event 6: Interaction with game materials *Action:* The player can not divide the number obtained with the dice roll among two or more tokens; for example, if a player rolls a 6, she cannot move one token 4 squares and another 2. *Reaction:* The player can move only one of her dice along the squares in a clockwise direction according to the number obtained in the last roll. *Consequences:* According to the positioning of her tokens on the game board, the player increases or reduces her chances of reaching the end of the game more quickly, thus winning the game.	This event is eliminated.

	Event 10 – Relations among players *Action:* A player draws a Team card. *Reaction:* All the players participate at the same time. The first player to complete the activity successfully wins extra points. *Consequences:* If the player who wins has a token on the Start square, it is moved directly to the fast track. The player who drew the Team card does not loose her turn. She completes another learning activity right after participating in the team card with the other players.
	Event 11 - Interaction with game materials *Action:* A player draws a Free Start card. *Reaction:* The player uses or does not use the card. *Consequences:* If she uses the card, one of her tokens in placed in the Start square and the player completes a learning activity. If the player does not use the card, the card is banked, protecting any tokens currently positioned in the Start square. If all the player's tokens are already in play, the card has no effect. In both cases, the player increases her chances of winning.
	Event 12 - Interaction with game materials *Action:* A player draws an Exact Roll card. *Reaction:* The player uses or does not use the card. *Consequences:* If the player uses the card, one of her tokens (except any on the Start square) is moved to the center of the board If the player does not use the card, it is banked to avoid the card being useless in the case of having only a token on the Start square. In both cases, the player increases her chances of winning.
	Event13 - Interaction with game materials *Action:* A player draws a Back to Start card. *Reaction:* The player uses or does not use the card. *Consequences*: One of her tokens returns to the Start square if she uses the card. The card is banked if she does not use it. This is done to avoid sending a token back to the personal space if there is one already in the Start square and the card is not made useless because the player has just one token in play already placed on the Start square. If the token positioned on the Start square is eaten before the Back to Start card can be used, the card is deleted. In both cases, the player increases her chances of winning.
	Event 14 - Interaction with game materials *Action:* A player draws an Access to the fast track card. *Reaction:* The player either uses or does not use the card. *Consequences:* If she does use the card, one of her players leaves the regular track and jumps to the fast track without requiring the player to complete a learning activity from the *Start* square. If she does not use the card, it is banked as the card is useless while a player's tokens are all on the fast track already.
Event 7: Interaction with game materials *Action:* The player obtains the exact number needed to land in the center of the board. *Reaction:* The player can move her token all the way to the middle of the board. *Consequences:* The token, entering the final zone, is removed from the board. The player thus increases her chances of reaching the end of the game and winning.	**Event 15 - Interaction with game materials** *Action:* One of the players removes her fourth token from the board. *Reaction:* The game ends. *Consequences:* The player with the highest score wins the game.
	Event 16 - Interaction with game materials *Action:* The allotted time runs out. *Reaction:* The game ends. *Consequences:* The player with the highest score wins.

APPENDIX B

Modifications of Rules for the *Parcheesi* Generic Educational Game Shell

Original *Parcheesi* game rules	Modified rules for the *Parcheesi* GEGS
	1. The game is played with a minimum of two players who each form a team or a maximum of 16 players organized into four teams. All other variations of team set-ups are possible.
	2. Before beginning the game, teams decide how the game will end: • When all 4 tokens of one team reach the center of the board and the team answers the learning activity correctly. • When the allotted time for the game runs out.
1. Four tokens, the same color as the corner, are placed in the personal space.	3. To begin the game, the system records the number of teams and their members. An equal number of four token sets is assigned to each team and are positioned automatically in each team's personal space.
	4. Each team clicks the dice in a random order to determine who will start the game. The team that rolls the highest number starts the game.
2. In order to get to the Start square in the personal space, a player must roll a 6. A player obtaining a 6 is rewarded with an extra roll.	5. A team must obtain a double (1-1, 2-2, 3-3, 4-4, 5-5, 6-6) in order to move one of its four tokens to the *Start* square. The team clicks the token it wishes to move first (the blue or red one for example). Once the token has been moved to the *Start* square, the team must immediately respond to a learning activity in the category corresponding to the color of the token: 1. If a team succeeds in **the first activity** when its token is in the *Start* square, it rolls the dice and the team's token moves along the fast track and advances the number of squares determined by the last roll of the dice. 2. If the team does not succeed in **the first activity**, the token stays on the *Start* square and the team waits for the next turn to try again. 3. If on the following turn, the team does succeed in **the second activity** when its token is in the *Start* square, this token moves along the regular track. 4. If the team does not succeed in **the second activity**, the token stays in the *Start* square and waits for the next turn until it succeeds.
3. The token moves along the arms of the cross in a clockwise direction (counter-clockwise for the Indian version).	6. Once a team has managed to move a token, turns will consist of the following: • The team responds to a learning activity corresponding to the color of the token it has moved in the previous turn. • If the team succeeds in the activity within the allotted time for the question, the team clicks on the dice and the token of their choice moves along the number of squares determined by the last roll. The team can also decide to free a new token if the results obtained allow it. Two tokens of the same team cannot be placed on the same square; this means that a team with a token on the *Start* square will not be able to free any new tokens until this first one has been moved. • If the team fails an activity, it cannot click the dice and must wait until it has correctly answered a question in this same category in the following turn before clicking the dice. • Once one of these possible outcomes has taken place, it is the following team's turn.

	7. When a team moves a token (on the fast track or regular track) and this team lands on a *Start* square, it must answer a learning activity, even if the token passes the square. Success in the learning activity determines the track that the token will follow, whether on the current turn or the next. If the team succeeds in the activity, the token will continue on the fast track. If the team fails, the token will move along the regular track. The same rule applies if the team's token arrives by an exact number on the *Start* square. In the case of a success, the team does not click the dice but its token will access the fast track during the next turn, even if the team chooses to move another token on its turn after succeeding in a learning activity When a token crosses the *Start* square before heading to the center of the board, the team must once again respond to a learning activity. If it fails, the token stays where it is and the team will have to answer the next learning activity correctly before heading to the center of the board. If the team succeeds in the activity and the token's travel was obstructed by the *Start* square, the token is free to continue its trajectory towards the center of the board.
	8. Each team that succeeds in a learning activity gains points. The point system varies according to the time taken to complete the activity.
4. If a token lands on a square already occupied by an opponent, the opponent's token is sent back to the personal space. The token, once sent back, cannot come back into play until the player rolls a 6.	9. A token that stops in a square already occupied by another token sends this token back to the *Start* square. If the *Start* square is already occupied by a token, that token is sent back to the personal space.
5. A token can only enter the final zone by rolling the exact number needed. For example, if a token is 5 squares from the finish and the player rolls a 6, the player must wait until the next turn to move this token. The player may however move another token if she currently has one active (freed from the personal space).	10. Tokens may land in the center of the board only if the exact number of squares between it and the finish is the number obtained in the roll. The center counts as one square. Once the token has arrived in the center, the token is taken off the board and that team is awarded 200 points.
	11. When a team has rolled the dice and obtained a number greater than the number of squares between a token and the final square, there are two options: • Leave the token where it is until the exact number needed is obtained and click another token to move it along the track according to the number obtained. • Move the token ahead to the center and then back the remaining number of squares according to the number obtained in the roll. For example: if a player's token is two squares from the center and the team rolls a 5, this token moves forward 3 squares and then back 2. • The token that moves back along the central track cannot go back further than the first square on of the central track. If the token lands on this square while moving backwards and is still required to move further, it begins to move back to towards the center of the board again.
6. Different rolls can be used to move different tokens. A roll can never be divided; for example, a 6 cannot be used to move one token forward 4 squares and another one 2 squares.	
	12. When a team draws a Team card, all the teams in the game participate. The first team to complete the activity successfully gains extra points. If this team has a token in the *Start* square, it moves directly to the fast track. The team that drew the *Team* card does not miss a turn. This team responds to a new learning activity immediately after participating in the *Team* card with the other teams.

	13. When a team draws a *Chance* card, the following actions are possible: • **Free Start**. This card allows the team to put a token (of their choice) on the *Start* square. This means the team must complete immediately a learning activity. If the team's *Start* square is already occupied by one of their tokens or if all their tokens are active, the team can keep the *Chance* card in their bank and use it at any time to place a token in the *Start* square. • **Exact Roll**. This card allows a team to move a token (any token in play, except one from the *Start* square) to the center of the board. If the team has only one token in play and it is on the Start square, then the team can bank the card to be used later • **Back to Start.** This card sends a token back to the Start square. If the square is already occupied by another token, this token is sent back to the personal space of the team it belongs to. If the team only has one token in play when it picks the card and this token is on the Start square, the card is banked and the token must turn around the first time it is moved (it will be moved to the *Start* square). If the token is eaten before the **Back to Start** card can be used, the card is deleted. • **Access to the Fast Track.** This card allows a team to move the token that made them pick a card from the regular track to the fast track without completing a learning activity when it comes up to the *Start* square. • **A maximum of two *Chance* cards** can be banked per team. If one team has two *Chance* cards in the bank, each new card selected replaces the oldest card in the bank.
7. A token that enters the final square is removed from the board. The first player to get all her tokens to the final square wins.	14. The game ends: • Once a team has retired all 4 tokens and correctly answered the final learning activity. If a team draws a *Team* card for the final learning activity, it wins only if it succeeds in the activity. If the team does not answer correctly, it must wait until the following turn to complete a new learning activity and win the game. • Once the allotted time has run out. The team with the highest score wins.

Chapter 24
Usability Guidelines for a Generic Educational Game Shell

Louise Sauvé
Télé-université, Canada

ABSTRACT

This chapter discusses usability rules for avoiding defects in the media design for Generic Educational Game Shell (GEGS) components, including visual interfaces, text, and sound. These rules served as a guide for the Web design of the Parcheesi™ GEGS and the games that it generates. The first section of the chapter deals with the screen, text, color, windows, images, and video as well as sound used in the input forms of the GEGS. The final section discusses some errors to be avoided in the interface design.

INTRODUCTION

Media design for the interface of a generic educational game shell (GEGS) makes use of familiar production techniques and tools, including computer graphics, layout design, and programming. An interface is a (hardware and software) device that enables an exchange of information between two systems. In concrete terms, an interface can be defined as everything that helps a human being understand and manipulate a machine. It is the central point of exchange between the person and the machine and has a physical layer (screen, keyboard, mouse, etc.) and a software component which intervenes between the machine and the user (Martial, 2000). This chapter focuses on the design of a GEGS interface, particularly its ergonomic aspects.

Ergonomics covers the body of science related to how humans use tools and machines for maximum comfort, security, and effectiveness (Wisner, 1972). In the case of computer interfaces such as for a GEGS, the ergonomist finds and implements solutions to inform and guide the user to minimize as much as possible the software's cognitive (information) load. (Millrand & Martial, 2001, p. 74).

The importance of a well-constructed interface is widely recognized, yet the literature on user interfaces for digital games is scarce (Kellner, 2008). To establish guidelines for the creation of a GEGS interface, we relied primarily on studies in ergonom-

DOI: 10.4018/978-1-61520-731-2.ch024

ics for web environments (e.g., Dufresne, 2009; Livet, 2007; Millerand & Martial, 200; Nielson, 2000). For the GEGS interface to be efficient, it must meet two criteria: it must be useful—that is, adapted to user needs and preferences—and usable, that is, easy to teach and to use. Since the target users of the GEGS are young students, the organization of the GEGS should be linear and logical, consistent with the educational process of creating the elements of a game. According to Millerand and Martial (2001), this organization is well-suited for web-based educational sites or tutorials.

In this chapter, we examine media usability rules that helped us to avoid deficiencies in the *Parcheesi* GEGS user interface, notably regarding visual, textual, and sound design. These media rules[i] served as a guide for the web layout of the GEGS and the games it generates. The first section of the chapter deals with the screen, text, color, windows, images, video, and sound. The final section discusses some errors to be avoided in the interface design for a GEGS.

GEGS INTERFACE DESIGN GUIDELINES

The Screen

The display's graphic design helps the user to focus on what is important. For Kellner (2008), a visual interface is problematic if it fails to highlight essential elements that the user needs to see. To avoid overload and emphasize the basics, here are some general rules[ii]:

- The team started formatting the GEGS by respecting the visual space limitations of the screen. In general, it is best to keep text brief—preferably to what can be viewed on a single screen. Long text on a computer monitor reduces motivation, and it is often not read. A web page should be more or less equivalent in length to a printed page, including pictures or video clips. It must be short to eliminate, or at least minimize, scrolling, maximize visibility, and minimize download time. A page should also be readable without horizontal scrolling. In the GEGS, template contents generally fit within a 1024 X 768 display and require very little scrolling.
- Well-positioned navigational tools give the user a certain amount of control over the interface. Avoid positioning them only at the bottom of the page, where they fall outside the field of vision for users with small screens. In the GEGS, both the navigation bar (1) and the design toolbar (2) are always visible to the user, as illustrated in Figure 1.
- Important information is highlighted with graphics and text, for example flashing and asterisks. All forms include asterisks (Figure 1) to let the user know that some form items must be completed for the game to be functional.
- Known symbols are used to show an action or an obvious function. They are the same on all interface pages and are located close to the requested action. The question mark, for example, brings up information bulletins, as in Figure 1, where "?" located next to the Title item in Figure 1 explains how to write a game title and shows examples.
- Forms and blank information sections help to avoid confusion by giving examples of answers or providing help. This help can take different forms: guides, information bulletins, forms for questions, an online assistant who can be reached by email or telephone, etc. In the GEGS, the fill-in boxes offer answer examples (Figure 1), as well as information bulletins and an easily-printable pdf guide to the use of the game creation forms.
- The user must get needed information with no more than three clicks, a rule that all

Figure 1. Location of the navigation tools

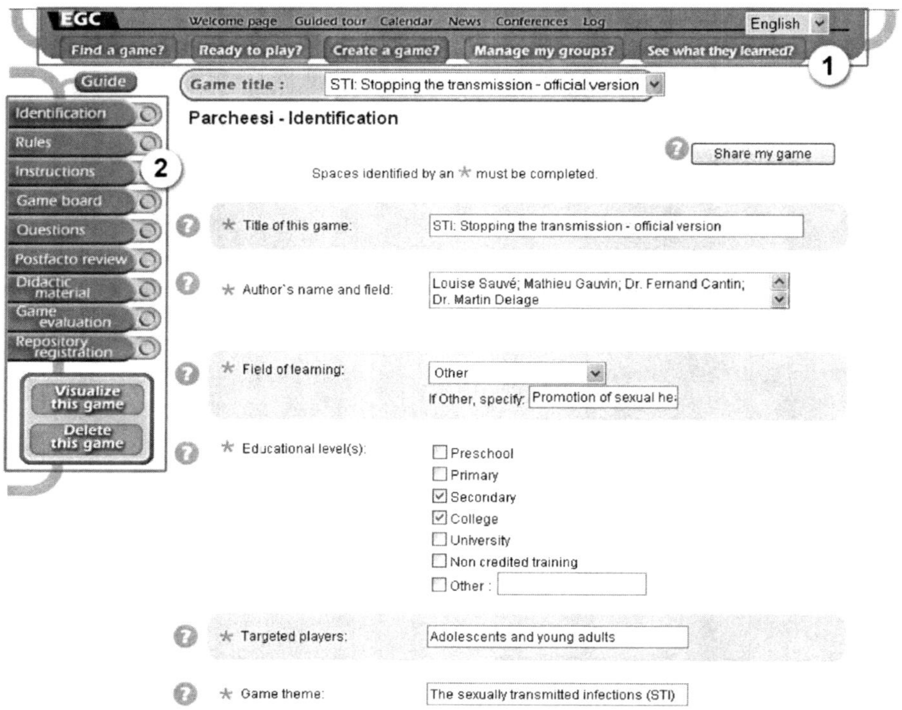

GEGS forms obey. For example, in Figure 2, a second click is enough to access all information bulletin contents.

How a web page displays will vary from user to user, depending on the size and definition of the screen, the configuration of the navigator (mouse, touchpad, etc.) and the computer equipment. It is therefore important to limit the zone of display to a predetermined frame that supports a display standard across computers.

Text

A legible interface is a necessary element of any digital product (Ergolab, 2003), especially for a young learner (Kellner, 2008). The text font must take into account the principles of on-screen legibility. According to Klare (1984, p. 681), the legibility of a text depends on three factors:

- whether the reader is interested in and values the writing. This aspect refers to the interests and skills that a learner has or must develop in order to make reading easier or more effective. We will not develop this point here.
- ease of comprehension due to the style of writing. This aspect, called editorial legibility, is defined by language level and vocabulary used, length and structure of sentences, and organizational elements that emphasize core information and give the reader a coherent understanding of the text.
- typographical legibility. This aspect pertains to the visual aspect of the text, including its organization, presentation style, and placement on the web page.

Several guidelines were used for the layout of text on a web page display to ensure editorial and typographical legibility:

- Position text for easy viewing. Text should be arranged in paragraphs or units of information separately for better comprehension. Overall, the difference between the title of the text and the paragraphs must be distinct.
- Left-justified text increases the reading rate. For beginners, a text without gaps and right-margin alignment appears more legible.
- Use font and background colors to support readability.
- Use different fonts and point sizes for emphasis.
- Avoid overflow of text beyond the screen.
- Use only one font per page, except when using special effects.
- Use a point size of 12 or higher, and a common font, such as Arial. Remember that the choice and size of font must support reading on the screen.
- Avoid using all upper case letters in the body of your text, because this impedes readability. Reserve upper case letters for the first letter of a sentence, words in a list or a warning, or for the title of a button, page, or rubric.
- Use underlining only for hypertext links.

To make the templates easier to read, the GEGS text is aligned to the left, and the font used is Arial. Body text is 12 point; titles are 14. Upper case letters are used for the titles of all the headers on the site for greater clarity.

The drafting of the instructions, the rules and the contents of the GEGS is based on certain principles adapted from Dessaint (1995, p. 130):

- Write in short sentences (20 to 25 words, maximum of 80 characters)
- Limit the sentences to one idea apiece
- Keep paragraphs short (5 to 6 lines)
- Use a conversational tone
- Add specific examples to explain a rule or an instruction
- Use positive sentences
- Introduce new vocabulary sparingly, and define the new words in pop-up windows or information bubbles
- Use the minimum of qualifying adverbs and adjectives
- Be objective, varied and simple
- Place the important words at the beginning of a sentence

Color

To use color effectively, several authors[iii] recommend the following guidelines:

- Use colors to facilitate reading and decoding of pages by the user. Colors are used in general either to link elements, or to differentiate between them. For example, in the GEGS forms, all titles are in navy blue, which contrasts with the background, and augments readability.
- Maintain a strong contrast between the foreground text and the background for optimal readability. Avoid using a dark background because it tires the eye and can print badly.
- Avoid textured or decorative fonts, and combinations such as yellow lettering on a white background, or red or blue letters on black background as these are difficult to read.
- Emphasize key information by bolding text, or changing the color, as the shown in Figure 3.
- Use color to distinguish mandatory from optional information. In the GEGS templates, fields marked with a bright orange asterisk (Figure 1) are mandatory.
- Opt for visual simplicity, using a maximum of three or four colors per screen. Select a

Figure 2. Use of an information bubble and a pop-up window

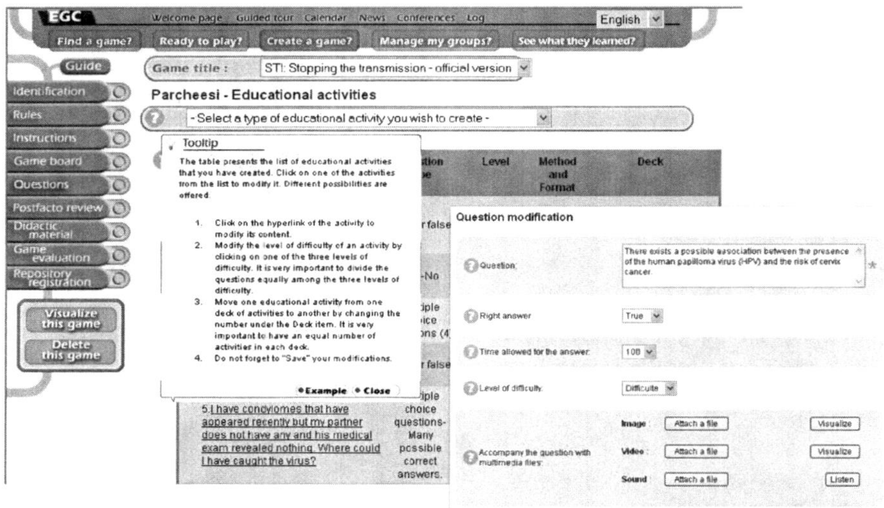

neutral color for the background that will contrast with the text. All the GEGS templates were color- coded for the types of content. Text body is blue, with navy blue for titles and sub-titles, for example. Titles in the table of contents, and the navigation buttons are pale blue with a scroll-over of bright orange.

Windows

Several authors[iv] recommend pop-up windows (no more than four), and defined zones within a screen. Shneiderman and Plaisant (2004) suggest a structure with titles, subtitles, followed by more detailed pages. Others suggest dividing the screen into a maximum of four parts. For the GEGS templates, the team opted to define three zones:

- The space in the top eighth of the screen contains the navigation bar and is present on all screens
- At the left margin, one-eighth of the screen displays the tool bars linked to each menu
- The remaining screen displays the main content, which changes depending on the user's selection from the table of contents, the tool bar, or the navigation bar

Each window, section, and page must be clearly identifiable. The GEGS displays only one level of pop-up screen to optimize visual space without overloading it. This screen appears consistently either as a window or as an information bubble, as shown in Figure 2.

Sound

Several principles guided our choices for integrating sound (Sauvé, 1995, p. 293-295). The use of intonation, inflection, expression, rhythm, volume, noise, and timbre of voice elicits certain responses which can be used for educational purposes, such as communicating mood or emotion, suggesting intimate communication, or encouraging focus on parts of the game or learning activities. Compared to written text, spoken text influences cognition (increases clarity and significance) and motivation by showing the student the importance of each

Figure 3. Objects highlighted when pointed to with the mouse

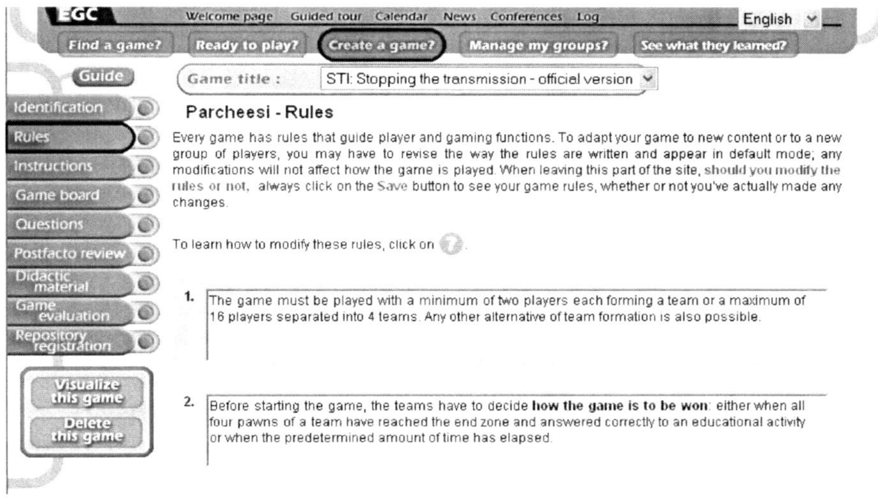

word. The contents of sound clips and talking text can motivate the student and increase her/his interest in the game's subject matter. The *Parcheesi* GEGS offers the following options:

- Introduce the game with a welcome message from the authors and creators of the game
- Use sound clips to guide the player through the game or through the rules
- Access written rules by a simple click
- Highlight the important aspects of the game with sound effects or music. Music can be used to announce the beginning of a game, as a theme or soundtrack element, can suggest a place, a space, communicate feelings or an atmosphere, and create a bond or a bridge between two parts of the game
- Supplement another medium, for example by providing instructions while supporting visual illustrations, as in adding video clips to illustrate questions, answers and feedback

Sound is of limited effectiveness for presenting large amounts of information or long lists, or for explaining abstract concepts or describing objects in two or three dimensions (procedures, progressions, space, time, etc.). Sound is also a difficult medium for conveying information when prior knowledge is required. Certain students do not like to learn through audio, while others do not have this skill, for various reasons (auditory acuity and discrimination, knowledge of vocabulary, etc.). The game shell should therefore offer the user the option of interacting with the content either in print or as an audio clip.

Images and Video Clips

The GEGS game board provides the option of including images (photos, drawings, graphs, figures) or short video clips (30 seconds or less) to illustrate a situation or give a demonstration or an explanation. Guidelines include the following[v]:

- Choose images that clearly illustrate the desired content or topic, introducing all its important aspects
- Use images that can be adjusted to fit the game board. Some pictures in JPEG format allow major modifications
- Focus on the relevant details in an image. Too many details will obscure the key points of the image, while too few will diminish the image's significance

- Avoid long download times for an image or video. If the estimated download time exceeds 10 seconds, warn the user of this wait
- Display pictures and video inside a screen window. If an image is large, it should open in a new window.
- Position videos on pages which contain little text information. The screen dimension should allow good visibility for any action taking place in the video clip. Keep the controls of the multimedia elements (replay, adjust volume, etc.) accessible at all times.

MEDIA DESIGN ERRORS IN A GEGS

Here are some media design errors to avoid while designing and building a game shell:

- poor quality materials such as inaudible sound clips, illegible charts, video displays which are too small, too slow to load, blurry, or too dark
- web pages with too many colors (more than six) or in which colors are used without coherence. Such excess inhibits reading of the pages and becomes a source of annoyance for users
- an inappropriate writing style for the target user, e.g., too informal or too formal for the age group or context
- a game board that is too large for the player's screen, which will prevent him from playing efficiently
- game actions that are difficult to carry out with a keyboard and that require technologies or materials not readily available in schools
- video clips, images, or 3D animation that requires too much memory (RAM), thus slowing down the game and reducing player interest and motivation

CONCLUSION

Information is part of our daily life, but it is not synonymous with simplicity. It is not enough to go on a web site to understand it, no more than it is enough to buy software to be able to make it work. They both have to be designed to be easy to use! (Usabilis, 2008, p.1).

Whether it is the choice of colors, fonts, organization of screen elements, navigation, or the text, visuals or sound of a web page, these guidelines, recommended by game and computer ergonomics experts, assure us that the GEGS and the games it generates are friendly, useful, simple, and rewarding.

Respecting these rules is important in developing online applications. Delays and difficulties during the creation of a GEGS can cost up to 80 percent of the project's budget to fix (Usabilis, 2008). Better knowledge of effective use of a web environment and of user needs allows us to avoid mistakes and the cost of correcting them. However, only a formative evaluation of the GEGS will allow us to measure its efficacy, and optimize its navigation by game developers.

ACKNOWLEDGMENT

We would like to thank the development team, under the direction of Louise Sauvé, for the online *Parcheesi* GEGS: Louis Poulette, Marc-André Girard, Daniel Paquet, Mélanie Gravel, Jean-François Paré, and Annie Lachance.

REFERENCES

Adams, E., & Rollings, A. (2003). *On game design.* Indianapolis, IN: New Riders Publishing.

Bailey, H. J., & Milheim, W. D. (1991). A comprehensive model for designing video based materials. In *Proceedings of the Ninth Conference on Interactive Instruction Delivery, Orlando, Florida* (pp. 26-33). Warrenton, VA: Society for Applied Learning Technology.

Chevallier, S. (2003). *D'une démarche ergonomique pour le développement des logiciels de loisir* [On an ergonomic process for the development of entertainment software]. Retrieved May 15, 2005 from http://www.hyperpsy.levillage.org/IMG/pdf/DemarcheErgo06.pdf

Clark, J. (2002). *Building accessible websites*. Indianapolis, IN: New Riders Publishing.

Dessaint, M. P. (1995). Lire, écrire et être lu [Reading, writing and readability]. In M. P. Dessaint (Ed.), *Guide de planification, de rédaction et d'édition pour la conception de cours à distance* [Guide to planning, writing, and editing for the design of a distance education course] (pp. 83-140). Québec, QC, Canada: Presses de l'Université du Québec.

Dufresne, A. (2009). *Introduction aux principes ergonomiques* (web site). Retrieved May 29, 2009 from http://lrcm.com.umontreal.ca/dufresne/bta/ergo/frame1.html

Ergolab (2003). *Faciliter la lecture d'informations sur le web* [Facilating the lecture with information on the web]. Retrieved May 29, 2009 from http://www.ergolab.net/articles/faciliter-lecture-informations-web.html

Ergolab (2004). *Accessibilité visuelle des interfaces web* [Accessibility of web interfaces]. Retrieved June 6, 2009 from http://www.ergolab.net/articles/accessibilite-visuelle-web.html

Fahy, P. J. (2004). Media characteristics and online learning technology. In T. Anderson & F. Elloumi (Eds). *Theory and practice of online learning* (pp. 137-174). Athabasca, AB, Canada: Athasbasca University.

Faiola, T. (1990). Principles and guidelines for a screen display interface. *The Videodiscs Monitor*, *8*(2), 27–29.

Faiola, T., & Deblois, M. L. (1988). Designing a visual factors-based screen display interface: The new role of the graphic technologist . *Educational Technology*, *28*(8), 12–21.

Garner, K. H. (1990). 20 rules for arranging text on a screen. *CBT Directions*, *3*(5), 13–17.

Gilbert, K. R. (1997). Teaching on the Internet: the World Wide Web as a course delivery system. In N. Millichap (Ed.), *Beginnings: Initial experiences in teaching via distance education.* Indianapolis, IN: Indiana Partnership for Statewide Education (IPSE).

Hannafin, M. J., & Hooper, S. (1989). An integrated framework for CBI screen design and layout. *Computers in Human Behavior*, *5*(3), 155–165. doi:10.1016/0747-5632(89)90009-5

Harvey, D. (1999). *La multimédiatisation de l'enseignement* [The multimediazation of learning]. Paris: Harmattan.

Hazen, M. (1985). Instructional software design principles. *Educational Technology*, *25I*(11), 18–23.

Hoekma, J. (1983). Interactive videodisc: A new architecture . *Performance & Instruction*, *22*(9), 6–9. doi:10.1002/pfi.4150220905

Johnson, D., & Wiles, J. (2003). Effective affective user interface design in games. *Ergonomics*, *46*(13-14), 1332–1345. doi:10.1080/00140130310001610865

Jonassen, D. H., Hannum, W. H., & Tessmer, M. (1989). *Handbook of task analysis procedures.* New York: Praeger.

Kellner, C. (2000). La *médiation par le cédérom « ludo-éducatif ». Approche communicationnelle* [Mediation by educational game CD-ROM: Communicative approach]. Unpublished Ph.D. dissertation in information science and communication, University of Metz.

Kellner, C. (2008). Utiliser les potentialités du multimédia interactif. [Utilize the potentiaql of interactive multimedia]. In *Actes du colloque scientifique Ludovia - 2008* (pp. 160-170). Ax les Thermes – Ariège, France: Institut de Recherche en Informatique de Toulouse and Laboratoire de Recherche en Audiovisuel.

Klare, G. R. (1984). Readability. In P. D. Pearson (Ed.), *Handbook of reading research* (pp. 681-744). New York: Longman.

Kox, K., & Walker, D. (1993). *User interface design* (2nd ed.). Toronto, ON, Canada: Prentice Hall.

Krug, S. (2001). *Don't make me think: A common sense approach to Web usability.* Indianapolis IN: New Riders Publishing.

Laberge, N., & Sauvé, L. (1998). *Les environnements multimédia interactifs sur l'inforoute. Critères à respecter pour l'interface – utilisateur* [Multimedia interactive environments on the Internet: Criteria for the user interface] (Research Report). Québec, QC, Canada: SAVIE.

Lebrun, N., & Berthelot, S. (1996). *Pour une approche multimédiatique de l'enseignement* [For a multimedia approach to teaching]. Montréal, QC, Canada: Éditions Nouvelles.

Livet, A. (2007). *Étude sur l'évolution ergonomique des logiciels de conception* [Study of the ergonomic evolution of computer design]. Unpublished report for the first year of the Master's of Cognitive Science. Bron, France: Université Lyon II.

Martial, O. (2000). *Méthodologie de conception d'application centrée sur l'utilisateur* User-centered application design]. Course manual. Montréal, QC, Canada: CRIM Formation, Centre de recherche informatique de Montréal.

Messin, A. (2008). L'usage d'Internet par les jeunes adultes: quelles compétences? [Use of the Internet by young adults: What competencies?] In *Actes du colloque scientifique Ludovia - 2008* (pp. 204-214). Ax les Thermes – Ariège, France: Institut de Recherche en Informatique de Toulouse et Laboratoire de Recherche en Audiovisuel.

Milheim, W. D., & Lavix, C. (1992). Screen design for computer-based training and interactive video: Practical suggestions and overall guidelines. *Performances & Instruction, 31*(5), 13–21. doi:10.1002/pfi.4170310507

Millerand, F., & Martial, O. (2001). *Guide pratique de conception et d'évaluation ergonomique de sites Web* [Practical guide to the design and evaluation of Web sites]. Montréal, QC, Canada: Centre de recherche informatique de Montréal. Available at http://www.crim.ca/files/documents/services/rd/GuideErgonomique.PDF

Najjar, L. J. (2001). Principles of educational multimedia user interface design. In R. W. Swezey & D. H. Andrews (Eds.), *Readings in training and simulation: A 30-year perspective* (pp. 146-158). Santa Monica, CA: Human Factors and Ergonomics Society.

Nielsen, J. (2000). *Designing Web usability: The practice of simplicity.* Indianapolis, IN: New Riders Publishing.

Nogier, J. F. (2005). *Ergonomie du logiciel et design web. Le manuel des interfaces utilisateur* [Computer ergonomics and web design: The manual of user interfaces]. Paris: Dunod.

Pagulayan, R. J., Keefer, K., Wixon, D., Romero, R. L., & Fuller, T. (2003). User-centered design in games. In A. Jacko Julie & A. Sears (Eds.), *The human-computer interaction handbook. Fundamentals, evolving technologies, and emerging applications* (pp. 883-906). Mahwah, N.J.: Lawrence Erlbaum Associates Inc.

Pearrow, M. (2007). *Web usability handbook* (2nd ed.). Boston, MA: Charles River Media.

Rambally, G. K., & Rambally, R. S. (1987). Human factors in CAI design. *Computers & Education*, *11*(2), 149–153. doi:10.1016/0360-1315(87)90009-1

Rollings, A., & Morris, D. (2005). *Conception et architecture des jeux vidéo* [Design and architecture of video games]. Paris: Vuibert Informatique.

Rovick, A. A. (1985). Writing computer lessons. *The Physiologist*, *28*(3), 173–176.

Salen, K., & Zimmerman, E. (2003). *Rules of play: Game design fundamentals*. Cambridge, MA: The MIT Press.

Sauvé, L. (1995). Les médias: des outils indispensables pour réduire la distance [Media: Indispensable tools for distance education]. In M.P. Dessaint (Ed.), *Guide de planification, de rédaction et d'édition pour la conception de cours à distance* (pp. 279-342). Québec, QC, Canada: Les presses de l'Universitaire du Québec.

Sauvé, L. (2006). *Guide de rédaction d'un devis de conception: quelques règles médiatiques* [Guide for writing a design plan: Media rules]. Québec, QC, Canada: SAVIE.

Sauvé, L., & Power, M. IsaBelle, C., Samson, D., & St-Pierre, C. (2002). *Rapport final - Jeux-cadres sur l'inforoute: Multiplicateurs de jeux pédagogiques francophones* [Final report – Frame games on the Internet: Multipliers of francophone learning games.] Report for partnership, Bureau des technologies d'apprentissage. Québec, QC, Canada: SAVIE.

Shneiderman, B., & Plaisant, C. (2004). *Designing the user interface: Strategies for effective Human-Computer interaction* (4th ed.). Boston, MA: Addison Wesley.

Strickland, R. M., & Poe, S. E. (1989). Developing a CAI graphics simulation model: Guidelines. *T.H.E. Journal*, *16*(7), 88–92.

Thoa, E. (2004). *Ergonomie et jeu vidéo* [Ergonomics and video games].Retrieved April 12, 2008 from http://www.usabilis.com/articles/2004/ergonomie-jeu.htm.

Thoa, E. (2004). *Ergonomie et jeu vidéo* [Ergonomics and video games]. Retrieved April 12, 2008 from http://www.usabilis.com/articles/2004/ergonomie-jeu.htm

Usabilis (2008). *Ergonomie informatique* [Information ergonomics]. Retrieved December 12, 2008 from http://www.usabilis.com/methode/ergonomienformatique.htm. Paris:Usabilis.

Usabilis (2009). *Ergonomie informatique* [Information ergonomics]. Available at http://www.usabilis.com/methode/ergonomienformatique.htm. Paris: Usabilis.

Vanderdonckt, J., & Mariage, C. (2000, October). *Introduction à la conception ergonomique des pages Web* [Introduction to ergonomic design for web pages]. Tutorial presented at the ERGO-IHM'2000 International Conference.

Wisner, A. (1972). *Textes généraux sur l'ergonomie* [General text on ergonomics]. Paris: Laboratoire de physiologie du travail et d'ergonomie.

ADDITIONAL READING

Nogier, J. F. (2005). *Ergonomie du logiciel et design web. Le manuel des interfaces utilisateur* [Ergonomics for software and web design: The manual for user interfaces]. Paris: Dunod.

KEY TERMS AND DEFINITIONS

Educational Game: A fictitious, fantasy, or imaginary situation in which players, placed in conflict with others or assembled in a team against an external opponent, are governed by rules determining their actions with a view to achieving learning objectives and a goal determined by the game, either to win or to seek revenge.

Interface: A device enabling exchanges of information between two systems. A computer interface includes all components, such as screen, keyboard, mouse, etc., and software, to help users accomplish a given set of tasks effectively.

Usability: The degree to which a product can be used by specific users to accomplish a given set of tasks effectively, and to their satisfaction.

Utility: The capacity of an object or application to help realize its user's objectives.

ENDNOTES

i Sources referred to in developing our guidelines include: Adams and Rollings (2003), Bailey and Milheim (1991), Chevallier (2003), Dufresne (2000), Faiola (1990), Faiola and Deblois (1988), Garner (1990), Gilbert (1997), Hannafin and Hooper (1989), Harvey (1999), Hazen (1985), Hoekma (1983), Johnson and Wiles (2001), Jonassen, Hannum, and Tessmer (1989), Kellner (2000), Kox and Walker (1993), Laberge and Sauvé (1998), Livet (2007), Messin (2008), Millerand and Martial (2001), Milheim and Lavix (1992), Najjar (2001), Pagulayan et al. (2003), Pearrow (2007), Rambally and Rambally (1987). Rollings and Morris (2005), Rovick (1985), Salen and Zimmerman (2003), Sauvé et al. (2002), Shneiderman and Plaisant (2004), Strickland and Poe (1989), Vanderdonckt and Mariage (2000).

ii Chevallier (2003), Dufresne (2000), Krug (2001), Millerand and Martial (2001), Nogier (2005), Sauvé (2006), Shneiderman and Plaisant (2004), Vanderdonckt and Mariage (2000).

iii Bailey and Milheim (1991), Clark (2002), Ergolab (2004), Fahy (2004), Faiola (1990), Millerand and Martial (2001), Nogier (2005), Rambally and Rambally (1987), Sauvé (2006), Strickland and Poe (1987), Vanderdonckt and Mariage (2000).

iv Dufresne (2000), Jonassen et al.(1989), Nogier (2005), Rambally and Rambally (1987), Sauvé (2006), Shneiderman and Plaisant (2004).

v Hoekma (1983), Lebrun and Berthelot (1996), Millerand and Martial (2001), Nogier (2005), Sauvé (2006), Thoa (2004).

Chapter 25
Validation of a Generic Educational Game Shell

Louise Sauvé
Télé-université, Canada

ABSTRACT

This chapter describes the process of validation of a generic educational game shell (GEGS) with the target users for whom it was created, based on the trial method known as Learner Verification and Revision (LVR). It describes the validation objectives and evaluation criteria (pedagogic and ergonomic) used to develop the measurement instruments. It also describes the methodology for a trial conducted with nine pre-service (student) teachers, finishing with the validation results and resulting revisions to the GEGS.

INTRODUCTION

The importance of taking into account the user's point of view in the creation of Internet-based learning environments has been increasingly studied (Koohang, 2004; Nielsen, 1993; Sing & Der-Thanq, 2004). Validation is a process intended to show that a procedure, technique or activity accomplishes its desired results (Thulal, 2003; Wikipédia, 2008). In the case of validation of a web environment such as a generic educational game shell (GEGS), it is a process of ensuring that the shell's results (i.e., the educational games developed by game builders) will consistently correspond to their specifications as entered and will meet predetermined quality criteria. Identifying delays and difficulties encountered by game builders during the creation of an educational game, and finding solutions to them, improves the usability of the GEGS (Nogier, 2005; Usabilis, 2008). Validation, the fourth stage of the process of creating a GEGS, allows us to measure the degree of user friendliness, utility, and ease of use for its target audience (i.e., teachers) as well as whether it meets the teachers' pedagogical requirements sufficiently to be used in class or for online teaching.

This chapter first introduces the *Learner Verification and Revision (LVR)* method, which guided

DOI: 10.4018/978-1-61520-731-2.ch025

our validation process. It then describes the validation of our *Parcheesi*™ GEGS, including the formulation of validation objectives and questions, analysis factors, development of measurement instruments (used before, during, and after the trial), the quantitative and qualitative modes of analyses used, and the ethical disclosure and consent procedures. Finally, results of the trial are outlined, and recommendations for improvements to the GEGS are presented.

THE VALIDATION METHOD

The *Learner Verification and Revision (LVR)* method (Komoski, 1979; 1984), which focuses on the user, is characterized by flexibility and is well adapted to the context in which the product will be used (Nguyen et al., 2008). It allowed us to identify and correct errors and problems and to effectively validate a prototype in the course of development with a sample of the target users for whom the GEGS was created. This method, based on user trials, has also been used in game development research (Kandaswany, Stolovitch, & Thiagarajan, 1976; Stolovitch, 1982; Thiagarajan, 1978), and for other online GEGSs (Sauvé et al., 2002; Sauve & Samson, 2004).

In this method, the three phases of the target population trial are:

- The *preparation* phase, consisting of: (1) establishing the objectives and the evaluation criteria; (2) choosing the evaluation tools; (3) writing out, testing and if necessary, revising the evaluation tools; (4) contacting and informing the target population (teachers and trainers), and (5) giving them the materials required for the trial.
- The *verification* phase, including: (1) examining and manipulating the various parts of the product, and (2) collecting the users' comments using measurement instruments before, during and after the development of the product (an online educational game).
- The *decision* phase, consisting of (1) compiling, processing and analyzing the results; (2) making any necessary revisions, and (3) revising, if necessary, the GEGS in light of the information gathered from the users.

We describe in the following sections how this method was applied in the creation of the *Parcheesi* GEGS.

THE *PARCHEESI* GEGS USER TRIAL

The *Parcheesi* GEGS user trial aimed to: (1) measure the relevance and the adaptability of the game to the teachers' pedagogical requirements, and (2) measure the degree of user-friendliness, usefulness and ease of use of the online GEGS. Participants were nine pre-service teachers studying preschool and elementary education in October, 2007. This trial was intended to answer the following two questions:

1. What are the pedagogical requirements to which educational game environments must conform in order to stimulate use and development of educational games by teachers and trainers?
2. What is the degree of user-friendliness, usefulness and ease of use of the *Parcheesi* GEGS design for teachers?

Variables and Evaluation Criteria

To answer these questions, evaluation criteria were identified, as shown in Table 1. We based our choice of criteria on the recommendations of Agence Fonds social européen (2005), Bibeau et Delisle (2001), Centre de ressources Le Préau (2002), Gerhardt-Powals (1996), Kennedy, Petrovic, & Keppell (1998), Kirakowski, Claridge, & Whitehand (1998), Najjar (2001),

Table 1. Parcheesi GEGS evaluation criteria

Variables Studied	Evaluation Criteria
User-friendliness, usefulness and ease of design of the GEGS	*Ease of navigation in the environment:* table of contents, navigation bar, navigation help button, etc.
	Usefulness: number of instructions used for creation (contextual help and Creation Guide) and ease of use of the templates in creating a game.
	Pedagogical readability of the web page contents while in author mode to ensure ease of game design.
	Time spent creating the game, preparation and design: (1) time taken to formulate the questions and the types of answers before creation; (2) time spent completing the different templates, and (3) time spent using different information bubbles as well as the guide during the creative process.
	Ease of execution of the design process: types of individual difficulties encountered and participant reactions during the design process.
	Flexibility during the creative process: choice of order when selecting templates.
Relevance and adaptability of games, in regards to pedagogical requirements of teachers, developed using the GEGS	*Game adaptability*: the game objectives and contents meet the objectives and contents suggested by school programs.
	Accessibility: availability at all times, in the classroom and at home, ease of online access, and only a reasonable amount of reading needed to understand the rules and instructions.
	User-friendliness: ease of use of the game, even for beginners.
	Game interactivity: whether the game gives the learner a chance to interact as the game progresses, e.g., choosing answers that best fit the questions asked in the game, stating an answer orally to be corrected by other players, voting for other players, voting to determine whether an answer is right or wrong, placing tokens according to a team strategy, receiving feedback for an answer or an action committed.
	The game's impact on learning: the game's ability to support the acquisition and integration of knowledge, the development of problem solving competencies, communication and cooperation abilities, human relations and encourages reflection on the part of the learner.
	Motivation: learner motivation for the subject matter being studied indicates the game's capacity to stimulate and maintain learner interest in the subject matter at hand.
	Appropriateness of game contents to the level of knowledge of the learners: the game's capacity to draw from the learner's prior knowledge in the hopes of engaging them in the learning process.
	Aesthetics and the game's currency: up-to-date images, videos and illustrations in the game adapted to the target population.

Nogier (2005), Nokelainen (2005), Turk (2001), and Usabilis (2008). These criteria refer to factors which can affect the pedagogical and technological quality of the online learning environment.

Measurement Instruments

The measurement instruments used to collect information from the target population included:

- a *questionnaire on teacher's pedagogical requirements for online games*, completed before the game trial. The purpose of this questionnaire was to determine which attributes of online games were considered important by teachers. A scale of one to five was used where 1 = very important and 5 = not at all important.
- two methods of *observation* during the process of creating a game with the GEGS: (1) the *OpenVULab* software (Wideman et al., 2007; also see Chapter 13 of this volume), which records the actions of each participant and captures screenshots, used throughout the trial process (Figure 1), and (2) real-time observation done by two research assistants during the sample population's trial of the GEGS. To analyze this data, an observation grid was developed to collect both the qualitative and the

Figure 1. Screenshot taken during the trial with the OpenVULab software

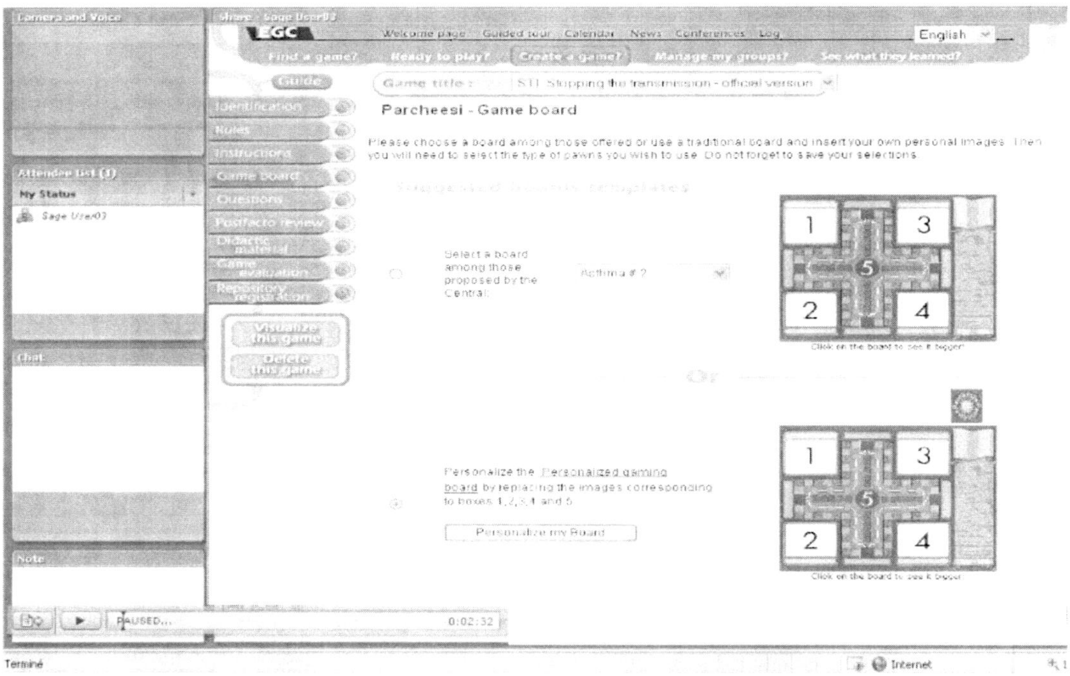

quantitative data regarding the ease of use, user-friendliness and potential difficulties for teacher candidates with the GEGS. The data collected was concerned with (1) data-processing competencies needed to use the GEGS; (2) the user-friendliness of the GEGS based on the number of information bubbles which were used for each template and their degree of help as indicated by the ease of use of the GEGS; (3) the time taken to prepare and develop the game (time used to prepare the formulation of the questions and the type of answer before the design, time to fill out the various forms, timing of use of the various information bubbles and the guide); (4) ease of execution of the game creation process, as indicated by the types of individual difficulties encountered, and the reactions of the participants during the trial, and (5) the flexibility of the game during the creative phase, highlighted by the possibility of choosing the order of the template development.

- a *questionnaire on user-friendliness and relevance,* completed by the participants after the trial, dealing with: (1) ease of use of the templates and help tools during the creation and modification of a game; (2) the users' degree of satisfaction with the clarity and the user-friendliness of the GEGS's various templates, and (3) the presence of certain attributes expected of online games in the *Parcheesi* GEGS.
- a *group interview protocol,* making it possible for all the participants to express their opinions on difficulties encountered during the creation of their game with the *Parcheesi* GEGS. This was completed following participants' design and construction of their online games.

Parcheesi GEGS Templates

Creation of a game using the *Parcheesi* GEGS requires creators to follow a series of steps. Each step is organized by templates which must be completed. The *Identification* template (Figure 1) is the only step which must be completed in order (before the others). The templates are:

- the *Identification* template, which includes fields such as the title of the game, the author (s) of the game, the level of study for which the game is designed, the topic and goal of the game, the type of material used, the maximum number of players, the duration, and the language of the game;
- the *Rules* template, providing default rules but the rules can be modified to best suit the learning contents (Figure 2);
- the *Instructions* template, which provides default instructions offered by the GEGS but the instructions can be modified to suit the learning contents;
- the *Game Board* template, which presents a selection of boards to choose from and gives the option of creating a personalized board;
- the *Pedagogical Materials* template, which makes it possible for the designer to integrate, if necessary, additional materials for the game;
- the *Questions* template, the central and most important part of the game's creative process. Game creators must write out a minimum of 40 questions specifying questions, answers, feedback and links to the material to be learned, distributed into four categories. The ideal range is somewhere between 48 and 64 questions;
- the *Synthesis and Reflection* template, offering the use of either the default reflective questions on the game and its contents or the addition of questions by the designer according to the learning objectives;
- the *Registration of the Game in the Database* template, which allows the game

Figure 2. Rules template

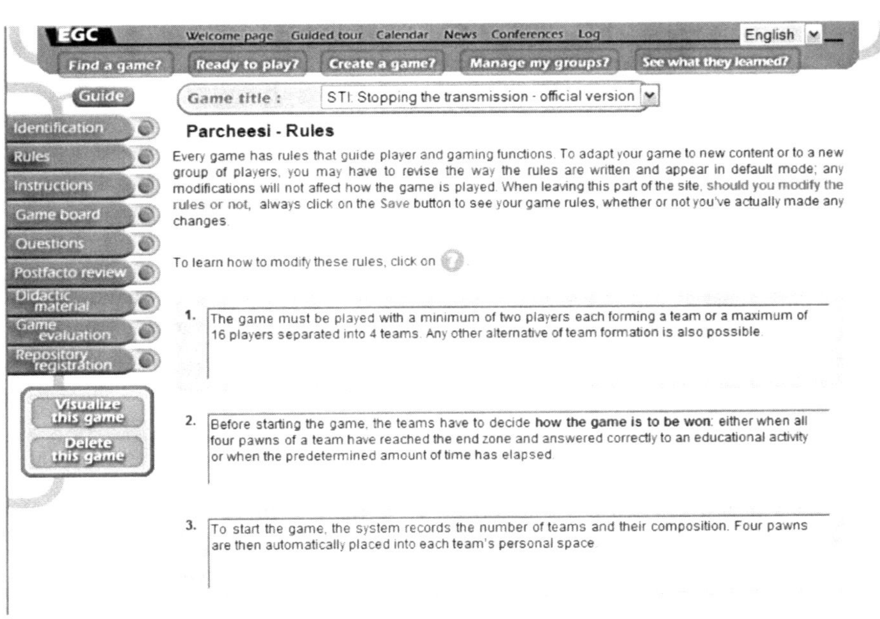

Figure 3. Green (here shown as gray) and red (here shown as white) buttons on the toolbar

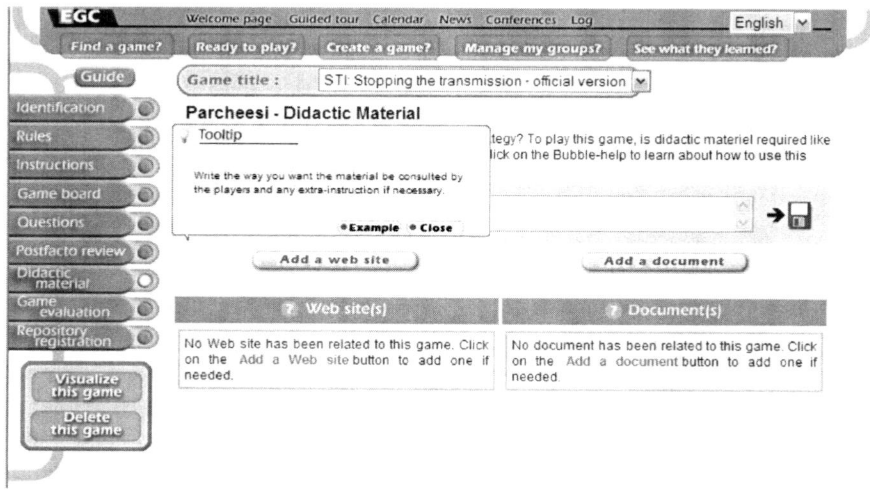

to be described and shared with the other members of the *Carrefour virtuel de jeux éducatifs/ Educational Games Central* community;

- the *Game Evaluation* template, offering the option of using the default game evaluation items or items modified to meet the evaluation goals of the designers.

To create a game using the GEGS and to make it available to other teachers and students, the designer must complete all of the GEGS's templates. When a form has been completed and the system requirements have been met, the red button which is displayed in the template tool bar turns to green (Figure 3). Once all the buttons are green they indicate that all the GEGS's templates have been completed, allowing the designer to create a game at her/his own pace and to make the game available only when it is complete.

Two other mechanisms were also integrated into the GEGS to facilitate creation of a game or its deletion if it becomes obsolete:

- the *Visualization* button, allowing the game to be previewed at any point during the creation process;
- the *Delete Game* button, allowing the game and all associated information to be deleted.

Data Analysis Methods

The quantitative information was analyzed using various descriptive techniques such as frequencies, average, and percentages). For the qualitative data, an observation grid was developed to organize the data into six sections: the behavior and competencies of teachers in the use of data processing, the reading of information bubbles by the participants for each template, the duration of template use, the flexibility of the steps, individual difficulties encountered, and the pre-service teachers' reactions during the trial. These sections made it possible to examine the user-friendliness, utility, and ease of use of the GEGS and to create design profiles of the participants in the experiment.

Conduct of the Trial

The trial was carried out in October, 2007 over two sessions of approximately two hours each.

One week before the trial, participants completed a pre-trial measurement instrument. During the two trial sessions, they each built a game using the *Parcheesi* GEGS. At the end of the second trial session, the participants completed a questionnaire and answered some questions in a focus group.

Ethical Disclosure and Consent

All participants signed consent forms describing their tasks during the trial and the confidentiality of the data to be gathered, both in terms of internal and external publications.

FORMATIVE EVALUATION RESULTS

The results of this formative evaluation provided useful feedback on many dimensions that helped us to refine and improve the *Parcheesi* GEGS as a tool to help educators to develop and use educational games that meet their learning requirements.

User-Friendliness, Utility, and Ease of Use

To measure the degree of user-friendliness, of utility and ease of use of the GEGS, various aspects were observed during the trial: (1) the degree of user-friendliness of the GEGS and its information bubbles; (2) the time used to prepare and create a game; (3) the flexibility of the game creation process; and finally, (4) game creation ease of execution.

User-Friendliness

Results showed that the majority of the templates were considered easy to use and the degree of pedagogical readability based on several indicators (quality of language, structure of the tool bar, ease of navigation) was very good.

The easiest templates to use, according to trial participants, were those that came with preset default parameters or text, such as the *Instructions*, *Rules*, *Synthesis and Reflections*, and the *Game Evaluation* template. The templates deemed more difficult to use were the *Game Board*, *Questions*, *Registration of the Game in the Database*, and *Pedagogical Materials* templates. Many users required the help of the information bubbles and took additional time to complete the last four templates mentioned. The participants also noted difficulties using certain templates, including the following:

- For the *Game Board* template, the only difficulty encountered was in inserting images in the game board. Two of the participants did not understand that only jpg and gif formatted images could be used. They tried unsuccessfully to insert images in Word format, which led them to the use of the information bubbles to help solve their problem. This issue reveals the technical expertise necessary to customize the game board and the importance of offering a choice of pre-developed game boards in the GEGS.
- For the *Registration of the Game in the Database* template, the only problems stemmed from the users' lack of knowledge of certain terms together with their failure to read certain information bubbles.
- For the *Pedagogical Materials* template, designers who did not wish to insert additional materials had problems activating the completion button. The needed explanation was provided in an often-ignored information bubble. To correct this situation, it may be necessary to insert additional information on completing the template on the template itself rather than as an information bubble.
- For the *Questions* template, a greater number of participants had to consult the information bubbles during the drafting of their first question. However, once they understood the functioning of the entry

mechanism for questions, answers and feedback, other questions were completed without difficulty.
- Lastly, the *Identification* template, in spite of the number of tasks necessary for completion, was seen as being very easy to complete by all the participants, as were the *Visualization* and *Delete Game* buttons.

User-Friendliness of the Information Bubbles

In order to better understand how to create a game, game builders using the GEGS are provided with a guide (in pdf format) that is accessible at all times by clicking on a toolbar icon. Small help capsules (information bubbles) are used in conjunction with the guide and are opened by a simple mouse click (Figure 3). Information bubbles are associated with template elements, explaining their functions and showing examples. Their use is optional and varies according to the needs of each game builder. During the trial process, we noted the usefulness and relevance of the information bubbles for the pre-service teachers.

Results showed that the use of the information bubbles did not necessarily depend on the GEGS's characteristics, but rather on the participants' competencies and level of understanding of the various template functions, as well as their curiosity or the degree of insecurity they felt during game creation. The designers generally found that the explanations provided by the information bubbles were clear and useful. They commented on the clarity of certain instructions and the relevance of certain examples (Table 2); they considered that the examples, for instance, should show more than one way of solving a problem, such as the information bubble which shows three ways of writing a game title.

It should be noted that the guide for creating a game was read outside the context of the trial sessions; the participants found the guide easy to use and suggested no changes at the time of the interview.

Game Creation Times

During the trial sessions, we measured (1) the time taken to prepare and design a game; (2) the time spent completing the various templates, and finally (3) the length of time spent using various information bubbles and the guide during game creation.

When designing the *Parcheesi* GEGS, we estimated that a teacher would spend between 120 and 160 minutes to create a game adapted to the needs of his students. This excludes time spent preparing game content—an estimated two to three hours of work (Sauvé et al., 2006).

Trial participants stated that they spent an average of two hours (120 minutes) to prepare the various types of questions and answers for their games; their average time to complete the templates was 105 minutes, while the longest time taken was 120 minutes. In fact, the *Questions* and *Game Board* templates required the most time. The majority of the designers took on average 80 minutes to enter 40 questions with various answer choices into the *Questions* template. Only two participants completed the form in less than one hour. Time spent completing the first learning activity was closely linked to high usage of information bubbles by students; the more the participants resorted to information bubbles at the beginning of the drafting of learning activities, the longer it took to complete the first question.

The time taken to complete the *Game Board* template varied. Participants who chose one of the GEGS's pre-designed game boards spent on average 3 minutes to complete this step, whereas those who created personalized game boards spent an average of 10 minutes to complete the template.

Finally, the average time an information bubble was used was 30 seconds. Participants spent an average of 20 minutes consulting the guide outside of the trial session.

Table 2. Parcheesi GEGS Revisions

Elements	Prescription	Revision
Game board template	Examine the accessibility of information on the topic of what types of images (jpg, gif) can be included in the game board.	In the instructions on image dimension, include a sentence explaining to designers that Word document format cannot be used to insert images. Additional instructions on converting the Word image into a jpg or gif file will be included using a hyperlink.
	Verify the possibility of transferring images as Word files into the game board. If it is possible, describe the method of image transfer from a Word document or as an Internet file for integration in the game board.	It is not possible to directly transfer images from a Word file ".doc". An explanation will be provided on converting doc files into HTML. Here is an example: *You can convert your image contained in a ".doc." file into an "HTML" file using Word. During the conversion, a repertoire is created of all the images in their original format.*
	Determine whether it is possible to transfer images found on the Internet to the questions and the game board.	Instructions will be given for web image transfer. Here is an example: *To save a web image, click the image with the right mouse button and select "Save image as... ". Be careful using images from web sites you did not create—you must get the author's permission to use the image unless it is a site with images that are not copyrighted.*
Questions template	Examine the location of information concerning the types of image to be included in the questions.	Include instructions above each type of question informing designers that it is not possible to directly include images from a Word file. Additional instructions will be provided in hyperlink form explaining the process of converting the Word file into jpg or gif.
	Determine whether it is possible to transfer images found on the Internet for their integration into the questions.	Instructions will be provided explaining the transfer of Web images. Here is an example: *To save a web image, right click your mouse on the image and select "Save image as... ". Be careful using images from web sites you did not create- you must get the author's permission to use the image unless it is a site with images that are not copyrighted.*
	Determine whether it is possible to transfer the images in Word to the questions. If so, explain the method of transfer of the images in a Word document or on the Internet for their integration into the questions.	It is not possible to directly transfer images from a Word file ".doc". An explanation will be provided on converting doc files into HTML. Here is an example: *You can convert your image contained in a ".doc." file into an "HTML" file using Word. During the conversion, a repertoire is created of all the images in their original format.*
	Verify whether the types of questions offered aid the development of the aptitudes and competencies of primary and secondary students.	Revisions to be made after additional studies.
Questions template	Check inconsistencies between the title in the table of contents, Questions, and the template's contents which in fact refers to Learning Activites.	Revise the template page to ensure consistent use of terms.
	When the designers begin creating their questions, no question is posted on the page. This creates confusion because of the instructions in the information-bubble about the *List of questions*. It is suggested that, as is the case with the other templates, short explanations to introduce the template be included.	Add to the *Questions* page the following text: *No question yet posted on this page. You must select one of the types of questions from the tab "Select a type of questions to create" in order to design one. Once the question has been created, it appears automatically on this page along with the other questions you will create. The list of your questions allows you to ensure you have met the minimum number of questions (8) in each of the 4 activity categories.*
The *Pedagogical materials* template	Explain how to complete the template if no pedagogical materials are to be included in the game.	Add the following phrase to the template page just after the first paragraph: *If this game requires no additional pedagogical materials, click on the tab (the disk icon) in order to signal that this step is complete and it will be saved.*
Registration of the game in the repertoire template	Specify and define the terms used in the information bubbles for this template, particularly the Game descriptor.	To define or clarify the term: "Game descriptor". Re-examine the other terms to improve the definitions and explanations.

continued next page

Table 2. continued

Elements	Prescription	Revision
Questions template information bubbles		
Information bubble *Select a type of question to be created from the selection*	The tab called "*Select a type of question to be created from the selection*" on the "Questions" page is not accompanied by an information bubble which specifies only "Type of questions" = different types of questions.	Add an information bubble to explain *Select a type of question to be created from the selection*. In this information bubble, explain the number of questions available to the designers as well as the impact of the choice of a question on the contents which will be integrated. Here is an example. *Thirteen types of questions are proposed. Click one of the types to select the template which will allow you to include contents. Once the type of question is selected, and the contents are integrated, the question is posted on the Questions list page. Note, the designer cannot transfer the contents of one question to another type of question. If she/he tries to do this, all the contents in the question's cells will be deleted.*
Information-bubble *Questions list*	Revise the information bubble on the *Questions list*. It does not allow the designer to understand its use or its role in synthesizing all the questions created by the designer.	Add to the information bubble instructions a complementary explanation on the use of the Questions list. Here is an example: *This page displays all the questions as you create them for the game. This list enables you to view, at any time, a particular question in order to modify it or delete it. Click on one of the questions listed to display the question created. Different possibilities are available once you have created a minimum of one question.*
Information-bubble: *Fill-in-the-blank questions*	Certain users considered this information bubble to be very detailed.	Display a short definition with an example, and give the option of finding a more detailed explanation by following a hyperlink.
Information bubble: *Multiple choice questions*	Contrary to the other information bubbles related to the multiple choice questions, this information bubble does not explain what a multiple choice question with multiple choice answers is.	Modify the information bubble instructions in order to include a short definition of the type of question and to review the example.
Information bubble: *True or false questions*	Certain users considered this information bubble to be too detailed.	Present a short definition accompanied by an example, and give the option finding a more details explanation by hyperlink.
Information bubble: *Subject matter reference*	The participants do not understand the explanations and the example in the existing information bubble: *Subject matter reference (if necessary)* Example: *General Chemistry, page 55.*	Re-examine the instructions and the example in the information bubble in order to specify the function of "*Subject matter reference*"

Flexibility Throughout the Creative Process

The *Parcheesi* GEGS offers designers a high level of flexibility in choosing the order in which the templates can be completed. Only the *Identification* template must be completed first in order to progress to the other steps in the design process. The recorded analyses show that the participants preferred to follow the steps in the order suggested by the site.

Ease of Completing the Game Creation Process

Based on the average time taken by the participants to create a game (105 minutes), results of observing the game creation process, and comments in the collective interview, we observed that the participants see the process as easy to execute. In order to improve the process, participants made some suggestions that were noted in the preceding sections, especially in regard to the clarity of explanations and examples in the information bubbles, but also about the tool which validates the completion of the *Pedagogical Requirements* template.

Quantitative and qualitative data analysis of the trial confirmed that the *Parcheesi* GEGS is very much appreciated for its user-friendliness, its usefulness and its ease of completion.

Relevance and Adaptability of Games Created with the GEGS

The results of our trial confirm the findings of O' Neill (2004) in that the eight requirements of teachers for the use of learning resources are the same as those of our participants for choosing online educational games.

First, the respondents are most sensitive to requirements directly associated with the learning process, such as: (1) the potential correspondence between the objectives and the contents of the game and the objectives and contents of the school curriculum, and (2) the impact the games can have on learning and motivation as indicated by the game's capacity to stimulate and maintain the interest of the learner. Our results show as well that the educational games built with the *Parcheesi* GEGS fulfilled the teaching requirements of the respondents in terms of degree of user-friendliness, motivation, and aesthetic elements. The GEGS also generated a very high degree of satisfaction with regards to accessibility interactivity. The least satisfactory aspect of the game, according to respondents, was its lack of adaptability to various aptitudes and the competencies of the target population. It is interesting to note that this aspect of the educational game is highly related to the content that the teachers themselves build into the questions. We might hypothesize that they missed using the GEGS question types that support development of aptitudes and competencies.

As for the possible use of the games in their teaching, the results of the trial show that, in spite of their youth and their openness to information and communication technologies, and to games, the use of these tools is still regarded by teacher candidates as inferior to traditional forms of teaching and is not seen as a form of teaching in and of itself.

PARCHEESI GEGS REVISIONS

Based on the trial results (Sauvé & Hanca, 2007), Table 2 illustrates several suggestions for minor GEGS revisions intended to facilitate the game creation process.

The suggested corrections were made to the *Parcheesi* GEGS.

CONCLUSION

In order to ensure the quality of the *Parcheesi* GEGS in terms user-friendliness, usefulness, and meeting teachers' pedagogical requirements, a validation trial was carried out with nine pre-service teachers. Five measurement instruments allowed us to answer the specific questions included in the trial:

- What is the degree of user-friendliness, utility, and ease of design of the *Parcheesi GEGS* for teachers?
- What pedagogical requirements must educational game environment designs respond to in order to support the use and development of educational games by teachers and trainers?

In answer to the first question, the participants considered the *Parcheesi* GEGS to be user-friendly, useful and easy to use. They reported that the majority of its templates are easy to use and that their level of pedagogical readability is very high in language quality, the structure of the contents, and the ease of navigation. Certain templates, such as the *Game Board, Questions,*

Registration in the Database, and *Pedagogical Materials* require the use of information bubbles to facilitate the creative process. As for the information bubbles, the participants identified some issues, and the GEGS instructions and examples were revised to increase their clarity.

In regards to the second question, the results correspond to O'Neill's (2004) findings. The eight requirements of teachers for the use of educational resources are the same as those required by the participants when choosing online educational games. Participants considered that the games they developed fulfill their teaching requirements for user-friendliness, adaptability, motivational elements, impact on learning and aesthetical elements. They also concluded that accessibility and interactivity were successful features of the game. However, the games achieved a weaker result in terms of suitability to the aptitudes and competencies of the target population. It is interesting to note that this aspect of the educational game is interconnected with the content the teachers themselves build into the questions.

These findings resulted in the following recommendations:

- Given that the target users of the *Parcheesi* GEGS do not always have the needed technological competencies in using design software and video, we proposed self-training modules on these competencies for teachers interested in developing multimedia games.
- Since the *Parcheesi* GEGS allows the development of games which meet seven of the eight requirements of educational resources, it was recommended to communicate the results of the study to teachers in order to encourage them to create games adapted to their teaching needs.
- Because the 13 types of questions included in the GEGS do not meet participant needs related to the development of all skills needed by their target learners, follow-up studies were recommended to examine the contribution of new types of questions or learning activities to the GEGS.
- Since participants requested information bulletins (just-in-time information) during game creation, it was recommended to include such a mechanism in future educational game creation environments.
- Given the difficulties encountered in completing some forms, it was recommended to include additional instructions and examples for game builders.

Of course, the step of formative valuation also has a cost, estimated at about 6% of the total development budget (Nielsen, 1993). This investment is relatively small in relation to the importance of product quality and client satisfaction.

ACKNOWLEDGMENT

We would like to thank the development team, under the direction of Louise Sauvé, for the online *Parcheesi* GEGS: Louis Poulette, Marc-André Girard, Daniel Paquet, Mélanie Gravel, Jean-François Paré and Annie Lachance.

REFERENCES

Agence Fonds social européen (2005). *Guide méthodologique d'auto-évaluation et de validation des produits Equal* [Methodological guide to self-evaluation and validation of EQUAL products]. Agence Fonds social européen. Brussels: Agence Fonds social européen, Beligique, Francophone et Germanophone. Retrieved May 30, 2009 from http://www.equal-france.com/virtual/30/Documents/pdf/BfrGuide AutoEvalPdts.pdf

Bibeau, R., & Delisle, C. (2001). *Critères de qualité pour l'évaluation d'un site web* [Quality criteria for evaluating a web site]. Retrieved March 15, 2005 from http://concours2002.educationquebec.qc.ca/qualite2002.htm

Centre de ressources Le Préau (2002). *Quel modèle qualité pour la e-formation? Les normes qualités existantes répondent-elles aux besoins des acteurs de la e-formation?* [What quality model for e-learning? The quality norms that respond to the needs of the e-learning users?]. Retrieved May 15, 2002 from http://www.preau.ccip.fr/qualite/index.php

Chinien, C. (1990). Examination of cognitive style FD/FI as a learner selection criterion in formative evaluation. *Canadian Journal of Educational Communication*, *19*(1), 19–39.

Doak, C. C., Doak, L. G., & Root, J. H. (1996). *Teaching patients with low literacy skills* (2nd ed.). Philadelphia: J. B. Lippincott.

Gerhardt-Powals, J. (1996). Cognitive engineering principles for enhancing human-computer performance. *International Journal of Human-Computer Interaction*, *8*(2), 189–211. doi:10.1080/10447319609526147

Kandaswamy, S., Stolovitch, H., & Thiagarajan, S. (1976). Learner verification and revision: An experimental comparison of two methods. *Audio-visual . Communication Review*, *24*(3), 316–328.

Kennedy, G., Petrovic, T., & Keppell, M. (1998). The development of multimedia evaluation criteria and a program of evaluation for computer aided learning. In *Proceedings, ASCILITE '98* (pp. 407-415). Retrieved September 9, 2008 from http://www.ascilite.org.au/conferences/wollongong98/asc98-pdf/kennedypetrovickeppel.pdf

Kirakowski, J., Claridge, N., & Whitehand, R. (1998). Human centered measures of success in web site design. In *Proceedings, 4th Conference on Human Factors and the Web* (pp. 24-27). Basking Ridge, NJ: AT&T Labs.

Komoski, K. (1984). Formative evaluation. The empirical improvement of learning materials. *Performance & Instruction Journal*, *22*(5), 3–4. doi:10.1002/pfi.4150220504

Komoski, P. K. (1979). Counterpoint: Learner verification of instructional materials. *Educational Evaluation and Policy Analysis*, *1*(3), 101–103.

Koohang, A. (2004). A study of users' perceptions toward e-learning courseware usability. *International Journal on E-Learning*, *3*(2), 10–17.

Maddrell, J. (2008). *Article Review: IDT 848 Evaluation study abstracts*. Norfolk, VA: Old Dominion University. Retrieved March 10, 2009 from designedtoinspire.com/drupal/files/Article-Summary%20Maddrell.doc.

Najjar, L. J. (2001). Principles of educational multimedia user interface design. In R. W. Swezey & D. H. Andrews (Eds.), *Readings in training and simulation: A 30-year perspective* (pp. 146-158). Santa Monica, CA: Human Factors and Ergonomics Society.

Nguyen, T., Chang, V., Chang, E., Jacob, C., & Turk, A. (2008). A contingent method for usability evaluation of Web-based learning systems. In K. McFerrin, R. Weber, R. Carlsen, & D. A. Willis (Eds). *Proceedings of the Society for Information Technology & Teacher Education Annual International Conference (19th International Conference of SITE 2008)* (pp. 579-585). Chesapeake, VA: AACE.

Nielsen, J. (1993). *Usability engineering*. Boston: Academic Press, Inc.

Nogier, J. F. (2005). *Designing ease of use*. Usabilis: Web & Software Usability Consulting. Retrieved June 7, 2007 from http://www.usabilis.com/gb/index.html

Nokelainen, P. (2005). The technical and pedagogical usability criteria for digital learning material. In *Proceedings of the 2005 World Conference on Educational Multimedia, Hypermedia and Telecommunications* (pp. 1011-1016). Chesapeake, VA: AACE.

O'Neil, M. (2004). *Final report on gaps in resources available to deliver history and social studies curricula in Canada*. Toronto, ON, Canada: Historica Foundation.

Perron, L., & Bordeleau, P. (1994). Modèle de développement d'ensembles didactiques d'intégration pédagogique de l'ordinateur [Development model for integrating pedogogy and the computer]. In P. Bordeleau (Ed.), *Des outils pour apprendre avec l'ordinateur* (pp. 513-553). Montréal, QC, Canada: Les Éditions Logiques.

Sauvé, L., & Hanca, G. (2007). *Validation d'une coquille générique de jeu éducatif auprès des enseignants: Parchési* [Validation with teachers of a generic educational game shell: *Parcheesi*] (Research report). Québec, QC, Canada: SAGE and SAVIE.

Sauvé, L., & Power, M. IsaBelle, C., Samson, D., & St-Pierre, C. (2002). *Rapport final - Jeux-cadres sur l'inforoute: Multiplicateurs de jeux pédagogiques francophones* [Final report – Frame games on the Internet: Multipliers of francophone learning games.] Report for partnership, Bureau des technologies d'apprentissage. Québec, QC, Canada: SAVIE.

Sauvé, L., Renaud, L., & Kaszap, M. IsaBelle, C., Gauvin, M., Rodriguez, A. et al., (2006). *Modélisation du jeu-cadre Parchési* [Designing the frame game *Parcheesi*]. Québec, QC, Canada: SAVIE and SAGE.

Sauvé, L., & Samson, D. (2004). *Rapport d'évaluation de la coquille générique du Jeu de l'oie du projet* [Evaluation report for the generic game shell Mother Goose]. Report for the project Jeux génériques: multiplicateurs de contenu multimédia éducatif canadien sur l'inforoute. Québec, QC, Canada: SAVIE & Fonds Inukshuk inc.

Sing, C. C., & Der-Thanq, V. (2004). A review on usability evaluation methods for instructional multimedia: An analytical framework. *International Journal of Instructional Media, 31*(3), 229–238.

Stolovitch, H. D. (1982). Applications of the intermediate technology of learner verification and revision (LVR) for adapting international instructional resources to meet local needs. *Performance & Instruction, 21*(7), 16–22. doi:10.1002/pfi.4170210708

Thiagarajan, S. (1978). Instructional product verification and revision: 20 questions and 200 speculations . *Educational Technology Research and Development, 26*(2), 1042–1629.

Thulal, A. N. (2003). *Application of software testing in e-learning*. Delhi: Department of Information Technology, Amity School of Engineering and Technology. Retrieved May 29, 2009 from http://www.jmi.nic.in/Events/witsa2003/Amrit-NathThulal.pdf

Turk, A. (2001). Towards contingent usability evaluation of WWW sites. In [Perth, Australia: CHISIG, Ergonomics Society of Australia.]. *Proceedings of Australian International Conference on Computer-Human Interaction OZCHI, 2001*, 161–167.

Usabilis (2008). *Ergonomie informatique* [Information ergonomics]. Retrieved December 12, 2008 from http://www.usabilis.com/methode/ergonomienformatique.htm

Wideman, H. H., Owston, R. D., Brown, C., Kushniruk, A., Ho, F., & Pitts, K. C. (2007). Unpacking the potential of educational gaming: A new tool for gaming research. *Simulation & Gaming, 38*(1), 10–30. doi:10.1177/1046878106297650

Wikipédia. (2008). *La validation* [Validation]. Retrieved May 29, 2009 from http://fr.wikipedia.org/wiki/Validation

ADDITIONAL READING

Doak, C. C., Doak, L. G., & Root, J. H. (1996). *Teaching patients with low literacy skills* (2nd ed.). Philadephia: J. B. Lippincott. Chapter 10: Learner Verification and Revision of Materials (pp. 167-185); Appendix D: Learner Verification and Revision (pp. 203-206).

KEY TERMS AND DEFINITIONS

Generic Educational Game Shell (GEGS): An online design environment that allows teachers and trainers to create games by providing all the tools needed to: (1) set the game parameters; (2) create instructions and rules that direct player actions; (3) create pedagogical material; (4) set the criteria that determine the end of the game and the winner, and (5) detail the tools required for revision and evaluation of the game, in order to ensure that the game is updated regularly and that learning is maximized.

Usability: The degree to which a product can be used by specific users to accomplish a given set of tasks effectively and to their satisfaction.

Validation: Aims at determining whether a product is coherent, pertinent, and innovative in comparison with solutions traditionally used in the sector where it is implemented and transferable. "Transferable" means the transmission of the product to another person, or to another organism. This validation is made with two types of evaluators: users and domain experts.

Chapter 26
Formative Evaluation of an Online Educational Game

Louise Sauvé
Télé-université, Canada

Lise Renaud
University of Québec in Montreal, Canada

Jérôme Elissalde
University of Québec in Montreal, Canada

Gabriela Hanca
Télé-université, Canada

ABSTRACT

This chapter discusses the creation of an educational game about sexually transmitted infections. STIs: Stopping the Transmission was created using the Parcheesi™ generic educational game shell (GEGS). It also presents the validation of the game with experts, followed by its trial with secondary school students to measure the effectiveness of the motivational mechanisms provided by the shell and its adequacy in meeting teachers' pedagogic requirements.

INTRODUCTION

Formative evaluation, the fifth and final stage in creating a GEGS, consists of trials of an educational game created with the GEGS, with game and content experts, and with the game's target learners. To accomplish this evaluation, the game designers must specify the formative evaluation framework, develop measurement instruments for experts and target learners, validate the game content and revise it if necessary, and finally conduct trials with target learners to measure the pedagogic and technological aspects of the online educational game.

This chapter describes the steps in the formative evaluation process. In the first part, we discuss the game *STIs: Stopping the Transmission,* developed using the *Parcheesi* GEGS. The game was created by doctors with expertise in health promotion and prevention of sexually transmitted infections (STIs). The second part presents the validation by experts of the relevance and accuracy of the game's design and learning content. In the third and last part, we describe a trial of the game, conducted with 14- and

DOI: 10.4018/978-1-61520-731-2.ch026

15-year-old students. Two aspects are examined: the effects of the game's motivational support tools, including feedback, challenge, competition, and active participation, and the game's ergonomic quality (design, user friendliness, and readability) from the point of view of the learners.

THE GAME—*STIS: STOPPING THE TRANSMISSION*

Two doctors joined our research team to develop a game on sexually transmitted infections (STIs) using the *Parcheesi* GEGS. The game was called *STIs: Stopping the Transmission*. They focused on developing cognitive questions related to four aspects of STIs:

- **Prevention:** Eleven questions teach the best ways to break the cycle of transmitting STIs, such as types of condoms, identifying high risk behavior, etc.
- **Prevalence:** Eleven questions report the current situation, the high number of infected cases and STI carriers, and information concerning the infections themselves (their nature and seen or unseen effects)
- **STI transmission:** Eighteen questions deal with the ways in which different STIs can be transmitted and call into question widespread popular beliefs
- **Treatment:** How certain STIs can be treated, managed, or cured, how STI transmission can be prevented, and some questions address what steps should be taken when someone believes he/she has been exposed to an STI

56 questions were created using various question types: yes/no, true/false, multiple choice (2, 3 or 4 possible answers), fill-in-the-blank sentences, and logical sequence questions. Images, sound clips and videos were also used in some questions, as shown in Figure 1.

Figure 1. Multimedia question example

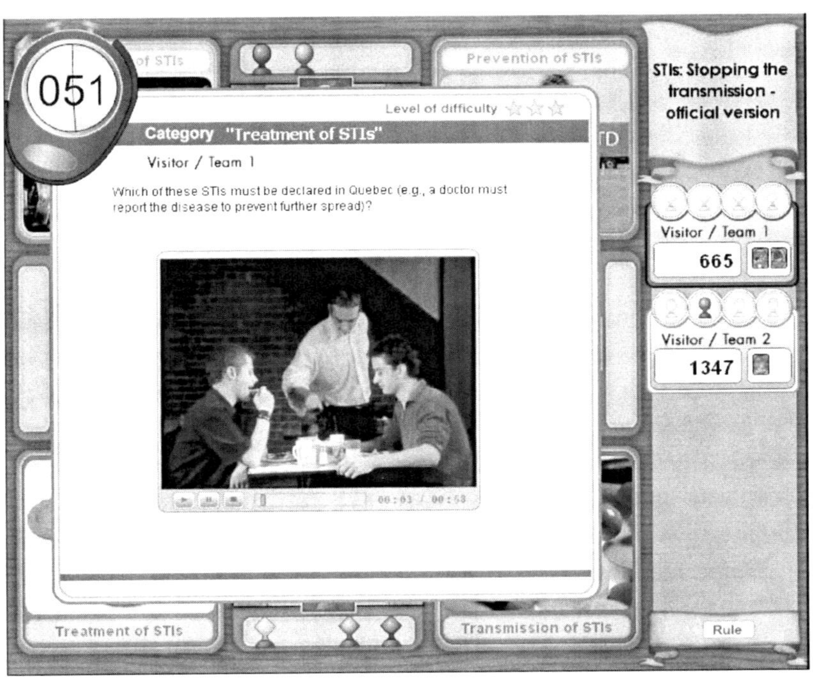

Figure 2. Example of a role-play activity

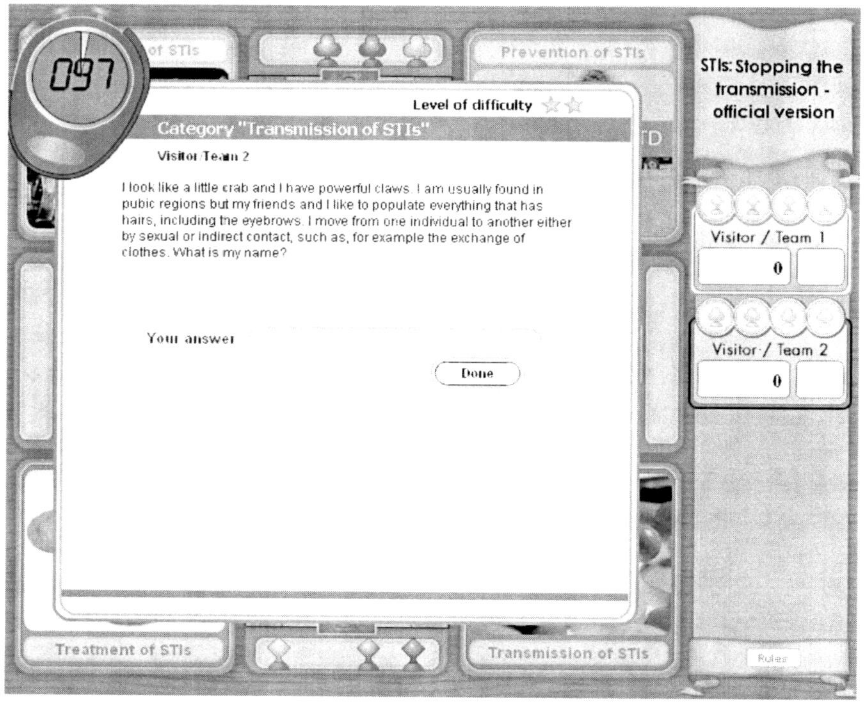

Based on these questions, the research team then designed 19 affective questions in the form of open-ended questions and questions requiring a certain task:

- 12 role-play questions, involving dialogue between one or more players, or spontaneous answers based on scenarios, to encourage an understanding of how and why the players would act a certain way in a given situation (Figure 2)
- 7 model-type questions require the player to observe a model or an example which she/he must imitate to acquire the desired behaviour. The model shown explains in concrete terms specifically what behaviors are expected and how these should be developed. In the game, these questions provide realistic demonstrations (correct or incorrect). For example, two cards show the back of a condom wrapper, one with an outdated expiration date and the other with a valid date. The player must indicate whether the date is good or not. For every correct answer, the player is given positive reinforcement. For every error, the player is given feedback to help her/him succeed the next time

Finally, the game board was edited to incorporate images related to the four aspects dealt with in the game (Figure 3).

Once the game was developed, we submitted it for evaluation by experts and the target population, as described in the rest of this chapter.

METHODOLOGY

Our formative evaluation used the Learner Verification and Revision (LVR) methodology (Komoski, 1979; 1984), which focuses on the

Figure3. Game board for STIs: Stopping the Transmission

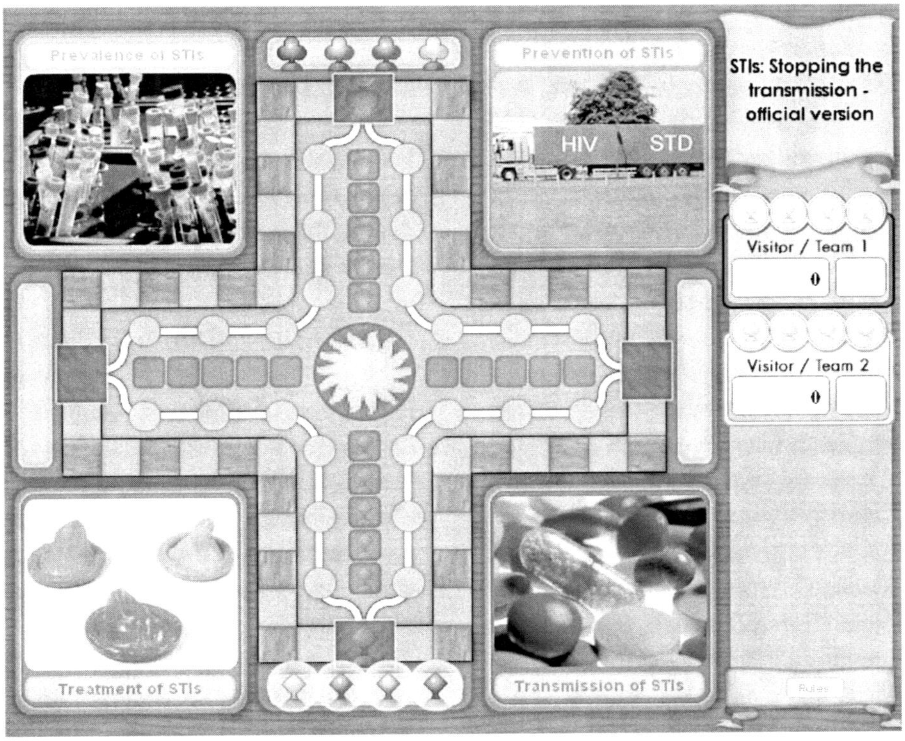

user, is characterized by flexibility, and is well adapted to the context in which the product will be used (Nguyen et al., 2008). LVR involves expert testing to detect errors and problems, which are then corrected (Chinien, 1990; Doak, Doak & Root, 1996; Maddrell, 2008; Perron & Bordeleau, 1994; Thulal, 2003), and efficient validation of a prototype with a restricted sample of the target audience. This method, also known as an educational trial, has been used for game development research (Kandaswamy, Stolovitch, & Thiagarajan, 1976; Stolovitch, 1982; Stolovitch & Thiagarajan, 1976; Thiagarajan, 1978), and for other online GEGSs (Sauvé et al., 2002; Sauvé & Samson, 2004).

The three phases of the expert and target population trials were:

- The *preparation* phase, consisting of: (1) establishing objectives and evaluation criteria; (2) choosing the evaluation tools; (3) writing, testing and if necessary, revising the evaluation tools; (4) contacting and informing content and learning experts and the target population (learner) sample; and (5) providing them with the materials required for the trial.
- The *verification* phase, including; (1) examining and manipulating the various parts of the product (the *Parcheesi* GEGS); and (2) collecting the experts' and users' comments using measurement instruments.
- The *decision* phase, consisting of: (1) compiling, processing, and analyzing the results; (2) making any necessary revisions; and (3) revising, if necessary, the product (the GEGS) in light of the information gathered from the experts and users.

EXPERT EVALUATION

Evaluation by experts allows measurement of the technical aspects, content, and relevant pedagogical aspects of an educational game. This evaluation can be carried out at various points in the development process; it can be done while producing a product with the aim of improving it, when selecting an educational game for a health education program, or at regular intervals after using a game in order to decide whether it should be withdrawn from a program of studies if it is no longer effective, or no longer meets the needs for which it was originally intended (Sauvé, 1990).

The doctors working on the *STIs: Stopping the Transmission* game designed it for 16- to 24-year-olds. To ensure that the game was relevant for the target group, we asked ten experts to evaluate its design and content (Renaud, Sauvé, & Ellisalde, 2007). In this section, we present the experts, evaluation criteria, and evaluation results.

The Experts

To carry out the game's evaluation, ten experts were consulted in a group interview. These people were selected for their expertise in regards to the target group, the subject matter, and the pedagogical and technological aspects involved in gameplay. The group included a sexologist specializing in adolescents, a university sexologist, an ergonomics expert, an educational technologist and a software programmer.

Evaluation Criteria

The experts evaluated both the game's design and its content. For design, they examined the game's playability, the intuitive dimensions of its interface, and the game dynamics. For content, the experts examined the accuracy of the information conveyed by the game and the match between its content and its target learners. They also looked at the complexity and degree of difficulty of the game's learning activities. Table 1 lists the specific evaluation criteria used in the expert review.

Expert Evaluation Results

The results are presented based on the target population (secondary school students), the game design, the learning material, and question complexity and difficulty.

Target Population

The experts found that the *STIs: Stopping the Transmission* game targeted too wide a population (from grade 9 students through the first two years of postsecondary education). In their opinion, the contents of the game were better suited to students at the postsecondary level, and particularly for those studying sexology or medicine. They proposed that the question content first be developed for postsecondary students and then modified for secondary school learners.

Game Design

While the structure of the game was found to be interesting and motivating, the experts deemed that the game board (colors and images) were aimed more at students at the postsecondary level and would be less interesting to teenagers. Some experts suggested that the tokens be modified to match the game subject matter. For example, four kinds of condoms could be used: ribbed, contoured, beaded, and those with widened tips.

There were few comments about the intuitive aspect of the game. The experts considered the instructions to be clear enough to guide the players through the game. They did note that unless the players read the rules of the game (available at any time), certain actions are not completely intuitive, particularly the color of the tokens and the corresponding categories of questions, token movement between the two tracks, and clicking on the feedback pop-up to activate the next part

Table 1. Expert evaluation criteria

Evaluation Criteria	Interview Chart Items
Game Design	
Playability	• Game board • Token
Intuitive interface	• Instruction clarity • Rule clarity • Ease of navigation
Game dynamics	• Types of questions • Chance cards • Voting system • Point system
Content	
Accuracy of information provided by the game	• Content that supports the goals of the game • Identification of potential gaps or non-pertinent information • Established information structure • Objectives specific to this type of game
Appropriateness of content in relation to the target population	• Content pertinent to target population • Possible exploitable points • Interest in using the game with young adults • Proposed target population
Complexity and difficulty of questions	• Pedagogical strength of questions and answers • Eventual question content modifications (content and form) • Complexity of vocabulary and wording of contents

of the game. Some experts suggested posting the rules in pdf format.

The experts considered the varying question types (multiple-choice, open-ended answer, true/false, yes/no, fill in the blank, logical sequence, matching, and performance questions) as one of the game's strengths. The Chance cards were also seen as helping to maintain user interest. The questions and scenarios (interaction and situational) included a voting system that gave the user an active part to play.

However, the experts advised that all the questions should offer multimedia content to appeal to teenagers.

The suggestions made by experts were taken into account. A new game board was designed and the tokens were adapted to suit the target users (Figure 4). New instructions appeared as the game progressed to explain the three actions which did not seem intuitive:

- You have selected the red token, so you must answer the questions which match this color
- Click on the feedback once you have finished reading it
- Congratulations! Your answer is correct and your token will now advance to the fast track

Learning Content

The experts considered the game's title to be representative of its content and the information conveyed in the questions to be scientifically correct. They noted, however, that certain key elements of sexual education for secondary school students were absent from the game, e.g.:

- There is no cure for HIV. Medications only reduce the effects
- There are condoms for women

Figure 4. Revised game board

- A dental dam may be used for oral sex
- Oral sex is not limited to fellatio, as it includes also cunnilingus, and less frequently, oral/anal contact
- Testing for STIs is often as simple as a blood test

They also recommended that the game should include:

- a summary of the various condoms and their potential uses
- a clear explanation of what the human papillomavirus (HPV) is, and a clear link between HPV and condylomas
- a question which encourages learning the list of STIs
- an explanation of genital herpes

The experts specified that this game was an appropriate tool for teenagers aged 14 to 17 to acquire new knowledge. However, it would be review material for older, postsecondary students. They also considered that the subject matter of certain questions was more or less representative of the concerns and beliefs of students at the secondary level. Several suggestions led to changes and a reorientation to the target population of the trial (secondary school students). Lastly, they suggested including a list of questions and answers, as well as a glossary of the most common terms. For postsecondary students, the game objectives were revised according to the experts' comments.

Question Complexity and Level of Difficulty

All the experts mentioned the relevance of the topic of the game and its importance as a tool for teaching young people about sexually transmitted infections. STIs are an increasingly alarming issue in North America, and certain infections (syphilis in particular) are sharply increasing. The effort to educate young people on the subject matter of

Table 2. Example of a modified game question

Before Expert Evaluation	Recommendations	After Expert Evaluation
Polyurethane condoms contribute to a reduction of sensation more than latex condoms. • True • False	An explanation of different the types of protection should precede the question Reword the sentence, as there is some opposition between the terms "contribute to" and "diminish". It is suggested that an explanation accompany the correct answer feedback as well as the incorrect answer feedback.	Two types of condoms are commercially available: latex (the most common) and polyurethane, (found mostly in drug stores). Polyurethane condoms usually diminish sensation compared to latex ones. • True • False
Correct Answer Feedback: Congratulations! That answer is correct!		**Correct Answer Feedback:** Congratulations! That answer is correct! Synthetic condoms transfer body heat better than latex ones. However, they are more expensive.
Incorrect Answer Feedback: The correct answer is "False". Synthetic condoms transfer body heat better than latex ones. However, they are more expensive.		**Incorrect Answer Feedback:** The correct answer is "False". Synthetic condoms transfer body heat better than latex ones. However, they are more expensive.

STIs was commended. However, the complexity of the questions drew comments from all users. Question formulation was appropriate for young adults and did not need revision.

Keeping in mind that the game was geared towards teaching students at the secondary level, the experts recommended changes to the language and/ or media in 60 of the 75 activities to improve their relevance or format. The experts noted that five questions from the game were not correctly classified, vocabulary was not always consistent, questions and illustrations of five questions were more or less similar and could lead to confusion, and the videos, which were suited to postsecondary students, needed to be revised for students at the secondary level.

Game Shell Revisions as a Result of Expert Feedback

All of the suggested corrections: images and videos were implemented, and the wording of some questions was corrected, as illustrated in Table 2. Finally, a new version of the game was put online that addressed the experts' comments.

TRIAL BY THE TARGET POPULATION

In order to ensure that educational games based on the *Parcheesi* GEGS support learning and fulfill pedagogical requirements, we had the revised game *STIs: Stopping the Transmission* tested by 173 secondary level students. The game trial examined two aspects: its learning support mechanisms and its ergonomics from the user's point of view. Here we describe the trial and present its results (adapted from Sauvé, Renaud & Hanca, 2008).

Trial Objectives

The objectives of this trial were (1) to determine the effect of the game's learning support mechanisms on participants' motivation and interest and (2) to determine the game's ergonomic quality. Table 3 outlines the evaluation criteria and measurement items used.

Target Population

To carry out the trial of the *STIs: Stopping the Transmission* game, we organized our student population sample into five classroom groups, taking into account the difficulties of running testing

Table 3. Evaluation criteria according to trial objectives

Criteria	Measurement items
Support Mechanisms	
Feedback	Instant feedback linked to each learning activity Navigational feedback Feedback on the results of the learning activity
Challenge	Maintaining an uncertain game outcome Integrated goals pertaining to reaching the different tracks (slow or fast)
Competition	The score obtained in each round Winner/ loser
Active Participation	Refers to engaging the learner and the learner's active role during the game Player actions influencing progress of the game
Ergonomics	
User-friendliness	Understanding and comprehension of game elements: instructions and rules, game progress, animations Technological competencies required to play the game Font size and color
Pedagogical Read-ability	Vocabulary used for the questions and feedback Displayed images and videos
Game Design	Game board format Display location of points, team and player names, stopwatch, and learning content (questions) Access to rules Choice of tokens and movement on the game board

in schools. In order to ensure that the students are of the "digital native" generation as described by Prensky (2006), we examined their computer and Internet knowledge as well as their perceptions on the importance of Internet and communication technologies (ITC) and learning games using our *Questionnaire sur les compétences en TIC et en JEUX* (Questionnaire on competencies in ITC and games). The evaluation criteria took into account the work of Koohang (2004), Turk (2001), and Webster (2002), whose research suggests that a learner's characteristics such as prior experience with the Internet and computer, cognitive style, and culture may affect his or her rating of the impact of certain usability factors affecting a web-based learning system.

Measurement Tools

One week before game trial, the students were told about the research and signed a consent form for the experiment. They then completed the questionnaire, which gathered socio-demographic and school information, students' knowledge of games and the Internet as a means of learning (7 statements), and their perceptions concerning the importance of ITC and learning games (11 statements).

The game trial was carried out over two sessions of approximately 1.5 hours each. During the trial, the students were invited to play the game in groups of three. Navigation directions helped participants reach the online game. Certain player actions such as the number of correct or incorrect answers were recorded in real time by the game's integrated data system.

Immediately after playing the game, students completed a questionnaire on the technological aspects and learning mechanisms of the game. The first part of this questionnaire asked about the students' opinions of the game's design (9 statements), pedagogical readability (6 statements), and user-friendliness (5 statements). Three open-ended questions made it possible to collect their comments for each criterion. The second part of the questionnaire measured the students' opinions of the impact of the game's learning support mechanisms on their motivation and interest: the feedback accompanying each learning activity (8 statements), the navigation and results of a learning activity (8 statements), the level of difficulty (5 statements), the competitive element (5 statements), and their active participation in the game (10 statements). Three open-ended questions collected their comments on the game's learning support mechanisms.

The quantitative information was treated using various descriptive analysis techniques (frequency, average, percentages, etc). The qualitative data was gathered by subject and documented in relation to the quantitative results.

The Population Sample

Five groups of Grade 9 students, a total of 173, took part in the experiment; 54.9% were boys and 45.1% were girls. The sample included 110 (63.6%) 14-year-olds and 63 (36.4%) 15-year-olds.

In general, the students had a very high degree of familiarity with computers and the Internet and showed a very low degree of stress when it comes to their use. However, they more often played traditional games than on CD-ROM or online. They generally expressed a positive attitude, or at least a neutral one, when faced with the use of games for learning. A small proportion (7 out of 173) was openly against their use. Boys and girls demonstrated similar experiences in the use of the various forms of educational games at school. However, boys displayed a more positive attitude than girls toward the use of learning games.

With one exception, all the participants had a computer in their home. Less than two thirds of the students use it to play online games and very few students spend more than 13 hours per week playing games on the computer. Boys reported spending more time playing online games than girls. In general, the students in our sample represented typical youth of the digital native generation described by Prensky (2006).

Learning Support Mechanisms

Learning support mechanisms in the game, including feedback, navigation and motivation, elements of competition and challenge, as well as active learner participation, were measured and produced the following results:

Feedback

Many studies stress the importance of feedback in an online game for stimulating motivation in young people. Feedback comes as a response to an action carried out by the learner. It is a correction method accompanied by notes and comments to guide and help the learner to further his/her knowledge or to change certain behaviors. Three types of feedback were integrated into the *STIs: Stopping the Transmission* game to encourage and motivate learners: consequential feedback, provided in links with each task; feedback related to navigation; and feedback on the results of a learning activity.

Trial results showed a very high degree of student appreciation for the three types of feedback. Statistics showed that 91.4% of the students strongly agreed or agreed that the messages posted under the lower parts of their answers helped them to understand their errors. More than 86% strongly agreed or agreed with their answers to open-ended questions being corrected by peers and concurred that this provided a fair evaluation process, while 85% of the students considered the thumbs up and thumbs down images to be satisfactory instant feedback on their answers. The game thus fulfilled student expectations of instant feedback in relation to individual learning activities.

I learned a lot when the answers to the questions were given. It enabled me to earn points, the same question came back and I knew the answer. (boy)

It was more than a game for me. It allowed me to understand why my answers wrong. (girl)

It is important to note that the students preferred formal feedback, including graphics (the thumbs up or down) over abstract or direct feedback from their fellow classmates. More than 91% strongly agreed or agreed with being corrected by the thumbs up or down, versus 86.1% who appreciated peer correction.

For me the thumbs up meant I had won and that my answer was right! (boy)

When the others were evaluating me it wasn't easy to tell if I had answered correctly. Good thing I could read the answer after I had answered the question. (girl)

For navigation feedback, results showed that instructions, posted as the game progressed, were appreciated (84.5%) more than just the rules of the game (75.7%). It should be noted that rules are posted only when the player clicks on the Rules icon located on the right at the bottom of the screen.

I like it better when it pops up at the right time. I don't like reading the game rules - it's boring. (boy)

I really liked the explanations which popped up to tell me what to do when I was playing. I felt like I was working well with the computer and the game. (girl)

I knew how to display the rules, but I didn't take the time to read everything before playing. I didn't think I would have to because explanations kept popping up as I was playing. (boy)

Finally, students using the "See what I learned" game option to examine their correct and incorrect answers expressed a high appreciation (83.8%) for this type of feedback but made no comments on it.

The results of this trial enabled us to confirm that any educational game should provide a variety of feedback (pertaining to learning, motivation and results) in order to support the player's interest in learning.

Challenge

Challenge occurs when a player's actions trigger reactions from the opponent, thus adding a competitive element (Kirriemur & MacFarlane, 2004). Four mechanisms adding to feelings of an uncertain outcome of the game were built into the generic game shell in order to maintain the challenge element: (1) taking into account preliminary knowledge, (2) the degree of difficulty of questions and learning activities, (3) distribution of Chance cards, and (4) goals associated with the different tracks (slow or fast routes).

Results in the *STIs: Stopping the Transmission* game showed that a strong majority of players (89.0% strongly agree or agree) appreciated that the game took into account their prior knowledge and that this could lead to gaining points. They were, however, divided as to the determinants of the questions' degree of difficulty, which could reduce their chances of gaining points. 44% agreed, and 56% disagreed with the fact that the questions on sexually transmitted infections were too difficult. The boys (73.7%) especially found the questions more difficult than did the girls (45.9%).

While the Good luck/ Bad luck cards evened out the odds of winning, the boys in particular did not seem to enjoy this element of the game. More than 53% disagreed or strongly disagreed with having Good luck/ Bad luck cards balance out the odds between players. For these students, winning seemed to be the main point of the game.

My token had almost reached the center when I picked a Chance card, I'd say it was more of a "bad luck" card because I had to start all over. It's not fair. (boy)

The only problem I found was whether or not there should be Chance cards. It "spices" up the game a little, but on the other hand it can determine the outcome of the game based on luck. (girl)

Certain comments concerning the Good luck/ Bad luck cards dealt with one of the mechanisms of reinforcement set up in the game format. The students considered the repeat questions to be a double-edged sword.

It's fun when "we" get the same questions again but it's frustrating when it's "the other team." (boy)

The same questions reoccur frequently. It's fun if I can remember the answers others gave, but it's not cool when I can't remember. I understood that I have to remember the questions if I want to win! It isn't easy! (boy)

I'm good at remembering the answers. I got the best score in my group because the same questions kept coming back. (girl)

The option of taking different tracks to victory in the game was appreciated by the students. Slightly more than 80% agreed or strongly agreed that the fast track was a positive element in maintaining interest in the game. They considered the two available tracks to be assets that increased the competitive element of the game, and found that this encouraged players to provide the right answers.

I really liked that my right answers got me to the fast track, it was very exciting when my token moved faster. (girl)

When I figured out that the right answers would get my token to the fast track, I paid attention to others' answers and I started to read the corrections as they popped up after having answered. Since the same questions kept coming back I increased my chances of winning. (boy)

Competition

In *Parcheesi* games, players compete to be the first to reach the center, winning the game. Starting with the basic *Parcheesi* game shell, we added competitive elements between players; the score obtained during each round and other means lead to a win. These mechanisms are intended to stimulate students' motivation and interest in learning through the game.

The students agreed or strongly agreed (68.8%) that allotting points based on the time taken to answer a question added to the competitive element. The boys especially appreciated this type of competition (83.4%) in comparison with the girls (45.1%).

The majority of the students (82%) agreed that returning their token to the Start square reduced their chances to win even if they answered the questions correctly. For 64.1%, having a game time limit increased their chances of winning compared to playing the complete game. A large majority of girls (73.4%) agreed or strongly agreed with this statement, while 54.9% of the boys reported this view.

I didn't know how much time was left in the game, it was annoying! I wanted to win. (boy)

Active Participation

The idea of "active participation" emphasizes action rather than passive observation during the learning process. This enables the learner to use his/her acquired knowledge in a structured situation and encourages the development of new knowledge and skills. In other words, the questions provide opportunities for the learner to use existing knowledge or skills, as in everyday life. Two indicators were measured at the end of the trial: (1) the engagement and active role of the learner during the game, and (2) the actions required of the player in order for the game to progress.

The game *STIs: Stopping the Transmission* forces students to take an active approach to their learning. Results showed that a majority (86.7%) of the students strongly agreed or agreed that the questions offered by the game enabled them to take part in their learning, that they enjoyed playing the game (83.8%) and finally, that they enjoyed competing with other players in the game (85.1%). 73.4% of participants stated that their engagement level with the game was high, and rated it 8, 9 and 10 on a scale of 1-10.

I very much enjoyed the game and this allowed me to learn more about STIs. (boy)

I believe the game allowed me to learn more about STIs. I liked the game because learning like this is more fun than studying out of a book. The game was very well made. (girl)

I had fun with my friends and I would like to learn this way in all my classes. (girl)

Very good for learning. Call me when you want to play online. (boy)

With regard to game progress through player actions, results show that most participants (75.7%) felt that they controlled the outcome of the game with their answers and the choices they made. 81.5% liked that the other players could not play if they did not perform the required actions. A large majority of the students (89.3%) stated that their degree of participation was high and indicated an 8, 9 or 10 on a scale of 1-10. These results confirmed that the more a game supports the active participation of the learner, the more the learner is inclined to learn the subject matter.

Game Format Design, Pedagogical Readability, and User-Friendliness

The second goal of the trial was to measure the ergonomic quality of the educational game. This evaluation was based on three criteria: design, pedagogical readability, and user-friendliness. Table 3 describes the indicators used for measurement.

Game Design

Results showed a very high level of satisfaction with the game design but a slightly lower level of satisfaction with the location of the stopwatch on the screen (78.2%). Students strongly agreed or agreed that the game design elements, namely the game board (80.9%), visible tokens (98.3%), player or team name display (95.8%), accessible game rules (85%), display of questions above the game board (89.1%), and selectable tokens and token movement (87.3%) were appropriate and supported the game's objectives. 73.8% of the students rated the overall game design as 8, 9 and 10 on a scale of 1-10. This confirms that the students appreciated the game design factors brought to their attention.

It was incredibly cool. I wanted to play as soon as I arrived at school.(girl)

Very good game. Good design, dynamic. (boy)

Some comments made by students concerning the game's approach and visual aspect corresponded to statements by Oblinger and Oblinger (2005) on teenager learning expectations, namely the inclusion of video and audio clips, as well as images in the questions (11/173), a lower number of turns necessary before moving a token out to the Start square (8/173), the importance of displaying the remaining time in a game with a predetermined time limit (6/173) and the increased movement speed of tokens on the game board (5/173).

Very well structured, allowed us to learn while playing instead of from a book. More animations, more videos, I like games with more animations. (boy)

The tokens move too slowly! I like fast-paced games! It took too long for my tokens to get to the Start square! (boy)

Pedagogical Readability

Results showed a very high degree of pedagogical readability in the game. The participants strongly agreed or agreed that the vocabulary used in the questions (87.9%) and feedback (90.2%), the way pictures were displayed (77.4%), the video image and sound quality (79.8%), and the font size and color (86.8%) were among many characteristics of the game that were understandable and appropriate to the game's goals. 74.8% of participants students rated the overall pedagogical readability of the game as 8, 9 and 10. This confirms that the students appreciated the elements of the game's readability that were brought to their attention.

Only two students commented on the readability of the game. They mentioned that the fonts used should be larger, which led us to think that these students perhaps had reading or vision difficulties.

User-Friendliness

Results show that *STIs: Stopping the Transmission* was seen as a very user-friendly game. The students strongly agreed or agreed that the instructions and help tips (89.7%) as well as the rules (85%) were easy to understand, that the graphics facilitated game play (83.8%), that the actions required did not require any advanced technological abilities (87.9%), and that, in general, playing the game was easy to understand (89.6%).

Some comments were made about the game being user-friendly. 22 students stated their appreciation for the choice of tokens (the brightly colored condoms). Seven students found the tokens moved too slowly. Two students suggested adding more interesting and entertaining images. One student mentioned difficulties with the rules and instructions without being more specific, while another considered them clear and easy to understand. Two students suggested adding animations without being more specific, while three others made positive remarks on the quality of the animations already in the game.

I loved this game! The animations and especially the sound effects were exceptional! It was really educational and fun. I also liked that the tokens were in the shape of condoms. They were brightly colored. It was SUPER! I want to play again at home with my friends! (girl)

The game was in fact very long. Many questions were repeated. However, we learned a great deal because by the end, we had answered all the questions many times—the information sunk in. Thanks, good luck! (1 girl, 2 boys)

Revising the Generic Game Shell as a Result of Student Feedback

To follow up on the trial, some modifications were made to the game shell, as described in Table 4.

CONCLUSION

STIs: Stopping the Transmission is an educational game developed by two doctors collaborating with the project research team. To ensure that this game fulfilled the pedagogical requirements of the curriculum for which it was intended, we engaged a panel of ten experts (sexologists, edu-

Table 4. Student suggestions and revisions for the Parcheesi GEGS

Comments and Suggestions	Proposed Revision
More images and videos incorporated in the questions, relating to the subject.	Incorporate information for the developers into the conceptual page of the game shell so that they can integrate a maximum number of images and videos to better communicate with digital generation users.
It's important to show the player how much time is left in the game if the end is based on a timer.	Add a tool to the game which displays the remaining time when playing in a time-based game.
Token movement is too slow.	Possibly increase the movement speed of token on the game board.
Reduce the number of turns before the game gets underway.	Reduce the number of times the dice are rolled from three to one to ensure the boys' interest is maintained.

cational technologists, and computer specialists) on the subject of the game's design and content. Following the experts' analysis, the game was revised and tested in February 2008 by a sample of 173 Grade 9 students, aged 14 and 15. Participants, both girls and boys, had a very high degree of familiarity with computers. However, a larger proportion of boys demonstrated a positive attitude towards the use of the Internet and games as learning tools.

Results from the experts' evaluation revealed that the game the doctors created was better suited to adults than adolescents. It was also noted that the game allowed cognitive learning on the subjects of prevention, prevalence, transmission, and treatment of sexually transmitted infections, and that the information on STIs was scientifically accurate. The objectives were well-suited to students at the secondary level (acquisition of knowledge), but should be readjusted for adult users (checking what was learned). Several recommendations and suggestions were made to adapt the game to secondary students. The pedagogical experts recommended changes and reworded questions to better suit a younger population. All the question changes suggested by the experts were taken into account, and a new version of the game was created. This evaluation of the game, focusing on both the pedagogical aspect and the target population, enabled us to adapt the game to suit the language level and interests of the target population on the one hand, and on the other hand, to better integrate it into the curriculum and context in which the game will be used.

Results from the trial of the *STIs: Stopping the Transmission* game showed that adolescents had a high level of appreciation for the motivational support mechanisms built in to the generic game shell. They reported that the mechanisms of feedback, challenge, competition, and active participation were effective, since they found the game to be highly engaging and motivating. It is to be stressed that only the Good luck/Bad luck cards mechanism was seen more negatively; some of the students, especially the boys, wanted to win quickly, and certain Good luck/Bad luck cards (e.g. the Back to Square One card) prevented this outcome. The Chance cards kept the outcome of the game uncertain.

As for the ergonomics of the game, results showed that students had a very high level of appreciation for the design, user-friendliness, and pedagogical readability of the game. The game board was seen as visually appealing, as were the various elements—tokens, rules, instructions, stopwatch, and questions. The game's instructions, rules and game play were reported as easy to understand. The question content was interesting and questions used a vocabulary appropriate for Grade 9 students. Lastly, the game did not require students to have any specific technological competencies.

Several students made positive comments, noting that the game is stimulating, instructive, interesting, and dynamic; this showed that the game reached the teenage participant audience, who came to regard it as a fun and stimulating way to learn. It fit in well with the educational process, as it allowed teens to learn about a subject which is sometimes difficult to broach in the classroom environment.

The teens, especially the boys, were regular users of graphics-loaded, fast-paced, online games. The majority of their comments on the game design reflect this. They asked for more animations, photographs and videos, faster movement of the tokens, fewer turns before moving a token out to the Start Square, etc.

Several constructive criticisms and suggestions were taken into account, and the generic game shell was revised in consequence. In closing, here are some terms used by the students which express the interest and excitement generated by the *STIs: Stopping the Transmission* game:

"masterly", "super", "original", "fascinating", "cool", "motivating", "fun", "informative", "enjoyable", "excellent", "captivating", "well organized."

The expert trials remind us of the necessity of expert feedback, as much as target group feedback for improving game design. The *Parcheesi* GEGS made it possible for health practitioners, eager to make their knowledge available, to develop a web-based educational game in only a few hours. However, scientific knowledge is not sufficient for building a game for young people. Notions of presentation, language, target learners' concerns, learning progression, and the context of game use must also be taken into account so that the game content is well adapted and effective for learning Thanks to our validation process, the game *STIs: Stopping the Transmission* was completely redone to respond to the comments of the experts.

Our trial with target learners confirmed the importance of mechanisms to support students' motivation and learning. It also reinforced the importance of following ergonomic guidelines during the development of a GEGS or a game.

ACKNOWLEDGMENT

We would like to thank Dr. Fernand Cantin from the *Centre Médical des Carrières* and Dr. Martin Delage from the *Clinique Médicale St- Augustin* for their involvement in the development of the *STIs: Stopping the Transmission* game.

REFERENCES

Chinien, C. (1990). Examination of cognitive style FD/FI as a learner selection criterion in formative evaluation. *Canadian Journal of Educational Communication*, *19*(1), 19–39.

Doak, C. C., Doak, L. G., & Root, J. H. (1996). *Teaching patients with low literacy skills* (2nd ed.). Chapter 10: Learner verification and revision of materials. Philadelphia, PA: J. B. Lippincott.

Kandaswamy, S., Stolovitch, H., & Thiagarajan, S. (1976). Learner verification and revision: An experimental comparison of two methods. *Audio-visual . Communication Review*, *24*(3), 316–328.

Kirriemur, J., & McFarlane, A. (2004*). Literature review in games and learning.* Bristol, UK: NESTA Futurelab.

Komoski, P. K. (1979). Counterpoint: Learner verification of instructional materials. *Educational Evaluation and Policy Analysis*, *1*(3), 101–103.

Komoski, P. K. (1984). Formative evaluation. The empirical improvement of learning materials. *Performance & Instruction Journal*, *22*(5), 3–4. doi:10.1002/pfi.4150220504

Koohang, A. (2004). A study of users' perceptions toward e-learning courseware usability. *International Journal on E-Learning*, *3*(2), 10–17.

Maddrell, J. (2008). *Article Review: IDT848 Evaluation study abstracts*. Norfolk, VA: Old Dominion University. Retrieved March 10, 2009 from http://designedtoinspire.com/drupal/files/ArticleSummary%20Maddrell.doc

Nguyen, T., Chang, V., Chang, E., Jacob, C., & Turk, A. (2008). A contingent method for usability evaluation of web-based learning systems. In K. McFerrin, R. Weber, R. Carlsen, & D. A. Willis (Eds), *Proceedings of the Society for Information Technology & Teacher Education Annual International Conference (19th International Conference of SITE 2008)* (pp. 579-585). Chesapeake, VA: AACE.

Oblinger, D., & Oblinger, J. L. (2005). *Educating the Net generation.* Washington, DC: Educause.

Perron, L., & Bordeleau, P. (1994). Modèle de développement d'ensembles didactiques d'intégration pédagogique de l'ordinateur [Development model for integrating pedogogy and the computer]. In P. Bordeleau (Ed.), *Des outils pour apprendre avec l'ordinateur* (pp. 513-553). Montréal, QC, Canada: Les Éditions Logiques.

Prensky, M. (2006). *Don't bother me Mom – I'm learning!* St. Paul, MN: Paragon House.

Renaud, L., Sauvé, L., & Ellisalde, J. (2007). *Évaluation du jeu « ITS: Stopper la transmission » auprès d'experts* [Expert evaluation of the game STIs: Stopping the Transmission] (Research report). Québec, QC, Canada: SAGE and SAVIE.

Sauvé, L. (1990). Comment évaluer une simulation et un jeu de simulation [How to evaluate a simulation and a simulation game]. In L. Renaud & L. Sauvé, *Simulation et jeu de simulation: outils éducatifs appliqués à la santé* (pp. 195-232). Montréal, QC, Canada: Éducation Agence d'Arc Inc.

Sauvé, L., & Power, M. IsaBelle, C., Samson, D., & St-Pierre, C. (2002). *Rapport final - Jeux-cadres sur l'inforoute: Multiplicateurs de jeux pédagogiques francophones* [Final report – Frame games on the Internet: Multipliers of francophone learning games]. Report for partnership, Bureau des technologies d'apprentissage. Québec, QC, Canada: SAVIE.

Sauvé, L., Renaud, L., & Hanca, G. (2008). *Étude de cas du projet: Apprendre par les jeux* [Case study: Learning with games] (Research report). Québec, QC, Canada: SAGE and SAVIE.

Sauvé, L., & Samson, D. (2004). *Rapport d'évaluation de la coquille générique du Jeu de l'oie du projet* [Evaluation report for the generic game shell Mother Goose]. Report for the project Jeux génériques: multiplicateurs de contenu multimédia éducatif canadien sur l'inforoute. Québec, QC, Canada: SAVIE and Fonds Inukshuk Inc.

Stolovitch, H. D. (1982). Applications of the intermediate technology of learner verification and revision (LVR) for adapting international instructional resources to meet local needs. *Performance & Instruction, 21*(7), 16–22. doi:10.1002/pfi.4170210708

Thiagarajan, S. (1978). Instructional product verification and revision: 20 questions and 200 speculations. *Educational Technology Research and Development, 26*(2), 1042–1629.

Thulal, A. N. (2003). *Application of software testing in e-learning.* Delhi, India: Department of Information Technology, Amity School of Engineering and Technology. Retrieved May 29, 2009 from http://www.jmi.nic.in/Events/witsa2003/AmritNathThulal.pdf

Turk, A. (2001). Towards contingent usability evaluation of WWW sites. In [Baulkham Hills, NSW, Australia: Ergonomics Society of Australia.]. *Proceedings of the Australian International Conference on Computer-Human Interaction OZCHI, 2001*, 161–167.

Webster, R. (2002). *Metacognition and the autonomous learner: Student reflections on cognitive profiles and learning environment development.* Perth, Australia: Edith Cowan University. Retrieved September 9, 2006 from http://www.csd.uwa.edu.au/iced2002/publication/Ray_Webster.pdf

ADDITIONAL READING

Stolovitch, H. D. (1982). Applications of the intermediate technology of learner verification and revision (LVR) for adapting international instructional resources to meet local needs. *Performance & Instruction*, *21*(7), 16–22. doi:10.1002/pfi.4170210708

Vedros, R. G. Improving Textbooks: LVR Florida Style. ERIC document ED275755. Retrieved June 4, 2009 from www.eric.ed.gov/ERICDocs/data/ericdocs2sql/content_storage_01/0000019b/80/2f/85/ed.pdf

Williams, B. O. Designing & conducting formative evaluation. Retrieved on June 4, 2009 from https://www.courses.psu.edu/trdev/trdev518_bow100/D_C10present/

KEY TERMS AND DEFINITIONS

Active Participation: Emphasizes action rather than passive observation during the learning process, encouraging the learner to use his/her acquired knowledge in a structured situation.

Challenge: Occurs when a player's actions result in opponent reactions, leading to a fight or competition.

Competition: A key feature of games with a single player (who opposes himself in order to improve his performance with every challenge) and those that include several players (who oppose each other to achieve the same purpose).

Cooperation: The capacity to enter into relationships with others, to negotiate, to discuss, to collaborate, to share feelings and ideas, to develop links and friendships, and, finally to develop team spirit (including a desire for competitiveness).

Educational Game: A fictitious, fantasy or imaginary situation in which players, placed in conflict with others or assembled in a team against an external opponent, are governed by rules determining their actions with a view to achieving learning objectives and a goal determined by the game, either to win or to seek revenge.

Feedback: A mechanism that indicates to the learner whether or not he has a satisfactory answer. It comes in response to an action by the learner, suggests a correction, and expresses a value judgment which should be well-reasoned and argued. Its purpose is to help the learner to deepen her knowledge or to change her behavior and to indicate to her how to do so.

Learning: The acquisition of knowledge or skills with the help of experience, practice or study. Learning results include knowledge, attitudes and skills acquired by students.

Learner Verification and Revision (LVR): A methodology for measuring technical aspects, content, and relevant pedagogical aspects of an educational game. This type of evaluation can be carried out at various points in the development process: while producing a product with the aim of improving it; when selecting an educational game for a specific program; or when deciding if a game should be withdrawn from a program of studies.

Compilation of References

Abaza, M., & Steyn, O. (2008). Role of computer serious games in education and training. In K. McFerrin, R. Weber, R. Carlsen, & D. A. Willis (Eds), *Proceedings of 19th International Conference Annual of Society for Information Technology & Teacher Education* (pp. 1592-1599). Chesapeake, VA: AACE.

Abel, G. G., Jordan, A., Hand, C. G., Holland, L. A., & Phipps, A. (2001). Classification models of child molesters utilizing the Abel Assessment for Sexual Interest. *Child Abuse & Neglect*, *25*(1), 703–718. doi:10.1016/S0145-2134(01)00227-7

Abelson, R. P. (1981). Psychological status of the script concept. *The American Psychologist*, *36*(7), 715–729. doi:10.1037/0003-066X.36.7.715

Abt, C. (1968). Games for learning. In S.S. Boocock, & E. O. Schild (Eds.), *Simulation games in learning* (pp. 65-92). Beverly Hills, CA: Sage Publications.

Academy of Interactive Arts & Sciences (AIAS). (2006, February 9). *9th Annual Interactive Achievement Awards.* Retrieved February 14, 2008, from http://www.interactive.org/awards.php?winners&year=2006&cat=200625#200625

Adams, E., & Rollings, A. (2003). *On game design.* Indianapolis, IN: New Riders Publishing.

Adams, W. K., Reid, S., LeMaster, R., McKagan, S. B., Perkins, K. K., & Dubson, M. (2008a). A study of educational simulations part I – Engagement and learning. *Journal of Interactive Learning Research*, *19*(3), 397–419.

Adams, W. K., Reid, S., LeMaster, R., McKagan, S. B., Perkins, K. K., & Dubson, M. (2008b). A study of educational simulations part II – Interface design. *Journal of Interactive Learning Research*, *19*(4), 551–557.

Agence Fonds social européen (2005). *Guide méthodologique d'auto-évaluation et de validation des produits Equal* [Methodological guide to self-evaluation and validation of EQUAL products].Agence Fonds social européen. Brussels: Agence Fonds social européen, Beligique, Francophone et Germanophone. Retrieved May 30, 2009 from http://www.equal-france.com/virtual/30/Documents/pdf/BfrGuide AutoEvalPdts.pdf

Aktouf, O. (1987). *Méthodologie des sciences sociales et approche qualitative des organisations* [A qualitative approach to social science and organizational research]. Québec, QC, Canada: Presses de l'Université du Québec.

Albanese, M. A. (1993). Problem-based learning: A review of literature on its outcomes and implementation issues. *Academic Medicine*, *68*(1), 52–81. doi:10.1097/00001888-199301000-00012

Alberto, P. A., Cihak, D. F., & Gama, R. I. (2005). Use of static picture prompts versus video modeling during simulation instruction. *Research in Developmental Disabilities*, *26*(4), 327–339. doi:10.1016/j.ridd.2004.11.002

Aldrich, C. (2004). *Simulations and the future of learning.* San Francisco, CA: Pfeiffer.

Alessi, S., & Trollip, S. (2001). *Multimedia for learning: Methods and development* (3rd ed.). Boston, MA: Allyn & Bacon.

Alinier, G., Hunt, B., Gordon, R., & Harwood, C. (2006). Effectiveness of intermediate-fidelity simulation training technology in undergraduate nursing education. *Journal of Advanced Nursing, 54*(3), 359–369. doi:10.1111/j.1365-2648.2006.03810.x

Allanson, J., & Mariani, J. (1999). Mind over virtual matter: Using virtual environments for neurofeedback training. In *Proceedings, IEEE Virtual Reality 1999* (pp. 270-273). New York: IEEE. doi 10.1109/VR.1999.756961.

Allard, S. (2008, March 15). Moins de crayons, plus de ballons [Fewer pencils, more balls]. *La Presse*, 2-3.

Alvarez, J. (2007). *Du jeu video au serious game: Approches culturelle, pragmatique et formelle* [Video games as serious games: Cultural, pragmatic and formal approaches]. Unpublished Ph.D. dissertation, Université Toulouse, Toulouse, France.

Alvarez, M. C., & Risko, V. J. (1989). *Schema activation, construction, and application.* ERIC Document Reproduction Service No. ED312611. Retrieved from ERIC database.

American Psychiatric Association (APA). (1994). *Diagnostic and statistical manual of mental disorders* (4th edition). Washington, DC: APA.

American Psychological Association's Board of Educational Affairs (APABEA). (1997). *The 14 learning-centred psychological principles.* Retrieved December 8, 2006 from http://www.apa.org/ed/lcp.html

Anadon, M. (1990). *Les rapports sciences/société et représentations scolaires* [Science and social reports and scholarly representations]. Québec, QC, Canada: Presses d'université du Québec.

Anderson, C. A. (2004). An update on the effects of playing violent video games. *Journal of Adolescence, 27*(1), 113–122. doi:10.1016/j.adolescence.2003.10.009

Anderson, C. A., & Bushman, B. J. (2001). Effects of violent video games on aggressive behavior, aggressive cognition, aggressive affect, physiological arousal, and prosocial behavior: A meta-analytic review of the scientific literature. *Psychological Science, 12*(5), 353–359. doi:10.1111/1467-9280.00366

Anderson, C. A., & Bushman, B. J. (2002). Human aggression. *Annual Review of Psychology, 53*(1), 27–51. doi:10.1146/annurev.psych.53.100901.135231

Anderson, C. A., & Carnagey, N. L. (2004). Violent evil and the general aggression model. In A. Miller (Ed.), The social psychology of good and evil (pp. 168-192). New York: Guilford Publications.

Anderson, C. A., & Dill, K. E. (2000). Video games and aggressive thoughts, feelings, and behavior in the laboratory and in life. *Journal of Personality and Social Psychology, 78*(4), 772–790. doi:10.1037/0022-3514.78.4.772

Anderson, C. A., & Ford, C. M. (1986). Affect of the video game player: Short-term effects of highly and mildly aggressive video games. *Personality and Social Psychology Bulletin, 12*(4), 390–402. doi:10.1177/0146167286124002

Anderson, L. R., & Stafford, S. L. (2006). Does crime pay? A classroom demonstration of monitoring and enforcement. *Southern Economic Journal, 72*(4), 1016–1025.

Andrieu, B., & Bourgeois, I. (2003). Interaction enseignant-élèves au cours des TPE, les dynamiques du processus de structuration des connaissances [Teacher-student interaction during independent study projects: Dynamics in the process of structuring knowledge]. In C. Larcher & A. Crindal (Eds.), *Structuration des connaissances et nouveaux dispositifs d'enseignement* (pp. 40-45). Paris: Institut national de recherche pédagogique.

Apkan, J. P. (2002). Which comes first: Computer simulation of dissection or a traditional laboratory practical method of dissection? *Electronic Journal of Science Education, 6*(4), 1–20.

Apperley, T. H. (2006). Genre and game studies: Toward a critical approach to video game genres. *Simulation & Gaming, 37*(1), 6–23. doi:10.1177/1046878105282278

Aristotle, , & Janko, R. (1987). [*With the tractatus coislinianus: A hypothetical reconstruction of poetics II, the fragments of the on poets.*] [R. Janko Trans.] [. Indianapolis, IN: Hackett Publishing Company.]. *Poetics*, I.

Armory, A., Naicker, K., Vincent, J., & Adams, C. (1999). The use of computer games as an educational tool: Identification of appropriate game types and game elements. *British Journal of Educational Technology, 30*(4), 311–321. doi:10.1111/1467-8535.00121

Armstrong, L. (2007). *Le suicide chez les jeunes: le temps d'agir* [Youth suicide: The time to act]. *Le forum de l'Express.* Available at http://www.lexpress.to/forum/157/

Arthur, D., Malone, S., & Nir, O. (2002). Optimal overbooking. *The UMAP Journal, 23*(3), 283–300.

Arya, A., & DiPaola, S. (2004, April). *Face as a multimedia object.* Paper presented at the 5th International Workshop on Image Analysis for Multimedia Interactive Services (WIAMIS 2004), Lisbon, Portugal.

Arya, A., & DiPaola, S. (2007). Face modeling and animation language for the MPEG-4 XMT Framework. *IEEE Transactions on Multimedia, 9*(6), 1137–1146. doi:10.1109/TMM.2007.902862

Arya, A., Enns, J., Jefferies, L., & DiPaola, S. (2006). Facial actions as visual cues for personality. *Computer Animation and Virtual Worlds (CAVW). Journal, 17*(3-4), 371–382.

Asakawa, T., & Gilbert, N. (2003). Synthesizing experiences: Lessons to be learned from Internet-mediated simulation games. *Simulation & Gaming, 34*(1), 10–22. doi:10.1177/1046878102250455

Asal, V. (2005). Playing games with international relations. *International Studies Perspectives, 6*, 359–373. doi:10.1111/j.1528-3577.2005.00213.x

Ascione, F. R. (1988). *Intermediate Attitude Scale: Assessment of third through sixth graders' attitudes toward the treatment of animals.* Logan, UT: Wasatch Institute for Research Evaluation.

Ascione, F. R. (1992). Enhancing children's attitudes about the humane treatment of animals: Generalization to human-directed empathy. *Anthrozoo, 5*(3), 176–191.

Ascione, F. R., & Weber, C. V. (1996). Children's attitudes about the humane treatment of animals and empathy: One-year follow up of a school-based intervention. *Anthrozoo, 9*(4), 188–195.

Asgari, M., & Kaufman, D. (2008). Motivation, learning, and game design. In R.E. Ferdig (Ed.), *Handbook of research on effective electronic gaming in education.* Hershey, PA: Information Science Reference.

Asgari, M., & Kaufman, D. M. (2004, September). *Intrinsic motivation and game design.* Paper presented by the first author at the 35th Ann. Conf. of the International Simulation and Gaming Association (ISAGA), and Conjoint Conference of Swiss, Austrian, German Simulation & Gaming Association (SAGSAGA), Munich, Germany.

Asimov, I. (1951) *The Foundation trilogy: Three classics of science fiction*, New York: Doubleday Books

Astolfi, J.-P. (1997). *L'erreur, un outil pour enseigner* [The error – a learning tool]. Paris: ESF.

Atake, K. (2003). *Using games to teach English in a Japanese junior high school.* ERIC Document Reproduction Service No. ED47948.

Bailey, H. J., & Milheim, W. D. (1991). A comprehensive model for designing video based materials. In *Proceedings of the Ninth Conference on Interactive Instruction Delivery, Orlando, Florida* (pp. 26-33). Warrenton, VA: Society for Applied Learning Technology.

Bain, C., & Newton, C. (2003). Art games: Pre-service art educators construct learning experiences for the elementary art classroom. *Art Education, 56*(5), 33–40.

Bakhtin, M. M. (1981). *The dialogic imagination: Four essays by M. M. Bakhtin.* M. Holquist (Ed.), C. Emerson & M. Holquist (Trans.). Austin, TX: University of Texas Press.

Bakhtin, M. M. (1986). *Speeck Genres and other late essays.* C. Emerson & M. Holquist (Eds.), V. W. McGee (Trans.). Austin, TX: University of Texas Press.

Baldaro, B., Tuozzi, G., Codispoti, M., & Montebarocci, O. (2004). Aggressive and non-violent videogames: short-term psychological and cardiovascular effects on habitual players. *Stress and Health, 20*(4), 203–208. doi:10.1002/smi.1015

Bali, L. R. (1979). Long-term effect of relaxation on blood pressure and anxiety levels of essential hypertensive males: A controlled study. *Psychosomatic Medicine, 41*(8), 637-646. Retrieved from http://www.psychosomaticmedicine.org/cgi/reprint/41/8/637.pdf

Bandura, A. (1977). Self-efficacy: Toward a unifying theory of behavioral change. *Psychological Review, 84*, 191–215. doi:10.1037/0033-295X.84.2.191

Bandura, A. (1977). Social learning theory. New York: Prentice Hall.

Bandura, A. (1986). *L'apprentissage social* [Social learning theory]. Brussels, Belgium: Éditions Margada.

Bandura, A. (1986). *Social foundations of thought and action: A social cognitive theory.* Englewood Cliffs, NJ: Prentice Hall.

Bandura, A. (2001). Social Cognitive Theory: An agentic perspective. *Annual Review of Psychology, 52*(1), 1–26. doi:10.1146/annurev.psych.52.1.1

Bantock, N. (1991). *Griffin & Sabine: An extraordinary correspondence*. San Francisco: Chronicle Books.

Bantock, N. (1992). *Sabine's notebook: In which the extraordinary correspondence of Griffin & Sabine continues.* Vancouver, BC, Canada: Raincoast Books.

Bantock, N. (1993). *The golden mean: In which the extraordinary correspondence of Griffin & Sabine concludes.* Vancouver, BC, Canada: Raincoast Books.

Bantock, N. (1997). *Ceremony of innocence* (Macintosh/Windows edition). Wiltshire: Real World Multimedia.

Barab, S., Arici, A., & Jackson, C. (2005). Eat your vegetables & do your homework: A design-based investigation of enjoyment and meaning in learning. *Educational Technology Research and Development, 65*(1), 15–21.

Barab, S., Thomas, M., Dodge, T., Carteaux, R., & Tuzun, H. (2005). Making learning fun: Quest Atlantis, a game without guns. *Educational Technology Research and Development, 53*(1), 86–107. doi:10.1007/BF02504859

Baranowski, T., Baranowski, J., Cullen, K. W., Marsh, T., Islam, N., & Zakeri, I. (2003). Squire's Quest! Dietary outcome evaluation of a multimedia game. *American Journal of Preventive Medicine, 24*(1), 52–61. doi:10.1016/S0749-3797(02)00570-6

Barber, K. (1998). *Canadian Oxford dictionary.* Toronto, ON, Canada: Oxford University Press.

Barnaud, C., Promburom, T., Trebuil, G., & Bousquet, F. (2007). An evolving simulation/gaming process to facilitate adaptive watershed management in northern mountainous Thailand. *Simulation & Gaming, 38*(3), 398–420. doi:10.1177/1046878107300670

Barrows, H. (2000). *Problem-based learning applied to medical education.* Springfield, IL: Southern Illinois University School of Medicine.

Barrows, H. S. (1984). A specific problem-based, self-directed learning method designed to teach medical problem-solving skills, and enhance knowledge retention and recall. In H. G. Schmidt, & M. L. De Volder (Eds.), *Tutorials in problem-based learning: A new direction in teaching the health professional.* Maastricht, The Netherlands: Vaan Gorcum.

Barrows, H. S. (1985). *How to design a problem-based curriculum for the preclinical years.* New York: Springer Publishing Company.

Barrows, H., & Tamblyn, R. (1980). *Problem-based learning: An approach to medical education.* New York: Springer Publishing Company.

Barwood, H. (2000). *Games as interactive storytelling.* Message posted to http://web.mit.edu/cms/games/storytelling.html

Bastien, C., & Rubio, R. (2001). *La conception de formulaires en ligne* [Design of online forms]. Retrieved March 15, 2005 from http://www.lergonome.org/dev/pages/article_5.asp

Battista, S., Cassalino, F., & Lande, C. (1999). MPEG-4: A multimedia standard for the third millennium. *Multimedia, 6*(4), 74–83. doi:. doi:10.1109/93.809236

Baumann, S. B., & Sayette, S. A. (2006). Smoking cues in a virtual world provoke craving in cigarette smokers. *Psychology of Addictive Behaviors, 20*(4), 484–489. doi:10.1037/0893-164X.20.4.484

Bayne-Smith, M., Fardy, P. S., Azzollini, A., Magel, J., Schmitz, K. H., & Agin, D. (2004). Improvements in heart health behaviors and reduction in coronary artery disease risk factors in urban teenaged girls through a school-based intervention: The PATH program. *American Journal of Public Health, 94*(9), 1538–1543. doi:10.2105/AJPH.94.9.1538

Bean, M. (2006). *What is a simulation*? Staff article for Forio Business Simulations. Retrieved from http://forio.com/resources/what-is-a-simulation

Beaufils, B. (2006). *Intelligence artificielle et intelligence collective: Théorie des jeux* [Artificial intelligence and collective intelligence: Theory of games. Lille: Laboratoire d'Informatique Fondamentale de Lille. Retrieved from http://www2.lifl.fr/~beaufils/mri/theorie_des_jeux.bruno-3.pdf

Beck, J. C., & Wade, M. (2004). *Got game: How a new generation of gamers is reshaping business forever.* Boston, MA: Harvard Business School Press.

Beck, J. C., & Wade, M. (2006). *The kids are alright: How the gamer generation is changing the workplace.* Boston, MA: Harvard Business School Press.

Becker, H. J. (1992). Computer-based integrated learning systems in the elementary and middle grades: A critical review and synthesis of evaluation reports. *Journal of Educational Computing Research, 8*(1), 1–41. doi:10.2190/23BC-ME1W-V37U-5TMJ

Becker, H. S. (1998). *Tricks of the trade: How to think about your research while you're doing it.* Chicago: University of Chicago Press.

Becker, K. (2007). Battle of the titans: Mario vs. MathBlaster. In C. Montgomerie & J. Seale (Eds.), *Proceedings of World Conference on Educational Multimedia, Hypermedia and Telecommunications 2007* (pp. 2707-2716). Chesapeake, VA: AACE.

Becta (2006). *Engagement and motivation in games development processes.* Research report. Available at www.becta.org.uk.

Becta. (2001). *Computer games in education project.* Retrieved May 20, 2009 from http://partners.becta.org.uk/index.php?section=rh&&catcode=&rid=13595

Bello, A., Knowlton, E., & Chaffin, J. (2007). Interactive videoconferencing as a medium for special education: Knowledge acquisition in preservice teacher education. *Intervention in School and Clinic, 43*(1), 38–46. doi:10.1177/10534512070430010501

Berger, A. (2006, January 31). 'Neverwinter Nights' in the classroom. *University of Minnesota News.* Retrieved June 16, 2008 from http://www1.umn.edu/umnnews/Feature_Stories/22Neverwinter_Nights22_in_the_classroom.html

Bergeron, B. (2006). *Developing serious games.* Hingham, MA: Charles River Media.

Bergeron, G. (2007). La richesse pédagogique de l'interactivité [The learning richness of interactivity]. *Correspondance, 13* (2), Available at http://www.ccdmd.qc.ca/correspo/Corr13-2/Richesse.html

Bergin, R. A., & Fors, U. G. H. (2003). Interactive simulated patient: An advanced tool for student-activated learning in medicine and healthcare. *Computers & Education, 40*(4), 361–376. doi:10.1016/S0360-1315(02)00167-7

Berkowitz, L. (1990). On the formation and regulation of anger and aggression: A cognitive neoassociationistic analysis. *The American Psychologist, 45*(4), 494–503. doi:10.1037/0003-066X.45.4.494

Bertrand, L. (1989). *Les effets de l'utilisation de la bureautique sur le développement des connaissances: Représentations discursives d'usagers* [The effects of the use of office automation on the development of knowledge: Discursive representations of users]. Unpublished doctoral dissertation, Laval University, Québec, QC, Canada.

Bertrand, Y. (1998). *Théories contemporaines de l'éducation* [Contemporary theories of education] (4th ed.). Montréal & Lyon: Éditions Nouvelles et Chronique Sociale.

Bibeau, R., & Delisle, C. (2001). *Critères de qualité pour l'évaluation d'un site web* [Quality criteria for evaluating a web site]. Retrieved March 15, 2005 from http://concours2002.educationquebec.qc.ca/qualite2002.htm

Biocca, F. (1995). *Communication in the age of virtual reality.* Mahwah, NJ: Lawrence Erlbaum Associates Inc.

Biofeedback Consultants. (2008). *EEG biofeedback: New York ripple effect.* Retrieved May 8, 2008, from http://www.therippleeffect.org/biofeedback_new_york.html#yonkers

Bizzocchi, J. (2001). *Ceremony of innocence: A case study in the emergent poetics of interactive narrative.* Unpublished M.Sc. thesis, Comparative Media Studies, Massachusetts Institute of Technology, Cambridge, MA.

Bizzocchi, J. (2003, May). *Ceremony of innocence and the subversion of interface: Cursor transformation as a narrative device.* Paper presented at the Digital Arts and Culture 2003: Streaming Wor(l)Ds, Royal Melbourne Institute of Technology, Melbourne, Australia.

Bizzocchi, J., & Woodbury, R. F. (2003). A case study in the design of interactive narrative: The subversion of the interface. *Simulation & Gaming, 34*(4), 550–568. doi:. doi:10.1177/1046878103258204

Blanton, W. E., Moorman, G. B., Hayes, B. A., & Warner, M. L. (1997). Effects of participation in the Fifth Dimension on far transfer. *Journal of Educational Computing Research, 16*, 371–396.

Blasi, L., & Asfonso, B. (2006). Increasing the transfer of simulation technology from R&D into school settings: An approach to evaluation from overarching vision to individual artifact in education. *Simulation & Gaming, 37*(2), 245–267. doi:10.1177/1046878105284449

Bloom, B. S. (1956) *Taxonomy of educational objectives: The classification of educational goals. Handbook 1: Cognitive domain.* New York: David McKay Company Inc.

Bloomer, J. (1973). What have simulation and gaming got to do with programmed learning and educational technology? *Programmed Learning and Educational Technology, 10*(4), 224–234.

Blouin, M., & Bergeron, C. (1997). *Dictionnaire de la réadaptation, tome 2:termes d'intervention et d'aides techniques* [Dictionary of rehabilitation, volume 2: Terms of intervention and technical help] (p. 32). Québec, QC, Canada: Les Publications du Québec.

Boethel, M., & Dimock, V. (1999). *Constructing knowledge with technology: A review of the literature.* Austin, TX: Southwest Educational Development Laboratory.

Bogdan, R., & Biklen, S. K. (1998). *Qualitative research for education: An introduction to theory and methods.* Boston, MA: Allyn & Bacon.

Bordwell, D., & Thompson, K. (1996). *Film art: An introduction* (5th ed.). New York: McGraw-Hill.

Borges, M. A. F., & Baranauskas, M. C. C. (1998). A user-centred approach to the design of an expert system for training. *British Journal of Educational Technology, 29*(1), 25–34. doi:10.1111/1467-8535.00043

Bos, N., Shami, N. S., & Naab, S. (2006). A globalization simulation to teach corporate social responsibility: Design features and analysis of student reasoning. *Simulation & Gaming, 37*(1), 56–72. doi:10.1177/1046878106286187

Bottino, R. M., Ferlino, L., Ott, M., & Tavella, M. (2006). Developing strategic and reasoning abilities with computer games at primary school level. *Computers & Education, 49*(4), 1272–1286. doi:10.1016/j.compedu.2006.02.003

Boulet, G. (2002). *Interactivité et communication médiatisée* [Interactivity and media communication]. Retrieved June 12, 2005 from http://cueep100.univ-lille1.fr/utic/Enseigner,%20 Former/interactivite.pdf

Bourgeault, G. (2004). *Éthiques, dit et non dit, contredit, interdit* [Ethics, said and not said, contradicted, forbidden]. Quebec, QC, Canada: Presses de l'Université du Québec.

Bradley, P. (2006). The history of simulation in medical education and possible future directions. *Medical Education, 40*(3), 254–262. doi:10.1111/j.1365-2929.2006.02394.x

Brand, S. (1968). *Whole Earth Catalog.* Menlo Park, CA: Portola Institute.

Brandon-Hall. (2006). *Online simulations 2006.* Retrieved January 23rd, 2008 from http://www.brandon-hall.com/publications/simkb/simkb.shtml

Bransford, J. D., Brown, A. L., & Cocking, R. R. (2000). *How people learn: Brain, mind, experience, and school* (expanded edition) Washington, DC: National Academy Press.

Brewer, M. (2000). Research design and issues of validity. In H. Reis & C. Judd (Eds.), *Handbook of research methods in social and personality psychology.* Cambridge, UK: Cambridge University Press.

Bricker, L., Tanimoto, S., Rothenberg, A., Hutama, D., & Wong, T. (1995). Multiplayer activities which develop mathematical coordination. In *Proceedings of CSCL'95* (pp. 32-39). New York: ACM Press.

Bridge, P., Appleyard, R. M., Ward, J. W., Philips, R., & Beavis, A. W. (2007). The development and evaluation of a virtual radiotherapy treatment machine using an immersive visualisation environment. *Computers & Education, 49*(2), 481–494. doi:10.1016/j.compedu.2005.10.006

Brien, R. (1981). *Design pédagogique* [Pedagogic design]. Ste-Foy, QC, Canada: Les Éditions St-Yves.

Brien, R. (2006). *Science cognitive et formation* [Training and cognitive science]. Québec, QC, Canada: Presses de l'Université du Québec.

British Educational Communications and Technology Agency (Becta). (2001). *Computer games in education project: Report.* Coventry, UK: Becta. Retrieved July 12, 2007, from http://partners.becta.org9.uk/index.php?section=rh&rid=13595.

British Educational Communications and Technology Agency (Becta). (2006). *Engagement and motivation in games development processes*, Version 1. Retrieved from http://partners.becta.org.uk/page_documents/partners/cge_games_development.pdf

Brookfield, S. (1987). Developing critical thinkers: *Challenging adults to explore alternative ways of thinking and acting* (1st edition). San Francisco, CA.: Jossey-Bass.

Brougère, G. (1999). Some elements relating to children's play and adult simulation/gaming. *Simulation & Gaming, 30*(2), 134–146. doi:10.1177/104687819903000204

Brown, A. L., & Campione, J. C. (1995). Concevoir une communauté de jeunes élèves: leçons théoriques et pratiques [Designing a community for young students: Theoretical and practical lessons]. *Revue française de pédagogie, 111*(avril-mai-juin), 11-33.

Brown, J. S., Collins, A., & Duguid, P. (1989). Situated cognition and the culture of learning. *Educational Researcher, 18*, 32–42.

Browne, K. D., & Hamilton-Giachritsis, C. (2005). The influence of violent media on children and adolescents: A public-health approach. *Lancet, 365*(9460), 702–710.

Brozik, D., & Zapalska, A. (1999). Interactive classroom economics: The market game. *Social Studies, 90*(6), 278–282. doi:10.1080/00377999909602431

Bruner, J. (1990). *Acts of meaning.* Cambridge, MA: Harvard University Press.

Bryant, B. (1982). An index of empathy for children and adolescents. *Child Development, 53*, 413–425. doi:10.2307/1128984

Bryce, D. A., King, N. J., Graebner, C. F., & Myers, J. H. (1998). Evaluation of a diagnostic reasoning program (DxR): Exploring student perceptions and addressing faculty concerns. *Journal of Interactive Media in Education, 98*(1). Available at www-jime.open.ac.uk/98/1

Bryce, J., & Rutter, J. (2005). Gendered gaming in gendered space. In J. Raessens & J. Goldstein (Eds.), *Handbook of computer games studies* (pp. 301-310). Cambridge, MA: The MIT Press.

Bryson, M., & de Castell, S. (1993). En/Gendering equity. *Educational Theory, 43*(4), 341–355. doi:10.1111/j.1741-5446.1993.00341.x

Buber, M. (1948). *Between man and man.* New York: Macmillan.

Bullinger, A. H., Mueller-Spahn, F., Mager, R., Stoermer, R., Kuntze, M. F., & Wurst, F. (2001). Virtual reality in future diagnoses and treatment. *The World Journal of Biological Psychiatry*, (Suppl. 1), 194S.

Burnham, D., & Fieser, J. (2006). René Descartes (1596-1650). *In International Encyclopedia of Philosophy.* Retrieved June 12, 2008 from http://www.iep.utm.edu/d/descarte.htm

Butler, J. (1990). Performative acts and gender constitution: An essay in phenomenology and feminist theory. In S. Case (Ed.), *Performing feminisms: Feminist critical theory and theatre.* Baltimore: Johns Hopkins University Press.

Butler, J. (1999). *Gender trouble: Feminism and the subversion of identity.* New York: Routledge.

Butler, K. A., & Lumpe, A. (2008). Student use of scaffolding software: Relationships with motivation and conceptual understanding. *Journal of Science Education and Technology, 17*(5), 427–436. doi:10.1007/s10956-008-9111-9

Caillois, R. (1958) *Les jeux et les hommes* [Games and men]. Paris: Gallimard.

Campbell, S. R. with the ENL Group. (2007). The ENGRAMMETRON: Establishing an educational neuroscience laboratory. *Simon Fraser University Educational Review, 1,* 17–29.

Canto-Sperber, M. (2001) *L'inquiétude morale et la vie humaine* [Moral unease and human life]. Paris: Presses universitaires de France.

Carless, S. (2005, September 1). Nintendo reveals impressive U.S. Nintendogs™ figures. *Gamasutra.* Retrieved February 14, 2008, from http://www.gamasutra.com/php-bin/news_index.php?story=6393

Carlson, S. (2003, August 15). Can Grand Theft Auto inspire professors? Educators say the virtual worlds of video games help students think more broadly. *Chronicle of Higher Education, 49*(49), A31. Retrieved June 16, 2008 from http://chronicle.com/free/v49/i49/49a03101.htm

Carnagey, N. L., Anderson, C. A., & Bushman, B. J. (2007). The effect of video game violence on physiological desensitization to real-life violence. *Journal of Experimental Social Psychology, 43*(3), 489–496. doi:10.1016/j.jesp.2006.05.003

Carr, D. (2005). Context, gaming pleasures and gendered preferences. *Simulation & Gaming, 36*(4), 464–482. doi:10.1177/1046878105282160

Casile, M., & Wheeler, J. V. (2005). The magnetic sentences industry game: A competitive in-class experience of business-level strategy. *Journal of Management Education, 29*(5), 696–713. doi:10.1177/1052562905277315

Cassell, J., Pelachaud, C., Badler, N., Steedman, M., Achorn, B., Becket, T., et al. (1994). Animated conversation: Rule-based generation of facial expression, gesture and spoken intonation for multiple conversational agents. In *Proceedings of ACM SIGGRAPH '94.* Available at http://citeseer.ist.psu.edu/cassell94animated.html

Cassell, J., Vilhjlmsson, H., & Bickmore, T. (2001). BEAT: The Behavior Expression Animation Toolkit. In *Proceedings of ACM SIGGRAPH 2001.* Available at http://citeseer.ist.psu.edu/cassell01beat.html.

Cassells, J., & Jenkins, H. (Eds.). (1998). *From Barbie to Mortal Kombat.* Boston: The MIT Press.

Castillo, F. (1987). *Le chemin des écoliers: l'éducation à la santé en milieu scolaire* [The long way round: Health education in the schools]. Brussels, Belgium: De Boeck Université.

Centre de ressources Le Préau (2002). *Quel modèle qualité pour la e-formation? Les normes qualités existantes répondent-elles aux besoins des acteurs de la e-formation?* [What quality model for e-learning? The quality norms that respond to the needs of the e-learning users?]. Retrieved May 15, 2002 from http://www.preau.ccip.fr/qualite/index.php

Chamberland, G., & Provost, G. (1996). *Jeu, simulation et jeu de rôle* [Games, simulations, and role-playing games]. Québec, QC, Canada: Presses de l'Université du Québec.

Chamberland, G., Lavoie, L., & Marquis, D. (1995). *20 formules pédagogiques* [20 pedagogical forms]. Quebec, QC, Canada: Presses de l'Université du Québec.

Chamberland, G., Lavoie, L., & Marquis, D. (1995). *20 formules pédagogiques* [20 pedagogic templates]. Ste-Foy, QC, Canada: Les Presses de l'Université du Québec.

Chapman, M. L. (1999). Situated, social, active: Rewriting genre in the elementary classroom. *Written Communication, 16*(4), 469–490. doi:10.1177/0741088399016004003

Charriere, P., & Magnin, M. C. (1998). Simulations globales avec Internet: un atout majeur pour les départements de langues [Global simulations with the Internet: A major trump card for language departments]. *The French Review*, *72*(2), 320–328.

Chasse, D., & Lefebvre, S. (2001). *ABC des notes de cours.* BAP- COSTIC. Available at http://www.cours.polymtl.ca/costic/atel_ndec_elec/sld001.htm

Cherry, R. A., Williams, J., George, J., & Ali, J. (2007). The effectiveness of a human patient simulator in the ATLS Shock Skills Station. *The Journal of Surgical Research*, *139*(2), 229–235. doi:10.1016/j.jss.2006.08.010

Chevallier, S. (2003). *D'une démarche ergonomique pour le développement des logiciels de loisir* [On an ergonomic process for the development of entertainment software]. Retrieved May 15, 2005 from http://www.hyperpsy.levillage.org/IMG/pdf/DemarcheErgo06.pdf

Chinien, C. (1990). Examination of cognitive style FD/FI as a learner selection criterion in formative evaluation. *Canadian Journal of Educational Communication*, *19*(1), 19–39.

Chomienne, M. (2007). *The video teleconference: A valuable academic tool.* Quebec, QC, Canada: profweb. Available at http://www.profweb.qc.ca/en/reports/the-video-teleconference-a-valuable-academic-tool/the-issue/dossier/32/index.html

Christopher, E. M. (1999). Simulations and games as subversive activities. *Simulation & Gaming*, *30*(4), 441–455. doi:10.1177/104687819903000403

Cioffi, J., Purcal, N., & Arundell, F. (2005). A pilot study to investigate the effect of a simulation strategy on the clinical decision making of midwifery students. *The Journal of Nursing Education*, *44*(3), 131–134.

Clark, J. (2002). *Building accessible websites.* Indianapolis, IN: New Riders Publishing.

Clark, R. (1989). Current progress and future directions for research in instructional technology. *Educational Technology Research and Development*, *37*(1), 57–66. doi:10.1007/BF02299046

Claudet, J. G. (1998). Using multimedia case simulations for professional growth of school leaders: Administrator Case Simulation Project. *T.H.E. Journal*, *25*(11), 82–86.

Clocksin, B. D., Watson, D. L., & Ransdell, L. (2002). Understanding youth obesity and media use: Implications for future intervention programs. *QUEST*, *54*, 259–275.

Coco, A., Woodward, I., Shaw, K., Cody, A., Lupton, G., & Peake, A. (2001). Bingo for beginners: A game strategy for facilitating active learning. *Teaching Sociology*, *29*(4), 492–503. doi:10.2307/1318950

Cohen, B., Evers, S., Manske, S., Bercovitz, K., & Edward, H. G. (2003). Smoking, physical activity and breakfast consumption among secondary school students in a southwestern Ontario community. *Canadian Journal of Public Health*, *94*(1), 41–44.

Coleman, J. S. (1968). Social processes and social simulation games. In S. S. Boocock, & E. O. Schild (Eds.), *Simulation games in learning* (pp. 29-51). Beverly Hills, CA: Sage Publications.

Coleridge, S. T. (1817). *Biographia literaria or, biographical sketches of my literary life and opinions.* New York: Kirk and Mercein.

Coles, C. D., Strickland, D. C., Padgett, L., & Bellmoff, L. (2007). Games that "work": Using computer games to teach alcohol-affected children about fire and street safety. *Research in Developmental Disabilities*, *28*(5), 518–530. doi:10.1016/j.ridd.2006.07.001

Colliver, J. A. (2000). Effectiveness of problem-based learning curricula: Research and theory. *Academic Medicine*, *75*(3), 259–266. doi:10.1097/00001888-200003000-00017

Committee on Quality of Health Care in America (CQHCA) Institute of Medicine. (1999). *To err is human: Building a safer health system.* Washington, DC: National Academy Press.

Cook, D. A., & Dupras, D. M. (2004). A practical guide to developing effective web-based learning. *Journal of General Internal Medicine: Official Journal of the Society for Research and Education in Primary Care Internal Medicine*, *19*(6), 698–707.

Cooper, T. (2006). *The responsible administrator: An approach to ethics for the administrative role* (5th edition). San Francisco CA: Jossey-Bass.

Coppé, M., & Schoonbroodt, C. (1992). *Guide pratique d'éducation pour la santé: réflexion, expérimentation et 50 fiches à l'usage des formateurs* [Practical Guide for Health Education: Reflection, Experimentation, and 50 Index Cards to Help the Trainer]. Brussels, Belgium: De Boeck Université.

Corbeil, P. (1999). Learning from the children: Practical and theoretical reflections on playing and learning. *Simulation & Gaming*, *30*(2), 163–180. doi:10.1177/104687819903000206

Cordova, D. I. (1993). *The effects of personalization and choice on students' intrinsic motivation and learning.* Unpublished Ph.D. dissertation, Stanford University.

Cordova, D. I., & Lepper, M. R. (1996). Intrinsic motivation and the process of learning: Beneficial effects of contextualization, personalization, and choice. *Journal of Educational Psychology*, *88*(4), 715–730. doi:10.1037/0022-0663.88.4.715

Cornell Management Game. (2006). Retrieved August 31, 2006 from http://www.cms-training.com/

Corson, D. L., Young, C. A., McManus, A., & Erdem, M. (2006). Overcoming managers' perceptual shortcuts through improvisational theater games. *Journal of Management Development*, *25*(3-4), 298–315. doi:10.1108/02621710610655792

Crawford, C. (1984). *The art of computer game design.* Berkeley, CA: Osborne/McGraw-Hill.

Crawford, C. (2003). *The art of interactive design: A euphonious and illuminating guide to building successful software.* San Francisco: No Starch Press.

Crawford, D. B. (1999). Managing the process of review: Playing "Baseball" in class. *Intervention in School and Clinic*, *35*(2), 93–95. doi:10.1177/105345129903500205

Crichton, M. T., Flin, R., & Rattray, W. A. R. (2000). Training decision makers – Tactical decision games. *Journal of Contingencies and Crisis Management*, *8*(4), 208–217. doi:10.1111/1468-5973.00141

Crookall, D. (1995) Simulation/ Gaming: A guide to the literature. In D. Crookall & K. Arai (Eds.), *Simulation and gaming across disciplines and cultures: ISAGA at a watershed* (pp. 151-177). Thousand Oaks, CA: Sage Publications.

Crookall, D., Greenblat, C. S., Coote, A., Klabbers, J. H. G., & Watson, D. R. (1987). *Simulation-gaming in the late 1980s.* Oxford, UK: Pergamon Press.

Crooks, S. M., & Eucker, T. R. (2001). "Fab 13": The learning factory. *Performance Improvement Quarterly*, *14*(2), 108–124.

Crowley, K., & Jacobs, M. (2002). Islands of expertise and the development of family scientific literacy. In K. Crowley, K. Knutson & K. Leinhardt (Eds.), *Learning conversations in museums* (1st ed., pp. 289-325). Mahwah, NJ: Lawrence Erlbaum Associates Inc.

Cruickshank, D. R., & Telfer, T. A. (1980). Classroom games and simulations. *Theory into Practice*, *19*(1), 75–80. doi:10.1080/00405848009542875

Cruz-Neira, C., Sandin, D. J., DeFanti, T. A., Kenyon, R., & Hart, J. C. (1992). The CAVE, Audio Visual Experience Automatic Virtual Environment. *Communications of the ACM*, *35*(6), 64–72. doi:10.1145/129888.129892

Csikszentmihalyi, M. (1975). Play and intrinsic rewards. *Journal of Humanistic Psychology*, *15*(3), 41–63. doi:10.1177/002216787501500306

Csikszentmihalyi, M. (1990). *Flow: The psychology of optimal experience.* New York: Harper and Row.

Cuban, L. (2001). *Oversold and overused: Computers in the classroom.* Cambridge, MA: Harvard University Press.

Dahl, A. (2009). Visioconférence en éducation: Exploite-t-on son potentiel pédagogique? [Videoconferencing in education: Are we exploiting its learning potential?]. *Revue DistanceS*, *11*(1), 1–16.

Darabi, A., Nelson, D. W., & Palanki, S. (2007). Acquisition of troubleshooting skills in a computer simulation: Worked example vs. conventional problem solving instructional strategies. *Computers in Human Behavior*, *23*(4), 1809–1819. doi:10.1016/j.chb.2005.11.001

Das, D. A., Grimmer, K. A., Sparnon, A. L., McRae, S. E., & Thomas, B. H. (2005). The efficacy of playing a virtual reality game in modulating pain for children with acute burn injuries: A randomized controlled trial. *BMC Pediatrics*, *4*(27). doi:.doi:10.1186/1471-2431-5-1

Davey, G. C. L. (1994). Self-reported fears to common indigenous animals in an adult U.K. population: The role of disgust sensitivity. *The British Journal of Psychology*, *85*(4), 541–554.

de Castell, S., & Bryson, M. (1998). Re-tooling play: Dystopia, dysphoria, and difference. In J. Cassell & H. Jenkins (Eds.), *From Barbie to Mortal Kombat* (pp. 232-261). Cambridge, MA: The MIT Press.

de Castell, S., & Jenson, J. (2002, October). *Designing for interactivity in theory and practice.* Paper presented at the annual meeting of the American Association for Research in Education (AREA), New Orleans, LA.

de Castell, S., & Jenson, J. (2003). Serious play. *Journal of Curriculum Studies*, *35*(6), 649–655. doi:10.1080/0022027032000145552

de Castell, S., & Jenson, J. (2006). Contagion: A preview of content design. In *Proceedings of the IMAGINE Network Conf.*, Banff, AB, Canada.

de Castell, S., Jenson, J., & Taylor, N. (2007). Digital games for education: When meanings play. In *Proceedings, 2007 Conference of the Digital Games Research Association (DiGRA), Situated Play*, Tokyo, Japan. Available at http://www.digra.org/dl/db/07312.45210.pdf

De Freitas, S. (2006). Learning in immersive worlds. A review of game based learning. London: JISC e-Learning Programme.

de Freitas, S., Savill-Smith, C., & Attewell, J. (2006). *Computer games and simulations for adult learning: Case studies from practice.* London: Learning and Skills Research Centre, University of London.

De Grandmont, N. (2005). *Pédagogie du jeu...philosophie du ludique* [Game pedagogy...ludic philosophy]. Available at http://cf.geocities.com/ndegrandmont/index.htm.

de Jong, T., & van Joolingen, W. R. (1998). Scientific discovery with computer simulations of conceptual domains. *Review of Educational Research*, *68*(2), 179–210.

De Vecchi, G. (1993). Des représentations, oui, pour en faire quoi ? [Representations, yes, for what?] *Cahiers pédagogiques, 312,* 55-57.

Deci, E. L., & Ryan, R. M. (1985). *Intrinsic motivation and self-determination in human behavior.* New York: Plenum.

Deci, E., Schwartz, A. J., Sheinman, L., & Ryan, R. M. (1981). An instrument to assess adults' orientations toward control versus autonomy with children: Reflections on intrinsic motivation and perceived competence. *Journal of Educational Psychology*, *73*(5), 642–650. doi:10.1037/0022-0663.73.5.642

DeMaria, R. (2007). *Reset: Changing the way we look at video games.* San Francisco: Berrett-Koehler Publishers, Inc.

Demetriadis, S., Karoulis, A., & Pombortis, A. (1999). "Graphical" jog through: Expert based methodology for user interface evaluation, applied in the case of an educational simulation interface. *Computers & Education*, *32*(4), 285–299. doi:10.1016/S0360-1315(99)00009-3

Dempsey, J. V., Haynes, L. L., Lucassen, B. A., & Casey, M. S. (2002). Forty simple computer games and what they could mean to educators. *Simulation & Gaming*, *33*(2), 157–168. doi:10.1177/1046878102332003

Dempsey, J. V., Lucassen, B. A., Haynes, L. L., & Casey, M. S. (1996). *Instructional applications of computer games.* New York: American Educational Research Association.

Dempsey, J. V., Lucassen, B., & Rasmussen, K. (1996). *The instructional gaming literature: Implications and 99 sources.* Technical Report 96-1. College of Education, University of South Alabama. Retrieved March 7,

2001, from http://www.coe.usouthal.edu/TechReports/notes.html

Dempsey, J., Lucassen, B., Gilley, W., & Rasmussen, K. (1993). Since Malone's theory of intrinsically motivating instruction: What's the score in the gaming literature? *Journal of Educational Technology Systems*, *22*(2), 173–183.

Denner, J., Werner, L., Bean, S., & Campe, S. (2005). The Girls Creating Games Program: Strategies for engaging middle school girls in information technology. *Frontiers: A Journal of Women's Studies. Special Issue on Gender and IT*, *26*(1), 90–98.

Depover, C., Giardina, M., & Marton, P. (1998). *Les environnements d'apprentissages multimédia - Analyse et conception* [Multimedia learning environments – Analysis and Design]. Paris: L'Harmatan.

Derrida, J. (1978). *Writing and difference* (A. Bass, Trans.). Chicago: University of Chicago Press.

Desgagné, S. (1997). Le concept de recherche collaborative: idée d'un rapprochement entre chercheurs universitaires et practiciens enseignants [The concept of collaborative research: The idea of a rapprochement between university researchers and practicing teachers]. *Revue des Sciences de l'Education*, *23*(2), 371–394.

Dessaint, M. P. (1995). Évaluer*:* de la mesure avant toute chose. [Evaluation: Measure above all] In M.P. Dessaint (Ed.). *La conception de cours. Guide de planification et de rédaction* [Course design: Guide to planning and writing] (pp. 207-247). Québec, QC, Canada: Les presses de l'Université du Québec.

Dessaint, M. P. (1995). Lire, écrire et être lu [Reading, writing and readability]. In M. P. Dessaint (Ed.), *Guide de planification, de rédaction et d'édition pour la conception de cours à distance* [Guide to planning, writing, and editing for the design of a distance education course] (pp. 83-140). Québec, QC, Canada: Presses de l'Université du Québec.

Dewey, J. (1910). *How we think.* Boston: D.C. Heath & Co.

Diabetes in Control. (2003). *Glucoboy moves closer to reality.* Retrieved May 20, 2009 from www.diabetesincontrol.com/issue173/np.shtml

Dias, J., Paiva, A., Vala, M., Aylett, R., Woods, S., Zoll, C., & Hall, L. (2006). Empathic characters in computer-based personal and social education. In M. Pivec (Ed.), *Affective and emotional aspects of human-computer interaction.* Amsterdam, Netherlands: IOS Press.

Dick, W., & Carey, L. (1996). *The systematic design of instruction* (4th edition). New York: Harper Collins College Publishers.

Dickey, M. D. (2005). Engaging by design: How engagement strategies in popular computer and video games can inform instructional design. *Educational Technology Research and Development*, *53*(2), 67–83. doi:10.1007/BF02504866

Dill, K. E., & Dill, J. C. (1998). Video game violence: A review of the empirical literature. *Aggression and Violent Behavior*, *3*(4), 407–428. doi:10.1016/S1359-1789(97)00001-3

DiPaola, S. (1991). Extending the range of facial types. *Visualization and Computer Animation*, *2*(4), 129–131. doi:10.1002/vis.4340020406

DiPaola, S. (2002). *FaceSpace*: A facial spatial-domain toolkit. In *Proceedings of the IEEE Symposium on Information Visualization 2002 (InfoViz 2002)* (pp. 49-55).

DiPaola, S., & Akai, C. (2007). Blending science knowledge and AI gaming techniques for experiential learning, *Loading... -. Journal of the Canadian Games Studies Association*, *1*(1), 40–45.

DiPaola, S., & Collins, C. (2003). A social metaphor-based 3D virtual environment. In *Proceedings, International Conference on Computer Graphics and Interactive Techniques: ACM SIGGRAPH 2003 Educators' Program.* doi 10.1145/965106.965134.

DiPaola, S., Akai, C., & Kraus, B. (2007). Experiencing belugas: Developing an action selection-based aquarium interactive. [Special Issue on Action Selection]. *Journal of Adaptive Behavior, 15*(1), 99–113. doi:10.1177/1059712306076251

DiPaola, S., Chan, J., & Arya, A. (2005). Simulating face to face collaboration for interactive learning systems. In G. Richards (Ed.), *Proceedings of World Conference on E-Learning in Corporate, Government, Healthcare, and Higher Education 2005* (pp. 1998-2003). Chesapeake, VA: Association for the Advancement of Computing in Education (AACE).

DiPaola, S., Dorash, D., & Brandt, G. (2004). Ratava's Line: Emergent learning and design using collaborative virtual worlds. In *Proceedings, International Conference on Computer Graphics and Interactive Techniques: ACM SIGGRAPH 2004 Educators' Program.* doi 10.1145/1186107.1186136.

Doak, C. C., Doak, L. G., & Root, J. H. (1996). *Teaching patients with low literacy skills* (2nd ed.). Philadelphia: J. B. Lippincott.

Dobson, M., Burgoyne, D., & Le Blanc, D. (2004). Transforming tensions in learning technology design: Operationalizing activity theory. *Canadian Journal of Learning Technologies, 30*(1), 20–45.

Dobson, M., Ha, D., Ciavarro, C., & Mulligan, D. (2005). From real-world data to game-world experience: A method for developing plausible and engaging learning games. In S. de Castell & J. Jenson (Eds.), *Proceedings of the Digital Games Research Association Conference (DIGRA 2005): Changing Views: Worlds in Play*, Vancouver, BC, Canada. Retrieved December 20th, 2007 from http://citeseer.ist.psu.edu/737505.html

Dobson, M., Pengelly, M., Sime, J.-A., Albaladejo, S., Garcia, E., Gonzales, F., et al. (2002). Situated learning with co-operative agent simulations in team training. In M. Dobson (Ed.), *Computers in Human Behavior (*special issue) (pp. 457-573). Amsterdam, The Netherlands: Elsevier Science.

Docherty, C., Hoy, D., Topp, H., & Trinder, K. (2005). eLearning techniques supporting problem based learning in clinical simulation. *International Journal of Medical Informatics, 74*(7-8), 527–533. doi:10.1016/j.ijmedinf.2005.03.009

Doise, W., & Mugny, G. (1981). *Le développement social de l'intelligence* [The social development of intelligence]. Paris: InterÉditions.

Dong, U. C., & Kwonki, Y. (2008). Validating a simulation for improving teacher's motivating skills. In K. McFerrin, R. Weber, R. Carlsen, & D. A. Willis (Eds), *Proceedings of 19th International Conference Annual of Society for Information Technology & Teacher Education* (pp. 1640-1645). Chesapeake, VA; AACE.

Downes, T. (1988). *Children's use of computers in their homes.* Unpublished Ph.D. dissertation, University of Western Sydney, Australia.

Duchowski, A., Medlin, E., & Cournia, N. (2002). 3-D eye movement analysis. *Behavior Research Methods, Instruments, & Computers, 34*(4), 573–591.

Duffy, T. M., & Jonassen, D. H. (1992) *Constructivism and the technology of instruction: A conversation.* Hillsdale, NJ: Lawrence Erlbaum Associates Inc.

Duffy, T. M., Dueber, B., & Hawley, C. L. (1998). Critical thinking in a distributed environment: A pedagogical base for the design of conferencing systems. In C. J. Bonk & K. S. King (Eds.), *Electronic collaborators: Learner-centered technologies for literacy, apprenticeship, and discourse* (pp. 51-78). Mahwah, NJ: Lawrence Erlbaum Associates Inc.

Duffy, T., & Cunningham, D. (1996). Constructivism: Implications for the design and delivery of instruction. In D. H. Jonassen (Ed.), *Handbook of research for educational communications and technology* (pp. 170-198). New York: Simon and Schuster.

Dufresne, A. (2009). *Introduction aux principes ergonomiques* (web site). Retrieved May 29, 2009 from http://lrcm.com.umontreal.ca/dufresne/bta/ergo/frame1.html

Dumas, J. S. (2003). User-based evaluations. In J. A. Jacko & A. Sears (Eds.), *The human-computer interaction handbook: Fundamentals, evolving technologies, and emerging applications* (pp. 1093-117). Mahwah, NJ: Lawrence Erlbaum Associates Inc.

Dyck, J., Pinelle, D., Brown, B., & Gutwin, C. (2003). Learning from games: HCI design innovations in entertainment software. In *Proceedings of the Conference on Human-Computer Interaction and Computer Graphics (GI'03), Halifax, Canada* (pp. 237-246). San Francisco, CA: Morgan Kaufmann.

Eaves, R. H., & Flagg, A. J. (2001). The U.S. Air Force pilot simulated medical unit: A teaching strategy with multiple applications. *The Journal of Nursing Education, 40*(3), 110–115.

Ebner, N., & Efron, Y. (2005, July). Using tomorrow's headlines for today's training: Creating pseudo-reality in conflict resolution simulation games. *Negotiation Journal, 21*(3), 377–393. doi:10.1111/j.1571-9979.2005.00070.x

Eccles, J., & Wigfield, A. (2002). Motivational beliefs, values, and goals. *Annual Review of Psychology, 53*, 109–132. doi:10.1146/annurev.psych.53.100901.135153

Eder-Van Hook, J. (2004). *Building a national agenda for simulation-based medical education.* Fort Detrick, MD: Telemedicine and Advanced Technology Research Center (TATRC), U.S. Army Medical Research and Materiel Command. Available at http://www.medsim.org/articles/AIMS_2004_Report_Simulation-based_Medical_Training.pdf

EEG Spectrum International Inc. (2007). *Biofeedback for anxiety and panic.* Retrieved June 26, 2008, from: http://www.eegspectrum.com/Applications/Intro/UltimateSelf-Help/SpecificApplications/

Egenfeldt-Nielsen, S. (2005). *Beyond edutainment: Exploring the educational potential of computer games.* Unpublished PhD dissertation, IT University Copenhagen, Denmark.

Eglesz, D., Fekete, I., Kiss, O. E., & Izso, L. (2005). Computer games are fun? On professional games and players' motivations. *Educational Media International, 42*(2), 117–124. doi:10.1080/09523980500060274

Ekman, P., & Friesen, W. V. (1978). *Facial Action Coding System: A technique for the animation of facial movement.* Palo Alto, CA: Consulting Psychologists Press Inc.

Ellis, S. R. (1995). Virtual environments and environmental instruments. In K. Carr & R. England (Eds.), *Simulated and virtual realities: Elements of perception* (pp. 11-51). London: Taylor & Francis.

Entertainment Software Association (ESA). (2006). Essential facts about games and youth violence. Washington, DC: Entertainment Software Association. Retrieved March 4, 2008 from http://www.theesa.com/archives/2006EF%20Youth%20Violence.pdf

Entertainment Software Association of Canada. (2008). *Essential facts about the Canadian computer and video game industry 2008.* Montreal, QC, Canada: Ipsos Reid.

Ergolab (2003). *Faciliter la lecture d'informations sur le web* [Facilating the lecture with information on the web]. Retrieved May 29, 2009 from http://www.ergolab.net/articles/faciliter-lecture-informations-web.html

Ergolab (2003). *Feedback et rapport homme-ordinateur* [Human-computer feedback and rapport]. Retrieved April 27, 2008 from http://www.ergolab.net/articles/feedback-erogonomie.html

Ergolab (2004). *Accessibilité visuelle des interfaces web* [Accessibility of web interfaces]. Retrieved June 6, 2009 from http://www.ergolab.net/articles/accessibilite-visuelle-web.html

Ermi, L., & Mäyra, F. (2007). Fundamental components of the game play experience: Analyzing immersion. In S. de Castell, & J. Jenson (Eds.), *Worlds in play: International perspectives on digital games research* (pp. 37-53). New York: Peter Lang Publishing.

Eron, L. D. (2001). Seeing is believing: How viewing violence alters attitudes and aggressive behavior. In A. C. Bohart & D. J. Stipek (Eds.), Constructive and destructive behavior: Implications for family, school, and society (pp. 49-60). Washington, DC: American Psychological Association.

Eslinger, E., White, B., Frederiksen, J., & Brobst, J. (2008). Supporting inquiry processes with an interactive learning environment: Inquiry Island. *Journal of Science Education and Technology, 17*(6), 610–617. doi:10.1007/s10956-008-9130-6

Evans, D. R. (1979). *Games and simulations in literacy training*. Teheran: Hulton Educational Publications.

Evry, H. (2004). *Beginning game graphics*. Boston: Course Technology, Incorporated.

Eyraud, E. (1998). Le jeu dans l'apprentissage d'une langue vivante: Application à l'espagnol [The game in learning a living language: Application to Spanish]. *Bulletin APLV* – Strasbourg summary no. 60. Summary of unpublished master's thesis, LCE (Langue et Civilisation Etrangère) d'espagnol, Université Paris X Nanterre. Available from http://averreman.free.fr/aplv/num60-jeu-espagnol.htm

Facer, K. (2002). *Computer games and learning: Why do we think it's worth talking about computer games and learning in the same breath?* (Discussion paper). London, UK. Futurelab. Retrieved May 30, 2009 from http://www.futurelab.org.uk/resources/documents/discussion_papers/Computer_Games_and_Learning_discpaper.pdf

Facer, K., Stanton, D., Joiner, R., Reid, J., Hull, R., & Kirk, D. (2004). Savannah: Mobile gaming and learning? *Journal of Computer Assisted Learning, 20*(6), 399–409. doi:10.1111/j.1365-2729.2004.00105.x

Fahy, P. J. (2004). Media characteristics and online learning technology. In T. Anderson & F. Elloumi (Eds). *Theory and practice of online learning* (pp. 137-174). Athabasca, AB, Canada: Athasbasca University.

Faiola, T. (1990). Principles and guidelines for a screen display interface. *The Videodiscs Monitor, 8*(2), 27–29.

Faiola, T., & Deblois, M. L. (1988). Designing a visual factors-based screen display interface: The new role of the graphic technologist. *Educational Technology, 28*(8), 12–21.

Falstein, N. (2004, May). The flow channel. *Game Developer Magazine, 11*(5), 52a.

Farkas, G. M., Sine, L. F., & Evans, I. M. (1979). The effects of distraction, performance demand, stimulus explicitness and personality on objective and subjective measures of male sexual arousal. *Behaviour Research and Therapy, 17*, 25–32. doi:10.1016/0005-7967(79)90047-0

Federation of American Scientists (FAS). (2006). *Harnessing the power of video games for learning: Final report on the Summit on Educational Games*. Available at http://www.fas.org/gamesummit/Resources/Summit%20on%20Educational%20Games.pdf

Feinstein, A. H., Mann, S., & Corsun, D. L. (2002). Charting the experiential territory: Clarifying definitions and uses of computer simulation, games, and role play. *Journal of Management Development, 21*(10), 732–744. doi:10.1108/02621710210448011

Feldon, D. F., & Kafai, Y. B. (2008). Mixed methods for mixed reality: Understanding users' avatar activities in virtual worlds. *Educational Technology Research and Development, 56*(5-6), 575–593. doi:10.1007/s11423-007-9081-2

Ferdig, R. E. (2007). Preface: Learning and teaching with electronic games. *Journal of Educational Multimedia and Hypermedia, 16*(3), 217–223.

Ferguson, C. J. (2007). Evidence for publication bias in video game violence affects literature: A meta-analytic review. *Aggression and Violent Behavior, 12*(4), 470–482. doi:10.1016/j.avb.2007.01.001

Fertig, G. (2001). Hard times and new deals: Teaching fifth graders about the Great Depression. *Social Education, 65*(1), 34–40.

Feshbach, N. D. (1978). Studies on empathic behavior in children. In B. A. Maher (Ed.), *Progress in experimental personality research 8* (pp. 1-47). New York: Academic Press.

Feshbach, N. D. (1979). Empathy training: A field study in affective education. In S. Feshbach & A. Fraczek (Eds.), *Aggression and behavior change* (pp. 234-249). New York: Praeger Publishers.

Feshbach, N. D. (1982). Sex differences in empathy. In N. Eisenberg (Ed.), *The development of prosocial behavior* (pp. 315-338). New York: Academic Press.

Fielding, M. (1976). Against competition: In praise of malleable analysis and the subversion of philosophy. *Journal of Philosophy of Education, 10*(1), 124–146. doi:10.1111/j.1467-9752.1976.tb00008.x

Fink, L. D. (2003). *Creating significant learning experiences: An integrated approach to designing college courses.* San Francisco: Jossey-Bass.

Fischer, L., & Smith, G. M. (1999). Statistical adequacy of The Abel Assessment for interest in paraphilias. *Sexual Abuse, 11*(1), 195–205. doi:10.1177/107906329901100303

Fishman, M. (1999). Evaluating the effects of a virtual environment (STARBRIGHT World) with hospitalized children. *Research on Social Work Practice, 9*(3), 365–382. doi:10.1177/104973159900900310

Flament, C., & Rouquette, M. L. (2003). *Anatomie des idées ordinaires: comment étudier les représentations sociales*[Anatomy of ordinary ideas: How to study social representations]. Paris: Armand Colin.

Foch'lay, B. (1997, July). *L'évaluation participative: une mise en œuvre du modèle de rationalité procédurale au service de la modernisation de l'action publique* [Participative evaluation: A process modelled on procedural rationality in the service of modernizing public action]. Paper presented at the conference of the Society for the Advancement of Socioeconomics (SASE), Montréal.

Forrester, J. W. (1971). *World dynamics.* Cambrige, MA: Wright Allen Press.

Foucault, M. (1990). *The history of sexuality, an introduction: Volume I.* New York: Vintage.

Fournier, M., Vincent, S. & Brougère, G.(2004). À quoi sert le jeu ? [What use are games?] *Sciences humaines, 152 (August-September),* 19-45.

Foxlin, E. (2002). Motion tracking requirements and technologies. In K. Stanney (Ed.) *Handbook of virtual environments: Design, implementation, and applications* (pp.163-210). Mahwah, NJ: Lawrence Erlbaum Associates Inc.

Frasca, G. (2001). *Videogames of the oppressed: Videogames as a mean for critical thinking and debate.* Unpublished master's thesis, Georgia Institute of Technology, Atlanta GA.

Freedman, J. L. (2001, October). Evaluating the research on violent video games. Paper presented at the Playing by the Rules conference, University of Chicago Cultural Policy Center. Retrieved March 4, 2008 from http://culturalpolicy.uchicago.edu/conf2001/papers/freedman.html

Freeman, M. A., & Capper, J. M. (1999). Exploiting the web for education: An anonymous asynchronous role simulation. *Australian Journal of Educational Technology, 15*(1), 95–116.

Freund, K. (1963). A laboratory method for diagnosing predominance of homo- and hetero-erotic interest in the male. *Behaviour Research and Therapy, 1,* 85–93. doi:10.1016/0005-7967(63)90012-3

Fuchs, T., Birbaumer, N., Lutzenberger, W., Gruzelier, J. H., & Kaiser, J. (2003). Neurofeedback treatment for attention-deficit/hyperactivity disorder in children: A comparison with methylphenidate. *Applied Psychophysiology and Biofeedback, 28*(1), 1–12. doi:10.1023/A:1022353731579

Funge, J. Tu, X., & Terzopolous, D. (1999). Cognitive Modeling: Knowledge, reasoning, and planning for intelligent characters. In *Proceedings of ACM SIGGRAPH 1999* (pp. 29-38).

Funk, J. B., Baldacci, H. B., Pasold, T., & Baumgardner, J. (2004). Violence exposure in real life, video games, television, movies, and the Internet: Is there desensitization? *Journal of Adolescence, 27*(1), 23–39. doi:10.1016/j.adolescence.2003.10.005

Funk, J. B., Buchman, D. D., Jenks, J., & Bechtoldt, H. (2003). Playing violent video games, desensitization, and moral evaluation in children. *Journal of Applied Developmental Psychology, 24*(4), 413–436. doi:10.1016/S0193-3973(03)00073-X

Gaba, D. M., Howard, S. K., Fish, K. J., Smith, B. E., & Sowb, Y. A. (2001). Simulation-based training in anesthesia crisis resource management (ACRM): a decade of experience. *Simulation & Gaming, 32*(2), 175–193. doi:10.1177/104687810103200206

Gagné, R. M. (1976). *Les principes fondamentaux de l'apprentissage* [Fundamental principles of learning]. Montreal, QC, Canada: HRW.

Gagné, S. (2002). *Bilan de santé des jeunes: exercice à la baisse et médication à la hausse* [Youth check-up: Exercise falls and medication increases]. *Passeportsanté.net.* Available at http://www.passeportsante.net/fr/Actualites/Nouvelles/Fiche.aspx?doc=2002112000

Gallagher, A. G., & Cates, C. U. (2004). Approval of virtual reality training for carotid stenting: What this means for procedural-based medicine. *Journal of the American Medical Association, 292*(24), 3024–3026. doi:10.1001/jama.292.24.3024

Gallie, W. B. (1956). Essentially contested concepts. In. *Proceedings of the Aristotelian Society, 56*, 167–198.

Galloway, A. R. (2006). *Gaming: Essays on algorithmic culture.* Minneapolis, MN: University of Minnesota Press.

Game Developers Conference (2006). *6th Annual game developers' choice awards.* Retrieved February 16, 2008, from http://www.gamechoiceawards.com/archive/gdca_6th.htm

Games for Health. (2005). *Games for health blog.* Available at www.gamesforhealth.org

Garcia-Palacios, A., Hoffman, H. G., & See, S. K. (2001). Redefining therapeutic success with virtual reality exposure therapy. *Cyberpsychology & Behavior, 4*(3), 341–348. doi:10.1089/109493101300210231

Gardner, J. E. (1991). Can the Mario Bros. help? Nintendo games as an adjunct in psychotherapy with children. Psychotherapy: Theory, Research, Practice. *Training (New York, N.Y.), 28*(4), 667–670.

Garner, K. H. (1990). 20 rules for arranging text on a screen. *CBT Directions, 3*(5), 13–17.

Garris, R., Ahlers, R., & Driskell, J. E. (2002). Games, motivation, and learning: A research and practice model. *Simulation & Gaming, 33*(4), 441–467. doi:10.1177/1046878102238607

Garrison, D. R. (1991). Critical thinking and adult education: A conceptual model for developing critical thinking in adult learners. *International Journal of Lifelong Education, 10*(4), 287–303. doi:10.1080/0260137910100403

Garrison, D. R., & Anderson, T. (2003). *E-Learning in the 21st century: A framework for research and practice.* London/New York: Routledge Falmer.

Garrison, D. R., & Vaughan, N. (2008). *Blended learning in higher education: Framework, principles, and guidelines.* San Francisco, CA: Jossey-Bass.

Gauthier, B. (2005). *Recherche sociale de la problématique à la collecte de données* [Social research and the problem of data collection]. Québec, QC, Canada: Presses de l'Université du Québec.

Gayet, D. (2006). *Pédagogie et éducation familiale. Concepts et perspectives en sciences humaines* [Pedagogy and family education: Concepts and perspectives in the human sciences]. Paris:L'harmattan.

Gee, J. P. (2003). *What video games have to teach us about learning and literacy.* New York: Palgrave Macmillan.

Gee, J. P. (2004). *Learning by design: Good video games as learning machines.* Madison, WI: University of Wisconsin Academic ADL Co-Lab. Available at: http://www.academiccolab.org/resources/documents/Game%20Paper.pdf

Gee, J. P. (2004b). *Video games and the future of learning.* University of Wisconsin. Madison, WI: Academic Advanced Distributed Learning Co-Laboratory.

Gee, J. P. (2007). *Good video games and good learning. Collected essays on video games, learning, and literacy.* New York: Peter Lang.

Gentile, D. A., & Anderson, C. A. (2006). Violent video games: The effects on youth, and public policy implications. In N. Dowd, D. G. Singer, & R. F. Wilson (Eds.), Handbook of children, culture, and violence (pp. 225-246). Thousand Oaks, CA: Sage Publications.

Gentile, D. A., & Gentile, J. R. (2008). Violent video games as exemplary teachers: A conceptual analysis. *Journal of Youth and Adolescence, 37*(2), 127–141. doi:10.1007/s10964-007-9206-2

Gentile, D. A., & Walsh, D. A. (2002). A normative study of family media habits. *Journal of Applied Developmental Psychology, 23*(2), 157–178. doi:10.1016/S0193-3973(02)00102-8

Gentile, D. A., Lynch, P. J., Linder, J. R., & Walsh, D. A. (2004). The effects of violent video game habits on adolescent hostility, aggressive behaviors, and school performance. *Journal of Adolescence, 27*(1), 5–22. doi:10.1016/j.adolescence.2003.10.002

George, M. H. (1999). The role of animals in the emotional and moral development of children. In F. R. Ascione & P. Arkow (Eds.), *Child abuse, domestic violence, and animal abuse* (pp. 380-392). West Lafayette, IN: Purdue University Press.

Gerhardt-Powals, J. (1996). Cognitive engineering principles for enhancing human-computer performance. *International Journal of Human-Computer Interaction, 8*(2), 189–211. doi:10.1080/10447319609526147

Gibb, G. D., Bailey, J. R., Lambirth, T. T., & Wilson, W. P. (1983). Personality differences in high and low electronic video game users. *The Journal of Psychology, 114*(2), 159–165.

Gibbs, G. I. (1974). The use of simulations as achievement tests with programmed texts. *Programmed Learning and Educational Technology, 11*(4), 183–191.

Gibson, W. (1984) *Neuromancer*. New York: Ace Books.

Giddings, S. (2007). Playing with non-humans: Digital games as technocultural form. In S. de Castell & J. Jenson (Eds.), *Worlds in play: International perspectives on digital games research* (pp. 115-128). New York: Peter Lang.

Giddings, S., & Kennedy, H. W. (2008). Little Jesuses and *@#?-off robots: On cybernetics, aesthetics and not being very good at *Lego Star Wars*. In M. Swallwell & J. Wilson (Eds.), *The pleasures of computer gaming* (pp. 13-32). Jefferson, NC: McFarland.

Gilbert, K. R. (1997). Teaching on the Internet: the World Wide Web as a course delivery system. In N. Millichap (Ed.), *Beginnings: Initial experiences in teaching via distance education*. Indianapolis, IN: Indiana Partnership for Statewide Education (IPSE).

Gillespie, P. H. (1973). *Learning through simulation games*. Paramus, NJ: Paulist Press.

Gilly, M. (1988). Interactions entre pairs et constructions cognitives [Interaction between peers and cognitive constructions]. In A. N. Perret-Clermond, & M. Nicolet (Eds.), *Interagir et connaître. Enjeux et régulations sociales dans le développement cognitif* (pp. 19-28). Cousset, Switzerland: DelVal.

Giordan, A. (1983). *L'élève et/ou les connaissances scientifiques: approche didactique de la construction des concepts scientifiques par les élèves* [Students and scientific knowledge: The didactic approach to the construction of scientific concepts by students]. Berne, Switzerland: Peter Lang.

Glaser, B. (1992). *Basics of grounded theory analysis: Emergence vs. forcing*. Mill Valley, CA: Sociology Press.

Glaser, B. G., & Strauss, A. (1967). *The discovery of grounded theory: Strategies for qualitative research*. Chicago: Aldine.

Glasgow, D. V., Osbourne, A., & Croxen, J. (2003). An assessment tool for investigating paedophile sexual interest using viewing time: An application of single case research methodology. *British Journal of Learning Disabilities, 31*(2), 96–102. doi:10.1046/j.1468-3156.2003.00180.x

Golde, J. A., Strassberg, D. S., & Turner, C. M. (2000). Psychophysiologic assessment of erectile response and its suppression as a function of stimulus media and previous experience with plethysmography. *Journal of Sex Research, 37*(1), 53–59.

Goldenberg, D., Andrusyszyn, M. A., & Iwastw, C. (2005). The effect of classroom simulation on nursing students' self-efficacy related to health teaching. *The Journal of Nursing Education, 44*(7), 310–314.

Goldstein, A. P., & Michaels, G. Y. (1985). *Empathy: Development, training, and consequences*. Hillsdale, NJ: Lawrence Erlbaum Association Inc.

Gordon, S., & Gill, R. (1997). Cognitive task analysis. In C. Zsambok & G. Klein (Eds.), *Naturalistic decision making* (pp. 131-140). Mahwah, NJ: Lawrence Erlbaum Associates Inc.

Gorman, P. J. (2000). The future of medical education is no longer blood and guts, it is bits and bytes. *American Journal of Surgery, 180*(5), 353–356. doi:10.1016/S0002-9610(00)00514-6

Gosen, J., & Wabush, J. (1999). As teachers and researchers, where do we go from here? *Simulation & Gaming, 30*(3), 292–303. doi:10.1177/104687819903000305

Gosen, J., & Washbush, J. (2004). A review of scholarship on assessing experiential learning effectiveness. *Simulation & Gaming, 35*(2), 270–293. doi:10.1177/1046878104263544

Goupil, G., & Lusignan, G. (1993). *Apprentissage et enseignement en milieu scolaire* [Learning and teaching in the schools]. Montréal, QC, Canada: Gaëtan Morin.

Gradler, M. E. (2004). Games and simulations and their relationships to learning. In D. H. Jonassen (Ed.), *Handbook of research for educational communications and technology* (2nd ed, pp. 571-581). Mahwah, NJ: Lawrence Erlbaum Associates Inc.

Grady, K. (2002). *Adolescent literacy and content area reading.* ERIC Document Reproduction Service No. ED469930. Retrieved from ERIC database.

Grafinger, D. J. (1988). *Basics of instructional systems development.* INFO_LINE Issue 8803. Alexandria, VA: American Society for Training and Development.

Graner Ray, S. (2004). *Gender inclusive game design: Expanding the market.* Hingham, MA: Charles River Media.

Grant, J. (2002). Learning needs assessment: Assessing the need. *British Medical Journal, 324*(7330), 156–159. doi:10.1136/bmj.324.7330.156

Grassberger, P., & Procaccia, I. (1983). Characterization of strange attractors. *Physical Review Letters, 50*(5), 346–349. doi:10.1103/PhysRevLett.50.346

Grassberger, P., Schreiber, T., & Schaffrath, C. (1991). Nonlinear time sequence analysis. *International Journal of Bifurcation and Chaos in Applied Sciences and Engineering, 1*(3), 521–547. doi:10.1142/S0218127491000403

Gray, A. R., Topping, K. J., & Carcary, W. B. (1998). Individual and group learning of the Highway Code: Comparing board game and traditional methods. *Educational Research, 40*(1), 45–53.

Graybill, D., Kirsch, J. R., & Esselman, E. D. (1985). Effects of playing violent versus nonviolent video games on the aggressive ideation of aggressive and nonaggressive children. *Child Study Journal, 15*(3), 199–205.

Graybill, D., Strawniak, M., Hunter, T., & O'Leary, M. (1987). Effects of playing versus observing violent versus nonviolent video games on children's aggression. Psychology: A Journal of Human Behavior, 24(3), 1-8.

Gredler, M. (2004). Games and simulations and their relationships to learning. In D. H. Jonassen (Ed.), *Handbook of research on educational communications and technology* (2nd ed., pp. 571-582). Mahwah, NJ: Lawrence Erlbaum Associates Inc.

Gredler, M. E. (1992). *Designing and evaluating games and simulations: A process approach.* London: Kogan Page.

Green, C., & Bavelier, D. (2003, May 29). Action video game modifies visual selective attention. *Nature, 423*, 534–537. doi:10.1038/nature01647

Greenblat, C. S. (1988). Designing games and simulations. Thousand Oaks, CA: Sage Publications.

Griffin, L. L., & Butler, J. I. (2005). *Teaching games for understanding.* Champaign, IL: Human Kinetics.

Griffiths, M. (1999). Violent video games and aggression: A review of the literature. *Aggression and Violent Behavior, 4*(2), 203–212. doi:10.1016/S1359-1789(97)00055-4

Griffiths, M. (2002). The educational benefits of videogames. *Education and Health, 20*(3), 47–51.

Gros, B. (2007). Digital games in education: The design of games-based learning environments. *Journal of Research on Technology in Education*, *40*(1), 23–38.

Group, N. P. D. Inc. (2007). Press release: Amount of time kids spend playing video games is on the rise. Retrieved February 19, 2008 from http://www.npd.com/press/releases/press_071016a.html

Guilbert, L., & Ouellet, L. (1997). *Études de cas, apprentissage par problèmes* [Case studies: Problem-based learning]. Québec, QC, Canada: Presses de l'Université Laval.

Guillot, B. (2004). La psychothérapie assistée par ordinateur: PsyaO [Computer-assisted psychotherapy: PsyaO]. *Adolescence*, *22*(1), 53–58.

Gunning, T. (1990). The cinema of attractions. In A. Barker, & T. Elsaesser (Eds.), *Early cinema: Space, frame, narrative* (pp. 56-67). London: BFI Publishing.

Habgood, M. P. J. (2005, June). *Zombie Division: Intrinsic integration in digital learning games*. Paper presented at the 2005 Human Centred Technology Workshop, Brighton, UK.

Habgood, M. P. J. (2007). *The effective integration of digital games and learning content*. Unpublished Ph.D. dissertation, University of Nottingham. Retrieved from http://etheses.nottingham.ac.uk/archive/00000385/

Habgood, M. P. J., Ainsworth, S. E., & Benford, S. (2005). Endogenous fantasy and learning in digital games. *Simulation & Gaming*, *36*(4), 483–498. doi:10.1177/1046878105282276

Habgood, M. P. J., Ainsworth, S. E., & Benford, S. (2005, July). *Intrinsic fantasy: Motivation and affect in educational games made by children*. Paper presented at the AIED 2005 workshop on motivation and affect in educational software, Amsterdam. Available at http://www.informatics.sussex.ac.uk/users/gr20/aied05/index.htm

Halverson, R. (2005). What can K-12 school leaders learn from video games and gaming? *Innovate Online: Innovate Journal of Online Education, 1* (6). Available from http://www.innovateonline.info/index.php?view=article&id=81

Hamalainen, R. (2008). Designing and evaluating collaboration in a virtual game environment for vocational learning. *Computers & Education*, *50*(1), 98–109. doi:10.1016/j.compedu.2006.04.001

Hamalainen, R., Manninen, T., Jarvela, S., & Hakkinen, P. (2006). Learning to collaborate: Designing collaboration in a 3-D game environment. *The Internet and Higher Education*, *9*(1), 47–61. doi:10.1016/j.iheduc.2005.12.004

Hamilton, R. (2005). Nurses' knowledge and skill retention following cardiopulmonary resuscitation training: A review of the literature. *Journal of Advanced Nursing*, *51*(3), 288–297. doi:10.1111/j.1365-2648.2005.03491.x

Haninger, K., & Thompson, K. M. (2004). Content and ratings of teen-rated video games. *Journal of the American Medical Association*, *291*(7), 856–865. doi:10.1001/jama.291.7.856

Hannafin, M. J., & Hooper, S. (1989). An integrated framework for CBI screen design and layout. *Computers in Human Behavior*, *5*(3), 155–165. doi:10.1016/0747-5632(89)90009-5

Hartmann, T., & Klimmt, C. (2006). Gender and computer games: Exploring females' dislikes. *Journal of Computer-Mediated Communication, 11*(4), article 2. Available at http://jcmc.indiana.edu/vol11/issue4/hartmann.html

Harvey, D. (1999). *La multimédiatisation de l'enseignement* [The multimediazation of learning]. Paris: Harmattan.

Harvey, G., Trudeau, F., Morency, L., & Bordeleau, C. (2007). *L'éducation à la santé* [Health education]. Retrieved January 15, 2008 from http://www.uquebec.ca/edusante/

Hatch, T. F., & Pearson, T. G. (1998). Using environmental scans in educational needs assessment. *The Journal of Continuing Education in the Health Professions*, *18*(3), 179–184. doi:10.1002/chp.1340180308

Hawley, C. L., & Duffy, T. M. (1998). Design model for learner-centered, computer-based simulations. In N. J.

Maushak & C. Schlosser (Eds.). *20th annual proceedings: Selected research and development presentations at the 1998 convention of the Association for Educational Communications and Technology* (pp. 159-166). Ames, IA: Iowa State University.

Hays, R. T., & Singer, M. J. (1989). *Simulation fidelity in training system design: Bridging the gap between reality and training.* New York: Springer-Verlag.

Hazen, M. (1985). Instructional software design principles. *Educational Technology, 25I*(11), 18–23.

Henderson, L., Lemes, J., & Eshet, Y. (2000). Just playing a game? Education simulation software and cognitive outcomes. *Journal of Educational Computing Research, 22*(1), 105–130. doi:10.2190/EPJT-AHYQ-1LAJ-U8WK

Hertel, J. P., & Millis, B. J. (2002). *Using simulations to promote learning in higher education: An introduction.* Sterling, VA: Stylus Publishing.

Hills, M., & O'Neill, M. (2000, October). *Symposium à l'intention des enseignants en promotion de la santé et en santé Communautaire tenu durant la Conférence annuelle de l'Association canadienne de santé publique, Quebec.* [Symposium for teachers on health promotion and community health presented during the Annual Conference of the Canadian Association for Public Health] (Symposium report, J. Hills, translator). Available at http://www.utoronto.ca/chp/CCHPR/Ottawa_Symposium_fr_3.doc

Hingston, P., Combes, B., & Masek, M. (2006). Teaching an undergraduate AI course with games and simulation. In Z. Pan, R. Aylett, H. Diener, X. Jin, S. Gobel, & L. Li (Eds.), *Technologies for E-Learning and Digital Entertainment* (LNCS 3942, pp. 494-506). New York: Springer-Verlag.

Hoekma, J. (1983). Interactive videodisc: A new architecture. *Performance & Instruction, 22*(9), 6–9. doi:10.1002/pfi.4150220905

Hoffman, B., & Ritchie, D. (1997). Using multimedia to overcome the problems with problem-based learning. *Instructional Science, 25*(2), 97–115. doi:10.1023/A:1002967414942

Hoffman, M. L. (1982). The development of prosocial motivation: Empathy and guilt. In N. Eisenberg (Ed.), *The development of prosocial behavior* (pp. 281-313). New York: Academic Press.

Hoffman, M. L. (1987). The contribution of empathy to justice and moral judgment. In N. Eisenberg & J. Strayer (Eds.), *Empathy and its development* (pp. 47-80). Cambridge, UK: Cambridge University Press.

Hoffman, M. L. (2000). *Empathy and moral development.* Cambridge, UK: Cambridge University Press.

Hogle, J. G. (1996). *Considering games as cognitive tools: In search of effective "Edutainment"* (working paper). University of Georgia Department of Instructional Technology. Retrieved June 11, 2008 from http://twinpinefarm.com/pdfs/games.pdf.

Holton, D., Ahmed, A., Williams, H., & Hill, C. (2001). On the importance of mathematical play. *International Journal of Mathematical Education in Science and Technology, 32*(3), 401–415. doi:10.1080/00207390010022158

Hostetter, O., & Madison, J. (2002). *Video games - The necessity of incorporating video games as part of constructivist learning, Department of Educational Technology.* Retrieved November 5, 2004 from http://www.game-research.com/art_games_contructivist.asp

Hourst, B., & Thiagarajan, S. (2001) *Les jeux-cadres de Thiagi: techniques d'animation à l'usage du formateur* [Thiagi frame games: Animation techniques for trainers]. Paris: Les Éditions d'Organisation.

Hourst, B., & Thiagarajan, S. (2007). *Modèles de jeu de formation – Les jeux-cadres de Thiagi* [Game models for training – the frame games of Thiagi] (3rd edition). Paris: Éditions Eyrolles.

Howes, R. J. (1998). Plethysmographic assessment of incarcerated nonsexual offenders: A comparison with rapists. *Sexual Abuse: Journal of Research and Treatment, 10*(3), 183–194.

Huesmann, L. R. (2007). The impact of electronic media violence: Scientific theory and research. *The Journal of Adolescent Health, 41*(6Supplement 1), S6–S13. doi:10.1016/j.jadohealth.2007.09.005

Huizinga, J. (1938). *Homo ludens: A study of the play element in culture.* Boston: Beacon Press.

Hung, D., Chee, T. S., & Hedberg, J. G. (2005). A framework for fostering a community of practice: Scaffolding learners through an evolving continuum. *British Journal of Educational Technology, 36*(2), 159–176. doi:10.1111/j.1467-8535.2005.00450.x

Hunsaker, P. L. (2007). Using social simulations to assess and train potential leaders to make effective decisions in turbulent environments. *Career Development International, 12*(4), 341–360. doi:10.1108/13620430710756744

Hunter, M. K. (1991). *Doctors' stories: The narrative structure of medical knowledge.* Princeton, NJ: Princeton University Press.

Imel, Z., Baldwin, S., Bonus, K., & MacCoon, D. (2008). Beyond the individual: Group effects in mindfulness-based stress reduction. *Psychotherapy Research, 18*(6), 735–742. doi:10.1080/10503300802326038

Impact Games. (2008). *Peacemaker game.* Retrieved April 25, 2008 from http://www.peacemakergame.com/game.php

Inform Z-machine. (2005). *Inform Z-machine* (software program). Available at http://www.inform-fiction.org/zmachine/

Instituts de recherche en santé du Canada (2006). *Le suicide chez les jeunes: Le temps d'agir* Youth suicide: The time to act]. Available at http://www.cihr-irsc.gc.ca/f/32154.html

International Society for Presence Resarch (ISPR). (2000). *The Concept of Presence: Explication Statement.* Available at http://www.temple.edu/ispr/frame_explicat.htm

Internet World Stats. (2008). Canada Internet usage, broadband and telecommunications report. Retrieved April 19, 2009 from: http://www.internetworldstats.com/am/ca.htm

Ip, A., & Naidu, S. (2001). Experience-based pedagogical designs for E-learning. *Educational Technology, 41*(5), 53–58.

Irwin, A. R., & Gross, A. M. (1995). Cognitive tempo, violent video games, and aggressive behavior in young boys. *Journal of Family Violence, 10*(3), 337–350. doi:10.1007/BF02110997

IsaBelle. C., Kaszap, M., Sauvé, L., & Samson, D. (2005). Faciliter l'intégration des jeux éducatifs à l'aide de jeux-cadre [Facilitating the integration of educational games with the help of frame games]. In P.Tchounikine, M. Joab & L. Abrouk (eds.), *Environnements Informatiques pour l'Apprentissage Humain* (pp. 45-46). Montpellier, France: ATIEF, LIRMM Université de Montpellier CNRS.

IsaBelle. C., Kaszap, M., Sauvé, L., Renaud. L., Ngandu, M., & Leblanc, D. (2005). *Vision des élèves et des futurs enseignants du Québec et du Nouveau-Brunswick quant aux jeux et aux thèmes de la santé* [Vision of students and future teachers in Quebec and New Brunswick on games and health themes] (Research report). Ottawa, ON, Canada: University of Ottawa.

Issenberg, S. B., Mcgaghie, W. C., Petrusa, E. R., Gordon, D. L., & Scalese, R. J. (2005). Features and uses of high-fidelity medical simulations that lead to effective learning: A BEME systematic review. *Medical Teacher, 27*(1), 10–28. Available at http://www.beme-collaboration.org/beme/pages/reviews/issenberg.html. doi:10.1080/01421590500046924

Jacko, J. A., & Sears, A. (Eds.). (2003). *The human-computer interaction handbook: Fundamentals, evolving technologies, and emerging applications.* Mahweh, NJ: Lawrence Erlbaum Associates Inc.

Jacobs, J. W., & Dempsey, J. V. (1993). Simulation & gaming: Fidelity, feedback, and motivation. In J. V. Dempsey & G. C. Sales (Eds.), *Interactive instruction and feedback* (pp.197-227). Englewood Cliffs, NJ: Educational Technology Publications.

Jacobs, J., Caudell, T., Wilks, D., Keep, M. F., Mitchell, S., Buchanan, H., et al. (2003). Integration of advanced technologies to enhance problem-based learning over distance: Project TOUCH. *The Anatomical Record (Part B: New Anatomy), 270B*, 16-22

Jeffries, P. R. (2005). A framework for designing, implementing, and evaluating simulations used as teaching strategies in nursing. *Nursing Education Perspectives*, *26*(2), 96–103.

Jenkins, D. (2005, April 28). Japanese sales charts, week ending April 24th. *Gamasutra.* Retrieved February 14, 2008, from http://www.gamasutra.com/php-bin/news_index.php?story=5386

Jenkins, H. (2001). *From Barbie to Mortal Kombat: Further reflections.* Available at http://culturalpolicy.uchicago.edu/conf2001/papers/jenkins.html.

Jenkins, H. (2004). Game design as narrative architecture. In N. Wardrip-Fruin, & P. Harrigan (Eds.), *First person: New media as story, performance, and game* (pp. 118-130). Cambridge, MA: The MIT Press.

Jenson, J. de Castell, S., & Fisher, S. (2007). Girls playing games: Rethinking stereotypes. In *Proceedings of the 2007 conference on Future Play,* Toronto, Canada (pp. 9-16). New York: ACM.

Jenson, J., & de Castell, S. (2005). Her own boss: Gender and the pursuit of incompetent play. In S. de Castell & J. Jenson (Eds.), *Proceedings, 2005 Conference of the Digital Games Research Association (DiGRA), Changing Views: Worlds in Play.* Vancouver, Canada. Available at http://www.digra.org/dl/display_html?chid=http://www.digra.org/dl/db/06278.27455.pdf

Jenson, J., & de Castell, S. (2006). Keeping it real: Gender, equity & digital games. In J. Terkeurst & I. Paterson (Eds.), *Women & Games Conf. Proc. 2005* (pp. 106-115). Dundee, UK: Univ. of Abertay Press.

Johne, M. (2002, September 27). On-line simulations put e-learners into action. *The Globe and Mail*, B16.

Johnson, D., & Wiles, J. (2003). Effective affective user interface design in games. *Ergonomics*, *46*(13-14), 1332–1345. doi:10.1080/00140130310001610865

Johnson, L. A., Wohlgemuth, B., Cameron, C. A., Caughman, F., Koertge, T., & Barna, J. (1998). Dental interactive simulations corporation (DISC): Simulations for education, continuing education, and assessment. *Journal of Dental Education*, *62*(11), 919–928.

Johnson, L. A., Wohlgemuth, B., Cameron, C. A., Caughman, F., Koertge, T., & Barna, J. (1998). Dental interactive simulations corporation (DISC): Simulations for education, continuing education, and assessment. *Journal of Dental Education*, *62*(11), 919–928.

Jonassen, D. (1999). Designing constructivist learning environments. In C. Reigeluth (Ed.), *Instructional design theories and models: A new paradigm of instructional theory* (Vol. II, pp. 215-239). Mahwah, NJ: Lawrence Erlbaum Associates Inc.

Jonassen, D. H., & Jonassen, D. H. (2000). *Computers as mindtools for schools: Engaging critical thinking* (2nd ed.). Upper Saddle River, NJ: Merrill.

Jonassen, D. H., Hannum, W. H., & Tessmer, M. (1989). *Handbook of task analysis procedures.* New York: Praeger.

Jones, K. (1998). Hidden damage to facilitators and participants. *Simulation & Gaming*, *29*(2), 165–172. doi:10.1177/1046878198292003

Jones, M. G. (1997). *Learning to play, playing to learn: Lessons learned from computer games.* Paper presented at the annual conference of the Association for Educational Communications and Technology. Retrieved January 7, 2005 from http://www.gsu.edu/~wwwitr/docs/mjgames/

Juul, J. (2003). *The game, the player, the world: Looking for a heart of gameness.* Keynote presentation at DiGRA Level-up Conference, Utrecht, Belgium.

Juul, J. (2005). *Half-real: Video games between real rules and fictional worlds.* Cambridge, MA: The MIT Press.

Kafai, Y. B. (1995). *Minds in play: Computer game design as a context for children's learning.* Hillsdale, NJ: Lawrence Erlbaum Associates, Inc.

Kahn, P. H., Friedman, B., Perez-Granados, D. R., & Freier, N. G. (2006). Robotic pets in the lives of preschool children. *Interaction Studies: Social Behaviour and Communication in Biological and Artificial Systems*, *7*(3), 405–436. doi:10.1075/is.7.3.13kah

Kalmus, E., & Beech, A. R. (2005). Forensic assessment of sexual interest: A review. *Aggression and Violent Behavior, 10*(2), 193–217. doi:10.1016/j.avb.2003.12.002

Kamin, C. S., Deterding, R. D., Wilson, B., Armacost, M., & Breedon, T. (1999). The development of a collaborative distance learning program to facilitate pediatric problem-based learning. *Medical Education Online, 4*(2). Available at http://www.Med-Ed-Online.org

Kamin, C. S., O'Sullivan, P. S., Younger, M., & Deterding, R. (2001). Measuring critical thinking in problem-based learning discourse. *Teaching and Learning in Medicine, 13*(1), 27–35. doi:10.1207/S15328015TLM1301_6

Kamin, C., O'Sullivan, P., Deterding, R., & Younger, M. (2003). A comparison of critical thinking in groups of third-year medical students in text, video, and virtual PBL case modalities. *Academic Medicine, 78*(2), 204–211. doi:10.1097/00001888-200302000-00018

Kandaswamy, S., Stolovitch, H., & Thiagarajan, S. (1976). Learner verification and revision: An experimental comparison of two methods. *Audio-visual. Communication Review, 24*(3), 316–328.

Kaptelinin, V., & Cole, M. (2001). Individual and collective activities in educational computer game playing. In T. Koschmann & R. Hall (Eds), *CSCL2 Carrying forward the conversation* (pp. 303-316). Mahwah, NJ: Lawrence Erlbaum Associates Inc.

Kashibuchi, M., & Sakamoto, A. (2001). The educational effectiveness of a simulation/game in sex education. *Simulation & Gaming, 32*(3), 331–343. doi:10.1177/104687810103200304

Kasvi, J. J. (2000). Not just fun and games - Internet games as a training medium. In P. Kymäläinen & L. Seppänen (Eds.), *Cosiga - Learning with computerised simulation games* (pp. 23-34). HUT: Espoo.

Kasvi, J. J. J. (2000). Not just fun and games - Internet games as a training medium. In P. Kymäläinen & L. Seppänen (Eds.), *Cosiga - Learning with computerised simulation games* (pp. 23-34). HUT: Espoo.

Kaszap, M. IsaBelle, C., & Rail, S., (2005) *Analyse des programmes scolaires -Québec, Ontario, Nouveau-Brunswick* [Analysis of school programs in Quebec, Ontario and New Brunswick]. Research report. Québec, QC, Canada: Laval University.

Kaszap, M., & Rail, S. (2006, May). *Conception d'un jeu-cadre visant une socio construction des connaissances: Considérations théoriques et empiriques* [Conception of a frame game using a socio-constructivist approach to knowledge: Theoretical and empirical considerations. Paper presented at the 23e Congrès de l'AIPU, Association internationale de pédagogie universitaire, Monastir, Tunisia. Moscovici, S. (1961). *La psychanalyse, son image, son public* [Psychoanalysis, its image, its public]. Paris: PUF.

Kaszap, M., Rail, S., & Power, M. (2007). Web-based design for board games: Theoretical and empirical socioconstructivist considerations. *International Journal of Intelligent Games & Simulations, 4*(2), 16–22.

Katchabaw, J., Elliott, D., & Danton, S. (2005). Neomancer: An exercise in interdisciplinary academic game development. In S. de Castell & J. Jenson (Eds.), *Proceedings, 2005 Conference of the Digital Games Research Association (DiGRA), Changing Views: Worlds in Play.* Available at http://www.digra.org/dl/db/06275.08442.pdf

Kaufman, D. (2005). Collaborative Online Multimedia Problem-based Simulations (COMPS). In *Proceedings, XXIIIrd International Council for Innovation in Higher Education.* Belfast, UK.

Kaufman, D. M., & Mann, K. V. (1997). Basic sciences in problem-based learning and conventional curricula: Students' attitudes. *Medical Education, 31*(3), 177–180. doi:10.1111/j.1365-2923.1997.tb02562.x

Kaufman, D. M., Mann, K. V., & Jennett, P. A. (2000). *Teaching and learning in medical education: How theory can inform practice.* Edinburgh, UK: Association for the Study of Medical Education.

Kaufman, D., & Sauvé, L. (2003). *Literature review for an SSHRC grant proposal.* Vancouver, BC, Canada, and Quebec, QC, Canada: SAGE Project.

Kaufman, D., & Sauvé, L. (2004). Simulation and Advanced Gaming Environments (SAGE) for Learning;

A Pan-Canadian research project. In L. Cantoni & C. McLoughlin (Eds.), *Proceedings, ED-MEDIA 2004: World Conference on Educational Multimedia, Hypermedia & Telecommunications* (pp. 4568-4573). Norfolk, VA: Association for the Advancement of Computing in Education (AACE).

Kaufman, D., & Schell, R. (2007). Piloting a collaborative online multimedia PBL simulation. In C. Montgomerie & J. Seale (Eds.), *Proceedings of World Conference on Educational Multimedia, Hypermedia and Telecommunications 2007* (pp. 1834-1841). Chesapeake, VA: Association for the Advancement of Computing in Education (AACE).

Kaufman, D., Sauve, L., & Ireland, A. (2005). Simulation and advanced gaming environments: Exploring their learning impacts. Keynote paper in Q. Medhi, N. Gough & S. Natkin (Eds.), *Proceedings, CGAMES05 (7th International Conference on Computer Games)* (pp. 16-25). Wolverhampton, UK: School of Computing and Information Technology, University of Wolverhampton.

Kellar, M., Watters, C., & Duffy, J. (2005, June). *A comparison of motivational factors between game players.* Paper presented at the 2005 conference of the Digital Games Research Association (DiGRA), Vancouver, BC, Canada.

Kellner, C. (2000). La *médiation par le cédérom « ludo-éducatif ». Approche communicationnelle* [Mediation by educational game CD-ROM: Communicative approach]. Unpublished Ph.D. dissertation in information science and communication, University of Metz.

Kellner, C. (2008). Utiliser les potentialités du multimédia interactif. [Utilize the potentiaql of interactive multimedia]. In *Actes du colloque scientifique Ludovia - 2008* (pp. 160-170). Ax les Thermes – Ariège, France: Institut de Recherche en Informatique de Toulouse and Laboratoire de Recherche en Audiovisuel.

Kelly, D. (2008). Adaptive versus learner control in a multiple intelligence learning environment. *Journal of Educational Multimedia and Hypermedia, 17*(3), 307–336.

Kelly, H. (2005). Games, cookies, and the future of education. *Issues in Science and Technology, 21*(4), 33–41.

Kennedy, G., Petrovic, T., & Keppell, M. (1998). The development of multimedia evaluation criteria and a program of evaluation for computer aided learning. In *Proceedings, ASCILITE '98* (pp. 407-415). Retrieved September 9, 2008 from http://www.ascilite.org.au/conferences/wollongong98/asc98-pdf/kennedypetrovickeppel.pdf

Kenny, N. P., & Beagan, B. L. (2004). The patient as text: A challenge for problem-based learning. *Medical Education, 38*(10), 1071–1079. doi:10.1111/j.1365-2929.2004.01956.x

Ker, J., & Bradley, P. (2007). *Simulation in medical education.* Edinburgh, UK: Association for the Study of Medical Education (ASME).

Kiegaldie, D., & White, G. (2006). The virtual patient: Development, implementation and evaluation of an innovative computer simulation for postgraduate nursing students. *Journal of Educational Multimedia and Hypermedia, 15*(1), 31–47.

Kiegaldie, D., & White, G. (2006). The virtual patient: Development, implementation and evaluation of an innovative computer simulation for postgraduate nursing students. *Journal of Educational Multimedia and Hypermedia, 15*(1), 31–47.

Kiili, K. (2007). Foundation for problem-based gaming. *British Journal of Educational Technology, 38*(3), 394–404. doi:10.1111/j.1467-8535.2007.00704.x

Kinzie, M. B., Larsen, V. A., Bursh, J. B., & Baker, S. M. (1996). Frog dissection via the World-Wide Web: Implications for widespread delivery of instruction. *Educational Technology Research and Development, 44*(2), 59–69. doi:10.1007/BF02300541

Kirakowski, J., Claridge, N., & Whitehand, R. (1998). Human centered measures of success in web site design. In *Proceedings, 4th Conference on Human Factors and the Web* (pp. 24-27). Basking Ridge, NJ: AT&T Labs.

Kirkpatrick, D. L. (1994). *Evaluating training programs: The four levels.* San Francisco, CA: Berrett-Koehler.

Kirriemuir, J., & McFarlane, A. (2004). *Literature review in games and learning.* Bristol, UK: NESTA Futurelab.

Kirsh, S. J. (2003). The effects of violent video games on adolescents: The overlooked influence of development. *Aggression and Violent Behavior, 8*(4), 377–389. doi:10.1016/S1359-1789(02)00056-3

Kirshner, D., & Whitson, J. A. (Eds.). (1997). *Situated cognition: Social, semiotic, and psychological perspectives.* Mahwah, NJ: Lawrence Erlbaum Associates Inc.

Klare, G. R. (1984). Readability. In P. D. Pearson (Ed.), *Handbook of reading research* (pp. 681-744). New York: Longman.

Klein, C., Stagl, K. C., Salas, E., Parker, C., & Van Eynde, D. F. (2007). Returning to flight: Simulation-based training for the US National Aeronautics and Space Administration's Space Shuttle Mission Management Team. *International Journal of Training and Development, 11*(2), 132–138. doi:10.1111/j.1468-2419.2007.00274.x

Klopfer, E., & Yoon, S. (2005). Developing games and simulations for today and tomorrow's tech savvy youth. *TechTrends, 49*(3), 33–41. doi:10.1007/BF02763645

Knapp, B. (2004). Competency: An essential component of caring in nursing. *Nursing Administration Quarterly, 28*(4), 285–287.

Knoll, T., Trojan, L., Haecker, A., Alken, P., & Michel, M. S. (2005). Validation of computer-based training in ureterorenoscopy. *BJU International, 95*(9), 1276–1279. doi:10.1111/j.1464-410X.2005.05518.x

Ko, S. (2002). An empirical analysis of children's thinking and learning in a computer game context. *Educational Psychology, 22*(2), 219–233. doi:10.1080/01443410120115274

Kokol, P., Kokol, M., & Dinevski, D. (2005). Teaching evolution using visual simulations. *British Journal of Educational Technology, 36*(3), 563–566. doi:10.1111/j.1467-8535.2005.00483.x

Kolb, D. A. (1984). *Experiential learning: Experience as the source of learning and development.* Englewood Cliffs, NJ: Prentice-Hall.

Komoski, P. K. (1979). Counterpoint: Learner verification of instructional materials. *Educational Evaluation and Policy Analysis, 1*(3), 101–103.

Komoski, P. K. (1984). Formative evaluation. The empirical improvement of learning materials. *Performance & Instruction Journal, 22*(5), 3–4. doi:10.1002/pfi.4150220504

Koohang, A. (2004). A study of users' perceptions toward e-learning courseware usability. *International Journal on E-Learning, 3*(2), 10–17.

Koster, R. (2004). *A theory of fun for game design.* Scottsdale, AZ: Paraglyph Press.

Kox, K., & Walker, D. (1993). *User interface design* (2nd ed.). Toronto, ON, Canada: Prentice Hall.

Kriz, W. C., & Hense, J. U. (2006). Theory-oriented evaluation for the design of and research in gaming and simulation. *Simulation & Gaming, 37*(2), 268–283. doi:10.1177/1046878106287950

Krolikowska, K., Kronenberg, J., Maliszewska, K., Sendzimir, J., Magnuszewski, P., & Dunajski, A. (2007). Role-playing simulation as a communication tool in community dialogue: Karkonosze Mountains case study. *Simulation & Gaming, 38*(2), 195–210. doi:10.1177/1046878107300661

Krug, S. (2001). *Don't make me think: A common sense approach to Web usability.* Indianapolis IN: New Riders Publishing.

Kulhavy, R., & Stock, W. (1989). Feedback in written instruction: The place of the response certitude. *Educational Psychology Review, 1*, 279–308. doi:10.1007/BF01320096

Kushniruk, A. W., & Patel, V. L. (2004). Cognitive and usability engineering methods for the evaluation of clinical information systems. *Journal of Biomedical Informatics, 37*(1), 56–76. doi:10.1016/j.jbi.2004.01.003

Kutner, L., & Olson, C. (2008). Grand Theft Childhood: The surprising truth about violent video games and what parents can do. New York: Simon & Schuster.

Laberge, N., & Sauvé, L. (1998). *Les environnements multimédia interactifs sur l'inforoute. Critères à respecter pour l'interface – utilisateur* [Multimedia interactive environments on the Internet: Criteria for the user interface] (Research Report). Québec, QC, Canada: SAVIE.

Lainema, T., & Makkonen, P. (2003). Applying a constructivist approach to educational business games: Case REALGAME. *Simulation & Gaming*, *34*(1), 131–149. doi:10.1177/1046878102250601

Landry, R. (2003). La simulation sur ordinateur [Computer simulation]. In B. Gauthier (Ed), *Recherche sociale. De la problématique à la collecte de données* (pp. 469-501). Québec, QC, Canada: Presses de l'Université du Québec.

Lane, J. L., Slavin, S., & Ziv, A. (2001). Simulation in medical education: A review. *Simulation & Gaming*, *32*(3), 297–314. doi:10.1177/104687810103200302

Langlois, L. (2004). Responding ethically: Complex decision-making by school district superintendents. *International Studies in Educational Administration*, *32*(2), 78–93.

Langlois, L. (2005). Comment instaurer un processus décisionnel éthique chez le gestionnaire? [How can we instill an ethical decision process in management?]In L. Langlois, R. Blouin, S. Montreuil, & J. Sexton (Eds.), *Éthique et dilemmes dans les organisations* [Ethics and dilemas in organizations] (pp. 13-26). Ste-Foy, QC, Canada: Presses de l'Université Laval.

Langlois, L., & Starratt, J. (2001). Identification of superintendents' and school commissioners' ethical perspective: Data talking to the model. In *Selected Papers presented at the 6th Annual Leadership & Ethics Conference,* Charlottesville, VA.

Larsen, S. (2006). *The healing power of neurofeedback, the revolutionary LENS technique for restoring optimal brain function.* Rochester, VT: Healing Arts Press.

Latour, B. (2005). *Reassembling the social: An introduction to Actor-Network-Theory* Oxford, UK: Oxford University Press.

Laurillard, D. (1998). Multimedia and the learner's experience of narrative. *Computers & Education*, *31*(2), 229. doi:10.1016/S0360-1315(98)00041-4

Lave, J., & Wenger, E. (1991). *Situated cognition: Legitimate peripheral participation.* Cambridge, UK: Cambridge University Press.

Lawrence, R. (2004). Teaching data structures using competitive games. *IEEE Transactions on Education*, *47*(4), 459–467. doi:10.1109/TE.2004.825053

Laws, D. R. (2003). Penile plethysmography. Will we ever get it right? In T. Ward, D. R.Laws, & S. M. Hudson (Eds.), *Sexual deviance: Issues and controversies* (pp. 82-102). Thousand Oaks, CA: Sage Publications.

Laws, D. R., & Gress, C. L. Z. (2004). Seeing things differently: The viewing time alternative to penile plethysmography. *Legal and Criminological Psychology*, *9*(2), 183–196. doi:10.1348/1355325041719338

Laws, D. R., & Marshall, W. L. (2003). A brief history of behavioral and cognitive-behavioral approaches to sexual offenders, Part 1, Early developments. *Sexual Abuse*, *15*(2), 75–92. doi:10.1177/107906320301500201

Le Boterf, G. (2001). *Construire les competences individuelles et collectives* [Building individual and collective competencies]. Paris: Editions d'organisation.

Le Ny, J. F. (1968). L'apprentissage [Learning] [Chicago: Encyclopædia Britannica.]. *Encyclopaedia Universalis*, *2*, 173–175.

Lean, J., Moisier, J., Towler, M., & Abbey, C. (2006). Simulations and games: Use and barriers in higher education. *Active Learning in Higher Education*, *7*(3), 227–242. doi:10.1177/1469787406069056

Lebrun, N., & Berthelot, S. (1996). *Pour une approche multimédiatique de l'enseignement* [For a multimedia approach to teaching]. Montréal, QC, Canada: Éditions Nouvelles.

Lee, C. (2007). Diagnostic, predictive and compositional modeling with data mining in integrated learning environments. *Computers & Education*, *49*(3), 562–580. doi:10.1016/j.compedu.2005.10.010

Lee, Y., Terzopoulos, D., & Waters, K. (1995). Realistic modeling for facial animation. *Computer Graphics, 29*, 55–62. doi:10.1145/204362.204374

Legault, G. (1999). *Professionnalisme et deliberation éthique* [Professionalism and ethical deliberation.]. Quebec, QC, Canada: Presses de l'Université du Québec.

Legendre, R. (2005). *Dictionnaire actuel de l'éducation*. Montréal, QC, Canada: Guérin.

LeMay, P. (2008). Game and flow concepts for learning: some considerations. In K. McFerrin, R. Weber, R. Carlsen, & D. A. Willis (Eds), *Proceedings of the Society for Information Technology and Teacher Education International Conference 2008* (pp. 510-515). Chesapeake, VA: AACE.

Lenhart, A., Kahne, J., Middaugh, E., McGill, A. R., Evans, C., & Vitak, J. (2008). *Teens, video games, and civics: Teens' gaming experiences are diverse and include significant social interaction and civic engagement*. Washington, DC: Pew Internet & American Life Project. Available at http://www.pewinternet.org/Reports/2008/Teens-Video-Games-and-Civics.aspx

Lepper, M. R., & Malone, T. W. (1987). Intrinsic motivation and instructional effectiveness in computer-based education. In R. E. Snow & M. J. Farr (Eds.), *Aptitude, learning, and instruction: Vol. 3. Conative and affective process analyses* (pp. 255-286). Hillsdale, NJ: Lawrence Erlbaum Associates Inc.

Lesaigle, E. M., & Biers, D. W. (2000). Effect of type of information on real-time usability evaluation: Implications for remote usability testing. In *Proceedings of the IEA 2000/HFES 2000 Congress* (pp. 585-588). Santa Monica, CA: Human Factors and Ergonomics Society.

Levinson, B. M. (1972). *Pets and human development*. Springfield, IL: Charles C Thomas.

Levinson, B. M. (1978). Pets and personality development. *Psychological Reports, 42*, 1031–1038.

Lewin, K. (1951). *Field theory in social science: Selected theoretical papers*. New York: Harper.

Lhôte, J.-M. (1986). *Dictionnaire des jeux de société* [Dictionary of games in society]. Paris: Flammarion.

Lieberman, D. A. (1998). *Health education video games for children and adolescents: Theory, design, and research findings*. Paper presented at the annual meeting of the International Communication Association, Jerusalem.

Lieberman, D. A. (2001). Management of chronic pediatric diseases with interactive health games: Theory and research findings. *The Journal of Ambulatory Care Management, 24*(1), 26–38.

Lin, B. (2007). *Games, narrative and interface design*. Unpublished M.Sc. thesis, Simon Fraser University, Burnaby, BC, Canada.

Lin, B., Bizzocchi, J., & Budd, J. (2005, June). *Interface and narrative texture*. Paper presented at the 2005 conference of the Digital Games Research Association (DiGRA), Changing Views: Worlds in Play, Vancouver BC, Canada. Retrieved October 25, 2007 from http://www.digra.org/dl/

Lincoln, Y. S., & Guba, E. G. (1985). *Naturalistic inquiry*. Beverly Hills, CA: Sage Publications.

Linsk, N. T., & Tunney, K. (1997). Learning to care: Use of practice simulation to train health social workers. *Journal of Social Work Education, 33*(3), 473–489.

Lipman, M. (1995). À l'école de la pensée [At the school of thought]. Brussels, Belgium: De Boeck University.

Liu, A., Tendick, F., Cleary, K., & Kaufmann, C. (2003). A survey of surgical simulation: Applications, technology, and education. *Presence (Cambridge, Mass.), 12*(6), 599–614. doi:10.1162/105474603322955905

Livet, A. (2007). *Étude sur l'évolution ergonomique des logiciels de conception* [Study of the ergonomic evolution of computer design]. Unpublished report for the first year of the Master's of Cognitive Science. Bron, France: Université Lyon II.

Loe, T. W., Ferrell, L., & Mansfield, P. (2000). A review of empirical studies assessing ethical decision making in business. *Journal of Business Ethics, 25*(3), 185–204. doi:10.1023/A:1006083612239

Lombardi, J. (2007). *Cost of simulations*. Weblog. Retrieved November13th, 2007. http://jlombardi.blogspot.com/2007/10/cost-of-simulations.html

Looman, J., & Marshall, W. L. (2001). Phallometric assessments designed to detect arousal to children: The responses of rapists and child molesters. *Sexual Abuse*, *13*(1), 3–13. doi:10.1177/107906320101300102

Looy, V. Jan and Baetans, Jan. (2003). *Close reading new media: Analyzing electronic literature*. Leuven, Belgium: Leuven University Press.

Losier, M. (2003). *My vocabulary* (online game). Quebec, QC, Canada: Carrefour virtuel de jeux éducatifs. Available at http://www.savie.qc.ca/CarrefourJeux2/Site/Jeux/Concentration/Info_Concentration.asp?NoPartie=379

Lubar, J. F., Swartwood, M. O., Swartwood, J. N., & O'Donnell, P. H. (1995). Evaluation of the effectiveness of EEG neurofeedback training for ADHD in a clinical setting as measured by changes in T.O.V.A. scores, behavioral ratings, and WISC-R performance. *Biofeedback and Self-Regulation*, *20*(1), 83–99. doi:10.1007/BF01712768

Maddrell, J. (2008). *Article Review: IDT 848 Evaluation study abstracts*. Norfolk, VA: Old Dominion University. Retrieved March 10, 2009 from designedtoinspire.com/drupal/files/ArticleSummary%20Maddrell.doc.

Mager, R., Bullinger, A. H., Mueller-Spahn, F., Kuntze, M. F., & Stoermer, R. (2001). Real-time monitoring of brain activity in patients with specific phobia during exposure therapy, employing a stereoscopic virtual environment. *Cyberpsychology & Behavior*, *4*(4), 465–469. doi:10.1089/109493101750527024

Maier, F. H., & Grobler, A. (2000). What are we talking about? A taxonomy of computer simulations to support learning. *System Dynamics Review*, *16*(2), 135–148. doi:10.1002/1099-1727(200022)16:2<135::AID-SDR193>3.0.CO;2-P

Mallender, A. (1999). *Écrire pour le multimédia* [Writing for multimedia]. Montreal: Editions DUNOD. Retrieved July 17, 2002 from http://mediamatch.derby.ac.uk/french/design/default.htm

Malone, T. W. (1980). *What makes things fun to learn? A study of intrinsically motivating computer games*. Unpublished Ph.D. dissertation, Stanford University.

Malone, T. W., & Lepper, M. R. (1987). Intrinsic motivation and instructional effectiveness in computer-based education. In R. E. Snow & M. J. Farr (Eds.), *Aptitude, learning, and instruction: III. Conative and affective process analysis* (pp. 255-286). Hillsdale, NJ: Lawrence Erlbaum Associates, Inc.

Malone, T., & Lepper, M. (1987). Making learning fun: A taxonomy of intrinsic motivations of learning. In R. E. Snow & M. J. Farr (Eds.), *Aptitude, learning, and instruction: Vol. 3. Conative and affective process analyses* (pp. 223-253). Hillsdale, NJ: Lawrence Erlbaum Associates Inc.

Mann, K. V., & Kaufman, D. M. (1999). A comparative study of problem-based and conventional undergraduate curricula in preparing students for graduate medical education. *Academic Medicine: Journal of the Association of American Medical Colleges*, *74*(10Suppl), S4–S6.

Maria, J., & Lynne, A. (2006). Measurement of anxiety for patients with cardiac disease: A critical review and analysis. *The Journal of Cardiovascular Nursing*, *21*(5), 412–419.

Markey, C., Power, D., & Booker, G. (2003). Using structured games to teach early fraction concepts to students who are deaf or hard of hearing. *American Annals of the Deaf*, *148*(3), 251–258. doi:10.1353/aad.2003.0021

Marks, M., Lehr, D., & Brastow, R. (2006). Cooperation versus free riding in a threshold public goods classroom experiment. *The Journal of Economic Education*, *37*(2), 156–170. doi:10.3200/JECE.37.2.156-170

Marshall, W. L., & Fernandez, Y. M. (2000). Phallometric testing with sexual offenders: Limits to its value. *Clinical Psychology Review*, *20*(7), 807–822. doi:10.1016/S0272-7358(99)00013-6

Marshall, W. L., & Fernandez, Y. M. (2003). Sexual preferences: Are they useful in the assessment and treatment of sexual offenders? *Aggression and Violent Behavior*, *8*(2), 131–143. doi:10.1016/S1359-1789(01)00056-8

Martial, O. (2000). *Méthodologie de conception d'application centrée sur l'utilisateur* User-centered application design]. Course manual. Montréal, QC, Canada: CRIM Formation, Centre de recherche informatique de Montréal.

Marton, P. (1994). *La conception pédagogique de systèmes d'apprentissage multimédia interactif: fondements, méthodologie et problématique* [The pedagogic design of interactive multimedia learning systems: Fundamentals, methodology, and problems]. *Educatechnologiques, 1* (3). Available at http://www.sites.fse.ulaval.ca/reveduc/html/vol1/no3/concept.html

Mateas, M., & Stern, A. (2005). Build it to understand it: Ludology meets narratology in game design space. In S. de Castell & J. Jenson (Eds.), *Proceedings, 2005 Conference of the Digital Games Research Association (DiGRA), Changing Views: Worlds in Play* (pp. 299-310). Burnaby, BC, Canada: Simon Fraser University.

Mathews, V., Wang, Y., Kalnin, A. J., Mosier, K. M., Dunn, D. W., & Kronenberger, W. G. (2006, November). Short-term effects of violent video game playing: An fMRI study. Paper presented at the Annual Meeting of the Radiological Society of North America, Chicago, IL.

Mayer, R. E. (2001). *Multimedia learning.* New York: Cambridge University Press.

Mayer, R. E., & Chandler, P. (2001). When learning is just a click away: Does simple user interaction foster deeper understanding of multimedia mes*SAGE*s? *Journal of Educational Psychology, 93*(2), 390. doi:10.1037/0022-0663.93.2.390

Mayer, R., Ouellet, F., Saint-Jacques, M.-C., & Turcotte, D. (Eds.). (2000*). Méthodes de recherche en intervention sociale*. Boucherville, QC, Canada: Gaëtan Morin.

McConaghy, N. (1999). Unresolved issues in scientific sexology. *Archives of Sexual Behavior, 28*(4), 285–318. doi:10.1023/A:1018744628161

McGee, M. (2006). *Simulation in education: State of the field review.* Ottawa, ON, Canada: Canadian Council on Learning. Available at http://www.ccl-cca.ca/NR/rdonlyres/C8CB4C08-F7D3-4915-BDAA-C41250A43516/0/SFRSimulationinEducationJul06REV.pdf

McGrady, A. V., Yonker, R., Tan, S. Y., Fine, T., & Woerner, M. (1981). The effect of biofeedback-assisted relaxation training on blood pressure and selected biochemical parameters in patients with essential hypertension. *Biofeedback and Self-Regulation, 5*, 25–44.

McGriff, S. J. (2000). *Instructional system design (ISD): Using the ADDIE model.* Retrieved May 26, 2009 from http://ehopac.org/TransformationReports/ISD-ADDIEmodel.pdf

McKimm, J., Jollie, C., & Cantillon, P. (2003). ABC of learning and teaching: Web based learning. *British Medical Journal, 326*(7394), 870–873. doi:10.1136/bmj.326.7394.870

McSharry, P. E. (2005). The danger of wishing for chaos. *Nonlinear Dynamics Psychology and Life Sciences, 9*(4), 375–397.

Mechling, L. C., Gast, D. L., & Langone, J. (2002). Computer-based video instruction to teach persons with moderate intellectual disabilities to read grocery aisle signs and locate items. *The Journal of Special Education, 35*(4), 224–240. doi:10.1177/002246690203500404

Mediamark Research and Intelligence (MRI). (2007, December 19). Gaming nearly ubiquitous among kids online, one-third have email address. Press release on the 2007 American Kids Survey. Retrieved March 4, 2008 from http://www.marketingcharts.com/direct/gaming-nearly-ubiquitous-among-kids-online-one-third-have-email-address-2839/

Medley, C. F., & Horne, C. (2005). Using simulation technology for undergraduate nursing education. *The Journal of Nursing Education, 44*(1), 31–34.

Meirieu, P. (1990). La pédagogie différenciée est-elle dépassée? [Is differentiated pedagogy obsolete?]. *Cahiers pédagogiques, 286*(1), 48-53.

Meirieu, P. (1997). Plus que jamais la pédagogie différenciée [Differentiated pedagogy – more than ever?]. *Cahiers pédagogiques,* supplément no 3 (*Retours sur la pédagogie différenciée)*, 39 -40.

Meller, G. (1997). A typology of simulators for medical education. *Journal of Digital Imaging, 10*(3), 194–196. doi:10.1007/BF03168699

Melson, G. F. (2001). *Why the wild things are: Animals in the lives of children.* Cambridge, MA: Harvard University Press.

Melson, G. F., Kahn, P. H., Beck, A. M., Friedman, B., Roberts, T., & Garret, E. (2005). Robots as dogs? Children's interactions with the robotic dog AIBO and a live Australian shepherd. In G. C. van der Veer & C. Gale (Eds.), *Extended Abstracts Proceedings of the 2005 Conference on Human Factors in Computing Systems, CHI 2005,* (pp.,1649-1652). Retrieved from http://faculty.washington.edu/pkahn/articles/Robots_as_Dogs.pdf.

Merceron, A., & Yacef, K. (2004). Mining student data captured from a web-based tutoring tool: Initial exploration and results. *Journal of Interactive Learning Research, 15*(4), 319–346.

Messin, A. (2008). L'usage d'Internet par les jeunes adultes: quelles compétences? [Use of the Internet by young adults: What competencies?] In *Actes du colloque scientifique Ludovia - 2008* (pp. 204-214). Ax les Thermes – Ariège, France: Institut de Recherche en Informatique de Toulouse et Laboratoire de Recherche en Audiovisuel.

Michael, D., & Chen, S. (2006). *Serious games: Games that educate, train, and inform.* Boston MA: Thomson.

Miles, M. B., &t Huberman, M. A. (2003). *Analyse des données qualitatives* [Analysis of quantitative data] (2nd ed.). Paris: Deboeck.

Milheim, W. D., & Lavix, C. (1992). Screen design for computer-based training and interactive video: Practical suggestions and overall guidelines. *Performances & Instruction, 31*(5), 13–21. doi:10.1002/pfi.4170310507

Miller, M. A. (1992). Outcomes evaluation: Measuring critical thinking. *Journal of Advanced Nursing, 17*(12), 1401–1407. doi:10.1111/j.1365-2648.1992.tb02810.x

Millerand, F., & Martial, O. (2001). *Guide pratique de conception et d'évaluation ergonomique de sites Web* [Practical guide to the design and evaluation of Web sites]. Montréal, QC, Canada: Centre de recherche informatique de Montréal. Available at http://www.crim.ca/files/documents/services/rd/GuideErgonomique.PDF

Millians, D. (1999). Thirty years and more of simulations and games. *Simulation & Gaming, 30*(3), 352–355. doi:10.1177/104687819903000311

Milrad, M. (2002). Using construction kits, modeling tools and system dynamics simulations to support collaborative discovery learning. *Educational Technology and Society, 5*(4), 76–87.

Milrad, M. (2002). Using construction kits, modeling tools and system dynamics simulations to support collaborative discovery learning. *Educational Technology and Society, 5*(4), 76–87.

Minier, P. (2000). *Constructivisme* [Constructivism]. Available at http://wwwens.uqac.ca/~pminier/act1/constr.htm

Ministère de l'Éducation du Québec (2001). *Programme de formation de l'école québécoise. Éducation préscolaire. Enseignement Primaire* [Quebec elementary school curriculum]. Québec, QC, Canada: Government of Québec.

Ministère de l'Éducation du Québec (2003). *Programme de formation de l'école québécoise Enseignement secondaire, premier cycle* [Quebec secondary school curriculum, first level]. Québec, QC, Canada: Government of Québec.

Mitchell, A., & Savill-Smith, C. (2004). *The use of computer and video games for learning: A review of the literature.* Learning and Skills Development Agency. Retrieved May 20, 2009 from http://www.lsda.org.uk/files/PDF/1529.pdf

Moline, T. (2008). "I get competent pretty quickly": How adolescents play their way to cognitive self-efficacy. In K. McFerrin, R. Weber, R. Carlsen, & D. A. Willis, (eds)., *Proceedings of 19th International Conference Annual of Society for Information Technology & Teacher Education* (pp. 1213-1219). Chesapeake, VA: AACE.

Morgan, M., Gibbs, S., Maxwell, K., & Britten, N. (2002). Hearing children's voices: methodological issues in conducting focus groups with children aged 7-11 years. *Qualitative Research*, *2*(1), 5–20. doi:10.1177/1468794102002001636

Morton, P. G., & Tarvin, L. (2001). The pain game: Pain assessment, management, and related JCAHO Standards. *Journal of Continuing Education in Nursing*, *32*(5), 223–227.

Moseley, W. G. (2001). Computer assisted comprehension of distant worlds: understanding hunger dynamics in Africa. *The Journal of Geography*, *100*(1), 32–45. doi:10.1080/00221340108978415

Mott, B., Callaway, C., Zettlemoyer, L., Lee, S., & Lester, J. (1999). Towards narrative centered learning environments. In M. Mateas & P. Sengers (Eds.), *Narrative Intelligence: Papers from the 1999 Fall Symposium*, Technical Report FS-99-01 (pp. 78-82). Menlo Park, CA: American Association for Artificial Intelligence.

Moyer, P. S., & Bolyard, J. J. (2003). Classify and capture: Using Venn diagrams and Tangrams to develop abilities in mathematical reasoning and proof. *Mathematics Teaching in the Middle School*, *8*(6), 325–330.

Murray, J. H. (1997). *Hamlet on the holodeck: The future of narrative in cyberspace*. New York: Free Press.

Myers, G. (1998). *Children and animals: Social development and our connections to other species*. Boulder, CO: Westview Press.

Mzoughi, T., Herring, S. D., Foley, J. T., Morris, M. J., & Gilbert, P. J. (2007). WebTOP: A 3D interactive system for teaching and learning optics. *Computers & Education*, *49*(1), 110–129. doi:10.1016/j.compedu.2005.06.008

Nadeau, M. A. (1981) *L'évaluation des programmes d'études* [Evaluation of study programs]. Québec, QC, Canada: Presses de l'Université Laval.

Naidu, S. (2003). *Learning and teaching with technology: Principles and practices*. London: Kogan Page.

Naidu, S., & Oliver, M. (1996). Computer-supported collaborative problem-based learning: An instructional design architecture for virtual learning in nursing education. *Journal of Distance Education*, *11*(2), 1–22.

Naismith, L., Lonsdale, P., Vavoula, G., & Sharples, M. (2004). *Literature review in mobile technologies and learning*. Bristol, UK: Futurelab. Retrieved August 21, 2006 from http://www.futurelab.org.uk/download/pdfs/research/lit_reviews/futurelab_review_11.pdf

Najjar, L. J. (2001). Principles of educational multimedia user interface design. In R. W. Swezey & D. H. Andrews (Eds.), *Readings in training and simulation: A 30-year perspective* (pp. 146-158). Santa Monica, CA: Human Factors and Ergonomics Society.

Nassar, K. (2002). Simulation gaming in construction: ER, the Equipment Replacement Game. *Journal of Construction Education*, *7*(1), 16–30.

New Brunswick Ministry of Education. (2005). *Programme d'étude. Éducation personnelle et sociale 6ème à 8ème année* [Program of study: Personal and social education, grades 6 – 8]. Frederickton, NB, Canada: Government of New Brunswick.

Newman, D. R., Webb, B., & Cochrane, C. (1995). A content analysis method to measure critical thinking in face-to-face and computer supported group learning. *Interpersonal Computing and Technology*, *3*(2), 56–77.

Newmann, W. W., & Twigg, J. L. (2000). Active engagement of the intro IR student: A simulation approach. *PS: Political Science and Politic*, *33*(4), 835–842. doi:10.2307/420926

Nguyen, T., Chang, V., Chang, E., Jacob, C., & Turk, A. (2008). A contingent method for usability evaluation of Web-based learning systems. In K. McFerrin, R. Weber, R. Carlsen, & D. A. Willis (Eds). *Proceedings of the Society for Information Technology & Teacher Education Annual International Conference (19th International Conference of SITE 2008)* (pp. 579-585). Chesapeake, VA: AACE.

Nielsen, J. (1993). *Usability engineering*. Boston: Academic Press, Inc.

Nielsen, J. (2000). *Designing Web usability: The practice of simplicity*. Indianapolis, IN: New Riders Publishing.

Nintendo World Report. (2005, November 28). *Europe loves Nintendogs.* Retrieved February 14. 2008, from http://www.nintendoworldreport.com/newsArt.cfm?artid=10961.

Nintendo.com. (2008, February). *Game guide.* Retrieved February 17, 2008, from http://www.nintendo.com/games/guide#qhardware=DS.

Nisenbaum, H. L., Arger, P. H., Derman, R. M., & Ziv, A. (2000). Ultrasound simulator (UltraSim) as an evaluation tool of residents' scanning skills: pilot study. *Journ. of Ultrasound in Med., 19*(suppl), S13.

Nogier, J. F. (2005). *Designing ease of use.* Usabilis: Web & Software Usability Consulting. Retrieved June 7, 2007 from http://www.usabilis.com/gb/index.html

Nogier, J. F. (2005). *Ergonomie du logiciel et design web. Le manuel des interfaces utilisateur* [Computer ergonomics and web design: The manual of user interfaces]. Paris: Dunod.

Nokelainen, P. (2005). The technical and pedagogical usability criteria for digital learning material. In *Proceedings of the 2005 World Conference on Educational Multimedia, Hypermedia and Telecommunications* (pp. 1011-1016). Chesapeake, VA: AACE.

Norcross, J. C., Hedges, M., & Prochaska, J. O. (2002). The face of 2010: A Delphi poll on the future of psychotherapy. *Professional Psychology, Research and Practice, 33*(3), 316–322. doi:10.1037/0735-7028.33.3.316

North, M. M., North, S. M., & Coble, J. R. (2002). Virtual reality therapy: An effective treatment for psychological disorders. In K. M. Stanney (Ed.), *Handbook of virtual environments: Design, implementation, and applications* (pp. 1065-1078). Mahwah, NJ: Lawrence Erlbaum Associates Inc.

Norton-Meier, L. (2005). Joining the video-game literacy club: A reluctant mother tries to join the "flow.". *Journal of Adolescent & Adult Literacy, 48*(5), 428–432. doi:10.1598/JAAL.48.5.6

Nurmi, S. (2004). *Are simulations useful for learning?* Review article for ERNIST research project. Retrieved October 25, 2007, from http://insight-old.eun.org/eun.org2/eun/en/Insight_Research&Development/content.cfm?ov=33695&lang=en

O'Neil, M. (2004). *Final report on gaps in resources available to deliver history and social studies curricula in Canada.* Toronto, ON, Canada: Historica Foundation.

O'Rourke, B. (2008). The other C in CMC: What alternative data sources can tell us about text-based synchronous computer mediated communication and language learning. *Computer Assisted Language Learning, 21*(3), 227–251. doi:10.1080/09588220802090253

Oblinger, D. G., & Oblinger, J. L. (2005). *Educating the net generation.* Washington, DC: Educause.

Olsen, F. (2000). Computer models teach scientists what experiments can't. *The Chronicle of Higher Education, 46*(49), A49.

Ontario Ministry of Education. (1998). The Ontario curriculum for grades 1 through 8: Health and physical education. Available at http://www.edu.gov.on.ca

Orne, M. (1969). Demand characteristics and the concept of quasi-controls. In R. Rosenthal & R. Rosnow (Eds.), *Artifact in behavioral research* (pp. 143-179). New York: Academic Press.

Orrill, C. H. (2002). Supporting online PBL: Design considerations for supporting distributed problem solving. *Distance Education, 23*(1), 41–57. doi:10.1080/01587910220123973

Othmer, S. F., & Othmer, S. (1994). *EEG biofeedback training for PMS.* Retrieved February 5, 2008, from: http://members.aol.com/eegspectrm/articles/pms94.htm

Pagulayan, R. J., Keefer, K., Wixon, D., Romero, R. L., & Fuller, T. (2003). User-centered design in games. In A. Jacko Julie & A. Sears (Eds.), *The human-computer interaction handbook. Fundamentals, evolving technologies, and emerging applications* (pp. 883-906). Mahwah, N.J.: Lawrence Erlbaum Associates Inc.

Paivio, A. (1991). Dual coding theory: Retrospect and current status. *Canadian Journal of Psychology, 45*(3), 255–287. doi:10.1037/h0084295

Palermo, T. M., Valenzuela, D., & Stork, P. P. (2004). A randomized trial of electronic versus paper pain diaries in children: Impact on compliance, accuracy, and acceptability. *Pain*, *107*(3), 213–219. doi:10.1016/j.pain.2003.10.005

Palsson, O. S., & Pope, A. T. (2002). Morphing beyond recognition: The future of biofeedback technologies. *Biofeedback*, *30*(1), 14–18.

Pandit, N. (1996). *The creation of theory: A recent application of the grounded theory method.* Retrieved May 20, 2009 from http://www.nova.edu/ssss/QR/QR2-4/pandit.html

Papert, S. (1980). *Mind-storms: Children, computers, and powerful ideas.* New York: Basic Books Inc.

Papert, S. (1998, June). Does easy do it? Children, games, and learning. *Game Developer Magazine*, *4*, 88–91.

Paquelin, D. (2002). Analyse d'applications multimédias pour un usage pédagogique [Analysis of multimedia applications for pedagogic use]. *Apprentissage des langues et systèmes d'information et de communication (ALSIC)*, *5*(1), 3-32.

Paras, B. S., & Bizzocchi, J. (2005, June). *Game, motivation, and effective learning: An integrated model for educational game design.* Paper presented at the 2005 conference of the Digital Games Research Association (DiGRA), Changing Views: Worlds in Play, Vancouver, BC, Canada. Retrieved October 25, 2007 from http://www.digra.org/dl/db/06276.18065.pdf

Parke, F. I. (1972). Computer generated animation of faces. In *Proceedings of the ACM Annual Conference*, volume 1 (pp. 451-457). doi 10.1145/800193.569955.

Parke, F. I., & Waters, K. (2000). *Computer facial animation.* Natick, MA: A. K. Peters Ltd.

Parker, L. E., & Lepper, M. R. (1992). Effects of fantasy contexts on children's learning and motivation: Making learning more fun. *Journal of Personality and Social Psychology*, *62*(4), 625–633. doi:10.1037/0022-3514.62.4.625

Patel, A., Schieble, T., Davidson, M., Tran, M. C. J., & Schoenberg, C., Delphin, E. et al. (2006). Distraction with a hand-held video game reduces pediatric preoperative anxiety. *Paediatric Anaesthesia*, *16*(10), 1019–1027. doi:. doi:10.1111/j.1460-9592.2006.01914.x

Patton, M. Q. (1980). *Qualitative evaluation and research methods.* Beverly Hills, CA: Sage Publications.

Paul, E. S. (2000). Love of pets and love of people. In A. L. Podberscek., E. S. Paul & J. Serpell (Eds.), *Companion animals and us: Exploring the relationships between people and pets* (pp. 168-188). Cambridge, UK: Cambridge University Press.

PCman. (2005). *Free Airfox destroyer game.* Available at http://www.thepcmanwebsite.com/media/air_fox/airfox.shtml.

Pearce, C. (2005) Theory wars: An argument against arguments in the so-called ludology/narratology debate. In S. DeCastell & J. Jenson (Eds.), *Changing Views - Worlds in Play, Selected Papers of the 2005 Digital Games Research Association's Second International Conference* (pp. 41-45). Vancouver, BC, Canada: Simon Fraser University.

Pearrow, M. (2007). *Web usability handbook* (2nd ed.). Boston, MA: Charles River Media.

Pegden, C. D., Shannon, R. E., & Sadowski, R. P. (1995). *Introduction to simulation using SIMAN* (2nd ed.). Singapore: McGraw-Hill.

Pei, X.-S. (1998). Using interactive physics in planetary motion. *The Physics Teacher*, *36*(1), 42–43. doi:10.1119/1.879975

Pelletier, C. (2005, June). *Studying games in school: A framework for media education.* Paper presented at the 2005 conference of the Digital Games Research Association (DiGRA), Changing Views: Worlds in Play. Vancouver, BC, Canada.

Pelletier, C., & Oliver, M. (2006). Learning to play in digital games. *Learning, Media and Technology*, *31*(4), 329–342. doi:10.1080/17439880601021942

People for the Ethical Treatment of Animals (PETA), (2006). *2006 PETA Proggy award.*

Perez, B. E., & Gallardo, A. L. (2004, September). *Empleo de juegos de simulación empresarial como herramienta para la innovación docente: Experiencia en control de gestión de la Diplomatura de Turismo* [Managerial use of simulation games as tool for teaching innovation: Experience in a tourism diploma course]. Paper presented at the Asociación Española de Profesores Universitarios de Contabilidad (ASEPUC) IV Jornada de Docencia en Contabilidad, Seville.

Perron, B. (2004). Sign of a threat: The effects of warning systems in survival horror games. In A. Clarke (Ed.), *Proceedings, the Fourth International Conference on Computational Semiotics for Games and New Media (COSIGN 2004)* (pp. 132-141).

Perron, B. (2005, June). *A cognitive psychological approach to gameplay emotions.* Paper presented at the 2005 conference of the Digital Games Research Association (DiGRA), Changing Views: Worlds in Play, Vancouver BC, Canada. Retrieved October 25, 2007 from http://www.digra.org/dl/db/06276.58345.pdf

Perron, L., & Bordeleau, P. (1994). Modèle de développement d'ensembles didactiques d'intégration pédagogique de l'ordinateur [Development model for integrating pedogogy and the computer]. In P. Bordeleau (Ed.), *Des outils pour apprendre avec l'ordinateur* (pp. 513-553). Montréal, QC, Canada: Les Éditions Logiques.

Peters, V., & Vissers, G. (2004). A simple classification model for debriefing simulation games. *Simulation & Gaming, 35*(1), 70–84. doi:10.1177/1046878103253719

Peters, V., Vissers, G., & Heijne, G. (1998). The validity of games. *Simulation & Gaming, 29*(1), 20–30. doi:10.1177/1046878198291003

Petranek, C. F. (2000). Written debriefing: The next vital step in learning with simulations. *Simulation & Gaming, 31*(1), 108–118. doi:10.1177/104687810003100111

Pew Internet & American Life Project (PIALP). (2008). *Demographics of Internet users.* Washington, DC: Pew Research Center. Retrieved June 11, 2008 from http://www.pewinternet.org/trends/User_Demo_2.15.08.htm

Pillay, H., Brownlee, J., & Wilss, L. (1999). Cognition and recreational computer games: Implications for education technology. *Journal of Research on Computing in Education, 32*(1/2), 203–216.

Pittaway, L., & Cope, J. (2007). Simulating entrepreneurial learning: Integrating experiential and collaborative approaches to learning. *Management Learning, 38*(2), 211–219. doi:10.1177/1350507607075776

Plotkin, W. B., & Rice, K. M. (1981). Biofeedback as a placebo: Anxiety reduction facilitated by training in either suppression or enhancement of alpha brainwaves. *Journal of Consulting and Clinical Psychology, 49*(4), 590–596. doi:10.1037/0022-006X.49.4.590

Plous, S. (1987). Perceptual illusions and military realities: Results from a computer-simulated arms race. *The Journal of Conflict Resolution, 31*(1), 5–33. doi:10.1177/0022002787031001002

Polkinghorne, D. (1988). *Narrative knowing and the human sciences.* Albany NY: State University of New York Press.

Poole, S. (2000). *Trigger happy – Video games and the entertainment revolution.* New York: Arcade Publishing.

Power, M. (2008, March). *Responsible outreach in higher education: The Blended Online Learning Environment.* Paper presented at the American Educational Research Association Instructional Design SIG, New York.

Power, M., Langlois, L., & Gagnon, M.-F. (2005). Ethical Advisor 1.0: Judge for yourself. In S. de Castell & J. Jenson (Eds.), *Proceedings of the Digital Games Research Association Conference (DIGRA 2005): Changing Views: Worlds in Play,* Vancouver, BC, Canada. CD-ROM.

Prégent, R. (1990). *La préparation d'un cours* [Preparation of a course]. Montreal, QC, Canada: Éditions de l'École Polytechnique de Montréal.

Prensky, M. (2001). *Digital game-based learning.* New York and London: McGraw Hill.

Prensky, M. (2003). Escape from Planet Jar-Gon: Or what video games have to teach academics about teaching and writing. A review of *What Video Games Have To Teach Us About Learning and Literacy* by James Paul Gee. *On*

The Horizon, 11(3). Retrieved July 15, 2009 from http://www.marcprensky.com/writing/Prensky%20-%20Review%20of%20James%20Paul%20Gee%20Book.pdf

Prensky, M. (2004) Interactive pretending: An overview of simulation. Retrieved November 28, 2008 from http://www.marcprensky.com/writing/Prensky-Interactive_Pretending.pdf.

Prensky, M. (2005). Computer games and learning: Digital game-based learning. In J. Raessens & J. Goldstein (Eds.), *Handbook of computer game studies* (pp. 97-122). Cambridge, MA: The MIT Press.

Prensky, M. (2005a, December). Adopt and adapt: 21st-century schools need 21st-century technology. *Edutopia*. Available at http://www.edutopia.org/adopt-and-adapt

Prensky, M. (2005b). Engage me or enrage me: What today's learners demand. *EDUCAUSE Review*, (September-October): 60–64.

Prensky, M. (2006). *Don't bother me mom! I'm learning! How computer and video games are preparing your kids for 21st century success.* St. Paul, MN: Paragon House.

Pridemore, D., & Klein, J. (1991). Control of feedback in computer-based instruction. *Educational Technology Research and Development, 39*(4), 27–32. doi:10.1007/BF02296569

Probst, W., Villardier, L., & Sauvé, L. (2004). A real-time configurable web-based tool for teleconferencing and telelearning. In C. Crawford et al. (Eds.), *Proceedings of Society for Information Technology and Teacher Education International Conference 2004* (pp. 644-651). Chesapeake, VA: AACE.

Pronovost, G. (2007). *L'univers du temps libre et des valeurs chez les jeunes* [The universe of free time and youth values]. Québec, QC, Canada: Presses de l'Université du Québec.

Proulx, J., Cote, G., & Achille, P. A. (1993). Prevention of voluntary control of penile response in homosexual pedophiles during phallometric testing. *Journal of Sex Research, 30*(2), 140–147.

Quinsey, V. L., & Chaplin, T. C. (1988). Preventing faking in phallometric assessments of sexual preference. *Annals of the New York Acad. of Sciences, 528*, 49–58. doi:10.1111/j.1749-6632.1988.tb50849.x

Quivy, R., & Campenhoudt, L. V. (1988). *Manuel de recherche en sciences sociales* [Manual on research in the social sciences]. Paris: Dunod.

Rabecq-Mallard, M. M. (1969). *Histoire des jeux éducatifs* [History of educational games]. Paris: Nathan.

Racine, L., Legault, G., & Bégin, L. (1991). *L'éthique et l'ingénierie* [Ethics and engineering]. Montréal, QC, Canada: McGraw Hill.

Rail, S. (2005). *Premières phases de conception d'un jeu éducatif sur la santé des jeune* [First stages in the design of an educational game on health in youth]. Unpublished master's thesis. Québec, QC, Canada: Université Laval.

Rainey, L. (2006). *Digital 'natives' invade the workplace*. Washington, DC: Pew Research Center. Retrieved June 11, 2008, from http://www.pewinternet.org/ppt/New%20Workers%20--%20pewresearch.org%20version%20_final_.pdf

Rambally, G. K., & Rambally, R. S. (1987). Human factors in CAI design. *Computers & Education, 11*(2), 149–153. doi:10.1016/0360-1315(87)90009-1

Ramirez, L. L. (2001). They're taking me to Marrakesh! A seventh grade French class's fantasy trip to Morocco. *The French Review, 74*(3), 552–560.

Randel, J., Morris, B. A., Wetzel, C. D., & Whitehill, B. V. (1992). The effectiveness of games for educational purposes: A review of recent research. *Simulation & Gaming, 23*(3), 261–276. doi:10.1177/1046878192233001

Ravenscroft, A. (2007). Promoting thinking and conceptual change with digital dialogue games. *Journal of Computer Assisted Learning, 23*(6), 453–465. doi:10.1111/j.1365-2729.2007.00232.x

Read, J. C., MacFarlane, S. J., & Casey, C. (2002). Endurability, engagement and expectations: Measuring children's fun. In *Proceedings, Interaction Design and*

Children 2002 (pp. 189-198). Eindhoven, The Netherlands: Shaker Publishing. Super Nintendo Classics (n.d.). *Bronkie the Bronchiasaurus.* Retrieved July 2, 2009 from http://www.snesclassics.com/snes-archive/bronkie.php

Reeve, J. (1992). *Understanding motivation and emotion.* Fort Worth: Harcourt Brace Jovanovich.

Renaud, L. (1987). *Impact de certains éléments, à l'intérieur du jeu de simulation, sur les attitudes, les comportements et le transfert d'apprentissage des jeunes enfants face à la sécurité routièr* [The impact of certain simulation game elements on the attitudes, behaviors, and transfer of learning in young children about road safety]. Unpublished Ph.D. dissertation, Université de Montréal, Montreal, QC, Canada.

Renaud, L., & Sauvé, L. (1990). *Simulation et jeu de simulation: outils éducatifs appliqués à la santé* [Simulation and simulation games: Educational tools applied to health]. Montreal, QC, Canada: Éditions Agence d'Arc Inc.

Renaud, L., Sauvé, L., & Ellisalde, J. (2007). *Évaluation du jeu « ITS: Stopper la transmission » auprès d'experts* [Expert evaluation of the game STIs: Stopping the Transmission] (Research report). Québec, QC, Canada: SAGE and SAVIE.

Renaud, P. (2004, October). *Moving assessment of sexual interest into the 21st century: the potential of new information technology.* Invited presentation at the 23rd Annual Research and Treatment Conference (ATSA), Albuquerque, NM.

Renaud, P. (2006a). *Method for providing data to be used by a therapist for analyzing a patient behavior in a virtual environment.* US patent 7128577.

Renaud, P., Bouchard, S., & Proulx, R. (2002a). Behavioral avoidance dynamics in the presence of a virtual spider. *IEEE (Institute of Electrical and Electronics Engineers). Transactions in Information Technology and Biomedicine, 6*, 235–243. doi:10.1109/TITB.2002.802381

Renaud, P., Chartier, S., & Albert, G. (2008, accepted). Embodied and embedded: The dynamics of extracting perceptual visual invariants. In S. Guastello, M. Koopman, & D. Pincus (Eds.), *Chaos and complexity: Recent advances and future directions in the theory of nonlinear dynamical systems psychology.* Cambridge, UK: Cambridge University Press.

Renaud, P., Chartier, S., Albert, G., Cournoyer, L.-G., Proulx, J., & Bouchard, S. (2006b). Sexual presence as determined by fractal oculomotor dynamics. *Annual Review of Cybertherapy and Telemedicine, 4*, 87–94.

Renaud, P., Chartier, S., Albert, G., Décarie, J., Cournoyer, L.-G., & Bouchard, S. (2007). Presence as determined by fractal perceptual-motor dynamics. *Cyberpsychology & Behavior, 10*(1), 122–130. doi:10.1089/cpb.2006.9983

Renaud, P., Cusson, J.-F., Bernier, S., Décarie, J., Gourd, S.-P., & Bouchard, S. (2002b). Extracting perceptual and motor invariants using eye-tracking technologies in virtual immersions. In Proceedings of *HAVE'2002-IEEE (Institute of Electrical and Electronics Engineers) International Workshop on Haptic Virtual Environments and their Applications* (pp. 73-78). doi 10.1109/HAVE.2002.1106917.

Renaud, P., Decarie, J., Gourd, S. P., Paquin, L. C., & Bouchard, S. (2003). Eye-tracking in immersive environments: A general methodology to analyze affordance-based interactions from oculomotor dynamics. *Cyberpsychology & Behavior, 6*(5), 519–526. doi:10.1089/109493103769710541

Renaud, P., Proulx, J., Rouleau, J.-L., Bouchard, S., Bradford, J., Fedoroff, P., et al. (2006c, November). *Sexual and oculomotor biofeedback mediated by sexual stimuli presented in virtual reality.* Paper presented at the 49th annual meeting of the Society for the Scientific Study of Sexuality, Las Vegas.

Renaud, P., Proulx, J., Rouleau, J.-L., Bouchard, S., Madrigrano, G., & Bradford, J. (2005). The recording of observational behaviors in virtual immersion: A new clinical tool to address the problem of sexual preferences with paraphiliacs. *Annual Review of Cybertherapy and Telemedicine, 3*, 85–92.

Renaud, P., Rouleau, J.-L., Granger, L., Barsetti, I., & Bouchard, S. (2002c). Measuring sexual preferences in virtual reality: A pilot study. *Cyberpsychology & Behavior, 5*(1), 1–10. doi:10.1089/109493102753685836

Renaud, P., Singer, G., & Proulx, R. (2001). Head-tracking fractal dynamics in visually pursuing virtual objects. In W. Sulis, & I. Trofimova (Eds), *Nonlinear dynamics in life and social sciences* (pp. 333-346). Amsterdam: IOS Press NATO Science Series.

Repine, T., & Hemler, D. (1999). Outcrops in the classroom. *Science Teacher (Normal, Ill.), 66*(8), 29–33.

Rest, J., & Narvaez, D. (1994). *Moral development in the professions: Psychology and applied ethics.* Mahwah, NJ: Lawrence Erlbaum Associates Inc.

Retrieved February 10, 2008, from http://www.peta.org.uk/feat/proggy/2006/index.html

Reuss, R. L., & Gardulski, A. F. (2001). An interactive game approach to learning in historical geology and paleontology. *Journal of Geoscience Education, 49*(2), 120–129.

Reuss, R. L., & Gardulski, A. F. (2001). An interactive game approach to learning in historical geology and paleontology. *Journal of Geoscience Education, 49*(2), 120–129.

Reuters (2007). Video-game sales overtaking music. Retrieved February 14, 2008 from http://articles.moneycentral.msn.com/Investing/Extra/VideoGameSalesOvertakingMusic.aspx

Rheingold, H. (1991). *Virtual reality: The revolutionary technology of computer-generated artificial worlds - and how it promises and threatens to transform business and society.* New York: Summit Books.

Rice, K. M., Blanchard, E. B., & Purcell, M. (1993). Biofeedback treatments of generalized anxiety disorder: Preliminary results. *Biofeedback and Self-Regulation, 18*(2), 93–105. doi:10.1007/BF01848110

Rieber, L. P. (1991). Animation, incidental learning, and continuing motivation. *Journal of Educational Psychology, 83*(3), 318–328. doi:10.1037/0022-0663.83.3.318

Rieber, L. P. (1996). Seriously considering play: Designing interactive learning environments based on blending of microworlds, simulations and games. *Educational Technology Research and Development, 44*(1), 43–58. doi:10.1007/BF02300540

Rieber, L. P. (2001). Designing learning environments that excite serious play. In G. Kennedy, M. Keppell, C. McNaught, & T. Petrovic (Eds.), *Meeting at the crossroads. Proceedings of the 18th Annual Conference of the Australian Society for Computers in Learning in Tertiary Education* (pp. 1-10). Melbourne: Biomedical Multimedia Unit, the University of Melbourne.

Ripp, K. (2001). *Bead game simulation lesson plan.* Davis, CA: Foundation for Teaching Economics.

Ritchie, D. C., & Hoffman, B. (1996, June). *Using instructional design principles to amplify learning on the World Wide Web.* Paper presented at SITE 96 (Society for Information Technology and Teacher Education 7th World Conference). Retrieved Nov. 1, 2002 from http://edweb.sdsu.edu/clrit/learningtree/DCD/WWWInstrdesign/ WWWInstrDesign.html

Rittel, H. W. J., & Webber, M., M. M. (1973). Dilemmas in a general theory of planning. *Policy Sciences, 4,* 155–159. doi:10.1007/BF01405730

Riva, G. (2005). Virtual reality in psychotherapy [review]. *Cyberpsychology & Behavior, 8*(3), 220–230. doi:10.1089/cpb.2005.8.220

Rizzo, A., Buckwalter, J. G., Neumann, U., Chua, C., Van Rooyen, A., & Larson, P. (1999). Virtual environments for targeting cognitive processes: An overview of projects at the University of Southern California Integrated Media Systems. *Cyberpsychology & Behavior, 2*(2), 89–100. doi:10.1089/cpb.1999.2.89

Robinet, J.-M. (2003). Visioconférence: Perspectives scientifiques. [Visioconferencing: Scientific perspectives] (Web bibliography). Retrieved May 24, 2009 from http://users.belgacom.net/bn580601/visioconference.htm

Rodet, J. (2000). La rétroaction, support d'apprentissage ? [Feedback – a learning support?] *Revue du Conseil québécois de la formation à distance, 4*(2), 45-74.

Rodriguez, E. E. (1998). A proposal for experimental homework. *The Physics Teacher*, *36*(7), 435–437. doi:10.1119/1.879915

Rollings, A., & Morris, D. (2005). *Conception et architecture des jeux vidéo* [Design and architecture of video games]. Paris: Vuibert Informatique.

Romme, A. G. L. (2002). *Microworlds for management education and learning.* Working paper. Tilburg University, Tilburg, Netherlands. Available at http://www.unice.fr/sg/resources/articles/romme_2002_microworlds-management-ed-learning.pdf

Rosas, R., Nussbaum, M., Cumsille, P., Marianov, V., Correa, M., & Flores, P. (2003). Beyond Nintendo: Design and assessment of educational video games for first and second grade students. *Computers & Education*, *40*(1), 71–94. doi:10.1016/S0360-1315(02)00099-4

Rosenbaum, E., Klopfer, E., & Perry, J. (2007). On location learning: Authentic applied science with networked augmented realities. *Journal of Science Education and Technology*, *16*(1), 31–45. doi:10.1007/s10956-006-9036-0

Rosenzweig, S. (1942). The photoscope as an objective device for evaluating sexual interest. *Psychosomatic Medicine*, *4*, 150–158.

Ross, T. J. (2004). *Fuzzy logic with engineering applications.* Hoboken, NJ: Wiley.

Rossiter, M. (2002). *Narrative and stories in adult teaching and learning.* ERIC Document Reproduction Service No. ED473147. Retrieved from ERIC database.

Rothbaum, B. O., Hodges, L. F., Smith, S., Lee, J. H., & Price, L. (2000). A controlled study of virtual reality exposure therapy for the fear of flying. *Journal of Consulting and Clinical Psychology*, *68*(6), 1020–1026. doi:10.1037/0022-006X.68.6.1020

Rousseau, D., & Hayes-Roth, B. (1997). *Interacting with personality-rich characters.* Knowledge Systems Laboratory Report No. KSL 97-06, Stanford University, Palo Alto, CA.

Rovick, A. A. (1985). Writing computer lessons. *The Physiologist*, *28*(3), 173–176.

Ruben, B. D. (1999). Simulation, games, and experience-based learning: The quest for a new paradigm for teaching and learning. *Simulation & Gaming*, *30*(4), 498–505. doi:10.1177/104687819903000409

Rushbrook, S. (1986). "Messages" of video games: Social implications. Unpublished Ph.D. dissertation, University of California, Los Angeles.

Russell, J. A. (1980). A circumplex model of affect. *Journal of Personality and Social Psychology*, *39*, 1161–1178. doi:10.1037/h0077714

Saethang, T., & Kee, C. C. (1998). A gaming strategy for teaching the use of critical cardiovascular drugs. *Journal of Continuing Education in Nursing*, *29*(2), 61–65.

Salen, K., & Zimmerman, E. (2003). *Rules of play: Game design fundamentals.* Cambridge, MA: The MIT Press.

Saliés, T. G. (2002). Simulation/gaming in the EAP writing class: Benefits and drawbacks. *Simulation & Gaming*, *33*(3), 316–329. doi:10.1177/104687810203300306

Salopek, J. J. (1999). Stop playing games. *Training & Development*, *53*(2), 28–38.

Sandford, R., & Williamson, B. (2005). *Games and learning.* Bristol, UK: futurelab. Available at http://www.futurelab.org.uk/resources/publications_reports_articles/handbooks/Handbook133.

Sauvé, L. (1985). *Simulation et transfert d'apprentissage. Une étude sur les niveaux de fidélité pour le transfert d'apprentissage* [Simulation and the transfer of learning: A study of the level of fidelity for the transfer of learning. Unpublished Ph.D. dissertation, University of Montreal, Montreal, QC, Canada. Sauvé, L (2004). *Guide de recension des écrits. ApprentisSAGE par les jeux* [Guide for a literature review: Learning with games].Québec, QC, Canada: SAVIE.

Sauvé, L. (1990). Comment évaluer une simulation et un jeu de simulation [How to evaluate a simulation and a simulation game]. In L. Renaud & L. Sauvé, *Simulation et jeu de simulation: outils éducatifs appliqués à la santé* (pp. 195-232). Montréal, QC, Canada: Éducation Agence d'Arc Inc.

Sauvé, L. (1995). Les médias: des outils indispensables pour réduire la distance [Media: Indispensable tools for distance education]. In M.P. Dessaint (Ed.), *Guide de planification, de rédaction et d'édition pour la conception de cours à distance* (pp. 279-342). Québec, QC, Canada: Les presses de l'Universitaire du Québec.

Sauvé, L. (2002, May). *Jeux-cadres en ligne: un outil d'aide pour le concepteur d'environnement d'apprentissage* [Frame games online: A tool to help the learning environment designer]. Paper presented at Nouveau centenaire - nouveaux modèles: Colloque de l'ACDE/ICDE.

Sauvé, L. (2005). *La grille d'analyse de base des jeux numériques éducatifs* [Analysis grid for digital educational games] (Research report). Québec, QC, Canada: SAGE and SAVIE.

Sauvé, L. (2005). Open and distance educational gaming: Using generic frame games to accelerate game design. In A. Lionarakis (Ed.), *Applications of Pedagogy and Technology, Proceedings of 3rd International Conference on Open and Distance Learning (ICODL 2005)* (pp. 393-398). Patras, Greece: ICODL.

Sauvé, L. (2006). *Guide de rédaction d'un devis de conception: quelques règles médiatiques* [Guide for writing a design plan: Media rules]. Québec, QC, Canada: SAVIE.

Sauvé, L. (2006). *La scénarisation et la production du jeu éducatif* [Design and production of an educational game]. Québec, QC, Canada: Télé-université.

Sauvé, L. (2006). *Rapport de modélisation du jeu-cadre Parchési* [Report on modelling the frame-game Parcheesi] (Research report). Québec, QC, Canada: *SAGE* and SAVIE.

Sauvé, L., & Chamberland, G. (2000). *Jeux, jeux de simulation et jeux de rôle: une analyse exploratoire et pédagogique* [Games, simulation games and role-playing games: An exploratory pedogical analysis. Cours TEC 1280: Environnement d'apprentissage multimédia sur l'inforoute. Québec, QC, Canada: Télé-université. Sauvé, L., Renaud, L., Kaufman, D., & Marquis, J.-S. (2007). Distinguishing between games and simulations: A systematic review of the literature. *Journal of Educational Technology & Society, 10*(3), 244–256.

Sauvé, L., & Hanca, G. (2007). *Validation d'une coquille générique de jeu éducatif auprès des enseignants: Parchési* [Validation with teachers of a generic educational game shell: *Parcheesi*] (Research report). Québec, QC, Canada: SAGE and SAVIE.

Sauvé, L., & Power, M. IsaBelle, C., Samson, D., & St-Pierre, C. (2002). *Rapport final - Jeux-cadres sur l'inforoute: Multiplicateurs de jeux pédagogiques francophones: Un projet de partenariat* [Final report – Frame games on the Internet: Multipliers of francophone educational games]. Québec, QC, Canada: Bureau des technologies d'apprentissage (SAVIE).

Sauvé, L., & Samson, D. (2004). *Rapport d'évaluation de la coquille générique du Jeu de l'oie du projet Jeux génériques: multiplicateurs de contenu multimédia éducatif canadien sur l'inforoute* [Evaluation report on the Mother Goose generic game shell for the project Generic games: Multipliers of Canadian multimedia educational content on the Internet]. Québec, QC, Canada: SAVIE and Fonds Inukshuk inc.

Sauvé, L., & St-Pierre, C. (2003). *Recension des écrits sur les jeux éducatifs* [Review of the literature on educational games]. Research report. Québec, QC, Canada: Télé-université and SAVIE.

Sauve, L., & Viau, R. (2002). L'abandon et la persévérance dans l'enseignement à distance: l'importance de la relation enseignement – apprentissage [Abandonment and perseverance in distance education: The importance of relation education – training]. In *Nouveau centenaire - nouveaux modèles. Acte du Colloque de l'ACDE.* Available at http://www.cade-aced.ca/icdepapers/sauveviau.htm

Sauvé, L., Renaud, L., & Hanca, G. (2008). *Étude de cas du projet: Apprendre par les jeux* [Case study: Learning with games] (Research report). Québec, QC, Canada: SAGE and SAVIE.

Sauvé, L., Renaud, L., & Hanca, G. (2008a). *Étude de cas auprès des élèves du secondaire:apprentissage des*

ITS à l'aide d'un jeu éducatif en ligne [Case study of secondary school students: Learning about STIs with the aid of an online educational game]. Research report. Québec, QC, Canada: SAGE and SAVIE.

Sauvé, L., Renaud, L., & Hanca, G. (2008a). *Étude de cas du projet: Apprendre par les jeux* [Case study: Learning with games] (Research report). Québec, QC, Canada: *SAGE* and SAVIE.

Sauvé, L., Renaud, L., & Kaszap, M. IsaBelle, C, Samson, D., Doré-Bluteau, V.,et al. (2005b). *Revue systématique des écrits (1998-2004) sur les impacts du jeu, de la simulation et du jeu de simulation sur l'apprentissage* [Systematic review of the literature (1998-2004) on the impacts of games, simulations and simulation games on learning] (Research report). Québec, QC, Canada: SAGE and SAVIE.

Sauvé, L., Renaud, L., & Kaszap, M. IsaBelle, C., Gauvin, M., Rodriguez, A., & Simard, G. (2006) *Modélisation du jeu-cadre Parchesi* [Design of the frame game *Parcheesi*] (Research Report). Québec, QC, Canada: SAVIE and SAGE.

Sauvé, L., Renaud, L., & Kazsap, M. IsaBelle, C., Gauvin, M., & Simard, G. (2005). *Analyse de 40 jeux éducatifs (en ligne ou sur cédérom)* [Analysis of 40 educational games (on line and on CD-ROM)]. Research report. Québec, QC, Canada: SAGE and SAVIE.

Sauvé, L., Renaud, L., Kaufman, D., & Marquis, J. S. (2007). Distinguishing between games and simulations: A systematic review. *Educational Technology & Society, 10*(3), 247–256.

Sauvé, L., Renaud, L., Kaufman, D., & Sibomana, F. (2008). *Revue systématique des écrits (1998-2008) sur les impacts du jeu, de la simulation et du jeu de simulation sur l'apprentissage. Rapport final* [Systematic review of the literature on the impacts of games, simulations and simulation games. Final report]. Québec, QC, Canada: SAGE and SAVIE.

Sauvé, L., Renaud, L., Kaufman, D., Samson, D., Bluteau-Dore, V., Dumais, C., et al. (2005). *Revue systématique des écrits (1998-2004) sur les fondements conceptuels du jeu, de la simulation et du jeu de simulation.* [Systematic review of the literature (1998-2004) on the conceptual foundations of games, simulations, and simulation games]. Québec, QC, Canada: SAGE and SAVIE.

Sauvé, L., Villardier, L., Probst, W., Boyd, G., Kaufman, D., & Sanchez Arias, V. G. (2005). Playing and learning without borders: A real-time online play environment. In S. de Castell & J. Jenson (Eds.), *Online Proceedings, Digital Games Research Association (DiGRA) 2005 Conference, Changing Views:Worlds in Play.* Vancouver. Retrieved December 15, 2005 from www.digra.org/dl/.

Sauvé, L., Villardier, L., Probst, W., Sanchez Arias, V., Kaufman, D., & Power, M. (2005b). World play: Playing internationally in real time. In P. Kommers & G. Richards (Eds.), *Proceedings of World Conference on Educational Multimedia, Hypermedia and Telecommunications 2005* (pp. 4059-4065). Chesapeake, VA: AACE.

Sawyer, B. (2002). Serious games: Improving public policy through game-based learning and simulation. Washington, DC: Foresight and Governance Project, Woodrow Wilson International Center for Scholars. Retrieved Sept. 8, 2008 from http://www.seriousgames.org/images/seriousarticle.pdf

Sawyer, B. (2004, April*)* So what are serious games*?* Paper presented at the Computer Game Technology Conference 2004, Toronto, ON, Canada.

Sawyer, B. (2007, May). *Ben Sawyer talks about Serious Games at E3. Online*: http://seriousgames.ning.com/video/video/show?id=630751:Video:6502 (0'32" to 0'39").

Scardamalia, M., & Bereiter, C. (1992). Text-based and knowledge-based questioning by children. *Cognition and Instruction, 9*(3), 177–199. doi:10.1207/s1532690xci0903_1

Schaffer, D. W. (2005). Epistemic frames for epistemic games. *Computers & Education, 46*(3), 223–234. doi:10.1016/j.compedu.2005.11.003

Schaffer, D. W. (2006). *How computer games help children learn.* New York: Palgrave Macmillan.

Schaffer, D. W., Squire, K. R., Halverson, R., & Gee, J. P. (2005). Video games and the future of learning. *Phi Delta Kappan*, *87*(2), 105–111.

Schank, R. C. (2002). Every curriculum tells a story. *Tech Directions*, *62*(2), 25–29.

Schank, R. C., & Cleary, C. (1995). *Engines for education*. Hillsdale, NJ: Lawrence Erlbaum Associates Inc.

Schank, R., & Neaman, A. (2001). Motivation and failure in educational simulation design. In K. D. Forbus & P. J. Feltovich (Eds.), *Smart machines in education: The coming revolution in educational technology* (pp. 37-69). Cambridge, MA: The MIT Press.

Scheef, M., Pinto, J., Rahardja, K., Snibbe, S., & Tow, R. (2002). Experiences with Sparky, a Social Robot. In K. Dautenhahn, A.H. Bond, L. Canamero, & B. Edmonds (Eds.). *Socially intelligent agents: Creating relationships with computers and robots* (pp. 173-180). Norwell, MA: Kluwer Academic Publishers.

Scherpereel, C. M. (2005). Changing mental models: Business simulation exercises. *Simulation & Gaming*, *36*(5), 388–403. doi:10.1177/1046878104270005

Schiaffino, S., Garcia, P., & Amandi, A. (2008). eTeacher: Providing personalized assistance to E-learning students. *Computers & Education*, *51*(4), 1744–1754. doi:10.1016/j.compedu.2008.05.008

Schmidt, S. J. (2003). Active and cooperative learning using web-based simulations. *The Journal of Economic Education*, *34*(2), 151–167. doi:10.1080/00220480309595209

Schnotz, W., & Rasch, T. (2005). Enabling, facilitating, and inhibiting effects of animations in multimedia learning: Why reduction of cognitive load can have negative results on learning. *Educational Technology Research and Development*, *53*(3), 47–58. doi:10.1007/BF02504797

Schön, D. A. (1983). *The reflective practitioner: How professionals think in action*. New York: Basic Books.

Schön, D. A. (1987). *Educating the reflective practitioner*. San Francisco: Jossey-Bass.

Schrader, J., Young, M., & Zheng, D. (2006). Teacher's perceptions of video games: MMOGs and the future of preservice teacher education. *Innovate Journal of Online Education, 2* (3). Available from http://innovateonline.info/index.php?view=article&id=125

Schubert, T., Friedmann, F., & Regenbrecht, H. (2001). The experience of presence: Factor analytic insights. *Presence (Cambridge, Mass.)*, *10*(3), 266–281. doi:10.1162/105474601300343603

Schutte, N. S., Malouff, J. M., Post-Gorden, J. C., & Rodasta, A. L. (1988). Effects of playing videogames on children's aggressive and other behaviors. *Journal of Applied Social Psychology*, *18*(5), 454–460. doi:10.1111/j.1559-1816.1988.tb00028.x

Schuytema, P. (2007). *Game design: A practical approach*. Boston, MA: Charles River Media.

Schwabe, G., & Goth, C. (2005). Mobile learning with a mobile game: Design and motivational effects. *Journal of Computer Assisted Learning*, *21*(3), 204–216. doi:10.1111/j.1365-2729.2005.00128.x

Scott, D. (1995). The effect of video games on feelings of aggression. *Journal of Psychology: Interdisciplinary & Applied*, *129*(2), 121–132.

Sedic, K. (2007). Toward operationalization of 'flow' in mathematics learnware. *Computers in Human Behavior*, *23*(4), 2064–2092. doi:10.1016/j.chb.2006.11.001

Seto, M. C., & Barbaree, H. E. (1996). Sexual aggression as antisocial behavior: A developmental model. In D. Stoff, J. Brieling, & J. D. Maser (Eds.), *Handbook of antisocial behavior* (pp. 524-533). New York: Wiley.

Seydegart, K., Spears, G., & Zulinov, P. (2005). *Young Canadians in a wired world, Phase II*. Erin, ON, Canada: Erin Research Inc. Available at http://www.media-awareness.ca/english/research/ycww/index.cfm

Sha, L., Winne, P., & Campbell, S. R. (2009, April). *Personal factors underlying the relations between metacognitive judgments and control in self-regulated learning*. Paper presented at the annual meeting of the American Educational Research Association, San Diego, CA.

Shaffer, D. W. (2006). Epistemic frames for epistemic games. *Computers & Education, 46*(3), 223–234. doi:10.1016/j.compedu.2005.11.003

Shaffer, D. W. (2006). *How computer games help children learn.* New York: Palgrave Macmillan.

Shaffer, D. W., Gordon, J. A., & Bennett, N. L. (2004). Learning, testing, and the evaluation of learning environments in medicine: Global performance assessment in medical education. *Interactive Learning Environments, 12*(3), 167–178. doi:10.1080/10494820512331383409

Shaffer, D. W., Squire, K. R., Halverson, R., & Gee, J. P. (2004). *Video games and the future of learning,* Research report, University of Wisconsin-Madison and Academic Advanced Distributed Learning Co-Laboratory. Available at http://www.academiccolab.org/resources/gappspaper1.pdf.

Shaffer, D. W., Squire, K. R., Halverson, R., & Gee, J. P. (2005). *Video games and the future of learning.* WCER (Wisconsin Center for Education Research) Working Paper, No. 2005-4. Available at http://www.wcer.wisc.edu/publications/workingPapers/Working_Paper_No_2005_4.pdf

Shaftel, J., Pass, L., & Schnabel, S. (2005). Math games for adolescents. *Teaching Exceptional Children, 37*(3), 27–33.

Shapiro, R., & Shapiro, R. G. (2001, April). *Games to explain aspects of psychology.* Paper presented at the Annual Convention of the National Association of School Psychologists, Washington, DC.

Sheese, B. E., & Graziano, W. G. (2005). Deciding to defect: The effects of video game violence on co-operative behavior. *Psychological Science, 16*(5), 354–357. doi:10.1111/j.0956-7976.2005.01539.x

Shellman, S., & Turan, K. (2006). Confronting global issues: A multipurpose IR simulation. *Simulation & Gaming, 37*(1), 98–123. doi:10.1177/1046878105278924

Sherer, M. (1998). The effect of computerized simulation games on the moral development of junior and senior high-school students. *Computers in Human Behavior, 14*(2), 375–386. doi:10.1016/S0747-5632(98)00013-2

Shi, Y. (2000). The game PIG: Making decisions based on mathematical thinking. *Teaching Mathematics and Its Applications, 19*(1), 30–34. doi:10.1093/teamat/19.1.30

Shipulina, O. V., Campbell, S. R., & Cimen, O. A. (2009, April). *Electrooculography: Connecting mind, brain, and behavior in mathematics education research.* Paper presented at the annual meeting of the American Educational Research Association, San Diego, CA.

Shneiderman, B. (2004). Designing for fun: How to make user interfaces more fun. *Interactions (New York, N.Y.), 11*(5), 48–50. doi:10.1145/1015530.1015552

Shneiderman, B., & Plaisant, C. (2004). *Designing the user interface: Strategies for effective human-computer interaction* (4th ed.). Boston, MA: Addison-Wesley.

Shreve, J. (2005, April). Let the games begin. Video games, once confiscated in class, are now a key teaching tool if they're done right. *Edutopia,* 29-31.

Silvern, S. B., & Williamson, P. A. (1987). The effects of video game play on young children's aggression, fantasy, and prosocial behavior. *Journal of Applied Developmental Psychology, 8*(4), 453–462. doi:10.1016/0193-3973(87)90033-5

Simon, W. T., & Schouten, P. G. (1991). Plethysmography in the assessment and treatment of sexual deviance: An overview. *Archives of Sexual Behavior, 20,* 75–91. doi:10.1007/BF01543009

Sing, C. C., & Der-Thanq, V. (2004). A review on usability evaluation methods for instructional multimedia: An analytical framework. *International Journal of Instructional Media, 31*(3), 229–238.

Singer, B. (1984). Conceptualizing sexual arousal and attraction. *Journal of Sex Research, 20*(3), 230–240.

Skemp-Arlt, K. M. (2006). Body image dissatisfaction and eating disturbances among children and adolescents: Prevalence, risk factors, and prevention strategies. [JOPERD]. *Journal of Physical Education, Recreation & Dance, 77*(1), 45–51.

Skyworks Interactive® (2009). *Skyworks advergame development.* Hackensack, NJ: Skyworks Interactive.

Retrieved February 13, 2009 from http://www.skyworks.com.

Slater, M., & Wilbur, S. (1997). A framework for immersive virtual environments (FIVE): Speculations on the role of presence in virtual environments. *Presence (Cambridge, Mass.)*, *6*(6), 603–616.

Slater, M., Steed, A., & McCarthy, J. (1998). The influence of body movement on subjective presence in virtual environments. *Human Factors*, *40*(3), 469–477. doi:10.1518/001872098779591368

Smith, D. E. (1989). *The everyday world as problematic*. Lebanon, NH: Northeastern University Press.

Smith, G. M., & Fischer, L. (1999). Assessment of juvenile sex offenders: Reliability and validity of The Abel Assessment for interest in paraphilias. *Sexual Abuse*, *11*(3), 207–216. doi:10.1177/107906329901100304

Snider, M. (2003, March 3). Wired to another world: Online games like EverQuest and The Sims have become a new addiction. *Maclean's*, *116*(9), 23–25.

Soussi, A. (2003, March 9). War games becoming all too real. *Sunday Herald*. Retrieved August 31, 2006 from http://www.sundayherald.com/31960.

Spear, L. P. (2000). The adolescent brain and age-related behavioral manifestations. *Neuroscience and Biobehavioral Reviews*, *24*(4), 417–463. doi:10.1016/S0149-7634(00)00014-2

Spears, G., & Seydegart, K. (2003). *Kid's take on media survey: What 5700 Canadian kids say about TV, movies, video and computer games*. Toronto, ON, Canada: Canadian Teacher's Federation/Media Awareness Network.

Spears, G., & Seydegart, K. (2004). Kids' views on violence in the media. *Canadian Child and Adolescent Psychiatry Review*, *13*(1), 7–12.

Spinello, E. F., & Fischbach, R. (2004). Problem-based learning in public health instructions: A pilot study of an online simulation as a problem-based learning approach. *Education for Health*, *17*(3), 365–373. doi:10.1080/13576280400002783

Sprott, J. C. (2003). *Chaos and time-series analysis*. Oxford, UK: Oxford University Press.

Squire, K. (2002). Cultural framing of computer/video games. *Game Studies*, *2*(1). Available from http://www.gamestudies.org/0102/squire

Squire, K. (2004). *Replaying history: Learning world history through playing Civilization III*. Unpublished PhD dissertation, Indiana University. Retrieved June 11, 2008 from http://website.education.wisc.edu/kdsquire/dissertation.html

Squire, K. (2005), *Game-based learning: An X-learn perspective paper*. Sarasota Springs, NY: MASIE center: e-Learning Consortium.

Squire, K. (2005). Changing the game: What happens when video games enter the classroom? *Innovate Journal of Online Education*, *1*(6). Available from http://innovateonline.info/index.php?view=article&id=82&highlight=Squire

Squire, K. (2006). From content to context: Videogames as designed experience. *Educational Researcher*, *35*(8), 19–29. doi:10.3102/0013189X035008019

Squire, K., Jenkins, H., Holland, W., Miller, H., O'Driscoll, A., & Tan, K. P. (2003). Design principles of next-generation digital gaming for education. *Educational Technology*, *43*(5), 17–23.

Stadler, M. A. (1998). Demonstrating scientific reasoning. *Teaching of Psychology*, *25*(3), 205–206. doi:10.1207/s15328023top2503_11

Stanney, K. M., & Zyda, M. (2002). Virtual environments in the 21st century. In K.M. Stanney (Ed.), *Handbook of virtual environments: Design, implementation, and applications* (pp. 1-14). Mahwah, NJ: Lawrence Erlbaum Associates Inc.

Starratt, R. J. (1997). *Administrating meaning, administrating community, administrating excellence: The new fundamentals of educational administration*. New York: Merrill.

Statistics Canada. (2005). *Enquête sur la santé dans les collectivités canadiennes: Obésité chez les enfants et les adultes. In Le Quotidien* [Inquiry into the health of Canadian groups: Obesity in children and adults]. Retrieved October 17, 2006 from http://www.statcan.ca/Daily/Francais/050706/q050706a.htm

Statistics Canada. (2005). *Household Internet use at home by Internet activity*. Retrieved on April 19, 2009 from: http://www40.statcan.gc.ca/l01/cst01/comm09a-eng.htm

Statistics Canada. (2007). *Ressources éducatives journal annuel 2006-2007* [Annual education resources journal 2006-2007]. Retrieved November 7, 2007 from http://www.statcan.ca/francais/edu/lr2006/LR2006family_f.htm

Steinkuehler, C. A. (2004). Learning in massively multiplayer online games. In Y. B. Kafai, W. A. Sandoval, N. Enyedy, A. S. Nixon, & F. Herrera (Eds.), *Proceedings of the 6th International Conference on Learning Sciences (ICLS 2004)* (pp. 521-528). Mahwah, NJ: Lawrence Erlbaum Associates Inc.

Steinkuehler, C. A. (2006). Massively multiplayer online videogames as participation in a discourse. *Mind, Culture, and Activity*, *3*(1), 38–52. doi:10.1207/s15327884mca1301_4

Stephenson, N. (1992). *Snowcrash*. New York: Bantam Books.

Sternheimer, K. (2007). Do video games kill? *Contexts*, *6*(1), 13–17. doi:10.1525/ctx.2007.6.1.13

Stewart, K. M. (1997). Beyond entertainment: Using interactive games in web-based instruction. *Journal of Instruction Delivery Systems*, *1*(2), 18–20.

St-Germain, M., & Laveault, D. (1997). Factors of success of simulations and games: A systemic approach to the evaluation of an organization's impact on the user. *Simulation & Gaming*, *28*(3), 317–336. doi:10.1177/1046878197283006

STHC. (2007). *Quelques faits: Maladie mentale et toxicomanie au Canada* [Some facts: Mental Illness and drug dependency in Canada]. Guelph, ON, Canada: Société pour les troubles de l'humeur du Canada.

Stolovitch, H. D. (1981). Technology of simulation gaming for education and training. Retrieved May 13, 2003 from http://www.hsa-ltd.com/Articles.htm#2.

Stolovitch, H. D. (1982). Applications of the intermediate technology of learner verification and revision (LVR) for adapting international instructional resources to meet local needs. *Performance & Instruction*, *21*(7), 16–22. doi:10.1002/pfi.4170210708

Stolovitch, H. D. (1983). *Notes de cours: jeux de simulation* [Course notes: Simulation games]. Montreal, QC, Canada: Université de Montréal, Section de technologie éducationnelle.

Stolovitch, H. D., & Thiagarajan, S. (1980). *Frame games*. Englewood Cliffs, NJ: Educational Technology Publications.

Stover, W. J. (2007). Simulating the Cuban Missile Crisis: Crossing time and space in virtual reality. *International Studies Perspectives*, *8*(1), 111–120. doi:10.1111/j.1528-3585.2007.00272.x

Strauss, A. L., & Corbin, J. (1998). *Basics of qualitative research: Techniques and procedures for developing grounded theory* (2nd edition). Thousand Oaks, CA: Sage Publications.

Streufert, S., Satish, U., & Barach, P. (2001). Improving medical care: The use of simulation technology. *Simulation & Gaming*, *32*(2), 164–174. doi:10.1177/104687810103200205

Strickland, R. M., & Poe, S. E. (1989). Developing a CAI graphics simulation model: Guidelines. *T.H.E. Journal*, *16*(7), 88–92.

Swanson, M. A., & Ornelas, D. (2001). Health jeopardy: A game to market school health services. *The Journal of School Nursing*, *17*(3), 166–169. doi:10.1177/10598405010170030901

Taradi, K., Taradi, M., Kresimir, R., & Pokrajac, N. (2005). Blending problem-based learning with web technology positively impacts student learning outcomes in acid-base physiology. *Advances in Physiology Education*, *29*(1), 35–39. doi:10.1152/advan.00026.2004

Tardif, J. (1992). *Pour un enseignement stratégique: L'apport de la psychologie cognitive* [For a strategic education: The contribution of cognitive psychology]. Montréal, QC, Canada: Éditions Logiques.

Theiler, J., Eubank, S., Longtin, A., Galdrikian, B., & Farmer, J. D. (1992). Testing for nonlinearity in time series: The method of surrogate data. *Physica D. Nonlinear Phenomena, 58*(1-4), 77–94. doi:10.1016/0167-2789(92)90102-S

Thiagarajan, S. (1978). Instructional product verification and revision: 20 questions and 200 speculations. *Educational Technology Research and Development, 26*(2), 1042–1629.

Thiagarajan, S. (1998). The myths and realities of simulations in performance technology. *Educational Technology, 38*(5), 35–40.

Thoa, E. (2004). *Ergonomie et jeu vidéo* [Ergonomics and video games].Retrieved April 12, 2008 from http://www.usabilis.com/articles/2004/ergonomie-jeu.htm.

Thompson, K. (1999). *Storytelling in the new Hollywood: Understanding classical narrative technique*. Cambridge, MA: Harvard University Press.

Thulal, A. N. (2003). *Application of software testing in e-learning.* Delhi: Department of Information Technology, Amity School of Engineering and Technology. Retrieved May 29, 2009 from http://www.jmi.nic.in/Events/witsa2003/AmritNathThulal.pdf

Tinius, T. (2006). Measuring the effectiveness of neurotherapy. *Journal of Neurotherapy, 10*(1), 1–3. doi:10.1300/J184v10n01_01

Todorov, A., & Bargh, J. A. (2001). Automatic sources of aggression. *Aggression and Violent Behavior, 7*(1), 53–68. doi:10.1016/S1359-1789(00)00036-7

Tommelein, I. D., Riley, D., & Howell, G. A. (1998). Parade Game: Impact of work flow variability on succeeding trade performance. In *Proceedings, Sixth Annual Conference of the International Group for Lean Construction, IGLC-6,* Guaruja, Brazil.

Townsend, R. E., House, J. F., & Addario, D. (1975). A comparison of biofeedback-mediated relaxation and group therapy in the treatment of chronic anxiety. *The American Journal of Psychiatry, 132,* 598–601.

Trepagnier, S., Sebrechts, M. M., & Peterson, R. (2002). Atypical face gaze in autism. *Cyberpsychology & Behavior, 5*(3), 213–217. doi:10.1089/109493102760147204

Turcotte, S., Gaudreau, L., & Otis, J. (2007). Démarche de modélisation de l'intervention en éducation à la santé incluse en éducation physique [Steps in modeling an educational intervention for physical education]. *STAPS, 77,* 63–78. doi:10.3917/sta.077.0063

Turk, A. (2001). Towards contingent usability evaluation of WWW sites. In [Perth, Australia: CHISIG, Ergonomics Society of Australia.]. *Proceedings of Australian International Conference on Computer-Human Interaction OZCHI, 2001,* 161–167.

Turkle, S. (2005). *The second self – Computers and the human spirit* (20th anniversary edition). Cambridge, MA: The MIT Press.

Turkle, S. 1995. *Life on the screen.* New York: Simon and Shuster.

Tuzun, H. (2007). Blending video games with learning: Issues and challenges with classroom implementations in the Turkish context. *British Journal of Educational Technology, 38*(3), 465–477. doi:10.1111/j.1467-8535.2007.00710.x

Uhlmann, E., & Swanson, J. (2004). Exposure to violent video games increases automatic aggressiveness. *Journal of Adolescence, 27*(1), 41–52. doi:10.1016/j.adolescence.2003.10.004

Unsworth, G., Devilly, G. J., & Ward, T. (2007). The effect of playing violent video games on adolescents: Should parents be quaking in their boots? *Psychology, Crime & Law, 13*(4), 383–394. doi:10.1080/10683160601060655

Usabilis (2008). *Ergonomie informatique* [Information ergonomics]. Retrieved December 12, 2008 from http://www.usabilis.com/methode/ergonomienformatique.htm. Paris:Usabilis.

Usabilis (2009). *Ergonomie informatique* [Information ergonomics]. Available at http://www.usabilis.com/methode/ergonomienformatique.htm. Paris: Usabilis.

Usta, E., Akbas, O., Cakir, R., & Ozdemir, S. (2008). The effects of computer games on high school students' perception of confidence. In K. McFerrin et al. (Eds.), *Proceedings of Society for Information Technology and Teacher Education International Conference 2008* (pp. 1833-1840). Chesapeake, VA: AACE.

Valentine, T. (1999). Face-space models of face recognition. In M. J. Wenger, & J. T. Townsend (Eds.), *Computational, geometric, and process perspectives on facial cognition: Contexts and challenges* (pp. 83-113). Mahwah, NJ: Lawrence Erlbaum Associates Inc.

Van Eck, R. (2006). The effect of contextual pedagogical advisement and competition on middle-school students' attitude toward mathematics and mathematics instruction using a computer-based simulation game. *Journal of Computers in Mathematics and Science Teaching, 25*(1), 165–195.

Van Houcke, M., Vereecke, A., & Gemmel, P. (2005). The Project Scheduling Game (PSG): Simulating time/cost trade-offs in projects. *Project Management Journal, 36*(1), 51–59.

van Merriënboer, J. G., & Kirschner, P. A. (2007). *Ten steps to complex learning: A systematic approach to four-component instructional design*. London: Routledge.

Vanderdonckt, J., & Mariage, C. (2000, October). *Introduction à la conception ergonomique des pages Web* [Introduction to ergonomic design for web pages]. Tutorial presented at the ERGO-IHM'2000 International Conference.

Vandeventer, S. S., & While, J. A. (2002). Expert behavior in children's video game play. *Simulation & Gaming, 33*(1), 28–49. doi:10.1177/1046878102033001002

Vanhoucke, M., Vereecke, A., & Gemmel, P. (2005). The project scheduling game (PSG): Simulating time/cost trade-offs in projects. *Project Management Journal, 36*(1), 51–59.

Vernon, D. J. (2005). Can neurofeedback training enhance performance? An evaluation of the evidence with implications for future research. *Applied Psychophysiology and Biofeedback, 30*(4), 347–364. doi:10.1007/s10484-005-8421-4

Viau, R. (1994). *La motivation en contexte scolaire* [Motivation in the school context] (Édition québécoise). Montréal, QC, Canada: Éditions du Renouveau pédagogique.

Villardier, L., Sauvé, L., Probst, W., Kaufman, D., Boyd, G., Sanchez-Arias, V., et al. (2006, May). *ENJEUX-S: Un environment d'enseignement synchrone au service de la formation à distance* [*ENJEUX-S*: A synchronous learning envrionment for distance education]. Paper presented at the ACED/AMTEC Symposium, Montreal, QC, Canada.

Virilio, P. (1980). *Esthétique de la disparition*. Paris: Balland.

Virvou, M., Katsionis, G., & Manos, K. (2005). Combining software games with education: Evaluation of its educational effectiveness. *Educational Technology & Society, 8*(2), 54–65.

Visweswaran, K. (1994) *Fictions of feminist ethnography*. Minneapolis, MN: University of Minnesota Press.

Vockell, E. (2004). *Educational psychology: a practical approach*. Retrieved January 20, 2009 from http://education.calumet.purdue.edu/Vockell/EdPsyBook/

Vogel, J. J., Vogel, D. S., Cannon-Bowers, J., Bowers, C. A., Muse, K., & Wright, M. (2006). Computer gaming and interactive simulations for learning: A meta-analysis. *Journal of Educational Computing Research, 34*(3), 229–243. doi:10.2190/FLHV-K4WA-WPVQ-H0YM

Vorderer, P., Hartmann, T., & Klimmt, C. (2003). *Explaining the enjoyment of playing video games: The role of competition*. In *Proceedings of the second international conference on entertainment computing*. Available at http://portal.acm.org/citation.cfm?id=958735

Waal, B. D. (1995). *Motivations for video game play: A study of social, cultural and physiological factors.*

Unpublished Master's thesis, School of Communication, Simon Fraser University

Walkerdine, V. (1998). Children in cyberspace: A new frontier? In K. Lesnik-Oberstein (Ed.), *Children in culture: Approaches to childhood* (pp. 231-247). New York: St. Martin's.

Walkerdine, V. (2007). *Children, gender, video games: Towards a relational approach to multimedia*. New York: Palgrave Macmillan.

Walkerdine, V., Thomas, A., & Studdert, D. (1998). *Young children and video games: Dangerous pleasures and pleasurable danger.* Available at http://creativetechnology.salford.ac.uk/fuchs/projects/downloads/young_children_and_videogames.htm.

Walsh, D. A., & Gentile, D. A. (2001). A validity test of movie, television, and videogame ratings. *Pediatrics, 107*(6), 1302–1308. doi:10.1542/peds.107.6.1302

Wann, J. P., Rushton, S. K., Smyth, M., & Jones, D. (1997). Virtual environments for the rehabilitation of disorders of attention and movement. *Studies in Health Technology and Informatics, 44*, 157–164.

Warnes, E., & Allen, K. D. (2005). Biofeedback treatment of paradoxical vocal fold motion and respiratory distress in an adolescent girl. *Journal of Applied Behavior Analysis, 38*(4), 529–532. doi:10.1901/jaba.2005.26-05

Waters, K. (1987). A muscle model for animating 3D facial expression. *Computer Graphics, 21*(4), 17–24. doi:10.1145/37402.37405

Watters, C., & Duffy, J. (2005). Metalevel analysis of motivational factors for interface design. In K. Fisher & S. Erdelex (Eds.), *Theories of information behavior: A researcher's guide* (pp. 242-246). Medford, NJ: Information Today Press.

Watters, C., Oore, S., Shepherd, M., & Abouzied, A. Cox, A., Kellar, M., et al. (2006). Extending the use of games in health care. In *Proceedings of the 39th Annual Hawaii International Conference on the System Sciences (HICSS39) - volume 05* (p. 88.2). Washington, DC; IEEE Computer Society. doi: 10.1109/HICSS.2006.179.

Webster, R. (2002). *Metacognition and the autonomous learner: Student reflections on cognitive profiles and learning environment development.* Perth, Australia: Edith Cowan University. Retrieved September 9, 2006 from http://www.csd.uwa.edu.au/iced2002/publication/Ray_Webster.pdf

Weiner, B. (1985). An attributional theory of achievement motivation and emotion. *Psychological Review, 92*(4), 548–573. doi:10.1037/0033-295X.92.4.548

Whitehouse, B., & Turner, S. (2007). *Biofeedback technology in the Journey to Wild Divine.* Retrieved June 26, 2008 from http://www.alivematrix.info/html/scienceofbiofeedback.html

Wideman, H. H., Owston, R. D., Brown, C., Kushniruk, A., Ho, F., & Pitts, K. C. (2007). Unpacking the potential of educational gaming: A new tool for gaming research. *Simulation & Gaming, 38*(1), 10–30. doi:10.1177/1046878106297650

Wiederhold, B. K., & Rizzo, A. (2005). Virtual Reality and applied psychophysiology. *Applied Psychophysiology and Biofeedback, 30*(3), 183–187. doi:10.1007/s10484-005-6375-1

Wiederhold, B. K., & Wiederhold, M. D. (2004). *Virtual Reality therapy for anxiety disorders.* Washington D.C: American Psychological Association Press.

Wiederhold, B. K., Jang, D. P., Kim, S. I., & Wiederhold, M. D. (2002). Physiological monitoring as an objective tool in Virtual Reality therapy. *Cyberpsychology & Behavior, 5*(1), 77–82. doi:10.1089/109493102753685908

Wiggins, J. S., Trapnell, P., & Phillips, N. (1988). Psychometric and geometric characteristics of the revised Interpersonal Adjective Scale. *Multivariate Behavioral Research, 23*, 517–530. doi:10.1207/s15327906mbr2304_8

Wikipedia (2006). *Exergaming.* Retrieved September 2, 2006 from http://en.wikipedia.org/wiki/Exertainment

Wikipedia (2007). *Simulation.* Retrieved November 8, 2007 from http://en.wikipedia.org/wiki/Simulation

Wikipedia (2008). Deontological ethics. Retrieved June 12, 2008 from http://en.wikipedia.org/wiki/Deontology

Wikipédia. (2008). *Interaction*. Retrieved January 3, 2008 from http://fr.wikipedia.org/wiki/Interaction

Wikipédia. (2008). *La validation* [Validation]. Retrieved May 29, 2009 from http://fr.wikipedia.org/wiki/Validation

Wikipédia. (2008a). *Jeu* [Game]. Retrieved September12, 2008 from http://fr.wikipedia.org/wiki/Jeu.

Wikipédia. (2008b). *Serious Game*. Retrieved January 7, 2008 from http://fr.wikipedia.org/wiki/Serious_game

Wilder, J., Hung, G., Tremaine, M., & Kaur, M. (2002). Eye tracking in virtual environments. In K. M. Stanney (Ed.), *Handbook of virtual environments: Design, implementation, and applications* (pp. 211-222). Mahwah, NJ: Lawrence Erlbaum Associates Inc.

Wilkerson, L., & Feletti, G. (1989). Problem-based learning: One approach to increasing student participation. *New Directions for Teaching and Learning*, *37*, 51–60. doi:10.1002/tl.37219893707

Windschitl, M., & Andre, T. (1998). Using computer simulations to enhance conceptual change: The roles of constructivist instruction and student epistemological beliefs. *Journal of Research in Science Teaching*, *35*(2), 145–160. doi:10.1002/(SICI)1098-2736(199802)35:2<145::AID-TEA5>3.0.CO;2-S

Winters, F. I., Greene, J. A., & Costich, C. M. (2008). Self-regulation of learning within computer-based learning environments: A critical analysis. *Educational Psychology Review*, *20*(4), 429–444. doi:10.1007/s10648-008-9080-9

Wisner, A. (1972). *Textes généraux sur l'ergonomie* [General text on ergonomics]. Paris: Laboratoire de physiologie du travail et d'ergonomie.

Wissmann, J. L., & Tankel, K. (2001). Nursing student's use of a psychopharmacology game for client empowerment. *Journal of Professional Nursing*, *17*(2), 101–106. doi:10.1053/jpnu.2001.22274

Witmer, B. G., & Singer, M. J. (1998). Measuring presence in virtual environments: A Presence Questionnaire. *Presence (Cambridge, Mass.)*, *7*(3), 225–240. doi:10.1162/105474698565686

Witteveen, L., & Enserink, B. (2007). Visual problem appraisal - Kerala's Coast: A simulation for social learning about integrated coastal zone management. *Simulation & Gaming*, *38*(2), 278–295. doi:10.1177/1046878107300667

Wolfe, J., & Crookall, D. (1998). Developing a scientific knowledge of simulation/gaming. *Simulation & Gaming*, *29*(1), 7–19. doi:10.1177/1046878198291002

Woltjer, G. B. (2005). Decisions and macroeconomics: Development and implementation of a simulation game. *The Journal of Economic Education*, *36*(2), 139–144. doi:10.3200/JECE.36.2.139-144

Wood, D., Underwood, J., & Avis, P. (1999). Integrated learning systems in the classroom. *Computers & Education*, *33*(2-3), 91–108. doi:10.1016/S0360-1315(99)00027-5

Woods, B., Whitworth, E., Hadziomerovic, A., Fiset, J., & Dormann, C. Caquard, et al., (2005). Repurposing a computer role playing game for engaging learning. In P. Kommers & G. Richards (Eds.), *Proceedings of World Conference on Educational Multimedia, Hypermedia and Telecommunications 2005* (pp. 4430-4435). Chesapeake, VA: AACE.

Woolf, M. J. P. (Ed.). (2001). *The medium of the video game*. Austin, TX: University of Austin Press.

Yaoyuenyong, C., Hadikusumo, B. H. W., Ogunlana, S. O., & Siengthai, S. (2005). Virtual construction negotiation game – An interactive learning tool for project management negotiation skill training. *International Journal of Business & Management Education*, *13*(2), 21–36.

Yeo, G. K., & Tan, S. T. (1999). Toward a multilingual, experiential environment for learning decision technology. *Simulation & Gaming*, *30*(1), 70–82. doi:10.1177/104687819903000108

Yilmaz, L., Ören, T., & Aghaee, N.-G. (2006). Intelligent agents, simulation and gaming. *Simulation & Gaming*, *37*(3), 339–349. doi:10.1177/1046878106289089

Young, M. I. (1998/2005). Five faces of oppression. In A. E. Cudd & R. O. Andreasen (Eds.), *Feminist theory:*

A philosophical anthology. Malden, MA: Blackwell Publishing.

Zamansky, H. S. (1956). A technique for measuring homosexual tendencies. *Journal of Personality*, *24*(4), 436–448. doi:10.1111/j.1467-6494.1956.tb01280.x

Zhu, H., Zhou, X., & Yin, B. (2001). Visible simulation in medical education: Notes and discussion. *Simulation & Gaming*, *3*(3), 362–369. doi:10.1177/104687810103200306

Zillmann, D. (1988). Cognition- excitation dependencies in aggressive behavior. *Aggressive Behavior*, *14*(1), 51–64. doi:10.1002/1098-2337(1988)14:1<51::AID-AB2480140107>3.0.CO;2-C

Zimmerman, E. (2004). Narrative, interactivity, play and games - four naughty concepts in need of discipline. In N. Wardrip-Fruin, & P. Harrigan (Eds.), *First person: New media as story, performance, and game* (pp. 154-155). Cambridge, MA: The MIT Press.

Zyda, M. (2005). From visual simulation to virtual reality to games. *Computer*, *38*(9), 25–32. doi:10.1109/MC.2005.297

About the Contributors

David Kaufman received his doctorate from the University of British Columbia (UBC) in 1973. Since that time, he has held a number of academic and administrative positions. He has held faculty appointments in Faculties of Engineering, Computer Science, Medicine, and Education at Concordia University (Loyola campus), Dalhousie University, Simon Fraser University, and the University of British Columbia. He has also served as Coordinator of Research and Development for the former Educational Research Institute of British Columbia, Director of Course Design for the Open Learning Institute (British Columbia's distance education institution), and Director of the Medical Education Unit, and later, Director of Faculty Development in Dalhousie University's Faculty of Medicine. Dr. Kaufman is the 1998 recipient of Dalhousie University's Instructional Leadership Award for his efforts in promoting and enhancing teaching. In 2001, he was appointed Director of the Learning and Instructional Development Centre at Simon Fraser University, and has recently completed a seven-year term in that position. Since 2003, he has been a Professor in the Faculty of Education at Simon Fraser University. His academic work continues as he resumes teaching responsibilities in 2009. Dr. Kaufman has given more than 200 presentations at universities and conferences in North America, Europe, Asia, South America, South Africa, and the Caribbean. He has published extensively, with more than 100 published articles and chapters, and a co-edited book (*Distance Education in Canada*) to his credit. He is the co-author of *Educational Gameplay and Simulation Environments: Case Studies and Lessons Learned,* published by IGI Global. He is also a reviewer for many journals, professional associations, and funding agencies, and has recently completed a term as member of the Canada's Social Sciences and Humanities Research Council (SSHRC) Major Collaborative Research Initiative (MCRI) research grant committee. He currently sits on SSHRC's Standard Research Grant adjudication committee (Education and Social Sciences). Dr. Kaufman and his colleague, Dr. Louise Sauvé, recently completed an SSHRC Initiative on the New Economy, Collaborative Research Initiative grant of $3 million over four years on Simulation and Advanced Gaming Environments (SAGE) for Learning. Dr. Kaufman and his colleagues currently hold an SSHRC research grant and are continuing their work in this area.

Louise Sauvé, Professor at Télé-université, Quebec's distance education institution, received her doctorate in Educational Technology from the University of Montreal in 1985. Since then, she has held various administrative positions: Section Coordinator, Director of the Teaching and Research unit, Head of the Professional Council, and Director of Promotion and Learning on Demand. As President and Scientific Director since 1994 of the *Center for Expertise and Research in Lifelong Learning* (SAVIE), she has directed numerous multi-disciplinary and inter-institutional teams for which she has received major research grants and contracts. As a senior researcher, she has been awarded numerous awards throughout her career, notably the Prize for Excellence and Innovation in Educational Technology from the Canadian

Network for Innovation in 2008, and the Medal of the National Assembly of Quebec in 2006 for her research contribution to Quebec society, the Special Prize from the Quebec Minister of Education in 2006 for her educational contribution to Quebec society, the Certificate of Honour from RÉFAD in 2006 for her contributions to distance education, and an honorable mention for the Minister of Education's prize in 2005 for her distance learning course. Dr. Sauvé is co-author of a first book entitled *Simulation et jeu de simulation, outils éducatifs appliqués à la santé (Simulation and simulation games, educational tools applied to health)*. She is also co-author of *Educational Gameplay and Simulation Environments: Case Studies and Lessons Learned,* published by IGI Global. Creator of more than ten online learning environments, she has also directed 20 university-level distance education courses and produced more than 60 research reports. Dr. Sauvé has published more than 160 research papers, review articles, and book chapters. She has presented more than 250 scientific papers and workshops in North America, Europe, Asia, Central and South America, North Africa, and Australia. She also serves as a reviewer for several funding agencies and journals. Dr. Sauvé and her colleague Dr. Kaufman recently completed a $3 million, five-year project entitled *Simulation and Advanced Gaming Environments (SAGE) for Learning.* They currently hold an SSHRC research grant and are continuing their work in this area.

* * *

Mahboubeh Asgari is a researcher and Ph.D. candidate in Curriculum Theory and Implementation in the Faculty of Education at Simon Fraser University. She has a number of interests relating to teaching and learning, gaming and simulation for learning, and self and its relationship to learning. Her interest in the concept of self is focused on a 'natural' self versus a self that has been 'misrecognized,' as well as the importance of educational games for students' self- exploration and reflection on the misrecognized self. She has presented several papers at national and international game conferences, and has published three book chapters on digital games. Her latest paper, "Motivation, Learning, and Game Design" (co-authored with Dr. David Kaufman) was published in *Handbook of Research on Effective Electronic Gaming in Education* (R. E. Ferdig, Ed.), Information Science Reference.

Jim Bizzocchi is an Assistant Professor in the School of Interactive Arts and Technology at Simon Fraser University. Prof. Bizzocchi teaches courses in Narrative, Video, and New Media. His research interests include the future of the moving image, the design and experience of interactive narrative, and the development of educational games and simulations. He has presented at numerous academic conferences, and his work has been published in a variety of scholarly books, journals, and conference proceedings. He is a past president of the Canadian Association for Distance Education and has consulted widely on educational media and educational technology in Canada and internationally. He is a practicing video artist, whose work had been widely exhibited; his Ambient Video art works complement his scholarly writing on the future of the moving image.

Stéphane Bouchard received his Ph.D. at Laval University in 1995, after which he completed his first year of post-doctoral studies and took a faculty position at the University of Quebec in Outaouais (UQO). His work revolves around the effectiveness of cognitive-behavioral therapy in the treatment of anxiety disorders and the mechanisms underlying this effectiveness. For the past few years, he has specialized in the use of virtual reality and telepsychotherapy delivered through videoconferencing. He continues to hold a vital leadership position at the Cyberpsychology Lab at UQO, thanks to ongoing close collaboration in research and publication with other research team members and internationally.

John Bradford is the Associate Chief of the Integrated Forensic Program of the Royal Ottawa Health Care Group, Ottawa, Ontario. He is Head of the Division of Forensic Psychiatry, Faculty of Medicine, with a cross appointment as Professor in the School of Criminology, University of Ottawa. He is also a Professor in the Department of Psychiatry, Queen's University. Dr. Bradford is a graduate in Medicine and received a Diploma of Psychological Medicine, both from the University of Capetown, South Africa and holds specialist degrees in Psychiatry from South Africa, the UK, USA, and Canada. He also has a sub-specialty degree in Forensic Psychiatry from the USA. Dr. Bradford's research interests focus on the assessment and treatment of the paraphilias, as well as impulse control disorders. He has published more than 100 peer-reviewed papers and presented at more than 250 international and national conferences, co-authored three books, and contributed to book chapters relating to forensic psychiatry. His expertise in the field of forensic psychiatry is well-recognized by his peers, media, judiciary, and government. He has sat on task forces, expert panels, served as expert witness, and provided special consultation to national and international working groups. He is the recipient of several international awards and was awarded the designation of Fellow of the Canadian Psychiatric Association in 2008.

Christine Brown recently graduated from York University's Ph.D. program, where she participated in various research projects related to the use of games in education and served on the Board of Directors of the Institute for Research in Learning Technologies. Her research interests focus on examining the ways in which different technologies can be used successfully in educational settings, as well as teaching strategies that foster a sense of community for adult distance education students. She has been a lecturer for Ryerson University in the School of Business for the past thirteen years, and is Program Manager for the Business Systems Analysis course series. She has also conducted executive training and provided consulting services for various companies across Canada, and serves on the Board of Directors of the Canadian Mental Health Association, Durham, Ontario.

Stephen R. Campbell is Associate Professor and Director of the Educational Neuroscience Laboratory (ENGRAMMETRON) in the Faculty of Education at Simon Fraser University. Dr. Campbell's scholarly focus is on the historical and psychological development of mathematical thinking from an embodied perspective informed by Kant, Husserl, and Merleau-Ponty. His research incorporates methods of psychophysics and cognitive neuroscience as a means for operationalizing affective and cognitive models of mathematics anxiety and concept formation.

Sylvain Chartier received his B.A. degree from the University of Ottawa in 1993 and B.Sc. and Ph.D. degrees from the University of Quebec in Montreal in 1996 and 2004, respectively, all in psychology. He has been a Professor at the University of Ottawa since 2007 and he is currently the Director of the Laboratory for Computational Neurodynamics and Cognition (CONEC). He is the author or coauthor of more than 40 journal and conference papers in the area of neural networks and quantitative methods. His research interests are in the development of unsupervised and supervised recurrent associative memories. He is also interested in nonlinear time series analysis as well as cognition, perception, and statistics.

Suzanne de Castell is Professor and former Dean pro-tem in the Faculty of Education at Simon Fraser University. She is interested in relations between media and epistemology, between 'knowing' and 'tools of intellect' in relation to print literacy, new media studies, and game-based educational technologies. Her books include *Literacy Society and Schooling* (with Alan Luke and Kieran Egan), *Language,*

Authority and Criticism (with Alan and Carmen Luke), *Radical Interventions* (with Mary Bryson), and *Worlds in Play* (with Jen Jenson). Her current work is on the ludic epistemologies of game-based learning, exemplified in several projects: *Contagion*, a compelling game about public health, *Arundo Donax*, a gripping engagement with Baroque music, and *Epidemic*, a social networking site where your 'friends' are contacts you manage to infect. She co-edits the Canadian Game Studies journal, *Loading...*.

Steve DiPaola is an Associate Professor in the School of Interactive Arts and Technology at Simon Fraser University (SFU), where he directs the iVizLab (ivizlab.sfu.ca) that strives to make interactive systems bend more to the human experience by incorporating biological & cognitive models. Much of his work is on making computation models for gaming, art, and research purposes of very human ideals such as expression, emotion, behavior, and creativity. He came to SFU from Stanford University and before that the New York Institute of Technology Computer Graphics Lab, and has held leadership positions at Electronic Arts, Saatchi Innovation, and several Silicon Valley start-ups. His art has been exhibited internationally, including the AIR and Tibor de Nagy galleries in New York City, the Whitney Museum, the MIT Museum, and the Smithsonian. He has collaborated with Nam June Paik and Kraftwerk. His new media tools are used by artists and scientists alike. See dipaola.org.

Xin Du is a Learning and Organizational Development e-learning consultant at Viterra Inc. in Saskatoon, Canada. Her main responsibility at Viterra involves using educational technologies to enhance and support employee training, including designing and delivering e-learning solutions for performance improvement, developing e-learning strategies, and maintaining a learning website. She completed her M.A. degree in Educational Technology at the Faculty of Education at Simon Fraser University under the supervision of Drs. Stephen Campbell and David Kaufman.

Jérôme Elissalde, M.Sc., is a research agent in knowledge promotion and transfer for the Media and Health Research Group at the University of Quebec in Montreal. He completed a Master's degree in the production and diffusion of scientific knowledge at the University of Paris Diderot - Paris 7. For many years he has been interested in knowledge mobilization and the social circulation of knowledge.

J. Paul Fedoroff is Director of the Sexual Behaviors Clinic in the Integrated Forensic Program of the Royal Ottawa Mental Health Care Group. He is also Director of Forensic Research at the University of Ottawa Institute for Mental Health Research. His clinical and research interests focus on the assessment and treatment of people with problematic sexual behaviors. He has a special interest in sex offenders with intellectual disability.

Mathieu Gauvin recently completed a Master's degree in political philosophy and a diploma in college teaching at Laval University. He was a research assistant for the SAGE project (with the SAVIE group) and worked on a project called 'The Computerized Expression of Philosophy,' based at Laval University; both projects were funded by Canada's Social Science and Humanities Research Council. He has been associated with other projects including Revue PHARES, the student philosophy magazine at Laval University.

Anthony Gurr is a professional video game developer with 20 years experience developing video games in Canada, Japan, and the United States. His background includes working for well- known video game companies such as Acclaim Entertainment, Electronic Arts, Taito Corporation (Tokyo), and Westwood Studios. Anthony received his Bachelor of Education from the University of Victoria in 1983, specializing in educational classroom computing. Anthony is currently a graduate student in Educational Technology at Simon Fraser University, working on his Masters' thesis. He was a research associate for the *Simulations and Advanced Gaming Environments for Learning (SAGE) Project* and produced several short documentaries about video games and education. From 2001 to 2007, Anthony taught courses in video game design and development for the Art Institute of Vancouver, working with teams of post-secondary students to develop original game concepts. Many of these games received awards and international recognition for their playability and technical quality.

Gabriela Hanca completed a Postgraduate Diploma in Sociology at the University Conference of French-speaking Switzerland and is a doctoral student in Sociology at Laval University. Her extensive experience in research, analysis, and research reporting includes coordination of several research projects as part of her role at the Télé-université (SAVIE), and important contributions to the review of the *Program of Activities for the Prevention of Drug Addiction,* developed by the *Quebec Centre for Fight against Dependency.* She participated in the evaluation of the *Passport to Your Success* program against school-leaving for the community organization *Always Together.* Recently Ms. Hanca has held several positions as a research assistant at Laval University, benefiting from numerous grants. She was awarded the Prize for Excellence by the Laval Department of Social Sciences for 2007-08.

Alice Ireland is an independent educational and financial management consultant and former Executive Director of the *Simulation and Advanced Gaming Environments (SAGE) for Learning* Project. She holds a Ph.D. in Interdisciplinary Studies (Computer Science and Business Administration) and an M.B.A. from Dalhousie University, as well as an M.Sc. in mathematics from Carnegie-Mellon University. Her research, published and presented in Canadian and international venues, has focused on decision support systems for management and financial decision-making, in particular the mathematics and applications of financial simulations and optimization models. She has held faculty positions in Business Administration at Dalhousie and Saint Mary's Universities and administrative positions including Associate Dean in the Faculty of Management, Dalhousie University, and Research Manager for the TeleLearning Network of Centres of Excellence, based at Simon Fraser University. Prior to her academic work, Dr. Ireland worked in the private sector as a public accountant and systems analyst.

Claire IsaBelle is an Associate Professor in the Faculty of Education at the University of Ottawa. Her research work is focused on the training of school principals and on educational leadership in facilitating teacher education, particularly through their use of information and communication technologies to improve teaching and learning conditions for francophone linguistic and cultural development and health education. She is also interested in continuing education for school principals through collaborative work in the school environment.

Jennifer Jenson is Associate Professor of Pedagogy and Technology in the Faculty of Education at York University. She is currently co-editor of *Loading...: The Journal of the Canadian Game Studies Association* and president of the Canadian Game Studies Association. She has just completed a three-year study of gender and digital gameplay, and has begun another on novice players and new game controllers. She has published widely on education, technology, gender, design and development of digital games, and technology policy. She is co-editor with Suzanne de Castell of *Worlds in Play: International Perspectives on Digital Game Research* (Peter Lang Press, 2007) and lead author of *Policy Unplugged* (McGill-Queens University Press, 2007) with Chloe Brushwood Rose and Brian Lewis.

Margot Kaszap is Professor of Social Sciences Education in the Faculty of Education at Laval University and is a specialist in qualitative methodologies. Since 1996, she has participated in a research group on health literacy that has been awarded research grants from Canadian agencies including the National Literacy Secretariat (NLS), Social Sciences and Humanities Research Council (SSHRC), Canadian Council on Learning (CCL), Office of Learning Technologies (OLT), Industry Canada, Inukshuk Fund, and the Natural Sciences and Engineering Research Council of Canada (NSERC). She has presented at more than 80 conferences, published chapters in six books, has 22 refereed articles in journals and conference proceedings, 11 professional reviews, 19 research reports, many learning materials, and a handbook, *Learn NVivo 2.0,* on the treatment and analysis of qualitative data.

Hadi Kharrazi, M.D., is an Interdisciplinary Ph.D. candidate focused on health informatics with faculty from the Faculties of Computer Sciences and Medicine at Dalhousie University. He is a physician and holds a Masters in Health Informatics. Hadi believes that bridging the gap between medicine and computer sciences requires research in different areas, and therefore flexibility in research is an essential characteristic of health informatics researchers. His research interests include, but are not limited to, patient empowerment, behavioral change in patients through interactive systems, patient-centered decision support systems, human-computer interaction in medicine, and web-based personalized patient health records.

Lyse Langlois is a Professor in Industrial Relations (human resources management) at the Faculty of Social Sciences, Laval University. Dr. Langlois is a member of the Center for the Study of Leadership, Values & Ethics, Penn State University, USA, and on the Board of Directors of the Institute of Applied Ethics. She is a researcher for the Inter-university Research Centre on Globalization and Work (CRIMT). Her main interests are ethical leadership, decision-making, and ethics in human resource management.

Sageev Oore is an Associate Professor of Computer Science at Saint Mary's University, as well as an award-winning musician frequently heard on CBC radio and jazz festivals throughout Canada. Born in Israel, he grew up in Canada speaking English, Hebrew, French, and Polish. He completed undergraduate work at Dalhousie University and graduate studies in Computer Science at the University of Toronto. His research is supported by that Natural Sciences and Engineering Research Council of Canada and the Canadian Foundation for Innovation.

Ronald Owston is University Professor of Education and Founding Director of the Institute for Research on Learning Technologies at York University in Toronto, Canada. He has spoken at numerous national and international conferences and has published extensively on teaching and learning with technology in leading refereed journals. He was domain leader for methodology and tools research in the *Simulation and Advanced Gaming Environments (SAGE) for Learning* project, and in 2008 he led three field studies on the impact of games on students' literacy skill development. Currently, he is a researcher in the *Fluid Project* where he is heading the development of the Open Virtual Usability Lab

(OpenVULab), an open source tool for testing the usability and accessibility of websites remotely. His website is at http://ronowston.ca.

Nathaniel Payne is a graduate of the Faculty of Business Administration at Simon Fraser University (SFU). He has several years' experience in research, technical, and teaching assistantships in the Faculties of Business Administration and Education at SFU and worked as a research assistant on the SAGE project. He has written academic papers on video games and aggression, gender roles and gaming, and retail channel management, and supported research on communities of practice & intellectual property. Currently, Nathaniel is employed by the Faculty of Business Administration at SFU.

Michael Power is Programs Director and Assistant Professor in Educational Technology at the Faculty of Education at Laval University (www.fse.ulaval.ca/Michael.Power). He is founder of the www.bold-research.org research network, Deputy Director (Education) and researcher with the GeoEDUC3D project http://geoeduc3d.scg.ulaval.ca/, and researcher with the Inter-university Learning & Technology Research Center (CIRTA) http://www.cirta.org/. Dr. Power is also a member of the Editorial Review Board for the French-language scientific journal *Revue des sciences de l'éducation* and a reviewer for several other scientific journals. He is the author of *A Designer's Log: Case Studies in Instructional Design* to be published by Athabasca University Press in August 2009.

Wilfried G. Probst, Associate Researcher with the *Center for Expertise and Research in Lifelong Learning* (SAVIE) is Adjunct Professor in Computer Science at the University of Quebec in Montreal. For 30 years, his research has concerned pedagogical computer applications and tools to support learning and training. Currently, Dr. Probst works in the design and development of the components of a multi-agent system for the support of intelligent computer-assisted information searching; he is also interested in the development of interactive, multimedia, web-based learning environments. Dr. Probst is part of a technology and networks research team at the French-Canadian Centre of Network Expertise (Centre d'expertise réseautique francophone canadien, or CERF), contributing expertise on telematics and applications of the Internet.

Jean Proulx is Professor and Director of the School of Criminology and researcher at the International Centre of Comparative Criminology at the University of Montreal, His main research interests are personality profiles, sexual preferences, treatment issues, and recidivism risk factors among sexual murderers, rapists, child molesters, and incest offenders. Over the last twenty years, he has published four books and more than 100 book chapters or refereed articles in French and English. Since 1989, he has been active, both as researcher and clinical psychologist, in treatment programs for sex offenders at the Philippe-Pinel Institute, a maximum-security psychiatric institution.

Sylvie Rail obtained her bachelor's degree in elementary education in 1994. As a teacher and facilitator, she has been involved in a wide variety of educational activities for both children and adults. Her interest in creating pedagogical activities, combined with her desire to integrate new media, motivated her to complete a Master's degree in Educational Technology at Laval University in 2003, and she is now working as an educational technologist focused on creating multimedia learning environments. During the final year of her Master's program, she was employed at the SAVIE research centre to analyze and develop multimedia-based educational games on adolescent health. Since November 2005, she has worked as a learning designer and advisor at CGI, an international IT services firm.

Lise Renaud, Ph.D. (Health Education) is a Professor in the Department of Social and Public Communication at the University of Quebec in Montreal, where she leads the Research Group on Media and Health. As a Health Promotion specialist, she is especially interested in media and the links between the public health and media players. Her research concerns mechanisms supporting the integration of norms in matters of health. She is the author of many scientific articles, pedagogical manuals, and articles for the public.

Patrice Renaud is a Professor of Psychology in the Department of Psycho-Education and Psychology and Co-director of the Cyberpsychology Laboratory at the University of Quebec in Outaouais. He is also a member of the Hexagram Institute for Research / Creation in Media Arts and Technologies and a Researcher at the Institut Philippe-Pinel in Montreal, a maximum security psychiatric facility. He has a background in psychophysiology, cognitive ergonomics and clinical psychology.

Joanne-Lucine Rouleau: Following a first post-doctoral degree working at Queen's University and Kingston penitentiary with incarcerated sex offenders and a second one working with non-incarcerated sex offenders at Columbia University in New York City, Dr Joanne-Lucine Rouleau became a professor in the Department of Psychiatry at the Emory University in Atlanta Georgia. In 1990 she returned home as a professor at the University of Montreal in the Department of Psychology. In 1992 she founded the Centre d'Étude et de Recherche de l'Université de Montreal. Since 2002 this clinic has specialized in research, assessment, and treatment of high risk, high need sex offenders recently released from federal establishments.

Robyn Schell participated as a research assistant and research associate in the *Simulation and Advanced Gaming Environments (SAGE) for Learning* project for nearly four years. She has published several papers relating to the project on problem-based learning and simulations and narrative-based case studies for medical education. Robyn is a graduate of Simon Fraser University's Educational Technology Masters Program and is currently enrolled in the Educational Technology & Learning Design Ph.D. program, where she plans to conduct further research on the use of simulation for medical education. Robyn is now a project manager at Ambit Consulting, which supports the distributed medical program at the University of British Columbia in Vancouver, Canada. In this role, she is working with the Faculty of Medicine to create and implement an overall educational technology strategy.

Nick Taylor is a Ph.D. candidate in the Faculty of Education at York University. His academic interests include designing and researching educational games, exploring research methodologies for online gaming, and developing new media-based pedagogies. He has recently coordinated a project at a local school to instruct at-risk elementary school students in stop-motion animation, and participated in the development of an educational game instructing players in Baroque music and culture. His dissertation charts the emergence of a professional gaming industry in which young, mostly male gamers compete in team-based game play at large-scale tournaments for increasingly lucrative rewards. Using audio-visual ethnographic research methods, this study looks at competitive game play as embodied and gendered performances, within a discourse that frames gaming as 21st century sport.

Yueh-Feng (Lily) Tsai is a Ph.D. graduate from the Faculty of Education at Simon Fraser University (SFU). Her research interests are in educational technology and early childhood education. Lily also has a Master's of Education in Curriculum and Instruction from the University of Victoria, and a Bachelor of Arts in Mass Communications from Ming Chuan University in her native country of Taiwan. Lily has worked as a researcher and online distance educator at SFU, educational resource developer at Benesse Corporation, early childhood educator with preschools in Taiwan and Canada, and as a journalist and editor at Tzu Chi Newsmagazine. Lily has presented her work internationally at conferences including the American Educational Research Association annual meeting and E-Learn, the World Conference on E-Learning in Corporate, Government, Healthcare, & Higher Education.

Louis Villardier is a Professor in Educational Technology at the Télé-université, the distance learning component of the University of Quebec in Montreal, and a researcher at the Center for Expertise and Research in Lifelong Learning (SAVIE). Among his accomplishments are the development of the asynchronous generic platform *Ad@pWeb,* for which he was awarded the Quebec Minister of Education's Prize in 2000 and the Prize for Excellence from the Canadian Association for Distance Education in 2000; software for the development of online learning objects (OSLO); and prototypes for the ECHO videoconferencing system and the ENJEUX-S videoconferencing and remote game delivery system.

Carolyn Watters is a Professor in the Faculty of Computer Science and the Dean of the Faculty of Graduate Studies at Dalhousie University. As Co-director of Dalhousie's Web Information Filtering Lab, her research focuses on improving the way applications are designed for users of information on a wide range of devices from desktop to handheld. Her work is funded by the Natural Sciences and Engineering Research Council of Canada, the Canadian Institutes of Health Research, and the Social Sciences and Humanities Research Council of Canada. She has supervised many Master's and Ph.D. students and produced more than 125 peer-reviewed publications, spin-off companies, and product licenses.

Herbert Wideman is the Senior Researcher at the Institute for Research on Learning Technologies at York University. His research interests include the study of technology innovation in education as a vehicle for transforming educational practice, methodologies for assessing educational technology implementation and its impacts, and the pedagogical potential of educational computer games and simulations. He has been a co-investigator and collaborator on several major studies of innovative technology infusion into education at both the K-12 and university levels, and has published articles in a number of leading journals, including the *Journal of Research on Computing, Simulation & Gaming: An Interdisciplinary Journal,* and *Research in the Teaching of English.* Most recently he has been a co-principal investigator in a two-year study program investigating student game development as a means of promoting literacy, and co-author of an article in *Computers in Education* on that work.

Index

D

E

F

G

H

I

J

K

L

P

Q

R

S

T

U

V

W

X

Z